Calculus: An Applied Approach

Providence College: MTH 109

Ron Larson

CENGAGE
Learning·

Australia • Brazil • Japan • Korea • Mexico • Singapore • Spain • United Kingdom • United States

Calculus: An Applied Approach, Providence College: MTH 109

Calculus: An Applied Approach, Ninth Edition
Ron Larson

© 2013, 2009, 2066 Brooks/Cole, Cengage Learning. All rights reserved.

Executive Editors:
 Maureen Staudt
 Michael Stranz

Senior Project Development Manager:
 Linda deStefano

Marketing Specialist:
 Courtney Sheldon

Senior Production/Manufacturing Manager:
 Donna M. Brown

Production Editorial Manager:
 Kim Fry

Sr. Rights Acquisition Account Manager:
 Todd Osborne

For product information and technology assistance, contact us at
Cengage Learning Customer & Sales Support, 1-800-354-9706
For permission to use material from this text or product,
submit all requests online at **cengage.com/permissions**
Further permissions questions can be emailed to
permissionrequest@cengage.com

This book contains select works from existing Cengage Learning resources and was produced by Cengage Learning Custom Solutions for collegiate use. As such, those adopting and/or contributing to this work are responsible for editorial content accuracy, continuity and completeness.

Compilation © 2012 Cengage Learning
ISBN-13: 978-1-285-14261-6

ISBN-10: 1-285-14261-6

Cengage Learning
5191 Natorp Boulevard
Mason, Ohio 45040
USA
Cengage Learning is a leading provider of customized learning solutions with office locations around the globe, including Singapore, the United Kingdom, Australia, Mexico, Brazil, and Japan. Locate your local office at:
international.cengage.com/region.

Cengage Learning products are represented in Canada by Nelson Education, Ltd.
For your lifelong learning solutions, visit **www.cengage.com/custom.**
Visit our corporate website at **www.cengage.com.**

Printed at CLDPC, USA, 07-18

Brief Contents

Preface

Welcome to the Ninth Edition of *Calculus: An Applied Approach*! I am always excited about a new edition, but with this edition, I am even more excited. I had a single goal in mind with this revision—to provide you with a book that is both real and relevant. This book has a bright business-oriented design that complements the multitude of business and life sciences applications found throughout.

The theme for the revision is **"IT'S ALL ABOUT YOU."** The pedagogy of the book is rock solid and is based on years of teaching, years of writing, and years of feedback from instructors and students. Please pay special attention to the study aids with a red **U**. These study aids will help you learn calculus, use technology, refresh your algebra skills, and prepare for tests. For an overview of these aids, check out CALCULUS & YOU on page 0.

In each exercise set, quiz, and test, be sure to notice the reference to **CalcChat.com.** At this free site, you can download a step-by-step solution to any odd-numbered exercise. Also, you can talk to a tutor, free, during the hours posted at the site (20 hours a week in the summer, 40 hours a week during the school year).

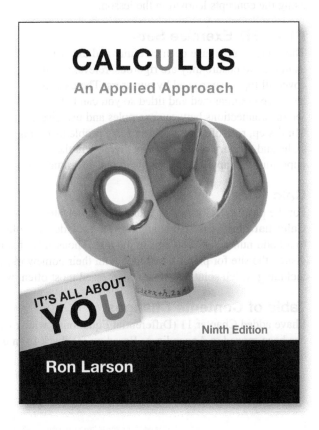

New To This Edition

NEW Chapter Opener
Each *Chapter Opener* highlights a real-life problem from an example in the chapter, showing a graph related to the data and describing the math concept used to solve the problem.

NEW Section Opener
Each *Section Opener* highlights a real-life problem in the exercises, showing a graph for the situation with a description of how you will use the math of the section to solve the problem.

NEW SUMMARIZE
The *Summarize* feature at the end of each section helps you organize the lesson's key concepts into a concise summary, providing you with a valuable study tool.

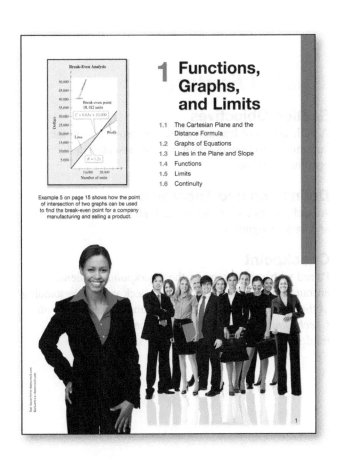

NEW HOW DO YOU SEE IT? Exercise

The *How Do You See It?* exercise in each section presents a real-life problem that you will solve by visual inspection using the concepts learned in the lesson.

REVISED Exercise Sets

The exercise sets have been carefully and extensively examined to ensure they are rigorous, relevant, and cover all topics suggested by our users. The exercises have been reorganized and titled so you can better see the connections between examples and exercises. Multi-step, real-life exercises reinforce problem-solving skills and mastery of concepts by giving you the opportunity to apply the concepts in real-life situations.

Calc Chat

For the past several years, an independent website—**CalcChat.com**—has been maintained to provide free solutions to all odd-numbered problems in the text. Thousands of students have visited the site for practice and help with their homework. For this edition, information from **CalcChat.com**, including which solutions students accessed most often, was used to help guide the revision of the exercises.

Table of Contents Changes

I have added Chapter 11 (Differential Equations), which was previously Appendix C. Chapter 0 (Precalculus Review) has been moved to Appendix A. Based on feedback from users, old Section 6.2 (Partial Fractions and Logistic Growth) has been removed.

60. **HOW DO YOU SEE IT?** The graph shows the cost and revenue equations for a product.

$C = 0.5x + 4000$

(10,000, 9000)

$R = 0.9x$

Dollars / Number of units

(a) For what numbers of units sold is there a loss for the company?

(b) For what number of units sold does the company break even?

(c) For what numbers of units sold is there a profit for the company?

Trusted Features

Section Objectives

A bulleted list of learning objectives provides you the opportunity to preview what will be presented in the upcoming section.

Definitions and Theorems

All definitions and theorems are highlighted for emphasis and easy recognition.

Checkpoint

Paired with every example, the *Checkpoint* problems encourage immediate practice and check your understanding of the concepts presented in the example. Answers to all *Checkpoint* problems appear at the back of the text to reinforce understanding of the skill sets learned.

Business Capsule

Business Capsules appear at the end of selected sections. These capsules and their accompanying research project highlight business situations related to the mathematical concepts covered in the chapter.

STUDY TIP

These hints and tips can be used to reinforce or expand upon concepts, help you learn how to study mathematics, caution you about common errors, address special cases, or show alternative or additional steps to a solution of an example.

TECH TUTOR

The *Tech Tutor* gives suggestions for effectively using tools such as calculators, graphing calculators, and spreadsheet programs to help deepen your understanding of concepts, ease lengthy calculations, and provide alternate solution methods for verifying answers obtained by hand.

ALGEBRA TUTOR

The *Algebra Tutor* appears throughout each chapter and offers algebraic support at point of use. This support is revisited in a two-page algebra review at the end of the chapter, where additional details of example solutions with explanations are provided.

Business Capsule

CitiKitty, Inc. was founded in 2005 by 26-year-old Rebecca Rescate after she moved into a small apartment in New York City with no place to hide her cat's litter box. Finding no easy-to-use cat toilet training kit, she created one, and CitiKitty was born with an initial investment of $20,000. Today the company flourishes with an expanded product line. Revenues in 2010 reached $350,000.

83. Research Project Use your school's library, the Internet, or some other reference source to find information about the start-up costs of beginning a business, such as the example above. Write a short paper about the company.

71. Project: Number of Stores For a project analyzing the numbers of Tiffany & Co. stores from 2000 through 2009, visit this text's website at *www.cengagebrain.com.*
(Source: Tiffany & Co.)

SKILLS WARM UP

The *Skills Warm Up* appears at the beginning of the exercise set for each section. These problems help you review previously learned skills that you will use in solving the section exercises.

Project

The projects at the end of selected sections involve in-depth applied exercises in which you will work with large, real-life data sets, often creating or analyzing models. These projects are offered online at *www.cengagebrain.com.*

Instructor Resources

Print

Complete Solutions Manual
ISBN-13: 978-1-133-36432-0
The *Complete Solutions Manual* provides worked-out solutions for all exercises in the text, including Checkpoints, Quiz Yourself, Test Yourself, and Tech Tutors.

Media

PowerLecture
ISBN-13: 978-1-133-36473-3
This comprehensive CD-ROM provides dynamic media tools designed to help you teach. PowerLecture includes Solution Builder, Diploma Computerized Testing, Microsoft® Powerpoint® lecture slides, and all art from the text.

Solution Builder
www.cengage.com/solutionbuilder
This online instructor database offers complete worked-out solutions of all exercises in the text. Solution Builder allows you to create customized, secure solutions printouts (in PDF format) matched exactly to the problems you assign in class.

Diploma Computerized Testing
Diploma is an easy-to-use assessment software containing hundreds of algorithmic questions derived from the text exercises. With Diploma, you can quickly create, customize, and deliver tests in both print and online formats. Diploma is available on the PowerLecture CD.

www.webassign.net
WebAssign's homework delivery system lets you deliver, collect, grade, and record assignments via the web. Enhanced WebAssign includes Cengage YouBook interactive eBook, Personal Study Plans, a Show My Work feature, Answer Evaluator, quizzes, videos, and more!

Cengage YouBook
YouBook is an interactive and customizable eBook! Containing all the content from the printed text, YouBook features a text edit tool that allows you to modify the textbook narrative as needed. With YouBook, you can quickly re-order entire sections and chapters or hide any content you don't teach to create an eBook that perfectly matches your syllabus. You can further customize the text by publishing web links. Additional media assets include: animated figures, video clips, highlighting, notes, and more! YouBook is available in Enhanced WebAssign.

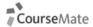

www.cengagebrain.com
Interested in a simple way to complement your text and course content with study and practice materials? CourseMate brings course concepts to life with interactive learning, study, and exam preparation tools that support the printed textbook. CourseMate includes Engagement Tracker, a first-of-its-kind tool that monitors student engagement. Watch student comprehension soar as your class works with both the printed text and text-specific website.

Student Resources

Print

Student Solutions Manual
ISBN-13: 978-1-133-11279-2

The *Student Solutions Manual* provides complete worked-out solutions to all odd-numbered exercises in the text. In addition, the solutions of all Checkpoint, Quiz Yourself, Test Yourself, and Tech Tutor exercises are included.

Media

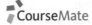

www.cengagebrain.com

Interested in a simple way to complement your text and course content with study and practice materials? CourseMate brings course concepts to life with interactive learning, study, and exam preparation tools that support the printed textbook. CourseMate includes: an interactive eBook, quizzes, flashcards, Excel guide, note-taking guide, videos, and more!

www.webassign.net

Enhanced WebAssign is an online homework system that lets instructors deliver, collect, grade, and record assignments via the web. Enhanced WebAssign includes Cengage YouBook interactive eBook, Personal Study Plans, a Show My Work feature, Answer Evaluator, quizzes, videos, and more! Be sure to check with your instructor to find out if Enhanced WebAssign is required for your course.

CengageBrain.com
To access additional course materials and companion resources, please visit *www.cengagebrain.com*. At the CengageBrain.com home page, search for the ISBN of your title (from the back cover of your book) using the search box at the top of the page. This will take you to the product page where free companion resources can be found.

Acknowledgements

I would like to thank my colleagues who have helped me develop this program. Their encouragement, criticisms, and suggestions have been invaluable to me.

Reviewers

Nasri Abdel-Aziz, *State University of New York College of Environmental Sciences and Forestry*

Alejandro Acuna, *Central New Mexico Community College*

Dona Boccio, *Queensborough Community College*

George Bradley, *Duquesne University*

Andrea Marchese, *Pace University*

Benselamonyuy Ntatin, *Austin Peay State University*

Maijian Qian, *California State University, Fullerton*

Judy Smalling, *St. Petersburg College*

Eddy Stringer, *Tallahassee Community College*

I would also like to thank the following reviewers, who have given me many useful insights to this and previous editions.

Carol Achs, *Mesa Community College;* Lateef Adelani, *Harris-Stowe State University, Saint Louis;* Frederick Adkins, *Indiana University of Pennsylvania;* Polly Amstutz, *University of Nebraska at Kearney;* George Anastassiou, *University of Memphis;* Judy Barclay, *Cuesta College;* Jean Michelle Benedict, *Augusta State University;* David Bregenzer, *Utah State University;* Ben Brink, *Wharton County Junior College;* Mary Chabot, *Mt. San Antonio College;* Jimmy Chang, *St. Petersburg College;* Joseph Chance, *University of Texas—Pan American;* John Chuchel, *University of California;* Derron Coles, *Oregon State University;* Miriam E. Connellan, *Marquette University;* William Conway, *University of Arizona;* Karabi Datta, *Northern Illinois University;* Keng Deng, *University of Louisiana at Lafayette;* Roger A. Engle, *Clarion University of Pennsylvania;* David French, *Tidewater Community College;* Randy Gallaher, *Lewis & Clark Community College;* Perry Gillespie, *Fayetteville State University;* Jose Gimenez, *Temple University;* Betty Givan, *Eastern Kentucky University;* Walter J. Gleason, *Bridgewater State College;* Shane Goodwin, *Brigham Young University of Idaho;* Mark Greenhalgh, *Fullerton College;* Harvey Greenwald, *California Polytechnic State University;* Karen Hay, *Mesa Community College;* Raymond Heitmann, *University of Texas at Austin;* Larry Hoehn, *Austin Peay State University;* William C. Huffman, *Loyola University of Chicago;* Arlene Jesky, *Rose State College;* Raja Khoury, *Collin County Community College;* Ronnie Khuri, *University of Florida;* Bernadette Kocyba, *J. Sergeant Reynolds Community College;* Duane Kouba, *University of California—Davis;* James A. Kurre, *The Pennsylvania State University;* Melvin Lax, *California State University—Long Beach;* Norbert Lerner, *State University of New York at Cortland;* Yuhlong Lio, *University of South Dakota;* Peter J. Livorsi, *Oakton Community College;* Ivan Loy, *Front Range Community College;* Peggy Luczak, *Camden County College;* Lewis D. Ludwig, *Denison University;* Samuel A. Lynch, *Southwest Missouri State University;* Augustine Maison, *Eastern Kentucky University;* Kevin McDonald, *Mt. San Antonio College;* Earl H. McKinney, *Ball State University;* Randall McNiece, *San Jacinto College;* Philip R. Montgomery, *University of Kansas;* John Nardo, *Oglethorpe University;* Mike Nasab, *Long Beach City College;* Karla Neal, *Louisiana State University;* James Osterburg, *University of Cincinnati;* Darla Ottman, *Elizabethtown Community & Technical College;* William Parzynski, *Montclair State University;* Scott Perkins, *Lake Sumter Community College;* Laurie Poe, *Santa Clara University;*

Adelaida Quesada, *Miami Dade College—Kendall;* Brooke P. Quinlan, *Hillsborough Community College;* David Ray, *University of Tennessee at Martin;* Rita Richards, *Scottsdale Community College;* Stephen B. Rodi, *Austin Community College;* Carol Rychly, *Augusta State University;* Yvonne Sandoval-Brown, *Pima Community College;* Richard Semmler, *Northern Virginia Community College— Annandale;* Bernard Shapiro, *University of Massachusetts—Lowell;* Mike Shirazi, *Germanna Community College;* Rick Simon, *University of La Verne;* Jane Y. Smith, *University of Florida;* Marvin Stick, *University of Massachusetts—Lowell;* DeWitt L. Sumners, *Florida State University;* Devki Talwar, *Indiana University of Pennsylvania;* Linda Taylor, *Northern Virginia Community College;* Stephen Tillman, *Wilkes University;* Jay Wiestling, *Palomar College;* Jonathan Wilkin, *Northern Virginia Community College;* Carol G. Williams, *Pepperdine University;* John Williams, *St. Petersburg College;* Ted Williamson, *Montclair State University;* Melvin R. Woodard, *Indiana University of Pennsylvania;* Carlton Woods, *Auburn University at Montgomery;* Jan E. Wynn, *Brigham Young University;* Robert A. Yawin, *Springfield Technical Community College;* Charles W. Zimmerman, *Robert Morris College*

My thanks to Robert Hostetler, The Pennsylvania State University, The Behrend College, Bruce Edwards, University of Florida, and David Heyd, The Pennsylvania State University, The Behrend College, for their significant contributions to previous editions of this text.

I would also like to thank the staff at Larson Texts, Inc. who assisted with proofreading the manuscript, preparing and proofreading the art package, and checking and typesetting the supplements.

On a personal level, I am grateful to my spouse, Deanna Gilbert Larson, for her love, patience, and support. Also, a special thanks goes to R. Scott O'Neil.

If you have suggestions for improving this text, please feel free to write to me. Over the past two decades I have received many useful comments from both instructors and students, and I value these comments very highly.

Ron Larson, Ph.D.
Professor of Mathematics
Penn State University
www.RonLarson.com

CALCULUS & YOU

Every feature in this text is designed to help you learn calculus. Whenever you see a red **U**, pay special attention to the study aid. These study aids represent years of experience in teaching students *just like you*.   Ron Larson

STUDY TIP

The expressions for $f(g(x))$ and $g(f(x))$ are different in Example 5. In general, the composite of f with g is not the same as the composite of g with f.

The *Study Tips* occur at point of use throughout the text. They represent **common questions** that students ask me, **insights** into understanding concepts, and **alternative ways to look at concepts**. For instance, the *Study Tip* at the left provides insight into the importance of order when working with composite functions.

TECH TUTOR

If you have access to a symbolic differentiation utility, try using it to confirm the derivatives shown in this section.

The *Tech Tutors* give suggestions on how you can use various types of technology to help understand the material. This includes **graphing calculators**, **computer graphing programs**, and **spreadsheet programs** such as Excel. For instance, the *Tech Tutor* at the left points out that some calculators and some computer programs are capable of symbolic differentiation.

ALGEBRA TUTOR xy

For help in evaluating the expressions in Example 2, see the review of order of operations on page 105.

Throughout years of teaching, I have found that the greatest stumbling block to success in calculus is a weakness in algebra. Each time you see an *Algebra Tutor*, please read it carefully. Then, flip ahead to the referenced page and give yourself a chance to enjoy a brief **algebra refresher**. It will be time well spent.

HOW DO YOU SEE IT?

The *How Do You See It?* question in each exercise set helps you **visually summarize concepts** without messy computations.

SUMMARIZE

The *Summarize* outline at the end of each section asks you to write each learning objective in **your own words**.

SKILLS WARM UP

The *Skills Warm Up* exercises that precede each exercise set will help you **review previously learned skills**.

SUMMARY AND STUDY STRATEGIES

The *Summary and Study Strategies,* coupled with the Review Exercises are designed to help you organize your thoughts as you **prepare for a chapter test**.

QUIZ YOURSELF

The *Quiz Yourself* occurs midway in each chapter. Take each of these quizzes as you would **take a quiz in class**.

TEST YOURSELF

The *Test Yourself* occurs at the end of each chapter. All questions are answered so you can **check your progress**.

Break-Even Analysis

Break-even point:
18,182 units

$C = 0.65x + 10,000$

Loss

Profit

$R = 1.2x$

Dollars

Number of units

Example 5 on page 15 shows how the point of intersection of two graphs can be used to find the break-even point for a company manufacturing and selling a product.

1 Functions, Graphs, and Limits

1.1 The Cartesian Plane and the Distance Formula

■ Plot points in a coordinate plane and represent data graphically.
■ Find the distance between two points in a coordinate plane.
■ Find the midpoint of a line segment connecting two points.
■ Translate points in a coordinate plane.

The Cartesian Plane

Just as you can represent real numbers by points on a real number line, you can represent ordered pairs of real numbers by points in a plane called the **rectangular coordinate system,** or the **Cartesian plane,** after the French mathematician René Descartes (1596–1650).

The Cartesian plane is formed by using two real number lines intersecting at right angles, as shown in Figure 1.1. The horizontal real number line is usually called the **x-axis,** and the vertical real number line is usually called the **y-axis.** The point of intersection of these two axes is the **origin,** and the two axes divide the plane into four parts called **quadrants.**

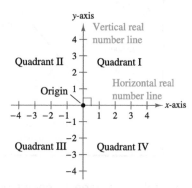

The Cartesian Plane

FIGURE 1.1

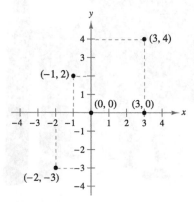

In Exercise 29 on page 9, you will use a line graph to estimate the Dow Jones Industrial Average.

Each point in the plane corresponds to an **ordered pair** (x, y) of real numbers x and y, called **coordinates** of the point. The **x-coordinate** represents the directed distance from the y-axis to the point, and the **y-coordinate** represents the directed distance from the x-axis to the point, as shown in Figure 1.2.

Directed distance from y-axis   Directed distance from x-axis

FIGURE 1.2

The notation (x, y) denotes both a point in the plane and an open interval on the real number line. The context will tell you which meaning is intended.

Example 1 **Plotting Points in the Cartesian Plane**

Plot the points

$$(-1, 2), \quad (3, 4), \quad (0, 0), \quad (3, 0), \quad \text{and} \quad (-2, -3).$$

SOLUTION To plot the point

$$(-1, 2)$$

x-coordinate ———⌐ ⌐——— y-coordinate

imagine a vertical line through -1 on the x-axis and a horizontal line through 2 on the y-axis. The intersection of these two lines is the point $(-1, 2)$. The other four points can be plotted in a similar way and are shown in Figure 1.3.

✓ **Checkpoint 1**

Plot the points

$$(-3, 2), \quad (4, -2), \quad (3, 1), \quad (0, -2), \quad \text{and} \quad (-1, -2).$$

FIGURE 1.3

Using a rectangular coordinate system allows you to visualize relationships between two variables. In Example 2, data is represented graphically by points plotted in a rectangular coordinate system. This type of graph is called a **scatter plot.**

Example 2   Sketching a Scatter Plot

The numbers E (in millions of people) of private-sector employees in the United States from 2000 through 2009 are shown in the table, where t represents the year. Sketch a scatter plot of the data.   *(Source: U.S. Bureau of Labor Statistics)*

t	2000	2001	2002	2003	2004	2005	2006	2007	2008	2009
E	111	111	109	108	110	112	114	115	114	108

STUDY TIP

In Example 2, $t = 1$ could have been used to represent the year 2000. In that case, the horizontal axis would not have been broken, and the tick marks would have been labeled 1 through 10 (instead of 2000 through 2009).

SOLUTION   To sketch a scatter plot of the data given in the table, you simply represent each pair of values by an ordered pair

$$(t, E)$$

and plot the resulting points, as shown in Figure 1.4. For instance, the first pair of values is represented by the ordered pair

$$(2000, 111).$$

Note that the break in the t-axis indicates that the numbers between 0 and 2000 have been omitted.

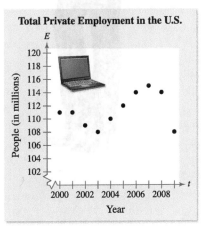

FIGURE 1.4

✓ Checkpoint 2

The numbers E (in thousands of people) of federal employees in the United States from 2000 through 2009 are shown in the table, where t represents the year. Sketch a scatter plot of the data.   *(Source: U.S. Bureau of Labor Statistics)*

t	2000	2001	2002	2003	2004	2005	2006	2007	2008	2009
E	2865	2764	2766	2761	2730	2732	2732	2734	2762	2828

The scatter plot in Example 2 is one way to represent the given data graphically. Another technique, a *bar graph*, is shown in Figure 1.5. Both graphical representations were created with a computer. If you have access to computer graphing software, try using it to represent graphically the data given in Example 2.

Another way to represent data is with a *line graph* (see Exercise 29).

FIGURE 1.5

The Distance Formula

Recall from the Pythagorean Theorem that, for a right triangle with hypotenuse of length c and sides of lengths a and b, you have

$$a^2 + b^2 = c^2 \qquad \text{Pythagorean Theorem}$$

as shown in Figure 1.6. Note that the converse is also true. That is, if $a^2 + b^2 = c^2$, then the triangle is a right triangle.

Suppose you want to determine the distance d between two points

$$(x_1, y_1) \quad \text{and} \quad (x_2, y_2)$$

in the plane. With these two points, a right triangle can be formed, as shown in Figure 1.7. The length of the vertical side of the triangle is

$$|y_2 - y_1|$$

and the length of the horizontal side is

$$|x_2 - x_1|.$$

By the Pythagorean Theorem, you can write

$$d^2 = |x_2 - x_1|^2 + |y_2 - y_1|^2$$
$$d = \sqrt{|x_2 - x_1|^2 + |y_2 - y_1|^2}$$
$$d = \sqrt{(x_2 - x_1)^2 + (y_2 - y_1)^2}.$$

This result is the **Distance Formula.**

Pythagorean Theorem
FIGURE 1.6

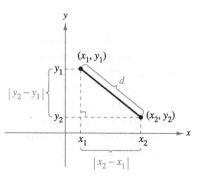

Distance Between Two Points
FIGURE 1.7

The Distance Formula

The distance d between the points (x_1, y_1) and (x_2, y_2) in the plane is

$$d = \sqrt{(x_2 - x_1)^2 + (y_2 - y_1)^2}.$$

Example 3 Finding a Distance

Find the distance between the points $(-2, 1)$ and $(3, 4)$.

SOLUTION Let $(x_1, y_1) = (-2, 1)$ and $(x_2, y_2) = (3, 4)$. Then apply the Distance Formula as shown.

$$\begin{aligned}
d &= \sqrt{(x_2 - x_1)^2 + (y_2 - y_1)^2} && \text{Distance Formula} \\
&= \sqrt{[3 - (-2)]^2 + (4 - 1)^2} && \text{Substitute for } x_1, y_1, x_2, \text{ and } y_2. \\
&= \sqrt{(5)^2 + (3)^2} && \text{Simplify.} \\
&= \sqrt{34} \\
&\approx 5.83 && \text{Use a calculator.}
\end{aligned}$$

So, the distance between the points is about 5.83 units. Note in Figure 1.8 that a distance of 5.83 looks about right.

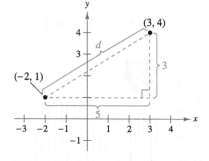

FIGURE 1.8

✓ Checkpoint 3

Find the distance between the points $(-2, 1)$ and $(2, 4)$.

Example 4 Verifying a Right Triangle

Use the Distance Formula to show that the points

$$(2, 1), \quad (4, 0), \quad \text{and} \quad (5, 7)$$

are vertices of a right triangle.

SOLUTION The three points are plotted in Figure 1.9. Using the Distance Formula, you can find the lengths of the three sides as shown below.

$$d_1 = \sqrt{(5 - 2)^2 + (7 - 1)^2} = \sqrt{9 + 36} = \sqrt{45}$$
$$d_2 = \sqrt{(4 - 2)^2 + (0 - 1)^2} = \sqrt{4 + 1} = \sqrt{5}$$
$$d_3 = \sqrt{(5 - 4)^2 + (7 - 0)^2} = \sqrt{1 + 49} = \sqrt{50}$$

Because

$$d_1^2 + d_2^2 = 45 + 5 = 50 = d_3^2$$

you can apply the converse of the Pythagorean Theorem to conclude that the triangle must be a right triangle.

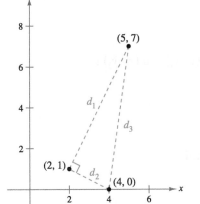

FIGURE 1.9

✓ **Checkpoint 4**

Use the Distance Formula to show that the points $(2, -1)$, $(5, 5)$, and $(6, -3)$ are vertices of a right triangle.

The figures provided with Examples 3 and 4 were not really essential to the solution. *Nevertheless*, it is strongly recommended that you develop the habit of including sketches with your solutions—even when they are not required.

Example 5 Finding the Length of a Pass

In a football game, a quarterback throws a pass from the 5-yard line, 20 yards from one sideline. The pass is caught by a wide receiver on the 45-yard line, 50 yards from the same sideline, as shown in Figure 1.10. How long was the pass?

SOLUTION You can find the length of the pass by finding the distance between the points $(20, 5)$ and $(50, 45)$.

$$d = \sqrt{(50 - 20)^2 + (45 - 5)^2} \qquad \text{Distance Formula}$$
$$= \sqrt{900 + 1600}$$
$$= 50 \qquad \text{Simplify.}$$

So, the pass was 50 yards long.

FIGURE 1.10

✓ **Checkpoint 5**

A quarterback throws a pass from the 10-yard line, 10 yards from one sideline. The pass is caught by a wide receiver on the 30-yard line, 25 yards from the same sideline. How long was the pass?

STUDY TIP

In Example 5, the scale along the goal line showing distance from the sideline does not normally appear on a football field. However, when you use coordinate geometry to solve real-life problems, you are free to place the coordinate system in any way that is convenient to the solution of the problem.

The Midpoint Formula

To find the **midpoint** of the line segment that joins two points in a coordinate plane, you can simply find the average values of the respective coordinates of the two endpoints.

The Midpoint Formula

The midpoint of the segment joining the points (x_1, y_1) and (x_2, y_2) is

$$\text{Midpoint} = \left(\frac{x_1 + x_2}{2}, \frac{y_1 + y_2}{2}\right).$$

Example 6   **Finding a Segment's Midpoint**

Find the midpoint of the line segment joining the points

$$(-5, -3) \quad \text{and} \quad (9, 3)$$

as shown in Figure 1.11.

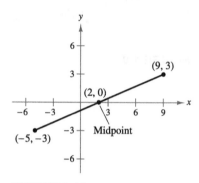

FIGURE 1.11

SOLUTION   Let $(x_1, y_1) = (-5, -3)$ and $(x_2, y_2) = (9, 3)$.

$$\text{Midpoint} = \left(\frac{x_1 + x_2}{2}, \frac{y_1 + y_2}{2}\right) = \left(\frac{-5 + 9}{2}, \frac{-3 + 3}{2}\right) = (2, 0)$$

✓**Checkpoint 6**

Find the midpoint of the line segment joining the points $(-6, 2)$ and $(2, 8)$.

Example 7   **Estimating Annual Sales**

Ford Motor Company had annual sales of about \$154 billion in 2007 and about \$106 billion in 2009. Without knowing any additional information, what would you estimate the 2008 annual sales to have been?   *(Source: Ford Motor Co.)*

SOLUTION   One solution to the problem is to assume that sales followed a linear pattern. Then you can estimate the 2008 sales by finding the midpoint of the segment connecting the points (2007, 154) and (2009, 106).

$$\text{Midpoint} = \left(\frac{2007 + 2009}{2}, \frac{154 + 106}{2}\right) = (2008, 130)$$

So, you would estimate the 2008 sales to have been \$130 billion, as shown in Figure 1.12. (The actual 2008 sales were \$129 billion.)

FIGURE 1.12

✓**Checkpoint 7**

CVS Caremark Corporation had annual sales of about \$76 billion in 2007 and about \$99 billion in 2009. What would you estimate the 2008 annual sales to have been?   *(Source: CVS Caremark Corp.)*

Translating Points in the Plane

Much of computer graphics consists of transformations of points in a coordinate plane. One type of transformation, a translation, is illustrated in Example 8. Other types of transformations include reflections, rotations, and stretches.

Example 8 Translating Points in the Plane

Figure 1.13(a) shows the vertices of a parallelogram. Find the vertices of the parallelogram after it has been translated four units to the right and two units down.

SOLUTION   To translate each vertex four units to the right, add 4 to each x-coordinate. To translate each vertex two units down, subtract 2 from each y-coordinate.

Original Point	*Translated Point*
$(1, 0)$	$(1 + 4, 0 - 2) = (5, -2)$
$(3, 2)$	$(3 + 4, 2 - 2) = (7, 0)$
$(3, 6)$	$(3 + 4, 6 - 2) = (7, 4)$
$(1, 4)$	$(1 + 4, 4 - 2) = (5, 2)$

The translated parallelogram is shown in Figure 1.13(b).

(a)   (b)

FIGURE 1.13

✓ **Checkpoint 8**

Find the vertices of the parallelogram in Example 8 after it has been translated two units to the left and four units down.

Many movies now use extensive computer graphics, much of which consists of transformations of points in two- and three-dimensional space. The photo above shows a character from *Avatar*. The movie's animators used computer graphics to design the scenery, characters, motion, and even the lighting throughout much of the film.

SUMMARIZE   (Section 1.1)

1. Describe the Cartesian plane *(page 2)*. For examples of plotting points in the Cartesian plane, see Examples 1 and 2.

2. State the Distance Formula *(page 4)*. For examples of using the Distance Formula to find the distance between two points, see Examples 3, 4, and 5.

3. State the Midpoint Formula *(page 6)*. For examples of using the Midpoint Formula to find the midpoint of a line segment, see Examples 6 and 7.

4. Describe how to translate points in the Cartesian plane *(page 7)*. For an example of translating points in the Cartesian plane, see Example 8.

In Exercises 1–6, simplify the expression.

1. $\sqrt{(3-6)^2 + [1-(-5)]^2}$

2. $\sqrt{(-2-0)^2 + [-7-(-3)]^2}$

3. $\dfrac{5+(-4)}{2}$

4. $\dfrac{-3+(-1)}{2}$

5. $\sqrt{27} + \sqrt{12}$

6. $\sqrt{8} - \sqrt{18}$

In Exercises 7–10, solve for x or y.

7. $\sqrt{(3-x)^2 + (7-4)^2} = \sqrt{45}$

8. $\sqrt{(6-2)^2 + (-2-y)^2} = \sqrt{52}$

9. $\dfrac{x+(-5)}{2} = 7$

10. $\dfrac{-7+y}{2} = -3$

Exercises 1.1

See www.CalcChat.com for worked-out solutions to odd-numbered exercises.

Plotting Points in the Cartesian Plane   In Exercises 1 and 2, plot the points in the Cartesian plane. *See Example 1.*

1. $(-5, 3)$, $(1, -1)$, $(-2, -4)$, $(2, 0)$, $(1, -6)$

2. $(0, -4)$, $(5, 1)$, $(-3, 5)$, $(2, -2)$, $(-6, -1)$

Finding a Distance and a Segment's Midpoint   In Exercises 3–12, (a) plot the points, (b) find the distance between the points, and (c) find the midpoint of the line segment joining the points. *See Examples 1, 3, and 6.*

3. $(3, 1)$, $(5, 5)$

4. $(-3, 2)$, $(3, -2)$

5. $\left(\frac{1}{2}, 1\right)$, $\left(-\frac{3}{2}, -5\right)$

6. $\left(\frac{2}{3}, -\frac{1}{3}\right)$, $\left(\frac{5}{6}, 1\right)$

7. $(2, 2)$, $(4, 14)$

8. $(-3, 7)$, $(1, -1)$

9. $(-5, -2)$, $(7, 3)$

10. $(2, -12)$, $(8, -4)$

11. $(0, -4.8)$, $(0.5, 6)$

12. $(5.2, 6.4)$, $(-2.7, 1.8)$

Verifying a Right Triangle   In Exercises 13–16, (a) find the length of each side of the right triangle and (b) show that these lengths satisfy the Pythagorean Theorem. *See Example 4.*

13.

14.

15.

16.

Verifying Figures   In Exercises 17–20, show that the points form the vertices of the given figure. (A rhombus is a quadrilateral whose sides have the same length.)

Vertices	Figure
17. $(0, 1)$, $(3, 7)$, $(4, -1)$	Right triangle
18. $(1, -3)$, $(3, 2)$, $(-2, 4)$	Isosceles triangle
19. $(0, 0)$, $(1, 2)$, $(2, 1)$, $(3, 3)$	Rhombus
20. $(0, 1)$, $(3, 7)$, $(4, 4)$, $(1, -2)$	Parallelogram

Finding Values   In Exercises 21 and 22, find the value(s) of x such that the distance between the points is 5.

21. $(1, 0)$, $(x, -4)$

22. $(2, -1)$, $(x, 2)$

Finding Values   In Exercises 23 and 24, find the value(s) of y such that the distance between the points is 8.

23. $(0, 0)$, $(3, y)$

24. $(5, 1)$, $(5, y)$

25. Sports A soccer player passes the ball from a point that is 18 yards from an endline and 12 yards from a sideline. The pass is received by a teammate who is 42 yards from the same endline and 50 yards from the same sideline, as shown in the figure. How long is the pass?

26. Sports The first soccer player in Exercise 25 passes the ball to another teammate who is 37 yards from the same endline and 33 yards from the same sideline. How long is the pass?

 Graphing Data In Exercises 27 and 28, use a graphing utility to graph a scatter plot, a bar graph, and a line graph to represent the data. Describe any trends that appear.

27. Consumer Trends The numbers (in millions) of cable high-speed Internet customers in the United States for 2000 through 2009 are shown in the table. *(Source: National Cable & Telecommunications Association)*

Year	2000	2001	2002	2003	2004
Customers	4.0	7.3	11.6	16.5	21.0

Year	2005	2006	2007	2008	2009
Customers	25.4	28.9	35.7	39.3	41.8

28. Consumer Trends The numbers (in millions) of cellular telephone subscribers in the United States for 2000 through 2009 are shown in the table. *(Source: CTIA-The Wireless Association)*

Year	2000	2001	2002	2003	2004
Subscribers	109.5	128.4	140.8	158.7	182.1

Year	2005	2006	2007	2008	2009
Subscribers	207.9	233.0	255.4	270.3	285.6

29. Dow Jones Industrial Average The graph shows the Dow Jones Industrial Average for common stocks. *(Source: Dow Jones, Inc.)*

(a) Estimate the Dow Jones Industrial Average for March 2009, July 2009, and July 2010.

(b) Estimate the percent increase or decrease in the Dow Jones Industrial Average from April 2010 to May 2010.

30. Home Sales The graph shows the median sales prices (in thousands of dollars) of existing one-family homes sold in the United States from 1994 through 2009. *(Source: National Association of Realtors)*

(a) Estimate the median sales prices of existing one-family homes for 1996, 2003, and 2008.

(b) Estimate the percent increase or decrease in the median value of existing one-family homes from 2001 to 2002.

The symbol indicates an exercise in which you are instructed to use graphing technology or a symbolic computer algebra system. The solutions of other exercises may also be facilitated by use of appropriate technology.

31. Revenue and Profit The revenues and profits of Buffalo Wild Wings for 2007 and 2009 are shown in the table. (a) Use the Midpoint Formula to estimate the revenue and profit in 2008. (b) Then use your school's library, the Internet, or some other reference source to find the actual revenue and profit for 2008. (c) Did the revenue and profit increase in a linear pattern from 2007 to 2009? Explain your reasoning. (d) What were the expenses during each of the given years? (e) How would you rate the growth of Buffalo Wild Wings from 2007 to 2009? *(Source: Buffalo Wild Wings, Inc.)*

Year	2007	2008	2009
Revenue (millions of $)	329.7		538.9
Profit (millions of $)	19.7		30.7

32. Revenue and Profit The revenues and profits of Cablevision Systems Corporation for 2007 and 2009 are shown in the table. (a) Use the Midpoint Formula to estimate the revenue and profit in 2008. (b) Then use your school's library, the Internet, or some other reference source to find the actual revenue and profit for 2008. (c) Did the revenue and profit increase in a linear pattern from 2007 to 2009? Explain your reasoning. (d) What were the expenses during each of the given years? (e) How would you rate the growth of Cablevision Systems Corporation from 2007 to 2009? *(Source: Cablevision Systems Corporation)*

Year	2007	2008	2009
Revenue (millions of $)	6484.5		7773.3
Profit (millions of $)	23.7		285.6

33. Economics The table shows the numbers of ear infections treated by doctors at HMO clinics of three different sizes: small, medium, and large.

Number of doctors	0	1	2	3	4
Cases per small clinic	0	20	28	35	40
Cases per medium clinic	0	30	42	53	60
Cases per large clinic	0	35	49	62	70

(a) On the same coordinate plane, show the relationship between doctors and treated ear infections using *three* line graphs, where the number of doctors is on the horizontal axis and the number of ear infections treated is on the vertical axis.

(b) Compare the three relationships.

(Source: Adapted from Taylor, Economics, Fifth Edition)

34. **HOW DO YOU SEE IT?** The scatter plot shows the numbers of pickup trucks sold in a city from 2006 to 2011.

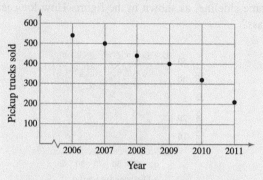

(a) In what year were 500 pickup trucks sold?

(b) About how many pickup trucks were sold in 2007?

(c) Describe the pattern shown by the data.

Translating Points in the Plane In Exercises 35 and 36, use the translation and the graph to find the vertices of the figure after it has been translated. *See Example 8.*

35. 3 units left and 5 units down

36. 2 units right and 4 units up

37. Using the Midpoint Formula Use the Midpoint Formula repeatedly to find the three points that divide the segment joining (x_1, y_1) and (x_2, y_2) into four equal parts.

38. Using the Midpoint Formula Use Exercise 37 to find the points that divide the line segment joining the given points into four equal parts.

(a) $(1, -2), (4, -1)$ (b) $(-2, -3), (0, 0)$

39. Using the Midpoint Formula Show that $\left(\frac{1}{3}[2x_1 + x_2], \frac{1}{3}[2y_1 + y_2]\right)$ is one of the points of trisection of the line segment joining (x_1, y_1) and (x_2, y_2). Then, find the second point of trisection by finding the midpoint of the segment joining

$$\left(\frac{1}{3}[2x_1 + x_2], \frac{1}{3}[2y_1 + y_2]\right) \quad \text{and} \quad (x_2, y_2).$$

40. Using the Midpoint Formula Use Exercise 39 to find the points of trisection of the line segment joining the given points.

(a) $(1, -2), (4, 1)$ (b) $(-2, -3), (0, 0)$

1.2 Graphs of Equations

In Exercise 62 on page 21, you will use a mathematical model to analyze the number of lung transplants in the United States.

■ Sketch graphs of equations by hand.
■ Find the *x*- and *y*-intercepts of graphs of equations.
■ Write the standard forms of equations of circles.
■ Find the points of intersection of two graphs.
■ Use mathematical models to model and solve real-life problems.

The Graph of an Equation

In Section 1.1, you used a coordinate system to represent graphically the relationship between two quantities. There, the graphical picture consisted of a collection of points in a coordinate plane (see Example 2 in Section 1.1).

Frequently, a relationship between two quantities is expressed as an equation. For instance, degrees on the Fahrenheit scale are related to degrees on the Celsius scale by the equation

$$F = \frac{9}{5}C + 32.$$

In this section, you will study some basic procedures for sketching the graphs of such equations. The **graph** of an equation is the set of all points that are solutions of the equation.

> ### Example 1   Sketching the Graph of an Equation
>
> Sketch the graph of $y = 7 - 3x$.
>
> **SOLUTION**   The simplest way to sketch the graph of an equation is the *point-plotting method*. With this method, you construct a table of values that consists of several solution points of the equation, as shown in the table below. For instance, when $x = 0$,
>
> $$y = 7 - 3(0) = 7$$
>
> which implies that $(0, 7)$ is a solution point of the equation.
>
> | x | 0 | 1 | 2 | 3 | 4 |
> |---|---|---|---|---|---|
> | $y = 7 - 3x$ | 7 | 4 | 1 | -2 | -5 |
>
> From the table, it follows that $(0, 7)$, $(1, 4)$, $(2, 1)$, $(3, -2)$, and $(4, -5)$ are solution points of the equation. After plotting these points, you can see that they appear to lie on a line, as shown in Figure 1.14. The graph of the equation is the line that passes through the five plotted points.

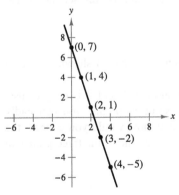

Solution Points for $y = 7 - 3x$
FIGURE 1.14

✓ **Checkpoint 1**

Sketch the graph of $y = 2x - 1$.

> **STUDY TIP**
>
> Even though the sketch shown in Figure 1.14 is referred to as the graph of $y = 7 - 3x$, it actually represents only a *portion* of the graph. The entire graph is a line that would extend off the page.

TECH TUTOR

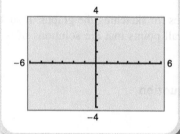

On most graphing utilities, the display screen is two thirds as high as it is wide. On such screens, you can obtain a graph with a true geometric perspective by using a *square setting*—one in which

$$\frac{\text{Ymax} - \text{Ymin}}{\text{Xmax} - \text{Xmin}} = \frac{2}{3}.$$

One such setting is shown below. Notice that the x and y tick marks are equally spaced on a square setting, but not on a *standard setting*.

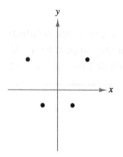

Example 2   **Sketching the Graph of an Equation**

Sketch the graph of $y = x^2 - 2$.

SOLUTION   Begin by constructing a table of values, as shown below.

x	-2	-1	0	1	2	3
$y = x^2 - 2$	2	-1	-2	-1	2	7

Next, plot the points given in the table, as shown in Figure 1.15(a). Finally, connect the points with a smooth curve, as shown in Figure 1.15(b).

(a)   (b)

FIGURE 1.15

✓ **Checkpoint 2**

Sketch the graph of $y = x^2 - 4$.

The graph shown in Example 2 is a **parabola.** The graph of any second-degree equation of the form

$$y = ax^2 + bx + c, \quad a \neq 0$$

has a similar shape. If $a > 0$, then the parabola opens upward, as shown in Figure 1.15(b), and if $a < 0$, then the parabola opens downward.

The point-plotting technique demonstrated in Examples 1 and 2 is easy to use, but it does have some shortcomings. With too few solution points, you can badly misrepresent the graph of a given equation. For instance, how would you connect the four points in Figure 1.16? Without further information, any one of the three graphs in Figure 1.17 would be reasonable.

FIGURE 1.16

FIGURE 1.17

Intercepts of a Graph

Some solution points have zero as either the *x*-coordinate or the *y*-coordinate. These points are called **intercepts** because they are the points at which the graph intersects the *x*- or *y*-axis.

Some texts denote the *x*-intercept as the *x*-coordinate of the point

$$(a, 0)$$

rather than the point itself. Unless it is necessary to make a distinction, when the term *intercept* is used in this text, it will mean either the point or the coordinate.

A graph may have no intercepts or several intercepts, as shown in Figure 1.18.

No *x*-intercept
One *y*-intercept

Three *x*-intercepts
One *y*-intercept

One *x*-intercept
Two *y*-intercepts

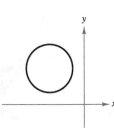

No intercepts

FIGURE 1.18

Finding Intercepts

1. To find **x-intercepts,** let *y* be zero and solve the equation for *x*.

2. To find **y-intercepts,** let *x* be zero and solve the equation for *y*.

Example 3 **Finding x- and y-Intercepts**

Find the *x*- and *y*-intercepts of the graph of $y = x^3 - 4x$.

SOLUTION To find the *x*-intercepts, let *y* be zero and solve for *x*.

$$x^3 - 4x = 0 \qquad \text{Let } y \text{ be zero.}$$
$$x(x^2 - 4) = 0 \qquad \text{Factor out common monomial factor.}$$
$$x(x + 2)(x - 2) = 0 \qquad \text{Factor.}$$
$$x = 0, -2, \text{ or } 2 \qquad \text{Solve for } x.$$

Because this equation has three solutions, you can conclude that the graph has three *x*-intercepts:

$$(0, 0), \quad (-2, 0), \quad \text{and} \quad (2, 0). \qquad \text{x-intercepts}$$

To find the *y*-intercepts, let *x* be zero and solve for *y*. Doing this produces

$$y = x^3 - 4x = 0^3 - 4(0) = 0.$$

This equation has only one solution, so the graph has one *y*-intercept:

$$(0, 0). \qquad \text{y-intercept}$$

(See Figure 1.19.)

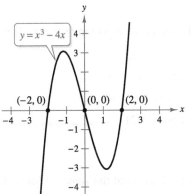

FIGURE 1.19

✓ Checkpoint 3

Find the *x*- and *y*-intercepts of the graph of $y = x^2 - 2x - 3$.

Circles

Throughout this course, you will learn to recognize several types of graphs from their equations. For instance, you should recognize that the graph of a second-degree equation of the form

$$y = ax^2 + bx + c, \quad a \neq 0$$

is a parabola (see Example 2). Another easily recognized graph is that of a **circle.**

Consider the circle shown in Figure 1.20. A point (x, y) is on the circle if and only if its distance from the center (h, k) is r. By the Distance Formula,

$$\sqrt{(x - h)^2 + (y - k)^2} = r.$$

By squaring both sides of this equation, you obtain the **standard form of the equation of a circle.**

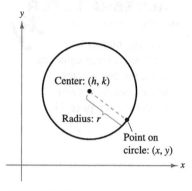

FIGURE 1.20

Standard Form of the Equation of a Circle

The **standard form of the equation of a circle** is

$$(x - h)^2 + (y - k)^2 = r^2. \qquad \text{Center at } (h, k)$$

The point (h, k) is the **center** of the circle, and the positive number r is the **radius** of the circle. The standard form of the equation of a circle whose center is the origin, $(h, k) = (0, 0)$, is

$$x^2 + y^2 = r^2. \qquad \text{Center at } (0, 0)$$

Example 4   **Finding the Equation of a Circle**

The point $(3, 4)$ lies on a circle whose center is at $(-1, 2)$. Find the standard form of the equation of this circle and sketch its graph.

SOLUTION   The radius of the circle is the distance between $(-1, 2)$ and $(3, 4)$.

$$
\begin{aligned}
r &= \sqrt{[3 - (-1)]^2 + (4 - 2)^2} & \text{Distance Formula} \\
&= \sqrt{(4)^2 + (2)^2} & \text{Simplify.} \\
&= \sqrt{16 + 4} & \text{Simplify.} \\
&= \sqrt{20} & \text{Radius}
\end{aligned}
$$

Using $(h, k) = (-1, 2)$ and $r = \sqrt{20}$, the standard form of the equation of the circle is

$$
\begin{aligned}
(x - h)^2 + (y - k)^2 &= r^2 & \text{Equation of a circle} \\
[x - (-1)]^2 + (y - 2)^2 &= \left(\sqrt{20}\right)^2 & \text{Substitute for } h, k, \text{ and } r. \\
(x + 1)^2 + (y - 2)^2 &= 20. & \text{Write in standard form.}
\end{aligned}
$$

The graph of the equation of the circle is shown in Figure 1.21. ▬▬▬

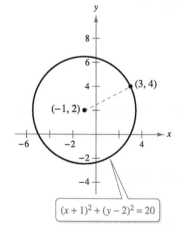

$$(x + 1)^2 + (y - 2)^2 = 20$$

FIGURE 1.21

✓ Checkpoint 4

The point $(1, 5)$ lies on a circle whose center is at $(-2, 1)$. Find the standard form of the equation of this circle and sketch its graph.

Points of Intersection

An ordered pair that is a solution of two different equations is called a **point of intersection** of the graphs of the two equations. For instance, Figure 1.22 shows that the graphs of

$$y = x^2 - 3 \quad \text{and} \quad y = x - 1$$

have two points of intersection: $(2, 1)$ and $(-1, -2)$. To find the points analytically, set the two y-values equal to each other and solve the equation

$$x^2 - 3 = x - 1$$

for x.

FIGURE 1.22

A common business application that involves points of intersection is **break-even analysis.** The marketing of a new product typically requires an initial investment. When sufficient units have been sold so that the total revenue has offset the total cost, the sale of the product has reached the **break-even point.** The **total cost** of producing x units of a product is denoted by C, and the **total revenue** from the sale of x units of the product is denoted by R. So, you can find the break-even point by setting the cost C equal to the revenue R and solving for x. In other words, the break-even point corresponds to the point of intersection of the cost and revenue graphs.

Example 5   Finding a Break-Even Point

A company manufactures a product at a cost of $0.65 per unit and sells the product for $1.20 per unit. The company's initial investment to produce the product was $10,000. Will the company break even when it sells 18,000 units? How many units must the company sell to break even?

SOLUTION   The total cost of producing x units of the product is given by

$$C = 0.65x + 10,000. \qquad \text{Cost equation}$$

The total revenue from the sale of x units is given by

$$R = 1.2x. \qquad \text{Revenue equation}$$

To find the break-even point, set the cost equal to the revenue and solve for x.

$$
\begin{aligned}
R &= C & \text{Set revenue equal to cost.} \\
1.2x &= 0.65x + 10,000 & \text{Substitute for } R \text{ and } C. \\
0.55x &= 10,000 & \text{Subtract } 0.65x \text{ from each side.} \\
x &= \frac{10,000}{0.55} & \text{Divide each side by 0.55.} \\
x &\approx 18,182 & \text{Use a calculator.}
\end{aligned}
$$

So, the company will not break even when it sells 18,000 units. The company must sell 18,182 units before it breaks even. This result is shown graphically in Figure 1.23. Note in Figure 1.23 that sales less than 18,182 units correspond to a loss for the company ($R < C$), whereas sales greater than 18,182 units correspond to a profit for the company ($R > C$).

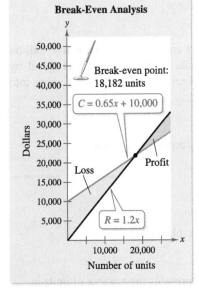

FIGURE 1.23

✓ **Checkpoint 5**

How many units must the company in Example 5 sell to break even when the selling price is $1.45 per unit?

Supply Curve
FIGURE 1.24

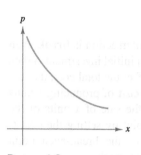

Demand Curve
FIGURE 1.25

Two types of equations that economists use to analyze a market are supply and demand equations. A **supply equation** shows the relationship between the unit price p of a product and the quantity supplied x. The graph of a supply equation is called a **supply curve.** (See Figure 1.24.) A typical supply curve rises because producers of a product want to sell more units when the unit price is higher.

A **demand equation** shows the relationship between the unit price p of a product and the quantity demanded x. The graph of a demand equation is called a **demand curve.** (See Figure 1.25.) A typical demand curve tends to show a decrease in the quantity demanded with each increase in price.

In an ideal situation, with no other factors present to influence the market, the production level should stabilize at the point of intersection of the graphs of the supply and demand equations. This point is called the **equilibrium point.** The x-coordinate of the equilibrium point is called the **equilibrium quantity** and the p-coordinate is called the **equilibrium price.** (See Figure 1.26.) You can find the equilibrium point by setting the demand equation equal to the supply equation and solving for x.

Equilibrium Point
FIGURE 1.26

Example 6   Finding the Equilibrium Point

The demand and supply equations for an e-book reader are given by

$$p = 195 - 5.8x \qquad \text{Demand equation}$$
$$p = 150 + 3.2x \qquad \text{Supply equation}$$

where p is the price in dollars and x represents the number of units in millions. Find the equilibrium point for this market.

SOLUTION   Begin by setting the demand equation equal to the supply equation.

$$195 - 5.8x = 150 + 3.2x \qquad \text{Set equations equal to each other.}$$
$$45 - 5.8x = 3.2x \qquad \text{Subtract 150 from each side.}$$
$$45 = 9x \qquad \text{Add } 5.8x \text{ to each side.}$$
$$5 = x \qquad \text{Divide each side by 9.}$$

So, the equilibrium point occurs when the demand and supply are each five million units. (See Figure 1.27.) The price that corresponds to this x-value is obtained by substituting $x = 5$ into either of the original equations. For instance, substituting into the demand equation produces

$$p = 195 - 5.8(5) = 195 - 29 = \$166.$$

Note that when you substitute $x = 5$ into the supply equation, you obtain

$$p = 150 + 3.2(5) = 150 + 16 = \$166.$$

Equilibrium Point

Price per unit (in dollars)

(5, 166) Supply

Demand

Number of units (in millions)

FIGURE 1.27

✓Checkpoint 6

The demand and supply equations for a Blu-ray disc player are

$$p = 136 - 3.5x \quad \text{and} \quad p = 112 + 2.5x$$

respectively, where p is the price in dollars and x represents the number of units in millions. Find the equilibrium point for this market.

Mathematical Models

In this text, you will see many examples of the use of equations as **mathematical models** of real-life phenomena. In developing a mathematical model to represent actual data, you should strive for two (often conflicting) goals—accuracy and simplicity.

 Example 7 **Using Mathematical Models**

The table shows the annual sales (in millions of dollars) for Dollar Tree and 99 Cents Only Stores from 2005 through 2009. In 2009, the publication *Value Line* listed the projected 2010 sales for the companies as $5770 million and $1430 million, respectively. How do you think these projections were obtained? *(Source: Dollar Tree, Inc. and 99 Cents Only Stores)*

Year	2005	2006	2007	2008	2009
t	5	6	7	8	9
Dollar Tree	3393.9	3969.4	4242.6	4644.9	5231.2
99 Cents Only Stores	1023.6	1104.7	1199.4	1302.9	1355.2

SOLUTION   The projections were obtained by using past sales to predict future sales. The past sales were modeled by equations that were found by a statistical procedure called least squares regression analysis. The models for the two companies are

$$S = 10.764t^2 + 284.31t + 1757.3, \quad 5 \le t \le 9 \qquad \text{Dollar Tree}$$

and

$$S = -3.486t^2 + 134.94t + 430.4, \quad 5 \le t \le 9. \qquad \text{99 Cents Only Stores}$$

Using $t = 10$ to represent 2010, you can predict the 2010 sales to be

$$S = 10.764(10)^2 + 284.31(10) + 1757.3 \approx 5676.8 \qquad \text{Dollar Tree}$$

and

$$S = -3.486(10)^2 + 134.94(10) + 430.4 \approx 1431.2. \qquad \text{99 Cents Only Stores}$$

These two projections are close to those projected by *Value Line*. The graphs of the two models are shown in Figure 1.28.

✓ Checkpoint 7

The table shows the annual revenues (in millions of dollars) for BJ's Wholesale Club from 2005 through 2009. In 2009, the publication *Value Line* listed the projected 2010 revenues for BJ's Wholesale Club as $11,150 million. How does this projection compare with the projection obtained using the model below? *(Source: BJ's Wholesale Club, Inc.)*

$$S = -17.393t^2 + 845.59t + 4097.7, \quad 5 \le t \le 9$$

Year	2005	2006	2007	2008	2009
t	5	6	7	8	9
Revenues	7949.9	8480.3	9005.0	10,027.0	10,187.0

To test the accuracy of a model, you can compare the actual data with the values given by the model. Try doing this for each model in Example 7.

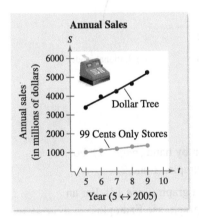

Annual Sales

FIGURE 1.28

ALGEBRA TUTOR
xy

For help in evaluating the expressions in Example 7, see the review of order of operations on page 70.

Much of your study of calculus will center around the behavior of the graphs of mathematical models. Figure 1.29 shows the graphs of six basic algebraic equations. Familiarity with these graphs will help you in the creation and use of mathematical models.

(a) Linear model

(b) Quadratic model

(c) Cubic model

(d) Square root model

(e) Absolute value model

(f) Rational model

FIGURE 1.29

SUMMARIZE (Section 1.2)

1. Describe how to sketch the graph of an equation by hand *(page 11)*. For examples of sketching a graph by hand, see Examples 1 and 2.

2. Describe how to find the *x*- and *y*-intercepts of a graph *(page 13)*. For an example of finding the *x*- and *y*-intercepts of a graph, see Example 3.

3. State the standard form of the equation of a circle *(page 14)*. For an example of finding the standard form of the equation of a circle, see Example 4.

4. Describe how to find a point of intersection of the graphs of two equations *(page 15)*. For examples of finding points of intersection, see Examples 5 and 6.

5. Describe break-even analysis *(page 15)*. For an example of break-even analysis, see Example 5.

6. Describe supply equations and demand equations *(page 16)*. For examples of a supply equation and a demand equation, see Example 6.

7. Describe a mathematical model *(page 17)*. For an example of a mathematical model, see Example 7.

SKILLS WARM UP 1.2   The following warm-up exercises involve skills that were covered in a previous course. You will use these skills in the exercise set for this section. For additional help, review Appendix Sections A.3 and A.4.

In Exercises 1–6, solve for y.

1. $5y - 12 = x$

2. $-y = 15 - x$

3. $x^3y + 2y = 1$

4. $x^2 + x - y^2 - 6 = 0$

5. $(x - 2)^2 + (y + 1)^2 = 9$

6. $(x + 6)^2 + (y - 5)^2 = 81$

In Exercises 7–10, evaluate the expression for the given value of x.

Expression	x-Value
7. $y = 5x$	$x = -2$
9. $y = 2x^2 + 1$	$x = 2$

Expression	x-Value
8. $y = 3x - 4$	$x = 3$
10. $y = x^2 + 2x - 7$	$x = -4$

In Exercises 11–14, factor the expression.

11. $x^2 - 3x + 2$

12. $x^2 + 5x + 6$

13. $y^2 - 3y + \frac{9}{4}$

14. $y^2 - 7y + \frac{49}{4}$

Exercises 1.2

See www.CalcChat.com for worked-out solutions to odd-numbered exercises.

Matching In Exercises 1–6, match the equation with its graph. [The graphs are labeled (a)–(f).]

1. $y = x - 2$

2. $y = -\frac{1}{2}x + 2$

3. $y = x^2 + 2x$

4. $y = \sqrt{9 - x^2}$

5. $y = |x| - 2$

6. $y = x^3 - x$

(a)

(b)

(c)

(d)

(e)

(f)

Sketching the Graph of an Equation In Exercises 7–22, sketch the graph of the equation. Use a graphing utility to verify your results. *See Examples 1, 2, and 3.*

7. $y = 2x + 3$

8. $y = -3x + 2$

9. $y = x^2 - 3$

10. $y = x^2 + 6$

11. $y = (x - 1)^2$

12. $y = (5 - x)^2$

13. $y = x^3 + 2$

14. $y = 1 - x^3$

15. $y = -\sqrt{x - 1}$

16. $y = \sqrt{x + 1}$

17. $y = |x + 1|$

18. $y = -|x - 2|$

19. $y = \dfrac{1}{x - 3}$

20. $y = \dfrac{1}{x + 1}$

21. $x = y^2 - 4$

22. $x = 4 - y^2$

Finding x- and y-Intercepts In Exercises 23–32, find the x- and y-intercepts of the graph of the equation. *See Example 3.*

23. $2x - y - 3 = 0$

24. $4x - 2y - 5 = 0$

25. $y = x^2 + x - 2$

26. $y = x^2 - 4x + 3$

27. $y = \sqrt{4 - x^2}$

28. $y = \sqrt{x + 9}$

29. $y = \dfrac{x^2 - 4}{x - 2}$

30. $y = \dfrac{x^2 + 3x}{2x}$

31. $x^2y - x^2 + 4y = 0$

32. $2x^2y + 8y - x^2 = 1$

Finding the Equation of a Circle　In Exercises 33–40, find the standard form of the equation of the circle and sketch its graph. *See Example 4.*

33. Center: $(0, 0)$; radius: 4
34. Center: $(0, 0)$; radius: 5
35. Center: $(2, -1)$; radius: 3
36. Center: $(-4, 3)$; radius: 2
37. Center: $(-1, 1)$; solution point: $(-1, 5)$
38. Center: $(3, -2)$; solution point: $(-1, 1)$
39. Endpoints of a diameter: $(-6, -8)$, $(6, 8)$
40. Endpoints of a diameter: $(0, -4)$, $(6, 4)$

Finding Points of Intersection　In Exercises 41–48, find the points of intersection (if any) of the graphs of the equations. Use a graphing utility to check your results.

41. $y = -x + 2, y = 2x - 1$
42. $y = -x + 7, y = \frac{3}{2}x - 8$
43. $y = -x^2 + 15, y = 3x + 11$
44. $y = x^2 + 2, y = x + 4$
45. $y = x^3, y = 2x$
46. $y = \sqrt{x}, y = x$
47. $y = x^4 - 2x^2 + 1, y = 1 - x^2$
48. $y = x^3 - 2x^2 + x - 1, y = -x^2 + 3x - 1$

Break-Even Point　In Exercises 49–54, C represents the total cost (in dollars) of producing x units of a product and R represents the total revenue (in dollars) from the sale of x units. How many units must the company sell to break even?　*See Example 5.*

49. $C = 0.85x + 35{,}000, R = 1.55x$
50. $C = 6x + 500{,}000, R = 35x$
51. $C = 8650x + 250{,}000, R = 9950x$
52. $C = 2.5x + 10{,}000, R = 4.9x$
53. $C = 6x + 5000, R = 10x$
54. $C = 130x + 12{,}600, R = 200x$

55. **Break-Even Analysis**　You are setting up a part-time business with an initial investment of $15,000. The unit cost of the product is $11.80, and the selling price is $19.30.

    (a) Find equations for the total cost C (in dollars) and total revenue R (in dollars) for x units.

    (b) Find the break-even point by finding the point of intersection of the cost and revenue equations.

    (c) How many units would yield a profit of $1000?

56. **Break-Even Analysis**　A 2010 Honda Accord costs $28,695 with a gasoline engine. A 2010 Toyota Camry costs $29,720 with a hybrid engine. The Accord gets 21 miles per gallon of gasoline and the Camry gets 34 miles per gallon of gasoline. Assume that the price of gasoline is $2.719.　*(Source: Consumer Reports)*

    (a) Show that the cost C_g (in dollars) of driving the Honda Accord x miles is
    $$C_g = 28{,}695 + \frac{2.719x}{21}$$
    and the cost C_h (in dollars) of driving the Toyota Camry x miles is
    $$C_h = 29{,}720 + \frac{2.719x}{34}.$$

    (b) Find the break-even point. That is, find the mileage at which the hybrid-powered Toyota Camry becomes more economical than the gasoline-powered Honda Accord.

57. **Supply and Demand**　The demand and supply equations for a handheld video game system are given by
    $$p = 240 - 4x \qquad \text{Demand equation}$$
    $$p = 135 + 3x \qquad \text{Supply equation}$$
    where p is the price (in dollars) and x represents the number of units (in thousands). Find the equilibrium point for this market.

58. **Supply and Demand**　The demand and supply equations for an MP3 player are given by
    $$p = 190 - 15x \qquad \text{Demand equation}$$
    $$p = 75 + 8x \qquad \text{Supply equation}$$
    where p is the price (in dollars) and x represents the number of units (in hundreds of thousands). Find the equilibrium point for this market.

59. **E-Book Spending**　The amounts of money y (in millions of dollars) spent on e-books in the United States in the years 2004 through 2009 are shown in the table.　*(Source: Association of American Publishers)*

Year	2004	2005	2006	2007	2008	2009
Amount	30	44	54	67	113	313

A mathematical model for the data is given by $y = 8.148t^3 - 139.71t^2 + 789.0t - 1416$, where t represents the year, with $t = 4$ corresponding to 2004.

    (a) Compare the actual amounts spent with those given by the model. How well does the model fit the data? Explain your reasoning.

    (b) Use the model to predict the amount spent in 2014.

60. **HOW DO YOU SEE IT?**   The graph shows the cost and revenue equations for a product.

(a) For what numbers of units sold is there a loss for the company?

(b) For what number of units sold does the company break even?

(c) For what numbers of units sold is there a profit for the company?

61. Associate's Degrees   A mathematical model for the numbers of associate's degrees conferred y (in thousands) from 2004 through 2008 is given by the equation $y = -1.50t^2 + 38.1t + 539$, where t represents the year, with $t = 4$ corresponding to 2004. *(Source: National Center for Education Statistics)*

(a) Use the model to complete the table.

Year	2004	2005	2006	2007	2008	2012
Degrees						

(b) This model was created using actual data from 2004 through 2008. How accurate do you think the model is in predicting the number of associate's degrees conferred in 2012? Explain your reasoning.

(c) Using this model, what is the prediction for the number of associate's degrees conferred in 2016? Do you think this prediction is valid?

62. Lung Transplants   A mathematical model for the numbers of lung transplants performed in the United States in the years 2005 through 2009 is given by $y = 22.36t^2 - 254.9t + 2127$, where y is the number of transplants and t represents the year, with $t = 5$ corresponding to 2005. *(Source: Organ Procurement and Transplantation Network)*

(a) Use a graphing utility or a spreadsheet to complete the table.

Year	2005	2006	2007	2008	2009
Transplants					

(b) Use your school's library, the Internet, or some other reference source to find the actual numbers of lung transplants in the years 2005 through 2009. Compare the actual numbers with those given by the model. How well does the model fit the data? Explain your reasoning.

(c) Using this model, what is the prediction for the number of transplants in 2015? Do you think this prediction is valid? What factors could affect this model's accuracy?

63. Making a Conjecture   Use a graphing utility to graph the equation $y = cx + 1$ for $c = 1, 2, 3, 4$, and 5. Then make a conjecture about the x-coefficient and the graph of the equation.

64. Break-Even Point   Define the break-even point for a business marketing a new product. Give examples of a linear cost equation and a linear revenue equation for which the break-even point is 10,000 units.

Finding Intercepts   In Exercises 65–70, use a graphing utility to graph the equation and approximate the x- and y-intercepts of the graph.

65. $y = 0.24x^2 + 1.32x + 5.36$

66. $y = -0.56x^2 - 5.34x + 6.25$

67. $y = \sqrt{0.3x^2 - 4.3x + 5.7}$

68. $y = \sqrt{-1.21x^2 + 2.34x + 5.6}$

69. $y = \dfrac{0.2x^2 + 1}{0.1x + 2.4}$ **70.** $y = \dfrac{0.4x - 5.3}{0.4x^2 + 5.3}$

71. Project: Number of Stores   For a project analyzing the numbers of Tiffany & Co. stores from 2000 through 2009, visit this text's website at *www.cengagebrain.com*. *(Source: Tiffany & Co.)*

1.3 Lines in the Plane and Slope

In Exercise 87 on page 32, you will use slope to analyze the average salaries of senior high school principals.

■ Use the slope-intercept form of a linear equation to sketch graphs.
■ Find slopes of lines passing through two points.
■ Use the point-slope form to write equations of lines.
■ Find equations of parallel and perpendicular lines.
■ Use linear equations to model and solve real-life problems.

Using Slope

The simplest mathematical model for relating two variables is the **linear equation**

$$y = mx + b. \qquad \text{Linear equation}$$

This equation is called *linear* because its graph is a line. (In this text, the term *line* is used to mean *straight line*.) By letting $x = 0$, you can see that the line crosses the y-axis at

$$y = b$$

as shown in Figure 1.30. In other words, the y-intercept is $(0, b)$. The steepness or slope of the line is m.

$$y = mx + b$$

Slope ——┘   └—— y-intercept

The **slope** of a nonvertical line is the number of units the line rises (or falls) vertically for each unit of horizontal change from left to right, as shown in Figure 1.30.

Positive slope, line rises.

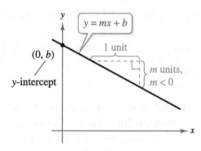

Negative slope, line falls.

FIGURE 1.30

A linear equation that is written in the form $y = mx + b$ is said to be written in **slope-intercept form.**

The Slope-Intercept Form of the Equation of a Line

The graph of the equation

$$y = mx + b$$

is a line whose slope is m and whose y-intercept is $(0, b)$.

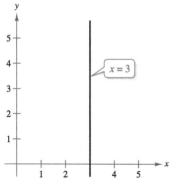

When the line is vertical, the slope is undefined.
FIGURE 1.31

A vertical line has an equation of the form

$$x = a. \qquad \text{Vertical line}$$

Because the equation of a vertical line cannot be written in the form $y = mx + b$, it follows that the slope of a vertical line is undefined, as indicated in Figure 1.31.

Once you have determined the slope and the y-intercept of a line, it is a relatively simple matter to sketch its graph.

Example 1 Graphing a Linear Equation

Sketch the graph of each linear equation.

a. $y = 2x + 1$

b. $y = 2$

c. $x + y = 2$

SOLUTION

a. This equation is written in slope-intercept form, $y = mx + b$. Because $b = 1$, the y-intercept is $(0, 1)$. Moreover, because the slope is $m = 2$, the line *rises* two units for each unit the line moves to the right, as shown in Figure 1.32(a).

b. By writing this equation in slope-intercept form

$$y = (0)x + 2$$

you can see that the y-intercept is $(0, 2)$ and the slope is zero. A zero slope implies that the line is horizontal—that is, it doesn't rise *or* fall, as shown in Figure 1.32(b).

c. By writing this equation in slope-intercept form

$x + y = 2$	Write original equation.
$y = -x + 2$	Subtract x from each side.
$y = (-1)x + 2$	Write in slope-intercept form.

you can see that the y-intercept is $(0, 2)$. Moreover, because the slope is $m = -1$, this line *falls* one unit for each unit the line moves to the right, as shown in Figure 1.32(c).

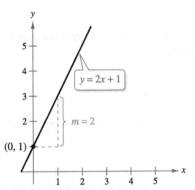

(a) When m is positive, the line rises from left to right.

(b) When m is zero, the line is horizontal.

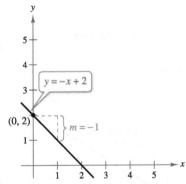

(c) When m is negative, the line falls from left to right.

FIGURE 1.32

✓ Checkpoint 1

Sketch the graph of each linear equation.

a. $y = 4x - 2$

b. $x = 1$

c. $2x + y = 6$

In real-life problems, the slope of a line can be interpreted as either a *ratio* or a *rate*. If the *x*-axis and *y*-axis have the same unit of measure, then the slope has no units and is a **ratio.** If the *x*-axis and *y*-axis have different units of measure, then the slope is a **rate** or **rate of change.**

 Example 2   Using Slope as a Ratio

The maximum recommended slope of a wheelchair ramp is $\frac{1}{12} \approx 0.083$. A business installs a wheelchair ramp that rises 22 inches over a horizontal length of 24 feet, as shown in Figure 1.33. Is the ramp steeper than recommended? *(Source: ADA Standards for Accessible Design)*

FIGURE 1.33

SOLUTION   The horizontal length of the ramp is 24 feet or $12(24) = 288$ inches. So, the slope of the ramp is

$$\text{Slope} = \frac{\text{vertical change}}{\text{horizontal change}}$$

$$= \frac{22 \text{ in.}}{288 \text{ in.}}$$

$$\approx 0.076.$$

So, the slope is not steeper than recommended.

✓**Checkpoint 2**

The business in Example 2 installs a second ramp that rises 27 inches over a horizontal length of 26 feet. Is the ramp steeper than recommended?

 Example 3   Using Slope as a Rate of Change

A manufacturing company determines that the total cost in dollars of producing *x* units of a product is

$$C = 25x + 3500.$$

Describe the practical significance of the *y*-intercept and slope of the line given by this equation.

SOLUTION   The *y*-intercept $(0, 3500)$ tells you that the cost of producing zero units is $3500. This is the **fixed cost** of production—it includes costs that must be paid regardless of the number of units produced. The slope, which is $m = 25$, tells you that the cost of producing each unit is $25, as shown in Figure 1.34. Economists call the cost per unit the **marginal cost.** If the production increases by one unit, then the "margin" or extra amount of cost is $25.

Production Cost

$C = 25x + 3500$

Marginal cost: $m = \$25$

Fixed cost: $3500

FIGURE 1.34

✓**Checkpoint 3**

A small business determines that the value of a copier *t* years after its purchase is $V = -300t + 1500$. Describe the practical significance of the *y*-intercept and slope of the line given by this equation.

Finding the Slope of a Line

Given an equation of a nonvertical line, you can find its slope by writing the equation in slope-intercept form. When you are not given an equation, you can still find the slope of a line. For instance, suppose you want to find the slope of the line passing through the points (x_1, y_1) and (x_2, y_2), as shown in Figure 1.35. As you move from left to right along this line, a change of $(y_2 - y_1)$ units in the vertical direction corresponds to a change of $(x_2 - x_1)$ units in the horizontal direction. These two changes are denoted by the symbols

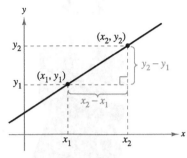

FIGURE 1.35

$$\Delta y = y_2 - y_1 = \text{the change in } y$$

and

$$\Delta x = x_2 - x_1 = \text{the change in } x.$$

(The symbol Δ is the Greek capital letter delta, and the symbols Δy and Δx are read as "delta y" and "delta x.") The ratio of Δy to Δx represents the slope of the line that passes through the points (x_1, y_1) and (x_2, y_2).

$$\text{Slope} = \frac{\Delta y}{\Delta x} = \frac{y_2 - y_1}{x_2 - x_1}$$

Be sure you see that Δx represents a single number, not the product of two numbers (Δ and x). The same is true for Δy.

The Slope of a Line Passing Through Two Points

The **slope** m of the nonvertical line passing through the points (x_1, y_1) and (x_2, y_2) is

$$m = \frac{\Delta y}{\Delta x} = \frac{y_2 - y_1}{x_2 - x_1}$$

where $x_1 \neq x_2$. Slope is not defined for vertical lines.

When this formula is used for slope, the *order of subtraction* is important. Given two points on a line, you may label either one of them as (x_1, y_1) and the other as (x_2, y_2). However, once you have done this, you must form the numerator and denominator using the same order of subtraction.

$$m = \frac{y_2 - y_1}{x_2 - x_1} \qquad m = \frac{y_1 - y_2}{x_1 - x_2} \qquad m = \frac{y_2 - y_1}{x_1 - x_2}$$

Correct Correct Incorrect

For instance, the slope of the line passing through the points $(3, 4)$ and $(5, 7)$ can be calculated as

$$m = \frac{7 - 4}{5 - 3} = \frac{3}{2}$$

or

$$m = \frac{4 - 7}{3 - 5} = \frac{-3}{-2} = \frac{3}{2}.$$

| Example 4 | **Finding the Slope of a Line** |

Find the slope of the line passing through each pair of points.

a. $(-2, 0)$ and $(3, 1)$ **b.** $(-1, 2)$ and $(2, 2)$

c. $(0, 4)$ and $(1, -1)$ **d.** $(3, 4)$ and $(3, 1)$

SOLUTION

a. Letting $(x_1, y_1) = (-2, 0)$ and $(x_2, y_2) = (3, 1)$, you obtain a slope of

$$m = \frac{y_2 - y_1}{x_2 - x_1} = \frac{1 - 0}{3 - (-2)} = \frac{1}{5}$$

◄——— Difference in y-values

◄——— Difference in x-values

as shown in Figure 1.36(a).

b. The slope of the line passing through $(-1, 2)$ and $(2, 2)$ is

$$m = \frac{2 - 2}{2 - (-1)} = \frac{0}{3} = 0.$$ See Figure 1.36(b).

c. The slope of the line passing through $(0, 4)$ and $(1, -1)$ is

$$m = \frac{-1 - 4}{1 - 0} = \frac{-5}{1} = -5.$$ See Figure 1.36(c).

d. The slope of the vertical line passing through $(3, 4)$ and $(3, 1)$ is not defined because division by zero is undefined. [See Figure 1.36(d).]

(a) Positive slope, line rises from left to right.

(b) Zero slope, line is horizontal.

(c) Negative slope, line falls from left to right.

(d) Vertical line, undefined slope.

FIGURE 1.36

✓**Checkpoint 4**

Find the slope of the line passing through each pair of points.

a. $(-3, 2)$ and $(5, 18)$

b. $(-2, 1)$ and $(-4, 2)$

c. $(2, -4)$ and $(-2, -4)$

Writing Linear Equations

When you know the slope of a line and the coordinates of one point on the line, you can find an equation for the line. For instance, in Figure 1.37, let (x_1, y_1) be a point on the line whose slope is m. If (x, y) is any other point on the line, then

$$\frac{y - y_1}{x - x_1} = m.$$

This equation, involving the variables x and y, can be rewritten in the form

$$y - y_1 = m(x - x_1)$$

which is the **point-slope form** of the equation of a line.

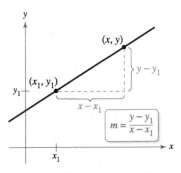

Any two points on a nonvertical line can be used to determine the slope of the line.

FIGURE 1.37

Point-Slope Form of the Equation of a Line

The equation of the line with slope m passing through the point (x_1, y_1) is

$$y - y_1 = m(x - x_1).$$

The point-slope form is most useful for *finding* the equation of a nonvertical line. You should remember this formula—it is used throughout the text.

Example 5 Using the Point-Slope Form

Find the equation of the line that has a slope of 3 and passes through the point $(1, -2)$.

SOLUTION   Use the point-slope form with $m = 3$ and $(x_1, y_1) = (1, -2)$.

$$y - y_1 = m(x - x_1) \qquad \text{Point-slope form}$$
$$y - (-2) = 3(x - 1) \qquad \text{Substitute for } m, x_1, \text{ and } y_1.$$
$$y + 2 = 3x - 3 \qquad \text{Simplify.}$$
$$y = 3x - 5 \qquad \text{Write in slope-intercept form.}$$

The slope-intercept form of the equation of the line is $y = 3x - 5$. The graph of this line is shown in Figure 1.38.

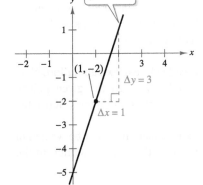

FIGURE 1.38

✓ Checkpoint 5

Find the equation of the line that has a slope of 2 and passes through the point $(-1, 2)$.

The point-slope form can be used to find an equation of the line passing through points (x_1, y_1) and (x_2, y_2). To do this, first find the slope of the line

$$m = \frac{y_2 - y_1}{x_2 - x_1}, \quad x_1 \neq x_2$$

and then use the point-slope form to obtain the equation

$$y - y_1 = \frac{y_2 - y_1}{x_2 - x_1}(x - x_1). \qquad \text{Two-point form}$$

This is sometimes called the **two-point form** of the equation of a line.

Example 6   **Predicting Diluted Earnings Per Share**

The diluted earnings per share (diluted EPS) for Tim Hortons, Inc. were $1.43 in 2007 and $1.55 in 2008. Using only this information, write a linear equation that gives the diluted EPS in terms of the year. Then predict the diluted EPS for 2009.   *(Source: Tim Hortons, Inc.)*

SOLUTION   Let $t = 7$ represent 2007. Then the two given values are represented by the data points

$$(7, 1.43)   \text{and}   (8, 1.55).$$

The slope of the line through these points is

$$m = \frac{1.55 - 1.43}{8 - 7} = 0.12.$$

Using the point-slope form, you can find the equation that relates the diluted EPS y and the year t to be

$$y = 0.12t + 0.59.$$

Using $t = 9$ to represent 2009, you can predict the 2009 diluted EPS to be

$$y = 0.12(9) + 0.59 = 1.08 + 0.59 = 1.67.$$

According to this equation, the diluted EPS in 2009 was $1.67, as shown in Figure 1.39. (In this case, the prediction is fairly good—the actual diluted EPS in 2009 was $1.64.)

FIGURE 1.39

✓ **Checkpoint 6**

The diluted EPS for Amazon.com was $0.45 in 2006 and $1.49 in 2008. Using only this information, write a linear equation that gives the diluted EPS in terms of the year. Then predict the diluted EPS for 2009.   *(Source: Amazon.com)*

(a) Linear Extrapolation

The prediction method illustrated in Example 6 is called **linear extrapolation.** Note in Figure 1.40(a) that an extrapolated point does not lie between the given points. When the estimated point lies between two given points, as shown in Figure 1.40(b), the procedure is called **linear interpolation.**

Because the slope of a vertical line is not defined, its equation cannot be written in slope-intercept form. However, every line has an equation that can be written in the **general form**

$$Ax + By + C = 0 \qquad \text{General form}$$

where A and B are not both zero. For instance, the vertical line given by $x = a$ can be represented by the general form

$$x - a = 0. \qquad \text{General form of vertical line}$$

The five most common forms of equations of lines are summarized below.

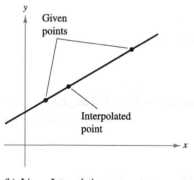

(b) Linear Interpolation

FIGURE 1.40

Equations of Lines

1. General form: $Ax + By + C = 0$

2. Vertical line: $x = a$

3. Horizontal line: $y = b$

4. Slope-intercept form: $y = mx + b$

5. Point-slope form: $y - y_1 = m(x - x_1)$

Parallel and Perpendicular Lines

Slope can be used to decide whether two nonvertical lines in a plane are parallel, perpendicular, or neither.

Parallel and Perpendicular Lines

1. Two distinct nonvertical lines are **parallel** if and only if their slopes are equal. That is, $m_1 = m_2$.

2. Two nonvertical lines are **perpendicular** if and only if their slopes are negative reciprocals of each other. That is, $m_1 = -1/m_2$.

Example 7 **Finding Parallel and Perpendicular Lines**

Find equations of the lines that pass through the point $(2, -1)$ and are (a) parallel to the line $2x - 3y = 5$ and (b) perpendicular to the line $2x - 3y = 5$.

SOLUTION By writing the given equation in slope-intercept form

$2x - 3y = 5$	Write original equation.
$-3y = -2x + 5$	Subtract $2x$ from each side.
$y = \dfrac{2}{3}x - \dfrac{5}{3}$	Write in slope-intercept form.

you can see that it has a slope of $m = \frac{2}{3}$, as shown in Figure 1.41.

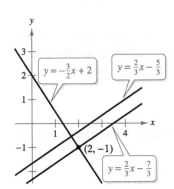

$y = -\frac{3}{2}x + 2$ $y = \frac{2}{3}x - \frac{5}{3}$

$(2, -1)$

$y = \frac{2}{3}x - \frac{7}{3}$

FIGURE 1.41

a. Any line parallel to the given line must also have a slope of $\frac{2}{3}$. So, the line through $(2, -1)$ that is parallel to the given line has the following equation.

$y - (-1) = \dfrac{2}{3}(x - 2)$	Write in point-slope form.
$y + 1 = \dfrac{2}{3}x - \dfrac{4}{3}$	Simplify.
$y = \dfrac{2}{3}x - \dfrac{4}{3} - 1$	Solve for y.
$y = \dfrac{2}{3}x - \dfrac{7}{3}$	Write in slope-intercept form.

b. Any line perpendicular to the given line must have a slope of $-\frac{3}{2}$ (because $-\frac{3}{2}$ is the negative reciprocal of $\frac{2}{3}$). So, the line through $(2, -1)$ that is perpendicular to the given line has the following equation.

$y - (-1) = -\dfrac{3}{2}(x - 2)$	Write in point-slope form.
$y + 1 = -\dfrac{3}{2}x + 3$	Simplify.
$y = -\dfrac{3}{2}x + 3 - 1$	Solve for y.
$y = -\dfrac{3}{2}x + 2$	Write in slope-intercept form.

TECH TUTOR

On a graphing utility, lines will not appear to have the correct slopes unless you use a viewing window that has a *square setting*. For instance, try graphing the lines in Example 7 using the standard setting $-10 \le x \le 10$ and $-10 \le y \le 10$. Then reset the viewing window with the square setting $-9 \le x \le 9$ and $-6 \le y \le 6$. On which setting do the lines $y = \frac{2}{3}x - \frac{5}{3}$ and $y = -\frac{3}{2}x + 2$ appear to be perpendicular?

✓**Checkpoint 7**

Find equations of the lines that pass through the point $(2, 1)$ and are (a) parallel to the line $2x - 4y = 5$ and (b) perpendicular to the line $2x - 4y = 5$.

Extended Application: Linear Depreciation

Most business expenses can be deducted the same year they occur. One exception to this is the cost of property that has a useful life of more than 1 year, such as buildings, cars, or equipment. Such costs must be **depreciated** over the useful life of the property. When the *same amount* is depreciated each year, the procedure is called **linear depreciation** or **straight-line depreciation.** The *book value* is the difference between the original value and the total amount of depreciation accumulated to date.

 Example 8 **Depreciating Equipment**

Your company has purchased a $12,000 machine that has a useful life of 8 years. The salvage value at the end of 8 years is $2000. Write a linear equation that describes the book value of the machine each year.

SOLUTION   Let V represent the value of the machine at the end of year t. You can represent the initial value of the machine by the ordered pair (0, 12,000) and the salvage value of the machine by the ordered pair (8, 2000). The slope of the line is

$$m = \frac{2000 - 12,000}{8 - 0} = \frac{-\$1250}{1 \text{ year}} \qquad m = \frac{V_2 - V_1}{t_2 - t_1}$$

which represents the annual depreciation in *dollars per year*. Using the point-slope form, you can write the equation of the line as shown.

$$V - 12,000 = -1250(t - 0) \qquad \text{Write in point-slope form.}$$
$$V = -1250t + 12,000 \qquad \text{Write in slope-intercept form.}$$

The graph of this equation is shown in Figure 1.42.

Straight-Line Depreciation

FIGURE 1.42

 Checkpoint 8

Write a linear equation for the machine in Example 8 when the salvage value at the end of 8 years is $1000.

SUMMARIZE   (Section 1.3)

1. State the slope-intercept form of the equation of a line *(page 22)*. For an example of an equation in slope-intercept form, see Example 1.

2. Explain how to decide whether the slope of a line is a ratio or a rate of change *(page 24)*. For an example of a slope that is a ratio, see Example 2. For an example of a slope that is a rate of change, see Example 3.

3. Explain how to find the slope of a line through two points *(page 25)*. For an example of finding the slope of a line through two points, see Example 4.

4. State the point-slope form of the equation of a line *(page 27)*. For examples of equations in point-slope form, see Examples 5 and 6.

5. Explain how to decide whether two lines are parallel, perpendicular, or neither *(page 29)*. For an example, see Example 7.

6. Describe a real-life example of how a linear equation can be used to analyze the depreciation of property *(page 30, Example 8)*.

SKILLS WARM UP 1.3   The following warm-up exercises involve skills that were covered in a previous course. You will use these skills in the exercise set for this section. For additional help, review Appendix Section A.3.

In Exercises 1 and 2, simplify the expression.

1. $\dfrac{5 - (-2)}{-3 - 4}$

2. $\dfrac{-7 - (-10)}{4 - 1}$

3. Evaluate $-\dfrac{1}{m}$ when $m = -3$.

4. Evaluate $-\dfrac{1}{m}$ when $m = \dfrac{6}{7}$.

In Exercises 5–10, solve for y in terms of x.

5. $-4x + y = 7$

6. $3x - y = 7$

7. $y - 2 = 3(x - 4)$

8. $y - (-5) = -1[x - (-2)]$

9. $y - (-3) = \dfrac{4 - (-3)}{2 - 1}(x - 2)$

10. $y - 1 = \dfrac{-3 - 1}{-7 - (-1)}[x - (-1)]$

Exercises 1.3

See www.CalcChat.com for worked-out solutions to odd-numbered exercises.

Estimating Slope   In Exercises 1–4, estimate the slope of the line.

1.

2.

3.

4.

Finding the Slope and y-Intercept   In Exercises 5–16, find the slope and y-intercept (if possible) of the equation of the line.

5. $y = x + 7$

6. $y = 4x + 3$

7. $5x + y = 20$

8. $2x + y = 40$

9. $7x + 6y = 30$

10. $2x + 3y = 9$

11. $3x - y = 15$

12. $2x - 3y = 24$

13. $x = 4$

14. $x + 5 = 0$

15. $y - 4 = 0$

16. $y + 1 = 0$

Graphing a Linear Equation   In Exercises 17–26, sketch the graph of the equation. Use a graphing utility to verify your result. *See Example 1.*

17. $y = -2$

18. $y = -4$

19. $y = -2x + 1$

20. $y = 3x - 2$

21. $6x + 3y = 18$

22. $4x + 5y = 20$

23. $2x - y - 3 = 0$

24. $x + 2y + 6 = 0$

25. $3x + 5y + 15 = 0$

26. $-5x + 2y - 20 = 0$

Finding the Slope of a Line   In Exercises 27–40, find the slope of the line passing through the pair of points. *See Example 4.*

27. $(0, -3), (9, 0)$

28. $(-2, 0), (1, 4)$

29. $(3, -4), (5, 2)$

30. $(1, 2), (-2, 2)$

31. $(4, -1), (2, 7)$

32. $\left(\frac{11}{3}, -2\right), \left(\frac{11}{3}, -10\right)$

33. $(-8, -3), (-8, -5)$

34. $(2, -1), (-2, -5)$

35. $(-2, 1), (4, -3)$

36. $(3, -5), (-2, -5)$

37. $\left(\frac{1}{4}, -2\right), \left(-\frac{3}{8}, 1\right)$

38. $\left(-\frac{3}{2}, -5\right), \left(\frac{5}{6}, 4\right)$

39. $\left(\frac{2}{3}, \frac{5}{2}\right), \left(\frac{1}{4}, -\frac{5}{6}\right)$

40. $\left(\frac{7}{8}, \frac{3}{4}\right), \left(\frac{5}{4}, -\frac{1}{4}\right)$

Finding Points on a Line   In Exercises 41–48, use the point on the line and the slope of the line to find three additional points through which the line passes. (There are many correct answers.)

	Point	Slope		Point	Slope
41.	$(2, 1)$	$m = 0$	**42.**	$(-3, -1)$	$m = 0$
43.	$(1, 7)$	$m = -3$	**44.**	$(7, -2)$	$m = 2$
45.	$(6, -4)$	$m = \frac{2}{3}$	**46.**	$(-1, -6)$	$m = -\frac{1}{2}$
47.	$(-8, 1)$	m is undefined.			
48.	$(-3, 4)$	m is undefined.			

Using Slope In Exercises 49–52, use the concept of slope to determine whether the three points are collinear.

49. $(-2, 1), (-1, 0), (2, -2)$

50. $(0, 4), (7, -6), (-5, 11)$

51. $(-2, -1), (0, 3), (2, 7)$

52. $(4, 1), (-2, -2), (8, 3)$

Using the Point-Slope Form In Exercises 53–62, find the equation of the line that passes through the given point and has the given slope. Then use the equation to sketch the line. *See Example 5.*

Point	*Slope*		*Point*	*Slope*
53. $(0, 3)$	$m = \frac{3}{4}$	**54.**	$(0, 0)$	$m = \frac{2}{3}$

55. $(-1, 2)$ m is undefined.

56. $(0, 4)$ m is undefined.

57. $(-2, 7)$ $m = 0$ **58.** $(-2, 4)$ $m = 0$

59. $(0, -2)$ $m = -4$ **60.** $(-1, -4)$ $m = -2$

61. $\left(0, \frac{2}{3}\right)$ $m = \frac{3}{4}$ **62.** $\left(0, -\frac{2}{3}\right)$ $m = \frac{1}{6}$

Writing an Equation of a Line In Exercises 63–74, find the equation of the line that passes through the points. Then use the equation to sketch the line.

63. $(4, 3), (0, -5)$ **64.** $(-3, -4), (1, 4)$

65. $(0, 0), (-1, 3)$ **66.** $(-3, 6), (1, 2)$

67. $(2, 3), (2, -2)$ **68.** $(6, 1), (10, 1)$

69. $(3, -1), (-2, -1)$ **70.** $(2, 5), (2, -10)$

71. $\left(-\frac{1}{3}, 1\right), \left(-\frac{2}{3}, \frac{5}{6}\right)$ **72.** $\left(\frac{7}{8}, \frac{3}{4}\right), \left(\frac{5}{4}, -\frac{1}{4}\right)$

73. $\left(-\frac{1}{2}, 4\right), \left(\frac{1}{2}, 8\right)$ **74.** $(4, -1), \left(\frac{1}{4}, -5\right)$

75. Write an equation of the vertical line with x-intercept at 3.

76. Write an equation of the horizontal line through $(0, -5)$.

77. Write an equation of the line with y-intercept at -10 and parallel to all horizontal lines.

78. Write an equation of the line with x-intercept at -5 and parallel to all vertical lines.

 Finding Parallel and Perpendicular Lines In Exercises 79–86, find equations of the lines through the given point (a) parallel to the given line and (b) perpendicular to the given line. Then use a graphing utility to graph all three equations in the same viewing window using a square setting. *See Example 7.*

Point	*Line*		*Point*	*Line*
79. $(-3, 2)$	$x + y = 7$	**80.**	$(2, 1)$	$4x - 2y = 3$
81. $\left(-\frac{2}{3}, \frac{7}{8}\right)$	$3x + 4y = 7$	**82.**	$\left(\frac{7}{8}, \frac{3}{4}\right)$	$5x + 3y = 0$
83. $(-1, 0)$	$y + 3 = 0$	**84.**	$(2, 5)$	$y + 4 = 0$
85. $(1, 1)$	$x - 2 = 0$	**86.**	$(12, -3)$	$x + 4 = 0$

 87. Average Salary The graph shows the average salaries (in dollars) of senior high school principals from 1996 through 2008. *(Source: Educational Research Service)*

(a) Determine the time periods in which the average salary increased the greatest and the least.

(b) Find the slope of the line segment connecting the points for the years 1996 and 2008.

(c) Interpret the meaning of the slope in part (b) in the context of the problem.

 88. Revenue The graph shows the revenue (in billions of dollars) for Verizon Communications for the years 2003 through 2009. *(Source: Verizon Communications)*

(a) Determine the years in which the revenue increased the greatest and the least.

(b) Find the slope of the line segment connecting the points for the years 2003 and 2009.

(c) Interpret the meaning of the slope in part (b) in the context of the problem.

89. Temperature Conversion   Write a linear equation that expresses the relationship between the temperature in degrees Celsius C and the temperature in degrees Fahrenheit F. Use the fact that water freezes at $0°C$ $(32°F)$ and boils at $100°C$ $(212°F)$.

90. Chemistry   Use the result of Exercise 89 to answer the following.

(a) A person has a temperature of $102.2°F$. What is this temperature on the Celsius scale?

(b) The temperature in a room is $76°F$. What is this temperature on the Celsius scale?

91. Population   The resident population of Wisconsin (in thousands) was 5511 in 2004 and 5655 in 2009. Assume that the relationship between the population y and the year t is linear. Let $t = 0$ represent 2000. *(Source: U.S. Census Bureau)*

(a) Write a linear model for the data. What is the slope and what does it tell you about the population?

(b) Use the model to estimate the population in 2006.

(c) Use your school's library, the Internet, or some other reference source to find the actual population in 2006. How close was your estimate?

(d) Do you think your model could be used to predict the population in 2015? Explain.

92. Linear Depreciation   A small business purchases a piece of equipment for $1025. After 5 years the equipment will be outdated, having no value.

(a) Write a linear equation giving the value y (in dollars) of the equipment in terms of the time t (in years), $0 \le t \le 5$.

(b) Use a graphing utility to graph the equation.

(c) Move the cursor along the graph and estimate (to two-decimal-place accuracy) the value of the equipment when $t = 3$.

(d) Move the cursor along the graph and estimate (to two-decimal-place accuracy) the time when the value of the equipment will be $600.

93. Personal Income   Personal income (in billions of dollars) in the United States was 9937 in 2004 and 12,175 in 2009. Assume that the relationship between the personal income y and the time t (in years) is linear. Let $t = 0$ represent 2000. *(Source: U.S. Bureau of Economic Analysis)*

(a) Write a linear model for the data.

(b) Estimate the personal income in 2006.

(c) Estimate the personal income in 2011.

(d) Use your school's library, the Internet, or some other reference source to find the actual personal income in 2006 and 2011. How close were your estimates?

94. Choosing a Job   As a salesperson, you receive a monthly salary of $2000, plus a commission of 7% of sales. You are offered a new job at $2300 per month, plus a commission of 5% of sales.

(a) Write linear equations for your monthly wage W (in dollars) in terms of your monthly sales S (in dollars) for your current job and for your job offer.

(b) Use a graphing utility to graph each equation and find the point of intersection. What does it signify?

(c) You think you can sell $20,000 worth of a product per month. Should you change jobs? Explain.

95. Profit Analysis   A business manufactures a product at a cost of $50 per unit and sells the product for $120 per unit. The company's initial investment to produce the product is $350,000.

(a) Write linear equations giving the total cost C (in dollars) of producing x units and the revenue R (in dollars) from selling x units.

(b) Use the formula for profit, $P = R - C$, to write an equation for the profit derived from x units produced and sold.

(c) The company estimates it can sell 13,000 units. What will be the company's profit or loss?

96. HOW DO YOU SEE IT?   Match the description of the situation with its graph. Then write the equation of the line. [The graphs are labeled (i), (ii), (iii), and (iv).]

(a) You are paying $10 per week to repay a $100 loan.

(b) An employee is paid $12.50 per hour plus $1.50 for each unit produced per hour.

(c) A sales representative receives $30 per day for food plus $0.51 for each mile traveled.

(d) A computer that was purchased for $600 depreciates $100 per year.

QUIZ YOURSELF

See www.CalcChat.com for worked-out solutions to odd-numbered exercises.

Take this quiz as you would take a quiz in class. When you are done, check your work against the answers given in the back of the book.

In Exercises 1–3, (a) plot the points, (b) find the distance between the points, and (c) find the midpoint of the line segment joining the points.

1. $(3, -2), (-3, 1)$ **2.** $\left(\frac{1}{4}, -\frac{3}{2}\right), \left(\frac{1}{2}, 2\right)$ **3.** $(-12, 4), (6, -2)$

4. Use the Distance Formula to show that the points $(4, 0)$, $(2, 1)$, and $(-1, -5)$ are vertices of a right triangle.

5. The resident population of Georgia (in thousands) was 9534 in 2007 and 9829 in 2009. Use the Midpoint Formula to estimate the population in 2008. *(Source: U.S. Census Bureau)*

In Exercises 6–8, sketch the graph of the equation and label the intercepts.

6. $y = 5x + 2$ **7.** $y = x^2 + x - 6$ **8.** $y = |x - 3|$

In Exercises 9–11, find the standard form of the equation of the circle and sketch its graph.

9. Center: $(0, 0)$; radius: 9

10. Center: $(-1, 0)$; radius: 6

11. Center: $(2, -2)$; solution point: $(-1, 2)$

12. A business manufactures a product at a cost of $4.55 per unit and sells the product for $7.19 per unit. The company's initial investment to produce the product was $12,500. How many units must the company sell to break even?

In Exercises 13–15, find the equation of the line that passes through the given point and has the given slope. Then use the equation to sketch the line.

13. $(0, -3); m = \frac{1}{2}$ **14.** $(1, 1); m = 2$ **15.** $(6, 5); m = -\frac{1}{3}$

In Exercises 16–18, find the equation of the line that passes through the points. Then use the equation to sketch the line.

16. $(1, -1), (-4, 5)$ **17.** $(-2, 3), (-2, 2)$ **18.** $\left(\frac{5}{2}, 2\right), (0, 2)$

19. Find equations of the lines that pass through the point $(3, -5)$ and are

(a) parallel to the line $x + 4y = -2$.

(b) perpendicular to the line $x + 4y = -2$.

20. A company had sales of $1,330,000 in 2007 and $1,800,000 in 2011. The company's sales can be modeled by a linear equation. Predict the sales in 2015 and 2018.

21. A company reimburses its sales representatives $175 per day for lodging and meals, plus $0.55 per mile driven. Write a linear equation giving the daily cost C (in dollars) in terms of x, the number of miles driven.

22. Your annual salary was $34,600 in 2009 and $37,800 in 2011. Assume your salary can be modeled by a linear equation.

(a) Write a linear equation giving your salary S (in dollars) in terms of the year t. Let $t = 9$ represent 2009.

(b) Use the linear model to predict your salary in 2015.

1.4 Functions

- Decide whether the relationship between two variables is a function.
- Find the domains and ranges of functions.
- Use function notation and evaluate functions.
- Combine functions to create other functions.
- Find inverse functions algebraically.

Functions

In many common relationships between two variables, the value of one of the variables depends on the value of the other variable. Here are some examples.

1. The sales tax on an item depends on its selling price.

2. The distance an object moves in a given amount of time depends on its speed.

3. The area of a circle depends on its radius.

Consider the relationship between the total revenue R and the sale of x units of a product sold for $1.25 per unit. This relationship can be expressed by the equation

$$R = 1.25x.$$

In this equation, the value of R depends on the choice of x. Because of this, R is the **dependent variable** and x is the **independent variable.**

Most of the relationships that you will study in this course have the property that for a given value of the independent variable, there corresponds exactly one value of the dependent variable. Such a relationship is a **function.**

In Exercise 67 on page 46, you will use a function to estimate the amounts spent on prescription drugs in the United States.

Definition of Function

A **function** is a relationship between two variables such that to each value of the independent variable there corresponds exactly one value of the dependent variable.

The **domain** of the function is the set of all values of the independent variable for which the function is defined. The **range** of the function is the set of all values taken on by the dependent variable.

As illustrated in Figure 1.43, a function can be thought of as a machine that inputs values of the independent variable and outputs values of the dependent variable.

Although functions can be described by various means such as tables, graphs, and diagrams, they are most often specified by formulas or equations. For instance, the equation

$$y = 4x^2 + 3$$

describes y as a function of x. For this function, x is the independent variable and y is the dependent variable.

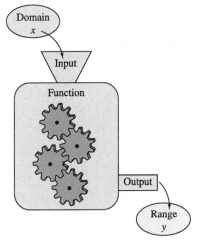

FIGURE 1.43

TECH TUTOR

Many graphing utilities have an *equation editor* feature that requires an equation to be written in "$y =$" form in order to be entered. So, the procedure used in Example 1, isolating the dependent variable on the left side, is also useful for graphing equations with a graphing utility. Note that to graph an equation in which y is not a function of x, such as a circle, you usually have to enter two or more equations into the graphing utility.

Example 1   **Deciding Whether Equations Are Functions**

Decide whether each equation defines y as a function of x.

a. $x + y = 1$ **b.** $x^2 + y^2 = 1$

c. $x^2 + y = 1$ **d.** $x + y^2 = 1$

SOLUTION   To decide whether an equation defines a function, it is helpful to isolate the dependent variable on the left side. For instance, to decide whether the equation $x + y = 1$ defines y as a function of x, write the equation in the form

$$y = 1 - x.$$

From this form, you can see that for any value of x, there is exactly one value of y. So, y is a function of x.

Original Equation	Rewritten Equation	Test: Is y a function of x?
a. $x + y = 1$	$y = 1 - x$	Yes, each value of x determines exactly one value of y.
b. $x^2 + y^2 = 1$	$y = \pm\sqrt{1 - x^2}$	No, some values of x determine two values of y.
c. $x^2 + y = 1$	$y = 1 - x^2$	Yes, each value of x determines exactly one value of y.
d. $x + y^2 = 1$	$y = \pm\sqrt{1 - x}$	No, some values of x determine two values of y.

Note that the equations that assign two values ($\pm$) to the dependent variable for a given value of the independent variable do not define functions of x. For instance, in part (b), when $x = 0$, the equation $y = \pm\sqrt{1 - x^2}$ indicates that $y = +1$ or $y = -1$. Figure 1.44 shows the graphs of the four equations.

(a)

(b)

(c)

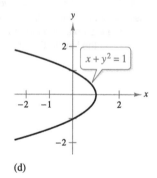

(d)

FIGURE 1.44

✓ Checkpoint 1

Decide whether each equation defines y as a function of x.

a. $x - y = 1$ **b.** $x^2 + y^2 = 4$ **c.** $y^2 + x = 2$ **d.** $x^2 - y = 0$

When the graph of a function is sketched, the standard convention is to let the horizontal axis represent the independent variable. When this convention is used, the test described in Example 1 has a nice graphical interpretation called the **Vertical Line Test.** This test states that if every vertical line intersects the graph of an equation at most once, then the equation defines y as a function of x. For instance, in Figure 1.44, the graphs in parts (a) and (c) pass the Vertical Line Test, but those in parts (b) and (d) do not.

The Domain and Range of a Function

The domain of a function may be described explicitly, or it may be *implied* by an equation used to define the function. For example, the function given by

$$y = \frac{1}{x^2 - 4}$$

has an implied domain that consists of all real numbers x except $x = \pm 2$. These two values are excluded from the domain because division by zero is undefined.

Another type of implied domain is that used to avoid even roots of negative numbers, as indicated in Example 2.

Example 2 Finding the Domain and Range of a Function

Find the domain and range of each function.

a. $y = \sqrt{x - 1}$

b. $y = \begin{cases} 1 - x, & x < 1 \\ \sqrt{x - 1}, & x \geq 1 \end{cases}$

SOLUTION

a. Because $\sqrt{x - 1}$ is not defined for $x - 1 < 0$ (that is, for $x < 1$), it follows that the domain of the function is the interval

$$x \geq 1 \text{ or } [1, \infty).$$

To find the range, observe that $\sqrt{x - 1}$ is never negative. Moreover, as x takes on the various values in the domain, y takes on all nonnegative values. So, the range is the interval

$$y \geq 0 \text{ or } [0, \infty)$$

as shown in Figure 1.45(a).

b. Because this function is defined for $x < 1$ *and* for $x \geq 1$, the domain is the entire set of real numbers. This function is called a **piecewise-defined function** because it is defined by two or more equations over a specified domain. When $x \geq 1$, the function behaves as in part (a). For $x < 1$, the values of $1 - x$ are positive. So, the range of the function is

$$y \geq 0 \text{ or } [0, \infty)$$

as shown in Figure 1.45(b).

(a)

(b)

FIGURE 1.45

✓ Checkpoint 2

Find the domain and range of each function.

a. $y = \sqrt{x + 1}$ **b.** $y = \begin{cases} x^2, & x \leq 0 \\ \sqrt{x}, & x > 0 \end{cases}$

A function is **one-to-one** when to each value of the dependent variable in the range there corresponds exactly one value of the independent variable in the domain. For instance, the function in Example 2(a) is one-to-one, whereas the function in Example 2(b) is not one-to-one.

Geometrically, a function is one-to-one when every horizontal line intersects the graph of the function at most once. This geometrical interpretation is the **Horizontal Line Test** for one-to-one functions. So, a graph that represents a one-to-one function must satisfy *both* the Vertical Line Test and the Horizontal Line Test.

Function Notation

When using an equation to define a function, you generally isolate the dependent variable on the left. For instance, writing the equation $x + 2y = 1$ as

$$y = \frac{1 - x}{2}$$

indicates that y is the dependent variable. In **function notation,** this equation has the form

$$f(x) = \frac{1 - x}{2}. \qquad \text{Function notation}$$

The independent variable is x, and the name of the function is "f." The symbol $f(x)$ is read as "f of x," and it denotes the value of the dependent variable. For instance, the value of f when $x = 3$ is

$$f(3) = \frac{1 - (3)}{2} = \frac{-2}{2} = -1.$$

The value $f(3)$ is called a **function value,** and it lies in the range of f. This means that the point $(3, f(3))$ lies on the graph of f. One of the advantages of function notation is that it allows you to be less wordy. For instance, instead of asking "What is the value of y when $x = 3$?" you can ask "What is $f(3)$?"

Example 3   Evaluating a Function

Find the values of the function

$$f(x) = 2x^2 - 4x + 1$$

when x is -1, 0, and 2. Is f one-to-one?

SOLUTION   You can evaluate f at the given values of x as shown.

$$x = -1: f(-1) = 2(-1)^2 - 4(-1) + 1 = 2 + 4 + 1 = 7$$
$$x = 0: \quad f(0) = 2(0)^2 - 4(0) + 1 = 0 - 0 + 1 = 1$$
$$x = 2: \quad f(2) = 2(2)^2 - 4(2) + 1 = 8 - 8 + 1 = 1$$

Because two different values of x yield the same value of $f(x)$, the function is *not* one-to-one, as shown in Figure 1.46.

STUDY TIP

You can use the Horizontal Line Test to determine whether the function in Example 3 is one-to-one. Because the line $y = 1$ intersects the graph of the function twice, the function is *not* one-to-one.

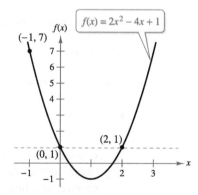

FIGURE 1.46

✓ Checkpoint 3

Find the values of $f(x) = x^2 - 5x + 1$ when x is 0, 1, and 4. Is f one-to-one?

Example 3 suggests that the role of the variable x in the equation

$$f(x) = 2x^2 - 4x + 1$$

is simply that of a placeholder. Informally, f could be defined by the equation

$$f(\quad) = 2(\quad)^2 - 4(\quad) + 1.$$

To evaluate $f(-2)$, simply place -2 in each set of parentheses.

$$f(-2) = 2(-2)^2 - 4(-2) + 1 = 8 + 8 + 1 = 17$$

Although f is often used as a convenient function name and x as the independent variable, you can use other symbols. For instance, the following equations all define the same function.

$f(x) = x^2 - 4x + 7$	Function name is f, independent variable is x.
$f(t) = t^2 - 4t + 7$	Function name is f, independent variable is t.
$g(s) = s^2 - 4s + 7$	Function name is g, independent variable is s.

Example 4   Evaluating a Function

Given $f(x) = x^2 + 7$, evaluate each expression.

a. $f(x + \Delta x)$ **b.** $\dfrac{f(x + \Delta x) - f(x)}{\Delta x}$

SOLUTION

a. To evaluate f at $x + \Delta x$, substitute $x + \Delta x$ for x in the original function.

$$\begin{aligned} f(x + \Delta x) &= (x + \Delta x)^2 + 7 \\ &= x^2 + 2x\,\Delta x + (\Delta x)^2 + 7 \end{aligned}$$

b. Using the result of part (a), you can write

$$\begin{aligned} \frac{f(x + \Delta x) - f(x)}{\Delta x} &= \frac{[(x + \Delta x)^2 + 7] - (x^2 + 7)}{\Delta x} \\ &= \frac{x^2 + 2x\,\Delta x + (\Delta x)^2 + 7 - x^2 - 7}{\Delta x} \\ &= \frac{2x\,\Delta x + (\Delta x)^2}{\Delta x} \\ &= \frac{\Delta x(2x + \Delta x)}{\Delta x} \\ &= 2x + \Delta x, \quad \Delta x \neq 0. \end{aligned}$$

✓ **Checkpoint 4**

Given $f(x) = x^2 + 3$, evaluate each expression.

a. $f(x + \Delta x)$ **b.** $\dfrac{f(x + \Delta x) - f(x)}{\Delta x}$

In Example 4(b), the expression

$$\frac{f(x + \Delta x) - f(x)}{\Delta x} \qquad \text{Difference quotient}$$

is called a *difference quotient* and has a special significance in calculus. You will learn more about this in Chapter 2.

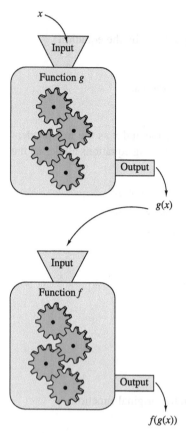

FIGURE 1.47

Combinations of Functions

Two functions can be combined in various ways to create new functions. For instance, given $f(x) = 2x - 3$ and $g(x) = x^2 + 1$, you can form the following functions.

$$f(x) + g(x) = (2x - 3) + (x^2 + 1) = x^2 + 2x - 2 \qquad \text{Sum}$$

$$f(x) - g(x) = (2x - 3) - (x^2 + 1) = -x^2 + 2x - 4 \qquad \text{Difference}$$

$$f(x)g(x) = (2x - 3)(x^2 + 1) = 2x^3 - 3x^2 + 2x - 3 \qquad \text{Product}$$

$$\frac{f(x)}{g(x)} = \frac{2x - 3}{x^2 + 1} \qquad \text{Quotient}$$

You can combine two functions in yet another way called a **composition.** The resulting function is called a **composite function.** For instance, given $f(x) = x^2$ and $g(x) = x + 1$, the composite of f with g is

$$f(g(x)) = f(x + 1) = (x + 1)^2.$$

This composition is denoted by $f \circ g$ and is read as "f composed with g."

Definition of Composite Function

Let f and g be functions. The function given by

$$(f \circ g)(x) = f(g(x))$$

is the **composite** of f with g. The **domain** of $f \circ g$ is the set of all x in the domain of g such that $g(x)$ is in the domain of f, as indicated in Figure 1.47.

The composite of f with g may not be equal to the composite of g with f, as shown in the next example.

Example 5   Forming Composite Functions

Given $f(x) = 2x - 3$ and $g(x) = x^2 + 1$, find each composite function.

a. $f(g(x))$ **b.** $g(f(x))$

SOLUTION

a. The composite of f with g is given by

$$\begin{aligned}
f(g(x)) &= 2(g(x)) - 3 && \text{Evaluate } f \text{ at } g(x).\\
&= 2(x^2 + 1) - 3 && \text{Substitute } x^2 + 1 \text{ for } g(x).\\
&= 2x^2 + 2 - 3 && \text{Distributive Property}\\
&= 2x^2 - 1. && \text{Simplify.}
\end{aligned}$$

b. The composite of g with f is given by

$$\begin{aligned}
g(f(x)) &= (f(x))^2 + 1 && \text{Evaluate } g \text{ at } f(x).\\
&= (2x - 3)^2 + 1 && \text{Substitute } 2x - 3 \text{ for } f(x).\\
&= 4x^2 - 12x + 9 + 1 && \text{Expand.}\\
&= 4x^2 - 12x + 10. && \text{Simplify.}
\end{aligned}$$

STUDY TIP

The expressions for $f(g(x))$ and $g(f(x))$ are different in Example 5. In general, the composite of f with g is not the same as the composite of g with f.

✓**Checkpoint 5**

Given $f(x) = 2x + 1$ and $g(x) = x^2 + 2$, find each composite function.

a. $f(g(x))$ **b.** $g(f(x))$

Inverse Functions

Informally, the inverse function of f is another function g that "undoes" what f has done. For instance, subtraction can be used to undo addition, and division can be used to undo multiplication.

$$x \qquad f(x) \qquad g(f(x)) = x$$

Definition of Inverse Function

Let f and g be two functions such that

$$f(g(x)) = x \text{ for each } x \text{ in the domain of } g$$

and

$$g(f(x)) = x \text{ for each } x \text{ in the domain of } f.$$

Under these conditions, the function g is the **inverse function** of f. The function g is denoted by f^{-1}, which is read as "f-inverse." So,

$$f(f^{-1}(x)) = x \qquad \text{and} \qquad f^{-1}(f(x)) = x.$$

The domain of f must be equal to the range of f^{-1}, and the range of f must be equal to the domain of f^{-1}.

Do not be confused by the use of the superscript -1 to denote the inverse function f^{-1}. In this text, whenever f^{-1} is written, it *always* refers to the inverse function of f and *not* to the reciprocal of $f(x)$.

Example 6 Finding Inverse Functions Informally

Find the inverse function of each function informally.

a. $f(x) = 2x$ **b.** $f(x) = x + 4$

SOLUTION

a. The function f *multiplies* each input by 2. To "undo" this function, you need to *divide* each input by 2. So, the inverse function of $f(x) = 2x$ is

$$f^{-1}(x) = \frac{x}{2}.$$

b. The function f *adds* 4 to each input. To "undo" this function, you need to *subtract* 4 from each input. So, the inverse function of $f(x) = x + 4$ is

$$f^{-1}(x) = x - 4.$$

Check that f and f^{-1} are inverse functions by showing that $f(f^{-1}(x)) = x$ and $f^{-1}(f(x)) = x$.

✓ Checkpoint 6

Find the inverse function of each function informally.

a. $f(x) = \frac{1}{5}x$ **b.** $f(x) = x - 6$

The graphs of f and f^{-1} are mirror images of each other (with respect to the line $y = x$), as shown in Figure 1.48. Try using a graphing utility with a *square setting* to confirm this for each of the functions given in Example 6.

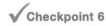

The graph of f^{-1} is a reflection of the graph of f in the line $y = x$.

FIGURE 1.48

The functions in Example 6 are simple enough so that their inverse functions can be found by inspection. The next example demonstrates a strategy for finding the inverse functions of more complicated functions.

Example 7   Finding an Inverse Function

Find the inverse function of $f(x) = \sqrt{2x - 3}$.

SOLUTION Begin by replacing $f(x)$ with y. Then, interchange x and y and solve for y.

$$f(x) = \sqrt{2x - 3} \qquad \text{Write original function.}$$
$$y = \sqrt{2x - 3} \qquad \text{Replace } f(x) \text{ with } y.$$
$$x = \sqrt{2y - 3} \qquad \text{Interchange } x \text{ and } y.$$
$$x^2 = 2y - 3 \qquad \text{Square each side.}$$
$$x^2 + 3 = 2y \qquad \text{Add 3 to each side.}$$
$$\frac{x^2 + 3}{2} = y \qquad \text{Divide each side by 2.}$$

So, the inverse function has the form

$$f^{-1}(\quad) = \frac{(\quad)^2 + 3}{2}.$$

Using x as the independent variable, you can write

$$f^{-1}(x) = \frac{x^2 + 3}{2}, \quad x \geq 0.$$

In Figure 1.49, note that the domain of f^{-1} coincides with the range of f.

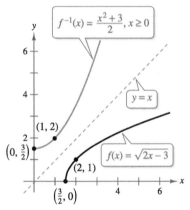

$$f^{-1}(x) = \frac{x^2 + 3}{2}, x \geq 0$$

$y = x$

$(1, 2)$

$(0, \frac{3}{2})$

$(2, 1)$

$f(x) = \sqrt{2x - 3}$

$(\frac{3}{2}, 0)$

FIGURE 1.49

✓ Checkpoint 7

Find the inverse function of $f(x) = x^2 + 2$ for $x \geq 0$.   ▨

After you have found an inverse function, you should check your results. You can check your results *graphically* by observing that the graphs of f and f^{-1} are reflections of each other in the line

$$y = x.$$

You can check your results *algebraically* by evaluating $f(f^{-1}(x))$ and $f^{-1}(f(x))$—both should be equal to x.

Check that $f(f^{-1}(x)) = x$

$$f(f^{-1}(x)) = f\left(\frac{x^2 + 3}{2}\right)$$
$$= \sqrt{2\left(\frac{x^2 + 3}{2}\right) - 3}$$
$$= \sqrt{x^2}$$
$$= x, \quad x \geq 0$$

Check that $f^{-1}(f(x)) = x$

$$f^{-1}(f(x)) = f^{-1}\left(\sqrt{2x - 3}\right)$$
$$= \frac{\left(\sqrt{2x - 3}\right)^2 + 3}{2}$$
$$= \frac{2x}{2}$$
$$= x, \quad x \geq \frac{3}{2}$$

TECH TUTOR

A graphing utility can help you check that the graphs of f and f^{-1} are reflections of each other in the line $y = x$. To do this, graph $y = f(x)$, $y = f^{-1}(x)$, and $y = x$ in the same viewing window, using a square setting.

Not every function has an inverse function. In fact, for a function to have an inverse function, it must be one-to-one.

Example 8   A Function That Has No Inverse Function

Show that the function

$$f(x) = x^2 - 1$$

has no inverse function. (Assume that the domain of f is the set of all real numbers.)

SOLUTION   Begin by sketching the graph of f, as shown in Figure 1.50. Note that

$$f(2) = (2)^2 - 1 = 3$$

and

$$f(-2) = (-2)^2 - 1 = 3.$$

So, f does not pass the Horizontal Line Test, which implies that it is not one-to-one and therefore has no inverse function. The same conclusion can be obtained by trying to find the inverse function of f algebraically.

$f(x) = x^2 - 1$	Write original function.
$y = x^2 - 1$	Replace $f(x)$ with y.
$x = y^2 - 1$	Interchange x and y.
$x + 1 = y^2$	Add 1 to each side.
$\pm\sqrt{x + 1} = y$	Take square root of each side.

The last equation does not define y as a function of x, and so f has no inverse function.

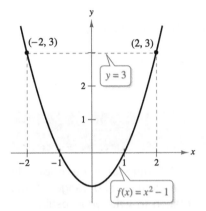

f is not one-to-one and has no inverse function.

FIGURE 1.50

✓ **Checkpoint 8**

Show that the function

$$f(x) = x^2 + 4$$

has no inverse function.

SUMMARIZE   (Section 1.4)

1. State the definition of a function *(page 35)*. For an example of a function, see Example 1.

2. Explain the meanings of domain and range *(page 37)*. For an example of a domain and a range, see Example 2.

3. Explain the meaning of function notation *(page 38)*. For examples of function notation, see Examples 3 and 4.

4. State the definition of a composite function *(page 40)*. For an example of a composite function, see Example 5.

5. State the definition of an inverse function *(page 41)*. For examples of inverse functions, see Examples 6 and 7.

6. State when a function does not have an inverse function *(page 43)*. For an example of a function that does not have an inverse function, see Example 8.

SKILLS WARM UP 1.4 The following warm-up exercises involve skills that were covered in a previous course. You will use these skills in the exercise set for this section. For additional help, review Appendix Sections A.3 and A.5.

In Exercises 1–6, simplify the expression.

1. $5(-1)^2 - 6(-1) + 9$

2. $(-2)^3 + 7(-2)^2 - 10$

3. $(x - 2)^2 + 5x - 10$

4. $(3 - x) + (x + 3)^3$

5. $\dfrac{1}{1 - (1 - x)}$

6. $1 + \dfrac{x - 1}{x}$

In Exercises 7–12, solve for y in terms of x.

7. $2x + y - 6 = 11$

8. $5y - 6x^2 - 1 = 0$

9. $(y - 3)^2 = 5 + (x + 1)^2$

10. $y^2 - 4x^2 = 2$

11. $x = \dfrac{2y - 1}{4}$

12. $x = \sqrt[3]{2y - 1}$

Exercises 1.4

See www.CalcChat.com for worked-out solutions to odd-numbered exercises.

Deciding Whether Equations Are Functions In Exercises 1–8, decide whether the equation defines y as a function of x. *See Example 1.*

1. $x^2 + y^2 = 16$

2. $x + y^2 = 4$

3. $\frac{1}{2}x - 6y = -3$

4. $3x - 2y + 5 = 0$

5. $x^2 + y = 4$

6. $x^2 + y^2 + 2x = 0$

7. $y = |x + 2|$

8. $x^2y - x^2 + 4y = 0$

Vertical Line Test In Exercises 9–12, use the Vertical Line Test to determine whether y is a function of x.

9. $x^2 + y^2 = 9$

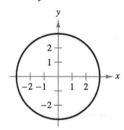

10. $x - xy + y + 1 = 0$

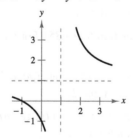

11. $x^2 = xy - 1$

12. $x = |y|$

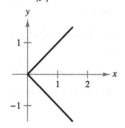

Finding the Domain and Range of a Function In Exercises 13–16, find the domain and range of the function. Use interval notation to write your result. *See Example 2.*

13. $f(x) = x^3$

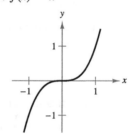

14. $f(x) = \sqrt{2x - 3}$

15. $f(x) = 4 - x^2$

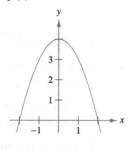

16. $f(x) = |x - 2|$

Finding the Domain and Range of a Function In Exercises 17–24, find the domain and range of the function. Use a graphing utility to verify your results. *See Example 2.*

17. $f(x) = 2x^2 - 5x + 1$

18. $f(x) = 5x^3 + 6x^2 - 1$

19. $f(x) = \dfrac{|x|}{x}$

20. $f(x) = \sqrt{9 - x^2}$

21. $f(x) = \dfrac{x}{\sqrt{x - 4}}$

22. $f(x) = \begin{cases} 3x + 2, & x < 0 \\ 2 - x, & x \geq 0 \end{cases}$

23. $f(x) = \dfrac{x - 2}{x + 4}$

24. $f(x) = \dfrac{x^2}{1 - x}$

Evaluating a Function In Exercises 25–28, evaluate the function at the specified values of the independent variable. Simplify the results. *See Example 3.*

25. $f(x) = 3x - 2$

    (a) $f(0)$ (b) $f(5)$ (c) $f(x - 1)$

26. $f(x) = x^2 - 4x + 1$

    (a) $f(-1)$ (b) $f\left(\frac{1}{2}\right)$ (c) $f(c + 2)$

27. $g(x) = 1/x$

    (a) $g\left(\frac{1}{4}\right)$ (b) $g(-4)$ (c) $g(x + 4)$

28. $f(x) = |x| + 4$

    (a) $f(-2)$ (b) $f(2)$ (c) $f(x + 2)$

Evaluating a Function In Exercises 29–34, evaluate the difference quotient and simplify the result. *See Example 4.*

29. $f(x) = x^2 - 5x + 2$ **30.** $h(x) = x^2 + x + 3$

$$\frac{f(x + \Delta x) - f(x)}{\Delta x}$$ $$\frac{h(2 + \Delta x) - h(2)}{\Delta x}$$

31. $g(x) = \sqrt{x + 1}$ **32.** $f(x) = \dfrac{1}{\sqrt{x}}$

$$\frac{g(x + \Delta x) - g(x)}{\Delta x}$$ $$\frac{f(x) - f(2)}{x - 2}$$

33. $f(x) = \dfrac{1}{x - 2}$ **34.** $f(x) = \dfrac{1}{x + 4}$

$$\frac{f(x + \Delta x) - f(x)}{\Delta x}$$ $$\frac{f(x + \Delta x) - f(x)}{\Delta x}$$

Combinations of Functions In Exercises 35–38, find (a) $f(x) + g(x)$, (b) $f(x) - g(x)$, (c) $f(x) \cdot g(x)$, (d) $f(x)/g(x)$, (e) $f(g(x))$, and (f) $g(f(x))$, if defined. *See Example 5.*

35. $f(x) = 2x - 5$ **36.** $f(x) = x^2 + 5$

    $g(x) = 5$ $g(x) = \sqrt{1 - x}$

37. $f(x) = x^2 + 1$ **38.** $f(x) = \dfrac{x}{x + 1}$

    $g(x) = x - 1$ $g(x) = x^3$

39. Composite Functions Given $f(x) = \sqrt{x}$ and $g(x) = x^2 - 1$, find the composite functions.

    (a) $f(g(1))$ (b) $g(f(1))$

    (c) $g(f(0))$ (d) $f(g(-4))$

    (e) $f(g(x))$ (f) $g(f(x))$

40. Composite Functions Given $f(x) = 1/x$ and $g(x) = x^2 - 1$, find the composite functions.

    (a) $f(g(2))$ (b) $g(f(2))$

    (c) $f(g(-3))$ (d) $g(f(1/\sqrt{2}))$

    (e) $f(g(x))$ (f) $g(f(x))$

Finding Inverse Functions Informally In Exercises 41–44, find the inverse function of *f* informally. Verify your results by showing that $f(f^{-1}(x)) = x$ and $f^{-1}(f(x)) = x$. *See Example 6.*

41. $f(x) = 4x$

42. $f(x) = \frac{1}{3}x$

43. $f(x) = x + 12$

44. $f(x) = x - 3$

Finding an Inverse Function In Exercises 45–56, find the inverse function of *f*. *See Example 7.*

45. $f(x) = 2x - 3$ **46.** $f(x) = 7 - x$

47. $f(x) = \frac{3}{2}x + 1$ **48.** $f(x) = -6x - 4$

49. $f(x) = x^5$ **50.** $f(x) = x^3$

51. $f(x) = \dfrac{1}{x}$ **52.** $f(x) = -\dfrac{2}{x}$

53. $f(x) = \sqrt{9 - x^2}, \quad 0 \le x \le 3$

54. $f(x) = \sqrt{x^2 - 4}, \quad x \ge 2$

55. $f(x) = x^{2/3}, \quad x \ge 0$

56. $f(x) = x^{3/5}$

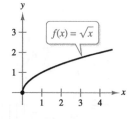

Determine Whether a Function Is One-to-One In Exercises 57–62, use a graphing utility to graph the function. Then use the Horizontal Line Test to determine whether the function is one-to-one. If it is, find its inverse function.

57. $f(x) = 3 - 7x$ **58.** $f(x) = \sqrt{x - 2}$

59. $f(x) = x^2$ **60.** $f(x) = x^4$

61. $f(x) = |x + 3|$ **62.** $f(x) = -5$

63. Graphing a Function Use the graph of $f(x) = \sqrt{x}$ below to sketch the graph of each function.

    (a) $y = \sqrt{x} + 2$

    (b) $y = -\sqrt{x}$

    (c) $y = \sqrt{x - 2}$

    (d) $y = \sqrt{x + 3}$

    (e) $y = \sqrt{x - 4} - 1$

    (f) $y = 2\sqrt{x}$

64. Graphing a Function Use the graph of $f(x) = |x|$ below to sketch the graph of each function.

    (a) $y = |x| + 3$

    (b) $y = -\frac{1}{2}|x|$

    (c) $y = |x - 2|$

    (d) $y = |x + 1| - 1$

    (e) $y = 2|x|$

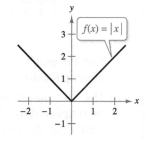

65. Writing a Function Use the graph of $f(x) = x^2$ to write an equation for each function whose graph is shown.

(a)

(−3, 0)

(b)

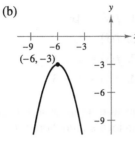

(−6, −3)

66. Writing a Function Use the graph of $f(x) = x^3$ to write an equation for each function whose graph is shown.

(a)

(2, 1)

(b)

(1, −2)

67. Prescription Drugs The amounts d (in billions of dollars) spent on prescription drugs in the United States from 1997 through 2008 (see figure) can be approximated by the model

$$d(t) = \begin{cases} 15.35t - 32.2, & 7 \le t \le 11 \\ -0.687t^2 + 33.57t - 146.5, & 12 \le t \le 18 \end{cases}$$

where t represents the year, with $t = 7$ corresponding to 1997. *(Source: U.S. Centers for Medicare & Medicaid Services)*

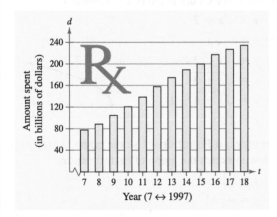

Year (7 ↔ 1997)

(a) Use the graph to estimate the amounts spent on prescription drugs in 2000, 2003, and 2007.

(b) Use the model to find the amounts spent on prescription drugs in 2000, 2003, and 2007. How well does the model fit the data? Explain your reasoning.

 68. **HOW DO YOU SEE IT?** An electronically controlled thermostat in a home is programmed to lower the temperature automatically during the night. The temperature in the house T (in degrees Fahrenheit) is given in terms of t, the time in hours on a 24-hour clock (see figure).

Time (in hours)

(a) Explain why T is a function of t.

(b) Approximate $T(4)$ and $T(15)$.

(c) The thermostat is reprogrammed to produce a temperature H for which

$$H(t) = T(t - 1).$$

How does this change the temperature?

(d) The thermostat is reprogrammed to produce a temperature H for which

$$H(t) = T(t) - 1.$$

How does this change the temperature?

69. Owning a Business You own two restaurants. From 2005 through 2011, the sales R_1 (in thousands of dollars) for one restaurant can be modeled by

$$R_1 = 690 - 8t - 0.8t^2, \quad t = 5, 6, 7, 8, 9, 10, 11$$

where $t = 1$ represents 2001. During the same seven-year period, the sales R_2 (in thousands of dollars) for the second restaurant can be modeled by

$$R_2 = 458 + 0.78t, \quad t = 5, 6, 7, 8, 9, 10, 11.$$

Write a function that represents the total sales for the two restaurants. Use a graphing utility to graph the total sales function.

70. Births and Deaths From 1990 to 2007, the total numbers of births B (in thousands) and deaths D (in thousands) in the United States can be approximated by the models

$$B(t) = -0.151t^3 + 8.00t^2 - 85.0t + 4176$$

and

$$D(t) = -1.25t^2 + 38.5t + 2136$$

where t represents the year, with $t = 0$ corresponding to 1990. Find $B(t) - D(t)$ and interpret this function. *(Source: U.S. National Center for Health Statistics)*

71. Cost The inventor of a new game believes that the variable cost for producing the game is $1.95 per unit. The fixed cost is $6000.

(a) Express the total cost C as a function of x, the number of games sold.

(b) Find a formula for the average cost per unit

$$\overline{C} = \frac{C}{x}.$$

(c) The selling price for each game is $4.95. How many units must be sold before the average cost per unit falls below the selling price?

72. Demand The demand function for a commodity is

$$p = \frac{14.75}{1 + 0.01x}, \quad x \ge 0$$

where p is the price per unit and x is the number of units sold.

(a) Find x as a function of p.

(b) Find the number of units sold when the price is $10.

73. Cost The weekly cost C of producing x units in a manufacturing process is given by $C(x) = 70x + 500$. The number of units x produced in t hours is given by $x(t) = 40t$.

(a) Find and interpret $C(x(t))$.

(b) Find the cost of 4 hours of production.

(c) After how much time does the cost of production reach $18,000?

74. Revenue For groups of 80 or more people, a charter bus company determines the rate r (in dollars per person) according to the formula

$$r = 15 - 0.05(n - 80), \quad n \ge 80$$

where n is the number of people.

(a) Express the revenue R for the bus company as a function of n.

(b) Complete the table.

n	100	125	150	175	200	225	250
R							

(c) Would you use the formula for the rate? Explain your reasoning.

75. Cost, Revenue, and Profit A company invests $98,000 for equipment to produce a new product. Each unit of the product costs $12.30 and is sold for $17.98. Let x be the number of units produced and sold.

(a) Write the total cost C as a function of x.

(b) Write the revenue R as a function of x.

(c) Write the profit P as a function of x.

Courtesy of CitiKitty Inc.

76. Profit A manufacturer charges $90 per unit for units that cost $60 to produce. To encourage large orders from distributors, the manufacturer will reduce the price by $0.01 per unit for each unit in excess of 100 units. (For example, an order of 101 units would have a price of $89.99 per unit, and an order of 102 units would have a price of $89.98 per unit.) This price reduction is discontinued when the price per unit drops to $75.

(a) Express the price per unit p as a function of the order size x.

(b) Express the profit P as a function of the order size x.

Graphing Functions In Exercises 77–82, use a graphing utility to graph the function. Then use the *zoom* and *trace* features to find the zeros of the function. Is the function one-to-one?

77. $f(x) = 9x - 4x^2$

78. $h(x) = 6x^3 - 12x^2 + 4$

79. $g(t) = \dfrac{t + 3}{1 - t}$

80. $f(x) = 2\left(3x^2 - \dfrac{6}{x}\right)$

81. $g(x) = x^2\sqrt{x^2 - 4}$

82. $f(x) = (x + 3)^3$

Business Capsule

CitiKitty, Inc. was founded in 2005 by 26-year-old Rebecca Rescate after she moved into a small apartment in New York City with no place to hide her cat's litter box. Finding no easy-to-use cat toilet training kit, she created one, and CitiKitty was born with an initial investment of $20,000. Today the company flourishes with an expanded product line. Revenues in 2010 reached $350,000.

83. Research Project Use your school's library, the Internet, or some other reference source to find information about the start-up costs of beginning a business, such as the example above. Write a short paper about the company.

1.5 Limits

■ Find limits of functions graphically and numerically.

■ Understand the definition of the limit of a function and use the properties of limits to evaluate limits of functions.

■ Use different analytic techniques to evaluate limits of functions.

■ Evaluate one-sided limits.

■ Recognize unbounded behavior of functions.

The Limit of a Function

In everyday language, people refer to a speed limit, a wrestler's weight limit, the limit of one's endurance, or stretching a spring to its limit. These phrases all suggest that a limit is a bound, which on some occasions may not be reached but on other occasions may be reached or exceeded.

Consider a spring that will break only when a weight of 10 pounds or more is attached. To determine how far the spring will stretch without breaking, you could attach increasingly heavier weights and measure the spring length s for each weight w, as shown in Figure 1.51. If the spring length approaches a value of L, then it is said that "the limit of s as w approaches 10 is L." A mathematical limit is much like the limit of a spring. The notation for a limit is

$$\lim_{x \to c} f(x) = L$$

which is read as "the limit of $f(x)$ as x approaches c is L."

In Exercise 75 on page 59, you will use a limit to analyze the cost of removing pollutants from a small lake.

What is the limit of s as w approaches 10 pounds?

FIGURE 1.51

Example 1 Finding a Limit

Find the limit: $\lim_{x \to 1} (x^2 + 1)$.

SOLUTION Let $f(x) = x^2 + 1$. From the graph of f in Figure 1.52, it appears that $f(x)$ approaches 2 as x approaches 1 from either side, and you can write

$$\lim_{x \to 1} (x^2 + 1) = 2.$$

The table yields the same conclusion. Notice that as x gets closer and closer to 1, $f(x)$ gets closer and closer to 2.

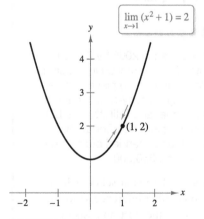

$$\lim_{x \to 1} (x^2 + 1) = 2$$

(1, 2)

FIGURE 1.52

	x approaches 1.				x approaches 1.		
x	0.900	0.990	0.999	1.000	1.001	1.010	1.100
$f(x)$	1.810	1.980	1.998	2.000	2.002	2.020	2.210
	$f(x)$ approaches 2.				$f(x)$ approaches 2.		

✓ **Checkpoint 1**

Find the limit: $\lim_{x \to 1} (2x + 4)$.

(a)

(b)

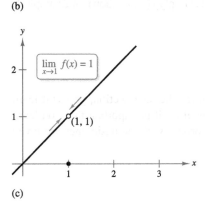

(c)

FIGURE 1.53

Example 2   **Finding Limits Graphically and Numerically**

Find the limit.

$$\lim_{x \to 1} f(x)$$

a. $f(x) = \dfrac{x^2 - 1}{x - 1}$ **b.** $f(x) = \dfrac{|x - 1|}{x - 1}$ **c.** $f(x) = \begin{cases} x, & x \neq 1 \\ 0, & x = 1 \end{cases}$

SOLUTION

a. From the graph of f in Figure 1.53(a), it appears that $f(x)$ approaches 2 as x approaches 1 from either side. A missing point is denoted by the open dot on the graph. This conclusion is reinforced by the table. Be sure you see that *it does not matter that $f(x)$ is undefined when $x = 1$.* The limit depends only on values of $f(x)$ near 1, not at 1.

	x approaches 1.				x approaches 1.		
x	0.900	0.990	0.999	1.000	1.001	1.010	1.100
$f(x)$	1.900	1.990	1.999	?	2.001	2.010	2.100

$f(x)$ approaches 2. $f(x)$ approaches 2.

b. From the graph of f in Figure 1.53(b), you can see that $f(x) = -1$ for all values to the left of $x = 1$ and $f(x) = 1$ for all values to the right of $x = 1$. So, $f(x)$ is approaching a different value from the left of $x = 1$ than it is from the right of $x = 1$. In such situations, you can conclude that *the limit does not exist.* This conclusion is reinforced by the table.

	x approaches 1.				x approaches 1.		
x	0.900	0.990	0.999	1.000	1.001	1.010	1.100
$f(x)$	-1.000	-1.000	-1.000	?	1.000	1.000	1.000

$f(x)$ approaches -1. $f(x)$ approaches 1.

c. From the graph of f in Figure 1.53(c), it appears that $f(x)$ approaches 1 as x approaches 1 from either side. This conclusion is reinforced by the table. It does not matter that $f(1) = 0$. The limit depends only on values of $f(x)$ near 1, not at 1.

	x approaches 1.				x approaches 1.		
x	0.900	0.990	0.999	1.000	1.001	1.010	1.100
$f(x)$	0.900	0.990	0.999	?	1.001	1.010	1.100

$f(x)$ approaches 1. $f(x)$ approaches 1.

✓ Checkpoint 2

Find the limit.

$$\lim_{x \to 2} f(x)$$

a. $f(x) = \dfrac{x^2 - 4}{x - 2}$ **b.** $f(x) = \dfrac{|x - 2|}{x - 2}$ **c.** $f(x) = \begin{cases} x^2, & x \neq 2 \\ 0, & x = 2 \end{cases}$

TECH TUTOR

You can use a graphing utility to estimate the limit of a function. One way is to estimate the limit numerically by creating a table of values using the *table* feature. Another way is to graph the function and use the *zoom* and *trace* features to estimate the limit graphically.

Definition of the Limit of a Function and Properties of Limits

There are three important ideas to learn from Examples 1 and 2.

1. Saying that the limit of $f(x)$ approaches L as x approaches c means that the value of $f(x)$ may be made *arbitrarily close* to the number L by choosing x closer and closer to c.

2. If $f(x)$ approaches the same number from *either side* of c, then the limit of $f(x)$ as x approaches c exists. However, if $f(x)$ approaches a different number from the right side of c than it does from the left side, then the limit of $f(x)$ as x approaches c *does not exist.* [See Example 2(b).]

3. The value of $f(x)$ when $x = c$ has no bearing on the existence or nonexistence of the limit of $f(x)$ as x approaches c. For instance, in Example 2(a), the limit of $f(x)$ exists as x approaches 1 even though the function f is not defined at $x = 1$.

Definition of the Limit of a Function

If $f(x)$ becomes arbitrarily close to a single number L as x approaches c from either side, then

$$\lim_{x \to c} f(x) = L$$

which is read as "the **limit** of $f(x)$ as x approaches c is L."

Many times the limit of $f(x)$ as x approaches c is simply $f(c)$, as shown in Example 1. Whenever the limit of $f(x)$ as x approaches c is

$$\lim_{x \to c} f(x) = f(c) \qquad \text{Substitute } c \text{ for } x.$$

the limit can be evaluated by **direct substitution.** (In the next section, you will learn that a function that has this property is *continuous at c.*) It is important that you learn to recognize the types of functions that have this property. Some basic ones are given in the following list.

Some Basic Limits

Let b and c be real numbers, and let n be a positive integer.

1. $\lim\limits_{x \to c} b = b$ 2. $\lim\limits_{x \to c} x = c$ 3. $\lim\limits_{x \to c} x^n = c^n$ 4. $\lim\limits_{x \to c} \sqrt[n]{x} = \sqrt[n]{c}$

In Property 4, if n is even, then c must be positive.

Example 3   **Evaluating Basic Limits**

a. $\lim\limits_{x \to 2} 3 = 3$ b. $\lim\limits_{x \to -4} x = -4$

c. $\lim\limits_{x \to 2} x^3 = 2^3 = 8$ d. $\lim\limits_{x \to 9} \sqrt{x} = \sqrt{9} = 3$

✓ **Checkpoint 3**

Find the limit.

a. $\lim\limits_{x \to 1} 5$ b. $\lim\limits_{x \to 6} x$ c. $\lim\limits_{x \to 5} x^2$ d. $\lim\limits_{x \to -8} \sqrt[3]{x}$

By combining the basic limits from the preceding page with the properties of limits shown below, you can find limits for a wide variety of algebraic functions.

Properties of Limits

Let b and c be real numbers, let n be a positive integer, and let f and g be functions with the following limits.

$$\lim_{x \to c} f(x) = L \quad \text{and} \quad \lim_{x \to c} g(x) = K$$

1. Scalar multiple: $\lim_{x \to c} [bf(x)] = bL$

2. Sum or difference: $\lim_{x \to c} [f(x) \pm g(x)] = L \pm K$

3. Product: $\lim_{x \to c} [f(x) \cdot g(x)] = LK$

4. Quotient: $\lim_{x \to c} \dfrac{f(x)}{g(x)} = \dfrac{L}{K}$, provided $K \neq 0$

5. Power: $\lim_{x \to c} [f(x)]^n = L^n$

6. Radical: $\lim_{x \to c} \sqrt[n]{f(x)} = \sqrt[n]{L}$

In Property 6, if n is even, then L must be positive.

TECH TUTOR

Symbolic computer algebra systems are capable of evaluating limits. Try using a computer algebra system to evaluate the limit given in Example 4.

Example 4   **Finding the Limit of a Polynomial Function**

Find the limit: $\lim_{x \to 2} (x^2 + 2x - 3)$.

SOLUTION

$$
\begin{aligned}
\lim_{x \to 2} (x^2 + 2x - 3) &= \lim_{x \to 2} x^2 + \lim_{x \to 2} 2x - \lim_{x \to 2} 3 && \text{Apply Property 2.}\\
&= \lim_{x \to 2} x^2 + 2 \lim_{x \to 2} x - \lim_{x \to 2} 3 && \text{Apply Property 1.}\\
&= 2^2 + 2(2) - 3 && \text{Use direct substitution.}\\
&= 5
\end{aligned}
$$

✓ **Checkpoint 4**

Find the limit: $\lim_{x \to 1} (2x^2 - x + 4)$.

In Example 4, note that the limit (as $x \to 2$) of the *polynomial function*

$$p(x) = x^2 + 2x - 3$$

is simply the value of p at $x = 2$.

$$\lim_{x \to 2} p(x) = p(2) = 2^2 + 2(2) - 3 = 4 + 4 - 3 = 5$$

This is an illustration of the following important result, which states that the limit of a polynomial function can be evaluated by direct substitution.

The Limit of a Polynomial Function

If p is a polynomial function and c is any real number, then

$$\lim_{x \to c} p(x) = p(c).$$

Techniques for Evaluating Limits

You have learned several techniques for evaluating limits. Another technique is shown in Example 5.

Example 5   Finding the Limit of a Function

Find the limit.

$$\lim_{x \to 1} \frac{x^3 - 1}{x - 1}$$

SOLUTION   Note that the numerator and denominator are zero when $x = 1$. This implies that $x - 1$ is a factor of both, and you can divide out this common factor.

$$\frac{x^3 - 1}{x - 1} = \frac{(x - 1)(x^2 + x + 1)}{x - 1} \qquad \text{Factor numerator.}$$

$$= \frac{(x - 1)(x^2 + x + 1)}{x - 1} \qquad \text{Divide out common factor.}$$

$$= x^2 + x + 1, \quad x \neq 1 \qquad \text{Simplify.}$$

So, the rational function $(x^3 - 1)/(x - 1)$ and the polynomial function $x^2 + x + 1$ agree for all values of x other than $x = 1$, and you can apply the Replacement Theorem.

$$\lim_{x \to 1} \frac{x^3 - 1}{x - 1} = \lim_{x \to 1} (x^2 + x + 1) = 1^2 + 1 + 1 = 3$$

Figure 1.54 illustrates this result graphically. Note that the two graphs are identical except that the graph of g contains the point $(1, 3)$, whereas this point is missing on the graph of f. (In the graph of f in Figure 1.54, the missing point is denoted by an open dot.)

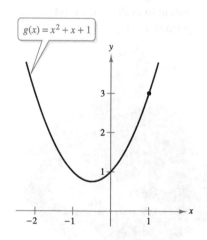

$f(x) = \dfrac{x^3 - 1}{x - 1}$

$g(x) = x^2 + x + 1$

FIGURE 1.54

✓ Checkpoint 5

Find the limit.

$$\lim_{x \to 2} \frac{x^3 - 8}{x - 2}$$

The technique used to evaluate the limit in Example 5 is called the **dividing out** technique. The validity of this technique stems from the fact that when two functions agree at all but a single number c, the functions must have identical limit behavior at $x = c$. This technique is further demonstrated in the next example.

Example 6   Using the Dividing Out Technique

For $\lim\limits_{x \to -3} \dfrac{x^2 + x - 6}{x + 3}$, direct substitution fails because both the numerator and the denominator are zero when $x = -3$.

$$\lim_{x \to -3} \frac{x^2 + x - 6}{x + 3} \qquad \begin{array}{l} \longleftarrow \lim\limits_{x \to -3} (x^2 + x - 6) = 0 \\[4pt] \longleftarrow \lim\limits_{x \to -3} (x + 3) = 0 \end{array}$$

Because the limits of both the numerator and the denominator are zero when $x = -3$, they must have a *common factor* of $x + 3$. So, for all $x \ne -3$, you can divide out this factor and find the limit as shown.

$$\begin{aligned}
\lim_{x \to -3} \frac{x^2 + x - 6}{x + 3} &= \lim_{x \to -3} \frac{(x - 2)(x + 3)}{x + 3} && \text{Factor numerator.} \\[4pt]
&= \lim_{x \to -3} \frac{(x - 2)(x + 3)}{x + 3} && \text{Divide out common factor.} \\[4pt]
&= \lim_{x \to -3} (x - 2) && \text{Simplify.} \\[4pt]
&= -3 - 2 && \text{Direct substitution} \\[4pt]
&= -5 && \text{Simplify.}
\end{aligned}$$

This result is shown graphically in Figure 1.55. Note that the graph of f coincides with the graph of $g(x) = x - 2$, except that the graph of f has a hole at $(-3, -5)$.

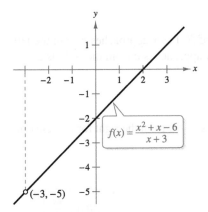

f is undefined when $x = -3$.

FIGURE 1.55

✔ **Checkpoint 6**

Find the limit: $\lim\limits_{x \to 3} \dfrac{x^2 + x - 12}{x - 3}$.

Example 7   Finding a Limit of a Function

Find the limit: $\lim\limits_{x \to 0} \dfrac{\sqrt{x + 1} - 1}{x}$.

SOLUTION   Direct substitution fails because both the numerator and the denominator are zero when $x = 0$. Rewrite the fraction by rationalizing the numerator.

$$\begin{aligned}
\frac{\sqrt{x + 1} - 1}{x} &= \left(\frac{\sqrt{x + 1} - 1}{x} \right)\left(\frac{\sqrt{x + 1} + 1}{\sqrt{x + 1} + 1} \right) \\[4pt]
&= \frac{(x + 1) - 1}{x\left(\sqrt{x + 1} + 1\right)} \\[4pt]
&= \frac{x}{x\left(\sqrt{x + 1} + 1\right)} \\[4pt]
&= \frac{1}{\sqrt{x + 1} + 1}, \quad x \ne 0
\end{aligned}$$

Now, using the Replacement Theorem, you can evaluate the limit as shown.

$$\lim_{x \to 0} \frac{\sqrt{x + 1} - 1}{x} = \lim_{x \to 0} \frac{1}{\sqrt{x + 1} + 1} = \frac{1}{\sqrt{0 + 1} + 1} = \frac{1}{1 + 1} = \frac{1}{2}$$

✔ **Checkpoint 7**

Find the limit: $\lim\limits_{x \to 0} \dfrac{\sqrt{x + 4} - 2}{x}$.

STUDY TIP

When you try to evaluate a limit and both the numerator and denominator are zero, remember that you must rewrite the fraction so that the new denominator does not have 0 as its limit. One way to do this is to divide out common factors, as shown in Example 6. Another technique is to rationalize the numerator, as shown in Example 7.

One-Sided Limits

In Example 2(b), you saw that one way in which a limit can fail to exist is when a function approaches a different value from the left of c than it approaches from the right of c. This type of behavior can be described more concisely with the concept of a **one-sided limit.**

$$\lim_{x \to c^-} f(x) = L \qquad \text{Limit from the left}$$

$$\lim_{x \to c^+} f(x) = L \qquad \text{Limit from the right}$$

The first of these two limits is read as "the limit of $f(x)$ as x approaches c from the left is L." The second is read as "the limit of $f(x)$ as x approaches c from the right is L."

Example 8   Finding One-Sided Limits

Find the limit as $x \to 0$ from the left and the limit as $x \to 0$ from the right for the function

$$f(x) = \frac{|2x|}{x}.$$

SOLUTION   From the graph of f, shown in Figure 1.56, you can see that

$$f(x) = -2$$

for all $x < 0$. So, the limit from the left is

$$\lim_{x \to 0^-} \frac{|2x|}{x} = -2. \qquad \text{Limit from the left}$$

Because

$$f(x) = 2$$

for all $x > 0$, the limit from the right is

$$\lim_{x \to 0^+} \frac{|2x|}{x} = 2. \qquad \text{Limit from the right}$$

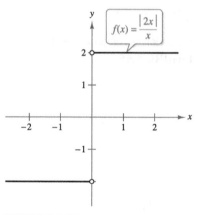

$$f(x) = \frac{|2x|}{x}$$

FIGURE 1.56

On most graphing utilities, the absolute value function is denoted by *abs*. You can verify the result in Example 8 by graphing

$$y = \frac{\text{abs}(2x)}{x}$$

in the viewing window $-3 \le x \le 3$ and $-3 \le y \le 3$.

✓ Checkpoint 8

Find each limit.

a. $\displaystyle \lim_{x \to 2^-} \frac{|x-2|}{x-2}$

b. $\displaystyle \lim_{x \to 2^+} \frac{|x-2|}{x-2}$

In Example 8, note that the function approaches different limits from the left and from the right. In such cases, the limit of $f(x)$ as $x \to c$ does not exist. For the limit of a function to exist as $x \to c$, *both* one-sided limits must exist and must be equal.

Existence of a Limit

If f is a function and c and L are real numbers, then

$$\lim_{x \to c} f(x) = L$$

if and only if both the left and right limits are equal to L.

Example 9   **Finding One-Sided Limits**

Find the limit of $f(x)$ as x approaches 1.

$$f(x) = \begin{cases} 4 - x, & x < 1 \\ 4x - x^2, & x > 1 \end{cases}$$

SOLUTION   Remember that you are concerned about the value of f near $x = 1$ rather than at $x = 1$. So, for $x < 1, f(x)$ is given by

$$4 - x$$

and you can use direct substitution to obtain

$$\lim_{x \to 1^-} f(x) = \lim_{x \to 1^-} (4 - x) = 4 - 1 = 3.$$

For $x > 1, f(x)$ is given by

$$4x - x^2$$

and you can use direct substitution to obtain

$$\lim_{x \to 1^+} f(x) = \lim_{x \to 1^+} (4x - x^2) = 4(1) - 1^2 = 4 - 1 = 3.$$

Because both one-sided limits exist and are equal to 3, it follows that

$$\lim_{x \to 1} f(x) = 3.$$

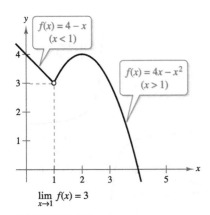

$$\lim_{x \to 1} f(x) = 3$$

FIGURE 1.57

The graph in Figure 1.57 confirms this conclusion.

✓**Checkpoint 9**

Find the limit of $f(x)$ as x approaches 0.

$$f(x) = \begin{cases} x^2 + 1, & x < 0 \\ 2x + 1, & x > 0 \end{cases}$$

Example 10   **Comparing One-Sided Limits**

An overnight delivery service charges \$18 for the first pound and \$2 for each additional pound. Let x represent the weight of a parcel and let $f(x)$ represent the shipping cost.

$$f(x) = \begin{cases} 18, & 0 < x \le 1 \\ 20, & 1 < x \le 2 \\ 22, & 2 < x \le 3 \end{cases}$$

Show that the limit of $f(x)$ as $x \to 2$ does not exist.

SOLUTION   The graph of f is shown in Figure 1.58. The limit of $f(x)$ as x approaches 2 from the left is

$$\lim_{x \to 2^-} f(x) = 20$$

whereas the limit of $f(x)$ as x approaches 2 from the right is

$$\lim_{x \to 2^+} f(x) = 22.$$

FIGURE 1.58

Because these one-sided limits are not equal, the limit of $f(x)$ as $x \to 2$ does not exist.

✓**Checkpoint 10**

Show that the limit of $f(x)$ as $x \to 1$ does not exist in Example 10.

Unbounded Behavior

Example 10 shows a limit that fails to exist because the limits from the left and right differ. Another important way in which a limit can fail to exist is when $f(x)$ increases or decreases without bound as x approaches c.

Example 11   An Unbounded Function

Find the limit (if possible): $\lim\limits_{x \to 2} \dfrac{3}{x - 2}$.

SOLUTION   From Figure 1.59, you can see that $f(x)$ decreases without bound as x approaches 2 from the left and $f(x)$ increases without bound as x approaches 2 from the right. Symbolically, you can write this as

$$\lim_{x \to 2^-} \frac{3}{x - 2} = -\infty$$

and

$$\lim_{x \to 2^+} \frac{3}{x - 2} = \infty.$$

Because f is unbounded as x approaches 2, the limit does not exist.

FIGURE 1.59

 Checkpoint 11

Find the limit (if possible): $\lim\limits_{x \to -2} \dfrac{5}{x + 2}$.

SUMMARIZE   (Section 1.5)

1. State the definition of the limit of a function *(page 50)*. For examples of limits, see Examples 1 and 2.

2. Make a list of the basic limits *(page 50)*. For examples of the basic limits, see Example 3.

3. Make a list of the properties of limits *(page 51)*. For an example of the use of these properties, see Example 4.

4. State the limit of a polynomial function *(page 51)*. For an example of the limit of a polynomial function, see Example 4.

5. Describe the dividing out technique *(page 52)*. For examples of the dividing out technique, see Examples 5 and 6.

6. Describe the rationalizing technique *(page 53)*. For an example of the rationalizing technique, see Example 7.

7. Describe a one-sided limit *(page 54)*. For examples of one-sided limits, see Examples 8, 9, and 10.

8. Describe the limit $\lim\limits_{x \to c} f(x)$ when $f(x)$ increases without bound as x approaches c *(page 56)*. For an example of an unbounded function, see Example 11.

SKILLS WARM UP 1.5 The following warm-up exercises involve skills that were covered in a previous course or in earlier sections. You will use these skills in the exercise set for this section. For additional help, review Appendix Section A.3, and Section 1.4.

In Exercises 1–4, simplify the expression by factoring.

1. $\dfrac{2x^3 + x^2}{6x}$ **2.** $\dfrac{x^5 + 9x^4}{x^2}$ **3.** $\dfrac{x^2 - 3x - 28}{x - 7}$ **4.** $\dfrac{x^2 + 11x + 30}{x + 5}$

In Exercises 5–8, evaluate the expression and simplify.

5. $f(x) = x^2 - 3x + 3$

    (a) $f(-1)$ (b) $f(c)$ (c) $f(x + h)$

6. $f(x) = \begin{cases} 2x - 2, & x < 1 \\ 3x + 1, & x \ge 1 \end{cases}$

    (a) $f(-1)$ (b) $f(3)$ (c) $f(t^2 + 1)$

7. $f(x) = x^2 - 2x + 2$ $\dfrac{f(1 + h) - f(1)}{h}$

8. $f(x) = 4x$ $\dfrac{f(2 + h) - f(2)}{h}$

In Exercises 9–12, find the domain and range of the function and sketch its graph.

9. $h(x) = -\dfrac{5}{x}$ **10.** $g(x) = \sqrt{25 - x^2}$ **11.** $f(x) = |x - 3|$ **12.** $f(x) = \dfrac{|x|}{x}$

In Exercises 13 and 14, determine whether y is a function of x.

13. $9x^2 + 4y^2 = 49$ **14.** $2x^2y + 8x = 7y$

Exercises 1.5

See www.CalcChat.com for worked-out solutions to odd-numbered exercises.

Finding Limits Graphically In Exercises 1–4, use the graph to find the limit. *See Examples 1 and 2.*

1.

  (a) $\displaystyle\lim_{x \to 0} f(x)$

  (b) $\displaystyle\lim_{x \to -1} f(x)$

2.

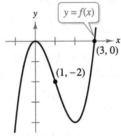

  (a) $\displaystyle\lim_{x \to 1} f(x)$

  (b) $\displaystyle\lim_{x \to 3} f(x)$

3.

  (a) $\displaystyle\lim_{x \to 0} g(x)$

  (b) $\displaystyle\lim_{x \to -1} g(x)$

4.

  (a) $\displaystyle\lim_{x \to -2} h(x)$

  (b) $\displaystyle\lim_{x \to 0} h(x)$

Finding Limits Numerically In Exercises 5–12, complete the table and use the result to estimate the limit. Use a graphing utility to graph the function to confirm your result. *See Examples 1 and 2.*

5. $\displaystyle\lim_{x \to 2} (2x + 5)$

x	1.9	1.99	1.999	2	2.001	2.01	2.1
$f(x)$				?			

6. $\displaystyle\lim_{x \to 2} (x^2 - 3x + 1)$

x	1.9	1.99	1.999	2	2.001	2.01	2.1
$f(x)$				?			

7. $\displaystyle\lim_{x \to 2} \dfrac{x - 2}{x^2 - 4}$

x	1.9	1.99	1.999	2	2.001	2.01	2.1
$f(x)$				?			

8. $\lim\limits_{x\to 2}\dfrac{x-2}{x^2-3x+2}$

x	1.9	1.99	1.999	2	2.001	2.01	2.1
$f(x)$				?			

9. $\lim\limits_{x\to 0}\dfrac{\sqrt{x+1}-1}{x}$

x	-0.1	-0.01	-0.001	0	0.001	0.01	0.1
$f(x)$				?			

10. $\lim\limits_{x\to 0}\dfrac{\sqrt{x+2}-\sqrt{2}}{x}$

x	-0.1	-0.01	-0.001	0	0.001	0.01	0.1
$f(x)$				?			

11. $\lim\limits_{x\to -4}\dfrac{\dfrac{1}{x+4}-\dfrac{1}{4}}{x}$

x	-4.1	-4.01	-4.001	-4	-3.999	-3.99	-3.9
$f(x)$				?			

12. $\lim\limits_{x\to -2}\dfrac{\dfrac{1}{2}-\dfrac{1}{x+2}}{2x}$

x	-2.1	-2.01	-2.001	-2	-1.999	-1.99	-1.9
$f(x)$				?			

Evaluating Basic Limits In Exercises 13–20, find the limit. *See Example 3.*

13. $\lim\limits_{x\to 3} 6$

14. $\lim\limits_{x\to 5} 4$

15. $\lim\limits_{x\to -2} x$

16. $\lim\limits_{x\to 10} x$

17. $\lim\limits_{x\to 7} x^2$

18. $\lim\limits_{x\to 3} x^3$

19. $\lim\limits_{x\to 16} \sqrt{x}$

20. $\lim\limits_{x\to -1} \sqrt[3]{x}$

Operations with Limits In Exercises 21 and 22, find the limit of (a) $f(x)+g(x)$, (b) $f(x)g(x)$, and (c) $f(x)/g(x)$, as x approaches c.

21. $\lim\limits_{x\to c} f(x) = 3$

$\lim\limits_{x\to c} g(x) = 9$

22. $\lim\limits_{x\to c} f(x) = \frac{3}{2}$

$\lim\limits_{x\to c} g(x) = \frac{1}{2}$

Operations with Limits In Exercises 23 and 24, find the limit of (a) $\sqrt{f(x)}$, (b) $[3f(x)]$, and (c) $[f(x)]^2$, as x approaches c.

23. $\lim\limits_{x\to c} f(x) = 16$

24. $\lim\limits_{x\to c} f(x) = 9$

Using Properties of Limits In Exercises 25–36, find the limit using direct substitution. *See Examples 3 and 4.*

25. $\lim\limits_{x\to -3} (2x+5)$

26. $\lim\limits_{x\to 0} (3x-2)$

27. $\lim\limits_{x\to 1} (1-x^2)$

28. $\lim\limits_{x\to 2} (-x^2+x-2)$

29. $\lim\limits_{x\to 3} \sqrt{x+6}$

30. $\lim\limits_{x\to 4} \sqrt[3]{x+4}$

31. $\lim\limits_{x\to -3} \dfrac{2}{x+2}$

32. $\lim\limits_{x\to -2} \dfrac{3x+1}{2-x}$

33. $\lim\limits_{x\to -2} \dfrac{x^2-1}{2x}$

34. $\lim\limits_{x\to 7} \dfrac{5x}{x+2}$

35. $\lim\limits_{x\to 5} \dfrac{\sqrt{x+11}+6}{x}$

36. $\lim\limits_{x\to 12} \dfrac{\sqrt{x-3}-2}{x}$

Finding Limits In Exercises 37–58, find the limit (if it exists). *See Examples 5, 6, 7, 9, and 11.*

37. $\lim\limits_{x\to -3} \dfrac{x^2-9}{x+3}$

38. $\lim\limits_{x\to -1} \dfrac{2x^2-x-3}{x+1}$

39. $\lim\limits_{x\to 2} \dfrac{2-x}{x^2-4}$

40. $\lim\limits_{t\to 1} \dfrac{t^2+t-2}{t^2-1}$

41. $\lim\limits_{x\to -2} \dfrac{x^3+8}{x+2}$

42. $\lim\limits_{x\to -1} \dfrac{x^3+1}{x+1}$

43. $\lim\limits_{\Delta x\to 0} \dfrac{2(x+\Delta x)-2x}{\Delta x}$

44. $\lim\limits_{\Delta x\to 0} \dfrac{4(x+\Delta x)-5-(4x-5)}{\Delta x}$

45. $\lim\limits_{\Delta t\to 0} \dfrac{(t+\Delta t)^2-5(t+\Delta t)-(t^2-5t)}{\Delta t}$

46. $\lim\limits_{\Delta t\to 0} \dfrac{(t+\Delta t)^2-4(t+\Delta t)+2-(t^2-4t+2)}{\Delta t}$

47. $\lim\limits_{x\to 4} \dfrac{\sqrt{x+5}-3}{x-4}$

48. $\lim\limits_{x\to 3} \dfrac{\sqrt{x+1}-2}{x-3}$

49. $\lim\limits_{x\to 0} \dfrac{\sqrt{x+5}-\sqrt{5}}{x}$

50. $\lim\limits_{x\to 0} \dfrac{\sqrt{x+2}-\sqrt{2}}{x}$

51. $\lim\limits_{x\to 2} f(x)$, where $f(x) = \begin{cases} 4-x, & x\neq 2 \\ 0, & x=2 \end{cases}$

52. $\lim\limits_{x\to 1} f(x)$, where $f(x) = \begin{cases} x^2+2, & x\neq 1 \\ 1, & x=1 \end{cases}$

53. $\lim\limits_{x\to 3} f(x)$, where $f(x) = \begin{cases} \frac{1}{3}x-2, & x\leq 3 \\ -2x+5, & x>3 \end{cases}$

54. $\lim\limits_{s\to 1} f(s)$, where $f(s) = \begin{cases} s, & s\leq 1 \\ 1-s, & s>1 \end{cases}$

55. $\lim\limits_{x\to-4} \dfrac{2}{x+4}$

56. $\lim\limits_{x\to5} \dfrac{4}{x-5}$

57. $\lim\limits_{x\to2} \dfrac{x-2}{x^2-4x+4}$

58. $\lim\limits_{t\to4} \dfrac{t+4}{t^2-16}$

Finding One-Sided Limits In Exercises 59 and 60, use a graph to find the limit from the left and the limit from the right. *See Example 8.*

59. $\lim\limits_{x\to-3^-} \dfrac{|x+3|}{x+3}$

$\lim\limits_{x\to-3^+} \dfrac{|x+3|}{x+3}$

60. $\lim\limits_{x\to6^-} \dfrac{|x-6|}{x-6}$

$\lim\limits_{x\to6^+} \dfrac{|x-6|}{x-6}$

Graphical, Numerical, and Analytic Analysis In Exercises 61–64, use a graphing utility to graph the function and estimate the limit. Use a table to reinforce your conclusion. Then find the limit by analytic methods.

61. $\lim\limits_{x\to1^-} \dfrac{2}{x^2-1}$

62. $\lim\limits_{x\to1^+} \dfrac{5}{1-x}$

63. $\lim\limits_{x\to-2^-} \dfrac{1}{x+2}$

64. $\lim\limits_{x\to0^-} \dfrac{x+1}{x}$

Finding Limits Graphically In Exercises 65–70, use the graph to find the limit (if it exists).

(a) $\lim\limits_{x\to c^+} f(x)$ (b) $\lim\limits_{x\to c^-} f(x)$ (c) $\lim\limits_{x\to c} f(x)$

65.

66.

67.

68.

69.

70.

Estimating Limits In Exercises 71–74, use a graphing utility to estimate the limit (if it exists).

71. $\lim\limits_{x\to2} \dfrac{x^2-5x+6}{x^2-4x+4}$

72. $\lim\limits_{x\to1} \dfrac{x^2+6x-7}{x^3-x^2+2x-2}$

73. $\lim\limits_{x\to-4} \dfrac{x^3+4x^2+x+4}{2x^2+7x-4}$

74. $\lim\limits_{x\to-2} \dfrac{4x^3+7x^2+x+6}{3x^2-x-14}$

75. Environment The cost C (in thousands of dollars) of removing $p\%$ of the pollutants from the water in a small lake is given by

$$C = \dfrac{25p}{100-p}, \quad 0 \le p < 100.$$

(a) Find the cost of removing 50% of the pollutants.

(b) What percent of the pollutants can be removed for $100 thousand?

(c) Evaluate $\lim\limits_{p\to100^-} C$. Explain your results.

76. HOW DO YOU SEE IT? The graph shows the cost C (in dollars) of making x photocopies at a copy shop.

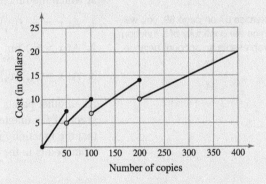

(a) Does $\lim\limits_{x\to50} C$ exist? Explain your reasoning.

(b) Does $\lim\limits_{x\to150} C$ exist? Explain your reasoning.

(c) You have to make 200 photocopies. Would it be better to make 200 or 201? Explain your reasoning.

77. Compound Interest Consider a certificate of deposit that pays 10% (annual percentage rate) on an initial deposit of $1000. The balance A after 10 years is $A = 1000(1 + 0.1x)^{10/x}$, where x is the length of the compounding period (in years).

(a) Use a graphing utility to graph A, where $0 \le x \le 1$.

(b) Use the *zoom* and *trace* features to estimate the balance for quarterly compounding and daily compounding.

(c) Use the *zoom* and *trace* features to estimate $\lim\limits_{x\to0^+} A$. What do you think this limit represents? Explain your reasoning.

1.6 Continuity

■ Determine the continuity of functions.
■ Determine the continuity of functions on a closed interval.
■ Use the greatest integer function to model and solve real-life problems.
■ Use compound interest models to solve real-life problems.

In Exercise 67 on page 69, you will examine the continuity of a function that represents an account balance.

Continuity

In mathematics, the term "continuous" has much the same meaning as it has in everyday use. To say that a function is continuous at

$$x = c$$

means that there is no interruption in the graph of f at c. That is, the graph of f

1. is unbroken at c.

2. has no holes, jumps, or gaps.

As simple as this concept may seem, its precise definition eluded mathematicians for many years. In fact, it was not until the early 1800's that a precise definition was finally developed.

Before looking at this definition, consider the function whose graph is shown in Figure 1.60. This figure identifies three values of x at which the function f is not continuous.

1. At $x = c_1$, $f(c_1)$ is not defined.

2. At $x = c_2$, $\lim_{x \to c_2} f(x)$ does not exist.

3. At $x = c_3$, $f(c_3) \neq \lim_{x \to c_3} f(x)$.

At all other points in the interval (a, b), the graph of f is uninterrupted, which implies that the function f is continuous at all other points in the interval (a, b).

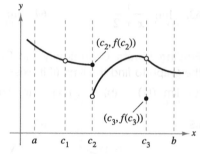

f is not continuous at $x = c_1, c_2, c_3$.

FIGURE 1.60

Definition of Continuity

Let c be a number in the interval (a, b), and let f be a function whose domain contains the interval (a, b). The function f is **continuous at the point c** when the following conditions are true.

1. $f(c)$ is defined.

2. $\lim_{x \to c} f(x)$ exists.

3. $\lim_{x \to c} f(x) = f(c)$.

If f is continuous at every point in the interval (a, b), then f is **continuous on the open interval (a, b).**

On the interval (a, b), the graph of f can be traced with a pencil.

FIGURE 1.61

Informally, you can say that a function is continuous on an interval when its graph on the interval can be traced using a pencil and paper without lifting the pencil from the paper, as shown in Figure 1.61.

Continuity of Polynomial and Rational Functions

1. A polynomial function is continuous at every real number.

2. A rational function is continuous at every number in its domain.

Example 1 Determining Continuity of a Polynomial Function

Discuss the continuity of each function.

a. $f(x) = x^2 - 2x + 3$ **b.** $f(x) = x^3 - x$ **c.** $f(x) = x^4 - 2x^2 + 1$

SOLUTION Each of these functions is a *polynomial function*. So, each is continuous on the entire real number line, as indicated in Figure 1.62.

(a)

(b)

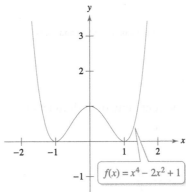

(c)

All three functions are continuous on $(-\infty, \infty)$.

FIGURE 1.62

✓ Checkpoint 1

Discuss the continuity of each function.

a. $f(x) = x^2 + x + 1$ **b.** $f(x) = x^3 + x$ **c.** $f(x) = x^4$

Polynomial functions are one of the most important types of functions used in calculus. Be sure you see from Example 1 that the graph of a polynomial function is continuous on the entire real number line and therefore has no holes, jumps, or gaps. Rational functions, on the other hand, need not be continuous on the entire real number line, as shown in Example 2.

Example 2   Determining Continuity of a Rational Function

Discuss the continuity of each function.

a. $f(x) = \dfrac{1}{x}$ **b.** $f(x) = \dfrac{x^2 - 1}{x - 1}$ **c.** $f(x) = \dfrac{1}{x^2 + 1}$

SOLUTION   Each of these functions is a rational function and is therefore continuous at every number in its domain.

a. The domain of $f(x) = 1/x$ consists of all real numbers except $x = 0$. So, this function is continuous on the intervals $(-\infty, 0)$ and $(0, \infty)$. [See Figure 1.63(a).]

b. The domain of $f(x) = (x^2 - 1)/(x - 1)$ consists of all real numbers except $x = 1$. So, this function is continuous on the intervals $(-\infty, 1)$ and $(1, \infty)$. [See Figure 1.63(b).]

c. The domain of $f(x) = 1/(x^2 + 1)$ consists of all real numbers. So, this function is continuous on the entire real number line. [See Figure 1.63(c).]

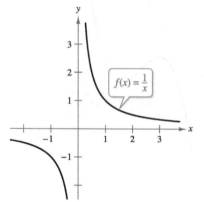

(a) Continuous on $(-\infty, 0)$ and $(0, \infty)$

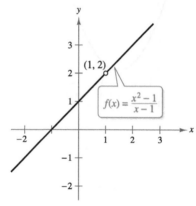

(b) Continuous on $(-\infty, 1)$ and $(1, \infty)$

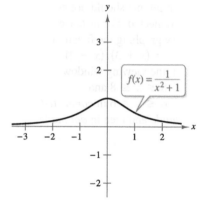

(c) Continuous on $(-\infty, \infty)$

FIGURE 1.63

TECH TUTOR

A graphing utility can give misleading information about the continuity of a function. For instance, try graphing the function from Example 2(b), $f(x) = (x^2 - 1)/(x - 1)$, in a standard viewing window. On most graphing utilities, the graph appears to be continuous at every real number. However, because $x = 1$ is not in the domain of f, you know that f is not continuous at $x = 1$. You can verify this on a graphing utility using the *trace* or *table* feature.

✓**Checkpoint 2**

Discuss the continuity of each function.

a. $f(x) = \dfrac{1}{x - 1}$

b. $f(x) = \dfrac{x^2 - 4}{x - 2}$

c. $f(x) = \dfrac{1}{x^2 + 2}$

Consider an open interval I that contains a real number c. If a function f is defined on I (except possibly at c), and f is not continuous at c, then f is said to have a **discontinuity** at c. Discontinuities fall into two categories: **removable** and **nonremovable.** A discontinuity at c is called removable when f can be made continuous by appropriately defining (or redefining) $f(c)$. For instance, the function in Example 2(b) has a removable discontinuity at $(1, 2)$. To remove the discontinuity, all you need to do is redefine the function so that $f(1) = 2$.

A discontinuity at $x = c$ is nonremovable when the function cannot be made continuous at $x = c$ by defining or redefining the function at $x = c$. For instance, the function in Example 2(a) has a nonremovable discontinuity at $x = 0$.

Continuity on a Closed Interval

The intervals discussed in Examples 1 and 2 are open. To discuss continuity on a closed interval, you can use the concept of one-sided limits, as defined in Section 1.5.

Definition of Continuity on a Closed Interval

Let f be defined on a closed interval $[a, b]$. If f is continuous on the open interval (a, b) and

$$\lim_{x \to a^+} f(x) = f(a) \quad \text{and} \quad \lim_{x \to b^-} f(x) = f(b)$$

then f is **continuous on the closed interval $[a, b]$**. Moreover, f is **continuous from the right** at a and **continuous from the left** at b.

Similar definitions can be made to cover continuity on intervals of the form $(a, b]$ and $[a, b)$, or on infinite intervals. For instance, the function

$$f(x) = \sqrt{x}$$

is continuous on the infinite interval $[0, \infty)$.

Example 3   Examining Continuity at an Endpoint

Discuss the continuity of

$$f(x) = \sqrt{3 - x}.$$

SOLUTION   Notice that the domain of f is the set $(-\infty, 3]$. Moreover, f is continuous from the left at $x = 3$ because

$$\lim_{x \to 3^-} f(x) = \lim_{x \to 3^-} \sqrt{3 - x}$$
$$= \sqrt{3 - 3}$$
$$= 0$$
$$= f(3).$$

For all $x < 3$, the function f satisfies the three conditions for continuity. So, you can conclude that f is continuous on the interval $(-\infty, 3]$, as shown in Figure 1.64.

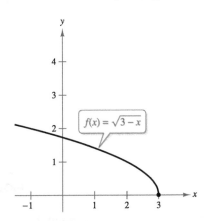

$f(x) = \sqrt{3 - x}$

FIGURE 1.64

STUDY TIP

When working with radical functions of the form

$$f(x) = \sqrt{g(x)}$$

remember that the domain of f coincides with the solution of $g(x) \geq 0$.

✓ **Checkpoint 3**

Discuss the continuity of

$$f(x) = \sqrt{x - 2}.$$

Example 4   Examining Continuity on a Closed Interval

Discuss the continuity of

$$g(x) = \begin{cases} 5 - x, & -1 \leq x \leq 2 \\ x^2 - 1, & 2 < x \leq 3 \end{cases}.$$

SOLUTION   The polynomial functions

$$5 - x$$

and

$$x^2 - 1$$

are continuous on the intervals $[-1, 2]$ and $(2, 3]$, respectively. So, to conclude that g is continuous on the entire interval

$$[-1, 3]$$

you need only to check the behavior of g when $x = 2$. You can do this by taking the one-sided limits when $x = 2$.

$$\lim_{x \to 2^-} g(x) = \lim_{x \to 2^-} (5 - x) = 5 - 2 = 3 \qquad \text{Limit from the left}$$

and

$$\lim_{x \to 2^+} g(x) = \lim_{x \to 2^+} (x^2 - 1) = 2^2 - 1 = 3 \qquad \text{Limit from the right}$$

Because these two limits are equal,

$$\lim_{x \to 2} g(x) = g(2) = 3.$$

So, g is continuous at $x = 2$ and, consequently, it is continuous on the entire interval

$$[-1, 3].$$

The graph of g is shown in Figure 1.65.

FIGURE 1.65

✓ Checkpoint 4

Discuss the continuity of

$$f(x) = \begin{cases} x + 2, & -1 \leq x < 3 \\ 14 - x^2, & 3 \leq x \leq 5 \end{cases}.$$

The Greatest Integer Function

Some functions that are used in business applications are **step functions.** For instance, the function in Example 10 in Section 1.5 is a step function. The **greatest integer function** is another example of a step function. This function is denoted by

$$[[x]] = \text{greatest integer less than or equal to } x.$$

For example,

$$[[-2.1]] = \text{greatest integer less than or equal to } -2.1 = -3$$
$$[[-2]] = \text{greatest integer less than or equal to } -2 = -2$$
$$[[1.5]] = \text{greatest integer less than or equal to } 1.5 = 1.$$

Note that the graph of the greatest integer function (Figure 1.66) jumps up one unit at each integer. This implies that the function is not continuous at each integer.

In real-life applications, the domain of the greatest integer function is often restricted to nonnegative values of x. In such cases, this function serves the purpose of **truncating** the decimal portion of x. For example, 1.345 is truncated to 1 and 3.57 is truncated to 3. That is,

$$[[1.345]] = 1 \quad \text{and} \quad [[3.57]] = 3.$$

 Example 5   Modeling a Cost Function

A bookbinding company produces 10,000 books in an eight-hour shift. The fixed cost *per shift* amounts to $5000, and the unit cost per book is $3. Using the greatest integer function, you can write the cost of producing x books as

$$C = 5000\left(1 + \left[\!\left[\frac{x-1}{10,000}\right]\!\right]\right) + 3x.$$

Sketch the graph of this cost function.

SOLUTION   Note that during the first eight-hour shift,

$$\left[\!\left[\frac{x-1}{10,000}\right]\!\right] = 0, \quad 1 \le x \le 10,000$$

which implies

$$C = 5000\left(1 + \left[\!\left[\frac{x-1}{10,000}\right]\!\right]\right) + 3x = 5000 + 3x.$$

During the second eight-hour shift,

$$\left[\!\left[\frac{x-1}{10,000}\right]\!\right] = 1, \quad 10,001 \le x \le 20,000$$

which implies

$$C = 5000\left(1 + \left[\!\left[\frac{x-1}{10,000}\right]\!\right]\right) + 3x$$
$$= 10,000 + 3x.$$

The graph of C is shown in Figure 1.67. Note the graph's discontinuities at $x = 10,000$, 20,000, and 30,000.

✓ Checkpoint 5

Use a graphing utility to graph the cost function in Example 5.

$f(x) = [[x]]$

Greatest Integer Function

FIGURE 1.66

Cost of Producing Books

$C = 5000\left(1 + \left[\frac{x-1}{10,000}\right]\right) + 3x$

Cost (in dollars)

First shift
Second shift
Third shift

10,000 20,000 30,000
Number of books

FIGURE 1.67

Extended Application: Compound Interest

Banks and other financial institutions differ on how interest is paid to an account. If the interest is added to the account so that future interest is paid on previously earned interest, then the interest is said to be **compounded.** For instance, a deposit of $10,000 is made in an account that pays 6% interest, compounded quarterly. Because the 6% is the annual interest rate, the quarterly rate is

$$\tfrac{1}{4}(0.06) = 0.015$$

or 1.5%. The balances during the first five quarters are shown below.

Quarter	Balance
1st	$10,000.00
2nd	$10,000.00 + (0.015)(10,000.00) = \$10,150.00$
3rd	$10,150.00 + (0.015)(10,150.00) = \$10,302.25$
4th	$10,302.25 + (0.015)(10,302.25) = \$10,456.78$
5th	$10,456.78 + (0.015)(10,456.78) = \$10,613.63$

 Example 6 **Graphing Compound Interest**

Sketch the graph of the balance in the account described above.

SOLUTION   Let A represent the balance in the account and let t represent the time, in years. You can use the greatest integer function to represent the balance, as shown.

$$A = 10,000(1 + 0.015)^{[\![4t]\!]}$$

From the graph shown in Figure 1.68, notice that the function has a discontinuity at each quarter. That is, A has discontinuities at

$$t = \frac{1}{4}, t = \frac{1}{2}, t = \frac{3}{4}, t = 1,$$

and

$$t = \frac{5}{4}.$$

Quarterly Compounding

FIGURE 1.68

✓**Checkpoint 6**

Write an equation that gives the balance of the account in Example 6 when the annual interest rate is 3%. Then sketch the graph of the equation.

SUMMARIZE   (Section 1.6)

1. State the definition of continuity *(page 60)*. For an example of a function that is continuous at every real number, see Example 1.

2. State the definition of continuity on a closed interval *(page 63)*. For an example of a function that is continuous on a closed interval, see Example 4.

3. State the definition of the greatest integer function *(page 65)*. For real-life examples of the greatest integer function, see Examples 5 and 6.

SKILLS WARM UP 1.6   The following warm-up exercises involve skills that were covered in a previous course or in earlier sections. You will use these skills in the exercise set for this section. For additional help, review Appendix Sections A.4 and A.5, and Section 1.5.

In Exercises 1–4, simplify the expression.

1. $\dfrac{x^2 + 6x + 8}{x^2 - 6x - 16}$

2. $\dfrac{x^2 - 5x - 6}{x^2 - 9x + 18}$

3. $\dfrac{2x^2 - 2x - 12}{4x^2 - 24x + 36}$

4. $\dfrac{x^3 - 16x}{x^3 + 2x^2 - 8x}$

In Exercises 5–8, solve for x.

5. $x^2 + 7x = 0$

6. $x^2 + 4x - 5 = 0$

7. $3x^2 + 8x + 4 = 0$

8. $x^3 + 5x^2 - 24x = 0$

In Exercises 9 and 10, find the limit.

9. $\lim\limits_{x \to 3} (2x^2 - 3x + 4)$

10. $\lim\limits_{x \to -2} (3x^3 - 8x + 7)$

Exercises 1.6

See www.CalcChat.com for worked-out solutions to odd-numbered exercises.

Determining Continuity In Exercises 1–10, determine whether the function is continuous on the entire real number line. Explain your reasoning. *See Examples 1 and 2.*

1. $f(x) = 5x^3 - x^2 + 2$

2. $f(x) = (x^2 - 1)^3$

3. $f(x) = \dfrac{3}{x^2 - 16}$

4. $f(x) = \dfrac{1}{9 - x^2}$

5. $f(x) = \dfrac{1}{4 + x^2}$

6. $f(x) = \dfrac{3x}{x^2 + 1}$

7. $f(x) = \dfrac{2x - 1}{x^2 - 8x + 15}$

8. $f(x) = \dfrac{x + 4}{x^2 - 6x + 5}$

9. $g(x) = \dfrac{x^2 - 4x + 4}{x^2 - 4}$

10. $g(x) = \dfrac{x^2 - 9x + 20}{x^2 - 16}$

Determining Continuity In Exercises 11–40, describe the interval(s) on which the function is continuous. Explain why the function is continuous on the interval(s). If the function has a discontinuity, identify the conditions of continuity that are not satisfied. *See Examples 1, 2, 3, 4, and 5.*

11. $f(x) = \dfrac{x^2 - 1}{x}$

12. $f(x) = \dfrac{1}{x^2 - 4}$

13. $f(x) = \dfrac{x^2 - 1}{x + 1}$

14. $f(x) = \dfrac{x^3 - 8}{x - 2}$

15. $f(x) = x^2 - 2x + 1$

16. $f(x) = 3 - 2x - x^2$

17. $f(x) = \dfrac{x}{x^2 - 1}$

18. $f(x) = \dfrac{x - 3}{x^2 - 9}$

19. $f(x) = \dfrac{x}{x^2 + 1}$

20. $f(x) = \dfrac{6}{x^2 + 3}$

21. $f(x) = \dfrac{x - 5}{x^2 - 9x + 20}$

22. $f(x) = \dfrac{x - 1}{x^2 + x - 2}$

23. $f(x) = \sqrt{4 - x}$

24. $f(x) = \sqrt{x - 1}$

25. $f(x) = \sqrt{x} + 2$

26. $f(x) = 3 - \sqrt{x}$

27. $f(x) = \begin{cases} -2x + 3, & -1 \le x \le 1 \\ x^2, & 1 < x \le 3 \end{cases}$

28. $f(x) = \begin{cases} \frac{1}{2}x + 1, & -3 \le x \le 2 \\ 3 - x, & 2 < x \le 4 \end{cases}$

29. $f(x) = \begin{cases} 3 + x, & x \le 2 \\ x^2 + 1, & x > 2 \end{cases}$

30. $f(x) = \begin{cases} x^2 - 4, & x \le 0 \\ 3x + 1, & x > 0 \end{cases}$

31. $f(x) = \dfrac{|x + 1|}{x + 1}$ **32.** $f(x) = \dfrac{|4 - x|}{4 - x}$

33. $f(x) = x\sqrt{x + 3}$ **34.** $f(x) = \dfrac{x + 1}{\sqrt{x}}$

35. $f(x) = [\![2x]\!] + 1$ **36.** $f(x) = \dfrac{[\![x]\!]}{2} + x$

37. $f(x) = [\![x - 1]\!]$ **38.** $f(x) = x - [\![x]\!]$

39. $h(x) = f(g(x))$, $f(x) = \dfrac{1}{\sqrt{x}}$, $g(x) = x - 1, x > 1$

40. $h(x) = f(g(x))$, $f(x) = \dfrac{1}{x - 1}$, $g(x) = x^2 + 5$

Determining Continuity   In Exercises 41–46, sketch the graph of the function and describe the interval(s) on which the function is continuous.

41. $f(x) = \dfrac{x^2 - 16}{x - 4}$ **42.** $f(x) = \dfrac{2x^2 + x}{x}$

43. $f(x) = \dfrac{x + 4}{3x^2 - 12}$ **44.** $f(x) = \dfrac{x^3 + x}{x}$

45. $f(x) = \begin{cases} x^2 + 1, & x < 0 \\ x - 1, & x \geq 0 \end{cases}$ **46.** $f(x) = \begin{cases} x^2 - 4, & x \leq 0 \\ 2x + 4, & x > 0 \end{cases}$

Determining Continuity on a Closed Interval   In Exercises 47–50, discuss the continuity of the function on the closed interval. If there are any discontinuities, determine whether they are removable.

Function	Interval
47. $f(x) = x^2 - 4x - 5$	$[-1, 5]$
48. $f(x) = \dfrac{5}{x^2 + 1}$	$[-2, 2]$
49. $f(x) = \dfrac{1}{x - 2}$	$[1, 4]$
50. $f(x) = \dfrac{x}{x^2 - 4x + 3}$	$[0, 4]$

Finding Discontinuities   In Exercises 51–56, use a graphing utility to graph the function. Use the graph to determine any x-value(s) at which the function is not continuous. Explain why the function is not continuous at the x-value(s).

51. $h(x) = \dfrac{1}{x^2 - x - 2}$

52. $k(x) = \dfrac{x - 4}{x^2 - 5x + 4}$

53. $f(x) = \begin{cases} 2x - 4, & x \leq 3 \\ x^2 - 2x, & x > 3 \end{cases}$

54. $f(x) = \begin{cases} 3x - 1, & x \leq 1 \\ x + 1, & x > 1 \end{cases}$

55. $f(x) = x - 2[\![x]\!]$

56. $f(x) = [\![2x - 1]\!]$

Making a Function Continuous   In Exercises 57 and 58, find the constant a (Exercise 57) and the constants a and b (Exercise 58) such that the function is continuous on the entire real number line.

57. $f(x) = \begin{cases} x^3, & x \leq 2 \\ ax^2, & x > 2 \end{cases}$

58. $f(x) = \begin{cases} 2, & x \leq -1 \\ ax + b, & -1 < x < 3 \\ -2, & x \geq 3 \end{cases}$

Writing   In Exercises 59 and 60, use a graphing utility to graph the function on the interval $[-4, 4]$. Does the graph of the function appear to be continuous on this interval? Is the function in fact continuous on $[-4, 4]$? Write a short paragraph about the importance of examining a function analytically as well as graphically.

59. $f(x) = \dfrac{x^2 + x}{x}$

60. $f(x) = \dfrac{x^3 - 8}{x - 2}$

61. Environmental Cost   The cost C (in millions of dollars) of removing x percent of the pollutants emitted from the smokestack of a factory can be modeled by

$$C = \frac{2x}{100 - x}.$$

(a) What is the implied domain of C? Explain your reasoning.

(b) Use a graphing utility to graph the cost function. Is the function continuous on its domain? Explain your reasoning.

(c) Find the cost of removing 75% of the pollutants from the smokestack.

62. **HOW DO YOU SEE IT?** The graph shows the number of gallons G of gasoline in a person's car after t days.

(a) On what days is the graph not continuous?

(b) What do you think happens on these days?

63. **Biology** The gestation period of rabbits is about 29 to 35 days. Therefore, the population of a form (rabbits' home) can increase dramatically in a short period of time. The table gives the population of a form, where t is the time in months and N is the rabbit population.

t	0	1	2	3	4	5	6
N	2	8	10	14	10	15	12

Graph the population as a function of time. Find any points of discontinuity in the function. Explain your reasoning.

64. **Owning a Franchise** You have purchased a franchise. You have determined a linear model for your revenue as a function of time. Is the model a continuous function? Would your actual revenue be a continuous function of time? Explain your reasoning.

65. **Consumer Awareness** The United States Postal Service first class mail rates for sending a letter are $0.44 for the first ounce and $0.20 for each additional ounce or fraction thereof up to 3.5 ounces. A model for the cost C (in dollars) of a first class mailing that weighs 3.5 ounces or less is given below. *(Source: United States Postal Service)*

$$C(x) = \begin{cases} 0.44, & 0 \le x \le 1 \\ 0.64, & 1 < x \le 2 \\ 0.84, & 2 < x \le 3 \\ 1.04, & 3 < x \le 3.5 \end{cases}$$

(a) Use a graphing utility to graph the function and then discuss its continuity. At what values is the function not continuous? Explain your reasoning.

(b) Find the cost of mailing a 2.5-ounce letter.

66. **Health Food** A co-op health food store charges $3.50 for the first pound of organically grown peanuts and $1.90 for each additional pound or fraction thereof.

(a) Use the greatest integer function to create a model for the cost C for x pounds of organically grown peanuts.

(b) Use a graphing utility to graph the function and then discuss its continuity.

67. **Compound Interest** A deposit of $7500 is made in an account that pays 6% compounded quarterly. The amount A in the account after t years is

$$A = 7500(1.015)^{[\![4t]\!]}, \quad t \ge 0.$$

(a) Is the graph continuous? Explain your reasoning.

(b) What is the balance after 2 years?

(c) What is the balance after 7 years?

68. **Salary Contract** A union contract guarantees a 9% yearly increase for 5 years. For a current salary of $28,500, the salaries for the next 5 years are given by

$$S = 28{,}500(1.09)^{[\![t]\!]}$$

where $t = 0$ represents the present year.

(a) Use the greatest integer function of a graphing utility to graph the salary function and then discuss its continuity.

(b) Find the salary during the fifth year (when $t = 5$).

69. **Inventory Management** The number of units in inventory in a small company is

$$N = 25\left(2\left[\![\frac{t+2}{2}\right]\!] - t\right), \quad 0 \le t \le 12$$

where the real number t is the time in months.

(a) Use the greatest integer function of a graphing utility to graph this function and then discuss its continuity.

(b) How often must the company replenish its inventory?

ALGEBRA TUTOR

Order of Operations

Much of the algebra in this chapter involves evaluation of algebraic expressions. When you evaluate an algebraic expression, you need to know the priorities assigned to different operations. These priorities are called the *order of operations*.

1. Perform operations inside *symbols of grouping or absolute value symbols,* starting with the innermost symbol.

2. Evaluate all *exponential* expressions.

3. Perform all *multiplications* and *divisions* from left to right.

4. Perform all *additions* and *subtractions* from left to right.

| Example 1 | Using Order of Operations |

Evaluate each expression.

a. $20 - 2 \cdot 3^2$ **b.** $3 + 8 \div 2 \cdot 2$ **c.** $7 - [(5 \cdot 3) + 2^3]$

d. $[36 \div (3^2 \cdot 2)] + 6$ **e.** $36 - [3^2 \cdot (2 \div 6)]$ **f.** $10 - 2(8 + |5 - 7|)$

SOLUTION

a. $20 - 2 \cdot 3^2 = 20 - 2 \cdot 9$ Evaluate exponential expression.

$= 20 - 18$ Multiply.

$= 2$ Subtract.

b. $3 + 8 \div 2 \cdot 2 = 3 + 4 \cdot 2$ Divide.

$= 3 + 8$ Multiply.

$= 11$ Add.

c. $7 - [(5 \cdot 3) + 2^3] = 7 - [15 + 2^3]$ Multiply inside parentheses.

$= 7 - [15 + 8]$ Evaluate exponential expression.

$= 7 - 23$ Add inside brackets.

$= -16$ Subtract.

d. $[36 \div (3^2 \cdot 2)] + 6 = [36 \div (9 \cdot 2)] + 6$ Evaluate exponential expression inside parentheses.

$= [36 \div 18] + 6$ Multiply inside parentheses.

$= 2 + 6$ Divide inside brackets.

$= 8$ Add.

e. $36 - [3^2 \cdot (2 \div 6)] = 36 - \left[3^2 \cdot \frac{1}{3}\right]$ Divide inside parentheses.

$= 36 - \left[9 \cdot \frac{1}{3}\right]$ Evaluate exponential expression.

$= 36 - 3$ Multiply inside brackets.

$= 33$ Subtract.

f. $10 - 2(8 + |5 - 7|) = 10 - 2(8 + |-2|)$ Subtract inside absolute value symbols.

$= 10 - 2(8 + 2)$ Evaluate absolute value.

$= 10 - 2(10)$ Add inside parentheses.

$= 10 - 20$ Multiply.

$= -10$ Subtract.

TECH TUTOR

Most scientific and graphing calculators use the same order of operations listed above. Try entering the expressions in Example 1 into your calculator. Do you get the same results?

Solving Equations

A second algebraic skill used in this chapter is solving an equation in one variable.

1. To solve a *linear equation,* you can add or subtract the same quantity to or from each side of the equation. You can also multiply or divide each side of the equation by the same *nonzero* quantity.

2. To solve a *quadratic equation,* you can take the square root of each side, use factoring, or use the Quadratic Formula.

3. To solve a *radical equation,* isolate the radical on one side of the equation and square each side of the equation.

4. To solve an *absolute value equation,* use the definition of absolute value to rewrite the equation as two equations.

Example 2   Solving Equations

Solve each equation.

a. $3x - 3 = 5x - 7$ **b.** $2x^2 = 10$

c. $2x^2 + 5x - 6 = 6$ **d.** $\sqrt{2x - 7} = 5$

e. $|3x + 6| = 9$

SOLUTION

a.
$$3x - 3 = 5x - 7 \qquad \text{Write original (linear) equation.}$$
$$-3 = 2x - 7 \qquad \text{Subtract } 3x \text{ from each side.}$$
$$4 = 2x \qquad \text{Add 7 to each side.}$$
$$2 = x \qquad \text{Divide each side by 2.}$$

b.
$$2x^2 = 10 \qquad \text{Write original (quadratic) equation.}$$
$$x^2 = 5 \qquad \text{Divide each side by 2.}$$
$$x = \pm\sqrt{5} \qquad \text{Take the square root of each side.}$$

c.
$$2x^2 + 5x - 6 = 6 \qquad \text{Write original (quadratic) equation.}$$
$$2x^2 + 5x - 12 = 0 \qquad \text{Write in general form.}$$
$$(2x - 3)(x + 4) = 0 \qquad \text{Factor.}$$
$$2x - 3 = 0 \implies x = \tfrac{3}{2} \qquad \text{Set first factor equal to zero.}$$
$$x + 4 = 0 \implies x = -4 \qquad \text{Set second factor equal to zero.}$$

d.
$$\sqrt{2x - 7} = 5 \qquad \text{Write original (radical) equation.}$$
$$2x - 7 = 25 \qquad \text{Square each side.}$$
$$2x = 32 \qquad \text{Add 7 to each side.}$$
$$x = 16 \qquad \text{Divide each side by 2.}$$

e.
$$|3x + 6| = 9 \qquad \text{Write original (absolute value) equation.}$$
$$3x + 6 = -9 \quad \text{or} \quad 3x + 6 = 9 \qquad \text{Rewrite equivalent equations.}$$
$$3x = -15 \quad \text{or} \quad 3x = 3 \qquad \text{Subtract 6 from each side.}$$
$$x = -5 \quad \text{or} \quad x = 1 \qquad \text{Divide each side by 3.}$$

STUDY TIP

Solving radical equations can sometimes lead to *extraneous solutions* (those that do not satisfy the original equation). For instance, squaring both sides of the following equation yields two possible solutions, one of which is extraneous.

$$\sqrt{x} = x - 2$$
$$x = x^2 - 4x + 4$$
$$0 = x^2 - 5x + 4$$
$$= (x - 4)(x - 1)$$
$$x - 4 = 0 \implies x = 4$$
(solution)
$$x - 1 = 0 \implies x = 1$$
(extraneous)

SUMMARY AND STUDY STRATEGIES

After studying this chapter, you should have acquired the following skills.
The exercise numbers are keyed to the Review Exercises that begin on page 74.
Answers to odd-numbered Review Exercises are given in the back of the text.*

Section 1.1	Review Exercises
■ Plot points in a coordinate plane.	*1, 2*
■ Find the distance between two points in a coordinate plane.	*3–8*
$d = \sqrt{(x_2 - x_1)^2 + (y_2 - y_1)^2}$	
■ Find the midpoint of a line segment connecting two points.	*9–14*
$\text{Midpoint} = \left(\dfrac{x_1 + x_2}{2}, \dfrac{y_1 + y_2}{2} \right)$	
■ Interpret real-life data that is presented graphically.	*15, 16*
■ Translate points in a coordinate plane.	*17, 18*

Section 1.2	
■ Sketch graphs of equations by hand.	*19–28*
■ Find the *x*- and *y*-intercepts of graphs of equations.	*29–32*
■ Find the standard forms of equations of circles.	*33–36*
$(x - h)^2 + (y - k)^2 = r^2$	
■ Find the points of intersection of two graphs.	*37–40*
■ Find the break-even point for a business.	*41, 42*
The break-even point occurs when the revenue *R* is equal to the cost *C*.	
■ Find the equilibrium points of supply equations and demand equations.	*43*
The equilibrium point is the point of intersection of the graphs of the supply and demand equations.	
■ Use mathematical models to model and solve real-life problems.	*44*

Section 1.3	
■ Use the slope-intercept form of a linear equation to sketch graphs of lines.	*45–52*
$y = mx + b$	
■ Find slopes of lines passing through two points.	*53–56*
$m = \dfrac{y_2 - y_1}{x_2 - x_1}$	
■ Use the point-slope form to write equations of lines and sketch graphs of lines.	*57–64*
$y - y_1 = m(x - x_1)$	

---

* A wide range of valuable study aids are available to help you master the material in this chapter. The *Student Solutions Manual* includes step-by-step solutions to all odd-numbered exercises to help you review and prepare. The student website at *www.cengagebrain.com* offers algebra help and a *Graphing Technology Guide*, which contains step-by-step commands and instructions for a wide variety of graphing calculators.

Section 1.3 (continued)

	Review Exercises
■ Find equations of parallel and perpendicular lines.	*65, 66*

Parallel lines: $m_1 = m_2$

Perpendicular lines: $m_1 = -\dfrac{1}{m_2}$

■ Use linear equations to solve real-life problems such as predicting future   *67, 68*
sales or creating a linear depreciation schedule.

Section 1.4

■ Use the Vertical Line Test to decide whether the relationship between   *69–72*
two variables is a function.

If every vertical line intersects the graph of an equation at most once,
then the equation defines y as a function of x.

■ Find the domains and ranges of functions.   *73–78*

■ Use function notation and evaluate functions.   *79, 80*

■ Combine functions to create other functions.   *81, 82*

■ Use the Horizontal Line Test to determine whether functions have inverse   *83–88*
functions. If they do, find the inverse functions.

A function is one-to-one when every horizontal line intersects the graph of
the function at most once. For a function to have an inverse function, it must
be one-to-one.

Section 1.5

■ Use a table to estimate limits.   *89–92*

■ Determine whether limits exist. If they do, find the limits.   *93–110*

Section 1.6

■ Determine whether functions are continuous at a point, on an open interval, and   *111–120*
on a closed interval.

■ Determine the constant such that f is continuous.   *121, 122*

■ Use analytic and graphical models of real-life data to solve real-life problems.   *123–126*

Study Strategies

■ **Use a Graphing Utility**   A graphing calculator or graphing software for a computer can help you in this course
in two important ways. As an *exploratory device*, a graphing utility allows you to learn concepts by allowing you
to compare graphs of equations. For instance, sketching the graphs of $y = x^2$, $y = x^2 + 1$, and $y = x^2 - 1$ helps
confirm that adding (or subtracting) a constant to (or from) a function shifts the graph of the function vertically. As
a *problem-solving tool*, a graphing utility frees you of some of the drudgery of sketching complicated graphs by hand.
The time that you save can be spent using mathematics to solve real-life problems.

■ **Use the Skills Warm-Up Exercises**   Each exercise set in this text begins with a set of skills warm-up exercises. You
should begin each homework session by quickly working all of these exercises. (All are answered in the back of the text.)
The "old" skills covered in these exercises are needed to master the "new" skills in the section exercise set. The skills
warm-up exercises remind you that mathematics is cumulative—to be successful in this course, you must retain "old" skills.

■ **Use the Additional Study Aids**   The additional study aids were prepared specifically to help you master the concepts
discussed in the text. They are the *Student Solutions Manual*, the student website, and the *Graphing Technology Guide*.

Review Exercises

See www.CalcChat.com for worked-out solutions to odd-numbered exercises.

Plotting Points in the Cartesian Plane In Exercises 1 and 2, plot the points in the Cartesian plane.

1. $(2, 3), (0, 6), (-5, 1), (4, -3), (-3, -1)$

2. $(1, -4), (-1, -2), (6, -5), (-2, 0), (5, 5)$

Finding a Distance In Exercises 3–8, find the distance between the two points.

3. $(0, 0), (5, 2)$

4. $(1, 2), (4, 3)$

5. $(-1, 3), (-4, 6)$

6. $(6, 8), (-3, 7)$

7. $\left(\frac{1}{4}, -8\right), \left(\frac{3}{4}, -6\right)$

8. $(-0.6, 3), (4, -1.8)$

Finding a Segment's Midpoint In Exercises 9–14, find the midpoint of the line segment connecting the two points.

9. $(5, 6), (9, 2)$

10. $(0, 0), (-4, 8)$

11. $(-10, 4), (-6, 8)$

12. $(7, -9), (-3, 5)$

13. $\left(-1, \frac{1}{5}\right), \left(6, \frac{3}{5}\right)$

14. $(6, 1.2), (-3.2, 5)$

Revenues, Costs, and Profits In Exercises 15 and 16, use the graph below, which gives the revenues, costs, and profits for Google from 2005 through 2009. *(Source: Google, Inc.)*

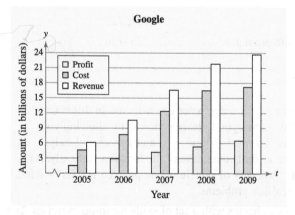

15. Write an equation that relates the revenue R, cost C, and profit P. Explain the relationship between the heights of the bars and the equation.

16. Estimate the revenue, cost, and profit for Google for each year.

Translating Points in the Plane In Exercises 17 and 18, use the translation and the graph to find the vertices of the figure after it has been translated.

17. 3 units left and 4 units up

18. 4 units right and 1 unit down

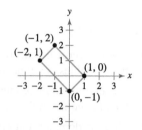

Sketching the Graph of an Equation In Exercises 19–28, sketch the graph of the equation.

19. $y = 4x - 12$

20. $y = 4 - 3x$

21. $y = x^2 + 5$

22. $y = 1 - x^2$

23. $y = |4 - x|$

24. $y = |2x - 3|$

25. $y = x^3 + 4$

26. $y = 2x^3 - 1$

27. $y = \sqrt{4x + 1}$

28. $y = \sqrt{2x}$

Finding x- and y-Intercepts In Exercises 29–32, find the x- and y-intercepts of the graph of the equation. Use a graphing utility to verify your results.

29. $4x + y + 3 = 0$

30. $3x - y + 6 = 0$

31. $y = x^2 + 2x - 8$

32. $y = (x - 1)^3 + 2(x - 1)^2$

Finding the Equation of a Circle In Exercises 33–36, find the standard form of the equation of the circle and sketch its graph.

33. Center: $(0, 0)$; radius: 8

34. Center: $(-5, -2)$; radius: 6

35. Center: $(0, 0)$; solution point: $\left(2, \sqrt{5}\right)$

36. Center: $(3, -4)$; solution point: $(-1, -1)$

Finding Points of Intersection In Exercises 37–40, find the point(s) of intersection (if any) of the graphs of the equations. Use a graphing utility to check your results.

37. $y = 2x + 13, \quad y = -5x - 1$

38. $y = x^2 - 5, \quad y = x + 1$

39. $y = x^3, \quad y = x$

40. $y = -x^2 + 4, \quad y = 2x - 1$

41. Break-Even Analysis A student organization wants to raise money by having a T-shirt sale. Each shirt costs $8. The silk screening costs $200 for the design, plus $2 per shirt. Each shirt will sell for $14.

(a) Find equations for the total cost C and the total revenue R for selling x shirts.

(b) Find the break-even point.

42. Break-Even Analysis You are starting a part-time business. You make an initial investment of $6000. The unit cost of the product is $6.50, and the selling price is $13.90.

(a) Find equations for the total cost C and the total revenue R for selling x units of the product.

(b) Find the break-even point.

43. Supply and Demand The demand and supply equations for a cordless screwdriver are given by

$p = 91.4 - 0.009x$ Demand equation

$p = 6.4 + 0.008x$ Supply equation

where p is the price in dollars and x represents the number of units. Find the equilibrium point for this market.

44. Wind Energy The table shows the annual amounts of U.S. consumption W (in trillion Btu) of wind energy for the years 2003 through 2008. *(Source: U.S. Energy Information Administration)*

Year	2003	2004	2005
Consumption	115	142	178

Year	2006	2007	2008
Consumption	264	341	546

A mathematical model for the data is given by

$W = 3.870t^3 - 45.04t^2 + 205.7t - 204$

where t represents the year, with $t = 3$ corresponding to 2003.

(a) Compare the actual consumptions with those given by the model. How well does the model fit the data? Explain your reasoning.

(b) Use the model to predict the consumption in 2014.

Finding the Slope and y-Intercept In Exercises 45–52, find the slope and y-intercept (if possible) of the equation of the line. Then sketch the graph of the equation.

45. $y = -x + 12$ **46.** $y = 3x - 1$

47. $3x + y = -2$ **48.** $2x - 4y = -8$

49. $y = -\frac{5}{3}$ **50.** $x = -3$

51. $-2x - 5y - 5 = 0$ **52.** $3.2x - 0.8y + 5.6 = 0$

Finding the Slope of a Line In Exercises 53–56, find the slope of the line passing through the pair of points.

53. $(0, 0), (7, 6)$ **54.** $(-1, 5), (-5, 7)$

55. $(10, 17), (-11, -3)$

56. $(-11, -3), (-1, -3)$

Using the Point-Slope Form In Exercises 57–60, find the equation of the line that passes through the given point and has the given slope. Then use the equation to sketch the line.

Point	Slope
57. $(3, -1)$	$m = -2$
58. $(-3, -3)$	$m = \frac{1}{2}$
59. $(1.5, -4)$	$m = 0$
60. $(8, 2)$	m is undefined.

Writing an Equation of a Line In Exercises 61–64, find the equation of the line that passes through the points. Then use the equation to sketch the line.

61. $(1, -7), (7, 5)$

62. $(2, 4), (8, 12)$

63. $(5, 7), (5, 14)$

64. $(4, -3), (-2, -3)$

Finding Parallel and Perpendicular Lines In Exercises 65 and 66, find the equation of the line passing through the given point and satisfying the given condition.

65. Point: $(-3, 6)$

(a) Slope is $\frac{7}{8}$.

(b) Parallel to the line $4x + 2y = 7$

(c) Passes through the origin

(d) Perpendicular to the line $3x - 2y = 2$

66. Point: $(1, -3)$

(a) Parallel to the x-axis

(b) Perpendicular to the x-axis

(c) Parallel to the line $-4x + 5y = -3$

(d) Perpendicular to the line $5x - 2y = 3$

67. Demand When a wholesaler sold a product at $32 per unit, sales were 750 units per week. After a price increase of $5 per unit, however, the sales dropped to 700 units per week. Assume that the relationship between the price p and the units sold per week x is linear.

(a) Write a linear equation expressing x in terms of p.

(b) Predict the number of units sold per week at a price of $34.50 per unit.

(c) Predict the number of units sold per week at a price of $42 per unit.

68. Linear Depreciation   A printing company purchases an advanced color copier/printer for $117,000. After 9 years, the equipment will be obsolete and have no value.

(a) Write a linear equation giving the value v (in dollars) of the equipment in terms of the time t (in years), $0 \leq t \leq 9$.

(b) Use a graphing utility to graph the equation.

(c) Move the cursor along the graph and estimate (to two-decimal-place accuracy) the value of the equipment after 4 years.

(d) Move the cursor along the graph and estimate (to two-decimal-place accuracy) the time when the value of the equipment will be $84,000.

Vertical Line Test   In Exercises 69–72, use the Vertical Line Test to determine whether y is a function of x.

69. $y = -x^2 + 2$ **70.** $x^2 + y^2 = 4$

71. $y^2 - \frac{1}{4}x^2 = 4$ **72.** $y = |x + 4|$

Finding the Domain and Range of a Function   In Exercises 73–78, find the domain and range of the function. Use a graphing utility to verify your results.

73. $f(x) = x^3 + 2x^2 - x + 2$

74. $f(x) = 2$

75. $f(x) = \sqrt{x + 1}$

76. $f(x) = -|x| + 3$

77. $f(x) = \dfrac{x - 3}{x^2 + x - 12}$

78. $f(x) = \begin{cases} 6 - x, & x < 2 \\ 3x - 2, & x \geq 2 \end{cases}$

Evaluating a Function   In Exercises 79 and 80, evaluate the function at the specified values of the independent variable. Simplify the result.

79. $f(x) = 3x + 4$

(a) $f(1)$ (b) $f(-5)$ (c) $f(x + 1)$

80. $f(x) = x^2 + 4x + 3$

(a) $f(0)$ (b) $f(3)$ (c) $f(x - 1)$

Combinations of Functions   In Exercises 81 and 82, find (a) $f(x) + g(x)$, (b) $f(x) - g(x)$, (c) $f(x) \cdot g(x)$, (d) $f(x)/g(x)$, (e) $f(g(x))$, and (f) $g(f(x))$, if defined.

81. $f(x) = 1 + x^2$, $g(x) = 2x - 1$

82. $f(x) = 2x - 3$, $g(x) = \sqrt{x + 1}$

Determine Whether a Function Is One-to-One In Exercises 83–88, use a graphing utility to graph the function. Then use the Horizontal Line Test to determine whether the function is one-to-one. If it is, find its inverse function.

83. $f(x) = 4x - 3$

84. $f(x) = \frac{3}{2}x$

85. $f(x) = -x^2 + \frac{1}{2}$

86. $f(x) = x^3 - 1$

87. $f(x) = |x + 1|$

88. $f(x) = 6$

Finding Limits Numerically   In Exercises 89–92, complete the table and use the result to estimate the limit. Use a graphing utility to graph the function to confirm your result.

89. $\lim\limits_{x \to 1} (4x - 3)$

x	0.9	0.99	0.999	1	1.001	1.01	1.1
$f(x)$				?			

90. $\lim\limits_{x \to 3} \dfrac{x - 3}{x^2 - 2x - 3}$

x	2.9	2.99	2.999	3	3.001	3.01	3.1
$f(x)$				?			

91. $\lim\limits_{x \to 0} \dfrac{\sqrt{x + 6} - 6}{x}$

x	-0.1	-0.01	-0.001	0	0.001	0.01	0.1
$f(x)$				?			

92. $\lim\limits_{x \to 7} \dfrac{\dfrac{1}{x - 7} - \dfrac{1}{7}}{x}$

x	6.9	6.99	6.999	7	7.001	7.01	7.1
$f(x)$				?			

Finding Limits   In Exercises 93–110, find the limit (if it exists).

93. $\lim\limits_{x \to 3} 8$

94. $\lim\limits_{x \to 4} x^2$

95. $\lim\limits_{x \to 2} (5x - 3)$

96. $\lim\limits_{x \to 5} (2x + 4)$

97. $\lim\limits_{x \to -1} \dfrac{x + 3}{6x + 1}$

98. $\lim\limits_{t \to 3} \dfrac{t}{t + 5}$

99. $\lim\limits_{t \to 0} \dfrac{t^2 + 1}{t}$

100. $\lim\limits_{t \to 2} \dfrac{t + 1}{t - 2}$

101. $\lim\limits_{x \to -2} \dfrac{x + 2}{x^2 - 4}$

102. $\lim\limits_{x \to 3^-} \dfrac{x^2 - 9}{x - 3}$

103. $\lim\limits_{x \to 0^+} \left(x - \dfrac{1}{x} \right)$

104. $\lim\limits_{x \to 1/2} \dfrac{2x - 1}{6x - 3}$

105. $\lim\limits_{x \to 0} \dfrac{[1/(x - 2)] - 1}{x}$

106. $\lim\limits_{s \to 0} \dfrac{\left(1/\sqrt{1 + s} \right) - 1}{s}$

107. $\lim\limits_{x \to 0} f(x)$, where $f(x) = \begin{cases} x + 5, & x \neq 0 \\ 3, & x = 0 \end{cases}$

108. $\lim\limits_{x \to -2} f(x)$, where $f(x) = \begin{cases} \frac{1}{2}x + 5, & x < -2 \\ -x + 2, & x \geq -2 \end{cases}$

109. $\lim\limits_{\Delta x \to 0} \dfrac{(x + \Delta x)^3 - (x + \Delta x) - (x^3 - x)}{\Delta x}$

110. $\lim\limits_{\Delta x \to 0} \dfrac{1 - (x + \Delta x)^2 - (1 - x^2)}{\Delta x}$

Determining Continuity   In Exercises 111–120, describe the interval(s) on which the function is continuous. Explain why the function is continuous on the interval(s). If the function has a discontinuity, identify the conditions of continuity that are not satisfied.

111. $f(x) = x + 6$

112. $f(x) = x^2 + 3x + 2$

113. $f(x) = \dfrac{1}{(x + 4)^2}$

114. $f(x) = \dfrac{x + 2}{x}$

115. $f(x) = \dfrac{3}{x + 1}$

116. $f(x) = \dfrac{x + 1}{2x + 2}$

117. $f(x) = [\![x + 3]\!]$

118. $f(x) = [\![x]\!] - 2$

119. $f(x) = \begin{cases} x, & x \leq 0 \\ x + 1, & x > 0 \end{cases}$

120. $f(x) = \begin{cases} x, & x \leq 0 \\ x^2, & x > 0 \end{cases}$

Making a Function Continuous   In Exercises 121 and 122, find the constant a such that the function is continuous on the entire real number line.

121. $f(x) = \begin{cases} -x + 1, & x \leq 3 \\ ax - 8, & x > 3 \end{cases}$

122. $f(x) = \begin{cases} x + 1, & x < 1 \\ 2x + a, & x \geq 1 \end{cases}$

123. Consumer Awareness   The cost C (in dollars) of purchasing x bottles of vitamins at a whole foods store is shown below.

$$C(x) = \begin{cases} 5.99x, & 0 < x \leq 5 \\ 4.99x, & 5 < x \leq 10 \\ 3.99x, & 10 < x \leq 15 \\ 2.99x, & x > 15 \end{cases}$$

(a) Use a graphing utility to graph the function and then discuss its continuity. At what values is the function not continuous? Explain your reasoning.

(b) Find the cost of purchasing 10 bottles.

124. Salary Contract   A union contract guarantees a 10% salary increase yearly for 3 years. For a current salary of $28,000, the salaries S (in thousands of dollars) for the next 3 years are given by

$$S(t) = \begin{cases} 28.00, & 0 < t \leq 1 \\ 30.80, & 1 < t \leq 2 \\ 33.88, & 2 < t \leq 3 \end{cases}$$

where $t = 0$ represents the present year. Does the limit of S exist as t approaches 2? Explain your reasoning.

125. Consumer Awareness   A pay-as-you-go cellular phone charges $1 for the first minute and $0.10 for each additional minute or fraction thereof.

(a) Use the greatest integer function to create a model for the cost C of a phone call lasting t minutes.

(b) Use a graphing utility to graph the function and then discuss its continuity.

126. Recycling   A recycling center pays $0.50 for each pound of aluminum cans. Twenty-four aluminum cans weigh one pound. A mathematical model for the amount A paid by the recycling center is

$$A = \frac{1}{2} \left[\!\!\left[\frac{x}{24} \right]\!\!\right]$$

where x is the number of cans.

(a) Use a graphing utility to graph the function and then discuss its continuity.

(b) How much does the recycling center pay out for 1500 cans?

TEST YOURSELF

See www.CalcChat.com for worked-out solutions to odd-numbered exercises.

Take this test as you would take a test in class. When you are done, check your work against the answers given in the back of the book.

In Exercises 1–3, (a) find the distance between the points, (b) find the midpoint of the line segment joining the points, (c) find the slope of the line passing through the points, (d) find an equation of the line passing through the points, and (e) sketch the graph of the equation.

1. $(1, -1), (-4, 4)$ 2. $(\frac{5}{2}, 2), (0, 2)$ 3. $(2, 3), (-4, 1)$

4. The demand and supply equations for a product are $p = 65 - 2.1x$ and $p = 43 + 1.9x$, respectively, where p is the price (in dollars) and x represents the number of units, in thousands. Find the equilibrium point for this market.

In Exercises 5–7, find the slope and y-intercept (if possible) of the equation of the line. Then sketch the graph of the equation.

5. $y = \frac{1}{5}x - 2$ 6. $x - \frac{7}{4} = 0$ 7. $-x - 0.4y + 2.5 = 0$

8. Write an equation of the line that passes through $(-1, -7)$ and is perpendicular to $-4x + y = 8$.

9. Write an equation of the line that passes through $(2, 1)$ and is parallel to $5x - 2y = 8$.

In Exercises 10–12, (a) graph the function and label the intercepts, (b) determine the domain and range of the function, (c) find the value of the function when x is -3, -2, and 3, and (d) determine whether the function is one-to-one.

10. $f(x) = 2x + 5$ 11. $f(x) = x^2 - x - 2$ 12. $f(x) = \sqrt{x + 5}$

In Exercises 13 and 14, find the inverse function of f.

13. $f(x) = 4x + 6$ 14. $f(x) = \sqrt[3]{8 - 3x}$

In Exercises 15–18, find the limit (if it exists).

15. $\lim\limits_{x \to 0} \dfrac{x - 2}{x + 2}$ 16. $\lim\limits_{x \to 5} \dfrac{x + 5}{x - 5}$

17. $\lim\limits_{x \to -3} \dfrac{x^2 + 2x - 3}{x^2 + 4x + 3}$ 18. $\lim\limits_{x \to 0} \dfrac{\sqrt{x + 9} - 3}{x}$

In Exercises 19–21, describe the interval(s) on which the function is continuous. Explain why the function is continuous on the interval(s). If the function has a discontinuity, identify the conditions of continuity that are not satisfied.

19. $f(x) = \dfrac{x^2 - 16}{x - 4}$ 20. $f(x) = \sqrt{5 - x}$ 21. $f(x) = \begin{cases} 1 - x, & x < 1 \\ x - x^2, & x \geq 1 \end{cases}$

22. The table lists the numbers of unemployed workers y (in thousands) in the United States for selected years. A mathematical model for the data is given by

$$y = 193.898t^3 - 3080.32t^2 + 15{,}478.5t - 16{,}925$$

where t represents the year, with $t = 4$ corresponding to 2004. *(Source: U.S. Bureau of Labor Statistics)*

(a) Compare the actual numbers of unemployed workers with those given by the model. How well does the model fit the data? Explain your reasoning.

(b) Use the model to predict the number of unemployed workers in 2014.

t	4	5	6
y	8149	7591	7001

t	7	8	9
y	7078	8924	14,265

Table for 22

McDonald's Revenue

Revenue (in millions of dollars)

Slope ≈ 1941

Year (4 ↔ 2004)

Example 11 on page 99 shows how differentiation can be used to find the rate of change in a company's revenue.

2 Differentiation

2.1 The Derivative and the Slope of a Graph

■ Identify tangent lines to a graph at a point.
■ Approximate the slopes of tangent lines to graphs at points.
■ Use the limit definition to find the slopes of graphs at points.
■ Use the limit definition to find the derivatives of functions.
■ Describe the relationship between differentiability and continuity.

In Exercise 13 on page 89, you will estimate and interpret the slope of the graph of a revenue function.

Tangent Line to a Graph

Calculus is a branch of mathematics that studies rates of change of functions. In this course, you will learn that rates of change have many applications in real life. In Section 1.3, you learned how the slope of a line indicates the rate at which the line rises or falls. For a line, this rate (or slope) is the same at every point on the line. For graphs other than lines, the rate at which the graph rises or falls changes from point to point. For instance, in Figure 2.1, the parabola is rising more quickly at the point (x_1, y_1) than it is at the point (x_2, y_2). At the vertex (x_3, y_3), the graph levels off, and at the point (x_4, y_4), the graph is falling.

The slope of a nonlinear graph changes from one point to another.
FIGURE 2.1

    To determine the rate at which a graph rises or falls at a *single point,* you can find the slope of the **tangent line** at the point. In simple terms, the tangent line to the graph of a function f at a point $P(x_1, y_1)$ is the line that best approximates the graph at that point, as shown in Figure 2.1. Figure 2.2 shows other examples of tangent lines.

Tangent Line to a Graph at a Point
FIGURE 2.2

    When Isaac Newton (1642–1727) was working on the "tangent line problem," he realized that it is difficult to define precisely what is meant by a tangent to a general curve. From geometry, you know that a line is tangent to a circle when the line intersects the circle at only one point, as shown in Figure 2.3. Tangent lines to a noncircular graph, however, can intersect the graph at more than one point. For instance, in the second graph in Figure 2.2, when the tangent line is extended, it intersects the graph at a point other than the point of tangency. In this section, you will see how the notion of a limit can be used to define a general tangent line.

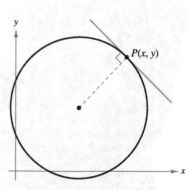

Tangent Line to a Circle
FIGURE 2.3

Slope of a Graph

Because a tangent line approximates the graph at a point, the problem of finding the slope of a graph at a point becomes one of finding the slope of the tangent line at the point.

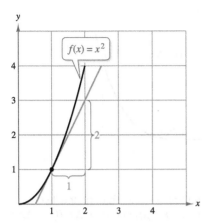

FIGURE 2.4

Example 1   Approximating the Slope of a Graph

Use the graph in Figure 2.4 to approximate the slope of the graph of

$$f(x) = x^2$$

at the point $(1, 1)$.

SOLUTION   From the graph of

$$f(x) = x^2$$

you can see that the tangent line at $(1, 1)$ rises approximately two units for each unit change in x. So, the slope of the tangent line at $(1, 1)$ is given by

$$\text{Slope} = \frac{\Delta y}{\Delta x} = \frac{\text{change in } y}{\text{change in } x} \approx \frac{2}{1} = 2.$$

Because the tangent line at the point $(1, 1)$ has a slope of about 2, you can conclude that the graph has a slope of about 2 at the point $(1, 1)$.

✔ **Checkpoint 1**

Use the graph to approximate the slope of the graph of

$$f(x) = x^3$$

at the point $(1, 1)$.

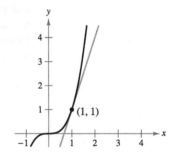

Example 2   Interpreting Slope

Figure 2.5 graphically depicts the average monthly temperature (in degrees Fahrenheit) in Duluth, Minnesota. Estimate the slope of this graph at the indicated point and give a physical interpretation of the result. *(Source: National Oceanic and Atmospheric Administration)*

SOLUTION   From the graph, you can see that the tangent line at the given point falls approximately 28 units for each two-unit change in x. So, you can estimate the slope at the given point to be

$$\text{Slope} = \frac{\Delta y}{\Delta x} = \frac{\text{change in } y}{\text{change in } x} \approx \frac{-28}{2} = -14 \text{ degrees per month.}$$

This means that you can expect the average daily temperatures in November to be about 14 degrees *lower* than the corresponding temperatures in October.

FIGURE 2.5

✔ **Checkpoint 2**

In Figure 2.5, for which months do the slopes of the tangent lines appear to be positive? Negative? Interpret these slopes in the context of the problem.

Slope and the Limit Process

In Examples 1 and 2, you approximated the slope of a graph at a point by making a careful graph and then "eyeballing" the tangent line at the point of tangency. A more precise method of approximating the slope of a tangent line makes use of a **secant line** through the point of tangency and a second point on the graph, as shown in Figure 2.6. If $(x, f(x))$ is the point of tangency and

$$(x + \Delta x, f(x + \Delta x))$$

is a second point on the graph of f, then the slope of the secant line through the two points is

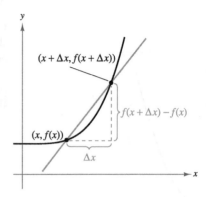

The Secant Line Through the Two Points $(x, f(x))$ and $(x + \Delta x, f(x + \Delta x))$
FIGURE 2.6

$$m = \frac{y_2 - y_1}{x_2 - x_1} \qquad \text{Formula for slope}$$

$$m_{\text{sec}} = \frac{f(x + \Delta x) - f(x)}{(x + \Delta x) - x} \qquad \frac{\text{Change in } y}{\text{Change in } x}$$

$$m_{\text{sec}} = \frac{f(x + \Delta x) - f(x)}{\Delta x}. \qquad \text{Slope of secant line}$$

The right side of this equation is called the **difference quotient.** The denominator Δx is the **change in x,** and the numerator is the **change in y.** The beauty of this procedure is that you obtain more and more accurate approximations of the slope of the tangent line by choosing points closer and closer to the point of tangency, as shown in Figure 2.7. Using the limit process, you can find the *exact* slope of the tangent line at $(x, f(x))$, which is also the slope of the graph of f at $(x, f(x))$.

FIGURE 2.7   As Δx approaches 0, the secant lines approach the tangent line.

Definition of the Slope of a Graph

The **slope** m of the graph of f at the point

$$(x, f(x))$$

is equal to the slope of the tangent line to the graph of f at $(x, f(x))$, and is given by

$$m = \lim_{\Delta x \to 0} m_{\text{sec}} = \lim_{\Delta x \to 0} \frac{f(x + \Delta x) - f(x)}{\Delta x}$$

provided this limit exists.

ALGEBRA TUTOR
xy

For help in evaluating the expressions in Examples 3–6, see the review of simplifying fractional expressions on page 158.

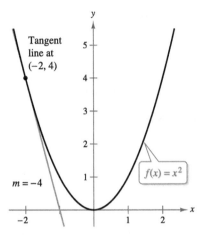

Tangent line at $(-2, 4)$

$m = -4$

$f(x) = x^2$

FIGURE 2.8

Example 3 **Finding Slope by the Limit Process**

Find the slope of the graph of

$$f(x) = x^2$$

at the point $(-2, 4)$.

SOLUTION Begin by finding an expression that represents the slope of a secant line at the point $(-2, 4)$.

$$m_{\text{sec}} = \frac{f(-2 + \Delta x) - f(-2)}{\Delta x} \qquad \text{Set up difference quotient.}$$

$$= \frac{(-2 + \Delta x)^2 - (-2)^2}{\Delta x} \qquad \text{Use } f(x) = x^2.$$

$$= \frac{4 - 4\,\Delta x + (\Delta x)^2 - 4}{\Delta x} \qquad \text{Expand terms.}$$

$$= \frac{-4\,\Delta x + (\Delta x)^2}{\Delta x} \qquad \text{Simplify.}$$

$$= \frac{\Delta x(-4 + \Delta x)}{\Delta x} \qquad \text{Factor and divide out.}$$

$$= -4 + \Delta x, \quad \Delta x \neq 0 \qquad \text{Simplify.}$$

Next, take the limit of m_{sec} as $\Delta x \to 0$.

$$m = \lim_{\Delta x \to 0} m_{\text{sec}} = \lim_{\Delta x \to 0} (-4 + \Delta x) = -4 + 0 = -4$$

So, the graph of f has a slope of -4 at the point $(-2, 4)$, as shown in Figure 2.8.

✓ **Checkpoint 3**

Find the slope of the graph of

$$f(x) = x^2$$

at the point $(2, 4)$.

Example 4 **Finding the Slope of a Graph**

Find the slope of the graph of $f(x) = -2x + 4$.

SOLUTION You know from your study of linear functions that the line given by $f(x) = -2x + 4$ has a slope of -2, as shown in Figure 2.9. This conclusion is consistent with the limit definition of slope.

$$m = \lim_{\Delta x \to 0} \frac{f(x + \Delta x) - f(x)}{\Delta x}$$

$$= \lim_{\Delta x \to 0} \frac{[-2(x + \Delta x) + 4] - (-2x + 4)}{\Delta x}$$

$$= \lim_{\Delta x \to 0} \frac{-2x - 2\,\Delta x + 4 + 2x - 4}{\Delta x}$$

$$= \lim_{\Delta x \to 0} \frac{-2\,\Delta x}{\Delta x}$$

$$= -2$$

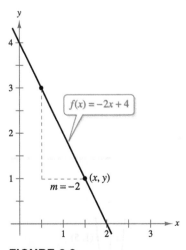

$f(x) = -2x + 4$

$m = -2$

(x, y)

FIGURE 2.9

✓ **Checkpoint 4**

Find the slope of the graph of $f(x) = 2x + 5$.

| Example 5 | Finding a Formula for the Slope of a Graph |

Find a formula for the slope of the graph of $f(x) = x^2 + 1$. What are the slopes at the points $(-1, 2)$ and $(2, 5)$?

SOLUTION

$$m_{sec} = \frac{f(x + \Delta x) - f(x)}{\Delta x}$$ Set up difference quotient.

$$= \frac{[(x + \Delta x)^2 + 1] - (x^2 + 1)}{\Delta x}$$ Use $f(x) = x^2 + 1$.

$$= \frac{x^2 + 2x \Delta x + (\Delta x)^2 + 1 - x^2 - 1}{\Delta x}$$ Expand terms.

$$= \frac{2x \Delta x + (\Delta x)^2}{\Delta x}$$ Simplify.

$$= \frac{\Delta x(2x + \Delta x)}{\Delta x}$$ Factor and divide out.

$$= 2x + \Delta x, \quad \Delta x \neq 0$$ Simplify.

Next, take the limit of m_{sec} as $\Delta x \to 0$.

$$m = \lim_{\Delta x \to 0} m_{sec}$$

$$= \lim_{\Delta x \to 0} (2x + \Delta x)$$

$$= 2x + 0$$

$$= 2x$$

Using the formula $m = 2x$, you can find the slopes at the specified points. At $(-1, 2)$ the slope is $m = 2(-1) = -2$, and at $(2, 5)$ the slope is $m = 2(2) = 4$. The graph of f is shown in Figure 2.10.

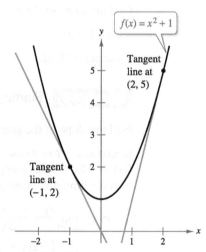

$f(x) = x^2 + 1$

Tangent line at (2, 5)

Tangent line at (−1, 2)

FIGURE 2.10

✓ **Checkpoint 5**

Find a formula for the slope of the graph of

$$f(x) = 4x^2 + 1.$$

What are the slopes at the points $(0, 1)$ and $(1, 5)$?

The Derivative of a Function

In Example 5, you started with the function

$$f(x) = x^2 + 1$$

and used the limit process to derive another function, $m = 2x$, that represents the slope of the graph of f at the point $(x, f(x))$. This derived function is called the **derivative** of f at x. It is denoted by $f'(x)$, which is read as "f prime of x."

Definition of the Derivative

The **derivative of f at x** is given by

$$f'(x) = \lim_{\Delta x \to 0} \frac{f(x + \Delta x) - f(x)}{\Delta x}$$

provided this limit exists. A function is **differentiable** at x when its derivative exists at x. The process of finding derivatives is called **differentiation.**

In addition to $f'(x)$, other notations can be used to denote the derivative of $y = f(x)$. The most common are

$$\frac{dy}{dx}, \quad y', \quad \frac{d}{dx}[f(x)], \quad \text{and} \quad D_x[y].$$

STUDY TIP

The notation dy/dx is read as "the derivative of y with respect to x," and using limit notation, you can write

$$\frac{dy}{dx} = \lim_{\Delta x \to 0} \frac{\Delta y}{\Delta x}$$

$$= \lim_{\Delta x \to 0} \frac{f(x + \Delta x) - f(x)}{\Delta x}$$

$$= f'(x).$$

Example 6 Finding a Derivative

Find the derivative of

$$f(x) = 3x^2 - 2x.$$

SOLUTION

$$f'(x) = \lim_{\Delta x \to 0} \frac{f(x + \Delta x) - f(x)}{\Delta x}$$

$$= \lim_{\Delta x \to 0} \frac{[3(x + \Delta x)^2 - 2(x + \Delta x)] - (3x^2 - 2x)}{\Delta x}$$

$$= \lim_{\Delta x \to 0} \frac{3x^2 + 6x\,\Delta x + 3(\Delta x)^2 - 2x - 2\,\Delta x - 3x^2 + 2x}{\Delta x}$$

$$= \lim_{\Delta x \to 0} \frac{6x\,\Delta x + 3(\Delta x)^2 - 2\,\Delta x}{\Delta x}$$

$$= \lim_{\Delta x \to 0} \frac{\Delta x(6x + 3\,\Delta x - 2)}{\Delta x}$$

$$= \lim_{\Delta x \to 0} (6x + 3\,\Delta x - 2)$$

$$= 6x + 3(0) - 2$$

$$= 6x - 2$$

So, the derivative of $f(x) = 3x^2 - 2x$ is

$$f'(x) = 6x - 2.$$

✓ **Checkpoint 6**

Find the derivative of

$$f(x) = x^2 - 5x.$$

In many applications, it is convenient to use a variable other than x as the independent variable. Example 7 shows a function that uses t as the independent variable.

Example 7   Finding a Derivative

Find the derivative of y with respect to t for the function

$$y = \frac{2}{t}.$$

SOLUTION   Consider $y = f(t)$, and use the limit process as shown.

$$\frac{dy}{dt} = \lim_{\Delta t \to 0} \frac{f(t + \Delta t) - f(t)}{\Delta t} \qquad \text{Set up difference quotient.}$$

$$= \lim_{\Delta t \to 0} \frac{\dfrac{2}{t + \Delta t} - \dfrac{2}{t}}{\Delta t} \qquad \text{Use } f(t) = 2/t.$$

$$= \lim_{\Delta t \to 0} \frac{\dfrac{2t - 2(t + \Delta t)}{t(t + \Delta t)}}{\Delta t} \qquad \text{Combine fractions in numerator.}$$

$$= \lim_{\Delta t \to 0} \frac{2t - 2t - 2\Delta t}{\Delta t(t)(t + \Delta t)} \qquad \text{Expand terms in numerator.}$$

$$= \lim_{\Delta t \to 0} \frac{-2\Delta t}{\Delta t(t)(t + \Delta t)} \qquad \text{Factor and divide out.}$$

$$= \lim_{\Delta t \to 0} \frac{-2}{t(t + \Delta t)} \qquad \text{Simplify.}$$

$$= \frac{-2}{t(t + 0)} \qquad \text{Direct substitution}$$

$$= -\frac{2}{t^2} \qquad \text{Simplify.}$$

So, the derivative of y with respect to t is

$$\frac{dy}{dt} = -\frac{2}{t^2}.$$

✓ Checkpoint 7

Find the derivative of y with respect to t for the function $y = 4/t$.   ▨

Remember that the derivative of a function gives you a formula for finding the slope of the tangent line at any point on the graph of the function. For instance, in Example 7 the slope of the tangent line to the graph of f at the point $(1, 2)$ is given by

$$f'(1) = -\frac{2}{1^2} = -2.$$

To find the slopes of the graph at other points, substitute the t-coordinate of the point into the derivative, as shown below.

Point	t-Coordinate	Slope
$(2, 1)$	$t = 2$	$m = f'(2) = -\dfrac{2}{2^2} = -\dfrac{1}{2}$
$(-2, -1)$	$t = -2$	$m = f'(-2) = -\dfrac{2}{(-2)^2} = -\dfrac{1}{2}$

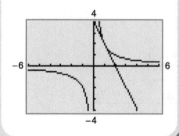

Differentiability and Continuity

Not every function is differentiable. Figure 2.11 shows some common situations in which a function will not be differentiable at a point—vertical tangent lines, discontinuities, and sharp turns in the graph. Each of the functions shown in Figure 2.11 is differentiable at every value of *x except x* = 0.

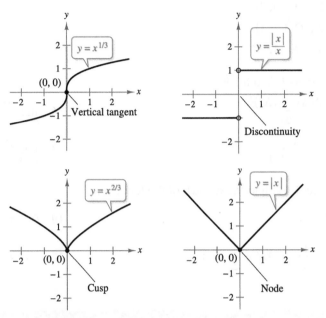

Functions That Are Not Differentiable at *x* = 0

FIGURE 2.11

In Figure 2.11, you can see that all but one of the functions are continuous at *x* = 0 but none are differentiable there. This shows that continuity is not a strong enough condition to guarantee differentiability. On the other hand, if a function is differentiable at a point, then it must be continuous at that point. This important result is stated in the following theorem.

Differentiability Implies Continuity

If a function *f* is differentiable at *x* = *c*, then *f* is continuous at *x* = *c*.

SUMMARIZE   (Section 2.1)

1. Describe a tangent line and how it can be used to approximate the slope of a graph at a point *(page 80)*. For an example of a tangent line, see Example 1.

2. State the definition of the slope of a graph using the limit process *(page 82)*. For examples of finding the slope of a graph using the limit process, see Examples 3, 4, and 5.

3. State the definition of the derivative of a function *(page 85)*. For examples of the derivative of a function, see Examples 6 and 7.

4. Describe the relationship between differentiability and continuity *(page 87)*. For an example showing that continuity does not guarantee differentiability, see Figure 2.11.

SKILLS WARM UP 2.1   The following warm-up exercises involve skills that were covered in earlier sections. You will use these skills in the exercise set for this section. For additional help, review Sections 1.3, 1.4, and 1.5.

In Exercises 1–4, find an equation of the line containing P and Q.

1. $P(2, 1)$, $Q(2, 4)$

2. $P(2, 2)$, $Q(-5, 2)$

3. $P(2, 0)$, $Q(3, -1)$

4. $P(3, 5)$, $Q(-1, -7)$

In Exercises 5–8, find the limit.

5. $\lim\limits_{\Delta x \to 0} \dfrac{2x\Delta x + (\Delta x)^2}{\Delta x}$

6. $\lim\limits_{\Delta x \to 0} \dfrac{3x^2\Delta x + 3x(\Delta x)^2 + (\Delta x)^3}{\Delta x}$

7. $\lim\limits_{\Delta x \to 0} \dfrac{1}{x(x + \Delta x)}$

8. $\lim\limits_{\Delta x \to 0} \dfrac{(x + \Delta x)^2 - x^2}{\Delta x}$

In Exercises 9–12, find the domain of the function.

9. $f(x) = 3x$

10. $f(x) = \dfrac{1}{x - 1}$

11. $f(x) = \dfrac{1}{5}x^3 - 2x^2 + \dfrac{1}{3}x - 1$

12. $f(x) = \dfrac{6x}{x^3 + x}$

Exercises 2.1

See www.CalcChat.com for worked-out solutions to odd-numbered exercises.

Sketching Tangent Lines   In Exercises 1–6, trace the graph and sketch the tangent lines at (x_1, y_1) and (x_2, y_2).

Approximating the Slope of a Graph   In Exercises 7–12, estimate the slope of the graph at the point (x, y). (Each square on the grid is 1 unit by 1 unit.) *See Example 1.*

1.

2.

3.

4.

5.

6.

7.

8.

9.

10.

11.

12.

13. Revenue The graph represents the revenue R (in millions of dollars) for Under Armour from 2004 through 2009, where t represents the year, with $t = 4$ corresponding to 2004. Estimate and interpret the slopes of the graph for the years 2005 and 2007. *(Source: Under Armour, Inc.)*

Under Armour

Revenue (in millions of dollars)

Year (4 ↔ 2004)

14. Sales The graph represents the sales S (in millions of dollars) for Scotts Miracle-Gro Company from 2003 through 2009, where t represents the year, with $t = 3$ corresponding to 2003. Estimate and interpret the slopes of the graph for the years 2006 and 2008. *(Source: Scotts Miracle-Gro Company)*

Scotts Miracle-Gro Company

Sales (in millions of dollars)

Year (3 ↔ 2003)

15. Temperature The graph represents the average monthly temperature F (in degrees Fahrenheit) in Blacksburg, Virginia for one year, where t represents the month, with $t = 1$ corresponding to January, $t = 2$ corresponding to February, and so on. Estimate and interpret the slopes of the graph at $t = 3$, 7, and 10. *(Source: National Oceanic and Atmospheric Administration)*

Average Temperature in Blacksburg

Temperature (in degrees Fahrenheit)

Month (1 ↔ January)

 16. HOW DO YOU SEE IT? Two long distance runners starting out side by side begin a 10,000-meter run. Their distances are given by $s = f(t)$ and $s = g(t)$, where s is measured in thousands of meters and t is measured in minutes.

10,000-Meter Run

Distance (in thousands of meters)

Time (in minutes)

(a) Which runner is running faster at t_1?

(b) What conclusion can you make regarding their rates at t_2?

(c) What conclusion can you make regarding their rates at t_3?

(d) Which runner finishes the race first? Explain.

Finding the Slope of a Graph In Exercises 17–26, use the limit definition to find the slope of the tangent line to the graph of f at the given point. *See Examples 3, 4, and 5.*

17. $f(x) = -1$; $(0, -1)$

18. $f(x) = 6$; $(-2, 6)$

19. $f(x) = 8 - 3x$; $(2, 2)$

20. $f(x) = 6x + 3$; $(1, 9)$

21. $f(x) = 2x^2 - 3$; $(2, 5)$

22. $f(x) = 4 - x^2$; $(2, 0)$

23. $f(x) = x^3 - x$; $(2, 6)$

24. $f(x) = x^3 + 2x$; $(1, 3)$

25. $f(x) = 2\sqrt{x}$; $(4, 4)$

26. $f(x) = \sqrt{x + 1}$; $(8, 3)$

Finding a Derivative In Exercises 27–40, use the limit definition to find the derivative of the function. *See Examples 6 and 7.*

27. $f(x) = 3$

28. $f(x) = -2$

29. $f(x) = -5x$

30. $f(x) = 4x + 1$

31. $g(s) = \frac{1}{3}s + 2$

32. $h(t) = 6 - \frac{1}{2}t$

33. $f(x) = 4x^2 - 5x$

34. $f(x) = 2x^2 + 7x$

35. $h(t) = \sqrt{t - 1}$

36. $f(x) = \sqrt{x + 2}$

37. $f(t) = t^3 - 12t$

38. $f(t) = t^3 + t^2$

39. $f(x) = \dfrac{1}{x + 2}$

40. $g(s) = \dfrac{1}{s - 1}$

Finding an Equation of a Tangent Line In Exercises 41–48, use the limit definition to find an equation of the tangent line to the graph of f at the given point. Then verify your results by using a graphing utility to graph the function and its tangent line at the point.

41. $f(x) = \frac{1}{2}x^2; (2, 2)$ **42.** $f(x) = -x^2; (-1, -1)$

43. $f(x) = (x - 1)^2; (-2, 9)$

44. $f(x) = 2x^2 - 1; (0, -1)$

45. $f(x) = \sqrt{x} + 1; (4, 3)$ **46.** $f(x) = \sqrt{x + 2}; (7, 3)$

47. $f(x) = \frac{1}{x}; (1, 1)$ **48.** $f(x) = \frac{1}{x - 3}; (2, -1)$

Finding an Equation of a Tangent Line In Exercises 49–52, find an equation of the line that is tangent to the graph of f and parallel to the given line.

Function	Line
49. $f(x) = -\frac{1}{4}x^2$	$x + y = 0$
50. $f(x) = x^2 - 7$	$2x + y = 0$
51. $f(x) = -\frac{1}{3}x^3$	$9x + y - 6 = 0$
52. $f(x) = x^2 - x$	$x + 2y - 6 = 0$

Determining Differentiability In Exercises 53–58, describe the x-values at which the function is differentiable. Explain your reasoning.

53. $y = |x + 3|$ **54.** $y = |x^2 - 9|$

55. $y = (x - 3)^{2/3}$ **56.** $y = \sqrt{x - 1}$

57. $y = \dfrac{x^2}{x^2 - 4}$ **58.** $y = \begin{cases} x^3 + 3, & x < 0 \\ x^3 - 3, & x \geq 0 \end{cases}$

Writing a Function Using Derivatives In Exercises 59 and 60, identify a function f that has the given characteristics. Then sketch the function.

59. $f(0) = 2; f'(x) = -3$ for $-\infty < x < \infty$

60. $f(-2) = f(4) = 0; f'(1) = 0;$
$f'(x) < 0$ for $x < 1; f'(x) > 0$ for $x > 1$

 Graphical, Numerical, and Analytic Analysis In Exercises 61–64, use a graphing utility to graph f on the interval $[-2, 2]$. Complete the table by graphically estimating the slopes of the graph at the given points. Then evaluate the slopes analytically and compare your results with those obtained graphically.

x	-2	$-\frac{3}{2}$	-1	$-\frac{1}{2}$	0	$\frac{1}{2}$	1	$\frac{3}{2}$	2
$f(x)$									
$f'(x)$									

61. $f(x) = \frac{1}{4}x^3$ **62.** $f(x) = \frac{3}{4}x^2$

63. $f(x) = -\frac{1}{2}x^3$ **64.** $f(x) = -\frac{3}{2}x^2$

 Graphing a Function and Its Derivative In Exercises 65–68, find the derivative of the given function f. Then use a graphing utility to graph f and its derivative in the same viewing window. What does the x-intercept of the derivative indicate about the graph of f?

65. $f(x) = x^2 - 4x$ **66.** $f(x) = 2 + 6x - x^2$

67. $f(x) = x^3 - 3x$ **68.** $f(x) = x^3 - 6x^2$

True or False? In Exercises 69–72, determine whether the statement is true or false. If it is false, explain why or give an example that shows it is false.

69. The slope of the graph of $y = x^2$ is different at every point on the graph of f.

70. If a function is continuous at a point, then it is differentiable at that point.

71. If a function is differentiable at a point, then it is continuous at that point.

72. A tangent line to a graph can intersect the graph at more than one point.

73. Writing Use a graphing utility to graph the two functions

$$f(x) = x^2 + 1 \quad \text{and} \quad g(x) = |x| + 1$$

in the same viewing window. Use the *zoom* and *trace* features to analyze the graphs near the point $(0, 1)$. What do you observe? Which function is differentiable at this point? Write a short paragraph describing the geometric significance of differentiability at a point.

2.2 Some Rules for Differentiation

- ■ Find the derivatives of functions using the Constant Rule.
- ■ Find the derivatives of functions using the Power Rule.
- ■ Find the derivatives of functions using the Constant Multiple Rule.
- ■ Find the derivatives of functions using the Sum and Difference Rules.
- ■ Use derivatives to answer questions about real-life situations.

The Constant Rule

In Section 2.1, you found derivatives by the limit process. This process is tedious, even for simple functions, but fortunately there are rules that greatly simplify differentiation. These rules allow you to calculate derivatives without the *direct* use of limits.

In Exercise 74 on page 102, you will use differentiation to find the rate of change in a company's sales.

The Constant Rule

The derivative of a constant function is zero. That is,

$$\frac{d}{dx}[c] = 0, \quad c \text{ is a constant.}$$

PROOF Let $f(x) = c$. Then, by the limit definition of the derivative, you can write

$$f'(x) = \lim_{\Delta x \to 0} \frac{f(x + \Delta x) - f(x)}{\Delta x} = \lim_{\Delta x \to 0} \frac{c - c}{\Delta x} = \lim_{\Delta x \to 0} 0 = 0.$$

So, $\frac{d}{dx}[c] = 0$.

Note in Figure 2.12 that the Constant Rule is equivalent to saying that the slope of a horizontal line is zero. An interpretation of the Constant Rule says that the tangent line to a constant function is the function itself. For instance, the equation of the tangent line to $f(x) = 4$ at $x = -1$ is

$$y = 4.$$

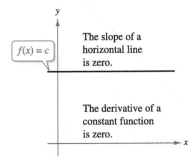

The slope of a horizontal line is zero.

The derivative of a constant function is zero.

FIGURE 2.12

Example 1 **Finding Derivatives of Constant Functions**

a. $\frac{d}{dx}[7] = 0$

b. If $f(x) = 0$, then $f'(x) = 0$.

c. If $y = 2$, then $\frac{dy}{dx} = 0$.

d. If $g(t) = -\frac{3}{2}$, then $g'(t) = 0$.

✓ Checkpoint 1

Find the derivative of each function.

a. $f(x) = -2$ **b.** $y = \pi$ **c.** $g(w) = \sqrt{5}$ **d.** $s(t) = 320.5$

The Power Rule

The binomial expansion process is used in proving a special case of the Power Rule.

$$(x + \Delta x)^2 = x^2 + 2x\,\Delta x + (\Delta x)^2$$

$$(x + \Delta x)^3 = x^3 + 3x^2\,\Delta x + 3x(\Delta x)^2 + (\Delta x)^3$$

$$(x + \Delta x)^n = x^n + nx^{n-1}\,\Delta x + \underbrace{\frac{n(n-1)x^{n-2}}{2}(\Delta x)^2 + \cdots + (\Delta x)^n}_{(\Delta x)^2 \text{ is a factor of these terms.}}$$

The (Simple) Power Rule

$$\frac{d}{dx}[x^n] = nx^{n-1}, \quad n \text{ is any real number.}$$

PROOF   This proof is limited to the case in which n is a positive integer. Let $f(x) = x^n$. Using the binomial expansion, you can write

$$
\begin{aligned}
f'(x) &= \lim_{\Delta x \to 0} \frac{f(x + \Delta x) - f(x)}{\Delta x} \qquad \text{Definition of derivative}\\[2mm]
&= \lim_{\Delta x \to 0} \frac{(x + \Delta x)^n - x^n}{\Delta x}\\[2mm]
&= \lim_{\Delta x \to 0} \frac{x^n + nx^{n-1}\,\Delta x + \dfrac{n(n-1)x^{n-2}}{2}(\Delta x)^2 + \cdots + (\Delta x)^n - x^n}{\Delta x}\\[2mm]
&= \lim_{\Delta x \to 0} \left[nx^{n-1} + \frac{n(n-1)x^{n-2}}{2}(\Delta x) + \cdots + (\Delta x)^{n-1} \right]\\[2mm]
&= nx^{n-1} + 0 + \cdots + 0\\[2mm]
&= nx^{n-1}.
\end{aligned}
$$

For the Power Rule, the case in which $n = 1$ is worth remembering as a separate differentiation rule. That is,

$$\frac{d}{dx}[x] = 1. \qquad \text{The derivative of } x \text{ is 1.}$$

This rule is consistent with the fact that the slope of the line given by $y = x$ is 1. (See Figure 2.13.)

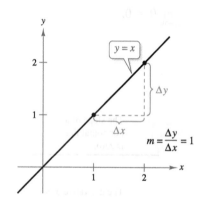

The slope of the line $y = x$ is 1.
FIGURE 2.13

Example 2   Applying the Power Rule

Original Function	Derivative
a. $f(x) = x^3$	$f'(x) = 3x^2$
b. $y = \dfrac{1}{x^2} = x^{-2}$	$\dfrac{dy}{dx} = (-2)x^{-3} = -\dfrac{2}{x^3}$
c. $g(t) = t$	$g'(t) = 1$

✓ **Checkpoint 2**

Find the derivative of each function.

a. $f(x) = x^4$ **b.** $y = \dfrac{1}{x^3}$ **c.** $g(w) = w^2$

In Example 2(b), note that *before* differentiating, you should rewrite $1/x^2$ as x^{-2}. Rewriting is the first step in *many* differentiation problems.

| Original Function: $y = \dfrac{1}{x^2}$ | Rewrite: $y = x^{-2}$ | Differentiate: $\dfrac{dy}{dx} = (-2)x^{-3}$ | Simplify: $\dfrac{dy}{dx} = -\dfrac{2}{x^3}$ |

Remember that the derivative of a function f is another function that gives the slope of the graph of f at any point at which f is differentiable. So, you can use the derivative to find slopes, as shown in Example 3.

Example 3   Finding the Slope of a Graph

Find the slopes of the graph of

$$f(x) = x^2$$

at $x = -2, -1, 0, 1,$ and 2.

SOLUTION   Begin by using the Power Rule to find the derivative of f.

$$f'(x) = 2x \qquad \text{Derivative}$$

You can use the derivative to find the slopes of the graph of f, as shown.

x-Value	*Slope of Graph of f*
$x = -2$	$m = f'(-2) = 2(-2) = -4$
$x = -1$	$m = f'(-1) = 2(-1) = -2$
$x = 0$	$m = f'(0) = 2(0) = 0$
$x = 1$	$m = f'(1) = 2(1) = 2$
$x = 2$	$m = f'(2) = 2(2) = 4$

The graph of f is shown in Figure 2.14.

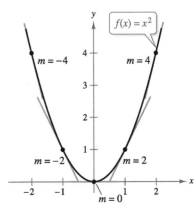

FIGURE 2.14

✓ Checkpoint 3

Find the slopes of the graph of

$$f(x) = x^3$$

at $x = -1, 0,$ and 1.

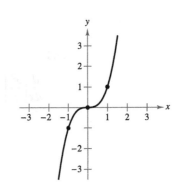

The Constant Multiple Rule

To prove the Constant Multiple Rule, the following property of limits is used.

$$\lim_{x \to a} cg(x) = c \left[\lim_{x \to a} g(x) \right]$$

The Constant Multiple Rule

If f is a differentiable function of x, and c is a real number, then

$$\frac{d}{dx}[cf(x)] = cf'(x), \quad c \text{ is a constant.}$$

PROOF Apply the definition of the derivative to produce

$$\frac{d}{dx}[cf(x)] = \lim_{\Delta x \to 0} \frac{cf(x + \Delta x) - cf(x)}{\Delta x} \qquad \text{Definition of derivative}$$

$$= \lim_{\Delta x \to 0} c \left[\frac{f(x + \Delta x) - f(x)}{\Delta x} \right]$$

$$= c \left[\lim_{\Delta x \to 0} \frac{f(x + \Delta x) - f(x)}{\Delta x} \right]$$

$$= cf'(x).$$

Informally, the Constant Multiple Rule states that constants can be factored out of the differentiation process.

$$\frac{d}{dx}[cf(x)] = c \frac{d}{dx}[f(x)] = cf'(x).$$

The usefulness of this rule is often overlooked, especially when the constant appears in the denominator, as shown below.

$$\frac{d}{dx}\left[\frac{f(x)}{c} \right] = \frac{d}{dx}\left[\frac{1}{c} f(x) \right]$$

$$= \frac{1}{c}\left(\frac{d}{dx}[f(x)] \right)$$

$$= \frac{1}{c} f'(x).$$

To use the Constant Multiple Rule efficiently, look for constants that can be factored out *before* differentiating. For example,

$$\frac{d}{dx}[5x^2] = 5\frac{d}{dx}[x^2] \qquad \text{Factor out 5.}$$

$$= 5(2x) \qquad \text{Differentiate.}$$

$$= 10x \qquad \text{Simplify.}$$

and

$$\frac{d}{dx}\left[\frac{x^2}{5} \right] = \frac{1}{5}\left(\frac{d}{dx}[x^2] \right) \qquad \text{Factor out } \tfrac{1}{5}.$$

$$= \frac{1}{5}(2x) \qquad \text{Differentiate.}$$

$$= \frac{2}{5}x. \qquad \text{Simplify.}$$

Example 4 **Using the Power and Constant Multiple Rules**

Find the derivative of (a) $y = 2x^{1/2}$ and (b) $f(t) = \dfrac{4t^2}{5}$.

SOLUTION

a. Using the Constant Multiple Rule and the Power Rule, you can write

$$\frac{dy}{dx} = \frac{d}{dx}[2x^{1/2}] = \underbrace{2\frac{d}{dx}[x^{1/2}]}_{\substack{\text{Constant} \\ \text{Multiple Rule}}} = 2\underbrace{\left(\frac{1}{2}x^{-1/2}\right)}_{\substack{\text{Power} \\ \text{Rule}}} = x^{-1/2} = \frac{1}{\sqrt{x}}.$$

b. Begin by rewriting $f(t)$ as

$$f(t) = \frac{4t^2}{5} = \frac{4}{5}t^2.$$

Then, use the Constant Multiple Rule and the Power Rule to obtain

$$f'(t) = \frac{d}{dt}\left[\frac{4}{5}t^2\right] = \frac{4}{5}\left(\frac{d}{dt}[t^2]\right) = \frac{4}{5}(2t) = \frac{8}{5}t.$$

✓**Checkpoint 4**

Find the derivative of (a) $y = 4x^2$ and (b) $f(x) = 16x^{1/2}$.

You may find it helpful to combine the Constant Multiple Rule and the Power Rule into one combined rule.

$$\frac{d}{dx}[cx^n] = cnx^{n-1}, \quad n \text{ is a real number, } c \text{ is a constant.}$$

For instance, in Example 4(b), you can apply this combined rule to obtain

$$\frac{d}{dt}\left[\frac{4}{5}t^2\right] = \left(\frac{4}{5}\right)(2)(t) = \frac{8}{5}t.$$

The three functions in the next example are simple, yet errors are frequently made in differentiating functions involving constant multiples of the first power of x. Keep in mind that

$$\frac{d}{dx}[cx] = c, \quad c \text{ is a constant.}$$

Example 5 **Applying the Constant Multiple Rule**

Original Function	*Derivative*
a. $y = -\dfrac{3x}{2}$	$y' = -\dfrac{3}{2}$
b. $y = 3\pi x$	$y' = 3\pi$
c. $y = -\dfrac{x}{2}$	$y' = -\dfrac{1}{2}$

✓**Checkpoint 5**

Find the derivative of (a) $y = \dfrac{t}{4}$ and (b) $y = -\dfrac{2x}{5}$.

Parentheses can play an important role in the use of the Constant Multiple Rule and the Power Rule. In Example 6, be sure you understand the mathematical conventions involving the use of parentheses.

Example 6   Using Parentheses When Differentiating

	Original Function	*Rewrite*	*Differentiate*	*Simplify*
a.	$y = \dfrac{5}{2x^3}$	$y = \dfrac{5}{2}(x^{-3})$	$y' = \dfrac{5}{2}(-3x^{-4})$	$y' = -\dfrac{15}{2x^4}$
b.	$y = \dfrac{5}{(2x)^3}$	$y = \dfrac{5}{8}(x^{-3})$	$y' = \dfrac{5}{8}(-3x^{-4})$	$y' = -\dfrac{15}{8x^4}$
c.	$y = \dfrac{7}{3x^{-2}}$	$y = \dfrac{7}{3}(x^2)$	$y' = \dfrac{7}{3}(2x)$	$y' = \dfrac{14x}{3}$
d.	$y = \dfrac{7}{(3x)^{-2}}$	$y = 63(x^2)$	$y' = 63(2x)$	$y' = 126x$

✓ Checkpoint 6

Find the derivative of each function.

a. $y = \dfrac{9}{4x^2}$

b. $y = \dfrac{9}{(4x)^2}$

When differentiating functions involving radicals, you should rewrite the function with rational exponents. For instance, you should rewrite

$$y = \sqrt[3]{x} \quad \text{as} \quad y = x^{1/3}$$

and you should rewrite

$$y = \dfrac{1}{\sqrt[3]{x^4}} \quad \text{as} \quad y = x^{-4/3}.$$

Example 7   Differentiating Radical Functions

	Original Function	*Rewrite*	*Differentiate*	*Simplify*
a.	$y = \sqrt{x}$	$y = x^{1/2}$	$y' = \left(\dfrac{1}{2}\right)x^{-1/2}$	$y' = \dfrac{1}{2\sqrt{x}}$
b.	$y = \dfrac{1}{2\sqrt[3]{x^2}}$	$y = \dfrac{1}{2}x^{-2/3}$	$y' = \dfrac{1}{2}\left(-\dfrac{2}{3}\right)x^{-5/3}$	$y' = -\dfrac{1}{3x^{5/3}}$
c.	$y = \sqrt{2x}$	$y = \sqrt{2}(x^{1/2})$	$y' = \sqrt{2}\left(\dfrac{1}{2}\right)x^{-1/2}$	$y' = \dfrac{1}{\sqrt{2x}}$

✓ Checkpoint 7

Find the derivative of each function.

a. $y = \sqrt{5x}$

b. $y = \sqrt[4]{x}$

The Sum and Difference Rules

To differentiate $y = 3x + 2x^3$, you would probably write

$$y' = 3 + 6x^2$$

without questioning your answer. The validity of differentiating a sum or difference of functions term by term is given by the Sum and Difference Rules.

The Sum and Difference Rules

The derivative of the sum or difference of two differentiable functions is the sum or difference of their derivatives.

$$\frac{d}{dx}[f(x) + g(x)] = f'(x) + g'(x) \qquad \text{Sum Rule}$$

$$\frac{d}{dx}[f(x) - g(x)] = f'(x) - g'(x) \qquad \text{Difference Rule}$$

PROOF Let $h(x) = f(x) + g(x)$. Then, you can prove the Sum Rule as shown.

$$h'(x) = \lim_{\Delta x \to 0} \frac{h(x + \Delta x) - h(x)}{\Delta x} \qquad \text{Definition of derivative}$$

$$= \lim_{\Delta x \to 0} \frac{f(x + \Delta x) + g(x + \Delta x) - f(x) - g(x)}{\Delta x}$$

$$= \lim_{\Delta x \to 0} \frac{f(x + \Delta x) - f(x) + g(x + \Delta x) - g(x)}{\Delta x}$$

$$= \lim_{\Delta x \to 0} \left[\frac{f(x + \Delta x) - f(x)}{\Delta x} + \frac{g(x + \Delta x) - g(x)}{\Delta x} \right]$$

$$= \lim_{\Delta x \to 0} \frac{f(x + \Delta x) - f(x)}{\Delta x} + \lim_{\Delta x \to 0} \frac{g(x + \Delta x) - g(x)}{\Delta x}$$

$$= f'(x) + g'(x)$$

So,

$$\frac{d}{dx}[f(x) + g(x)] = f'(x) + g'(x).$$

The Difference Rule can be proved in a similar manner.

The Sum and Difference Rules can be extended to the sum or difference of any finite number of functions. For instance, if $y = f(x) + g(x) + h(x)$, then $y' = f'(x) + g'(x) + h'(x)$.

STUDY TIP

Look back at Example 6 on page 85. Notice that the example asks for the derivative of the difference of two functions. Compare the result with the one obtained in Example 8(b) at the right.

Example 8 Using the Sum and Difference Rules

Original Function	*Derivative*
a. $y = x^3 + 4x^2$	$y' = 3x^2 + 8x$
b. $f(x) = 3x^2 - 2x$	$f'(x) = 6x - 2$

✓ **Checkpoint 8**

Find the derivative of each function.

a. $f(x) = 2x^2 + 5x$ **b.** $y = x^4 - 2x$

With the differentiation rules listed in this section, you can differentiate any polynomial function.

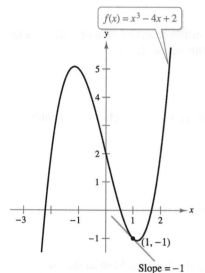

FIGURE 2.15

Example 9   Finding the Slope of a Graph

Find the slope of the graph of $f(x) = x^3 - 4x + 2$ at the point $(1, -1)$.

SOLUTION   The derivative of $f(x)$ is

$$f'(x) = 3x^2 - 4.$$

So, the slope of the graph of f at $(1, -1)$ is

$$\text{Slope} = f'(1) = 3(1)^2 - 4 = 3 - 4 = -1$$

as shown in Figure 2.15.

✓ **Checkpoint 9**

Find the slope of the graph of $f(x) = x^2 - 5x + 1$ at the point $(2, -5)$.

Example 9 illustrates the use of the derivative for determining the shape of a graph. A rough sketch of the graph of $f(x) = x^3 - 4x + 2$ might lead you to think that the point $(1, -1)$ is a minimum point of the graph. After finding the slope at this point to be -1, however, you can conclude that the minimum point (where the slope is 0) is farther to the right. (You will study techniques for finding minimum and maximum points in Section 3.2.)

Example 10   Finding an Equation of a Tangent Line

Find an equation of the tangent line to the graph of

$$g(x) = -\frac{1}{2}x^4 + 3x^3 - 2x$$

at the point $\left(-1, -\frac{3}{2}\right)$.

SOLUTION   The derivative of $g(x)$ is $g'(x) = -2x^3 + 9x^2 - 2$, which implies that the slope of the graph at the point $\left(-1, -\frac{3}{2}\right)$ is

$$\begin{aligned}
\text{Slope} &= g'(-1) \\
&= -2(-1)^3 + 9(-1)^2 - 2 \\
&= 2 + 9 - 2 \\
&= 9
\end{aligned}$$

as shown in Figure 2.16. Using the point-slope form, you can write the equation of the tangent line at $\left(-1, -\frac{3}{2}\right)$ as shown.

$$y - \left(-\frac{3}{2}\right) = 9[x - (-1)] \qquad \text{Point-slope form}$$

$$y + \frac{3}{2} = 9x + 9 \qquad \text{Simplify.}$$

$$y = 9x + \frac{15}{2} \qquad \text{Equation of tangent line}$$

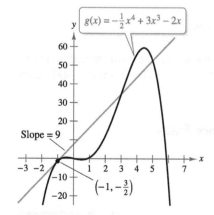

FIGURE 2.16

✓ **Checkpoint 10**

Find an equation of the tangent line to the graph of $f(x) = -x^2 + 3x - 2$ at the point $(2, 0)$.

Application

There are many applications of the derivative that you will study in this textbook. In Example 11, you will use a derivative to find the rate of change of a company's revenue with respect to time.

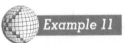 **Example 11** Modeling Revenue

From 2004 through 2009, the revenue R (in millions of dollars) for McDonald's can be modeled by

$$R = -130.769t^3 + 2296.47t^2 - 11{,}493.5t + 35{,}493, \quad 4 \le t \le 9$$

where t represents the year, with $t = 4$ corresponding to 2004. At what rate was McDonald's revenue changing in 2006? *(Source: McDonald's Corporation)*

SOLUTION One way to answer this question is to find the derivative of the revenue model with respect to time.

$$\frac{dR}{dt} = -392.307t^2 + 4592.94t - 11{,}493.5, \quad 4 \le t \le 9$$

In 2006 (at $t = 6$), the rate of change of the revenue with respect to time is given by

$$\frac{dR}{dt} = -392.307(6)^2 + 4592.94(6) - 11{,}493.5 \approx 1941.$$

Because R is measured in millions of dollars and t is measured in years, it follows that the derivative dR/dt is measured in millions of dollars per year. So, at the end of 2006, McDonald's revenue was increasing at a rate of about \$1941 million per year, as shown in Figure 2.17.

McDonald's Revenue

Slope ≈ 1941

Year (4 ↔ 2004)

FIGURE 2.17

✓ **Checkpoint 11**

From 2000 through 2010, the sales per share S (in dollars) for Microsoft Corporation can be modeled by

$$S = 0.0330t^2 + 0.208t + 2.13, \quad 0 \le t \le 10$$

where t represents the year, with $t = 0$ corresponding to 2000. At what rate was Microsoft's sales per share changing in 2002? *(Source: Microsoft Corporation)*

SUMMARIZE (Section 2.2)

1. State the Constant Rule *(page 91)*. For an example of the Constant Rule, see Example 1.

2. State the Power Rule *(page 92)*. For examples of the Power Rule, see Examples 2 and 3.

3. State the Constant Multiple Rule *(page 94)*. For examples of the Constant Multiple Rule, see Examples 4, 5, 6, and 7.

4. State the Sum Rule *(page 97)*. For an example of the Sum Rule, see Example 8.

5. State the Difference Rule *(page 97)*. For an example of the Difference Rule, see Example 8.

6. Describe a real-life example of how differentiation can be used to analyze the rate of change of a company's revenue *(page 99, Example 11)*.

SKILLS WARM UP 2.2   The following warm-up exercises involve skills that were covered in a previous course. You will use these skills in the exercise set for this section. For additional help, review Appendix Sections A.3 and A.4.

In Exercises 1 and 2, evaluate each expression when $x = 2$.

1. (a) $2x^2$ (b) $(2x)^2$ (c) $2x^{-2}$

2. (a) $\dfrac{1}{(3x)^2}$ (b) $\dfrac{1}{4x^3}$ (c) $\dfrac{(2x)^{-3}}{4x^{-2}}$

In Exercises 3–6, simplify the expression.

3. $4(3)x^3 + 2(2)x$

4. $\frac{1}{2}(3)x^2 - \frac{3}{2}x^{1/2}$

5. $\left(\frac{1}{4}\right)x^{-3/4}$

6. $\frac{1}{3}(3)x^2 - 2\left(\frac{1}{2}\right)x^{-1/2} + \frac{1}{3}x^{-2/3}$

In Exercises 7–10, solve the equation.

7. $3x^2 + 2x = 0$

8. $x^3 - x = 0$

9. $x^2 + 8x - 20 = 0$

10. $x^2 - 10x - 24 = 0$

Exercises 2.2

See www.CalcChat.com for worked-out solutions to odd-numbered exercises.

Finding Derivatives In Exercises 1–24, find the derivative of the function. *See Examples 1, 2, 4, 5, and 8.*

1. $y = 3$

2. $f(x) = -8$

3. $y = x^5$

4. $f(x) = \dfrac{1}{x^5}$

5. $h(x) = 3x^3$

6. $h(x) = 2x^5$

7. $y = \dfrac{2x^3}{3}$

8. $g(t) = \dfrac{3t^2}{4}$

9. $f(x) = 4x$

10. $g(x) = 3x$

11. $y = 8 - x^3$

12. $y = t^2 - 6$

13. $f(x) = 4x^2 - 3x$

14. $g(x) = x^2 + 4x^3$

15. $f(t) = -3t^2 + 2t - 4$

16. $y = x^3 - 9x^2 + 2$

17. $s(t) = t^3 - 2t + 4$

18. $y = 2x^3 - x^2 + 3x - 1$

19. $g(x) = x^{2/3}$

20. $h(x) = x^{5/2}$

21. $y = 4t^{4/3}$

22. $f(x) = 10x^{1/2}$

23. $y = 4x^{-2} + 2x^2$

24. $s(t) = 4t^{-1} + 1$

Using Parentheses When Differentiating In Exercises 25–30, find the derivative. *See Example 6.*

Function	Rewrite	Differentiate	Simplify
25. $y = \dfrac{2}{7x^4}$			
26. $y = \dfrac{2}{3x^2}$			
27. $y = \dfrac{1}{(4x)^3}$			
28. $y = \dfrac{\pi}{(3x)^2}$			
29. $y = \dfrac{4}{(2x)^{-5}}$			
30. $y = \dfrac{4x}{x^{-3}}$			

Differentiating Radical Functions In Exercises 31–36, find the derivative. *See Example 7.*

Function	Rewrite	Differentiate	Simplify
31. $y = 6\sqrt{x}$			
32. $y = \dfrac{3\sqrt{x}}{4}$			
33. $y = \dfrac{1}{5\sqrt[5]{x}}$			
34. $y = \dfrac{3}{2\sqrt[4]{x^3}}$			
35. $y = \sqrt{3x}$			
36. $y = \sqrt[3]{6x^2}$			

Finding the Slope of a Graph In Exercises 37–44, find the slope of the graph of the function at the given point. *See Examples 3 and 9.*

37. $y = x^{3/2}$

(1, 1)

38. $y = x^{-1}$

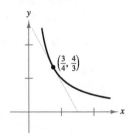

$\left(\frac{3}{4}, \frac{4}{3}\right)$

39. $f(t) = t^2; (4, 16)$ **40.** $f(x) = x^{-1/3}; \left(8, \frac{1}{2}\right)$

41. $f(x) = 2x^3 + 8x^2 - x - 4; (-1, 3)$

42. $f(x) = 3x^4 - 5x^3 + 6x^2 - 10x; (1, -6)$

43. $f(x) = -\frac{1}{2}x(1 + x^2); (1, -1)$

44. $f(x) = 3(5 - x)^2; (5, 0)$

Finding an Equation of a Tangent Line In Exercises 45–50, (a) find an equation of the tangent line to the graph of the function at the given point, (b) use a graphing utility to graph the function and its tangent line at the point, and (c) use the derivative feature of a graphing utility to confirm your results. *See Example 10.*

45. $y = -2x^4 + 5x^2 - 3; (1, 0)$

46. $y = x^3 + x; (-1, -2)$

47. $f(x) = \sqrt[3]{x} + \sqrt[5]{x}; (1, 2)$

48. $f(x) = \dfrac{1}{\sqrt[3]{x^2}} - x; (-1, 2)$

49. $y = 3x\left(x^2 - \dfrac{2}{x}\right); (2, 18)$

50. $y = (2x + 1)^2; (0, 1)$

Finding Derivatives In Exercises 51–62, find $f'(x)$.

51. $f(x) = x^2 - \dfrac{4}{x} - 3x^{-2}$

52. $f(x) = x^2 - 3x - 3x^{-2} + 5x^{-3}$

53. $f(x) = x^2 - 2x - \dfrac{2}{x^4}$ **54.** $f(x) = x^2 + 4x + \dfrac{1}{x}$

55. $f(x) = x^{4/5} + x$ **56.** $f(x) = x^{1/3} - 1$

57. $f(x) = x(x^2 + 1)$

58. $f(x) = (x^2 + 2x)(x + 1)$

59. $f(x) = \dfrac{2x^3 - 4x^2 + 3}{x^2}$

60. $f(x) = \dfrac{2x^2 - 3x + 1}{x}$

61. $f(x) = \dfrac{4x^3 - 3x^2 + 2x + 5}{x^2}$

62. $f(x) = \dfrac{-6x^3 + 3x^2 - 2x + 1}{x}$

Finding Horizontal Tangent Lines In Exercises 63–66, determine the point(s), if any, at which the graph of the function has a horizontal tangent line.

63. $y = -x^4 + 3x^2 - 1$ **64.** $y = x^3 + 3x^2$

65. $y = \frac{1}{2}x^2 + 5x$ **66.** $y = x^2 + 2x$

Exploring Relationships In Exercises 67 and 68, (a) sketch the graphs of f and g, (b) find $f'(1)$ and $g'(1)$, (c) sketch the tangent line to each graph at $x = 1$, and (d) explain the relationship between f' and g'.

67. $f(x) = x^3$ **68.** $f(x) = x^2$

$g(x) = x^3 + 3$ $g(x) = 3x^2$

Exploring Relationships In Exercises 69–72, the relationship between f and g is given. Explain the relationship between f' and g'.

69. $g(x) = f(x) + 6$ **70.** $g(x) = 2f(x)$

71. $g(x) = -5f(x)$ **72.** $g(x) = 3f(x) - 1$

73. Revenue The revenue R (in millions of dollars) for Under Armour from 2004 through 2009 can be modeled by

$$R = -5.1509t^3 + 103.166t^2 - 526.15t + 985.4$$

where t is the year, with $t = 4$ corresponding to 2004. *(Source: Under Armour, Inc.)*

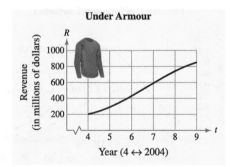

Under Armour

(a) Find the slopes of the graph for the years 2005 and 2007.

(b) Compare your results with those obtained in Exercise 13 in Section 2.1.

(c) Interpret the slope of the graph in the context of the problem.

74. Sales   The sales S (in millions of dollars) for Scotts Miracle-Gro Company from 2003 through 2009 can be modeled by $S = 5.45682t^4 - 136.9359t^3 + 1219.018t^2 - 4294.73t + 7078.4$, where t is the year, with $t = 3$ corresponding to 2003.   *(Source: Scotts Miracle-Gro Company)*

(a) Find the slopes of the graph for the years 2006 and 2008.

(b) Compare your results with those obtained in Exercise 14 in Section 2.1.

(c) Interpret the slope of the graph in the context of the problem.

75. Psychology: Migraine Prevalence   The graph illustrates the prevalence of migraine headaches in males and females in selected income groups. *(Source: Adapted from Sue/Sue/Sue, Understanding Abnormal Behavior, Seventh Edition)*

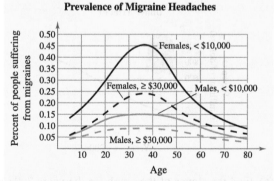

(a) Write a short paragraph describing your general observations about the prevalence of migraines in females and males with respect to age group and income bracket.

(b) Describe the graph of the derivative of each curve, and explain the significance of each derivative. Include an explanation of the units of the derivatives, and indicate the time intervals in which the derivatives would be positive and negative.

76.   HOW DO YOU SEE IT?   The attendance for four high school basketball games is given by $s = f(t)$, and the attendance for four high school football games is given by $s = g(t)$, where $t = 1$ corresponds to the first game.

(a) Which attendance rate, f' or g', is greater at game 1?

(b) What conclusion can you make regarding the attendance rates, f' and g', at game 3?

(c) What conclusion can you make regarding the attendance rates, f' and g', at game 4?

(d) Which sport do you think would have a greater attendance for game 5? Explain your reasoning.

77. Cost   The marginal cost for manufacturing an electrical component is $7.75 per unit, and the fixed cost is $500. Write the cost C as a function of x, the number of units produced. Show that the derivative of this cost function is a constant and is equal to the marginal cost.

78. Political Fundraiser   A politician raises funds by selling tickets to a dinner for $500. The politician pays $150 for each dinner and has fixed costs of $7000 to rent a dining hall and wait staff. Write the profit P as a function of x, the number of dinners sold. Show that the derivative of the profit function is a constant and is equal to the increase in profit from each dinner sold.

Finding Horizontal Tangent Lines   In Exercises 79 and 80, use a graphing utility to graph f and f' over the given interval. Determine any points at which the graph of f has horizontal tangents.

Function	Interval
79. $f(x) = 4.1x^3 - 12x^2 + 2.5x$	$[0, 3]$
80. $f(x) = x^3 - 1.4x^2 - 0.96x + 1.44$	$[-2, 2]$

True or False?   In Exercises 81 and 82, determine whether the statement is true or false. If it is false, explain why or give an example that shows it is false.

81. If $f'(x) = g'(x)$, then $f(x) = g(x)$.

82. If $f(x) = g(x) + c$, then $f'(x) = g'(x)$.

2.3 Rates of Change: Velocity and Marginals

■ Find the average rates of change of functions over intervals.
■ Find the instantaneous rates of change of functions at points.
■ Find the marginal revenues, marginal costs, and marginal profits for products.

Average Rate of Change

In Sections 2.1 and 2.2, you studied the two primary applications of derivatives.

1. **Slope** The derivative of f is a function that gives the slope of the graph of f at a point $(x, f(x))$.

2. **Rate of Change** The derivative of f is a function that gives the rate of change of $f(x)$ with respect to x at the point $(x, f(x))$.

In this section, you will see that there are many real-life applications of rates of change. A few are velocity, acceleration, population growth rates, unemployment rates, production rates, and water flow rates. Although rates of change often involve change with respect to time, you can investigate the rate of change of one variable with respect to any other related variable.

When determining the rate of change of one variable with respect to another, you must be careful to distinguish between *average* and *instantaneous* rates of change. The distinction between these two rates of change is comparable to the distinction between the slope of the secant line through two points on a graph and the slope of the tangent line at one point on the graph.

In Exercise 13 on page 114, you will use the graph of a function to estimate the rate of change of the number of visitors to a national park.

Definition of Average Rate of Change

If $y = f(x)$, then the **average rate of change** of y with respect to x on the interval $[a, b]$ is

$$\text{Average rate of change} = \frac{f(b) - f(a)}{b - a} = \frac{\Delta y}{\Delta x}.$$

Note that $f(a)$ is the value of the function at the *left* endpoint of the interval, $f(b)$ is the value of the function at the *right* endpoint of the interval, and $b - a$ is the width of the interval, as shown in Figure 2.18.

STUDY TIP

In real-life problems, it is important to list the units of measure for a rate of change. The units for $\Delta y/\Delta x$ are "y-units" per "x-units." For example, if y is measured in miles and x is measured in hours, then $\Delta y/\Delta x$ is measured in *miles per hour*.

FIGURE 2.18

Example 1   **Medicine**

The concentration C (in milligrams per milliliter) of a drug in a patient's bloodstream is monitored over 10-minute intervals for 2 hours, where t is measured in minutes, as shown in the table.

t	0	10	20	30	40	50	60	70	80	90	100	110	120
C	0	2	17	37	55	73	89	103	111	113	113	103	68

Find the average rate of change of C over each interval.

a. $[0, 10]$

b. $[0, 20]$

c. $[100, 110]$

SOLUTION

a. For the interval $[0, 10]$, the average rate of change is

$$\frac{\Delta C}{\Delta t} = \frac{2 - 0}{10 - 0} = \frac{2}{10} = 0.2 \text{ milligram per milliliter per minute.}$$

b. For the interval $[0, 20]$, the average rate of change is

$$\frac{\Delta C}{\Delta t} = \frac{17 - 0}{20 - 0} = \frac{17}{20} = 0.85 \text{ milligram per milliliter per minute.}$$

c. For the interval $[100, 110]$, the average rate of change is

$$\frac{\Delta C}{\Delta t} = \frac{103 - 113}{110 - 100} = \frac{-10}{10} = -1 \text{ milligram per milliliter per minute.}$$

Notice in Figure 2.19 that the average rate of change is positive when the concentration increases and negative when the concentration decreases.

Drug Concentration in Bloodstream

FIGURE 2.19

✓**Checkpoint 1**

Use the table in Example 1 to find the average rate of change of C over each interval.

a. $[0, 120]$

b. $[90, 100]$

c. $[90, 120]$

The rates of change in Example 1 are in milligrams per milliliter per minute because the concentration is measured in milligrams per milliliter and the time is measured in minutes.

$$\frac{\Delta C}{\Delta t} = \frac{2 - 0}{10 - 0} = \frac{2}{10} = 0.2 \text{ milligram per milliliter per minute}$$

A common application of an average rate of change is to find the **average velocity** of an object that is moving in a straight line. That is,

$$\text{Average velocity} = \frac{\text{change in distance}}{\text{change in time}}.$$

This formula is demonstrated in Example 2.

Example 2 Finding an Average Velocity

A free-falling object is dropped from a height of 100 feet. *Neglecting air resistance,* the height h (in feet) of the object at time t (in seconds) is given by

$$h = -16t^2 + 100. \qquad \text{(See Figure 2.20.)}$$

Find the average velocity of the object over each interval.

a. $[1, 2]$ **b.** $[1, 1.5]$ **c.** $[1, 1.1]$

SOLUTION You can use the position equation $h = -16t^2 + 100$ to determine the heights at

$$t = 1, 1.1, 1.5, \text{ and } 2$$

as shown in the table.

t (in seconds)	0	1	1.1	1.5	2
h (in feet)	100	84	80.64	64	36

a. For the interval $[1, 2]$, the object falls from a height of 84 feet to a height of 36 feet. So, the average velocity is

$$\frac{\Delta h}{\Delta t} = \frac{36 - 84}{2 - 1} = \frac{-48}{1} = -48 \text{ feet per second.}$$

b. For the interval $[1, 1.5]$, the average velocity is

$$\frac{\Delta h}{\Delta t} = \frac{64 - 84}{1.5 - 1} = \frac{-20}{0.5} = -40 \text{ feet per second.}$$

c. For the interval $[1, 1.1]$, the average velocity is

$$\frac{\Delta h}{\Delta t} = \frac{80.64 - 84}{1.1 - 1} = \frac{-3.36}{0.1} = -33.6 \text{ feet per second.}$$

✓ Checkpoint 2

The height h (in feet) of a free-falling object at time t (in seconds) is given by

$$h = -16t^2 + 180.$$

Find the average velocity of the object over each interval.

a. $[0, 1]$ **b.** $[1, 2]$ **c.** $[2, 3]$

STUDY TIP

In Example 2, the average velocities are negative because the object is moving downward.

---

h

100
90
80
70
60
50
40
30
20
10

Height (in feet)

○ $t = 0$
○ $t = 1$
○ $t = 1.1$
◇ $t = 1.5$

↓

● $t = 2$
Falling object

Some falling objects have considerable air resistance. Other falling objects have negligible air resistance. When modeling a falling-body problem, you must decide whether to account for air resistance or neglect it.

FIGURE 2.20

Instantaneous Rate of Change and Velocity

Suppose in Example 2 you wanted to find the rate of change of h at the instant $t = 1$ second. Such a rate is called an **instantaneous rate of change.** You can approximate the instantaneous rate of change at $t = 1$ by calculating the average rate of change over smaller and smaller intervals of the form $[1, 1 + \Delta t]$, as shown in the table. From the table, it seems reasonable to conclude that the instantaneous rate of change of the height at $t = 1$ is -32 feet per second.

Δt approaches 0.

Δt	1	0.5	0.1	0.01	0.001	0.0001	0
$\dfrac{\Delta h}{\Delta t}$	-48	-40	-33.6	-32.16	-32.016	-32.0016	-32

$\dfrac{\Delta h}{\Delta t}$ approaches -32.

STUDY TIP

The limit in the definition of instantaneous rate of change is the same as the limit in the definition of the derivative of f at x. This is the second major interpretation of the derivative—as an *instantaneous rate of change in one variable with respect to another*. Recall that the first interpretation of the derivative is as the slope of the graph of f at x.

Definition of Instantaneous Rate of Change

The **instantaneous rate of change** (or simply **rate of change**) of $y = f(x)$ at x is the limit of the average rate of change on the interval

$$[x, x + \Delta x]$$

as Δx approaches 0.

$$\lim_{\Delta x \to 0} \frac{\Delta y}{\Delta x} = \lim_{\Delta x \to 0} \frac{f(x + \Delta x) - f(x)}{\Delta x}$$

If y is a distance and x is time, then the rate of change is a **velocity.**

Example 3   Finding an Instantaneous Rate of Change

Find the velocity of the object in Example 2 at $t = 1$.

SOLUTION   From Example 2, you know that the height of the falling object is given by

$h = -16t^2 + 100.$ Position function

By taking the derivative of this position function, you obtain the velocity function.

$h'(t) = -32t$ Velocity function

The velocity function gives the velocity at *any* time. So, at $t = 1$, the velocity is

$h'(1) = -32(1)$

$= -32$ feet per second.

✓**Checkpoint 3**

The height of the object in Checkpoint 2 is given by

$h = -16t^2 + 180.$

Find the velocities of the object at

a. $t = 1.75.$

b. $t = 2.$

The general **position function** for a free-falling object, neglecting air resistance, is

$$h = -16t^2 + v_0 t + h_0 \qquad \text{Position function}$$

where h is the height (in feet), t is the time (in seconds), v_0 is the initial velocity (in feet per second), and h_0 is the initial height (in feet). Remember that the model assumes that positive velocities indicate upward motion and negative velocities indicate downward motion. The derivative

$$h' = -32t^2 + v_0 \qquad \text{Velocity function}$$

is the **velocity function.** The absolute value of the velocity is the **speed** of the object.

 Example 4 **Finding the Velocity of a Diver**

At time $t = 0$, a diver jumps from a diving board that is 32 feet high, as shown in Figure 2.21. Because the diver's initial velocity is 16 feet per second, the position of the diver is given by

$$h = -16t^2 + 16t + 32. \qquad \text{Position function}$$

a. When does the diver hit the water?

b. What is the diver's velocity at impact?

SOLUTION

a. To find the time at which the diver hits the water, let $h = 0$ and solve for t.

$$-16t^2 + 16t + 32 = 0 \qquad \text{Set } h \text{ equal to 0.}$$
$$-16(t^2 - t - 2) = 0 \qquad \text{Factor out common factor.}$$
$$-16(t + 1)(t - 2) = 0 \qquad \text{Factor.}$$
$$t = -1 \ \text{ or } \ t = 2 \qquad \text{Solve for } t.$$

The solution $t = -1$ does not make sense in the problem because it would mean that the diver hits the water 1 second before jumping. So, you can conclude that the diver hits the water at $t = 2$ seconds.

b. The velocity at time t is given by the derivative

$$h' = -32t + 16. \qquad \text{Velocity function}$$

The velocity at time $t = 2$ is

$$h' = -32(2) + 16 = -48 \text{ feet per second.}$$

FIGURE 2.21

✓**Checkpoint 4**

At time $t = 0$, a diver jumps from a diving board that is 12 feet high with initial velocity 16 feet per second. The diver's position function is $h = -16t^2 + 16t + 12$.

a. When does the diver hit the water?

b. What is the diver's velocity at impact?

In Example 4, note that the diver's initial velocity is $v_0 = 16$ feet per second (upward) and the diver's initial height is $h_0 = 32$ feet.

Initial velocity is 16 feet per second.
Initial height is 32 feet.

$$h = -16t^2 + 16t + 32$$

Rates of Change in Economics: Marginals

Another important use of rates of change is in the field of economics. Economists refer to *marginal profit, marginal revenue,* and *marginal cost* as the rates of change of the profit, revenue, and cost with respect to *x*, the number of units produced or sold. An equation that relates these three quantities is

$$P = R - C$$

where *P*, *R*, and *C* represent the following quantities.

$$P = \text{total profit}, \quad R = \text{total revenue}, \quad \text{and} \quad C = \text{total cost}$$

The derivatives of these quantities are called the **marginal profit, marginal revenue,** and **marginal cost,** respectively.

$$\frac{dP}{dx} = \text{marginal profit}$$

$$\frac{dR}{dx} = \text{marginal revenue}$$

$$\frac{dC}{dx} = \text{marginal cost}$$

In many business and economics problems, the number of units produced or sold is restricted to nonnegative integer values, as indicated in Figure 2.22. (Of course, it could happen that a sale involves half or quarter units, but it is hard to conceive of a sale involving $\sqrt{2}$ units.) The variable that denotes such units is called a **discrete variable.**

Function of a Discrete Variable

FIGURE 2.22

To analyze a function of a discrete variable *x*, you can temporarily assume that *x* is a **continuous variable** and is able to take on any real value in a given interval, as indicated in Figure 2.23. Then, you can use the methods of calculus to find the *x*-value that corresponds to the marginal revenue, maximum profit, minimum cost, or whatever is called for. Finally, you should round the solution to the nearest sensible *x*-value— cents, dollars, units, or days, depending on the context of the problem.

Function of a Continuous Variable

FIGURE 2.23

Example 5   **Finding the Marginal Profit**

The profit derived from selling x units of an alarm clock is given by

$$P = 0.0002x^3 + 10x.$$

a. Find the marginal profit for a production level of 50 units.

b. Compare the marginal profit with the actual gain in profit obtained by increasing the production level from 50 to 51 units.

SOLUTION

a. The profit is $P = 0.0002x^3 + 10x$. The marginal profit is given by the derivative

$$\frac{dP}{dx} = 0.0006x^2 + 10.$$

When $x = 50$, the marginal profit is

$$\frac{dP}{dx} = 0.0006(50)^2 + 10 \qquad \text{Substitute 50 for } x.$$

$$= 0.0006(2500) + 10$$

$$= 1.5 + 10$$

$$= \$11.50 \text{ per unit.} \qquad \text{Marginal profit for } x = 50$$

b. For $x = 50$, the actual profit is

$$P = 0.0002(50)^3 + 10(50) \qquad \text{Substitute 50 for } x.$$

$$= 0.0002(125,000) + 500$$

$$= 25 + 500$$

$$= \$525.00 \qquad \text{Actual profit for } x = 50$$

and for $x = 51$, the actual profit is

$$P = 0.0002(51)^3 + 10(51) \qquad \text{Substitute 51 for } x.$$

$$= 0.0002(132,651) + 510$$

$$\approx 26.53 + 510$$

$$= \$536.53. \qquad \text{Actual profit for } x = 51$$

So, the additional profit obtained by increasing production from 50 to 51 units is

$$536.53 - 525.00 = \$11.53. \qquad \text{Extra profit for one unit}$$

Note that the actual profit increase of $11.53 (when x increases from 50 to 51 units) can be approximated by the marginal profit of $11.50 per unit (when $x = 50$), as shown in Figure 2.24.

Marginal Profit

$P = 0.0002x^3 + 10x$

FIGURE 2.24

✔ **Checkpoint 5**

Find the marginal profit in Example 5 for a production level of 100 units. Compare this with the actual gain in profit by increasing production from 100 to 101 units. ■

STUDY TIP

In Example 5, the marginal profit gives a good approximation of the actual change in profit because the graph of P is nearly straight over the interval $50 \le x \le 51$. You will study more about the use of marginals to approximate actual changes in Section 3.8.

The profit function in Example 5 is unusual in that the profit continues to increase as long as the number of units sold increases. In practice, it is more common to encounter situations in which sales can be increased only by lowering the price per item. Such reductions in price will ultimately cause the profit to decline.

The number of units x that consumers are willing to purchase at a given price per unit p is given by the **demand function**

$$p = f(x).$$ Demand function

The total revenue R is then related to the price per unit and the quantity demanded (or sold) by the equation

$$R = xp.$$ Revenue function

 Example 6 **Finding a Demand Function**

The table shows the numbers x (in millions) of prerecorded high-definition DVDs sold in the United States and the average unit prices p (in dollars) from 2006 through 2009. Use this information to find the demand function and the total revenue function. *(Source: SNL Kagan)*

Year	2006	2007	2008	2009
x	1.2	9.8	22.7	54.0
p	23.75	23.38	22.21	20.43

TECH TUTOR

Another way to find a linear model for the demand function in Example 6 is to use the *linear regression* feature of a graphing utility or a spreadsheet software program. Use a graphing utility or a spreadsheet software program to find the demand function and compare your results with those in Example 6. You will learn more about linear regression in Section 7.7. (Consult the user's manual of a graphing utility or a spreadsheet software program for specific instructions.)

SOLUTION Begin by making a scatter plot of the data using the ordered pairs (x, p), as shown in Figure 2.25. From the graph, it appears that a linear model would be a good fit for the data. To find a linear model for the demand function, use any two points, such as $(1.2, 23.75)$ and $(54.0, 20.43)$. The slope of the line through these points is

$$m = \frac{20.43 - 23.75}{54.0 - 1.2}$$

$$= \frac{-3.32}{52.8}$$

$$\approx -0.063.$$

Prerecorded DVDs

p — Average price per unit (in dollars)

Number of units sold (in millions)

FIGURE 2.25

Using the point-slope form of a line, you can approximate the equation of the demand function to be $p = -0.063x + 23.83$. The total revenue function for prerecorded high-definition DVDs is

$$R = xp = x(-0.063x + 23.83) = -0.063x^2 + 23.83x.$$

 Checkpoint 6

Repeat Example 6 given that in 2010 an estimated 104.2 million prerecorded high-definition DVDs were sold at an average unit price of $17.88. To find a linear model for the demand function, use the points $(1.2, 23.75)$ and $(104.2, 17.88)$. *(Source: SNL Kagan)*

Example 7   **Finding the Marginal Revenue**

A fast-food restaurant has determined that the monthly demand for its hamburgers is given by

$$p = \frac{60,000 - x}{20,000}.$$

Figure 2.26 shows that as the price decreases, the quantity demanded increases. The table shows the demands for hamburgers at various prices.

x	60,000	50,000	40,000	30,000	20,000	10,000	0
p	$0.00	$0.50	$1.00	$1.50	$2.00	$2.50	$3.00

Find the increase in revenue per hamburger for monthly sales of 20,000 hamburgers. In other words, find the marginal revenue when $x = 20,000$.

SOLUTION   Because the demand is given by

$$p = \frac{60,000 - x}{20,000}$$

and the revenue is given by $R = xp$, you have

$$R = xp \qquad \text{Formula for revenue}$$

$$= x\left(\frac{60,000 - x}{20,000}\right) \qquad \text{Substitute for } p.$$

$$= \frac{1}{20,000}(60,000x - x^2). \qquad \text{Revenue function}$$

By differentiating, you can find the marginal revenue to be

$$\frac{dR}{dx} = \frac{1}{20,000}(60,000 - 2x).$$

So, at $x = 20,000$, the marginal revenue is

$$\frac{dR}{dx} = \frac{1}{20,000}(60,000 - 2x) \qquad \text{Marginal revenue}$$

$$= \frac{1}{20,000}[60,000 - 2(20,000)] \qquad \text{Substitute 20,000 for } x.$$

$$= \frac{1}{20,000}(60,000 - 40,000) \qquad \text{Multiply.}$$

$$= \frac{1}{20,000}(20,000) \qquad \text{Subtract.}$$

$$= \$1 \text{ per unit.} \qquad \text{Marginal revenue when } x = 20,000$$

So, for monthly sales of 20,000 hamburgers, you can conclude that the increase in revenue per hamburger is $1.

✓**Checkpoint 7**

Find the revenue function and marginal revenue for a demand function of

$$p = 2000 - 4x.$$

Find the marginal revenue when $x = 250$.

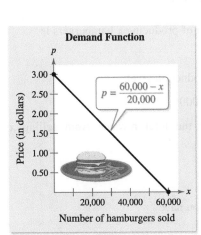

Demand Function

$$p = \frac{60,000 - x}{20,000}$$

As the price decreases, more hamburgers are sold.

FIGURE 2.26

STUDY TIP

Writing a demand function in the form $p = f(x)$ is a convention used in economics. From a consumer's point of view, it might seem more reasonable to think that the quantity demanded is a function of the price. Mathematically, however, the two points of view are equivalent because a typical demand function is one-to-one and so has an inverse function. For instance, in Example 7, you could write the demand function as $x = 60,000 - 20,000p$.

Example 8 **Finding the Marginal Profit**

For the fast-food restaurant in Example 7, the cost of producing x hamburgers is

$$C = 5000 + 0.56x, \quad 0 \le x \le 50,000.$$

Find the profit and the marginal profit for each production level.

a. $x = 20,000$ **b.** $x = 24,400$ **c.** $x = 30,000$

SOLUTION From Example 7, you know that the total revenue from selling x hamburgers is

$$R = \frac{1}{20,000}(60,000x - x^2).$$

Because the total profit is given by $P = R - C$, you have

$$P = \frac{1}{20,000}(60,000x - x^2) - (5000 + 0.56x)$$

$$= 3x - \frac{x^2}{20,000} - 5000 - 0.56x$$

$$= 2.44x - \frac{x^2}{20,000} - 5000. \qquad \text{See Figure 2.27.}$$

So, the marginal profit is

$$\frac{dP}{dx} = 2.44 - \frac{x}{10,000}.$$

Using these formulas, you can compute the profit and marginal profit.

Production	Profit	Marginal Profit
a. $x = 20,000$	$P = \$23,800.00$	$2.44 - \dfrac{20,000}{10,000} = \$0.44$ per unit
b. $x = 24,400$	$P = \$24,768.00$	$2.44 - \dfrac{24,400}{10,000} = \$0.00$ per unit
c. $x = 30,000$	$P = \$23,200.00$	$2.44 - \dfrac{30,000}{10,000} = -\$0.56$ per unit

Profit Function

$$P = 2.44x - \frac{x^2}{20,000} - 5000$$

Profit (in dollars)

Number of hamburgers sold

FIGURE 2.27

✓**Checkpoint 8**

From Example 8, compare the marginal profit when 10,000 units are produced with the actual increase in profit from 10,000 units to 10,001 units.

SUMMARIZE (Section 2.3)

1. State the definition of average rate of change *(page 103)*. For examples of average rate of change, see Examples 1 and 2.

2. State the definition of instantaneous rate of change *(page 106)*. For examples of an instantaneous rate of change, see Examples 3 and 4.

3. Describe a real-life example of how rates of change can be used in the field of economics *(pages 109–112, Examples 5, 6, 7, and 8)*.

SKILLS WARM UP 2.3

The following warm-up exercises involve skills that were covered in earlier sections. You will use these skills in the exercise set for this section. For additional help, review Sections 2.1 and 2.2.

In Exercises 1–4, evaluate the expression.

1. $\dfrac{-63 - (-105)}{21 - 7}$

2. $\dfrac{-37 - 54}{16 - 3}$

3. $\dfrac{24 - 33}{9 - 6}$

4. $\dfrac{40 - 16}{18 - 8}$

In Exercises 5–12, find the derivative of the function.

5. $y = 4x^2 - 2x + 7$

6. $y = -3t^3 + 2t^2 - 8$

7. $s = -16t^2 + 24t + 30$

8. $y = -16x^2 + 54x + 70$

9. $A = \frac{1}{10}(-2r^3 + 3r^2 + 5r)$

10. $y = \frac{1}{9}(6x^3 - 18x^2 + 63x - 15)$

11. $y = 12x - \dfrac{x^2}{5000}$

12. $y = 138 + 74x - \dfrac{x^3}{10,000}$

Exercises 2.3

See www.CalcChat.com for worked-out solutions to odd-numbered exercises.

1. Research and Development The table shows the amounts A (in billions of dollars) spent on Research and Development in the United States from 1980 through 2008, where t is the year, with $t = 0$ corresponding to 1980. Approximate the average rate of change of A during each period.
(Source: U.S. National Science Foundation)

(a) 1980–1985   (b) 1985–1990
(c) 1990–1995   (d) 1995–2000
(e) 2000–2005   (f) 1980–2008
(g) 1990–2008   (h) 2000–2008

t	0	1	2	3	4	5	6	7
A	63	72	81	90	102	115	120	126

t	8	9	10	11	12	13	14
A	134	142	152	161	165	166	169

t	15	16	17	18	19	20	21
A	184	197	212	226	245	267	277

t	22	23	24	25	26	27	28
A	276	288	299	322	347	373	398

2. Trade Deficit The graph shows the values I (in billions of dollars) of goods imported to the United States and the values E (in billions of dollars) of goods exported from the United States from 1980 through 2009. Approximate the average rates of change of I and E during each period.
(Source: U.S. International Trade Administration)

(a) Imports: 1980–1990   (b) Exports: 1980–1990
(c) Imports: 1990–2000   (d) Exports: 1990–2000
(e) Imports: 2000–2009   (f) Exports: 2000–2009
(g) Imports: 1980–2009   (h) Exports: 1980–2009

Finding Rates of Change   In Exercises 3–12, use a graphing utility to graph the function and find its average rate of change over the interval. Compare this rate with the instantaneous rates of change at the endpoints of the interval.

3. $f(t) = 3t + 5; [1, 2]$ **4.** $h(x) = 2 - x; [0, 2]$

5. $h(x) = x^2 - 4x + 2; [-2, 2]$

6. $f(x) = x^2 - 6x - 1; [-1, 3]$

7. $f(x) = 3x^{4/3}; [1, 8]$ **8.** $f(x) = x^{3/2}; [1, 4]$

9. $f(x) = \dfrac{1}{x}; [1, 4]$ **10.** $f(x) = \dfrac{1}{\sqrt{x}}; [1, 4]$

11. $g(x) = x^4 - x^2 + 2; [1, 3]$

12. $g(x) = x^3 - 1; [-1, 1]$

13. Consumer Trends   The graph shows the number of visitors V (in thousands) to a national park during a one-year period, where $t = 1$ represents January.

Visitors to a National Park

Month (1 ↔ January)

(a) Estimate the rate of change of V over the interval $[9, 12]$ and explain your results.

(b) Over what interval is the average rate of change approximately equal to the rate of change at $t = 8$? Explain your reasoning.

14. Medicine   The graph shows the estimated number of milligrams of a pain medication M in the bloodstream t hours after a 1000-milligram dose of the drug has been given.

Pain Medication in Bloodstream

Hours

(a) Estimate the one-hour interval over which the average rate of change is the greatest.

(b) Over what interval is the average rate of change approximately equal to the rate of change at $t = 4$? Explain your reasoning.

15. Velocity   The height s (in feet) at time t (in seconds) of a ball thrown upward from the top of a building is given by

$$s = -16t^2 + 30t + 250.$$

Find the average velocity over each indicated interval and compare this velocity with the instantaneous velocity at the endpoints of the interval.

(a) $[0, 1]$ (b) $[1, 2]$ (c) $[2, 3]$ (d) $[3, 4]$

16. Chemistry: Wind Chill   At $0°$ Celsius, the heat loss H (in kilocalories per square meter per hour) from a person's body can be modeled by

$$H = 33\left(10\sqrt{v} - v + 10.45\right)$$

where v is the wind speed (in meters per second).

(a) Find $\dfrac{dH}{dv}$ and interpret its meaning in this situation.

(b) Find the rates of change of H when $v = 2$ and $v = 5$.

17. Velocity   The height s (in feet) at time t (in seconds) of a silver dollar dropped from the top of a building is given by $s = -16t^2 + 555$.

(a) Find the average velocity over the interval $[2, 3]$.

(b) Find the instantaneous velocities when $t = 2$ and $t = 3$.

(c) How long will it take the coin to hit the ground?

(d) Find the velocity of the coin when it hits the ground.

18. Velocity   A ball is thrown straight down from the top of a 210-foot building with an initial velocity of -18 feet per second.

(a) Find the position and velocity functions for the ball.

(b) Find the average velocity over the interval $[1, 2]$.

(c) Find the instantaneous velocities when $t = 1$ and $t = 2$.

(d) How long will it take the ball to hit the ground?

(e) Find the velocity of the ball when it hits the ground.

Marginal Cost   In Exercises 19–22, find the marginal cost for producing x units. (The cost is measured in dollars.)

19. $C = 205,000 + 9800x$

20. $C = 150,000 + 7x^3$

21. $C = 55,000 + 470x - 0.25x^2, 0 \le x \le 940$

22. $C = 100\left(9 + 3\sqrt{x}\right)$

Marginal Revenue   In Exercises 23–26, find the marginal revenue for producing x units. (The revenue is measured in dollars.)

23. $R = 50x - 0.5x^2$ **24.** $R = 30x - x^2$

25. $R = -6x^3 + 8x^2 + 200x$

26. $R = 50(20x - x^{3/2})$

Marginal Profit In Exercises 27–30, find the marginal profit for producing x units. (The profit is measured in dollars.)

27. $P = -2x^2 + 72x - 145$

28. $P = -0.25x^2 + 2000x - 1,250,000$

29. $P = 0.0013x^3 + 12x$

30. $P = -0.5x^3 + 30x^2 - 164.25x - 1000$

31. **Marginal Cost** The cost C (in dollars) of producing x units of a product is given by

$$C = 3.6\sqrt{x} + 500.$$

(a) Find the additional cost when the production increases from 9 to 10 units.

(b) Find the marginal cost when $x = 9$.

(c) Compare the results of parts (a) and (b).

32. **Marginal Revenue** The revenue R (in dollars) from renting x apartments can be modeled by

$$R = 2x(900 + 32x - x^2).$$

(a) Find the additional revenue when the number of rentals is increased from 14 to 15.

(b) Find the marginal revenue when $x = 14$.

(c) Compare the results of parts (a) and (b).

33. **Marginal Profit** The profit P (in dollars) from selling x laptop computers is given by

$$P = -0.04x^2 + 25x - 1500.$$

(a) Find the additional profit when the sales increase from 150 to 151 units.

(b) Find the marginal profit when $x = 150$.

(c) Compare the results of parts (a) and (b).

34. **Marginal Profit** The profit P (in dollars) from selling x units of a product is given by

$$P = 36,000 + 2048\sqrt{x} - \frac{1}{8x^2}, \quad 150 \leq x \leq 275.$$

Find the marginal profit for each of the following sales.

(a) $x = 150$ (b) $x = 175$ (c) $x = 200$

(d) $x = 225$ (e) $x = 250$ (f) $x = 275$

35. **Population Growth** The population P (in thousands) of Japan from 1980 through 2010 can be modeled by

$$P = -15.56t^2 + 802.1t + 117,001$$

where t is the year, with $t = 0$ corresponding to 1980. *(Source: U.S. Census Bureau)*

(a) Evaluate P for $t = 0$, 5, 10, 15, 20, 25, and 30. Explain these values.

(b) Determine the population growth rate, dP/dt.

(c) Evaluate dP/dt for the same values as in part (a). Explain your results.

36. **Health** The temperature T (in degrees Fahrenheit) of a person during an illness can be modeled by the equation

$$T = -0.0375t^2 + 0.3t + 100.4$$

where t is time in hours since the person started to show signs of a fever.

(a) Use a graphing utility to graph the function. Be sure to choose an appropriate window.

(b) Do the slopes of the tangent lines appear to be positive or negative? What does this tell you?

(c) Evaluate the function for $t = 0$, 4, 8, and 12.

(d) Find dT/dt and explain its meaning in this situation.

(e) Evaluate dT/dt for $t = 0$, 4, 8, and 12.

37. **Economics** Use the information in the table to find the models and answer the questions below.

Quantity produced and sold (Q)	Price (p)	Total revenue (TR)	Marginal revenue (MR)
0	160	0	—
2	140	280	130
4	120	480	90
6	100	600	50
8	80	640	10
10	60	600	-30

(a) Use the *regression* feature of a graphing utility to find a quadratic model that relates the total revenue (TR) to the quantity produced and sold (Q).

(b) Using derivatives, find a model for marginal revenue from the model you found in part (a).

(c) Calculate the marginal revenue for all values of Q using your model in part (b), and compare these values with the actual values given. How good is your model? *(Source: Adapted from Taylor, Economics, Fifth Edition)*

38. **Profit** The monthly demand function p and cost function C for x newspapers at a newsstand are given by

$$p = 5 - 0.001x \quad \text{and} \quad C = 35 + 1.5x.$$

(a) Find the monthly revenue R as a function of x.

(b) Find the monthly profit P as a function of x.

(c) Complete the table.

x	600	1200	1800	2400	3000
dR/dx					
dP/dx					
P					

39. Marginal Profit When the price of a glass of lemonade at a lemonade stand was $1.75, 400 glasses were sold. When the price was lowered to $1.50, 500 glasses were sold. Assume that the demand function is linear and that the marginal and fixed costs are $0.10 and $25, respectively.

(a) Find the profit P as a function of x, the number of glasses of lemonade sold.

(b) Use a graphing utility to graph P, and comment about the slopes of P when $x = 300$ and $x = 700$.

(c) Find the marginal profits when 300 glasses of lemonade are sold and when 700 glasses of lemonade are sold.

40. Marginal Profit When the admission price for a baseball game was $6 per ticket, 36,000 tickets were sold. When the price was raised to $7, only 33,000 tickets were sold. Assume that the demand function is linear and that the marginal and fixed costs for the ballpark owners are $0.20 and $85,000, respectively.

(a) Find the profit P as a function of x, the number of tickets sold.

(b) Use a graphing utility to graph P, and comment about the slopes of P when $x = 18,000$ and $x = 36,000$.

(c) Find the marginal profits when 18,000 tickets are sold and when 36,000 tickets are sold.

41. Fuel Cost A car is driven 15,000 miles a year and gets x miles per gallon. Assume that the average fuel cost is $2.95 per gallon.

(a) Find the annual cost of fuel C as a function of x.

(b) Find dC/dx and explain its meaning in this situation.

(c) Use the functions to complete the table.

x	10	15	20	25	30	35	40
C							
dC/dx							

(d) Who would benefit more from a 1 mile per gallon increase in fuel efficiency—the driver who gets 15 miles per gallon or the driver who gets 35 miles per gallon? Explain.

42. Gasoline Sales The number N of gallons of regular unleaded gasoline sold by a gasoline station at a price of p dollars per gallon is given by $N = f(p)$.

(a) Describe the meaning of $f'(2.959)$.

(b) Is $f'(2.959)$ usually positive or negative? Explain.

43. Dow Jones Industrial Average The table shows the year-end closing prices p of the Dow Jones Industrial Average (DJIA) from 1995 through 2009, where t is the year, with $t = 5$ corresponding to 1995. *(Source: Dow Jones Industrial Average)*

t	5	6	7	8
p	5117.12	6448.26	7908.24	9181.43

t	9	10	11	12
p	11,497.12	10,786.85	10,021.50	8341.63

t	13	14	15	16
p	10,453.92	10,783.01	10,717.50	12,463.15

t	17	18	19
p	13,264.82	8776.39	10,428.05

(a) Determine the average rate of change in the value of the DJIA from 1995 through 2009.

(b) Estimate the instantaneous rate of change in 1998 by finding the average rate of change from 1996 to 2000.

(c) Estimate the instantaneous rate of change in 1998 by finding the average rate of change from 1997 to 1999.

(d) Compare your answers for parts (b) and (c). Which interval do you think produced the best estimate for the instantaneous rate of change in 1998?

44. HOW DO YOU SEE IT? Many populations in nature exhibit logistic growth, which consists of four phases, as shown in the figure. Describe the rate of growth of the population in each phase, and give possible reasons as to why the rates might be changing from phase to phase. *(Source: Adapted from Levine/Miller, Biology: Discovering Life, Second Edition)*

2.4 The Product and Quotient Rules

In Exercise 63 on page 125, you will use the Quotient Rule to find the rate of change of a population of bacteria.

- Find the derivatives of functions using the Product Rule.
- Find the derivatives of functions using the Quotient Rule.
- Use derivatives to answer questions about real-life situations.

The Product Rule

In Section 2.2, you saw that the derivative of a sum or difference of two functions is simply the sum or difference of their derivatives. The rules for the derivative of a product or quotient of two functions are not as simple.

The Product Rule

The derivative of the product of two differentiable functions is equal to the first function times the derivative of the second plus the second function times the derivative of the first.

$$\frac{d}{dx}[f(x)g(x)] = f(x)g\,'(x) + g(x)f'(x)$$

PROOF   Some mathematical proofs, such as the proof of the Sum Rule, are straightforward. Others involve clever steps that may not appear to follow clearly from a prior step. The proof below involves such a step—adding and subtracting the same quantity. (This step is shown in color.) Let $F(x) = f(x)g(x)$.

$$F'(x) = \lim_{\Delta x \to 0} \frac{F(x + \Delta x) - F(x)}{\Delta x}$$

$$= \lim_{\Delta x \to 0} \frac{f(x + \Delta x)g(x + \Delta x) - f(x)g(x)}{\Delta x}$$

$$= \lim_{\Delta x \to 0} \frac{f(x + \Delta x)g(x + \Delta x) - f(x + \Delta x)g(x) + f(x + \Delta x)g(x) - f(x)g(x)}{\Delta x}$$

$$= \lim_{\Delta x \to 0} \left[f(x + \Delta x) \frac{g(x + \Delta x) - g(x)}{\Delta x} + g(x) \frac{f(x + \Delta x) - f(x)}{\Delta x} \right]$$

$$= \lim_{\Delta x \to 0} f(x + \Delta x) \frac{g(x + \Delta x) - g(x)}{\Delta x} + \lim_{\Delta x \to 0} g(x) \frac{f(x + \Delta x) - f(x)}{\Delta x}$$

$$= \lim_{\Delta x \to 0} f(x + \Delta x) \cdot \lim_{\Delta x \to 0} \frac{g(x + \Delta x) - g(x)}{\Delta x} + \lim_{\Delta x \to 0} g(x) \cdot \lim_{\Delta x \to 0} \frac{f(x + \Delta x) - f(x)}{\Delta x}$$

$$= f(x)g\,'(x) + g(x)f'(x)$$

STUDY TIP

Rather than trying to remember the formula for the Product Rule, it can be more helpful to remember its verbal statement:

the first function times the derivative of the second plus the second function times the derivative of the first.

Example 1   Using the Product Rule

Find the derivative of $y = (3x - 2x^2)(5 + 4x)$.

SOLUTION   Using the Product Rule, you can write

$$\frac{dy}{dx} = \overbrace{(3x - 2x^2)}^{\text{First}} \overbrace{\frac{d}{dx}[5 + 4x]}^{\substack{\text{Derivative} \\ \text{of second}}} + \overbrace{(5 + 4x)}^{\text{Second}} \overbrace{\frac{d}{dx}[3x - 2x^2]}^{\substack{\text{Derivative} \\ \text{of first}}}$$

$$= (3x - 2x^2)(4) + (5 + 4x)(3 - 4x)$$

$$= (12x - 8x^2) + (15 - 8x - 16x^2)$$

$$= 15 + 4x - 24x^2.$$

✓ **Checkpoint 1**

Find the derivative of $y = (4x + 3x^2)(6 - 3x)$.

In general, the derivative of the product of two functions is not equal to the product of the derivatives of the two functions. To see this, compare the product of the derivatives of

$$f(x) = 3x - 2x^2 \quad \text{and} \quad g(x) = 5 + 4x$$

with the derivative found in Example 1.

In the next example, notice that the first step in differentiating is *rewriting the original function*.

TECH TUTOR

If you have access to a symbolic differentiation utility, try using it to confirm several of the derivatives in this section.

Example 2   Using the Product Rule

Find the derivative of $f(x) = \left(\dfrac{1}{x} + 1\right)(x - 1)$.

SOLUTION   Rewrite the function. Then use the Product Rule to find the derivative.

$$f(x) = \left(\frac{1}{x} + 1\right)(x - 1) \qquad \text{Write original function.}$$

$$= (x^{-1} + 1)(x - 1) \qquad \text{Rewrite function.}$$

$$f'(x) = (x^{-1} + 1)\frac{d}{dx}[x - 1] + (x - 1)\frac{d}{dx}[x^{-1} + 1] \qquad \text{Product Rule}$$

$$= (x^{-1} + 1)(1) + (x - 1)(-x^{-2})$$

$$= \frac{1}{x} + 1 - \frac{x - 1}{x^2}$$

$$= \frac{x + x^2 - x + 1}{x^2} \qquad \text{Write with common denominator.}$$

$$= \frac{x^2 + 1}{x^2} \qquad \text{Simplify.}$$

✓ **Checkpoint 2**

Find the derivative of

$$f(x) = \left(\frac{1}{x} + 1\right)(2x + 1).$$

You now have two differentiation rules that deal with products—the Constant Multiple Rule and the Product Rule. The difference between these two rules is that the Constant Multiple Rule is used when one of the factors is a constant

$$F(x) = c f(x) \qquad \text{Use Constant Multiple Rule.}$$

whereas the Product Rule is used when both of the factors are variable quantities

Variable quantity   Variable quantity

$$F(x) = f(x) g(x). \qquad \text{Use Product Rule.}$$

The next example compares these two rules.

Example 3   Comparing Differentiation Rules

Find the derivative of each function.

a. $y = 2x(x^2 + 3x)$

b. $y = 2(x^2 + 3x)$

SOLUTION

a. Because both factors are variable quantities, use the Product Rule.

$$y = 2x(x^2 + 3x)$$

$$\frac{dy}{dx} = (2x) \frac{d}{dx}[x^2 + 3x] + (x^2 + 3x) \frac{d}{dx}[2x] \qquad \text{Product Rule}$$

$$= (2x)(2x + 3) + (x^2 + 3x)(2)$$

$$= 4x^2 + 6x + 2x^2 + 6x$$

$$= 6x^2 + 12x$$

b. Because one of the factors is a constant, use the Constant Multiple Rule.

$$y = 2(x^2 + 3x)$$

$$\frac{dy}{dx} = 2 \frac{d}{dx}[x^2 + 3x] \qquad \text{Constant Multiple Rule}$$

$$= 2(2x + 3)$$

$$= 4x + 6$$

> **STUDY TIP**
>
> You could calculate the derivative in Example 3(a) without the Product Rule. For instance,
>
> $$y = 2x(x^2 + 3x) = 2x^3 + 6x^2$$
>
> and
>
> $$\frac{dy}{dx} = 6x^2 + 12x.$$

✓ **Checkpoint 3**

Find the derivative of each function.

a. $y = 3x(2x^2 + 5x)$

b. $y = 3(2x^2 + 5x)$

The Product Rule can be extended to products that have more than two factors. For example, if f, g, and h are differentiable functions of x, then

$$\frac{d}{dx}[f(x)g(x)h(x)] = f'(x)g(x)h(x) + f(x)g'(x)h(x) + f(x)g(x)h'(x).$$

The Quotient Rule

In Section 2.2, you saw that by using the Constant Rule, the Power Rule, the Constant Multiple Rule, and the Sum and Difference Rules, you were able to differentiate any polynomial function. By combining these rules with the Quotient Rule, you can now differentiate any *rational* function.

> **The Quotient Rule**
>
> The derivative of the quotient of two differentiable functions is equal to the denominator times the derivative of the numerator minus the numerator times the derivative of the denominator, all divided by the square of the denominator.
>
> $$\frac{d}{dx}\left[\frac{f(x)}{g(x)}\right] = \frac{g(x)f'(x) - f(x)g'(x)}{[g(x)]^2}, \quad g(x) \neq 0$$

PROOF Begin by letting

$$F(x) = \frac{f(x)}{g(x)}.$$

As in the proof of the Product Rule, a key step in this proof is adding and subtracting the same quantity.

$$F'(x) = \lim_{\Delta x \to 0} \frac{F(x + \Delta x) - F(x)}{\Delta x}$$

$$= \lim_{\Delta x \to 0} \frac{\dfrac{f(x + \Delta x)}{g(x + \Delta x)} - \dfrac{f(x)}{g(x)}}{\Delta x}$$

$$= \lim_{\Delta x \to 0} \left[\left(\frac{g(x)f(x + \Delta x)}{g(x)g(x + \Delta x)} - \frac{f(x)g(x + \Delta x)}{g(x)g(x + \Delta x)}\right) \div \Delta x\right]$$

$$= \lim_{\Delta x \to 0} \left[\frac{g(x)f(x + \Delta x) - f(x)g(x + \Delta x)}{g(x)g(x + \Delta x)} \cdot \frac{1}{\Delta x}\right]$$

$$= \lim_{\Delta x \to 0} \frac{g(x)f(x + \Delta x) - f(x)g(x + \Delta x)}{\Delta x\, g(x)g(x + \Delta x)}$$

$$= \lim_{\Delta x \to 0} \frac{g(x)f(x + \Delta x) - f(x)g(x) + f(x)g(x) - f(x)g(x + \Delta x)}{\Delta x\, g(x)g(x + \Delta x)}$$

$$= \frac{\displaystyle\lim_{\Delta x \to 0} \frac{g(x)[f(x + \Delta x) - f(x)]}{\Delta x} - \lim_{\Delta x \to 0} \frac{f(x)[g(x + \Delta x) - g(x)]}{\Delta x}}{\displaystyle\lim_{\Delta x \to 0} [g(x)g(x + \Delta x)]}$$

$$= \frac{g(x)\left[\displaystyle\lim_{\Delta x \to 0} \frac{f(x + \Delta x) - f(x)}{\Delta x}\right] - f(x)\left[\displaystyle\lim_{\Delta x \to 0} \frac{g(x + \Delta x) - g(x)}{\Delta x}\right]}{\displaystyle\lim_{\Delta x \to 0} [g(x)g(x + \Delta x)]}$$

$$= \frac{g(x)f'(x) - f(x)g'(x)}{[g(x)]^2}$$

From the Quotient Rule, you can see that the derivative of a quotient is not, in general, the quotient of the derivatives. That is,

$$\frac{d}{dx}\left[\frac{f(x)}{g(x)}\right] \neq \frac{f'(x)}{g'(x)}.$$

ALGEBRA TUTOR
xy

When applying the Quotient Rule, it is suggested that you enclose all factors and derivatives in symbols of grouping, such as parentheses. Also, pay special attention to the subtraction required in the numerator. For help in simplifying expressions like the one in Example 4, see the *Chapter 2 Algebra Tutor* on page 159, Example 2(d).

Example 4   Using the Quotient Rule

Find the derivative of $y = \dfrac{x-1}{2x+3}$.

SOLUTION   Apply the Quotient Rule, as shown.

$$\frac{dy}{dx} = \frac{(2x+3)\dfrac{d}{dx}[x-1] - (x-1)\dfrac{d}{dx}[2x+3]}{(2x+3)^2}$$

$$= \frac{(2x+3)(1) - (x-1)(2)}{(2x+3)^2}$$

$$= \frac{2x+3 - 2x+2}{(2x+3)^2}$$

$$= \frac{5}{(2x+3)^2}$$

✓ **Checkpoint 4**

Find the derivative of $y = \dfrac{x+4}{5x-2}$.

Example 5   Finding an Equation of a Tangent Line

Find an equation of the tangent line to the graph of

$$y = \frac{2x^2 - 4x + 3}{2 - 3x}$$

at $x = 1$.

SOLUTION   Apply the Quotient Rule, as shown.

$$\frac{dy}{dx} = \frac{(2-3x)\dfrac{d}{dx}[2x^2 - 4x + 3] - (2x^2 - 4x + 3)\dfrac{d}{dx}[2-3x]}{(2-3x)^2}$$

$$= \frac{(2-3x)(4x-4) - (2x^2 - 4x + 3)(-3)}{(2-3x)^2}$$

$$= \frac{-12x^2 + 20x - 8 - (-6x^2 + 12x - 9)}{(2-3x)^2}$$

$$= \frac{-12x^2 + 20x - 8 + 6x^2 - 12x + 9}{(2-3x)^2}$$

$$= \frac{-6x^2 + 8x + 1}{(2-3x)^2}$$

When $x = 1$, the value of the function is $y = -1$ and the slope is $m = 3$. Using the point-slope form of a line, you can find the equation of the tangent line to be $y = 3x - 4$. The graph of the function and the tangent line is shown in Figure 2.28.

$y = \dfrac{2x^2 - 4x + 3}{2 - 3x}$

FIGURE 2.28

✓ **Checkpoint 5**

Find an equation of the tangent line to the graph of

$$y = \frac{x^2 - 4}{2x + 5}$$

at $x = 0$. Sketch the line tangent to the graph at $x = 0$.

Example 6   Rewriting Before Differentiating

Find the derivative of

$$y = \frac{3 - (1/x)}{x + 5}.$$

SOLUTION Begin by rewriting the function. Then apply the Quotient Rule and simplify the result.

$$y = \frac{3 - (1/x)}{x + 5}$$ Write original function.

$$= \frac{x[3 - (1/x)]}{x(x + 5)}$$ Multiply numerator and denominator by x.

$$= \frac{3x - 1}{x^2 + 5x}$$ Rewrite.

$$\frac{dy}{dx} = \frac{(x^2 + 5x)(3) - (3x - 1)(2x + 5)}{(x^2 + 5x)^2}$$ Apply Quotient Rule.

$$= \frac{(3x^2 + 15x) - (6x^2 + 13x - 5)}{(x^2 + 5x)^2}$$

$$= \frac{-3x^2 + 2x + 5}{(x^2 + 5x)^2}$$ Simplify.

✓**Checkpoint 6**

Find the derivative of $y = \dfrac{3 - (2/x)}{x + 4}$.

Not every quotient needs to be differentiated by the Quotient Rule. For instance, each quotient in the next example can be considered as the product of a constant and a function of x. In such cases, the Constant Multiple Rule is more efficient than the Quotient Rule.

Example 7   Using the Constant Multiple Rule

Original Function	Rewrite	Differentiate	Simplify
a. $y = \dfrac{x^2 + 3x}{6}$	$y = \dfrac{1}{6}(x^2 + 3x)$	$y' = \dfrac{1}{6}(2x + 3)$	$y' = \dfrac{1}{3}x + \dfrac{1}{2}$
b. $y = \dfrac{5x^4}{8}$	$y = \dfrac{5}{8}x^4$	$y' = \dfrac{5}{8}(4x^3)$	$y' = \dfrac{5}{2}x^3$
c. $y = \dfrac{-3(3x - 2x^2)}{7x}$	$y = -\dfrac{3}{7}(3 - 2x)$	$y' = -\dfrac{3}{7}(-2)$	$y' = \dfrac{6}{7}$
d. $y = \dfrac{9}{5x^2}$	$y = \dfrac{9}{5}(x^{-2})$	$y' = \dfrac{9}{5}(-2x^{-3})$	$y' = -\dfrac{18}{5x^3}$

✓**Checkpoint 7**

Find the derivative of each function.

a. $y = \dfrac{x^2 + 4x}{5}$ **b.** $y = \dfrac{3x^4}{4}$

Application

 Example 8   **Rate of Change of Systolic Blood Pressure**

As blood moves from the heart through the major arteries out to the capillaries and back through the veins, the systolic blood pressure continuously drops. Consider a person whose systolic blood pressure P (in millimeters of mercury) is given by

$$P = \frac{25t^2 + 125}{t^2 + 1}, \quad 0 \le t \le 10$$

where t is measured in seconds. At what rate is the blood pressure changing 5 seconds after blood leaves the heart?

SOLUTION   Begin by applying the Quotient Rule.

$$P = \frac{25t^2 + 125}{t^2 + 1} \qquad \text{Write original function.}$$

$$\frac{dP}{dt} = \frac{(t^2 + 1)(50t) - (25t^2 + 125)(2t)}{(t^2 + 1)^2} \qquad \text{Quotient Rule}$$

$$= \frac{50t^3 + 50t - 50t^3 - 250t}{(t^2 + 1)^2}$$

$$= -\frac{200t}{(t^2 + 1)^2} \qquad \text{Simplify.}$$

When $t = 5$, the rate of change is

$$\frac{dP}{dt} = -\frac{200(5)}{26^2} \approx -1.48 \text{ millimeters per second.}$$

So, the pressure is *dropping* at a rate of 1.48 millimeters per second at $t = 5$ seconds.

✓**Checkpoint 8**

In Example 8, find the rate at which systolic blood pressure is changing at each time shown in the table below. Describe the changes in blood pressure as the blood moves away from the heart.

t	0	1	2	3	4	5	6	7
$\dfrac{dP}{dt}$								

SUMMARIZE   (Section 2.4)

1. State the Product Rule *(page 117)*. For examples of the Product Rule, see Examples 1, 2, and 3.

2. State the Quotient Rule *(page 120)*. For examples of the Quotient Rule, see Examples 4, 5, and 6.

3. Describe a real-life example of how the Quotient Rule can be used to analyze the rate of change of systolic blood pressure *(page 123, Example 8)*.

SKILLS WARM UP 2.4   The following warm-up exercises involve skills that were covered in a previous course or earlier sections. You will use these skills in the exercise set for this section. For additional help, review Appendix Sections A.4 and A.5, and Section 2.2.

In Exercises 1–10, simplify the expression.

1. $(x^2 + 1)(2) + (2x + 7)(2x)$

2. $(2x - x^3)(8x) + (4x^2)(2 - 3x^2)$

3. $x(4)(x^2 + 2)^3(2x) + (x^2 + 4)(1)$

4. $x^2(2)(2x + 1)(2) + (2x + 1)^4(2x)$

5. $\dfrac{(2x + 7)(5) - (5x + 6)(2)}{(2x + 7)^2}$

6. $\dfrac{(x^2 - 4)(2x + 1) - (x^2 + x)(2x)}{(x^2 - 4)^2}$

7. $\dfrac{(x^2 + 1)(2) - (2x + 1)(2x)}{(x^2 + 1)^2}$

8. $\dfrac{(1 - x^4)(4) - (4x - 1)(-4x^3)}{(1 - x^4)^2}$

9. $(x^{-1} + x)(2) + (2x - 3)(-x^{-2} + 1)$

10. $\dfrac{(1 - x^{-1})(1) - (x - 4)(x^{-2})}{(1 - x^{-1})^2}$

In Exercises 11–14, find $f'(2)$.

11. $f(x) = 3x^2 - x + 4$

12. $f(x) = -x^3 + x^2 + 8x$

13. $f(x) = \dfrac{1}{x}$

14. $f(x) = x^2 - \dfrac{1}{x^2}$

Exercises 2.4

See www.CalcChat.com for worked-out solutions to odd-numbered exercises.

Using the Product Rule In Exercises 1–10, use the Product Rule to find the derivative of the function. *See Examples 1, 2, and 3.*

1. $f(x) = (2x - 3)(1 - 5x)$

2. $g(x) = (x - 4)(x + 2)$

3. $f(x) = (6x - x^2)(4 + 3x)$

4. $f(x) = (x^2 + 1)(2x + 5)$

5. $f(x) = x(x^2 + 3)$

6. $f(x) = x^2(3x^3 - 1)$

7. $h(x) = \left(\dfrac{2}{x} - 3\right)(x^2 + 7)$

8. $f(x) = (3 - x)\left(\dfrac{4}{x^2} - 5\right)$

9. $g(x) = (x^2 - 4x + 3)(x - 2)$

10. $g(x) = (x^2 - 2x + 1)(x^3 - 1)$

Using the Quotient Rule In Exercises 11–20, use the Quotient Rule to find the derivative of the function. *See Examples 4 and 6.*

11. $h(x) = \dfrac{x}{x - 5}$

12. $h(x) = \dfrac{x^2}{x + 3}$

13. $f(t) = \dfrac{2t^2 - 3}{3t + 1}$

14. $f(x) = \dfrac{x + 1}{x - 1}$

15. $f(t) = \dfrac{t^2 - 1}{t + 4}$

16. $g(x) = \dfrac{4x - 5}{x^2 - 1}$

17. $f(x) = \dfrac{x^2 + 6x + 5}{2x - 1}$

18. $f(x) = \dfrac{4x^2 - x + 1}{x + 2}$

19. $f(x) = \dfrac{6 + (2/x)}{3x - 1}$

20. $f(x) = \dfrac{5 - (1/x^2)}{x + 2}$

Using the Constant Multiple Rule In Exercises 21–30, find the derivative of the function. *See Example 7.*

Original Function	Rewrite	Differentiate	Simplify
21. $f(x) = \dfrac{x^3 + 6x}{3}$			
22. $f(x) = \dfrac{3x^2}{7}$			
23. $y = \dfrac{x^2 + 2x}{3}$			
24. $y = \dfrac{4x^{3/2}}{x}$			
25. $y = \dfrac{7}{3x^3}$			
26. $y = \dfrac{4}{5x^2}$			
27. $y = \dfrac{4x^2 - 3x}{8\sqrt{x}}$			
28. $y = \dfrac{5(3x^2 + 5x)}{8x}$			
29. $y = \dfrac{x^2 - 4x + 3}{2(x - 1)}$			
30. $y = \dfrac{x^2 - 4}{4(x + 2)}$			

Finding Derivatives In Exercises 31–44, find the derivative of the function. State which differentiation rule(s) you used to find the derivative.

31. $f(x) = (x^3 - 3x)(2x^2 + 3x + 5)$

32. $h(t) = (t^5 - 1)(4t^2 - 7t - 3)$

33. $f(x) = \dfrac{x^3 + 3x + 2}{x^2 - 1}$

34. $f(x) = (x^5 - 3x)\left(\dfrac{1}{x^2}\right)$

35. $f(x) = \dfrac{x^2 - x - 20}{x + 4}$

36. $h(t) = \dfrac{t + 2}{t^2 + 5t + 6}$

37. $g(t) = (2t^3 - 1)^2$

38. $f(x) = \sqrt[3]{x}(x + 1)$

39. $g(s) = \dfrac{s^2 - 2s + 5}{\sqrt{s}}$

40. $f(x) = \dfrac{x + 1}{\sqrt{x}}$

41. $f(x) = \dfrac{(x - 2)(3x + 1)}{4x + 2}$

42. $f(x) = \dfrac{(x + 1)(2x - 7)}{2x + 1}$

43. $g(x) = \left(\dfrac{x - 3}{x + 4}\right)(x^2 + 2x + 1)$

44. $f(x) = (3x^3 + 4x)(x - 5)(x + 1)$

Finding an Equation of a Tangent Line In Exercises 45–52, find an equation of the tangent line to the graph of the function at the given point. Then use a graphing utility to graph the function and the tangent line in the same viewing window. *See Example 5.*

Function	*Point*
45. $f(x) = (5x + 2)(x^2 + x)$	$(-1, 0)$
46. $h(x) = (x^2 - 1)^2$	$(-2, 9)$
47. $f(x) = x^3(x^2 - 4)$	$(1, -3)$
48. $f(x) = \sqrt{x}(x - 3)$	$(9, 18)$
49. $f(x) = \dfrac{x - 2}{x + 1}$	$\left(1, -\dfrac{1}{2}\right)$
50. $f(x) = \dfrac{2x + 1}{x - 1}$	$(2, 5)$
51. $f(x) = \dfrac{(3x - 2)(6x + 5)}{2x - 3}$	$(-1, -1)$
52. $g(x) = \dfrac{(x + 2)(x^2 + x)}{x - 4}$	$(1, -2)$

Finding Horizontal Tangent Lines In Exercises 53–56, find the point(s), if any, at which the graph of f has a horizontal tangent line.

53. $f(x) = \dfrac{x^2}{x - 1}$

54. $f(x) = \dfrac{x^2}{x^2 + 1}$

55. $f(x) = \dfrac{x^4}{x^3 + 1}$

56. $f(x) = \dfrac{x^4 + 3}{x^2 + 1}$

 Graphing a Function and Its Derivative In Exercises 57–60, use a graphing utility to graph f and f' on the interval $[-2, 2]$.

57. $f(x) = x(x + 1)$

58. $f(x) = x^2(x + 1)$

59. $f(x) = x(x + 1)(x - 1)$

60. $f(x) = x^2(x + 1)(x - 1)$

Demand In Exercises 61 and 62, use the demand function to find the rate of change in the demand x for the given price p.

61. $x = 275\left(1 - \dfrac{3p}{5p + 1}\right)$, $p = \$4$

62. $x = 300 - p - \dfrac{2p}{p + 1}$, $p = \$3$

63. Population Growth A population of bacteria is introduced into a culture. The number of bacteria P can be modeled by

$$P = 500\left(1 + \dfrac{4t}{50 + t^2}\right)$$

where t is the time (in hours). Find the rate of change of the population at $t = 2$.

64. Quality Control The percent P of defective parts produced by a new employee t days after the employee starts work can be modeled by

$$P = \dfrac{t + 1750}{50(t + 2)}.$$

Find the rates of change of P at (a) $t = 1$ and (b) $t = 10$.

65. Environment The model

$$f(t) = \dfrac{t^2 - t + 1}{t^2 + 1}$$

measures the level of oxygen in a pond, where t is the time (in weeks) after organic waste is dumped into the pond. Find the rates of change of f with respect to t at (a) $t = 0.5$, (b) $t = 2$, and (c) $t = 8$. Interpret the meaning of these values.

66. Physical Science The temperature T (in degrees Fahrenheit) of food placed in a refrigerator is modeled by

$$T = 10\left(\frac{4t^2 + 16t + 75}{t^2 + 4t + 10}\right)$$

where t is the time (in hours). What is the initial temperature of the food? Find the rates of change of T with respect to t at (a) $t = 1$, (b) $t = 3$, (c) $t = 5$, and (d) $t = 10$. Interpret the meaning of these values.

67. Cost The cost C of producing x units of a product is given by $C = x^3 - 15x^2 + 87x - 73$ for $4 \le x \le 9$.

(a) Use a graphing utility to graph the marginal cost function and the average cost function, C/x, in the same viewing window.

(b) Find the point of intersection of the graphs of dC/dx and C/x. Does this point have any significance?

68. HOW DO YOU SEE IT? The advertising manager for a new product determines that P percent of the potential market is aware of the product t weeks after the advertising campaign begins.

Market Awareness

(a) What happens to the percent of people who are aware of the product in the long run?

(b) What happens to the rate of change of the percent of people who are aware of the product in the long run?

69. Inventory Replenishment The ordering and transportation cost C per unit (in thousands of dollars) of the components used in manufacturing a product is given by

$$C = 100\left(\frac{200}{x^2} + \frac{x}{x + 30}\right), \quad 1 \le x$$

where x is the order size (in hundreds). Find the rate of change of C with respect to x for each order size. What do these rates of change imply about increasing the size of an order? Of the given order sizes, which would you choose? Explain.

(a) $x = 10$ (b) $x = 15$ (c) $x = 20$

70. Managing a Store You are managing a store and have been adjusting the price of an item. You have found that you make a profit of $50 when 10 units are sold, $60 when 12 units are sold, and $65 when 14 units are sold.

(a) Use the *regression* feature of a graphing utility to find a quadratic model that relates the profit P to the number of units sold x.

(b) Use a graphing utility to graph P.

(c) Find the point on the graph at which the marginal profit is zero. Interpret this point in the context of the problem.

Using Relationships In Exercises 71–74, use the given information to find $f'(2)$.

$$g(2) = 3 \quad \text{and} \quad g'(2) = -2$$
$$h(2) = -1 \quad \text{and} \quad h'(2) = 4$$

71. $f(x) = 2g(x) + h(x)$ **72.** $f(x) = 3 - g(x)$

73. $f(x) = g(x)h(x)$ **74.** $f(x) = \dfrac{g(x)}{h(x)}$

Business Capsule

In 1978 Ben Cohen and Jerry Greenfield used their combined life savings of $8000 to convert an abandoned gas station in Burlington, Vermont into their first ice cream shop. Today, Ben & Jerry's Homemade Holdings, Inc. has almost 800 scoop shops in 25 countries. The company's three-part mission statement emphasizes product quality, economic reward, and a commitment to the community. Ben & Jerry's contributes a minimum of $1.8 million annually through corporate philanthropy that is primarily employee led.

75. Research Project Use your school's library, the Internet, or some other reference source to find information on a company that is noted for its philanthropy and community commitment. (One such business is described above.) Write a short paper about the company.

QUIZ YOURSELF

See www.CalcChat.com for worked-out solutions to odd-numbered exercises.

Take this quiz as you would take a quiz in class. When you are done, check your work against the answers given in the back of the book.

In Exercises 1–3, use the limit definition to find the derivative of the function. Then find the slope of the tangent line to the graph of f at the given point.

1. $f(x) = 5x + 3; (-2, -7)$

2. $f(x) = \sqrt{x + 3}; (1, 2)$

3. $f(x) = x^2 - 2x; (3, 3)$

In Exercises 4–13, find the derivative of the function.

4. $f(x) = 12$

5. $f(x) = 19x + 9$

6. $f(x) = 5 - 3x^2$

7. $f(x) = 12x^{1/4}$

8. $f(x) = 4x^{-2}$

9. $f(x) = 2\sqrt{x}$

10. $f(x) = \dfrac{2x + 3}{3x + 2}$

11. $f(x) = (x^2 + 1)(-2x + 4)$

12. $f(x) = (x^2 + 3x + 4)(5x - 2)$

13. $f(x) = \dfrac{4x}{x^2 + 3}$

In Exercises 14–17, use a graphing utility to graph the function and find its average rate of change on the given interval. Compare this rate with the instantaneous rates of change at the endpoints of the interval.

14. $f(x) = x^2 - 3x + 1; [0, 3]$

15. $f(x) = 2x^3 + x^2 - x + 4; [-1, 1]$

16. $f(x) = \dfrac{1}{2x}; [2, 5]$

17. $f(x) = \sqrt[3]{x}; [8, 27]$

18. The profit P (in dollars) from selling x units of a product is given by

$$P = -0.0125x^2 + 16x - 600.$$

(a) Find the additional profit when sales increase from 175 to 176 units.

(b) Find the marginal profit when $x = 175$.

(c) Compare the results of parts (a) and (b).

In Exercises 19 and 20, find an equation of the tangent line to the graph of f at the given point. Then use a graphing utility to graph the function and the equation of the tangent line in the same viewing window.

19. $f(x) = 5x^2 + 6x - 1; (-1, -2)$

20. $f(x) = (x^2 + 1)(4x - 3); (1, 2)$

21. From 2003 through 2009, the sales per share S (in dollars) for Columbia Sportswear can be modeled by

$$S = -0.13556t^3 + 1.8682t^2 - 4.351t + 23.52, \quad 3 \le t \le 9$$

where t represents the year, with $t = 3$ corresponding to 2003. *(Source: Columbia Sportswear Company)*

(a) Find the rate of change of the sales per share with respect to the year.

(b) At what rate were the sales per share changing in 2004? in 2007? in 2008?

2.5 The Chain Rule

■ Find derivatives using the Chain Rule.
■ Find derivatives using the General Power Rule.
■ Write derivatives in simplified form.
■ Use derivatives to answer questions about real-life situations.
■ Review the basic differentiation rules for algebraic functions.

The Chain Rule

In this section, you will study one of the most powerful rules of differential calculus—the **Chain Rule.** This differentiation rule deals with composite functions and adds versatility to the rules presented in Sections 2.2 and 2.4. For example, compare the functions below. Those on the left can be differentiated without the Chain Rule, whereas those on the right are best done with the Chain Rule.

Without the Chain Rule	*With the Chain Rule*
$y = x^2 + 1$	$y = \sqrt{x^2 + 1}$
$y = x + 1$	$y = (x + 1)^{-1/2}$
$y = 3x + 2$	$y = (3x + 2)^5$
$y = \dfrac{x + 5}{x^2 + 2}$	$y = \left(\dfrac{x + 5}{x^2 + 2}\right)^2$
$y = \dfrac{x + 1}{x}$	$y = \sqrt{\dfrac{x + 1}{x}}$

In Exercise 71 on page 136, you will use the General Power Rule to find the rate of change of the balance in an account.

The Chain Rule

If $y = f(u)$ is a differentiable function of u, and $u = g(x)$ is a differentiable function of x, then $y = f(g(x))$ is a differentiable function of x, and

$$\frac{dy}{dx} = \frac{dy}{du} \cdot \frac{du}{dx}$$

or, equivalently,

$$\frac{d}{dx}[f(g(x))] = f'(g(x))g'(x).$$

Basically, the Chain Rule states that if y changes dy/du times as fast as u, and u changes du/dx times as fast as x, then y changes

$$\frac{dy}{du} \cdot \frac{du}{dx}$$

times as fast as x, as illustrated in Figure 2.29. One advantage of the

$$\frac{dy}{dx}$$

notation for derivatives is that it helps you remember differentiation rules, such as the Chain Rule. For instance, in the formula

$$\frac{dy}{dx} = \frac{dy}{du} \cdot \frac{du}{dx}$$

you can imagine that the du's divide out.

x

Input

Function g Output

Rate of change of u with respect to x is $\dfrac{du}{dx}$.

$u = g(x)$

u

Input

Function f Output

Rate of change of y with respect to u is $\dfrac{dy}{du}$.

$y = f(u) = f(g(x))$

Rate of change of y with respect to x is $\dfrac{dy}{dx} = \dfrac{dy}{du}\dfrac{du}{dx}$.

FIGURE 2.29

When applying the Chain Rule, it is helpful to think of the composite function $y = f(g(x))$ or $y = f(u)$ as having two parts—an *inside* and an *outside*—as illustrated below.

$$\text{Inside}$$
$$y = f(g(x)) = f(u)$$
$$\text{Outside}$$

The Chain Rule tells you that the derivative of $y = f(u)$ is the derivative of the outer function (at the inner function u) *times* the derivative of the inner function. That is,

$$y' = f'(u) \cdot u'.$$

Example 1   Decomposing Composite Functions

Write each function as the composition of two functions.

a. $y = \dfrac{1}{x + 1}$ **b.** $y = \sqrt{3x^2 - x + 1}$

SOLUTION   There is more than one correct way to decompose each function. One way for each is shown below.

$y = f(g(x))$	$u = g(x)$ *(inside)*	$y = f(u)$ *(outside)*
a. $y = \dfrac{1}{x + 1}$	$u = x + 1$	$y = \dfrac{1}{u}$
b. $y = \sqrt{3x^2 - x + 1}$	$u = 3x^2 - x + 1$	$y = \sqrt{u}$

✓ Checkpoint 1

Write each function as the composition of two functions, where $y = f(g(x))$.

a. $y = \dfrac{1}{\sqrt{x + 1}}$ **b.** $y = (x^2 + 2x + 5)^3$

Example 2   Using the Chain Rule

Find the derivative of $y = (x^2 + 1)^3$.

SOLUTION   To apply the Chain Rule, you need to identify the inside function u.

$$y = \overbrace{(x^2 + 1)}^{u}{}^3 = u^3$$

The inside function is $u = x^2 + 1$. By the Chain Rule, you can write the derivative as shown.

$$\frac{dy}{dx} = \overbrace{3(x^2 + 1)^2}^{\frac{dy}{du}}\overbrace{(2x)}^{\frac{du}{dx}} = 6x(x^2 + 1)^2$$

✓ Checkpoint 2

Find the derivative of $y = (x^3 + 1)^2$.

STUDY TIP

Try checking the result of Example 2 by expanding the function to obtain

$$y = x^6 + 3x^4 + 3x^2 + 1$$

and finding the derivative. Do you obtain the same answer?

The General Power Rule

The function in Example 2 illustrates one of the most common types of composite functions—a power function of the form

$$y = [u(x)]^n.$$

The rule for differentiating such functions is called the **General Power Rule,** and it is a special case of the Chain Rule.

The General Power Rule

If $y = [u(x)]^n$, where u is a differentiable function of x and n is a real number, then

$$\frac{dy}{dx} = n[u(x)]^{n-1}\frac{du}{dx}$$

or, equivalently,

$$\frac{d}{dx}[u^n] = nu^{n-1}u'.$$

PROOF   Apply the Chain Rule and the Simple Power Rule as shown.

$$\frac{dy}{dx} = \frac{dy}{du} \cdot \frac{du}{dx}$$

$$= \frac{d}{du}[u^n]\frac{du}{dx}$$

$$= nu^{n-1}\frac{du}{dx}$$

TECH TUTOR

If you have access to a symbolic differentiation utility, try using it to confirm the result of Example 3.

Example 3   Using the General Power Rule

Find the derivative of

$$y = (3x - 2x^2)^3.$$

SOLUTION   To apply the General Power Rule, you need to identify the inside function u.

$$y = \overbrace{(3x - 2x^2)}^{u}{}^3 = u^3$$

The inside function is

$$u = 3x - 2x^2.$$

So, by the General Power Rule,

$$\frac{dy}{dx} = \overset{n}{3}\overbrace{(3x - 2x^2)^2}^{u^{n-1}}\overbrace{\frac{d}{dx}[3x - 2x^2]}^{u'}$$

$$= 3(3x - 2x^2)^2(3 - 4x).$$

✓**Checkpoint 3**

Find the derivative of

$$y = (x^2 + 3x)^4.$$

Example 4 **Finding an Equation of a Tangent Line**

Find an equation of the tangent line to the graph of

$$y = \sqrt[3]{(x^2 + 4)^2}$$

at $x = 2$.

SOLUTION Begin by rewriting the function in rational exponent form.

$$y = (x^2 + 4)^{2/3} \qquad \text{Rewrite original function.}$$

Then, using the inside function, $u = x^2 + 4$, apply the General Power Rule.

$$\frac{dy}{dx} = \frac{2}{3}(x^2 + 4)^{-1/3}(2x) \qquad \text{Apply General Power Rule.}$$

$$= \frac{4x(x^2 + 4)^{-1/3}}{3}$$

$$= \frac{4x}{3\sqrt[3]{x^2 + 4}} \qquad \text{Write in radical form.}$$

When $x = 2$, $y = 4$ and the slope of the line tangent to the graph at $(2, 4)$ is $\frac{4}{3}$. Using the point-slope form, you can find the equation of the tangent line to be $y = \frac{4}{3}x + \frac{4}{3}$. The graph of the function and the tangent line is shown in Figure 2.30.

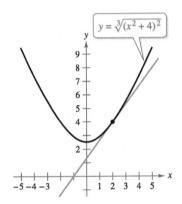

FIGURE 2.30

✓**Checkpoint 4**

Find an equation of the tangent line to the graph of $y = \sqrt[3]{(x + 4)^2}$ at $x = 4$.

Example 5 **Differentiating a Quotient with a Constant Numerator**

Find the derivative of

$$y = \frac{5}{(4x - 3)^2}.$$

SOLUTION Begin by rewriting the function in rational exponent form.

$$y = 5(4x - 3)^{-2} \qquad \text{Rewrite original function.}$$

Then, using the inside function, $u = 4x - 3$, apply the General Power Rule.

$$\frac{dy}{dx} = 5(-2)(4x - 3)^{-3}(4) \qquad \text{Apply General Power Rule.}$$

$$\underset{\substack{\text{Constant} \\ \text{Multiple Rule}}}{}$$

$$= -40(4x - 3)^{-3} \qquad \text{Simplify.}$$

$$= \frac{-40}{(4x - 3)^3} \qquad \text{Write with positive exponent.}$$

✓**Checkpoint 5**

Find the derivative of $y = \frac{4}{2x + 1}$.

> **STUDY TIP**
>
> The derivative of a quotient can sometimes be found more easily with the General Power Rule than with the Quotient Rule. This is especially true when the numerator is a constant, as shown in Example 5.

Simplification Techniques

Throughout this chapter, writing derivatives in simplified form has been emphasized. The reason for this is that most applications of derivatives require a simplified form. The next two examples illustrate some useful simplification techniques.

ALGEBRA TUTOR xy

In Example 6, note that you subtract exponents when factoring. That is, when $(1 - x^2)^{-1/2}$ is factored out of $(1 - x^2)^{1/2}$, the *remaining* factor has an exponent of $\frac{1}{2} - \left(-\frac{1}{2}\right) = 1$. So, $(1 - x^2)^{1/2}$ is equal to the product of $(1 - x^2)^{-1/2}$ and $(1 - x^2)^1$. For help in simplifying expressions like the one in Example 6, see the *Chapter 2 Algebra Tutor* on pages 158 and 159.

Example 6   Simplifying by Factoring Out Least Powers

Find the derivative of $y = x^2\sqrt{1 - x^2}$.

SOLUTION

$$
\begin{aligned}
y &= x^2\sqrt{1 - x^2} && \text{Write original function.} \\
&= x^2(1 - x^2)^{1/2} && \text{Rewrite function.} \\
y' &= x^2\frac{d}{dx}\left[(1 - x^2)^{1/2}\right] + (1 - x^2)^{1/2}\frac{d}{dx}\left[x^2\right] && \text{Product Rule} \\
&= x^2\left[\frac{1}{2}(1 - x^2)^{-1/2}(-2x)\right] + (1 - x^2)^{1/2}(2x) && \text{General Power Rule} \\
&= -x^3(1 - x^2)^{-1/2} + 2x(1 - x^2)^{1/2} && \text{Simplify.} \\
&= x(1 - x^2)^{-1/2}\left[-x^2(1) + 2(1 - x^2)\right] && \text{Factor.} \\
&= x(1 - x^2)^{-1/2}(2 - 3x^2) && \text{Simplify.} \\
&= \frac{x(2 - 3x^2)}{\sqrt{1 - x^2}} && \text{Write in radical form.}
\end{aligned}
$$

✓**Checkpoint 6**

Find and simplify the derivative of $y = x^2\sqrt{x^2 + 1}$.

STUDY TIP

In Example 7, try to find $f'(x)$ by applying the Quotient Rule to

$$f(x) = \frac{(3x - 1)^2}{(x^2 + 3)^2}.$$

Which method do you prefer?

Example 7   Differentiating a Quotient Raised to a Power

Find the derivative of

$$f(x) = \left(\frac{3x - 1}{x^2 + 3}\right)^2.$$

SOLUTION

$$
\begin{aligned}
f'(x) &= 2\left(\frac{3x - 1}{x^2 + 3}\right)\frac{d}{dx}\left[\frac{3x - 1}{x^2 + 3}\right] && \text{General Power Rule} \\
&= \left[\frac{2(3x - 1)}{x^2 + 3}\right]\left[\frac{(x^2 + 3)(3) - (3x - 1)(2x)}{(x^2 + 3)^2}\right] && \text{Quotient Rule} \\
&= \frac{2(3x - 1)(3x^2 + 9 - 6x^2 + 2x)}{(x^2 + 3)^3} && \text{Multiply.} \\
&= \frac{2(3x - 1)(-3x^2 + 2x + 9)}{(x^2 + 3)^3} && \text{Simplify.}
\end{aligned}
$$

✓**Checkpoint 7**

Find the derivative of

$$f(x) = \left(\frac{x + 1}{x - 5}\right)^2.$$

Application

Example 8   **Finding Rates of Change**

From 2000 through 2009, the revenue per share R (in dollars) for U.S. Cellular can be modeled by

$$R = (-0.009t^2 + 0.39t + 4.3)^2, \quad 0 \le t \le 9$$

where t is the year, with $t = 0$ corresponding to 2000. Use the model to approximate the rates of change in the revenue per share in 2001, 2002, and 2005. Would U.S. Cellular stockholders have been satisfied with the performance of this stock from 2000 through 2009? *(Source: U.S. Cellular)*

SOLUTION   The rate of change in R is given by the derivative dR/dt. You can use the General Power Rule to find the derivative.

$$\frac{dR}{dt} = 2(-0.009t^2 + 0.39t + 4.3)(-0.018t + 0.39)$$

$$= (-0.036t + 0.78)(-0.009t^2 + 0.39t + 4.3)$$

In 2001, the revenue per share was changing at a rate of

$$[-0.036(1) + 0.78][-0.009(1)^2 + 0.39(1) + 4.3] \approx \$3.48 \text{ per year.}$$

In 2002, the revenue per share was changing at a rate of

$$[-0.036(2) + 0.78][-0.009(2)^2 + 0.39(2) + 4.3] \approx \$3.57 \text{ per year.}$$

In 2005, the revenue per share was changing at a rate of

$$[-0.036(5) + 0.78][-0.009(5)^2 + 0.39(5) + 4.3] \approx \$3.62 \text{ per year.}$$

The graph of the revenue per share function R is shown in Figure 2.31. So, most stockholders would have been satisfied with the performance of this stock.

FIGURE 2.31

✓ **Checkpoint 8**

From 2000 through 2009, the sales per share S (in dollars) for Dollar Tree can be modeled by

$$S = (0.010t^2 + 0.27t + 3.1)^2, \quad 0 \le t \le 9$$

where t is the year, with $t = 0$ corresponding to 2000. Use the model to approximate the rate of change of sales per share in 2005. *(Source: Dollar Tree, Inc.)*

Review of Basic Differentiation Rules

You now have all the rules you need to differentiate *any* algebraic function. For your convenience, they are summarized below.

Summary of Basic Differentiation Rules

Let u and v be differentiable functions of x.

1. Constant Rule $\qquad\qquad\qquad$ $\dfrac{d}{dx}[c] = 0, \quad c$ is a constant.

2. Constant Multiple Rule $\qquad$ $\dfrac{d}{dx}[cu] = c\dfrac{du}{dx}, \quad c$ is a constant.

3. Sum and Difference Rules $\qquad$ $\dfrac{d}{dx}[u \pm v] = \dfrac{du}{dx} \pm \dfrac{dv}{dx}$

4. Product Rule $\qquad\qquad\qquad$ $\dfrac{d}{dx}[uv] = u\dfrac{dv}{dx} + v\dfrac{du}{dx}$

5. Quotient Rule $\qquad\qquad\qquad$ $\dfrac{d}{dx}\left[\dfrac{u}{v}\right] = \dfrac{v\dfrac{du}{dx} - u\dfrac{dv}{dx}}{v^2}$

6. Power Rules $\qquad\qquad\qquad$ $\dfrac{d}{dx}[x^n] = nx^{n-1}$

$\qquad\qquad\qquad\qquad\qquad$ $\dfrac{d}{dx}[u^n] = nu^{n-1}\dfrac{du}{dx}$

7. Chain Rule $\qquad\qquad\qquad$ $\dfrac{dy}{dx} = \dfrac{dy}{du} \cdot \dfrac{du}{dx}$

SUMMARIZE (Section 2.5)

1. State the Chain Rule *(page 128)*. For an example of the Chain Rule, see Example 2.

2. State the General Power Rule *(page 130)*. For examples of the General Power Rule, see Examples 3, 4, and 5.

3. Describe a real-life example of how the General Power Rule can be used to analyze the rate of change of a company's revenue per share *(page 133, Example 8)*.

4. Use the Summary of Basic Differentiation Rules to identify the differentiation rules illustrated by (a)–(f) below *(page 134)*.

(a) $\dfrac{d}{dx}[2x] = 2\dfrac{d}{dx}[x]$ $\qquad$ (b) $\dfrac{d}{dx}[x^4] = 4x^3$

(c) $\dfrac{d}{dx}[8] = 0$ $\qquad\qquad$ (d) $\dfrac{d}{dx}[x^2 + x] = \dfrac{d}{dx}[x^2] + \dfrac{d}{dx}[x]$

(e) $\dfrac{d}{dx}[x - x^3] = \dfrac{d}{dx}[x] - \dfrac{d}{dx}[x^3]$

(f) $\dfrac{d}{dx}[x(x + 1)] = (x)\dfrac{d}{dx}[x + 1] + (x + 1)\dfrac{d}{dx}[x]$

The following warm-up exercises involve skills that were covered in a previous course. You will use these skills in the exercise set for this section. For additional help, review Appendix Sections A.3 and A.4.

In Exercises 1–6, rewrite the expression with rational exponents.

1. $\sqrt[5]{(1 - 5x)^2}$

2. $\sqrt[4]{(2x - 1)^3}$

3. $\dfrac{1}{\sqrt{4x^2 + 1}}$

4. $\dfrac{1}{\sqrt[3]{x - 6}}$

5. $\dfrac{\sqrt{x}}{\sqrt[3]{1 - 2x}}$

6. $\dfrac{\sqrt{(3 - 7x)^3}}{2x}$

In Exercises 7–10, factor the expression.

7. $3x^3 - 6x^2 + 5x - 10$

8. $5x\sqrt{x} - x - 5\sqrt{x} + 1$

9. $4(x^2 + 1)^2 - x(x^2 + 1)^3$

10. $-x^5 + 3x^3 + x^2 - 3$

Exercises 2.5

See www.CalcChat.com for worked-out solutions to odd-numbered exercises.

Decomposing Composite Functions In Exercises 1–6, identify the inside function, $u = g(x)$, and the outside function, $y = f(u)$. *See Example 1.*

$y = f(g(x))$	$u = g(x)$	$y = f(u)$
1. $y = (6x - 5)^4$		
2. $y = (x^2 - 2x + 3)^3$		
3. $y = \sqrt{5x - 2}$		
4. $y = \sqrt{1 - x^2}$		
5. $y = \dfrac{1}{3x + 1}$		
6. $y = \dfrac{1}{\sqrt{x^2 - 3}}$		

Using the Chain Rule In Exercises 7–12, find dy/du, du/dx, and dy/dx. *See Example 2.*

7. $y = u^2,\ u = 4x + 7$

8. $y = u^3,\ u = 3x^2 - 2$

9. $y = \sqrt{u},\ u = 3 - x^2$

10. $y = 2\sqrt{u},\ u = 5x + 9$

11. $y = u^{2/3},\ u = 5x^4 - 2x$

12. $y = u^{-1},\ u = x^3 + 2x^2$

Choosing a Differentiation Rule In Exercises 13–20, match the function with the rule that you would use to find the derivative *most efficiently.*

(a) Simple Power Rule

(b) Constant Rule

(c) General Power Rule

(d) Quotient Rule

13. $f(x) = \dfrac{2}{1 - x^3}$

14. $f(x) = \dfrac{2x}{1 - x^3}$

15. $f(x) = \sqrt[3]{8^2}$

16. $f(x) = \sqrt[3]{x^2}$

17. $f(x) = \dfrac{x^2 + 2}{x}$

18. $f(x) = \dfrac{\sqrt{x}}{x^3 + 2x - 5}$

19. $f(x) = \dfrac{2}{x - 2}$

20. $f(x) = \dfrac{5}{x^2 + 1}$

Using the General Power Rule In Exercises 21–36, use the General Power Rule to find the derivative of the function. *See Examples 3 and 5.*

21. $y = (2x - 7)^3$

22. $g(x) = (4 - 2x)^3$

23. $f(x) = (5x - x^2)^{3/2}$

24. $y = (2x^3 + 1)^2$

25. $h(x) = (6x - x^3)^2$

26. $f(x) = (4x - x^2)^3$

27. $f(t) = \sqrt{t + 1}$

28. $g(x) = \sqrt{5 - 3x}$

29. $s(t) = \sqrt{2t^2 + 5t + 2}$

30. $y = \sqrt[3]{3x^3 + 4x}$

31. $y = \sqrt[3]{9x^2 + 4}$

32. $y = 2\sqrt{4 - x^2}$

33. $f(x) = \dfrac{2}{(2 - 9x)^3}$

34. $g(x) = \dfrac{3}{\sqrt{(x^2 + 8x)^3}}$

35. $f(x) = \dfrac{1}{\sqrt{x^2 + 25}}$

36. $y = \dfrac{1}{\sqrt[3]{(4 - x^3)^4}}$

 Finding an Equation of a Tangent Line In Exercises 37–42, find an equation of the tangent line to the graph of f at the point $(2, f(2))$. Then use a graphing utility to graph the function and the tangent line in the same viewing window. *See Example 4.*

37. $f(x) = 2(x^2 - 1)^3$

38. $f(x) = 3(9x - 4)^4$

39. $f(x) = \sqrt{4x^2 - 7}$

40. $f(x) = x\sqrt{x^2 + 5}$

41. $f(x) = \sqrt{x^2 - 2x + 1}$

42. $f(x) = (4 - 3x^2)^{-2/3}$

 Using Technology In Exercises 43–46, use a symbolic differentiation utility to find the derivative of the function. Graph the function and its derivative in the same viewing window. Describe the behavior of the function when the derivative is zero.

43. $f(x) = \dfrac{\sqrt{x} + 1}{x^2 + 1}$

44. $f(x) = \sqrt{\dfrac{2x}{x + 1}}$

45. $f(x) = \sqrt{\dfrac{x + 1}{x}}$

46. $f(x) = \sqrt{x}(2 - x^2)$

Finding Derivatives In Exercises 47–62, find the derivative of the function. State which differentiation rule(s) you used to find the derivative.

47. $y = \dfrac{1}{4 - x^2}$

48. $s(t) = \dfrac{1}{t^2 + 3t - 1}$

49. $y = -\dfrac{4}{(t + 2)^2}$

50. $f(x) = \dfrac{3x}{(x^3 - 4)^2}$

51. $f(x) = (2x - 1)(9 - 3x^2)$

52. $y = x^3(7x + 2)$

53. $y = \dfrac{1}{\sqrt{x + 2}}$

54. $g(x) = \dfrac{3}{\sqrt[3]{x^3 - 1}}$

55. $f(x) = x(3x - 9)^3$

56. $f(x) = x^3(x - 4)^2$

57. $y = x\sqrt{2x + 3}$

58. $y = t\sqrt{t + 1}$

59. $y = t^2\sqrt{t - 2}$

60. $y = \sqrt{x}(x - 2)^2$

61. $y = \left(\dfrac{6 - 5x}{x^2 - 1}\right)^2$

62. $y = \left(\dfrac{4x^2}{3 - x}\right)^3$

Finding an Equation of a Tangent Line In Exercises 63–70, find an equation of the tangent line to the graph of the function at the given point. Then use a graphing utility to graph the function and the tangent line in the same viewing window.

63. $f(t) = \dfrac{36}{(3 - t)^2}; \; (0, 4)$

64. $y = (4x^3 + 3)^2; \; (-1, 1)$

65. $f(x) = \sqrt[5]{3x^3 + 4x}; \; (2, 2)$

66. $s(x) = \dfrac{1}{\sqrt{x^2 - 3x + 4}}; \; \left(3, \tfrac{1}{2}\right)$

67. $f(t) = (t^2 - 9)\sqrt{t + 2}; \; (-1, -8)$

68. $y = \dfrac{2x}{\sqrt{x + 1}}; \; (3, 3)$

69. $f(x) = \dfrac{x + 1}{\sqrt{2x - 3}}; \; (2, 3)$ **70.** $y = \dfrac{x}{\sqrt{25 + x^2}}; \; (0, 0)$

71. Compound Interest You deposit $1000 in an account with an annual interest rate of r (in decimal form) compounded monthly. At the end of 5 years, the balance A is

$$A = 1000\left(1 + \frac{r}{12}\right)^{60}.$$

Find the rates of change of A with respect to r when (a) $r = 0.08$, (b) $r = 0.10$, and (c) $r = 0.12$.

72. Biology The number N of bacteria in a culture after t days is modeled by

$$N = 400\left[1 - \frac{3}{(t^2 + 2)^2}\right].$$

Find the rate of change of N with respect to t when (a) $t = 0$, (b) $t = 1$, (c) $t = 2$, (d) $t = 3$, and (e) $t = 4$. (f) What can you conclude?

73. Depreciation The value V of a machine t years after it is purchased is inversely proportional to the square root of $t + 1$. The initial value of the machine is $10,000.

(a) Write V as a function of t.

(b) Find the rate of depreciation when $t = 1$.

(c) Find the rate of depreciation when $t = 3$.

74. **HOW DO YOU SEE IT?** The cost C (in dollars) of producing x units of a product is

$$C = 60x + 1350.$$

For one week, management determined that the number of units produced x at the end of t hours was

$$x = -1.6t^3 + 19t^2 - 0.5t - 1.$$

The graph shows the cost C in terms of the time t.

Cost of Producing a Product

(a) Which is greater, the rate of change of the cost after 1 hour or the rate of change of the cost after 4 hours?

(b) Explain why the cost function is not increasing at a constant rate during the eight-hour shift.

75. Credit Card Rate The average annual rate r (in percent form) for commercial bank credit cards from 2003 through 2009 can be modeled by

$$r = \sqrt{2.8557t^4 - 72.792t^3 + 676.14t^2 - 2706t + 4096}$$

where t represents the year, with $t = 3$ corresponding to 2003. *(Source: Board of Governors of the Federal Reserve System)*

(a) Find the derivative of this model. Which differentiation rule(s) did you use?

(b) Use a graphing utility to graph the derivative on the interval $3 \le t \le 9$.

(c) Use the *trace* feature to find the year(s) during which the finance rate was changing the most.

(d) Use the *trace* feature to find the year(s) during which the finance rate was changing the least.

2.6 Higher-Order Derivatives

Position of a Ball

In Exercise 35 on page 142, you will use derivatives to find the velocity function and the acceleration function of a ball.

■ Find higher-order derivatives.
■ Find and use a position function to determine the velocity and acceleration of a moving object.

Second, Third, and Higher-Order Derivatives

The "standard" derivative f' is often called the **first derivative** of f. The derivative of f' is the **second derivative** of f and is denoted by f''.

$$\frac{d}{dx}[f'(x)] = f''(x) \qquad \text{Second derivative}$$

The derivative of f'' is the **third derivative** of f and is denoted by f'''.

$$\frac{d}{dx}[f''(x)] = f'''(x) \qquad \text{Third derivative}$$

By continuing this process, you obtain **higher-order derivatives** of f. Higher-order derivatives are denoted as follows.

Notation for Higher-Order Derivatives

1. 1st derivative: $\quad y', \quad f'(x), \quad \dfrac{dy}{dx}, \quad \dfrac{d}{dx}[f(x)], \quad D_x[y]$

2. 2nd derivative: $\quad y'', \quad f''(x), \quad \dfrac{d^2y}{dx^2}, \quad \dfrac{d^2}{dx^2}[f(x)], \quad D_x^2[y]$

3. 3rd derivative: $\quad y''', \quad f'''(x), \quad \dfrac{d^3y}{dx^3}, \quad \dfrac{d^3}{dx^3}[f(x)], \quad D_x^3[y]$

4. 4th derivative: $\quad y^{(4)}, \quad f^{(4)}(x), \quad \dfrac{d^4y}{dx^4}, \quad \dfrac{d^4}{dx^4}[f(x)], \quad D_x^4[y]$

5. nth derivative: $\quad y^{(n)}, \quad f^{(n)}(x), \quad \dfrac{d^ny}{dx^n}, \quad \dfrac{d^n}{dx^n}[f(x)], \quad D_x^n[y]$

Example 1 **Finding Higher-Order Derivatives**

Find the first five derivatives of

$$f(x) = 2x^4 - 3x^2.$$

SOLUTION

$$f(x) = 2x^4 - 3x^2 \qquad \text{Write original function.}$$
$$f'(x) = 8x^3 - 6x \qquad \text{First derivative}$$
$$f''(x) = 24x^2 - 6 \qquad \text{Second derivative}$$
$$f'''(x) = 48x \qquad \text{Third derivative}$$
$$f^{(4)}(x) = 48 \qquad \text{Fourth derivative}$$
$$f^{(5)}(x) = 0 \qquad \text{Fifth derivative}$$

✓ **Checkpoint 1**

Find the first four derivatives of $f(x) = 6x^3 - 2x^2 + 1$.

Example 2 **Finding Higher-Order Derivatives**

Find the value of $g'''(2)$ for the function

$$g(t) = -t^4 + 2t^3 + t + 4.$$

SOLUTION   Begin by differentiating three times.

$$g'(t) = -4t^3 + 6t^2 + 1 \qquad \text{First derivative}$$
$$g''(t) = -12t^2 + 12t \qquad \text{Second derivative}$$
$$g'''(t) = -24t + 12 \qquad \text{Third derivative}$$

Then, evaluate the third derivative of g at $t = 2$.

$$g'''(2) = -24(2) + 12$$
$$= -36 \qquad \text{Value of third derivative}$$

✓**Checkpoint 2**

Find the value of $g'''(1)$ for $g(x) = x^4 - x^3 + 2x$. ■

Examples 1 and 2 show how to find higher-order derivatives of *polynomial* functions. Note that with each successive differentiation, the degree of the polynomial drops by one. Eventually, higher-order derivatives of polynomial functions degenerate to a constant function. Specifically, the nth-order derivative of an nth-degree polynomial function

$$f(x) = a_n x^n + a_{n-1} x^{n-1} + \cdots + a_1 x + a_0$$

is the constant function

$$f^{(n)}(x) = n! a_n$$

where $n! = 1 \cdot 2 \cdot 3 \cdots n$. Each derivative of order higher than n is the zero function.

TECH TUTOR

Higher-order derivatives of nonpolynomial functions can be difficult to find by hand. If you have access to a symbolic differentiation utility, try using it to find higher-order derivatives.

Example 3 **Finding Higher-Order Derivatives**

Find the first four derivatives of $y = x^{-1}$.

SOLUTION

$$y = x^{-1} = \frac{1}{x} \qquad \text{Write original function.}$$

$$y' = (-1)x^{-2} = -\frac{1}{x^2} \qquad \text{First derivative}$$

$$y'' = (-1)(-2)x^{-3} = \frac{2}{x^3} \qquad \text{Second derivative}$$

$$y''' = (-1)(-2)(-3)x^{-4} = -\frac{6}{x^4} \qquad \text{Third derivative}$$

$$y^{(4)} = (-1)(-2)(-3)(-4)x^{-5} = \frac{24}{x^5} \qquad \text{Fourth derivative}$$

✓**Checkpoint 3**

Find the fourth derivative of

$$y = \frac{1}{x^2}.$$

Acceleration

In Section 2.3, you saw that the velocity of a free-falling object (neglecting air resistance) is given by the derivative of its position function. In other words, the rate of change of the position with respect to time is defined to be the velocity. In a similar way, the rate of change of the velocity with respect to time is defined to be the **acceleration** of the object.

$$s = f(t)$$ Position function

$$\frac{ds}{dt} = f'(t)$$ Velocity function

$$\frac{d^2s}{dt^2} = f''(t)$$ Acceleration function

To find the position, velocity, or acceleration at a particular time t, substitute the given value of t into the appropriate function, as illustrated in Example 4.

 Example 4   **Finding Acceleration**

A ball is thrown upward from the top of a 160-foot cliff, as shown in Figure 2.32. The initial velocity of the ball is 48 feet per second, which implies that the position function is

$$s = -16t^2 + 48t + 160$$

where the time t is measured in seconds. Find the height, velocity, and acceleration of the ball at $t = 3$.

SOLUTION   Begin by differentiating to find the velocity and acceleration functions.

FIGURE 2.32

$$s = -16t^2 + 48t + 160$$ Position function

$$\frac{ds}{dt} = -32t + 48$$ Velocity function

$$\frac{d^2s}{dt^2} = -32$$ Acceleration function

To find the height, velocity, and acceleration at $t = 3$, substitute $t = 3$ into each of the functions above.

Height $= -16(3)^2 + 48(3) + 160 = 160$ feet

Velocity $= -32(3) + 48 = -48$ feet per second

Acceleration $= -32$ feet per second squared

✓ **Checkpoint 4**

A ball is thrown upward from the top of an 80-foot cliff with an initial velocity of 64 feet per second, which implies that the position function is

$$s = -16t^2 + 64t + 80$$

where the time t is measured in seconds. Find the height, velocity, and acceleration of the ball at $t = 2$.

The acceleration due to gravity on the surface of the moon is only about one-sixth that exerted on the surface of Earth.

In Example 4, notice that the acceleration of the ball is -32 feet per second squared at any time t. This constant acceleration is due to the gravitational force of Earth and is called the **acceleration due to gravity.** Note that the negative value indicates that the ball is being pulled *down*—toward Earth.

Although the acceleration exerted on a falling object is relatively constant near Earth's surface, it varies greatly throughout our solar system. Large planets exert a much greater gravitational pull than do small planets or moons. The next example describes the motion of a free-falling object on the moon.

Example 5   Finding Acceleration on the Moon

An astronaut standing on the surface of the moon throws a rock upward. The height s (in feet) of the rock is given by

$$s = -\frac{27}{10}t^2 + 27t + 6$$

where t is measured in seconds. How does the acceleration due to gravity on the moon compare with that on Earth?

SOLUTION

$$s = -\frac{27}{10}t^2 + 27t + 6 \qquad \text{Position function}$$

$$\frac{ds}{dt} = -\frac{27}{5}t + 27 \qquad \text{Velocity function}$$

$$\frac{d^2s}{dt^2} = -\frac{27}{5} \qquad \text{Acceleration function}$$

So, the acceleration at any time is

$$-\frac{27}{5} = -5.4 \text{ feet per second squared}$$

—about one-sixth of the acceleration due to gravity on Earth. _____

✓ Checkpoint 5

The position function on Earth, where s is measured in meters, t is measured in seconds, v_0 is the initial velocity in meters per second, and h_0 is the initial height in meters, is

$$s = -4.9t^2 + v_0 t + h_0.$$

An object is thrown upward with an initial velocity of 2.2 meters per second from an initial height of 3.6 meters. What is the acceleration due to gravity on Earth in meters per second squared?

The position function described in Example 5 neglects air resistance, which is appropriate because the moon has no atmosphere—and *no air resistance*. This means that the position function for any free-falling object on the moon is given by

$$s = -\frac{27}{10}t^2 + v_0 t + h_0$$

where s is the height (in feet), t is the time (in seconds), v_0 is the initial velocity (in feet per second), and h_0 is the initial height (in feet). For instance, the rock in Example 5 was thrown upward with an initial velocity of 27 feet per second and had an initial height of 6 feet. This position function is valid for all objects, whether heavy ones such as hammers or light ones such as feathers.

Example 6 **Finding Velocity and Acceleration**

The velocity v (in feet per second) of a certain automobile starting from rest is

$$v = \frac{80t}{t + 5} \qquad \text{Velocity function}$$

where t is the time (in seconds). The positions of the automobile at 10-second intervals are shown in Figure 2.33. Find the velocity and acceleration of the automobile at 10-second intervals from $t = 0$ to $t = 60$.

$t = 0$
$t = 10$
$t = 20$
$t = 30$
$t = 40$
$t = 50$
$t = 60$

FIGURE 2.33

SOLUTION To find the acceleration function, differentiate the velocity function.

$$\frac{dv}{dt} = \frac{(t + 5)(80) - (80t)(1)}{(t + 5)^2} \qquad \text{Apply Quotient Rule.}$$

$$= \frac{400}{(t + 5)^2} \qquad \text{Acceleration function}$$

t (seconds)	0	10	20	30	40	50	60
v (ft/sec)	0	53.3	64.0	68.6	71.1	72.7	73.8
$\dfrac{dv}{dt}$ (ft/sec²)	16	1.78	0.64	0.33	0.20	0.13	0.09

In the table, note that the acceleration approaches zero as the velocity levels off. This observation should agree with your experience—when riding in an accelerating automobile, you do not feel the velocity, but you do feel the acceleration. In other words, you feel changes in velocity.

✓**Checkpoint 6**

Use a graphing utility to graph the velocity function and acceleration function in Example 6 in the same viewing window. Compare the graphs with the table in Example 6. As the velocity levels off, what does the acceleration approach?

SUMMARIZE (Section 2.6)

1. State the meaning of each derivative listed below (*page 137*). For examples of higher-order derivatives, see Examples 1, 2, and 3.

   (a) y'' (b) $f^{(4)}(x)$ (c) $\dfrac{d^3y}{dx^3}$

2. Describe a real-life example of how higher-order derivatives can be used to analyze the velocity and acceleration of an object (*page 139, Examples 4, 5, and 6*).

In Exercises 1–4, solve the equation.

1. $-16t^2 + 24t = 0$

2. $-16t^2 + 80t + 224 = 0$

3. $-16t^2 + 128t + 320 = 0$

4. $-16t^2 + 9t + 1440 = 0$

In Exercises 5–8, find dy/dx.

5. $y = x^2(2x + 7)$ **6.** $y = (x^2 + 3x)(2x^2 - 5)$ **7.** $y = \dfrac{x^2}{2x + 7}$ **8.** $y = \dfrac{x^2 + 3x}{2x^2 - 5}$

In Exercises 9 and 10, find the domain and range of f.

9. $f(x) = x^2 - 4$

10. $f(x) = \sqrt{x - 7}$

Exercises 2.6

Finding Higher-Order Derivatives In Exercises 1–12, find the second derivative of the function. *See Examples 1 and 3.*

1. $f(x) = 9 - 2x$

2. $f(x) = 4x + 15$

3. $f(x) = x^2 + 7x - 4$

4. $f(x) = 3x^2 + 4x$

5. $g(t) = \frac{1}{3}t^3 - 4t^2 + 2t$

6. $f(x) = -2x^5 + 3x^4 + 8x$

7. $f(t) = \dfrac{3}{4t^2}$

8. $g(t) = \dfrac{8}{t}$

9. $f(x) = 3(2 - x^2)^3$

10. $y = 4(x^2 + 5x)^3$

11. $f(x) = \dfrac{x + 1}{x - 1}$

12. $g(t) = -\dfrac{4}{(t + 2)^2}$

Finding Higher-Order Derivatives In Exercises 13–18, find the third derivative of the function. *See Examples 1 and 3.*

13. $f(x) = x^5 - 3x^4$

14. $f(x) = x^4 - 2x^3$

15. $f(x) = 5x(x + 4)^3$

16. $f(x) = (x^3 - 6)^4$

17. $f(x) = \dfrac{3}{16x^2}$

18. $f(x) = -\dfrac{2}{x}$

Finding Higher-Order Derivatives In Exercises 19–24, find the given value. *See Example 2.*

Function	Value
19. $g(t) = 5t^4 + 10t^2 + 3$	$g''(2)$
20. $f(x) = 9 - x^2$	$f''\left(-\sqrt{5}\right)$
21. $f(x) = \sqrt{4 - x}$	$f'''(-5)$
22. $f(t) = \sqrt{2t + 3}$	$f'''\left(\frac{1}{2}\right)$
23. $f(x) = (x^3 - 2x)^3$	$f''(1)$
24. $g(x) = (x^2 + 3x)^4$	$g''(-1)$

Finding Higher-Order Derivatives In Exercises 25–30, find the higher-order derivative. *See Examples 1 and 3.*

Given	Derivative
25. $f'(x) = 2x^2$	$f''(x)$
26. $f''(x) = 20x^3 - 36x^2$	$f'''(x)$
27. $f'''(x) = 2\sqrt{x - 1}$	$f^{(4)}(x)$
28. $f'''(x) = 4x^{-4}$	$f^{(5)}(x)$
29. $f^{(4)}(x) = (x^2 + 1)^2$	$f^{(6)}(x)$
30. $f''(x) = 2x^2 + 7x - 12$	$f^{(5)}(x)$

Using Derivatives In Exercises 31–34, find the second derivative and solve the equation $f''(x) = 0$.

31. $f(x) = x^3 - 9x^2 + 27x - 27$

32. $f(x) = (x + 2)(x - 2)(x + 3)(x - 3)$

33. $f(x) = x\sqrt{x^2 - 1}$

34. $f(x) = \dfrac{x}{x^2 + 3}$

35. Velocity and Acceleration A ball is propelled straight upward from ground level with an initial velocity of 144 feet per second.

(a) Write the position, velocity, and acceleration functions of the ball.

(b) Find the height, velocity, and acceleration at $t = 3$.

(c) When is the ball at its highest point? How high is this point?

(d) How fast is the ball traveling when it hits the ground? How is this speed related to the initial velocity?

36. Velocity and Acceleration A brick becomes dislodged from the top of the Empire State Building (at a height of 1250 feet) and falls to the sidewalk below.

(a) Write the position, velocity, and acceleration functions of the brick.

(b) How long does it take the brick to hit the sidewalk?

(c) How fast is the brick traveling when it hits the sidewalk?

37. Velocity and Acceleration The velocity (in feet per second) of an automobile starting from rest is modeled by $ds/dt = 90t/(t + 10)$. Create a table showing the velocity and acceleration at 10-second intervals during the first minute of travel. What can you conclude?

38. Stopping Distance A car is traveling at a rate of 66 feet per second (45 miles per hour) when the brakes are applied. The position function for the car is given by $s = -8.25t^2 + 66t$, where s is measured in feet and t is measured in seconds. Use this function to complete the table showing the position, velocity, and acceleration for each given value of t. What can you conclude?

t	0	1	2	3	4
s					
$\dfrac{ds}{dt}$					
$\dfrac{d^2s}{dt^2}$					

39. Derivatives of Polynomial Functions Consider the function $f(x) = x^2 - 6x + 6$.

(a) Use a graphing utility to graph f, f', and f'' in the same viewing window.

(b) What is the relationship among the degree of f and the degrees of its successive derivatives?

(c) Repeat parts (a) and (b) for $f(x) = 3x^3 - 9x$.

(d) In general, what is the relationship among the degree of a polynomial function and the degrees of its successive derivatives?

40. HOW DO YOU SEE IT? The graph shows the position, velocity, and acceleration functions of a particle. Identify each function. Explain your reasoning.

41. Modeling Data The table shows the revenues y (in millions of dollars) for eBay from 2004 to 2009, where t is the year, with $t = 4$ corresponding to 2004. *(Source: eBay Inc.)*

t	4	5	6	7	8	9
y	3271	4552	5970	7672	8541	8727

(a) Use a graphing utility to find a cubic model for the revenue $y(t)$ of eBay.

(b) Find the first and second derivatives of the function.

(c) Show that the revenue of eBay was increasing from 2005 to 2008.

(d) Find the year when the revenue was increasing at the greatest rate by solving $y''(t) = 0$.

42. Finding a Pattern Develop a general rule for

$$[x f(x)]^{(n)}$$

where f is a differentiable function of x.

True or False? In Exercises 43 and 44, determine whether the statement is true or false. If it is false, explain why or give an example that shows it is false.

43. If $y = f(x)g(x)$, then $y' = f'(x)g'(x)$.

44. If $f'(c)$ and $g'(c)$ are zero and $h(x) = f(x)g(x)$, then $h'(c) = 0$.

45. Project: Median Prices of U.S. Homes For a project analyzing the median prices of new privately owned homes in the United States from 2000 to 2009, visit this text's website at *www.cengagebrain.com*. *(Data Source: U.S. Census Bureau)*

2.7 Implicit Differentiation

Demand of a Product

■ Find derivatives explicitly.
■ Find derivatives implicitly.
■ Use derivatives to answer questions about real-life situations.

Explicit and Implicit Functions

So far in this text, most functions involving two variables have been expressed in the **explicit form**

$$y = f(x). \qquad \text{Explicit form}$$

That is, one of the two variables has been explicitly given in terms of the other. For example, in the equation

$$y = 3x - 5$$

the variable y is explicitly written as a function of x. Some functions, however, are not given explicitly and are only implied by a given equation, as shown in Example 1.

In Exercise 43 on page 150, you will use implicit differentiation to find the rate of change for a demand function.

Example 1   Finding a Derivative Explicitly

Find dy/dx for the equation

$$xy = 1.$$

SOLUTION   In this equation, y is **implicitly** defined as a function of x. One way to find dy/dx is first to solve the equation for y, then differentiate as usual.

$xy = 1$	Write original equation.
$y = \dfrac{1}{x}$	Solve for y.
$= x^{-1}$	Rewrite.
$\dfrac{dy}{dx} = -x^{-2}$	Differentiate with respect to x.
$= -\dfrac{1}{x^2}$	Simplify.

✓ **Checkpoint 1**

Find dy/dx for the equation

$$x^2 y = 1.$$

The procedure shown in Example 1 works well whenever you can easily write the given function explicitly. You cannot, however, use this procedure when you are unable to solve for y as a function of x. For instance, how would you find dy/dx for the equations

$$x^2 - 2y^3 + 4y = 2$$

and

$$x^2 + 2xy - y^3 = 5$$

where it is very difficult to express y as a function of x explicitly? To differentiate such equations, you can use a procedure called **implicit differentiation.**

Implicit Differentiation

To understand how to find dy/dx implicitly, you must realize that the differentiation is taking place *with respect to x*. This means that when you differentiate terms involving x alone, you can differentiate as usual. *But* when you differentiate terms involving y, you must apply the Chain Rule because you are assuming that y is defined implicitly as a differentiable function of x. Study the next example carefully. Note in particular how the Chain Rule is used to introduce the dy/dx factors in Examples 2(b) and 2(d).

Example 2   Applying the Chain Rule

Differentiate each expression with respect to x.

a. $3x^2$ **b.** $2y^3$

c. $x + 3y$ **d.** xy^2

SOLUTION

a. The only variable in this expression is x. So, to differentiate with respect to x, you can use the Simple Power Rule and the Constant Multiple Rule to obtain

$$\frac{d}{dx}[3x^2] = 6x.$$

b. This case is different. The variable in the expression is y, and yet you are asked to differentiate with respect to x. To do this, assume that y is a differentiable function of x and use the Chain Rule.

$$\frac{d}{dx}[2y^3] = \overset{cu^n}{} \quad \overset{c}{2} \quad \overset{n}{(3)} \quad \overset{u^{n-1}}{y^2} \quad \overset{u'}{\frac{dy}{dx}} \qquad \text{Chain Rule}$$

$$= 6y^2\frac{dy}{dx}$$

c. This expression involves both x and y. By the Sum Rule and the Constant Multiple Rule, you can write

$$\frac{d}{dx}[x + 3y] = 1 + 3\frac{dy}{dx}.$$

d. By the Product Rule and the Chain Rule, you can write

$$\frac{d}{dx}[xy^2] = x\frac{d}{dx}[y^2] + y^2\frac{d}{dx}[x] \qquad \text{Product Rule}$$

$$= x\left(2y\frac{dy}{dx}\right) + y^2(1) \qquad \text{Chain Rule}$$

$$= 2xy\frac{dy}{dx} + y^2.$$

✓ **Checkpoint 2**

Differentiate each expression with respect to x.

a. $4x^3$

b. $3y^2$

c. $x + 5y$

d. xy^3

Guidelines for Implicit Differentiation

Consider an equation involving x and y in which y is a differentiable function of x. You can use the steps below to find dy/dx.

1. Differentiate both sides of the equation *with respect to x*.

2. Write the result so that all terms involving dy/dx are on the left side of the equation and all other terms are on the right side of the equation.

3. Factor dy/dx out of the terms on the left side of the equation.

4. Solve for dy/dx by dividing both sides of the equation by the left-hand factor that does not contain dy/dx.

In Example 3, note that implicit differentiation can produce an expression for dy/dx that contains both x and y.

Example 3 Using Implicit Differentiation

Find dy/dx for the equation $y^3 + y^2 - 5y - x^2 = -4$.

SOLUTION

1. Differentiate both sides of the equation with respect to x.

$$\frac{d}{dx}[y^3 + y^2 - 5y - x^2] = \frac{d}{dx}[-4]$$

$$\frac{d}{dx}[y^3] + \frac{d}{dx}[y^2] - \frac{d}{dx}[5y] - \frac{d}{dx}[x^2] = \frac{d}{dx}[-4]$$

$$3y^2\frac{dy}{dx} + 2y\frac{dy}{dx} - 5\frac{dy}{dx} - 2x = 0$$

2. Collect the dy/dx terms on the left side of the equation and move all other terms to the right side of the equation.

$$3y^2\frac{dy}{dx} + 2y\frac{dy}{dx} - 5\frac{dy}{dx} = 2x$$

3. Factor dy/dx out of the left side of the equation.

$$\frac{dy}{dx}(3y^2 + 2y - 5) = 2x$$

4. Solve for dy/dx by dividing by $(3y^2 + 2y - 5)$.

$$\frac{dy}{dx} = \frac{2x}{3y^2 + 2y - 5}$$

✓ Checkpoint 3

Find dy/dx for the equation $y^2 + x^2 - 2y - 4x = 4$.

To see how you can use an implicit derivative, consider the graph shown in Figure 2.34. The derivative found in Example 3 gives a formula for the slope of the tangent line at a point on this graph. For instance, the slope at the point $(1, -3)$ is

$$\frac{dy}{dx} = \frac{2(1)}{3(-3)^2 + 2(-3) - 5} = \frac{1}{8}.$$

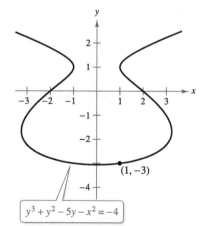

$y^3 + y^2 - 5y - x^2 = -4$

FIGURE 2.34

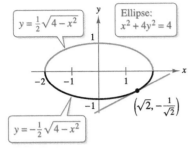

$y = \frac{1}{2}\sqrt{4 - x^2}$

Ellipse: $x^2 + 4y^2 = 4$

$y = -\frac{1}{2}\sqrt{4 - x^2}$

$\left(\sqrt{2}, -\frac{1}{\sqrt{2}}\right)$

Slope of tangent line is $\frac{1}{2}$.

FIGURE 2.35

Example 4 Finding the Slope of a Graph Implicitly

Find the slope of the tangent line to the ellipse given by $x^2 + 4y^2 = 4$ at the point $\left(\sqrt{2}, -1/\sqrt{2}\right)$, as shown in Figure 2.35.

SOLUTION

$$x^2 + 4y^2 = 4 \qquad \text{Write original equation.}$$

$$\frac{d}{dx}[x^2 + 4y^2] = \frac{d}{dx}[4] \qquad \text{Differentiate with respect to } x.$$

$$2x + 8y\frac{dy}{dx} = 0 \qquad \text{Implicit differentiation}$$

$$8y\frac{dy}{dx} = -2x \qquad \text{Subtract } 2x \text{ from each side.}$$

$$\frac{dy}{dx} = \frac{-2x}{8y} \qquad \text{Divide each side by } 8y.$$

$$\frac{dy}{dx} = -\frac{x}{4y} \qquad \text{Simplify.}$$

To find the slope at the given point, substitute $x = \sqrt{2}$ and $y = -1/\sqrt{2}$ into the derivative, as shown below.

$$\frac{dy}{dx} = -\frac{\sqrt{2}}{4\left(-1/\sqrt{2}\right)}$$

$$= \frac{1}{2}$$

> **STUDY TIP**
>
> To see the benefit of implicit differentiation, try reworking Example 4 using the explicit function
>
> $$y = -\frac{1}{2}\sqrt{4 - x^2}.$$
>
> The graph of this function is the lower half of the ellipse.

✓ **Checkpoint 4**

Find the slope of the tangent line to the circle $x^2 + y^2 = 25$ at the point $(3, -4)$. ▨

Example 5 Finding the Slope of a Graph Implicitly

Find the slope of the graph of $2x^2 - y^2 = 1$ at the point $(1, 1)$.

SOLUTION   Begin by finding dy/dx implicitly.

$$2x^2 - y^2 = 1 \qquad \text{Write original equation.}$$

$$4x - 2y\frac{dy}{dx} = 0 \qquad \text{Differentiate with respect to } x.$$

$$-2y\frac{dy}{dx} = -4x \qquad \text{Subtract } 4x \text{ from each side.}$$

$$\frac{dy}{dx} = \frac{2x}{y} \qquad \text{Divide each side by } -2y.$$

At the point $(1, 1)$, the slope of the graph is

$$\frac{dy}{dx} = \frac{2(1)}{1}$$

$$= 2$$

as shown in Figure 2.36. The graph is called a **hyperbola.**

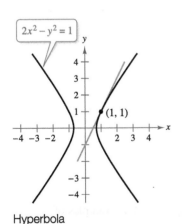

$2x^2 - y^2 = 1$

$(1, 1)$

Hyperbola

FIGURE 2.36

✓ **Checkpoint 5**

Find the slope of the graph of $x^2 - 9y^2 = 16$ at the point $(5, 1)$. ▨

Demand Function

FIGURE 2.37

Application

Example 6 **Using a Demand Function**

The demand function for a product is modeled by

$$p = \frac{3}{0.000001x^3 + 0.01x + 1}$$

where p is measured in dollars and x is measured in thousands of units, as shown in Figure 2.37. Find the rate of change of the demand x with respect to the price p when $x = 100$.

SOLUTION   To simplify the differentiation, begin by rewriting the function. Then, differentiate *with respect to p.*

$$p = \frac{3}{0.000001x^3 + 0.01x + 1}$$

$$0.000001x^3 + 0.01x + 1 = \frac{3}{p}$$

$$0.000003x^2\frac{dx}{dp} + 0.01\frac{dx}{dp} = -\frac{3}{p^2}$$

$$(0.000003x^2 + 0.01)\frac{dx}{dp} = -\frac{3}{p^2}$$

$$\frac{dx}{dp} = -\frac{3}{p^2(0.000003x^2 + 0.01)}$$

When $x = 100$, the price is

$$p = \frac{3}{0.000001(100)^3 + 0.01(100) + 1} = \$1.$$

So, when $x = 100$ and $p = 1$, the rate of change of the demand with respect to the price is

$$\frac{dx}{dp} = -\frac{3}{(1)^2[0.000003(100)^2 + 0.01]} = -75.$$

This means that when $x = 100$, the demand is dropping at the rate of 75 thousand units for each dollar increase in price.

✓**Checkpoint 6**

The demand function for a product is given by

$$p = \frac{2}{0.001x^2 + x + 1}.$$

Find dx/dp implicitly.

SUMMARIZE   (Section 2.7)

1. State the guidelines for implicit differentiation *(page 146)*. For examples of implicit differentiation, see Examples 2, 3, 4, and 5.

2. Describe a real-life example of how implicit differentiation can be used to analyze the rate of change of a product's demand *(page 148, Example 6)*.

SKILLS WARM UP 2.7   The following warm-up exercises involve skills that were covered in a previous course. You will use these skills in the exercise set for this section. For additional help, review Appendix Section A.3.

In Exercises 1–6, solve the equation for y.

1. $x - \dfrac{y}{x} = 2$

2. $\dfrac{4}{x - 3} = \dfrac{1}{y}$

3. $xy - x + 6y = 6$

4. $12 + 3y = 4x^2 + x^2 y$

5. $x^2 + y^2 = 5$

6. $x = \pm\sqrt{6 - y^2}$

In Exercises 7–9, evaluate the expression at the given point.

7. $\dfrac{3x^2 - 4}{3y^2}$, $(2, 1)$

8. $\dfrac{x^2 - 2}{1 - y}$, $(0, -3)$

9. $\dfrac{5x}{3y^2 - 12y + 5}$, $(-1, 2)$

Exercises 2.7

See www.CalcChat.com for worked-out solutions to odd-numbered exercises.

Finding Derivatives   In Exercises 1–12, find dy/dx. See Examples 1 and 3.

1. $xy = 4$

2. $3x^2 - y = 8x$

3. $y^2 = 1 - x^2$, $0 \le x \le 1$

4. $y^3 = 4x^3 + 2x$

5. $x^2 y^2 - 2x = 3$

6. $xy^2 + 4xy = 10$

7. $4y^2 - xy = 2$

8. $2xy^3 - x^2 y = 2$

9. $\dfrac{xy - y^2}{y - x} = 1$

10. $\dfrac{2x + y}{x - 5y} = 1$

11. $\dfrac{2y - x}{y^2 - 3} = 5$

12. $\dfrac{4y^2}{y^2 - 9} = x^2$

Finding the Slope of a Graph Implicitly   In Exercises 13–26, find the slope of the graph of the function at the given point. See Examples 4 and 5.

Equation	Point
13. $x^2 + y^2 = 16$	$(0, 4)$
14. $x^2 - y^2 = 25$	$(5, 0)$
15. $y + xy = 4$	$(-5, -1)$
16. $16x^2 + 25y^2 = 400$	$(5, 4)$
17. $x^3 - xy + y^2 = 4$	$(0, -2)$
18. $x^2 y + y^2 x = -2$	$(2, -1)$
19. $x^3 y^3 - y = x$	$(0, 0)$
20. $x^3 + y^3 = 6xy$	$\left(\frac{4}{3}, \frac{8}{3}\right)$
21. $x^{1/2} + y^{1/2} = 9$	$(16, 25)$
22. $x^{2/3} + y^{2/3} = 5$	$(8, 1)$
23. $\sqrt{xy} = x - 2y$	$(4, 1)$
24. $(x + y)^3 = x^3 + y^3$	$(-1, 1)$

Equation	Point
25. $y^2(x^2 + y^2) = 2x^2$	$(1, 1)$
26. $(x^2 + y^2)^2 = 8x^2 y$	$(2, 2)$

Finding the Slope of a Graph Implicitly   In Exercises 27–32, find the slope of the graph at the given point. See Examples 4 and 5.

27. $3x^2 - 2y + 5 = 0$

28. $4x^2 + 2y - 1 = 0$

29. $x^2 + y^2 = 4$

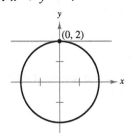

30. $4x^2 + 9y^2 = 36$

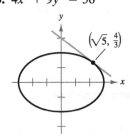

31. $(4 - x)y^2 = x^3$

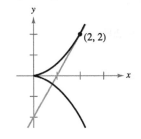

32. $x^2 - y^3 = 0$

Finding Derivatives Implicitly and Explicitly In Exercises 33 and 34, find dy/dx implicitly and explicitly (the explicit functions are shown on the graph) and show that the results are equivalent. Use the graph to estimate the slope of the tangent line at the labeled point. Then verify your result analytically by evaluating dy/dx at the point.

33. $x - y^2 - 1 = 0$ **34.** $4y^2 - x^2 = 7$

 Finding an Equation of a Tangent Line In Exercises 35–42, find equations of the tangent lines to the graph at the given points. Use a graphing utility to graph the equation and the tangent lines in the same viewing window.

Equation	*Points*
35. $x^2 + y^2 = 100$	$(8, 6)$ and $(-6, 8)$
36. $x^2 + y^2 = 9$	$(0, 3)$ and $\left(2, \sqrt{5}\right)$
37. $y^2 = 5x^3$	$\left(1, \sqrt{5}\right)$ and $\left(1, -\sqrt{5}\right)$
38. $4xy + x^2 = 5$	$(1, 1)$ and $(5, -1)$
39. $x^3 + y^3 = 8$	$(0, 2)$ and $(2, 0)$
40. $x + y^3 = 6xy^3 - 1$	$(-1, 0)$ and $(0, -1)$
41. $x^2y - 8 = -4y$	$(-2, 1)$ and $\left(6, \frac{1}{5}\right)$
42. $y^2 = \dfrac{x^3}{4 - x}$	$(2, 2)$ and $(2, -2)$

Demand In Exercises 43–46, find the rate of change of x with respect to p. *See Example 6.*

43. $p = \dfrac{2}{0.00001x^3 + 0.1x}, \quad x \ge 0$

44. $p = \dfrac{4}{0.000001x^2 + 0.05x + 1}, \quad x \ge 0$

45. $p = \sqrt{\dfrac{200 - x}{2x}}, \quad 0 < x \le 200$

46. $p = \sqrt{\dfrac{500 - x}{2x}}, \quad 0 < x \le 500$

47. Production Let x represent the units of labor and y the capital invested in a manufacturing process. When 135,540 units are produced, the relationship between labor and capital can be modeled by $100x^{0.75}y^{0.25} = 135,540$.

(a) Find the rate of change of y with respect to x when $x = 1500$ and $y = 1000$.

(b) The model used in this problem is called the *Cobb-Douglas production function*. Graph the model on a graphing utility and describe the relationship between labor and capital.

 48. **HOW DO YOU SEE IT?**   The graph shows the demand function for a product.

(a) What happens to the demand as the price increases?

(b) Over what interval is the rate of change of the demand with respect to the price decreasing?

49. Health: U.S. HIV/AIDS Epidemic The numbers (in thousands) of cases y of HIV/AIDS reported in the years 2004 through 2008 can be modeled by

$$y^2 - 1952.4 = 13.0345t^3 - 168.969t^2 + 465.66t$$

where t represents the year, with $t = 4$ corresponding to 2004. *(Source: U.S. Centers for Disease Control and Prevention)*

(a) Use a graphing utility to graph the model and describe the results.

(b) Use the graph to estimate the year during which the number of reported cases was decreasing at the greatest rate.

(c) Complete the table to estimate the year during which the number of reported cases was decreasing at the greatest rate. Compare this estimate with your answer in part (b).

t	4	5	6	7	8
y					
y'					

2.8 Related Rates

■ Examine related variables.
■ Solve related-rate problems.

Related Variables

In this section, you will study problems involving variables that are changing with respect to time. If two or more such variables are related to each other, then their rates of change with respect to time are also related.

For instance, suppose that x and y are related by the equation

$$y = 2x.$$

If both variables are changing with respect to time, then their rates of change will also be related.

In this simple example, you can see that because y always has twice the value of x, it follows that the rate of change of y with respect to time is always twice the rate of change of x with respect to time.

In Exercise 25 on page 157, you will use related rates to find the rate of change of the sales for a product.

Example 1   Examining Two Rates That Are Related

The variables x and y are differentiable functions of t and are related by the equation

$$y = x^2 + 3.$$

When $x = 1$, $dx/dt = 2$. Find dy/dt when $x = 1$.

SOLUTION   Use the Chain Rule to differentiate both sides of the equation with respect to t.

$$y = x^2 + 3 \qquad \text{Write original equation.}$$

$$\frac{d}{dt}[y] = \frac{d}{dt}[x^2 + 3] \qquad \text{Differentiate with respect to } t.$$

$$\frac{dy}{dt} = 2x\frac{dx}{dt} \qquad \text{Apply Chain Rule.}$$

When $x = 1$ and $dx/dt = 2$, you have

$$\frac{dy}{dt} = 2(1)(2)$$

$$= 4.$$

✓ Checkpoint 1

The variables x and y are differentiable functions of t and are related by the equation

$$y = x^3 + 2.$$

When $x = 1$, $dx/dt = 3$. Find dy/dt when $x = 1$.

Solving Related-Rate Problems

In Example 1, you were *given* the mathematical model.

$$\text{Given equation: } y = x^2 + 3$$

$$\text{Given rate: } \frac{dx}{dt} = 2 \text{ at } x = 1$$

$$\text{Find: } \frac{dy}{dt} \text{ at } x = 1$$

In the next example, you must *create* a mathematical model from a verbal description.

 Example 2   **Changing Area**

A pebble is dropped into a calm pool of water, causing ripples in the form of concentric circles, as shown in the photo. The radius r of the outer ripple is increasing at a constant rate of 1 foot per second. When the radius is 4 feet, at what rate is the total area A of the disturbed water changing?

SOLUTION   The variables r and A are related by the equation for the area of a circle, $A = \pi r^2$. To solve this problem, use the fact that the rate of change of the radius is given by dr/dt.

$$\text{Equation: } A = \pi r^2$$

$$\text{Given rate: } \frac{dr}{dt} = 1 \text{ at } r = 4$$

$$\text{Find: } \frac{dA}{dt} \text{ at } r = 4$$

Total area increases as the outer radius increases.

Using this model, you can proceed as in Example 1.

$A = \pi r^2$	Write original equation.
$\dfrac{d}{dt}[A] = \dfrac{d}{dt}[\pi r^2]$	Differentiate with respect to t.
$\dfrac{dA}{dt} = 2\pi r \dfrac{dr}{dt}$	Apply Chain Rule.

When $r = 4$ and $dr/dt = 1$, you have

$$\frac{dA}{dt} = 2\pi(4)(1) = 8\pi \qquad \text{Substitute 4 for } r \text{ and 1 for } dr/dt.$$

When the radius is 4 feet, the area is changing at a rate of 8π square feet per second.

✓ **Checkpoint 2**

As in Example 2, a pebble is dropped into the pool, but this time the radius r of the outer ripple is increasing at a rate of 2 feet per second. At what rate is the total area changing when the radius is 3 feet?

In Example 2, note that the radius changes at a *constant* rate ($dr/dt = 1$ for all t), but the area changes at a *nonconstant* rate.

When $r = 1$ ft	When $r = 2$ ft	When $r = 3$ ft	When $r = 4$ ft
$\dfrac{dA}{dt} = 2\pi$ ft²/sec	$\dfrac{dA}{dt} = 4\pi$ ft²/sec	$\dfrac{dA}{dt} = 6\pi$ ft²/sec	$\dfrac{dA}{dt} = 8\pi$ ft²/sec

The solution shown in Example 2 illustrates the steps for solving a related-rate problem.

Guidelines for Solving a Related-Rate Problem

1. Identify all *given* quantities and all quantities *to be determined*. If possible, make a sketch and label the quantities.

2. Write an equation that relates all variables whose rates of change are either given or to be determined.

3. Use the Chain Rule to differentiate both sides of the equation *with respect to time*.

4. *After* completing Step 3, substitute into the resulting equation all known values for the variables and their rates of change. Then solve for the required rate of change.

STUDY TIP

Be sure you notice the order of Steps 3 and 4 in the guidelines. Do not substitute the known values for the variables until after you have differentiated.

In Step 2 of the guidelines, note that you must write an equation that relates the given variables. To help you with this step, reference tables that summarize many common formulas are included in the appendices. For instance, the volume of a sphere of radius r is given by the formula

$$V = \frac{4}{3}\pi r^3$$

as listed in Appendix D.

The table below lists examples of the mathematical models for some common rates of change that can be used in the first step of the solution of a related-rate problem.

Verbal statement	Mathematical model
The velocity of a car after traveling for 1 hour is 50 miles per hour.	x = distance traveled $\frac{dx}{dt} = 50$ when $t = 1$
Water is being pumped into a swimming pool at a rate of 10 cubic feet per minute.	V = volume of water in pool $\frac{dV}{dt} = 10 \text{ ft}^3/\text{min}$
A population of bacteria is increasing at a rate of 2000 per hour.	x = number in population $\frac{dx}{dt} = 2000$ bacteria per hour
Revenue is increasing at a rate of $4000 per month.	R = revenue $\frac{dR}{dt} = 4000$ dollars per month
Profit is decreasing at a rate of $2500 per day.	P = profit $\frac{dP}{dt} = -2500$ dollars per day

Example 3   **Analyzing a Profit Function**

A company's profit P (in dollars) from selling x units of a product can be modeled by

$$P = 500x - \frac{1}{4}x^2. \qquad \text{Model for profit}$$

The sales are increasing at a rate of 10 units per day. Find the rate of change in the profit (in dollars per day) when 500 units have been sold.

SOLUTION   Because the sales are increasing at a rate of 10 units per day, you know that at time t the rate of change is $dx/dt = 10$. So, the problem can be stated as shown.

$$\text{Given rate: } \frac{dx}{dt} = 10$$

$$\text{Find: } \frac{dP}{dt} \text{ when } x = 500$$

To find the rate of change of the profit, use the model for profit that relates the profit P and the units of the product sold x.

$$\text{Equation: } P = 500x - \frac{1}{4}x^2$$

By differentiating both sides of the equation with respect to t, you obtain

$$\frac{d}{dt}[P] = \frac{d}{dt}\left[500x - \frac{1}{4}x^2\right] \qquad \text{Differentiate with respect to } t.$$

$$\frac{dP}{dt} = \left(500 - \frac{1}{2}x\right)\frac{dx}{dt}. \qquad \text{Apply Chain Rule.}$$

When $x = 500$ units and $dx/dt = 10$, the rate of change in the profit is

$$\frac{dP}{dt} = \left[500 - \frac{1}{2}(500)\right](10) = (500 - 250)(10) = 250(10) = \$2500 \text{ per day.}$$

The graph of the profit function (in terms of x) is shown in Figure 2.38.

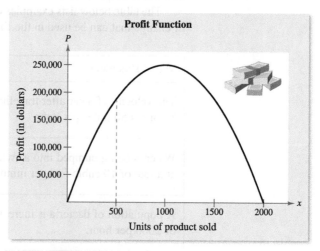

FIGURE 2.38

✓ **Checkpoint 3**

Find the rate of change in profit (in dollars per day) when 50 units have been sold, sales have increased at a rate of 10 units per day, and $P = 200x - \frac{1}{2}x^2$.

Example 4   **Increasing Production**

A company is increasing the production of a product at the rate of 200 units per week. The weekly demand function is modeled by

$$p = 100 - 0.001x$$

where p is the price per unit and x is the number of units produced in a week. Find the rate of change of the revenue with respect to time when the weekly production is 2000 units. Will the rate of change of the revenue be greater than $20,000 per week?

SOLUTION   Because production is increasing at a rate of 200 units per week, you know that at time t the rate of change is $dx/dt = 200$. So, the problem can be stated as shown.

Given rate: $\dfrac{dx}{dt} = 200$

Find: $\dfrac{dR}{dt}$ when $x = 2000$

To find the rate of change of the revenue, you must find an equation that relates the revenue R and the number of units produced x.

Equation: $R = xp = x(100 - 0.001x) = 100x - 0.001x^2$

By differentiating both sides of the equation with respect to t, you obtain

$R = 100x - 0.001x^2$ Write original equation.

$\dfrac{d}{dt}[R] = \dfrac{d}{dt}[100x - 0.001x^2]$ Differentiate with respect to t.

$\dfrac{dR}{dt} = (100 - 0.002x)\dfrac{dx}{dt}.$ Apply Chain Rule.

Using $x = 2000$ and $dx/dt = 200$, you have

$\dfrac{dR}{dt} = [100 - 0.002(2000)](200)$

$= \$19{,}200$ per week.

No, the rate of change of the revenue will not be greater than $20,000 per week.

✓**Checkpoint 4**

Find the rate of change of the revenue with respect to time for the company in Example 4 when the weekly demand function is

$$p = 150 - 0.002x.$$

SUMMARIZE   (Section 2.8)

1. Give a description of related variables *(page 151)*. For an example of two related variables, see Example 1.

2. State the guidelines for solving a related-rate problem *(page 153)*. For examples of solving related-rate problems, see Examples 2, 3, and 4.

3. Describe a real-life example of how related rates can be used to analyze the rate of change of a company's revenue *(page 155, Example 4)*.

SKILLS WARM UP 2.8   The following warm-up exercises involve skills that were covered in earlier sections. You will use these skills in the exercise set for this section. For additional help, review Section 2.7.

In Exercises 1–6, write a formula for the given quantity.

1. Area of a circle

2. Volume of a sphere

3. Surface area of a cube

4. Volume of a cube

5. Volume of a cone

6. Area of a triangle

In Exercises 7–10, find dy/dx by implicit differentiation.

7. $x^2 + y^2 = 9$ 8. $3xy - x^2 = 6$ 9. $x^2 + 2y + xy = 12$ 10. $x + xy^2 - y^2 = xy$

Exercises 2.8

See www.CalcChat.com for worked-out solutions to odd-numbered exercises.

Examining Two Rates That Are Related   In Exercises 1–4, assume that x and y are both differentiable functions of t. Use the given values to find (a) dy/dt and (b) dx/dt. See Example 1.

Equation	Find	Given
1. $y = \sqrt{x}$	(a) $\dfrac{dy}{dt}$ when $x = 4$,	$\dfrac{dx}{dt} = 3$
	(b) $\dfrac{dx}{dt}$ when $x = 25$,	$\dfrac{dy}{dt} = 2$
2. $y = 2(x^2 - 3x)$	(a) $\dfrac{dy}{dt}$ when $x = 3$,	$\dfrac{dx}{dt} = 2$
	(b) $\dfrac{dx}{dt}$ when $x = 1$,	$\dfrac{dy}{dt} = 5$
3. $xy = 4$	(a) $\dfrac{dy}{dt}$ when $x = 8$,	$\dfrac{dx}{dt} = 10$
	(b) $\dfrac{dx}{dt}$ when $x = 1$,	$\dfrac{dy}{dt} = -6$
4. $x^2 + y^2 = 25$	(a) $\dfrac{dy}{dt}$ when $x = 3, y = 4$,	$\dfrac{dx}{dt} = 8$
	(b) $\dfrac{dx}{dt}$ when $x = 4, y = 3$,	$\dfrac{dy}{dt} = -2$

5. **Area**   The radius r of a circle is increasing at a rate of 3 inches per minute. Find the rates of change of the area when (a) $r = 6$ inches and (b) $r = 24$ inches.

6. **Volume**   The radius r of a sphere is increasing at a rate of 3 inches per minute. Find the rates of change of the volume when (a) $r = 6$ inches and (b) $r = 24$ inches.

7. **Area**   Let A be the area of a circle of radius r that is changing with respect to time. If dr/dt is constant, is dA/dt constant? Explain your reasoning.

8. **Volume**   Let V be the volume of a sphere of radius r that is changing with respect to time. If dr/dt is constant, is dV/dt constant? Explain your reasoning.

9. **Volume**   A spherical balloon is inflated with gas at a rate of 10 cubic feet per minute. How fast is the radius of the balloon changing at the instant the radius is (a) 1 foot and (b) 2 feet?

10. **Volume**   The radius r of a right circular cone is increasing at a rate of 2 inches per minute. The height h of the cone is related to the radius by

$$h = 3r.$$

Find the rates of change of the volume when (a) $r = 6$ inches and (b) $r = 24$ inches.

11. **Cost, Revenue, and Profit**   A company that manufactures sport supplements calculates that its costs and revenue can be modeled by the equations

$$C = 125{,}000 + 0.75x \quad \text{and} \quad R = 250x - \frac{1}{10}x^2$$

where x is the number of units of sport supplements produced in 1 week. Production during one particular week is 1000 units and is increasing at a rate of 150 units per week. Find the rates at which the (a) cost, (b) revenue, and (c) profit are changing.

12. **Cost, Revenue, and Profit**   A company that manufactures pet toys calculates that its costs and revenue can be modeled by the equations

$$C = 75{,}000 + 1.05x \quad \text{and} \quad R = 500x - \frac{x^2}{25}$$

where x is the number of toys produced in 1 week. Production during one particular week is 5000 toys and is increasing at a rate of 250 toys per week. Find the rates at which the (a) cost, (b) revenue, and (c) profit are changing.

13. **Volume**   All edges of a cube are expanding at a rate of 3 centimeters per second. How fast is the volume changing when each edge is (a) 1 centimeter and (b) 10 centimeters?

14. Surface Area   All edges of a cube are expanding at a rate of 3 centimeters per second. How fast is the surface area changing when each edge is (a) 1 centimeter and (b) 10 centimeters?

15. Moving Point   A point is moving along the graph of $y = x^2$ such that dx/dt is 3 inches per second. Find dy/dt for (a) $x = -3$, (b) $x = 0$, (c) $x = 1$, and (d) $x = 3$.

16. Moving Point   A point is moving along the graph of $y = 1/(1 + x^2)$ such that dx/dt is 2 inches per second. Find dy/dt for (a) $x = -2$, (b) $x = 0$, (c) $x = 6$, and (d) $x = 10$.

17. Boating   A boat is pulled by a winch on a dock, and the winch is 12 feet above the deck of the boat (see figure). The winch pulls the rope at a rate of 4 feet per second. Find the speed of the boat when 13 feet of rope is out. What happens to the speed of the boat as it gets closer and closer to the dock?

Figure for 17   Figure for 18

18. Shadow Length   A man 6 feet tall walks at a rate of 5 feet per second away from a light that is 15 feet above the ground (see figure).

(a) When he is 10 feet from the base of the light, at what rate is the tip of his shadow moving?

(b) When he is 10 feet from the base of the light, at what rate is the length of his shadow changing?

19. Air Traffic Control   An airplane flying at an altitude of 6 miles passes directly over a radar antenna (see figure). When the airplane is 10 miles away ($s = 10$), the radar detects that the distance s is changing at a rate of 240 miles per hour. What is the speed of the airplane?

Figure for 19   Figure for 20

20. Baseball   A (square) baseball diamond has sides that are 90 feet long (see figure). A player 26 feet from third base is running at a speed of 30 feet per second. At what rate is the player's distance from home plate changing?

21. Air Traffic Control   An air traffic controller spots two airplanes at the same altitude converging to a point as they fly at right angles to each other. One airplane is 150 miles from the point and has a speed of 450 miles per hour. The other is 200 miles from the point and has a speed of 600 miles per hour.

(a) At what rate is the distance between the planes changing?

(b) How much time does the controller have to get one of the airplanes on a different flight path?

22. Advertising Costs   A retail sporting goods store estimates that weekly sales S and weekly advertising costs x are related by the equation $S = 2250 + 50x + 0.35x^2$. The current weekly advertising costs are $1500, and these costs are increasing at a rate of $125 per week. Find the current rate of change of weekly sales.

23. Environment   An accident at an oil drilling platform is causing a circular oil slick. The slick is 0.08 foot thick, and when the radius of the slick is 150 feet, the radius is increasing at the rate of 0.5 foot per minute. At what rate (in cubic feet per minute) is oil flowing from the site of the accident?

24. Profit   A company is increasing the production of a product at the rate of 25 units per week. The demand and cost functions for the product are given by $p = 50 - 0.01x$ and $C = 4000 + 40x - 0.02x^2$. Find the rate of change of the profit with respect to time when the weekly sales are $x = 800$ units. Use a graphing utility to graph the profit function, and use the *zoom* and *trace* features of the graphing utility to verify your result.

25. Sales   The profit for a product is increasing at a rate of $5600 per week. The demand and cost functions for the product are given by $p = 6000 - 25x$ and $C = 2400x + 5200$. Find the rate of change of sales with respect to time when the weekly sales are $x = 44$ units.

26. HOW DO YOU SEE IT?   The graph shows the demand and supply equations for a product, where x represents the number of units (in thousands) and p is the price (in dollars). Using the graph, (a) determine whether dp/dt is positive or negative given that dx/dt is negative, and (b) determine whether dx/dt is positive or negative given that dp/dt is positive.

ALGEBRA TUTOR

xy

Simplifying Algebraic Expressions

To be successful in using derivatives, you must be good at simplifying algebraic expressions. Here are some helpful simplification techniques.

1. Combine *like terms*. This may involve expanding an expression by multiplying factors.

2. Divide out *common factors* in the numerator and denominator of an expression.

3. Factor an expression.

4. Rationalize a denominator.

5. Add, subtract, multiply, or divide fractions.

TECH TUTOR

Symbolic algebra systems can simplify algebraic expressions. If you have access to such a system, try using it to simplify the expressions in this Algebra Tutor.

Example 1   **Simplifying Fractional Expressions**

a. $\dfrac{[3(x + \Delta x) + 5] - (3x + 5)}{\Delta x} = \dfrac{3x + 3\Delta x + 5 - 3x - 5}{\Delta x}$ Multiply factors and remove parentheses.

$= \dfrac{3\Delta x}{\Delta x}$ Combine like terms.

$= 3, \quad \Delta x \neq 0$ Divide out common factors.

b. $\dfrac{(x + \Delta x)^2 - x^2}{\Delta x} = \dfrac{x^2 + 2x(\Delta x) + (\Delta x)^2 - x^2}{\Delta x}$ Expand terms.

$= \dfrac{2x(\Delta x) + (\Delta x)^2}{\Delta x}$ Combine like terms.

$= \dfrac{\Delta x(2x + \Delta x)}{\Delta x}$ Factor.

$= 2x + \Delta x, \quad \Delta x \neq 0$ Divide out common factors.

c. $\dfrac{(x^2 - 1)(-2 - 2x) - (3 - 2x - x^2)(2)}{(x^2 - 1)^2}$

$= \dfrac{(-2x^2 - 2x^3 + 2 + 2x) - (6 - 4x - 2x^2)}{(x^2 - 1)^2}$ Expand terms.

$= \dfrac{-2x^2 - 2x^3 + 2 + 2x - 6 + 4x + 2x^2}{(x^2 - 1)^2}$ Remove parentheses.

$= \dfrac{-2x^3 + 6x - 4}{(x^2 - 1)^2}$ Combine like terms.

d. $2\left(\dfrac{2x + 1}{3x}\right)\left[\dfrac{3x(2) - (2x + 1)(3)}{(3x)^2}\right]$

$= 2\left(\dfrac{2x + 1}{3x}\right)\left[\dfrac{6x - (6x + 3)}{(3x)^2}\right]$ Multiply factors.

$= \dfrac{2(2x + 1)(6x - 6x - 3)}{(3x)^3}$ Multiply fractions and remove parentheses.

$= \dfrac{2(2x + 1)(-3)}{3(9)x^3}$ Combine like terms and factor.

$= \dfrac{-2(2x + 1)}{9x^3}$ Divide out common factors.

Example 2   **Simplifying Expressions with Powers**

Simplify each expression.

a. $(2x + 1)^2(6x + 1) + (3x^2 + x)(2)(2x + 1)(2)$

b. $(-1)(3x^2 - 2x)^{-2}(6x - 2)$

c. $(x)\left(\frac{1}{2}\right)(2x + 3)^{-1/2} + (2x + 3)^{1/2}(1)$

d. $\dfrac{x^2\left(\frac{1}{2}\right)(x^2 + 1)^{-1/2}(2x) - (x^2 + 1)^{1/2}(2x)}{x^4}$

SOLUTION

a. $(2x + 1)^2(6x + 1) + (3x^2 + x)(2)(2x + 1)(2)$

$= (2x + 1)[(2x + 1)(6x + 1) + (3x^2 + x)(2)(2)]$ Factor.

$= (2x + 1)[12x^2 + 8x + 1 + (12x^2 + 4x)]$ Multiply factors.

$= (2x + 1)(12x^2 + 8x + 1 + 12x^2 + 4x)$ Remove parentheses.

$= (2x + 1)(24x^2 + 12x + 1)$ Combine like terms.

b. $(-1)(3x^2 - 2x)^{-2}(6x - 2)$

$= \dfrac{(-1)(6x - 2)}{(3x^2 - 2x)^2}$ Rewrite as a fraction.

$= \dfrac{(-1)(2)(3x - 1)}{(3x^2 - 2x)^2}$ Factor.

$= \dfrac{-2(3x - 1)}{(3x^2 - 2x)^2}$ Multiply factors.

c. $(x)\left(\frac{1}{2}\right)(2x + 3)^{-1/2} + (2x + 3)^{1/2}(1)$

$= (2x + 3)^{-1/2}\left(\frac{1}{2}\right)[x + (2x + 3)(2)]$ Factor.

$= \dfrac{x + 4x + 6}{(2x + 3)^{1/2}(2)}$ Rewrite as a fraction.

$= \dfrac{5x + 6}{2(2x + 3)^{1/2}}$ Combine like terms.

d. $\dfrac{x^2\left(\frac{1}{2}\right)(x^2 + 1)^{-1/2}(2x) - (x^2 + 1)^{1/2}(2x)}{x^4}$

$= \dfrac{(x^3)(x^2 + 1)^{-1/2} - (x^2 + 1)^{1/2}(2x)}{x^4}$ Multiply factors.

$= \dfrac{(x^2 + 1)^{-1/2}(x)[x^2 - (x^2 + 1)(2)]}{x^4}$ Factor.

$= \dfrac{x[x^2 - (2x^2 + 2)]}{(x^2 + 1)^{1/2}x^4}$ Write with positive exponents.

$= \dfrac{x^2 - 2x^2 - 2}{(x^2 + 1)^{1/2}x^3}$ Divide out common factors and remove parentheses.

$= \dfrac{-x^2 - 2}{(x^2 + 1)^{1/2}x^3}$ Combine like terms.

STUDY TIP

All but one of the expressions in this Algebra Tutor are derivatives. Can you see what the original function is? Explain your reasoning.

SUMMARY AND STUDY STRATEGIES

After studying this chapter, you should have acquired the following skills.
The exercise numbers are keyed to the Review Exercises that begin on page 162.
Answers to odd-numbered Review Exercises are given in the back of the text.*

Section 2.1

	Review Exercises
■ Approximate the slope of the tangent line to a graph at a point.	*1–4*
■ Interpret the slope of a graph in a real-life setting.	*5–8*
■ Use the limit definition to find the slope of a graph at a point and the derivative of a function.	*9–24*

$$f'(x) = \lim_{\Delta x \to 0} \frac{f(x + \Delta x) - f(x)}{\Delta x}$$

■ Use the graph of a function to recognize points at which the function is not differentiable.	*25–28*

Section 2.2

■ Use the Constant Rule for differentiation.	*29, 30*

$$\frac{d}{dx}[c] = 0$$

■ Use the Power Rule for differentiation.	*31, 32*

$$\frac{d}{dx}[x^n] = nx^{n-1}$$

■ Use the Constant Multiple Rule for differentiation.	*33–36*

$$\frac{d}{dx}[cf(x)] = cf'(x)$$

■ Use the Sum and Difference Rules for differentiation.	*37–40*

$$\frac{d}{dx}[f(x) \pm g(x)] = f'(x) \pm g'(x)$$

■ Use derivatives to find the slope of a graph.	*41–44*
■ Use derivatives to write equations of tangent lines.	*45–48*
■ Use derivatives to answer questions about real-life situations.	*49, 50*

Section 2.3

■ Find the average rate of change of a function over an interval and the instantaneous rate of change at a point.	*51–54*

Average rate of change: $\dfrac{f(b) - f(a)}{b - a}$;   Instantaneous rate of change: $\lim\limits_{\Delta x \to 0} \dfrac{f(x + \Delta x) - f(x)}{\Delta x}$

■ Use derivatives to find the velocities of objects.	*55, 56*
■ Find the marginal revenues, marginal costs, and marginal profits for products.	*57–66*
■ Use derivatives to answer questions about real-life situations.	*67, 68*

---

* A wide range of valuable study aids are available to help you master the material in this chapter.
The *Student Solutions Manual* includes step-by-step solutions to all odd-numbered exercises to help
you review and prepare. The student website at *www.cengagebrain.com* offers algebra help and a
Graphing Technology Guide, which contains step-by-step commands and instructions for a wide
variety of graphing calculators. ■

Section 2.4

■ Use the Product Rule for differentiation.

$$\frac{d}{dx}[f(x)g(x)] = f(x)g'(x) + g(x)f'(x)$$

■ Use the Quotient Rule for differentiation.

$$\frac{d}{dx}\left[\frac{f(x)}{g(x)}\right] = \frac{g(x)f'(x) - f(x)g'(x)}{[g(x)]^2}$$

Section 2.5

■ Use the General Power Rule for differentiation.

$$\frac{d}{dx}[u^n] = nu^{n-1}u'$$

■ Use differentiation rules efficiently to find the derivative of any algebraic function, then simplify the result.

■ Use derivatives to answer questions about real-life situations.   (Sections 2.1–2.5)

Section 2.6

■ Find higher-order derivatives.

■ Find and use a position function to determine the velocity and acceleration of a moving object.

Section 2.7

■ Find derivatives implicitly.

■ Use implicit differentiation to write equations of tangent lines.

Section 2.8

■ Solve related-rate problems.

Study Strategies

■ **Simplify Your Derivatives**   You may ask if you have to simplify your derivatives. The answer is "Yes, if you expect to use them." In the next chapter, you will see that almost all applications of derivatives require that the derivatives be written in simplified form. It is not difficult to see the advantage of a derivative in simplified form. Consider, for instance, the derivative of

$$f(x) = \frac{x}{\sqrt{x^2 + 1}}.$$

The "raw form" produced by the Quotient and Chain Rules

$$f'(x) = \frac{(x^2 + 1)^{1/2}(1) - (x)\left(\frac{1}{2}\right)(x^2 + 1)^{-1/2}(2x)}{\left(\sqrt{x^2 + 1}\right)^2}$$

is obviously much more difficult to use than the simplified form

$$f'(x) = \frac{1}{(x^2 + 1)^{3/2}}.$$

■ **List Units of Measure in Applied Problems**   When using derivatives in real-life applications, be sure to list the units of measure for each variable. For instance, if R is measured in dollars and t is measured in years, then the derivative dR/dt is measured in dollars per year.

Review Exercises
See www.CalcChat.com for worked-out solutions to odd-numbered exercises.

Approximating the Slope of a Graph In Exercises 1–4, estimate the slope of the graph at the point (x, y). (Each square on the grid is 1 unit by 1 unit.)

1.

2.

3.

4.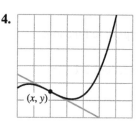

5. Sales The graph represents the sales S (in millions of dollars) for Tractor Supply Company for the years 2003 through 2009, where t represents the year, with $t = 3$ corresponding to 2003. Estimate and interpret the slopes of the graph for the years 2004 and 2007. *(Source: Tractor Supply Company)*

6. Farms The graph represents the amount of farm land L (in millions of acres) in the United States for the years 2004 through 2009, where t represents the year, with $t = 4$ corresponding to 2004. Estimate and interpret the slopes of the graph for the years 2005 and 2008. *(Source: U.S. Department of Agriculture)*

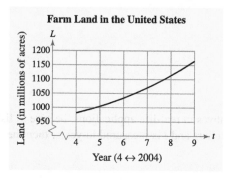

7. Consumer Trends The graph shows the number of visitors V (in thousands) to a national park during a one-year period, where $t = 1$ corresponds to January. Estimate and interpret the slopes of the graph at $t = 1, 8$, and 12.

8. White-Water Rafting Two white-water rafters leave a campsite simultaneously and start downstream on a 9-mile trip. Their distances from the campsite are given by $s = f(t)$ and $s = g(t)$, where s is measured in miles and t is measured in hours.

(a) Which rafter is traveling at a greater rate at t_1?

(b) What can you conclude about their rates at t_2?

(c) What can you conclude about their rates at t_3?

(d) Which rafter finishes the trip first? Explain your reasoning.

Finding the Slope of a Graph In Exercises 9–16, use the limit definition to find the slope of the tangent line to the graph of f at the given point.

9. $f(x) = -3x - 5; (-2, 1)$

10. $f(x) = 7x + 3; (-1, -4)$

11. $f(x) = x^2 - 4x; (1, -3)$

12. $f(x) = x^2 + 10; (2, 14)$

13. $f(x) = \sqrt{x + 9}; (-5, 2)$

14. $f(x) = \sqrt{x - 1}; (10, 3)$

15. $f(x) = \dfrac{1}{x - 5}; (6, 1)$ **16.** $f(x) = \dfrac{1}{x + 4}; (-3, 1)$

Finding a Derivative In Exercises 17–24, use the limit definition to find the derivative of the function.

17. $f(x) = 9x + 1$

18. $f(x) = 1 - 4x$

19. $f(x) = -\frac{1}{2}x^2 + 2x$

20. $f(x) = 4 - x^2$

21. $f(x) = \sqrt{x - 5}$

22. $f(x) = \sqrt{x} + 3$

23. $f(x) = \dfrac{5}{x}$

24. $f(x) = \dfrac{1}{x + 4}$

Determining Differentiability In Exercises 25–28, determine the x-values at which the function is differentiable. Explain your reasoning.

25. $y = \dfrac{x + 1}{x - 1}$

26. $y = -|x| + 3$

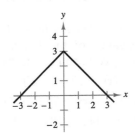

27. $y = \begin{cases} -x - 2, & x \le 0 \\ x^3 + 2, & x > 0 \end{cases}$

28. $y = (x + 1)^{2/3}$

Finding Derivatives In Exercises 29–40, find the derivative of the function.

29. $y = -6$

30. $f(x) = 5$

31. $f(x) = x^3$

32. $h(x) = \dfrac{1}{x^4}$

33. $f(x) = 4x^2$

34. $g(t) = 6t^5$

35. $f(x) = \dfrac{2x^4}{5}$

36. $y = 3x^{2/3}$

37. $g(x) = 2x^4 + 3x^2$

38. $f(x) = 6x^2 - 4x$

39. $y = x^2 + 6x - 7$

40. $y = 2x^4 - 3x^3 + x$

Finding the Slope of a Graph In Exercises 41–44, find the slope of the graph of the function at the given point.

41. $f(x) = 2x^{-1/2}; (4, 1)$

42. $y = \dfrac{3}{2x} + 3; \left(\dfrac{1}{2}, 6\right)$

43. $g(x) = x^3 - 4x^2 - 6x + 8; (-1, 9)$

44. $y = 2x^4 - 5x^3 + 6x^2 - x; (1, 2)$

 Finding an Equation of a Tangent Line In Exercises 45–48, (a) find an equation of the tangent line to the graph of the function at the given point, (b) use a graphing utility to graph the function and its tangent line at the point, and (c) use the *derivative* feature of a graphing utility to confirm your results.

45. $f(x) = 2x^2 - 3x + 1; (2, 3)$

46. $y = 11x^4 - 5x^2 + 1; (-1, 7)$

47. $f(x) = \sqrt{x} - \dfrac{1}{\sqrt{x}}; (1, 0)$

48. $f(x) = -x^2 - 4x - 4; (-4, -4)$

49. Sales The annual sales S (in millions of dollars) for Tractor Supply Company for the years 2003 through 2009 can be modeled by

$$S = -0.7500t^4 + 13.278t^3 - 74.50t^2 + 440.2t + 523$$

where t is the year, with $t = 3$ corresponding to 2003. *(Source: Tractor Supply Company)*

(a) Find the slopes of the graph for the years 2004 and 2007.

(b) Compare your results with those obtained in Exercise 5.

(c) Interpret the slope of the graph in the context of the problem.

50. Farms The amount of farm land L (in millions of acres) in the United States for the years 2004 through 2009 can be modeled by

$$L = 0.0991t^3 + 1.512t^2 + 4.01t + 933.9$$

where t is the year, with $t = 4$ corresponding to 2004. *(Source: U.S. Department of Agriculture)*

(a) Find the slopes of the graph for the years 2005 and 2008.

(b) Compare your results with those obtained in Exercise 6.

(c) Interpret the slope of the graph in the context of the problem.

Finding Rates of Change In Exercises 51–54, use a graphing utility to graph the function and find its average rate of change over the interval. Compare this rate with the instantaneous rates of change at the endpoints of the interval.

51. $f(t) = 4t + 3; [-3, 1]$

52. $f(x) = x^{2/3}; [1, 8]$

53. $f(x) = x^2 + 3x - 4; [0, 1]$

54. $f(x) = x^3 + x; [-2, 2]$

55. Velocity The height s (in feet) at time t (in seconds) of a ball thrown upward from the top of a 300-foot building with an initial velocity of 24 feet per second is given by

$$s = -16t^2 + 24t + 300.$$

(a) Find the average velocity on the interval $[1, 2]$.

(b) Find the instantaneous velocities when $t = 1$ and $t = 3$.

(c) How long will it take the ball to hit the ground?

(d) Find the velocity of the ball when it hits the ground.

56. Velocity A rock is dropped from a tower on the Brooklyn Bridge, 276 feet above the East River. Let t represent the time in seconds.

(a) Find the position and velocity functions for the rock.

(b) Find the average velocity over the interval $[0, 2]$.

(c) Find the instantaneous velocities at $t = 2$ and $t = 3$.

(d) How long will it take the rock to hit the water?

(e) Find the velocity of the rock when it hits the water.

Marginal Cost In Exercises 57–60, find the marginal cost for producing x units. (The cost is measured in dollars.)

57. $C = 2500 + 320x$

58. $C = 3x^3 + 24,000$

59. $C = 370 + 2.55\sqrt{x}$

60. $C = 475 + 5.25x^{2/3}$

Marginal Revenue In Exercises 61–64, find the marginal revenue for producing x units. (The revenue is measured in dollars.)

61. $R = 150x - 0.6x^2$

62. $R = 150x - \frac{3}{4}x^2$

63. $R = -4x^3 + 2x^2 + 100x$

64. $R = 4x + 10\sqrt{x}$

Marginal Profit In Exercises 65 and 66, find the marginal profit for producing x units. (The profit is measured in dollars.)

65. $P = -0.0002x^3 + 6x^2 - x - 2000$

66. $P = -\frac{1}{15}x^3 + 4000x^2 - 120x - 144,000$

67. Marginal Profit The profit P (in dollars) from selling x units of a product is given by

$$P = -0.05x^2 + 20x - 1000.$$

(a) Find the additional profit when the sales increase from 100 to 101 units.

(b) Find the marginal profit when $x = 100$ units.

(c) Compare the results of parts (a) and (b).

68. Population Growth The population P (in millions) of Brazil from 1980 through 2010 can be modeled by

$$P = -0.007t^2 + 2.78t + 123.6$$

where t represents the year, with $t = 0$ corresponding to 1980. *(Source: U.S. Census Bureau)*

(a) Evaluate P for $t = 0, 5, 10, 15, 20, 25,$ and 30. Explain these values.

(b) Determine the population growth rate, dP/dt.

(c) Evaluate dP/dt for the same values as in part (a). Explain your results.

Finding Derivatives In Exercises 69–90, find the derivative of the function. State which differentiation rule(s) you used to find the derivative.

69. $f(x) = x^3(5 - 3x^2)$

70. $y = (3x^2 + 7)(x^2 - 2x)$

71. $y = (4x - 3)(x^3 - 2x^2)$

72. $s = \left(4 - \frac{1}{t^2}\right)(t^2 - 3t)$

73. $g(x) = \dfrac{x}{x + 3}$

74. $f(x) = \dfrac{2 - 5x}{3x + 1}$

75. $f(x) = \dfrac{6x - 5}{x^2 + 1}$

76. $f(x) = \dfrac{x^2 + x - 1}{x^2 - 1}$

77. $f(x) = (5x^2 + 2)^3$

78. $f(x) = \sqrt[3]{x^2 - 1}$

79. $h(x) = \dfrac{2}{\sqrt{x + 1}}$

80. $g(x) = \sqrt{x^6 - 12x^3 + 9}$

81. $g(x) = x\sqrt{x^2 + 1}$ **82.** $g(t) = \dfrac{t}{(1 - t)^3}$

83. $f(x) = x(1 - 4x^2)^2$ **84.** $f(x) = \left(x^2 + \dfrac{1}{x}\right)^5$

85. $h(x) = [x^2(2x + 3)]^3$ **86.** $f(x) = [(x - 2)(x + 4)]^2$

87. $f(x) = x^2(x - 1)^5$ **88.** $f(s) = s^3(s^2 - 1)^{5/2}$

89. $h(t) = \dfrac{\sqrt{3t + 1}}{(1 - 3t)^2}$ **90.** $g(x) = \dfrac{(3x + 1)^2}{(x^2 + 1)^2}$

91. Physical Science The temperature T (in degrees Fahrenheit) of food placed in a freezer can be modeled by

$$T = \frac{1300}{t^2 + 2t + 25}$$

where t is the time (in hours).

(a) Find the rates of change of T at $t = 1, 3, 5,$ and 10.

(b) Graph the model on a graphing utility and describe the rate at which the temperature is changing.

92. Forestry According to the *Doyle Log Rule*, the volume V (in board-feet) of a log of length L (in feet) and diameter D (in inches) at the small end is

$$V = \left(\frac{D-4}{4}\right)^2 L.$$

Find the rates at which the volume is changing with respect to D for a 12-foot-long log whose smallest diameter is (a) 8 inches, (b) 16 inches, (c) 24 inches, and (d) 36 inches.

Finding Higher-Order Derivatives In Exercises 93–100, find the higher-order derivative.

Given	Derivative
93. $f(x) = 3x^2 + 7x + 1$	$f''(x)$
94. $f'(x) = 5x^4 - 6x^2 + 2x$	$f'''(x)$
95. $f'''(x) = -\dfrac{6}{x^4}$	$f^{(5)}(x)$
96. $f(x) = \sqrt{x}$	$f^{(4)}(x)$
97. $f'(x) = 7x^{5/2}$	$f''(x)$
98. $f(x) = x^2 + \dfrac{3}{x}$	$f''(x)$
99. $f''(x) = 6\sqrt[3]{x}$	$f'''(x)$
100. $f'''(x) = 20x^4 - \dfrac{2}{x^3}$	$f^{(5)}(x)$

101. Athletics A person dives from a 30-foot platform with an initial velocity of 5 feet per second (upward).

(a) Find the position function of the diver.

(b) How long will it take the diver to hit the water?

(c) What is the diver's velocity at impact?

(d) What is the diver's acceleration at impact?

102. Velocity and Acceleration The position function of a particle is given by

$$s = \frac{1}{t^2 + 2t + 1}$$

where s is the height (in feet) and t is the time (in seconds). Find the velocity and acceleration functions.

Finding Derivatives In Exercises 103–106, use implicit differentiation to find dy/dx.

103. $x^2 + 3xy + y^3 = 10$

104. $x^2 + 9xy + y^2 = 0$

105. $y^2 - x^2 + 8x - 9y - 1 = 0$

106. $y^2 + x^2 - 6y - 2x - 5 = 0$

Finding an Equation of a Tangent Line In Exercises 107–110, use implicit differentiation to find an equation of the tangent line to the graph of the function at the given point.

Equation	Point
107. $y^2 = x - y$	$(2, 1)$
108. $2\sqrt[3]{x} + 3\sqrt{y} = 10$	$(8, 4)$
109. $y^2 - 2x = xy$	$(1, 2)$
110. $y^3 - 2x^2y + 3xy^2 = -1$	$(0, -1)$

111. Area The radius r of a circle is increasing at a rate of 2 inches per minute. Find the rate of change of the area at (a) $r = 3$ inches and (b) $r = 10$ inches.

112. Moving Point A point is moving along the graph of $y = \sqrt{x}$ such that dx/dt is 3 centimeters per second. Find dy/dt for (a) $x = \frac{1}{4}$, (b) $x = 1$, and (c) $x = 4$.

113. Water Level A swimming pool is 40 feet long, 20 feet wide, 4 feet deep at the shallow end, and 9 feet deep at the deep end (see figure). Water is being pumped into the pool at the rate of 10 cubic feet per minute. How fast is the water level rising when there is 4 feet of water in the deep end?

114. Profit The demand and cost functions for a product can be modeled by

$$p = 211 - 0.002x$$

and

$$C = 30x + 1,500,000$$

where x is the number of units produced.

(a) Write the profit function for this product.

(b) Find the marginal profit when 80,000 units are produced.

(c) Graph the profit function on a graphing utility and use the graph to determine the price you would charge for the product. Explain your reasoning.

TEST YOURSELF

See www.CalcChat.com for worked-out solutions to odd-numbered exercises.

Take this test as you would take a test in class. When you are done, check your work against the answers given in the back of the book.

In Exercises 1 and 2, use the limit definition to find the derivative of the function. Then find the slope of the tangent line to the graph of f at the given point.

1. $f(x) = x^2 + 1; (2, 5)$ **2.** $f(x) = \sqrt{x} - 2; (4, 0)$

In Exercises 3–11, find the derivative of the function.

3. $f(t) = t^3 + 2t$ **4.** $f(x) = 4x^2 - 8x + 1$ **5.** $f(x) = x^{3/2}$

6. $f(x) = (x + 3)(x^2 + 2x)$ **7.** $f(x) = -3x^{-3}$ **8.** $f(x) = \sqrt{x}(5 + x)$

9. $f(x) = (3x^2 + 4)^2$ **10.** $f(x) = \sqrt{1 - 2x}$ **11.** $f(x) = \dfrac{(5x - 1)^3}{x}$

12. Find an equation of the tangent line to the graph of

$$f(x) = x - \frac{1}{x}$$

at the point $(1, 0)$. Then use a graphing utility to graph the function and the tangent line in the same viewing window.

13. The annual sales S (in billions of dollars) of CVS Caremark for the years 2004 through 2009 can be modeled by

$$S = -1.3241t^3 + 26.562t^2 - 155.81t + 314.3$$

where t represents the year, with $t = 4$ corresponding to 2004. *(Source: CVS Caremark Corporation)*

(a) Approximate the average rate of change for the years from 2005 through 2008.

(b) Find the instantaneous rates of change of the model for the years 2005 and 2008.

(c) Interpret the results of parts (a) and (b) in the context of the problem.

14. The monthly demand and cost functions for a product are given by

$$p = 1700 - 0.016x \quad \text{and} \quad C = 715{,}000 + 240x.$$

(a) Write the profit function for this product.

(b) Find the rate of change of the profit when the monthly sales are $x = 700$ units.

In Exercises 15–17, find the third derivative of the function.

15. $f(x) = 2x^2 + 3x + 1$ **16.** $f(x) = \sqrt{3 - x}$ **17.** $f(x) = \dfrac{2x + 1}{2x - 1}$

18. A ball is thrown straight upward from a height of 75 feet above the ground with an initial velocity of 30 feet per second. Write the position, velocity, and acceleration functions of the ball. Find the height, velocity, and acceleration when $t = 2$.

In Exercises 19–21, use implicit differentiation to find dy/dx.

19. $x + xy = 6$ **20.** $y^2 + 2x - 2y + 1 = 0$ **21.** $x^2 - 2y^2 = 4$

22. The radius r of a right circular cylinder is increasing at a rate of 0.25 centimeter per minute. The height h of the cylinder is related to the radius by $h = 20r$. Find the rate of change of the volume when (a) $r = 0.5$ centimeter and (b) $r = 1$ centimeter.

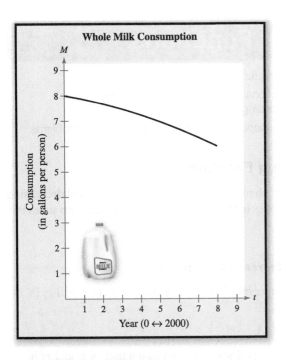

Whole Milk Consumption

Example 2 on page 169 shows how the derivative can be used to show that milk consumption decreased in the United States from 2000 through 2008.

3 Applications of the Derivative

3.1 Increasing and Decreasing Functions

■ Test for increasing and decreasing functions.
■ Find the critical numbers of functions and find the open intervals on which functions are increasing or decreasing.
■ Use increasing and decreasing functions to model and solve real-life problems.

Increasing and Decreasing Functions

A function is **increasing** when its graph moves up as x moves to the right and **decreasing** when its graph moves down as x moves to the right. The following definition states this more formally.

In Exercise 47 on page 176, you will use derivatives and critical numbers to find the intervals on which the profit from selling popcorn is increasing and decreasing.

Definition of Increasing and Decreasing Functions

A function f is **increasing** on an interval when, for any two numbers x_1 and x_2 in the interval,

$$x_2 > x_1 \quad \text{implies} \quad f(x_2) > f(x_1).$$

A function f is **decreasing** on an interval when, for any two numbers x_1 and x_2 in the interval,

$$x_2 > x_1 \quad \text{implies} \quad f(x_2) < f(x_1).$$

The function in Figure 3.1 is decreasing on the interval $(-\infty, a)$, constant on the interval (a, b), and increasing on the interval (b, ∞). Actually, from the definition of increasing and decreasing functions, the function shown in Figure 3.1 is decreasing on the interval $(-\infty, a]$ and increasing on the interval $[b, \infty)$. This text restricts the discussion to finding *open* intervals on which a function is increasing or decreasing.

The derivative of a function can be used to determine whether the function is increasing or decreasing on an interval.

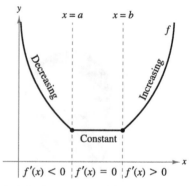

FIGURE 3.1

Test for Increasing and Decreasing Functions

Let f be differentiable on the interval (a, b).

1. If $f'(x) > 0$ for all x in (a, b), then f is increasing on (a, b).

2. If $f'(x) < 0$ for all x in (a, b), then f is decreasing on (a, b).

3. If $f'(x) = 0$ for all x in (a, b), then f is constant on (a, b).

STUDY TIP

The conclusions in the first two cases of testing for increasing and decreasing functions are valid even when $f'(x) = 0$ at a finite number of x-values in (a, b).

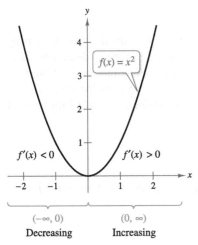

$f(x) = x^2$

$f'(x) < 0$ $f'(x) > 0$

$(-\infty, 0)$ $(0, \infty)$
Decreasing   Increasing

FIGURE 3.2

Example 1   Testing for Increasing and Decreasing Functions

Show that the function $f(x) = x^2$ is decreasing on the open interval $(-\infty, 0)$ and increasing on the open interval $(0, \infty)$.

SOLUTION   The derivative of f is

$$f'(x) = 2x.$$

On the open interval $(-\infty, 0)$, the fact that x is negative implies that $f'(x) = 2x$ is also negative. So, by the test for a decreasing function, you can conclude that f is *decreasing* on this interval. Similarly, on the open interval $(0, \infty)$, the fact that x is positive implies that $f'(x) = 2x$ is also positive. So, it follows that f is *increasing* on this interval, as shown in Figure 3.2.

✓ **Checkpoint 1**

Show that the function $f(x) = x^4$ is decreasing on the open interval $(-\infty, 0)$ and increasing on the open interval $(0, \infty)$.

Example 2   Modeling Consumption

From 2000 through 2008, the consumption M of whole milk in the United States (in gallons per person) can be modeled by

$$M = -0.015t^2 + 0.13t + 8.0, \quad 0 \le t \le 8$$

where $t = 0$ corresponds to 2000 (see Figure 3.3). Show that the consumption of whole milk was decreasing from 2000 to 2008. *(Source: U.S. Department of Agriculture)*

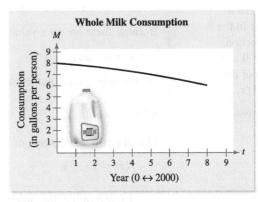

Whole Milk Consumption

x-axis: Year (0 ↔ 2000)
y-axis: Consumption (in gallons per person)

FIGURE 3.3

SOLUTION   The derivative of this model is $dM/dt = -0.030t + 0.13$. For the open interval $(0, 8)$, the derivative is negative. So, the function is decreasing, which implies that the consumption of whole milk was decreasing during the given time period.

✓ **Checkpoint 2**

From 2003 through 2008, the consumption F of fresh fruit in the United States (in pounds per person) can be modeled by

$$F = -0.7674t^2 + 2.872t + 277.87, \quad 3 \le t \le 8$$

where $t = 3$ corresponds to 2003. Show that the consumption of fresh fruit was decreasing from 2003 to 2008. *(Source: U.S. Department of Agriculture)*

$f'(c) = 0$

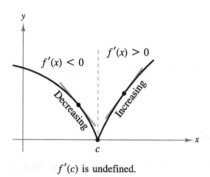

$f'(c)$ is undefined.

FIGURE 3.4

Critical Numbers and Their Use

In Example 1, you were given two intervals: one on which the function was decreasing and one on which it was increasing. Suppose you had been asked to determine these intervals. To do this, you could have used the fact that for a continuous function, $f'(x)$ can change signs only at x-values for which $f'(x) = 0$ or at x-values for which $f'(x)$ is undefined, as shown in Figure 3.4. These two types of numbers are called the **critical numbers** of f.

Definition of a Critical Number

If f is defined at c, then c is a critical number of f when $f'(c) = 0$ or when $f'(c)$ is undefined.

Example 3   **Finding Critical Numbers**

Find the critical numbers of

$$f(x) = 2x^3 - 9x^2.$$

SOLUTION   Begin by differentiating the function.

$$f(x) = 2x^3 - 9x^2 \qquad \text{Write original function.}$$
$$f'(x) = 6x^2 - 18x \qquad \text{Differentiate.}$$

To find the critical numbers of f, you must find all x-values for which $f'(x) = 0$ and all x-values for which $f'(x)$ is undefined.

$$6x^2 - 18x = 0 \qquad \text{Set } f'(x) \text{ equal to 0.}$$
$$6x(x - 3) = 0 \qquad \text{Factor.}$$
$$x = 0, x = 3 \qquad \text{Critical numbers}$$

Because there are no x-values for which f' is undefined, you can conclude that

$$x = 0 \quad \text{and} \quad x = 3$$

are the only critical numbers of f.

✓**Checkpoint 3**

Find the critical numbers of

$$f(x) = x^2 - x.$$

To determine the intervals on which a continuous function is increasing or decreasing, you can use the guidelines below.

Guidelines for Applying the Increasing/Decreasing Test

1. Find the derivative of f.

2. Locate the critical numbers of f and use these numbers to determine test intervals. That is, find all x for which $f'(x) = 0$ or $f'(x)$ is undefined.

3. Determine the sign of $f'(x)$ at one test value in each of the intervals.

4. Use the test for increasing and decreasing functions to decide whether f is increasing or decreasing on each interval.

Example 4   **Intervals on Which f Is Increasing or Decreasing**

Find the open intervals on which the function is increasing or decreasing.

$$f(x) = x^3 - \frac{3}{2}x^2$$

SOLUTION   Begin by finding the derivative of f. Then set the derivative equal to zero and solve for the critical numbers.

$f'(x) = 3x^2 - 3x$	Differentiate original function.
$3x^2 - 3x = 0$	Set derivative equal to 0.
$3x(x - 1) = 0$	Factor.
$x = 0, x = 1$	Critical numbers

Because there are no x-values for which f' is undefined, it follows that $x = 0$ and $x = 1$ are the only critical numbers. So, the intervals that need to be tested are

$$(-\infty, 0), (0, 1), \quad \text{and} \quad (1, \infty). \qquad \text{Test intervals}$$

The table summarizes the testing of these three intervals.

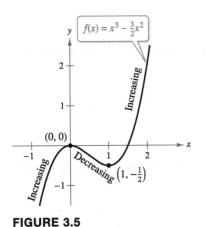

$f(x) = x^3 - \frac{3}{2}x^2$

Interval	$-\infty < x < 0$	$0 < x < 1$	$1 < x < \infty$
Test value	$x = -1$	$x = \frac{1}{2}$	$x = 2$
Sign of $f'(x)$	$f'(-1) = 6 > 0$	$f'(\frac{1}{2}) = -\frac{3}{4} < 0$	$f'(2) = 6 > 0$
Conclusion	Increasing	Decreasing	Increasing

FIGURE 3.5

The graph of f is shown in Figure 3.5. Note that the test values in the intervals were chosen for convenience—other x-values could have been used. ____

✓**Checkpoint 4**

Find the open intervals on which the function $f(x) = x^3 - 12x$ is increasing or decreasing.

TECH TUTOR

You can use the *trace* feature of a graphing utility to confirm the result of Example 4. Begin by graphing the function, as shown below. Then use the *trace* feature and move the cursor from left to right. In intervals on which the function is increasing, note that the y-values increase as the x-values increase, whereas in intervals on which the function is decreasing, the y-values decrease as the x-values increase.

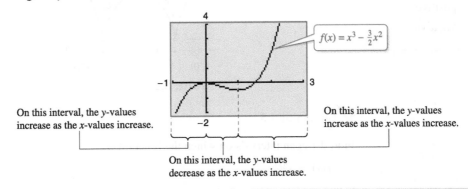

$f(x) = x^3 - \frac{3}{2}x^2$

On this interval, the y-values increase as the x-values increase.

On this interval, the y-values increase as the x-values increase.

On this interval, the y-values decrease as the x-values increase.

Not only is the function in Example 4 continuous on the entire real number line, it is also differentiable there. For such functions, the only critical numbers are those for which $f'(x) = 0$. The next example considers a continuous function that has *both* types of critical numbers—those for which $f'(x) = 0$ and those for which $f'(x)$ is undefined.

ALGEBRA TUTOR xy

For help on the algebra in Example 5, see Example 2(d) in the *Chapter 3 Algebra Tutor*, on page 243.

Example 5   **Intervals on Which *f* Is Increasing or Decreasing**

Find the open intervals on which the function

$$f(x) = (x^2 - 4)^{2/3}$$

is increasing or decreasing.

SOLUTION   Begin by finding the derivative of the function.

$$f'(x) = \frac{2}{3}(x^2 - 4)^{-1/3}(2x) \qquad \text{Differentiate.}$$

$$= \frac{4x}{3(x^2 - 4)^{1/3}} \qquad \text{Simplify.}$$

From this, you can see that the derivative is zero when $x = 0$ and the derivative is undefined when $x = \pm 2$. So, the critical numbers are

$$x = -2, \quad x = 0, \quad \text{and} \quad x = 2. \qquad \text{Critical numbers}$$

This implies that the test intervals are

$$(-\infty, -2), \quad (-2, 0), \quad (0, 2), \quad \text{and} \quad (2, \infty). \qquad \text{Test intervals}$$

The table summarizes the testing of these four intervals, and the graph of the function is shown in Figure 3.6.

Interval	$-\infty < x < -2$	$-2 < x < 0$	$0 < x < 2$	$2 < x < \infty$
Test value	$x = -3$	$x = -1$	$x = 1$	$x = 3$
Sign of $f'(x)$	$f'(-3) < 0$	$f'(-1) > 0$	$f'(1) < 0$	$f'(3) > 0$
Conclusion	Decreasing	Increasing	Decreasing	Increasing

STUDY TIP

To test the intervals in the table in Example 5, it is not necessary to *evaluate* $f'(x)$ at each test value—you only need to determine its sign. For instance, you can determine the sign of $f'(-3)$ as shown.

$$f'(-3) = \frac{4(-3)}{3(9 - 4)^{1/3}}$$

$$= \frac{\text{negative}}{\text{positive}}$$

$$= \text{negative}$$

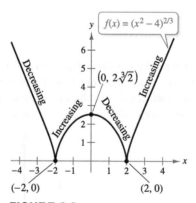

FIGURE 3.6

✓ **Checkpoint 5**

Find the open intervals on which the function

$$f(x) = x^{2/3}$$

is increasing or decreasing.

The functions in Examples 1 through 5 are continuous on the entire real number line. If there are isolated x-values at which a function is not continuous, then these x-values should be used along with the critical numbers to determine the test intervals.

Example 6   Testing a Function That Is Not Continuous

The function

$$f(x) = \frac{x^4 + 1}{x^2}$$

is not continuous at $x = 0$. Because the derivative of f

$$f'(x) = \frac{2(x^4 - 1)}{x^3}$$

is zero at $x = \pm 1$, you should use the following numbers to determine the test intervals.

$x = -1, x = 1$ Critical numbers

$x = 0$ Discontinuity

After testing $f'(x)$, you can determine that f is decreasing on the intervals $(-\infty, -1)$ and $(0, 1)$, and increasing on the intervals $(-1, 0)$ and $(1, \infty)$, as shown in Figure 3.7.

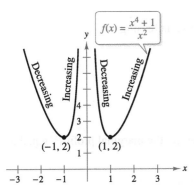

$f(x) = \dfrac{x^4 + 1}{x^2}$

FIGURE 3.7

✓ Checkpoint 6

Find the open invervals on which the function $f(x) = \dfrac{x^2 + 1}{x}$ is increasing or decreasing.

The converse of the test for increasing and decreasing functions is *not* true. For instance, it is possible for a function to be increasing on an interval even though its derivative is not positive at every point in the interval.

Example 7   Testing an Increasing Function

Show that $f(x) = x^3 - 3x^2 + 3x$ is increasing on the entire real number line.

SOLUTION   From the derivative of f

$$f'(x) = 3x^2 - 6x + 3 = 3(x - 1)^2$$

you can see that the only critical number is $x = 1$. So, the test intervals are $(-\infty, 1)$ and $(1, \infty)$. The table summarizes the testing of these two intervals. From Figure 3.8, you can see that f is increasing on the entire real number line, even though $f'(1) = 0$. To convince yourself of this, look back at the definition of an increasing function.

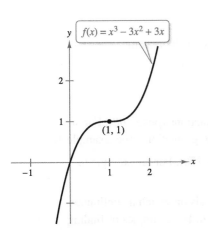

$f(x) = x^3 - 3x^2 + 3x$

FIGURE 3.8

Interval	$-\infty < x < 1$	$1 < x < \infty$
Test value	$x = 0$	$x = 2$
Sign of $f'(x)$	$f'(0) = 3(-1)^2 > 0$	$f'(2) = 3(1)^2 > 0$
Conclusion	Increasing	Increasing

✓ Checkpoint 7

Show that $f(x) = -x^3 + 2$ is decreasing on the entire real number line.

Application

 Example 8   **Profit Analysis**

A national toy distributor determines the cost and revenue models for one of its games.

$$C = 2.4x - 0.0002x^2, \quad 0 \le x \le 6000$$
$$R = 7.2x - 0.001x^2, \quad 0 \le x \le 6000$$

Determine the interval on which the profit function is increasing.

SOLUTION   The profit for producing x games is

$$P = R - C$$
$$= (7.2x - 0.001x^2) - (2.4x - 0.0002x^2)$$
$$= 4.8x - 0.0008x^2.$$

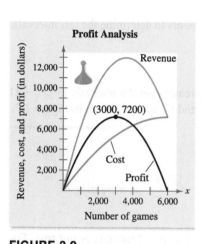

Profit Analysis

To find the interval on which the profit is increasing, set the marginal profit P' equal to zero and solve for x.

$$P' = 4.8 - 0.0016x \qquad \text{Differentiate profit function.}$$
$$4.8 - 0.0016x = 0 \qquad \text{Set } P' \text{ equal to 0.}$$
$$-0.0016x = -4.8 \qquad \text{Subtract 4.8 from each side.}$$
$$x = \frac{-4.8}{-0.0016} \qquad \text{Divide each side by } -0.0016.$$
$$x = 3000 \text{ games} \qquad \text{Simplify.}$$

On the interval $(0, 3000)$, P' is positive and the profit is *increasing*. On the interval $(3000, 6000)$, P' is negative and the profit is *decreasing*. The graphs of the cost, revenue, and profit functions are shown in Figure 3.9.

FIGURE 3.9

✓**Checkpoint 8**

A national distributor of pet toys determines the cost and revenue functions for one of its toys.

$$C = 1.2x - 0.0001x^2, \quad 0 \le x \le 6000$$
$$R = 3.6x - 0.0005x^2, \quad 0 \le x \le 6000$$

Determine the interval on which the profit function is increasing.

SUMMARIZE   (Section 3.1)

1. State the test for increasing and decreasing functions (*page 168*). For an example of testing for increasing and decreasing functions, see Example 1.

2. State the definition of a critical number (*page 170*). For an example of finding a critical number, see Example 3.

3. State the guidelines for determining the intervals on which a continuous function is increasing or decreasing (*page 170*). For examples of finding the intervals on which a function is increasing or decreasing, see Examples 4, 5, and 7.

4. Describe a real-life example of how testing for increasing and decreasing functions can be used to analyze the profit of a company (*page 174, Example 8*).

SKILLS WARM UP 3.1   The following warm-up exercises involve skills that were covered in a previous course or earlier sections. You will use these skills in the exercise set for this section. For additional help, review Appendix Section A.3, and Section 1.4.

In Exercises 1–4, solve the equation.

1. $x^2 = 8x$

2. $15x = \dfrac{5}{8}x^2$

3. $\dfrac{x^2 - 25}{x^3} = 0$

4. $\dfrac{2x}{\sqrt{1 - x^2}} = 0$

In Exercises 5–8, find the domain of the function.

5. $y = \dfrac{x + 3}{x - 3}$

6. $y = \dfrac{2}{\sqrt{1 - x}}$

7. $y = \dfrac{2x + 1}{x^2 - 3x - 10}$

8. $y = \dfrac{3x}{\sqrt{9 - 3x^2}}$

In Exercises 9–12, evaluate the expression when $x = -2$, 0, and 2.

9. $-2(x + 1)(x - 1)$

10. $4(2x + 1)(2x - 1)$

11. $\dfrac{2x + 1}{(x - 1)^2}$

12. $\dfrac{-2(x + 1)}{(x - 4)^2}$

Exercises 3.1

See www.CalcChat.com for worked-out solutions to odd-numbered exercises.

Using Graphs In Exercises 1–4, use the graph to estimate the open intervals on which the function is increasing or decreasing.

1. $f(x) = -(x + 1)^2$

2. $f(x) = \dfrac{x^3}{4} - 3x$

3. $f(x) = x^4 - 2x^2$

4. $f(x) = -(x^2 - 9)^{2/3}$

Finding Critical Numbers In Exercises 5–10, find the critical numbers of the function. *See Example 3.*

5. $f(x) = 4x^2 - 6x$

6. $f(x) = 3x^2 + 10$

7. $y = x^4 + 4x^3 + 8$

8. $g(x) = 2x^2 - 54x$

9. $f(x) = \sqrt{x^2 - 4}$

10. $y = \dfrac{x}{x^2 + 16}$

Intervals on Which f Is Increasing or Decreasing In Exercises 11–34, find the critical numbers and the open intervals on which the function is increasing or decreasing. Use a graphing utility to verify your results. *See Examples 4 and 5.*

11. $f(x) = 2x - 3$

12. $f(x) = 5 - 3x$

13. $y = x^2 - 6x$

14. $y = -x^2 + 2x$

15. $f(x) = -2x^2 + 4x + 3$

16. $f(x) = x^2 + 8x + 10$

17. $y = 3x^3 + 12x^2 + 15x$

18. $y = x^3 - 3x + 2$

19. $f(x) = x^4 - 2x^3$

20. $f(x) = \frac{1}{4}x^4 - 2x^2$

21. $g(x) = (x + 2)^2$

22. $y = (x - 2)^3$

23. $g(x) = -(x - 1)^2$

24. $y = x^3 - 6x^2$

25. $y = x^{1/3} + 1$

26. $y = x^{2/3} - 4$

27. $f(x) = \sqrt{x^2 - 1}$

28. $f(x) = \sqrt{9 - x^2}$

29. $g(x) = (x + 2)^{1/3}$

30. $g(x) = (x - 1)^{2/3}$

31. $f(x) = x\sqrt{x + 1}$

32. $h(x) = x\sqrt[3]{x - 1}$

33. $f(x) = \dfrac{x}{x^2 + 9}$

34. $f(x) = \dfrac{x^2}{x^2 + 4}$

Intervals on Which *f* Is Increasing or Decreasing   In Exercises 35–42, find the critical numbers and the open intervals on which the function is increasing or decreasing. (*Hint:* Check for discontinuities.) Sketch the graph of the function. *See Example 6.*

35. $f(x) = \dfrac{x+4}{x-5}$

36. $f(x) = \dfrac{x}{x+1}$

37. $f(x) = \dfrac{2x}{16-x^2}$

38. $f(x) = \dfrac{x^2}{x^2-9}$

39. $y = \begin{cases} 4-x^2, & x \le 0 \\ -2x, & x > 0 \end{cases}$

40. $y = \begin{cases} 3x+1, & x \le 1 \\ 5-x^2, & x > 1 \end{cases}$

41. $y = \begin{cases} 2x+1, & x \le -1 \\ x^2-2, & x > -1 \end{cases}$

42. $y = \begin{cases} -x^3+1, & x \le 0 \\ -x^2+2x, & x > 0 \end{cases}$

43. Sales   The sales S of Wal-Mart (in billions of dollars) from 2003 through 2009 can be modeled by

$$S = -1.598t^2 + 45.61t + 130.2, \quad 3 \le t \le 9$$

where t is the time in years, with $t = 3$ corresponding to 2003. Show that the sales were increasing from 2003 through 2009. *(Source: Wal-Mart Stores, Inc.)*

44. **HOW DO YOU SEE IT?**   Plots of the relative numbers of N_2 (nitrogen) molecules that have a given velocity at each of three temperatures (in degrees Kelvin) are shown in the figure. Identify the differences in the average velocities (indicated by the peaks of the curves) for the three temperatures, and describe the intervals on which the velocity is increasing and decreasing for each of the three temperatures. *(Source: Adapted from Zumdahl, Chemistry, Seventh Edition)*

Molecular Velocity

45. Medical Degrees   The number y of medical degrees conferred in the United States from 1970 through 2008 can be modeled by

$$y = 0.692t^3 - 50.11t^2 + 1119.7t + 7894, \ 0 \le t \le 38$$

where t is the time in years, with $t = 0$ corresponding to 1970. *(Source: U.S. National Center for Education Statistics)*

 (a) Use a graphing utility to graph the model. Then graphically estimate the years during which the model is increasing and the years during which it is decreasing.

(b) Use the test for increasing and decreasing functions to verify the result of part (a).

46. Cost   The ordering and transportation cost C (in hundreds of dollars) for an automobile dealership is modeled by

$$C = 10\left(\frac{1}{x} + \frac{x}{x+3}\right), \quad x \ge 1$$

where x is the number of automobiles ordered.

(a) Find the intervals on which C is increasing or decreasing.

(b) Use a graphing utility to graph the cost function.

(c) Use the *trace* feature to determine the order sizes for which the cost is $900. Assuming that the revenue function is increasing for $x \ge 0$, which order size would you use? Explain your reasoning.

47. Profit   The profit P (in dollars) made by a cinema from selling x bags of popcorn can be modeled by

$$P = 2.36x - \frac{x^2}{25,000} - 3500, \quad 0 \le x \le 50,000.$$

(a) Find the intervals on which P is increasing and decreasing.

(b) If you owned the cinema, what price would you charge to obtain a maximum profit from popcorn sales? Explain your reasoning.

48. Profit Analysis   A fast-food restaurant determines the cost and revenue models for its hamburgers.

$$C = 0.6x + 7500, \quad 0 \le x \le 50,000$$

$$R = \frac{1}{20,000}(65,000x - x^2), \quad 0 \le x \le 50,000$$

(a) Write the profit function for this situation.

(b) Determine the intervals on which the profit function is increasing and decreasing.

(c) Determine how many hamburgers the restaurant needs to sell to obtain a maximum profit. Explain your reasoning.

3.2 Extrema and the First-Derivative Test

Profit from Selling Soft Drinks

In Exercise 49 on page 185, you will use the First-Derivative Test to find the price of a soft drink that yields a maximum profit.

- ■ Recognize the occurrence of relative extrema of functions.
- ■ Use the First-Derivative Test to find the relative extrema of functions.
- ■ Find absolute extrema of continuous functions on a closed interval.
- ■ Find minimum and maximum values of real-life models and interpret the results in context.

Relative Extrema

You have used the derivative to determine the intervals on which a function is increasing or decreasing. In this section, you will examine the points at which a function changes from increasing to decreasing, or vice versa. At such a point, the function has a **relative extremum.** (The plural of extremum is *extrema*.) The **relative extrema** of a function include the **relative minima** and **relative maxima** of the function. For instance, the function shown in Figure 3.10 has a relative maximum at the left point and a relative minimum at the right point.

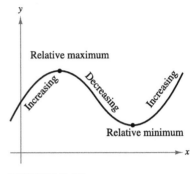

FIGURE 3.10

Definition of Relative Extrema

Let f be a function defined at c.

1. $f(c)$ is a **relative maximum** of f when there exists an interval (a, b) containing c such that $f(x) \leq f(c)$ for all x in (a, b).

2. $f(c)$ is a **relative minimum** of f when there exists an interval (a, b) containing c such that $f(x) \geq f(c)$ for all x in (a, b).

If $f(c)$ is a relative extremum of f, then the relative extremum is said to occur at $x = c$.

For a continuous function, the relative extrema must occur at critical numbers of the function, as shown in Figure 3.11.

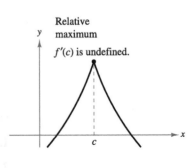

FIGURE 3.11

Occurrences of Relative Extrema

If f has a relative minimum or relative maximum at $x = c$, then c is a critical number of f. That is, either $f'(c) = 0$ or $f'(c)$ is undefined.

The First-Derivative Test

The discussion on the preceding page implies that in your search for relative extrema of a continuous function, you need to test only the critical numbers of the function. Once you have determined that c is a critical number of a function f, the **First-Derivative Test** for relative extrema enables you to classify $f(c)$ as a relative minimum, a relative maximum, or neither.

First-Derivative Test for Relative Extrema

Let f be continuous on the interval (a, b) in which c is the only critical number. If f is differentiable on the interval (except possibly at c), then $f(c)$ can be classified as a relative minimum, a relative maximum, or neither, as shown.

1. On the interval (a, b), if $f'(x)$ is negative to the left of $x = c$ and positive to the right of $x = c$, then $f(c)$ is a relative minimum.

2. On the interval (a, b), if $f'(x)$ is positive to the left of $x = c$ and negative to the right of $x = c$, then $f(c)$ is a relative maximum.

3. On the interval (a, b), if $f'(x)$ is positive on both sides of $x = c$ or negative on both sides of $x = c$, then $f(c)$ is neither a relative minimum nor a relative maximum.

A graphical interpretation of the First-Derivative Test is shown in Figure 3.12.

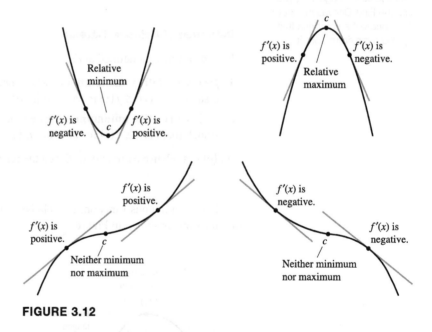

FIGURE 3.12

Guidelines for Finding Relative Extrema

1. Find the derivative of f.

2. Locate the critical numbers of f and use these numbers to determine the test intervals.

3. Test the sign of $f'(x)$ at an arbitrary number in each of the test intervals.

4. For each critical number c, use the First-Derivative Test to decide whether $f(c)$ is a relative minimum, a relative maximum, or neither.

Example 1 **Finding Relative Extrema**

Find all relative extrema of the function

$$f(x) = 2x^3 - 3x^2 - 36x + 14.$$

SOLUTION   Begin by finding the derivative of f.

$$f'(x) = 6x^2 - 6x - 36 \qquad \text{Differentiate.}$$

Next, find the critical numbers of f.

$$6x^2 - 6x - 36 = 0 \qquad \text{Set derivative equal to 0.}$$
$$6(x^2 - x - 6) = 0 \qquad \text{Factor out common factor.}$$
$$6(x - 3)(x + 2) = 0 \qquad \text{Factor.}$$
$$x = -2, x = 3 \qquad \text{Critical numbers}$$

Because $f'(x)$ is defined for all x, the only critical numbers of f are

$$x = -2 \quad \text{and} \quad x = 3. \qquad \text{Critical numbers}$$

Using these numbers, you can form the three test intervals

$$(-\infty, -2), (-2, 3), \quad \text{and} \quad (3, \infty). \qquad \text{Test intervals}$$

The testing of the three intervals is shown in the table.

Interval	$-\infty < x < -2$	$-2 < x < 3$	$3 < x < \infty$
Test value	$x = -3$	$x = 0$	$x = 4$
Sign of $f'(x)$	$f'(-3) = 36 > 0$	$f'(0) = -36 < 0$	$f'(4) = 36 > 0$
Conclusion	Increasing	Decreasing	Increasing

Using the First-Derivative Test, you can conclude that the critical number -2 yields a relative maximum [$f'(x)$ changes sign from positive to negative], and the critical number 3 yields a relative minimum [$f'(x)$ changes sign from negative to positive]. The graph of f is shown in Figure 3.13. The relative maximum is

$$f(-2) = 58$$

and the relative minimum is

$$f(3) = -67.$$

FIGURE 3.13

✓ Checkpoint 1

Find all relative extrema of

$$f(x) = 2x^3 - 6x + 1.$$

In Example 1, both critical numbers yielded relative extrema. In the next example, only one of the two critical numbers yields a relative extremum.

ALGEBRA TUTOR xy

For help on the algebra in Example 2, see Example 2(c) in the *Chapter 3 Algebra Tutor*, on page 243.

Example 2   Finding Relative Extrema

Find all relative extrema of the function $f(x) = x^4 - x^3$.

SOLUTION   From the derivative of the function

$$f'(x) = 4x^3 - 3x^2 = x^2(4x - 3)$$

you can see that the function has only two critical numbers: $x = 0$ and $x = \frac{3}{4}$. These numbers produce the test intervals $(-\infty, 0)$, $\left(0, \frac{3}{4}\right)$, and $\left(\frac{3}{4}, \infty\right)$, which are tested in the table.

Interval	$-\infty < x < 0$	$0 < x < \frac{3}{4}$	$\frac{3}{4} < x < \infty$
Test value	$x = -1$	$x = \frac{1}{2}$	$x = 1$
Sign of $f'(x)$	$f'(-1) = -7 < 0$	$f'\left(\frac{1}{2}\right) = -\frac{1}{4} < 0$	$f'(1) = 1 > 0$
Conclusion	Decreasing	Decreasing	Increasing

By the First-Derivative Test, it follows that f has a relative minimum at $x = \frac{3}{4}$, as shown in Figure 3.14. The relative minimum is

$$f\left(\frac{3}{4}\right) = -\frac{27}{256}.$$

$f(x) = x^4 - x^3$

$(0, 0)$

$\left(\frac{3}{4}, -\frac{27}{256}\right)$

Relative minimum

FIGURE 3.14

Note that the critical number $x = 0$ does not yield a relative extremum because $f'(x)$ is negative on both sides of $x = 0$.

✓ **Checkpoint 2**

Find all relative extrema of $f(x) = x^4 - 4x^3$.

Example 3   Finding Relative Extrema

Find all relative extrema of the function

$$f(x) = 2x - 3x^{2/3}.$$

SOLUTION   From the derivative of the function

$$f'(x) = 2 - \frac{2}{x^{1/3}} = \frac{2(x^{1/3} - 1)}{x^{1/3}}$$

you can see that $f'(1) = 0$ and f' is undefined at $x = 0$. So, the function has two critical numbers: $x = 1$ and $x = 0$. These numbers produce the test intervals $(-\infty, 0)$, $(0, 1)$, and $(1, \infty)$. By testing these intervals, you can conclude that f has a relative maximum at $(0, 0)$ and a relative minimum at $(1, -1)$, as shown in Figure 3.15.

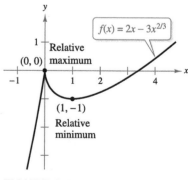

$f(x) = 2x - 3x^{2/3}$

Relative maximum $(0, 0)$

$(1, -1)$ Relative minimum

FIGURE 3.15

✓ **Checkpoint 3**

Find all relative extrema of $f(x) = 3x^{2/3} - 2x$.

Absolute Extrema

The terms *relative minimum* and *relative maximum* describe the *local* behavior of a function. To describe the *global* behavior of the function on an entire interval, you can use the terms **absolute maximum** and **absolute minimum.**

Definition of Absolute Extrema

Let f be defined on an interval I containing c.

1. $f(c)$ is an **absolute minimum of f** on I when $f(c) \leq f(x)$ for every x in I.

2. $f(c)$ is an **absolute maximum of f** on I when $f(c) \geq f(x)$ for every x in I.

The absolute minimum and absolute maximum values of a function on an interval are sometimes called simply the **minimum** and **maximum** of f on I.

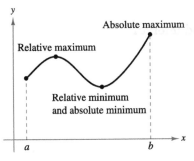

FIGURE 3.16

Be sure that you understand the distinction between relative extrema and absolute extrema. For instance, in Figure 3.16, the function has a relative minimum that also happens to be an absolute minimum on the interval $[a, b]$. The relative maximum of f, however, is not the absolute maximum on the interval $[a, b]$. The next theorem points out that if a continuous function has a closed interval as its domain, then it *must* have both an absolute minimum and an absolute maximum on the interval. From Figure 3.16, note that these extrema can occur at the endpoints of the interval.

Extreme Value Theorem

If f is continuous on a closed interval $[a, b]$, then f has both a minimum value and a maximum value on $[a, b]$.

Although a continuous function has just one minimum and one maximum value on a closed interval, either of these values can occur for more than one x-value. For instance, on the interval $[-3, 3]$, the function

$$f(x) = 9 - x^2$$

has a minimum value of zero at $x = -3$ *and* at $x = 3$, as shown in Figure 3.17.

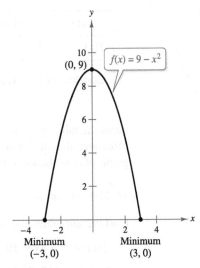

FIGURE 3.17

When looking for extrema of a function on a *closed* interval, remember that you must consider the values of the function at the endpoints as well as at the critical numbers of the function. You can use the guidelines below to find extrema on a closed interval.

Guidelines for Finding Extrema on a Closed Interval

To find the extrema of a continuous function f on a closed interval $[a, b]$, use the following steps.

1. Find the critical numbers of f in the open interval (a, b).

2. Evaluate f at each of its critical numbers in (a, b).

3. Evaluate f at each endpoint, a and b.

4. The least of these values is the minimum, and the greatest is the maximum.

Example 4   **Finding Extrema on a Closed Interval**

Find the minimum and maximum values of

$$f(x) = x^2 - 6x + 2$$

on the interval $[0, 5]$.

SOLUTION   Begin by differentiating the function.

$$f(x) = x^2 - 6x + 2 \qquad \text{Write original function.}$$
$$f'(x) = 2x - 6 \qquad \text{Differentiate.}$$

Next, find the critical numbers of f.

$$2x - 6 = 0 \qquad \text{Set derivative equal to 0.}$$
$$2x = 6 \qquad \text{Add 6 to each side.}$$
$$x = 3 \qquad \text{Solve for } x.$$

Because f' is defined for all x, you can conclude that the only critical number of f is $x = 3$. Because this number lies in the interval $[0, 5]$, you should evaluate f at this number *and* at the endpoints of the interval, as shown in the table.

x-value	Endpoint: $x = 0$	Critical number: $x = 3$	Endpoint: $x = 5$
$f(x)$	$f(0) = 2$	$f(3) = -7$	$f(5) = -3$
Conclusion	Maximum is 2.	Minimum is -7.	Neither maximum nor minimum

From the table, you can see that the minimum of f on the interval $[0, 5]$ is $f(3) = -7$. Moreover, the maximum of f on the interval $[0, 5]$ is $f(0) = 2$. This is confirmed by the graph of f, as shown in Figure 3.18.

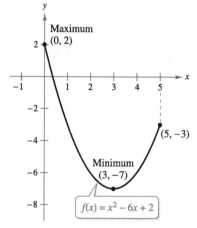

FIGURE 3.18

✓ **Checkpoint 4**

Find the minimum and maximum values of

$$f(x) = x^2 - 8x + 10$$

on the interval $[0, 7]$. Sketch the graph of f and label the minimum and maximum values.

Application

Finding the minimum and maximum values of a function is one of the most common applications of calculus.

Example 5   **Finding the Maximum Profit**

Recall the fast-food restaurant in Examples 7 and 8 in Section 2.3. The restaurant's profit function for hamburgers is given by

$$P = 2.44x - \frac{x^2}{20,000} - 5000, \quad 0 \le x \le 50,000.$$

Find the sales level that yields a maximum profit.

SOLUTION   To begin, find an equation for marginal profit.

$$\frac{dP}{dx} = 2.44 - \frac{x}{10,000} \qquad \text{Find marginal profit.}$$

Next, set the marginal profit equal to zero and solve for x.

$$2.44 - \frac{x}{10,000} = 0 \qquad \text{Set marginal profit equal to 0.}$$

$$-\frac{x}{10,000} = -2.44 \qquad \text{Subtract 2.44 from each side.}$$

$$x = 24,400 \text{ hamburgers} \qquad \text{Critical number}$$

In Figure 3.19, you can see that the critical number $x = 24,400$ corresponds to the sales level that yields a maximum profit. To find the maximum profit, substitute $x = 24,400$ into the profit function.

$$P = 2.44x - \frac{x^2}{20,000} - 5000$$

$$= 2.44(24,400) - \frac{(24,400)^2}{20,000} - 5000$$

$$= \$24,768$$

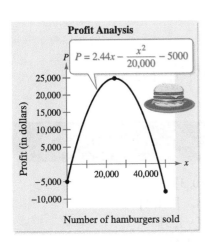

Profit Analysis

$$P = 2.44x - \frac{x^2}{20,000} - 5000$$

Profit (in dollars)

Number of hamburgers sold

FIGURE 3.19

✓ **Checkpoint 5**

Verify the results of Example 5 by completing the table.

x (units)	24,000	24,200	24,300	24,400	24,500	24,600	24,800
P (profit)							

SUMMARIZE   (Section 3.2)

1. State the First-Derivative Test *(page 178)*. For examples in which the First-Derivative Test is used, see Examples 1, 2, and 3.

2. State the guidelines for finding extrema on a closed interval *(page 182)*. For an example of finding the extrema of a function on a closed interval, see Example 4.

3. Describe a real-life example of how the First-Derivative Test can be used to find the sales level that yields a maximum profit for a company *(page 183, Example 5)*.

SKILLS WARM UP 3.2   The following warm-up exercises involve skills that were covered in earlier sections. You will use these skills in the exercise set for this section. For additional help, review Sections 2.2, 2.4, and 3.1.

In Exercises 1–6, solve the equation $f'(x) = 0$.

1. $f(x) = 4x^4 - 2x^2 + 1$

2. $f(x) = \frac{1}{3}x^3 - \frac{3}{2}x^2 - 10x$

3. $f(x) = 5x^{4/5} - 4x$

4. $f(x) = \frac{1}{2}x^2 - 3x^{5/3}$

5. $f(x) = \frac{x+4}{x^2+1}$

6. $f(x) = \frac{x-1}{x^2+4}$

In Exercises 7–10, use $g(x) = -x^5 - 2x^4 + 4x^3 + 2x - 1$ to determine the sign of the derivative.

7. $g'(-4)$

8. $g'(0)$

9. $g'(1)$

10. $g'(3)$

In Exercises 11 and 12, decide whether the function is increasing or decreasing on the given interval.

11. $f(x) = 2x^2 - 11x - 6$, $(3, 6)$

12. $f(x) = x^3 + 2x^2 - 4x - 8$, $(-2, 0)$

Exercises 3.2

See www.CalcChat.com for worked-out solutions to odd-numbered exercises.

Finding Relative Extrema In Exercises 1–12, find all relative extrema of the function. *See Examples 1, 2, and 3.*

1. $f(x) = -2x^2 + 4x + 3$

2. $f(x) = x^2 + 8x + 10$

3. $f(x) = x^2 - 6x$

4. $f(x) = -4x^2 + 4x + 1$

5. $f(x) = x^4 - 12x^3$

6. $g(x) = \frac{1}{5}x^5 - x$

7. $h(x) = -(x + 4)^3$

8. $h(x) = 2(x - 3)^3$

9. $f(x) = x^3 - 6x^2 + 15$

10. $f(x) = x^4 - 32x + 4$

11. $f(x) = 6x^{2/3} + 4x$

12. $f(x) = 3x - 36x^{1/3}$

 Finding Relative Extrema In Exercises 13–18, use a graphing utility to find graphically all relative extrema of the function.

13. $f(x) = 2x - 6x^{2/3}$

14. $f(t) = (t - 1)^{1/3}$

15. $g(t) = t - \frac{1}{2t^2}$

16. $f(x) = x + \frac{1}{x}$

17. $f(x) = \frac{x}{x+1}$

18. $h(x) = \frac{6}{x^2+2}$

Finding Extrema on a Closed Interval In Exercises 19–30, find the absolute extrema of the function on the closed interval. Use a graphing utility to verify your results. *See Example 4.*

19. $f(x) = 2(3 - x)$, $[-1, 2]$

20. $f(x) = \frac{1}{3}(2x + 5)$, $[0, 5]$

21. $f(x) = 5 - 2x^2$, $[0, 3]$

22. $f(x) = x^2 + 2x - 4$, $[-1, 1]$

23. $f(x) = x^3 - 3x^2$, $[-1, 3]$

24. $f(x) = x^3 - 12x$, $[0, 4]$

25. $h(s) = \frac{1}{3 - s}$, $[0, 2]$

26. $h(t) = \frac{t}{t-2}$, $[3, 5]$

27. $g(t) = \frac{t^2}{t^2+3}$, $[-1, 1]$

28. $g(x) = 4\left(1 + \frac{1}{x} + \frac{1}{x^2}\right)$, $[-4, 5]$

29. $h(t) = (t - 1)^{2/3}$, $[-7, 2]$

30. $g(x) = (x^2 - 4)^{2/3}$, $[-6, 3]$

Determining Types of Extrema In Exercises 31–34, approximate the critical numbers of the function shown in the graph. Determine whether the function has a relative maximum, a relative minimum, an absolute maximum, an absolute minimum, or none of these at each critical number on the interval shown.

31.

32.

33.

34.

 Finding Extrema on a Closed Interval In Exercises 35–38, use a graphing utility to find graphically the absolute extrema of the function on the closed interval.

35. $f(x) = 0.4x^3 - 1.8x^2 + x - 3$, $[0, 5]$

36. $f(x) = 3.2x^5 + 5x^3 - 3.5x$, $[0, 1]$

37. $f(x) = \frac{4}{3}x\sqrt{3 - x}$, $[0, 3]$

38. $f(x) = 4\sqrt{x} - 2x + 1$, $[0, 6]$

Finding Absolute Extrema In Exercises 39–42, find the absolute extrema of the function on the interval $[0, \infty)$.

39. $f(x) = x^2 + \dfrac{16}{x}$ **40.** $f(x) = \dfrac{8}{x + 1}$

41. $f(x) = \dfrac{2x}{x^2 + 4}$ **42.** $f(x) = 8 - \dfrac{4x}{x^2 + 1}$

Creating the Graph of a Function In Exercises 43 and 44, graph a function on the closed interval $[-2, 5]$ having the given characteristics. (There are many correct answers.)

43. Absolute maximum at $x = -2$

Absolute minimum at $x = 1$

Relative maximum at $x = 3$

44. Relative minimum at $x = -1$

Critical number at $x = 0$, but no extrema

Absolute maximum at $x = 2$

Absolute minimum at $x = 5$

45. Population The resident populations P (in millions) of the United States from 1790 through 2010 can be modeled by $P = 0.000006t^3 + 0.005t^2 + 0.14t + 4.6$, $-10 \le t \le 210$, where $t = 0$ corresponds to 1800. *(Source: U.S. Census Bureau)*

(a) Make a conjecture about the maximum and minimum populations of the United States from 1790 to 2010.

(b) Analytically find the maximum and minimum populations over the interval.

(c) Write a brief paragraph comparing your conjecture with your results in part (b).

46. **HOW DO YOU SEE IT?** The graph of the United States fertility rate shows the number of births per 1000 women in their lifetime according to the birth rate in that particular year. *(Source: U.S. National Center for Health Statistics)*

United States Fertility

(a) Around what year was the fertility rate the highest, and to how many births per 1000 women did this rate correspond?

(b) During which time periods was the fertility rate increasing most rapidly? most slowly?

(c) During which time periods was the fertility rate decreasing most rapidly? most slowly?

(d) Give some possible real-life reasons for fluctuations in the fertility rate.

47. Cost A retailer determines that the cost C of ordering and storing x units of a product can be modeled by

$$C = 3x + \frac{20,000}{x}, \quad 0 < x \le 200.$$

The delivery truck can carry at most 200 units per order. Find the order size that will minimize the cost. Use a graphing utility to verify your result.

48. Medical Science Coughing forces the trachea (windpipe) to contract, which in turn affects the velocity of the air passing through the trachea. The velocity of the air during coughing can be modeled by

$$v = k(R - r)r^2, \quad 0 \le r < R$$

where k is a constant, R is the normal radius of the trachea, and r is the radius during coughing. What radius r will produce the maximum air velocity?

49. Profit When soft drinks are sold for $1.00 per can at football games, approximately 6000 cans are sold. When the price is raised to $1.20 per can, the quantity demanded drops to 5600. The initial cost is $5000 and the cost per unit is $0.50. Assuming that the demand function is linear, what number of units and what price will yield a maximum profit?

3.3 Concavity and the Second-Derivative Test

- Determine the intervals on which the graphs of functions are concave upward or concave downward.
- Find the points of inflection of the graphs of functions.
- Use the Second-Derivative Test to find the relative extrema of functions.
- Find the points of diminishing returns of input-output models.

Concavity

You already know that locating the intervals over which a function f increases or decreases helps to describe its graph. In this section, you will see that locating the intervals on which f' increases or decreases can determine where the graph of f is curving upward or curving downward. This property of curving upward or downward is defined formally as the **concavity** of the graph of the function.

Definition of Concavity

Let f be differentiable on an open interval I. The graph of f is

1. **concave upward** on I when f' is increasing on the interval.

2. **concave downward** on I when f' is decreasing on the interval.

In Exercise 69 on page 194, you will use the Second-Derivative Test to find the production level that will minimize the average cost per unit.

In Figure 3.20, you can observe the following graphical interpretation of concavity.

1. A curve that is concave upward lies *above* its tangent line.

2. A curve that is concave downward lies *below* its tangent line.

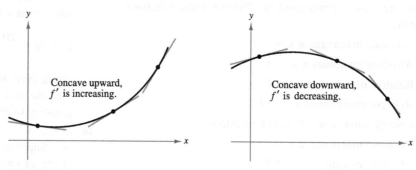

Concave upward, f' is increasing.

Concave downward, f' is decreasing.

FIGURE 3.20

To find the open intervals on which the graph of a function is concave upward or concave downward, you can use the second derivative of the function as follows.

Test for Concavity

Let f be a function whose second derivative exists on an open interval I.

1. If $f''(x) > 0$ for all x in I, then the graph of f is concave upward on I.

2. If $f''(x) < 0$ for all x in I, then the graph of f is concave downward on I.

Example 1   **Determining Concavity**

a. The graph of the function

$$f(x) = x^2 \qquad \text{Original function}$$

is concave upward on the entire real number line because its second derivative

$$f''(x) = 2 \qquad \text{Second derivative}$$

is positive for all x. (See Figure 3.21.)

b. The graph of the function

$$f(x) = \sqrt{x} \qquad \text{Original function}$$

is concave downward for $x > 0$ because its second derivative

$$f''(x) = -\frac{1}{4}x^{-3/2} \qquad \text{Second derivative}$$

is negative for all $x > 0$. (See Figure 3.22.)

Concave Upward
FIGURE 3.21

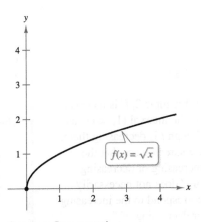

Concave Downward
FIGURE 3.22

✓**Checkpoint 1**

Find the second derivative of f and discuss the concavity of its graph.

a. $f(x) = -2x^2$

b. $f(x) = -2\sqrt{x}$

For a *continuous* function f, you can find the open intervals on which the graph of f is concave upward and concave downward as follows. [When there are x-values at which the function is not continuous, these values should be used, along with the points at which $f''(x) = 0$ or $f''(x)$ is undefined, to form the test intervals.]

Guidelines for Applying the Concavity Test

1. Locate the x-values at which $f''(x) = 0$ or $f''(x)$ is undefined.

2. Use these x-values to determine the test intervals.

3. Test the sign of $f''(x)$ in each test interval.

ALGEBRA TUTOR xy

For help on the algebra in Example 2, see Example 1(a) in the *Chapter 3 Algebra Tutor*, on page 242.

David Gilder/Shutterstock.com

Example 2   Applying the Test for Concavity

Determine the open intervals on which the graph of

$$f(x) = \frac{6}{x^2 + 3}$$

is concave upward or concave downward.

SOLUTION   Begin by finding the second derivative of f.

$$f(x) = 6(x^2 + 3)^{-1}$$ Rewrite original function.

$$f'(x) = 6(-1)(x^2 + 3)^{-2}(2x)$$ Chain Rule

$$= \frac{-12x}{(x^2 + 3)^2}$$ Simplify.

$$f''(x) = \frac{(x^2 + 3)^2(-12) - (-12x)(2)(x^2 + 3)(2x)}{(x^2 + 3)^4}$$ Quotient Rule

$$= \frac{-12(x^2 + 3) + 48x^2}{(x^2 + 3)^3}$$ Simplify.

$$= \frac{36(x^2 - 1)}{(x^2 + 3)^3}$$ Simplify.

From this, you can see that $f''(x)$ is defined for all real numbers and $f''(x) = 0$ when $x = \pm 1$. So, you can test the concavity of f by testing the intervals

$$(-\infty, -1), \quad (-1, 1), \quad \text{and} \quad (1, \infty).$$ Test intervals

The results are shown in the table and in Figure 3.23.

Interval	$-\infty < x < -1$	$-1 < x < 1$	$1 < x < \infty$
Test value	$x = -2$	$x = 0$	$x = 2$
Sign of $f''(x)$	$f''(-2) > 0$	$f''(0) < 0$	$f''(2) > 0$
Conclusion	Concave upward	Concave downward	Concave upward

STUDY TIP

In Example 2, f' is increasing on the interval $(1, \infty)$ even though f is decreasing there. Be sure you see that the increasing or decreasing of f' does not necessarily correspond to the increasing or decreasing of f.

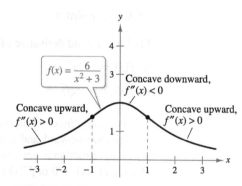

FIGURE 3.23

✓ Checkpoint 2

Determine the intervals on which the graph of

$$f(x) = \frac{12}{x^2 + 4}$$

is concave upward or concave downward.

Points of Inflection

If the tangent line to a graph exists at a point at which the concavity changes, then the point is a **point of inflection**. Three examples of inflection points are shown in Figure 3.24. (Note that the third graph has a vertical tangent line at its point of inflection.)

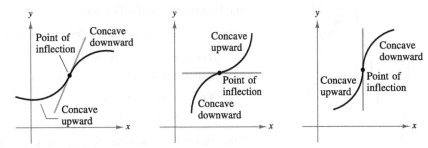

The graph *crosses* its tangent line at a point of inflection.

FIGURE 3.24

Definition of Point of Inflection

If the graph of a continuous function has a tangent line at a point where its concavity changes from upward to downward (or downward to upward), then the point is a **point of inflection.**

Because a point of inflection occurs where the concavity of a graph changes, it must be true that at such points the sign of f'' changes. So, to locate possible points of inflection, you need to determine only the values of x for which $f''(x) = 0$ or for which $f''(x)$ does not exist. This parallels the procedure for locating the relative extrema of f by determining the critical numbers of f.

Property of Points of Inflection

If $(c, f(c))$ is a point of inflection of the graph of f, then either $f''(c) = 0$ or $f''(c)$ is undefined.

Example 3 Finding a Point of Inflection

Discuss the concavity of the graph of $f(x) = 2x^3 + 1$ and find its point of inflection.

SOLUTION Differentiating twice produces the following.

$$f(x) = 2x^3 + 1 \qquad \text{Write original function.}$$
$$f'(x) = 6x^2 \qquad \text{Find first derivative.}$$
$$f''(x) = 12x \qquad \text{Find second derivative.}$$

Setting $f''(x) = 0$, you can determine that the only possible point of inflection occurs at $x = 0$. After testing the intervals $(-\infty, 0)$ and $(0, \infty)$, you can determine that the graph is concave downward on $(-\infty, 0)$ and concave upward on $(0, \infty)$. Because the concavity changes at $x = 0$, you can conclude that the graph of f has a point of inflection at $(0, 1)$, as shown in Figure 3.25.

$f(x) = 2x^3 + 1$

FIGURE 3.25

✓ **Checkpoint 3**

Discuss the concavity of the graph of $f(x) = -x^3$ and find its point of inflection. ■

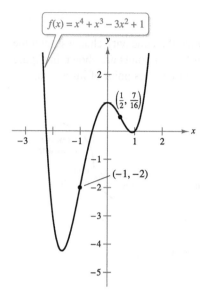

$$f(x) = x^4 + x^3 - 3x^2 + 1$$

Two Points of Inflection
FIGURE 3.26

Example 4 **Finding Points of Inflection**

Discuss the concavity of the graph of

$$f(x) = x^4 + x^3 - 3x^2 + 1$$

and find its points of inflection.

SOLUTION Begin by finding the second derivative of f.

$$f(x) = x^4 + x^3 - 3x^2 + 1 \qquad \text{Write original function.}$$
$$f'(x) = 4x^3 + 3x^2 - 6x \qquad \text{Find first derivative.}$$
$$f''(x) = 12x^2 + 6x - 6 \qquad \text{Find second derivative.}$$
$$= 6(2x - 1)(x + 1) \qquad \text{Factor.}$$

From this, you can see that the possible points of inflection occur at $x = \frac{1}{2}$ and $x = -1$. After testing the intervals $(-\infty, -1)$, $\left(-1, \frac{1}{2}\right)$, and $\left(\frac{1}{2}, \infty\right)$, you can determine that the graph is concave upward on $(-\infty, -1)$, concave downward on $\left(-1, \frac{1}{2}\right)$, and concave upward on $\left(\frac{1}{2}, \infty\right)$. Because the concavity changes at $x = -1$ and $x = \frac{1}{2}$, you can conclude that the graph of f has points of inflection at these x-values, as shown in Figure 3.26. The points of inflection are

$$(-1, -2) \quad \text{and} \quad \left(\frac{1}{2}, \frac{7}{16}\right).$$

✓**Checkpoint 4**

Discuss the concavity of the graph of

$$f(x) = x^4 - 2x^3 + 1$$

and find its points of inflection.

It is possible for the second derivative to be zero at a point that is *not* a point of inflection. For example, compare the graphs of

$$f(x) = x^3 \quad \text{and} \quad g(x) = x^4$$

as shown in Figure 3.27. Both second derivatives are zero when $x = 0$, but only the graph of f has a point of inflection at $x = 0$. This shows that before concluding that a point of inflection exists at a value of x for which $f''(x) = 0$, you must test to be certain that the concavity actually changes at that point.

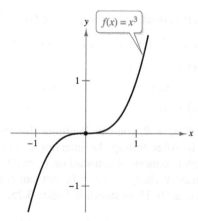

$f''(0) = 0$, and $(0, 0)$ is a point of inflection.

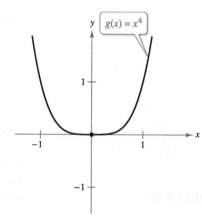

$g''(0) = 0$, but $(0, 0)$ is not a point of inflection.

FIGURE 3.27

The Second-Derivative Test

The second derivative can be used to perform a simple test for relative minima and relative maxima. If f is a function such that $f'(c) = 0$ and the graph of f is concave upward at $x = c$, then $f(c)$ is a relative minimum of f. Similarly, if f is a function such that $f'(c) = 0$ and the graph of f is concave downward at $x = c$, then $f(c)$ is a relative maximum of f, as shown in Figure 3.28.

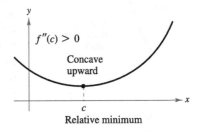

FIGURE 3.28

Second-Derivative Test

Let $f'(c) = 0$, and let f'' exist on an open interval containing c.

1. If $f''(c) > 0$, then $f(c)$ is a relative minimum.

2. If $f''(c) < 0$, then $f(c)$ is a relative maximum.

3. If $f''(c) = 0$, then the test fails. In such cases, you can use the First-Derivative Test to determine whether $f(c)$ is a relative minimum, a relative maximum, or neither.

Example 5 Using the Second-Derivative Test

Find the relative extrema of $f(x) = -3x^5 + 5x^3$.

SOLUTION Begin by finding the first derivative of f.

$$f'(x) = -15x^4 + 15x^2 = 15x^2(1 - x^2)$$

From this derivative, you can see that $x = 0$, $x = -1$, and $x = 1$ are the only critical numbers of f. Using the second derivative

$$f''(x) = -60x^3 + 30x = 30x(1 - 2x^2)$$

you can apply the Second-Derivative Test, as shown.

Point	$(-1, -2)$	$(0, 0)$	$(1, 2)$
Sign of $f''(x)$	$f''(-1) > 0$	$f''(0) = 0$	$f''(1) < 0$
Conclusion	Relative minimum	Test fails.	Relative maximum

Because the Second-Derivative Test fails at $(0, 0)$, you can use the First-Derivative Test and observe that f is positive on both sides of $x = 0$. So, $(0, 0)$ is neither a relative minimum nor a relative maximum. A test for concavity would show that $(0, 0)$ is a point of inflection. The graph of f is shown in Figure 3.29.

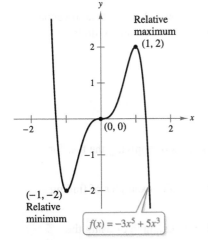

FIGURE 3.29

✓ **Checkpoint 5**

Find all relative extrema of $f(x) = x^4 - 4x^3 + 1$.

FIGURE 3.30

FIGURE 3.31

Extended Application: Diminishing Returns

In economics, the notion of concavity is related to the concept of **diminishing returns.** Consider a function

Output $\longrightarrow$ $\qquad$ $\longleftarrow$ Input

$$y = f(x)$$

where x measures input (in dollars) and y measures output (in dollars). In Figure 3.30, notice that the graph of this function is concave upward on the interval (a, c) and is concave downward on the interval (c, b). On the interval (a, c), each additional dollar of input returns more than the previous input dollar. By contrast, on the interval (c, b), each additional dollar of input returns less than the previous input dollar. The point $(c, f(c))$ is called the **point of diminishing returns.** An increased investment beyond this point is usually considered a poor use of capital.

Example 6 Exploring Diminishing Returns

By increasing its advertising cost x (in thousands of dollars) for a product, a company discovers that it can increase the sales y (in thousands of dollars) according to the model

$$y = -\frac{1}{10}x^3 + 6x^2 + 400, \quad 0 \le x \le 40.$$

Find the point of diminishing returns for this product.

SOLUTION   Begin by finding the first and second derivatives.

$$y' = 12x - \frac{3x^2}{10} \qquad \text{First derivative}$$

$$y'' = 12 - \frac{3x}{5} \qquad \text{Second derivative}$$

The second derivative is zero only when $x = 20$. By testing for concavity on the intervals $(0, 20)$ and $(20, 40)$, you can conclude that the graph has a point of diminishing returns when $x = 20$, as shown in Figure 3.31. So, the point of diminishing returns for this product occurs when \$20,000 is spent on advertising.

✓**Checkpoint 6**

Find the point of diminishing returns for the model below, where R is the revenue (in thousands of dollars) and x is the advertising cost (in thousands of dollars).

$$R = \frac{1}{20,000}(450x^2 - x^3), \quad 0 \le x \le 300$$

SUMMARIZE   (Section 3.3)

1. State the test for concavity (*page 186*). For examples of applying the test for concavity, see Examples 1 and 2.

2. State the definition of point of inflection (*page 189*). For examples of finding points of inflection, see Examples 3 and 4.

3. State the Second-Derivative Test (*page 191*). For an example of using the Second-Derivative Test, see Example 5.

4. Describe a real-life example of how the second derivative can be used to find the point of diminishing returns for a product (*page 192, Example 6*).

SKILLS WARM UP 3.3

The following warm-up exercises involve skills that were covered in earlier sections. You will use these skills in the exercise set for this section. For additional help, review Sections 2.2, 2.4, 2.5, 2.6, and 3.1.

In Exercises 1–6, find the second derivative of the function.

1. $f(x) = 4x^4 - 9x^3 + 5x - 1$

2. $g(s) = (s^2 - 1)(s^2 - 3s + 2)$

3. $g(x) = (x^2 + 1)^4$

4. $f(x) = (x - 3)^{4/3}$

5. $h(x) = \dfrac{4x + 3}{5x - 1}$

6. $f(x) = \dfrac{2x - 1}{3x + 2}$

In Exercises 7–10, find the critical numbers of the function.

7. $f(x) = 5x^3 - 5x + 11$

8. $f(x) = x^4 - 4x^3 - 10$

9. $g(t) = \dfrac{16 + t^2}{t}$

10. $h(x) = \dfrac{x^4 - 50x^2}{8}$

Exercises 3.3

See www.CalcChat.com for worked-out solutions to odd-numbered exercises.

Using Graphs In Exercises 1–4, state the signs of $f'(x)$ and $f''(x)$ on the interval $(0, 2)$.

1.

2.

3.

4.

Applying the Test for Concavity In Exercises 5–12, determine the open intervals on which the graph of the function is concave upward or concave downward. *See Examples 1 and 2.*

5. $f(x) = -3x^2$

6. $f(x) = -5\sqrt{x}$

7. $y = -x^3 + 3x^2 - 2$

8. $y = -x^3 + 6x^2 - 9x - 1$

9. $f(x) = \dfrac{x^2 - 1}{2x + 1}$

10. $f(x) = \dfrac{x^2 + 4}{4 - x^2}$

11. $f(x) = \dfrac{24}{x^2 + 12}$

12. $f(x) = \dfrac{x^2}{x^2 + 1}$

Finding Points of Inflection In Exercises 13–20, discuss the concavity of the graph of the function and find the points of inflection. *See Examples 3 and 4.*

13. $f(x) = x^3 - 9x^2 + 24x - 18$

14. $f(x) = -4x^3 - 8x^2 + 32$

15. $f(x) = 2x^3 - 3x^2 - 12x + 5$

16. $f(x) = \frac{1}{2}x^4 + 2x^3$

17. $g(x) = 2x^4 - 8x^3 + 12x^2 + 12x$

18. $g(x) = x^5 + 5x^4 - 40x^2$

19. $f(x) = x(6 - x)^2$

20. $f(x) = (x - 1)^3(x - 5)$

Using the Second-Derivative Test In Exercises 21–34, find all relative extrema of the function. Use the Second-Derivative Test when applicable. *See Example 5.*

21. $f(x) = 6x - x^2$

22. $f(x) = 9x^2 - x^3$

23. $f(x) = x^3 - 5x^2 + 7x$

24. $f(x) = x^4 + 8x^3 - 6$

25. $f(x) = x^{2/3} - 3$

26. $f(x) = x + \dfrac{4}{x}$

27. $f(x) = \sqrt{x^2 + 1}$

28. $f(x) = \sqrt{2x^2 + 6}$

29. $f(x) = \sqrt{9 - x^2}$

30. $f(x) = \sqrt{4 - x^2}$

31. $f(x) = \dfrac{8}{x^2 + 2}$

32. $f(x) = \dfrac{x}{x^2 + 16}$

33. $f(x) = \dfrac{x}{x - 1}$

34. $f(x) = \dfrac{x}{x^2 - 1}$

Finding Relative Extrema   In Exercises 35–38, use a graphing utility to estimate graphically all relative extrema of the function.

35. $f(x) = 5 + 3x^2 - x^3$ **36.** $f(x) = x^3 - 6x^2 + 7$

37. $f(x) = \frac{1}{2}x^4 - \frac{1}{3}x^3 - \frac{1}{2}x^2$

38. $f(x) = -\frac{1}{3}x^5 - \frac{1}{2}x^4 + x$

Using the Second-Derivative Test   In Exercises 39–50, find all relative extrema and points of inflection. Then use a graphing utility to graph the function.

39. $f(x) = x^3 - 12x$ **40.** $f(x) = x^3 - 3x$

41. $g(x) = \sqrt{x} + \dfrac{4}{\sqrt{x}}$ **42.** $f(x) = x^3 - \frac{3}{2}x^2 - 6x$

43. $f(x) = \frac{1}{4}x^4 - 2x^2$ **44.** $f(x) = 2x^4 - 8x + 3$

45. $g(x) = (x - 2)(x + 1)^2$ **46.** $g(x) = (x - 6)(x + 2)^3$

47. $g(x) = x\sqrt{x + 3}$ **48.** $g(x) = x\sqrt{9 - x}$

49. $f(x) = \dfrac{4}{1 + x^2}$

50. $f(x) = \dfrac{2}{x^2 - 1}$

Creating a Function   In Exercises 51–54, sketch a graph of a function f having the given characteristics. (There are many correct answers.)

51. $f(2) = f(4) = 0$ **52.** $f(2) = f(4) = 0$
$f'(x) < 0$ if $x < 3$ $f'(x) > 0$ if $x < 3$
$f'(3) = 0$ $f'(3)$ is undefined.
$f'(x) > 0$ if $x > 3$ $f'(x) < 0$ if $x > 3$
$f''(x) > 0$ $f''(x) > 0, x \neq 3$

53. $f(0) = f(2) = 0$ **54.** $f(0) = f(2) = 0$
$f'(x) > 0$ if $x < 1$ $f'(x) < 0$ if $x < 1$
$f'(1) = 0$ $f'(1) = 0$
$f'(x) < 0$ if $x > 1$ $f'(x) > 0$ if $x > 1$
$f''(x) < 0$ $f''(x) > 0$

Using Graphs   In Exercises 55 and 56, use the graph to sketch the graph of f'. Find the intervals on which (a) $f'(x)$ is positive, (b) $f'(x)$ is negative, (c) f' is increasing, and (d) f' is decreasing. For each of these intervals, describe the corresponding behavior of f.

55.

56.

Using the First Derivative   In Exercises 57–60, you are given f'. Find the intervals on which (a) $f'(x)$ is increasing or decreasing and (b) the graph of f is concave upward or concave downward. (c) Find the x-values of the relative extrema and inflection points of f.

57. $f'(x) = 2x + 5$ **58.** $f'(x) = 3x^2 - 2$

59. $f'(x) = -x^2 + 2x - 1$ **60.** $f'(x) = x^2 + x - 6$

Point of Diminishing Returns   In Exercises 61 and 62, find the point of diminishing returns for the function. For each function, R is the revenue (in thousands of dollars) and x is the amount spent (in thousands of dollars) on advertising. Use a graphing utility to verify your results. *See Example 6.*

61. $R = \dfrac{1}{50,000}(600x^2 - x^3), \quad 0 \le x \le 400$

62. $R = -\dfrac{4}{9}x^3 + 4x^2 + 12, \quad 0 \le x \le 5$

Productivity   In Exercises 63 and 64, consider a college student who works from 7 P.M. to 11 P.M. assembling mechanical components. The number N of components assembled after t hours is given by the function. At what time is the student assembling components at the greatest rate?

63. $N = -0.12t^3 + 0.54t^2 + 8.22t, \quad 0 \le t \le 4$

64. $N = \dfrac{20t^2}{4 + t^2}, \quad 0 \le t \le 4$

Comparing a Function and Its Derivatives   In Exercises 65–68, use a graphing utility to graph f, f', and f'' in the same viewing window. Graphically locate the relative extrema and points of inflection of the graph of f. State the relationship between the behavior of f and the signs of f' and f''.

65. $f(x) = \frac{1}{2}x^3 - x^2 + 3x - 5, \quad [0, 3]$

66. $f(x) = -\frac{1}{20}x^5 - \frac{1}{12}x^2 - \frac{1}{3}x + 1, \quad [-2, 2]$

67. $f(x) = \dfrac{2}{x^2 + 1}, \quad [-3, 3]$

68. $f(x) = \dfrac{x^2}{x^2 + 1}, \quad [-3, 3]$

69. Average Cost   A manufacturer has determined that the total cost C (in dollars) of operating a factory is $C = 0.5x^2 + 10x + 7200$, where x is the number of units produced. At what level of production will the average cost per unit be minimized? (The average cost per unit is C/x.)

70. Inventory Cost   The cost C (in dollars) of ordering and storing x units is $C = 2x + 300,000/x$. What order size will produce a minimum cost?

71. Home Sales   The median sales price p (in thousands of dollars) of new single-family houses sold in the United States from 1995 through 2009 can be modeled by

$p = -0.02812t^4 + 1.177t^3 - 17.02t^2 + 108.7t - 115$,

for $5 \le t \le 19$, where t is the year, with $t = 5$ corresponding to 1995.   *(Source: U.S. Census Bureau)*

(a) Use a graphing utility to graph the model on the interval $[5, 19]$.

(b) Use the graph in part (a) to estimate the year corresponding to the absolute minimum sales price.

(c) Use the graph in part (a) to estimate the year corresponding to the absolute maximum sales price.

(d) During approximately which year was the rate of increase of the sales price the greatest? the least?

72. HOW DO YOU SEE IT?   The graph shows the Dow Jones Industrial Average y on Black Monday, October 19, 1987, where $t = 0$ corresponds to 9:30 A.M., when the market opens, and $t = 6.5$ corresponds to 4 P.M., the closing time.
(Source: Wall Street Journal)

Black Monday

(a) Estimate the relative extrema and absolute extrema of the graph. Interpret your results in the context of the problem.

(b) Estimate the point of inflection of the graph on the interval $[1, 3]$. Interpret your result in the context of the problem.

73. Veteran Benefits   From 1995 through 2008, the number v of veterans (in thousands) receiving compensation and pension benefits for service in the armed forces can be modeled by

$v = -0.0687t^4 + 3.169t^3 - 45t^2 + 230.6t + 2950$

for $5 \le t \le 18$, where t is the year, with $t = 5$ corresponding to 1995.   *(Source: U.S. Department of Veterans Affairs)*

(a) Use a graphing utility to graph the model on the interval $[5, 18]$.

(b) Use the second derivative to determine the concavity of v.

(c) Find the point(s) of inflection of the graph of v.

(d) Interpret the meaning of the inflection point(s) of the graph of v.

74. Think About It   Let S represent monthly sales of a new digital audio player. Write a statement describing S' and S'' for each of the following.

(a) The rate of change of sales is increasing.

(b) Sales are increasing, but at a greater rate.

(c) The rate of change of sales is steady.

(d) Sales are steady.

(e) Sales are declining, but at a lower rate.

(f) Sales have bottomed out and have begun to rise.

Business Capsule

While working in New York City in 2004, Matthew Corrin noticed an abundance of fresh food bars and decided that if someone could successfully brand one, that person could create the "Starbucks of the fresh food business." With $275,000, he opened his first Freshii store in Toronto in 2005, and soon began developments for more. By the end of 2011, he will have 80–90 locations worldwide, with agreements signed for 400 additional stores in 25 cities and four countries. The mission of this eco-friendly chain is "to eliminate the excuse of people not eating fresh food because it isn't convenient," Corrin said.

75. Research Project   Use your school's library, the Internet, or some other reference source to research the financial history of a fast-growing company like the one discussed above. Gather data on the company's costs and revenues over a period of time, and use a graphing utility to graph a scatter plot of the data. Fit models to the data. Do the models appear to be concave upward or downward? Do they appear to be increasing or decreasing? Discuss the implications of your answers.

3.4 Optimization Problems

■ Solve real-life optimization problems.

Solving Optimization Problems

One of the most common applications of calculus is the determination of optimum (minimum or maximum) values. Before learning a general method for solving optimization problems, consider the next example.

  Example 1 **Finding the Maximum Volume**

A manufacturer wants to design an open box that has a square base and a surface area S of 108 square inches, as shown in Figure 3.32. What dimensions will produce a box with a maximum volume?

SOLUTION   Because the base of the box is square, the volume is

$$V = x^2h. \qquad \text{Primary equation}$$

This equation is called the **primary equation** because it gives a formula for the quantity to be optimized. The surface area of the box is

$$S = (\text{area of base}) + (\text{area of four sides})$$
$$108 = x^2 + 4xh. \qquad \text{Secondary equation}$$

Open Box with Square Base:
$S = x^2 + 4xh = 108$
FIGURE 3.32

Because V is to be optimized, it helps to express V as a function of just one variable. To do this, solve the secondary equation for h in terms of x to obtain

$$h = \frac{108 - x^2}{4x}$$

and substitute for h in the primary equation.

$$V = x^2h = x^2\left(\frac{108 - x^2}{4x}\right) = 27x - \frac{1}{4}x^3 \qquad \text{Function of one variable}$$

Before finding which x-value yields a maximum value of V, you need to determine the *feasible domain* of the function. That is, what values of x make sense in this problem? Because x must be nonnegative and the area of the base $(A = x^2)$ is at most 108, you can conclude that the feasible domain is

$$0 \le x \le \sqrt{108}. \qquad \text{Feasible domain}$$

Using the techniques described in the first three sections of this chapter, you can determine that $\left(\text{on the interval } 0 \le x \le \sqrt{108}\right)$ this function has an absolute maximum at $x = 6$ inches and $h = 3$ inches.

✓ **Checkpoint 1**

Use a graphing utility to graph the volume function

$$V = 27x - \frac{1}{4}x^3$$

from Example 1 on $0 \le x \le \sqrt{108}$. Verify that the function has an absolute maximum at $x = 6$. What is the maximum volume?

In Exercise 13 on page 202, you will use primary equations, secondary equations, and derivatives to find the dimensions of a box that will minimize the cost of making the box.

ALGEBRA TUTOR xy

For help on the algebra in Example 1, see Example 1(c) in the *Chapter 3 Algebra Tutor,* on page 242.

Cost of a Storage Box
Cost (in dollars)
Side length (in centimeters)

In studying Example 1, be sure that you understand the basic question that it asks. Remember that you are not ready to begin solving an optimization problem until you have clearly identified the problem. Once you are sure you understand what is being asked, you are ready to begin considering a method for solving the problem.

For instance, in Example 1, you should realize that there are infinitely many open boxes having 108 square inches of surface area. To begin solving this problem, you might ask yourself which basic shape would seem to yield a maximum volume. Should the box be tall, squat, or nearly cubical? You might even try calculating a few volumes, as shown in Figure 3.33, to see if you can get a better feeling for what the optimum dimensions should be.

Volume $= 74\frac{1}{4}$

Volume $= 92$

Volume $= 103\frac{3}{4}$

$3 \times 3 \times 8\frac{1}{4}$ $4 \times 4 \times 5\frac{3}{4}$ $5 \times 5 \times 4\frac{3}{20}$

Volume $= 108$

Volume $= 88$

$6 \times 6 \times 3$ $8 \times 8 \times 1\frac{3}{8}$

Which box has the greatest volume?

FIGURE 3.33

There are several steps in the solution of Example 1. The first step is to sketch a diagram and identify all *known* quantities and all quantities *to be determined*. The second step is to write a primary equation for the quantity to be optimized. Then, a secondary equation is used to rewrite the primary equation as a function of one variable. Finally, calculus is used to determine the optimum value. These steps are summarized below.

STUDY TIP

When performing Step 5, remember that to determine the maximum or minimum value of a continuous function f on a closed interval, you need to compare the values of f at its critical numbers with the values of f at the endpoints of the interval. The greatest of these values is the desired maximum, and the least is the desired minimum.

Guidelines for Solving Optimization Problems

1. Identify all given quantities and all quantities to be determined. If possible, make a sketch.

2. Write a **primary equation** for the quantity that is to be maximized or minimized. (A summary of several common formulas is given in Appendix D.)

3. Reduce the primary equation to one having a single independent variable. This may involve the use of a **secondary equation** that relates the independent variables of the primary equation.

4. Determine the feasible domain of the primary equation. That is, determine the values for which the stated problem makes sense.

5. Determine the desired maximum or minimum value by the calculus techniques discussed in Sections 3.1 through 3.3.

Example 2   Finding a Minimum Distance

Find the points on the graph of

$$y = 4 - x^2$$

that are closest to $(0, 2)$.

SOLUTION

1. Figure 3.34 shows that there are two points at a minimum distance from $(0, 2)$.

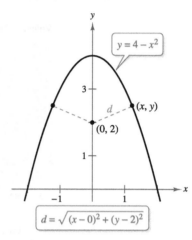

$$d = \sqrt{(x - 0)^2 + (y - 2)^2}$$

FIGURE 3.34

2. You are asked to minimize the distance d. So, you can use the Distance Formula to obtain a primary equation.

$$d = \sqrt{(x - 0)^2 + (y - 2)^2} \qquad \text{Primary equation}$$

3. Using the secondary equation $y = 4 - x^2$, you can rewrite the primary equation as a function of a single variable.

$$
\begin{aligned}
d &= \sqrt{x^2 + (4 - x^2 - 2)^2} && \text{Substitute } 4 - x^2 \text{ for } y. \\
&= \sqrt{x^2 + (2 - x^2)^2} && \text{Simplify.} \\
&= \sqrt{x^2 + 4 - 4x^2 + x^4} && \text{Expand binomial.} \\
&= \sqrt{x^4 - 3x^2 + 4} && \text{Combine like terms.}
\end{aligned}
$$

Because d is smallest when the expression under the radical is smallest, you simplify the problem by finding the minimum value of $f(x) = x^4 - 3x^2 + 4$.

4. The domain of f is the entire real number line.

5. To find the minimum value of $f(x)$, first find the critical numbers of f.

$$
\begin{aligned}
f'(x) &= 4x^3 - 6x && \text{Find derivative of } f. \\
0 &= 4x^3 - 6x && \text{Set derivative equal to 0.} \\
0 &= 2x(2x^2 - 3) && \text{Factor.} \\
x &= 0, \ x = \sqrt{\tfrac{3}{2}}, \ x = -\sqrt{\tfrac{3}{2}} && \text{Critical numbers}
\end{aligned}
$$

The First-Derivative Test verifies that $x = 0$ yields a relative maximum, whereas both $\sqrt{3/2}$ and $-\sqrt{3/2}$ yield a minimum. So, the points closest to $(0, 2)$ are

$$\left(\sqrt{\tfrac{3}{2}}, \tfrac{5}{2}\right) \quad \text{and} \quad \left(-\sqrt{\tfrac{3}{2}}, \tfrac{5}{2}\right).$$

✓ **Checkpoint 2**

Find the points on the graph of $y = 4 - x^2$ that are closest to $(0, 3)$.

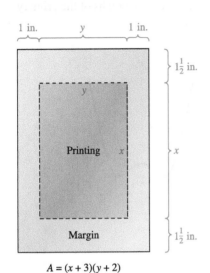

1 in.   y   1 in.

$1\frac{1}{2}$ in.

$1\frac{1}{2}$ in.

Printing   x

x

Margin

$A = (x + 3)(y + 2)$

FIGURE 3.35

Example 3   **Finding a Minimum Area**

A rectangular page will contain 24 square inches of print. The margins at the top and bottom of the page are $1\frac{1}{2}$ inches wide. The margins on each side are 1 inch wide. What should the dimensions of the page be to minimize the amount of paper used?

SOLUTION

1. A diagram of the page is shown in Figure 3.35.

2. Letting A be the area to be minimized, the primary equation is

    $$A = (x + 3)(y + 2).$$ Primary equation

3. The printed area inside the margins is given by

    $$24 = xy.$$ Secondary equation

    Solving this equation for y produces

    $$y = \frac{24}{x}.$$

    By substituting this result into the primary equation, you obtain

    $$A = (x + 3)\left(\frac{24}{x} + 2\right)$$ Write as a function of one variable.

    $$= (x + 3)\left(\frac{24 + 2x}{x}\right)$$ Rewrite second factor as a single fraction.

    $$= \frac{2x^2}{x} + \frac{30x}{x} + \frac{72}{x}$$ Multiply and separate into terms.

    $$= 2x + 30 + \frac{72}{x}.$$ Simplify.

4. Because x must be positive, the feasible domain is $x > 0$.

5. To find the minimum area, begin by finding the critical numbers of A.

    $$\frac{dA}{dx} = 2 - \frac{72}{x^2}$$ Find derivative of A.

    $$0 = 2 - \frac{72}{x^2}$$ Set derivative equal to 0.

    $$-2 = -\frac{72}{x^2}$$ Subtract 2 from each side.

    $$x^2 = 36$$ Simplify.

    $$x = \pm 6$$ Critical numbers

    Because $x = -6$ is not in the feasible domain, you need to consider only the critical number $x = 6$. Using the First-Derivative Test, it follows that A is a minimum when $x = 6$. So, the dimensions of the page should be

    $$x + 3 = 6 + 3 = 9 \text{ inches}   \text{by}   y + 2 = \frac{24}{6} + 2 = 6 \text{ inches.}$$

✓**Checkpoint 3**

A rectangular page will contain 54 square inches of print. The margins at the top and bottom of the page are $1\frac{1}{2}$ inches wide. The margins on each side are 1 inch wide. What should the dimensions of the page be to minimize the amount of paper used? ■

As applications go, the examples described in this section are fairly simple, and yet the resulting primary equations are quite complicated. Real-life applications often involve equations that are at least as complex as the ones in the examples. Remember that one of the main goals of this course is to enable you to use the power of calculus to analyze equations that at first glance seem formidable.

Also remember that once you have found the primary equation, you can use the graph of the equation to help solve the problem. For instance, the graphs of the primary equations in Examples 1 through 3 are shown in Figure 3.36.

Example 1

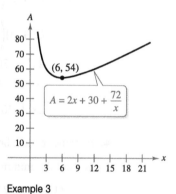

Example 2

Example 3

FIGURE 3.36

SUMMARIZE   (Section 3.4)

1. State what is meant by the primary equation of an optimization problem *(page 196)*. For examples of primary equations in optimization problems, see Examples 1, 2, and 3.

2. State what is meant by the feasible domain of a function *(page 196)*. For examples of feasible domains, see Examples 1, 2, and 3.

3. State what is meant by the secondary equation of an optimization problem *(page 197)*. For examples of secondary equations in optimization problems, see Examples 1, 2, and 3.

4. State the guidelines for solving optimization problems *(page 197)*. For examples of solving optimization problems, see Examples 2 and 3.

5. Describe a real-life example of how solving an optimization problem can be used to determine the dimensions of a page so that the amount of paper used is minimized *(page 199, Example 3)*.

SKILLS WARM UP 3.4   The following warm-up exercises involve skills that were covered in earlier sections. You will use these skills in the exercise set for this section. For additional help, review Section 3.1.

In Exercises 1–4, write a formula for the written statement.

1. The sum of one number and half a second number is 12.

2. The product of one number and twice another is 24.

3. The area of a rectangle is 24 square units.

4. The distance between two points is 10 units.

In Exercises 5–10, find the critical numbers of the function.

5. $y = x^2 + 6x - 9$

6. $y = 2x^3 - x^2 - 4x$

7. $y = 5x + \dfrac{125}{x}$

8. $y = 3x + \dfrac{96}{x^2}$

9. $y = \dfrac{x^2 + 1}{x}$

10. $y = \dfrac{x}{x^2 + 9}$

Exercises 3.4

See www.CalcChat.com for worked-out solutions to odd-numbered exercises.

Maximum Area   In Exercises 1 and 2, find the length and width of a rectangle that has the given perimeter and a maximum area.

1. Perimeter: 100 meters

2. Perimeter: P units

Minimum Perimeter   In Exercises 3 and 4, find the length and width of a rectangle that has the given area and a minimum perimeter.

3. Area: 64 square feet

4. Area: A square centimeters

5. Maximum Area   A rancher has 200 feet of fencing to enclose two adjacent rectangular corrals (see figure). What dimensions should be used so that the enclosed area will be a maximum?

6. Minimum Dimensions   A dairy farmer plans to enclose a rectangular pasture adjacent to a river. To provide enough grass for the herd, the pasture must contain 245,000 square meters. No fencing is required along the river. What dimensions will use the least amount of fencing?

7. Maximum Volume

(a) Verify that each of the rectangular solids shown in the figure has a surface area of 150 square inches.

(b) Find the volume of each solid.

(c) Determine the dimensions of a rectangular solid (with a square base) of maximum volume if its surface area is 150 square inches.

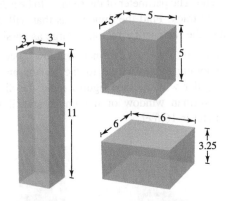

8. Maximum Volume   A rectangular solid with a square base has a surface area of 337.5 square centimeters.

(a) Determine the dimensions that yield the maximum volume.

(b) Find the maximum volume.

9. Minimum Surface Area   A rectangular solid with a square base has a volume of 8000 cubic inches.

(a) Determine the dimensions that yield the minimum surface area.

(b) Find the minimum surface area.

10. **HOW DO YOU SEE IT?** The graph shows the profit P (in thousands of dollars) of a company in terms of its advertising cost x (in thousands of dollars).

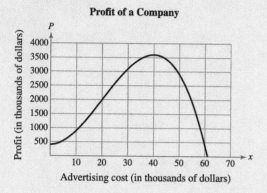

Profit of a Company

(a) Estimate the interval on which the profit is increasing.

(b) Estimate the interval on which the profit is decreasing.

(c) Estimate the amount of money the company should spend on advertising in order to yield a maximum profit.

(d) Estimate the point of diminishing returns.

11. Maximum Area An indoor physical fitness room consists of a rectangular region with a semicircle on each end. The perimeter of the room is to be a 200-meter running track. Find the dimensions that will make the area of the rectangular region as large as possible.

12. Maximum Area A Norman window is constructed by adjoining a semicircle to the top of an ordinary rectangular window (see figure). Find the dimensions of a Norman window of maximum area if the total perimeter is 16 feet.

13. Minimum Cost A storage box with a square base must have a volume of 80 cubic centimeters. The top and bottom cost $0.20 per square centimeter and the sides cost $0.10 per square centimeter. Find the dimensions that will minimize cost.

14. Minimum Surface Area A net enclosure for golf practice is open at one end (see figure). The volume of the enclosure is $83\frac{1}{3}$ cubic meters. Find the dimensions that require the least amount of netting.

Figure for 14

Figure for 15

15. Maximum Volume An open box is to be made from a six-inch by six-inch square piece of material by cutting equal squares from the corners and turning up the sides (see figure). Find the volume of the largest box that can be made.

16. Maximum Volume An open box is to be made from a three-foot by eight-foot rectangular piece of material by cutting equal squares from the corners and turning up the sides. Find the volume of the largest box that can be made in this manner.

17. Minimum Area A rectangular page is to contain 36 square inches of print. The margins at the top and bottom and on each side are to be $1\frac{1}{2}$ inches. Find the dimensions of the page that will minimize the amount of paper used.

18. Minimum Area A rectangular page is to contain 50 square inches of print. The margins at the top and bottom of the page are to be 2 inches wide. The margins on each side are to be 1 inch wide. Find the dimensions of the page that will minimize the amount of paper used.

19. Maximum Area A rectangle is bounded by the x- and y-axes and the graph of

$$y = \tfrac{1}{2}(6 - x)$$

(see figure). What length and width should the rectangle have so that its area is a maximum?

Figure for 19

Figure for 20

20. Minimum Length and Minimum Area A right triangle is formed in the first quadrant by the x- and y-axes and a line through the point $(1, 2)$ (see figure).

(a) Write the length L of the hypotenuse as a function of x.

(b) Use a graphing utility to approximate x graphically such that the length of the hypotenuse is a minimum.

(c) Find the vertices of the triangle such that its area is a minimum.

21. Maximum Area A rectangle is bounded by the x-axis and the semicircle $y = \sqrt{25 - x^2}$ (see figure). What length and width should the rectangle have so that its area is a maximum?

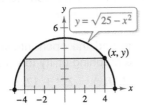

22. Maximum Area Find the dimensions of the largest rectangle that can be inscribed in a semicircle of radius r. (See Exercise 21.)

23. Minimum Surface Area You are designing a soft drink container that has the shape of a right circular cylinder. The container is supposed to hold 12 fluid ounces (1 fluid ounce is approximately 1.80469 cubic inches). Find the dimensions that will use a minimum amount of construction material.

24. Minimum Cost An energy drink container of the shape described in Exercise 23 must have a volume of 16 fluid ounces. The cost per square inch of constructing the top and bottom is twice the cost of constructing the lateral side. Find the dimensions that will minimize cost.

Finding a Minimum Distance In Exercises 25–28, find the points on the graph of the function that are closest to the given point. *See Example 2.*

25. $f(x) = x^2, \quad \left(2, \frac{1}{2}\right)$ **26.** $f(x) = (x + 1)^2, \quad (5, 3)$

27. $f(x) = \sqrt{x}, \quad (4, 0)$ **28.** $f(x) = \sqrt{x - 8}, \quad (12, 0)$

29. Maximum Volume A rectangular package to be sent by a postal service can have a maximum combined length and girth (perimeter of a cross section) of 108 inches. Find the dimensions of the package with maximum volume. Assume that the package's dimensions are x by x by y (see figure).

30. Minimum Surface Area A solid is formed by adjoining two hemispheres to the ends of a right circular cylinder. The total volume of the solid is 12 cubic inches. Find the radius of the cylinder that produces the minimum surface area.

31. Minimum Cost An industrial tank of the shape described in Exercise 30 must have a volume of 3000 cubic feet. The hemispherical ends cost twice as much per square foot of surface area as the sides. Find the dimensions that will minimize cost.

32. Minimum Time You are in a boat 2 miles from the nearest point on the coast. You are to go to point Q, located 3 miles down the coast and 1 mile inland (see figure). You can row at a rate of 2 miles per hour and you can walk at a rate of 4 miles per hour. Toward what point on the coast should you row in order to reach point Q in the least amount of time?

33. Minimum Area The sum of the circumference of a circle and the perimeter of a square is 16. Find the dimensions of the circle and square that produce a minimum total area.

34. Minimum Area The sum of the perimeters of an equilateral triangle and a square is 10. Find the dimensions of the triangle and square that produce a minimum total area.

35. Area Four feet of wire is to be used to form a square and a circle.

(a) Express the sum of the areas of the square and the circle as a function A of a side of the square x.

(b) What is the domain of A?

(c) Use a graphing utility to graph A on its domain.

(d) How much wire should be used for the square and how much for the circle in order to enclose the least total area? the greatest total area?

36. Maximum Yield A home gardener estimates that 16 apple trees will produce an average yield of 80 apples per tree. But because of the size of the garden, for each additional tree planted, the yield will decrease by four apples per tree. How many trees should be planted to maximize the total yield of apples? What is the maximum yield?

37. Farming A strawberry farmer will receive $30 per bushel of strawberries during the first week of harvesting. Each week after that, the value will drop $0.80 per bushel. The farmer estimates that there are approximately 120 bushels of strawberries in the fields, and that the crop is increasing at a rate of four bushels per week. When should the farmer harvest the strawberries to maximize their value? How many bushels of strawberries will yield the maximum value? What is the maximum value of the strawberries?

QUIZ YOURSELF

See www.CalcChat.com for worked-out solutions to odd-numbered exercises.

Take this quiz as you would take a quiz in class. When you are done, check your work against the answers given in the back of the book.

In Exercises 1–3, find the critical numbers and the open intervals on which the function is increasing or decreasing. Use a graphing utility to verify your results.

1. $f(x) = x^2 - 6x + 1$

2. $f(x) = 2x^3 + 12x^2$

3. $f(x) = \dfrac{x}{x^2 + 25}$

In Exercises 4–6, find all relative extrema of the function.

4. $f(x) = x^3 + 3x^2 - 5$

5. $f(x) = x^4 - 8x^2 + 3$

6. $f(x) = 2x^{2/3}$

In Exercises 7–9, find the absolute extrema of the function on the closed interval. Use a graphing utility to verify your results.

7. $f(x) = x^2 + 2x - 8, \quad [-2, 1]$

8. $f(x) = x^3 - 27x, \quad [-4, 4]$

9. $f(x) = \dfrac{x}{x^2 + 1}, \quad [0, 2]$

In Exercises 10 and 11, discuss the concavity of the graph of the function and find the points of inflection.

10. $f(x) = x^3 - 6x^2 + 7x$

11. $f(x) = x^4 - 24x^2$

In Exercises 12 and 13, use the Second-Derivative Test to find all relative extrema of the function.

12. $f(x) = 2x^3 + 3x^2 - 12x + 16$

13. $f(x) = 2x + \dfrac{18}{x}$

14. By increasing its advertising cost x for a product, a company discovers that it can increase the sales S according to the model

$$S = \frac{1}{3600}(360x^2 - x^3), \quad 0 \le x \le 240$$

where x and S are in thousands of dollars. Find the point of diminishing returns for this product.

15. A gardener has 200 feet of fencing to enclose a rectangular garden adjacent to a river (see figure). No fencing is needed along the river. What dimensions should be used so that the area of the garden will be a maximum?

Figure for 15

16. The resident population P (in thousands) of Maine from 2000 through 2009 can be modeled by

$$P = 0.001t^3 - 0.64t^2 + 10.3t + 1276, \quad 0 \le t \le 9$$

where t is the year, with $t = 0$ corresponding to 2000. *(Source: U.S. Census Bureau)*

(a) During which year(s) was the population increasing? decreasing?

(b) During which year, from 2000 through 2009, was the population the greatest? the least?

3.5 Business and Economics Applications

■ Solve business and economics optimization problems.
■ Find the price elasticity of demand for demand functions.
■ Recognize basic business terms and formulas.

Optimization in Business and Economics

The problems in this section are primarily optimization problems. So, the five-step procedure used in Section 3.4 is an appropriate strategy to follow.

Example 1 **Finding the Maximum Revenue**

A company has determined that its total revenue (in dollars) for a product can be modeled by

$$R = -x^3 + 450x^2 + 52,500x$$

where x is the number of units produced (and sold). What production level will yield a maximum revenue?

SOLUTION

1. A sketch of the revenue function is shown in Figure 3.37.

2. The primary equation is the given revenue function.

$$R = -x^3 + 450x^2 + 52,500x$$

3. Because R is already given as a function of one variable, you do not need a secondary equation.

4. The feasible domain of the primary equation is

$$0 \le x \le 546. \qquad \text{Feasible domain}$$

This is determined by finding the x-intercepts of the revenue function, as shown in Figure 3.37.

5. To maximize the revenue, find the critical numbers.

$$\frac{dR}{dx} = -3x^2 + 900x + 52,500 = 0 \qquad \text{Set derivative equal to 0.}$$

$$-3(x - 350)(x + 50) = 0 \qquad \text{Factor.}$$

$$x = 350, x = -50 \qquad \text{Critical numbers}$$

The only critical number in the feasible domain is $x = 350$. From the graph of the function, you can see that the production level of 350 units corresponds to a maximum revenue.

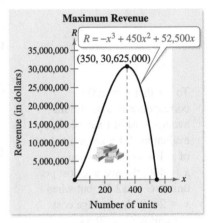

Maximum Revenue

$R = -x^3 + 450x^2 + 52,500x$

(350, 30,625,000)

Maximum revenue occurs when $dR/dx = 0$.

FIGURE 3.37

In Exercise 15 on page 212, you will use derivatives to find the price that yields a maximum profit.

✓ **Checkpoint 1**

Find the number of units that must be produced to maximize the revenue function $R = -x^3 + 150x^2 + 9375x$, where R is the total revenue (in dollars) and x is the number of units produced (and sold). What is the maximum revenue?

To study the effects of production levels on cost, one method economists use is the **average cost function** $\overline{C}$, which is defined as

$$\overline{C} = \frac{C}{x}$$

Average cost function

where $C = f(x)$ is the total cost function and x is the number of units produced.

Example 2 Finding the Minimum Average Cost

A company estimates that the cost (in dollars) of producing x units of a product can be modeled by

$$C = 800 + 0.04x + 0.0002x^2.$$

Find the production level that minimizes the average cost per unit.

SOLUTION

1. C represents the total cost, x represents the number of units produced, and $\overline{C}$ represents the average cost per unit.

2. The primary equation is

$$\overline{C} = \frac{C}{x}.$$

Primary equation

3. Substituting the given equation for C produces

$$\overline{C} = \frac{800 + 0.04x + 0.0002x^2}{x}$$

Substitute for C.

$$= \frac{800}{x} + 0.04 + 0.0002x.$$

Function of one variable

4. The feasible domain of this function is

$$x > 0$$

Feasible domain

because the company cannot produce a negative number of units.

5. You can find the critical numbers as shown.

$$\frac{d\overline{C}}{dx} = -\frac{800}{x^2} + 0.0002 = 0$$

Set derivative equal to 0.

$$0.0002 = \frac{800}{x^2}$$

$$x^2 = \frac{800}{0.0002}$$

Multiply each side by x^2 and divide each side by 0.0002.

$$x^2 = 4{,}000{,}000$$

$$x = \pm 2000$$

Critical numbers

By choosing the positive value of x and sketching the graph of $\overline{C}$, as shown in Figure 3.38, you can see that a production level of $x = 2000$ minimizes the average cost per unit.

Minimum Average Cost

$$\overline{C} = \frac{800}{x} + 0.04 + 0.0002x$$

Minimum average cost occurs when $d\overline{C}/dx = 0$.

FIGURE 3.38

✓ Checkpoint 2

Find the production level that minimizes the average cost per unit for the cost function

$$C = 400 + 0.05x + 0.0025x^2$$

where C is the cost (in dollars) of producing x units of a product.

Example 3   **Finding the Maximum Revenue**

A business sells 2000 units of a product per month at a price of $10 each. It can sell 250 more items per month for each $0.25 reduction in price. What price per unit will maximize the monthly revenue?

SOLUTION

1. Let x represent the number of units sold in a month, let p represent the price per unit, and let R represent the monthly revenue.

2. Because the revenue is to be maximized, the primary equation is

   $$R = xp.$$ Primary equation

3. A price of $p = \$10$ corresponds to $x = 2000$, and a price of $p = \$9.75$ corresponds to $x = 2250$. Using this information, you can use the two-point form to write the demand equation.

   $$p - 10 = \frac{10 - 9.75}{2000 - 2250}(x - 2000)$$ Two-point form

   $$p - 10 = -0.001(x - 2000)$$ Simplify.

   $$p = -0.001x + 12$$ Secondary equation

   Substituting this value into the revenue equation produces

   $$R = x(-0.001x + 12)$$ Substitute for p.

   $$= -0.001x^2 + 12x.$$ Function of one variable

4. The feasible domain of the revenue function is

   $$0 \le x \le 12{,}000.$$ Feasible domain

   This is determined by finding the x-intercepts of the revenue function.

5. To maximize the revenue, find the critical numbers.

   $$\frac{dR}{dx} = 12 - 0.002x = 0$$ Set derivative equal to 0.

   $$-0.002x = -12$$

   $$x = 6000$$ Critical number

   From the graph of R in Figure 3.39, you can see that this production level yields a maximum revenue. The price that corresponds to this production level is

   $$p = 12 - 0.001x$$ Demand function

   $$= 12 - 0.001(6000)$$ Substitute 6000 for x.

   $$= \$6.$$ Price per unit

Maximum Revenue

$R = 12x - 0.001x^2$

(6000, 36,000)

Revenue (in dollars)

40,000
30,000
20,000
10,000

4,000   8,000   12,000

Number of units

FIGURE 3.39

✓ **Checkpoint 3**

Find the price per unit that will maximize the monthly revenue for the business in Example 3 when it can sell only 200 more items per month for each $0.25 reduction in price.

In Example 3, the revenue function was written as a function of x. It could also have been written as a function of p. That is,

$$R = 1000(12p - p^2).$$

By finding the critical numbers of this function, you can determine that the maximum revenue occurs at $p = 6$.

ALGEBRA TUTOR xy

For help on the algebra in Example 4, see Example 2(b) in the *Chapter 3 Algebra Tutor*, on page 243.

Example 4   **Finding the Maximum Profit**

The marketing department of a business has determined that the demand for a product can be modeled by $p = 50/\sqrt{x}$, where p is the price per unit (in dollars) and x is the number of units. The cost (in dollars) of producing x units is given by $C = 0.5x + 500$. What price will yield a maximum profit?

SOLUTION

1. Let R represent the revenue, P the profit, p the price per unit, x the number of units, and C the total cost of producing x units.

2. Because you are maximizing the profit, the primary equation is

$$P = R - C. \qquad \text{Primary equation}$$

3. Because the revenue is $R = xp$, you can write the profit function as

$$
\begin{aligned}
P &= R - C \\
&= xp - (0.5x + 500) & \text{Substitute for } R \text{ and } C. \\
&= x\left(\frac{50}{\sqrt{x}}\right) - 0.5x - 500 & \text{Substitute for } p. \\
&= 50\sqrt{x} - 0.5x - 500. & \text{Function of one variable}
\end{aligned}
$$

4. The feasible domain of the function is $127 < x \le 7872$. (When x is less than 127 or greater than or equal to 7872, the profit is negative.)

5. To maximize the profit, find the critical numbers.

$$
\begin{aligned}
\frac{dP}{dx} &= \frac{25}{\sqrt{x}} - 0.5 = 0 & \text{Set derivative equal to 0.} \\
\frac{25}{\sqrt{x}} &= 0.5 & \text{Add 0.5 to each side.} \\
50 &= \sqrt{x} & \text{Isolate } x\text{-term on one side.} \\
2500 &= x & \text{Critical number}
\end{aligned}
$$

From the graph of the profit function shown in Figure 3.40, you can see that a maximum profit occurs at $x = 2500$. The price that corresponds to $x = 2500$ is

$$p = \frac{50}{\sqrt{x}} = \frac{50}{\sqrt{2500}} = \frac{50}{50} = \$1.00. \qquad \text{Price per unit}$$

✓ Checkpoint 4

Find the price that will maximize profit for the demand and cost functions

$$p = \frac{40}{\sqrt{x}} \quad \text{and} \quad C = 2x + 50$$

where p is the price per unit (in dollars), x is the number of units, and C is the cost (in dollars).

To find the maximum profit in Example 4, the equation $P = R - C$ was differentiated and set equal to zero. From the equation

$$\frac{dP}{dx} = \frac{dR}{dx} - \frac{dC}{dx} = 0$$

it follows that the maximum profit occurs when the marginal revenue is equal to the marginal cost, as shown in Figure 3.41.

Maximum Profit

$P = 50\sqrt{x} - 0.5x - 500$

(2500, 750)

Profit (in dollars)

Number of units

FIGURE 3.40

Marginal Revenue and Marginal Cost

$R = 50\sqrt{x}$

Maximum profit: $\dfrac{dR}{dx} = \dfrac{dC}{dx}$

$C = 0.5x + 500$

Revenue and cost (in dollars)

Number of units

FIGURE 3.41

Price Elasticity of Demand

One way in which economists measure the responsiveness of consumers to a change in the price of a product is with **price elasticity of demand.** For example, a drop in the price of fresh tomatoes might result in a much greater demand for fresh tomatoes; such a demand is called **elastic.** On the other hand, the demand for items such as coffee and gasoline is relatively unresponsive to changes in price; the demand for such items is called **inelastic.**

More formally, the elasticity of demand is the percent change of a quantity demanded x, divided by the percent change in its price p. You can develop a formula for price elasticity of demand using the approximation

$$\frac{\Delta p}{\Delta x} \approx \frac{dp}{dx}$$

which is based on the definition of the derivative. Using this approximation, you can write

$$\text{Price elasticity of demand} = \frac{\text{rate of change in demand}}{\text{rate of change in price}}$$

$$= \frac{\Delta x/x}{\Delta p/p}$$

$$= \frac{p/x}{\Delta p/\Delta x}$$

$$\approx \frac{p/x}{dp/dx}.$$

Definition of Price Elasticity of Demand

If $p = f(x)$ is a differentiable function, then the **price elasticity of demand** is given by

$$\eta = \frac{p/x}{dp/dx}$$

where η is the lowercase Greek letter eta. For a given price, the demand is **elastic** when $|\eta| > 1$, the demand is **inelastic** when $|\eta| < 1$, and the demand has **unit elasticity** when $|\eta| = 1$.

Price elasticity of demand is related to the total revenue function, as indicated in Figure 3.42 and the list below.

1. If the demand is *elastic*, then a decrease in price is accompanied by an increase in unit sales sufficient to increase the total revenue.

2. If the demand is *inelastic*, then a decrease in price is not accompanied by an increase in unit sales sufficient to increase the total revenue.

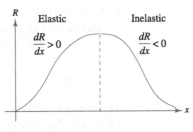

Revenue Curve

FIGURE 3.42

Demand Function of a Product

FIGURE 3.43

![globe icon] *Example 5*   **Comparing Elasticity and Revenue**

The demand function for a product is modeled by

$$p = 24 - 2\sqrt{x}, \quad 0 \le x \le 144$$

where p is the price per unit (in dollars) and x is the number of units. (See Figure 3.43.)

a. Determine when the demand is elastic, inelastic, and of unit elasticity.

b. Use the result of part (a) to describe the behavior of the revenue function.

SOLUTION

a. The price elasticity of demand is given by

$$\eta = \frac{p/x}{dp/dx} \qquad \text{Formula for price elasticity of demand}$$

$$= \frac{\dfrac{24 - 2\sqrt{x}}{x}}{\dfrac{-1}{\sqrt{x}}} \qquad \text{Substitute for } p/x \text{ and } dp/dx.$$

$$= \frac{\left(\dfrac{24 - 2\sqrt{x}}{x}\right)(-\sqrt{x})}{\left(\dfrac{-1}{\sqrt{x}}\right)(-\sqrt{x})} \qquad \text{Multiply numerator and denominator by } -\sqrt{x}.$$

$$= \frac{-24\sqrt{x} + 2x}{x} \qquad \text{Simplify.}$$

$$= -\frac{24\sqrt{x}}{x} + 2. \qquad \text{Rewrite as two fractions and simplify.}$$

The demand is of unit elasticity when $|\eta| = 1$. In the interval $[0, 144]$, the only solution of the equation

$$|\eta| = \left|-\frac{24\sqrt{x}}{x} + 2\right| = 1 \qquad \text{Unit elasticity}$$

is $x = 64$. So, the demand is of unit elasticity when $x = 64$. For x-values in the interval $(0, 64)$,

$$|\eta| = \left|-\frac{24\sqrt{x}}{x} + 2\right| > 1, \quad 0 < x < 64 \qquad \text{Elastic}$$

which implies that the demand is elastic when $0 < x < 64$. For x-values in the interval $(64, 144)$,

$$|\eta| = \left|-\frac{24\sqrt{x}}{x} + 2\right| < 1, \quad 64 < x < 144 \qquad \text{Inelastic}$$

which implies that the demand is inelastic when $64 < x < 144$.

b. From part (a), you can conclude that the revenue function R is increasing on the open interval $(0, 64)$, is decreasing on the open interval $(64, 144)$, and is a maximum when $x = 64$, as indicated in Figure 3.44.

Revenue Function of a Product

FIGURE 3.44

✓ **Checkpoint 5**

The demand function for a product is modeled by $p = 36 - 2\sqrt{x}, 0 \le x \le 324$, where p is the price per unit (in dollars) and x is the number of units. Determine when the demand is elastic, inelastic, and of unit elasticity.

Business Terms and Formulas

This section concludes with a summary of the basic business terms and formulas used in this section. A summary of the graphs of the demand, revenue, cost, and profit functions is shown in Figure 3.45.

Summary of Business Terms and Formulas

x = number of units produced (or sold)	η = price elasticity of demand
p = price per unit	$= \dfrac{p/x}{dp/dx}$
R = total revenue from selling x units $= xp$	$\dfrac{dR}{dx}$ = marginal revenue
C = total cost of producing x units	$\dfrac{dC}{dx}$ = marginal cost
P = total profit from selling x units $= R - C$	$\dfrac{dP}{dx}$ = marginal profit
$\overline{C}$ = average cost per unit $= \dfrac{C}{x}$	

Demand Function
Quantity demanded increases as price decreases.

Revenue Function
The low prices required to sell more units eventually result in a decreasing revenue.

Cost Function
The total cost to produce x units includes the fixed cost.

Profit Function
The break-even point occurs when $R = C$.

FIGURE 3.45

SUMMARIZE   (Section 3.5)

1. Describe a real-life example of how optimization can be used to find the maximum revenue for a product *(page 205, Example 1)*.

2. State the definition of the average cost function *(page 206)*. For an example of an average cost function, see Example 2.

3. State the definition of price elasticity of demand *(page 209)*. For an example of price elasticity of demand, see Example 5.

SKILLS WARM UP 3.5   The following warm-up exercises involve skills that were covered in a previous course or earlier sections. You will use these skills in the exercise set for this section. For additional help, review Appendix Sections A.2 and A.3, and Section 2.3.

In Exercises 1–4, evaluate the expression for $x = 150$.

1. $\left| -\dfrac{300}{x} + 3 \right|$ **2.** $\left| -\dfrac{600}{5x} + 2 \right|$ **3.** $\left| \dfrac{(20x^{-1/2})/x}{-10x^{-3/2}} \right|$ **4.** $\left| \dfrac{(4000/x^2)/x}{-8000x^{-3}} \right|$

In Exercises 5–10, find the marginal revenue, marginal cost, or marginal profit.

5. $C = 650 + 1.2x + 0.003x^2$ **6.** $P = 0.01x^2 + 11x$

7. $P = -0.7x^2 + 7x - 50$ **8.** $C = 1700 + 4.2x + 0.001x^3$

9. $R = 14x - \dfrac{x^2}{2000}$ **10.** $R = 3.4x - \dfrac{x^2}{1500}$

Exercises 3.5

See www.CalcChat.com for worked-out solutions to odd-numbered exercises.

Finding the Maximum Revenue   In Exercises 1–4, find the number of units x that produces a maximum revenue R. *See Example 1.*

1. $R = 800x - 0.2x^2$ **2.** $R = 48x^2 - 0.02x^3$

3. $R = 400x - x^2$ **4.** $R = 30x^{2/3} - 2x$

Finding the Minimum Average Cost   In Exercises 5–8, find the number of units x that produces the minimum average cost per unit $\overline{C}$. *See Example 2.*

5. $C = 0.125x^2 + 20x + 5000$

6. $C = 0.001x^3 + 5x + 250$

7. $C = 2x^2 + 255x + 5000$

8. $C = 0.02x^3 + 55x^2 + 1380$

Finding the Maximum Profit   In Exercises 9–12, find the price that will maximize profit for the demand and cost functions, where p is the price, x is the number of units, and C is the cost. *See Example 4.*

Demand Function	Cost Function
9. $p = 90 - x$	$C = 100 + 30x$
10. $p = 70 - 0.01x$	$C = 8000 + 50x + 0.03x^2$
11. $p = 50 - 0.1\sqrt{x}$	$C = 35x + 500$
12. $p = \dfrac{24}{\sqrt{x}}$	$C = 0.4x + 600$

    Average Cost   In Exercises 13 and 14, use the cost function to find the production level at which the average cost is a minimum. For this production level, show that the marginal cost and average cost are equal. Use a graphing utility to graph the average cost function and verify your results.

13. $C = 2x^2 + 5x + 18$ **14.** $C = x^3 - 6x^2 + 13x$

15. Maximum Profit   A commodity has a demand function modeled by

$$p = 80 - 0.2x$$

and a total cost function modeled by

$$C = 30x + 40$$

where x is the number of units.

(a) What price yields a maximum profit?

(b) When the profit is maximized, what is the average cost per unit?

16. Maximum Profit   A commodity has a demand function modeled by $p = 100 - 0.5x$, and a total cost function modeled by $C = 50x + 37.5$, where x is the number of units.

(a) What price yields a maximum profit?

(b) When the profit is maximized, what is the average cost per unit?

Maximum Profit   In Exercises 17 and 18, find the amount s spent on advertising (in thousands of dollars) that maximizes the profit P (in thousands of dollars). Find the point of diminishing returns.

17. $P = -2s^3 + 35s^2 - 100s + 200$

18. $P = -0.1s^3 + 6s^2 + 400$

19. Maximum Profit   The cost per unit of producing an MP3 player is $90. The manufacturer charges $150 per unit for orders of 100 or less. To encourage large orders, however, the manufacturer reduces the charge by $0.10 per player for each order in excess of 100 units. For instance, an order of 101 players would be $149.90 per player, an order of 102 players would be $149.80 per player, and so on. Find the largest order the manufacturer should allow to obtain a maximum profit.

20. Maximum Profit A real estate office handles a 50-unit apartment complex. When the rent is $580 per month, all units are occupied. For each $40 increase in rent, however, an average of one unit becomes vacant. Each occupied unit requires an average of $45 per month for service and repairs. What rent should be charged to obtain a maximum profit?

21. Maximum Revenue When a wholesaler sold a product at $40 per unit, sales were 300 units per week. After a price increase of $5, however, the average number of units sold dropped to 275 per week. Assuming that the demand function is linear, what price per unit will yield a maximum total revenue?

22. Maximum Profit Assume that the amount of money deposited in a bank is proportional to the square of the interest rate the bank pays on the money. Furthermore, the bank can reinvest the money at 12% simple interest. Find the interest rate the bank should pay to maximize its profit.

23. Minimum Cost A power station is on one side of a river that is 0.5 mile wide, and a factory is 6 miles downstream on the other side of the river (see figure). It costs $18 per foot to run overland power lines and $25 per foot to run underwater power lines. Write a cost function for running the power lines from the power station to the factory. Use a graphing utility to graph your function. Estimate the value of x that minimizes the cost. Explain your results.

24. Minimum Cost An offshore oil well is 1 mile off the coast. The oil refinery is 2 miles down the coast. Laying pipe in the ocean is twice as expensive as laying it on land. Find the most economical path for the pipe from the well to the oil refinery.

Minimum Cost In Exercises 25 and 26, find the speed v, in miles per hour, that will minimize costs on a 110-mile delivery trip. The cost per hour for fuel is C dollars, and the driver is paid W dollars per hour. (Assume there are no costs other than wages and fuel.)

25. Fuel cost: $C = \dfrac{v^2}{300}$

Driver: $W = \$12$

26. Fuel cost: $C = \dfrac{v^2}{500}$

Driver: $W = \$9.50$

Elasticity In Exercises 27–32, find the price elasticity of demand for the demand function at the indicated x-value. Is the demand elastic, inelastic, or of unit elasticity at the indicated x-value? Use a graphing utility to graph the revenue function, and identify the intervals of elasticity and inelasticity.

Demand Function	Quantity Demanded
27. $p = 600 - 5x$	$x = 60$
28. $p = 400 - 3x$	$x = 20$
29. $p = 5 - 0.03x$	$x = 100$
30. $p = 20 - 0.0002x$	$x = 30$
31. $p = \dfrac{500}{x + 2}$	$x = 23$
32. $p = \dfrac{500}{x^2} + 5$	$x = 5$

33. Elasticity The demand function for a product is modeled by

$$p = 20 - 0.02x, \quad 0 \le x \le 1000$$

where p is the price (in dollars) and x is the number of units.

(a) Determine when the demand is elastic, inelastic, and of unit elasticity.

(b) Use the result of part (a) to describe the behavior of the revenue function.

34. Elasticity The demand function for a product is given by $p = 800 - 4x$, $0 \le x \le 200$, where p is the price (in dollars) and x is the number of units.

(a) Determine when the demand is elastic, inelastic, and of unit elasticity.

(b) Use the result of part (a) to describe the behavior of the revenue function.

35. Minimum Cost The shipping and handling cost C of a manufactured product is modeled by

$$C = 4\left(\frac{25}{x^2} - \frac{x}{x - 10}\right), \quad 0 < x < 10$$

where C is measured in thousands of dollars and x is the number of units shipped (in hundreds). Use the *root* feature of a graphing utility to find the shipment size that minimizes the cost.

36. Minimum Cost The ordering and transportation cost C of the components used in manufacturing a product is modeled by

$$C = 8\left(\frac{2500}{x^2} - \frac{x}{x - 100}\right), \quad 0 < x < 100$$

where C is measured in thousands of dollars and x is the order size in hundreds. Use the *root* feature of a graphing utility to find the order size that minimizes the cost.

37. Revenue The demand for a car wash is $x = 900 - 45p$, where the current price is \$8. Can revenue be increased by lowering the price and thus attracting more customers? Use price elasticity of demand to determine your answer.

38. HOW DO YOU SEE IT? Match each graph with the function it best represents—a demand function, a revenue function, a cost function, or a profit function. Explain your reasoning. (The graphs are labeled a–d.)

39. Sales The sales S (in millions of dollars per year) for The Clorox Company for the years 2001 through 2010 can be modeled by

$$S = -1.893t^3 + 41.03t^2 - 58.6t + 3972, \quad 1 \le t \le 10$$

where t represents the year, with $t = 1$ corresponding to 2001.   *(Source: The Clorox Company)*

(a) During which year, from 2001 through 2010, were the company's sales increasing most rapidly?

(b) During which year were the sales increasing at the lowest rate?

(c) Find the rate of increase or decrease for each year in parts (a) and (b).

(d) Use a graphing utility to graph the sales function. Then use the *zoom* and *trace* features to confirm the results in parts (a), (b), and (c).

40. Sales The sales S (in billions of dollars) for Lockheed Martin Corporation from 2001 through 2010 can be modeled by

$$S = \frac{18.17 + 8.165t}{1 + 0.116t}, \quad 1 \le t \le 10$$

where t represents the year, with $t = 1$ corresponding to 2001.   *(Source: Lockheed Martin Corporation)*

(a) During which year, from 2001 through 2010, were the company's sales the greatest? the least?

(b) During which year were the sales increasing at the greatest rate? decreasing at the greatest rate?

(c) Use a graphing utility to graph the revenue function. Then use the *zoom* and *trace* features to confirm the results in parts (a) and (b).

41. Demand A demand function is modeled by

$$x = \frac{a}{p^m}$$

where a is a constant and $m > 1$. Show that $\eta = -m$. In other words, show that a 1% increase in price results in an m% decrease in the quantity demanded.

42. Think About It Throughout this text, it is assumed that demand functions are decreasing. Can you think of a product that has an increasing demand function? That is, can you think of a product that becomes more in demand as its price increases? Explain your reasoning, and sketch a graph of the function.

Business Capsule

The website vWorker.com is a marketplace that links freelance workers with employers looking to outsource jobs. The site's founder, Ian Ippolito, noticed that more and more companies were outsourcing rather than hiring full-time employees. He saw the potential in this trend, borrowed \$5000 from his parents, and turned the capital into an online business in 2001. Today his company is known as vWorker.com—for virtual worker—and it connects more than 150,000 employers with over 300,000 workers worldwide. Posting and bidding are free, but vWorker takes a percentage of the workers' final earnings. Only eight years after the company's debut, annual revenues reached \$2.5 million in 2009.

43. Research Project Choose a company with an innovative product or service like the one described above. Use your school's library, the Internet, or some other reference source to research the history of the company. Collect data about the revenue that the product or service has generated, and find a mathematical model of the data. Summarize your findings.

3.6 Asymptotes

■ Find the vertical asymptotes of functions and find infinite limits.
■ Find the horizontal asymptotes of functions and find limits at infinity.
■ Use asymptotes to answer questions about real-life situations.

In Exercise 61 on page 225, you will use limits at infinity to find the limit of an average cost function as the number of units produced increases.

Vertical Asymptotes and Infinite Limits

In the first three sections of this chapter, you studied ways in which you can use calculus to help analyze the graph of a function. In this section, you will study another valuable aid to curve sketching: the determination of vertical and horizontal asymptotes.

Recall from Section 1.5, Example 11, that the function

$$f(x) = \frac{3}{x - 2}$$

is unbounded as x approaches 2 (see Figure 3.46).

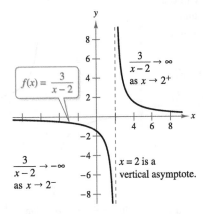

FIGURE 3.46

This type of behavior is described by saying that the line

$x = 2$ Vertical asymptote

is a **vertical asymptote** of the graph of f. The type of limit in which $f(x)$ approaches infinity (or negative infinity) as x approaches c from the left or from the right is an **infinite limit.** The infinite limits for the function $f(x) = 3/(x - 2)$ can be written as

$$\lim_{x \to 2^-} \frac{3}{x - 2} = -\infty$$

and

$$\lim_{x \to 2^+} \frac{3}{x - 2} = \infty.$$

Definition of Vertical Asymptote

If $f(x)$ approaches infinity (or negative infinity) as x approaches c from the right or from the left, then the line

$x = c$

is a **vertical asymptote** of the graph of f.

One of the most common instances of a vertical asymptote is the graph of a *rational function*—that is, a function of the form $f(x) = p(x)/q(x)$, where $p(x)$ and $q(x)$ are polynomials. If c is a real number such that $q(c) = 0$ and $p(c) \neq 0$, then the graph of f has a vertical asymptote at $x = c$. Example 1 shows four cases.

Example 1   Finding Infinite Limits

Limit from the left	*Limit from the right*	
a. $\displaystyle\lim_{x \to 1^-} \frac{1}{x-1} = -\infty$	$\displaystyle\lim_{x \to 1^+} \frac{1}{x-1} = \infty$	See Figure 3.47(a).
b. $\displaystyle\lim_{x \to 1^-} \frac{-1}{x-1} = \infty$	$\displaystyle\lim_{x \to 1^+} \frac{-1}{x-1} = -\infty$	See Figure 3.47(b).
c. $\displaystyle\lim_{x \to 1^-} \frac{-1}{(x-1)^2} = -\infty$	$\displaystyle\lim_{x \to 1^+} \frac{-1}{(x-1)^2} = -\infty$	See Figure 3.47(c).
d. $\displaystyle\lim_{x \to 1^-} \frac{1}{(x-1)^2} = \infty$	$\displaystyle\lim_{x \to 1^+} \frac{1}{(x-1)^2} = \infty$	See Figure 3.47(d).

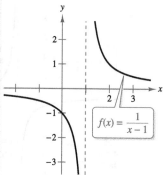

$$\lim_{x \to 1^-} \frac{1}{x-1} = -\infty \qquad \lim_{x \to 1^+} \frac{1}{x-1} = \infty$$

(a)

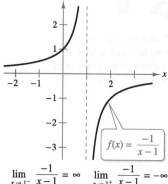

$$\lim_{x \to 1^-} \frac{-1}{x-1} = \infty \qquad \lim_{x \to 1^+} \frac{-1}{x-1} = -\infty$$

(b)

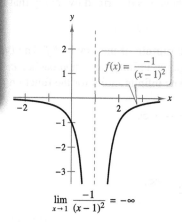

$$\lim_{x \to 1} \frac{-1}{(x-1)^2} = -\infty$$

(c)

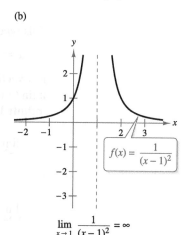

$$\lim_{x \to 1} \frac{1}{(x-1)^2} = \infty$$

(d)

FIGURE 3.47

 Checkpoint 1

Find each limit.

a. $\displaystyle\lim_{x \to 2^-} \frac{1}{x-2}$ **b.** $\displaystyle\lim_{x \to 2^+} \frac{1}{x-2}$ **c.** $\displaystyle\lim_{x \to -3^-} \frac{1}{x+3}$ **d.** $\displaystyle\lim_{x \to -3^+} \frac{1}{x+3}$

Each of the graphs in Example 1 has only one vertical asymptote. As shown in the next example, the graph of a rational function can have more than one vertical asymptote.

Example 2   Finding Vertical Asymptotes

Determine all vertical asymptotes of the graph of

$$f(x) = \frac{x + 2}{x^2 - 2x}.$$

SOLUTION   The possible vertical asymptotes correspond to the x-values for which the denominator is zero.

$x^2 - 2x = 0$	Set denominator equal to 0.
$x(x - 2) = 0$	Factor.
$x = 0, x = 2$	Zeros of denominator

Because the numerator of f is not zero at either of these x-values, you can conclude that the graph of f has two vertical asymptotes—one at $x = 0$ and one at $x = 2$, as shown in Figure 3.48.

✓ **Checkpoint 2**

Determine all vertical asymptotes of the graph of

$$f(x) = \frac{x + 4}{x^2 - 4x}.$$

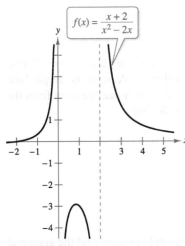

$$f(x) = \frac{x + 2}{x^2 - 2x}$$

Vertical Asymptotes at $x = 0$ and $x = 2$

FIGURE 3.48

Example 3   Finding Vertical Asymptotes

Determine all vertical asymptotes of the graph of

$$f(x) = \frac{x^2 + 2x - 8}{x^2 - 4}.$$

SOLUTION   First factor the numerator and denominator. Then divide out common factors.

$f(x) = \dfrac{x^2 + 2x - 8}{x^2 - 4}$	Write original function.
$= \dfrac{(x + 4)(x - 2)}{(x + 2)(x - 2)}$	Factor numerator and denominator.
$= \dfrac{(x + 4)(x - 2)}{(x + 2)(x - 2)}$	Divide out common factors.
$= \dfrac{x + 4}{x + 2}, \quad x \neq 2$	Simplify.

For all values of x other than $x = 2$, the graph of this simplified function is the same as the graph of f. So, you can conclude that the graph of f has only one vertical asymptote. This occurs at $x = -2$, as shown in Figure 3.49.

✓ **Checkpoint 3**

Determine all vertical asymptotes of the graph of

$$f(x) = \frac{x^2 + 4x + 3}{x^2 - 9}.$$

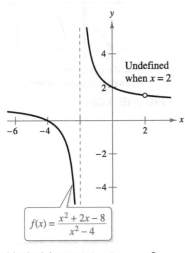

Undefined when $x = 2$

$$f(x) = \frac{x^2 + 2x - 8}{x^2 - 4}$$

Vertical Asymptote at $x = -2$

FIGURE 3.49

From Example 3, you know that the graph of

$$f(x) = \frac{x^2 + 2x - 8}{x^2 - 4}$$

has a vertical asymptote at $x = -2$. This implies that the limit of $f(x)$ as $x \to -2$ from the right (or from the left) is either ∞ or $-\infty$. But without looking at the graph, how can you determine that the limit from the left is *negative* infinity and the limit from the right is *positive* infinity? That is, why is the limit from the left

$$\lim_{x \to -2^-} \frac{x^2 + 2x - 8}{x^2 - 4} = -\infty \qquad \text{Limit from the left}$$

and why is the limit from the right

$$\lim_{x \to -2^+} \frac{x^2 + 2x - 8}{x^2 - 4} = \infty? \qquad \text{Limit from the right}$$

It is cumbersome to determine these limits analytically, and you may find the graphical method shown in Example 4 to be more efficient.

Example 4   Determining Infinite Limits

Find the limits.

$$\lim_{x \to 1^-} \frac{x^2 - 3x}{x - 1} \quad \text{and} \quad \lim_{x \to 1^+} \frac{x^2 - 3x}{x - 1}$$

SOLUTION   Begin by considering the function

$$f(x) = \frac{x^2 - 3x}{x - 1}.$$

Because the denominator is zero when $x = 1$ and the numerator is not zero when $x = 1$, it follows that the graph of the function has a vertical asymptote at $x = 1$. This implies that each of the given limits is either ∞ or $-\infty$. To determine which, use a graphing utility to graph the function, as shown in Figure 3.50. From the graph, you can see that the limit from the left is positive infinity and the limit from the right is negative infinity. That is,

$$\lim_{x \to 1^-} \frac{x^2 - 3x}{x - 1} = \infty \qquad \text{Limit from the left}$$

and

$$\lim_{x \to 1^+} \frac{x^2 - 3x}{x - 1} = -\infty. \qquad \text{Limit from the right}$$

From the left, $f(x)$ approaches positive infinity.

From the right, $f(x)$ approaches negative infinity.

FIGURE 3.50

✓ Checkpoint 4

Find the limits.

$$\lim_{x \to 2^-} \frac{x^2 - 4x}{x - 2} \quad \text{and} \quad \lim_{x \to 2^+} \frac{x^2 - 4x}{x - 2}$$

In Example 4, try evaluating $f(x)$ at x-values that are just barely to the left of 1. You will find that you can make the values of $f(x)$ arbitrarily large by choosing x sufficiently close to 1. For instance, $f(0.99999) \approx 199,999$.

Horizontal Asymptotes and Limits at Infinity

Another type of limit, called a **limit at infinity,** specifies a finite value approached by a function as x increases (or decreases) without bound.

Definition of Horizontal Asymptote

If f is a function and L_1 and L_2 are real numbers, then the statements

$$\lim_{x \to \infty} f(x) = L_1 \quad \text{and} \quad \lim_{x \to -\infty} f(x) = L_2$$

denote **limits at infinity.** The lines $y = L_1$ and $y = L_2$ are **horizontal asymptotes** of the graph of f.

Figure 3.51 shows two ways in which the graph of a function can approach one or more horizontal asymptotes. Note that it is possible for the graph of a function to cross its horizontal asymptote.

Limits at infinity share many of the properties of limits discussed in Section 1.5. When finding horizontal asymptotes, you can use the property that

$$\lim_{x \to \infty} \frac{1}{x^r} = 0, \quad r > 0 \quad \text{and} \quad \lim_{x \to -\infty} \frac{1}{x^r} = 0, \quad r > 0.$$

FIGURE 3.51

(The second limit assumes that x^r is defined when $x < 0$.)

Example 5   Finding Limits at Infinity

Find the limit: $\displaystyle \lim_{x \to \infty} \left(5 - \frac{2}{x^2}\right)$.

SOLUTION

$$\lim_{x \to \infty} \left(5 - \frac{2}{x^2}\right) = \lim_{x \to \infty} 5 - \lim_{x \to \infty} \frac{2}{x^2} \qquad \lim_{x \to \infty} [f(x) - g(x)] = \lim_{x \to \infty} f(x) - \lim_{x \to \infty} g(x)$$

$$= \lim_{x \to \infty} 5 - 2\left(\lim_{x \to \infty} \frac{1}{x^2}\right) \qquad \lim_{x \to \infty} cf(x) = c \lim_{x \to \infty} f(x)$$

$$= 5 - 2(0)$$

$$= 5$$

You can verify this limit by sketching the graph of

$$f(x) = 5 - \frac{2}{x^2}$$

as shown in Figure 3.52. Note that the graph has $y = 5$ as a horizontal asymptote to the right. By evaluating the limit

$$\lim_{x \to -\infty} \left(5 - \frac{2}{x^2}\right)$$

you can show that $y = 5$ is also a horizontal asymptote to the left.

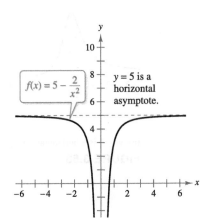

FIGURE 3.52

✓ **Checkpoint 5**

Find the limit: $\displaystyle \lim_{x \to \infty} \left(2 + \frac{5}{x^2}\right)$.

There is an easy way to determine whether the graph of a *rational* function has a horizontal asymptote. This shortcut is based on a comparison of the degrees of the numerator and denominator of the rational function.

Horizontal Asymptotes of Rational Functions

Let $f(x) = p(x)/q(x)$ be a rational function.

1. If the degree of the numerator is less than the degree of the denominator, then $y = 0$ is a horizontal asymptote of the graph of f (to the left and to the right).

2. If the degree of the numerator is equal to the degree of the denominator, then $y = a/b$ is a horizontal asymptote of the graph of f (to the left and to the right), where a and b are the leading coefficients of $p(x)$ and $q(x)$, respectively.

3. If the degree of the numerator is greater than the degree of the denominator, then the graph of f has no horizontal asymptote.

Example 6   Finding Horizontal Asymptotes

Find the horizontal asymptote of the graph of each function.

a. $y = \dfrac{-2x + 3}{3x^2 + 1}$ **b.** $y = \dfrac{-2x^2 + 3}{3x^2 + 1}$ **c.** $y = \dfrac{-2x^3 + 3}{3x^2 + 1}$

SOLUTION

a. Because the degree of the numerator is less than the degree of the denominator, $y = 0$ is a horizontal asymptote. [See Figure 3.53(a).]

b. Because the degree of the numerator is equal to the degree of the denominator, the line $y = -\frac{2}{3}$ is a horizontal asymptote. [See Figure 3.53(b).]

c. Because the degree of the numerator is greater than the degree of the denominator, the graph has no horizontal asymptote. [See Figure 3.53(c).]

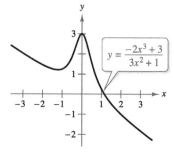

(a) $y = 0$ is a horizontal asymptote.   (b) $y = -\frac{2}{3}$ is a horizontal asymptote.   (c) No horizontal asymptote

FIGURE 3.53

✓ **Checkpoint 6**

Find the horizontal asymptote of the graph of each function.

a. $y = \dfrac{2x + 1}{4x^2 + 5}$ **b.** $y = \dfrac{2x^2 + 1}{4x^2 + 5}$ **c.** $y = \dfrac{2x^3 + 1}{4x^2 + 5}$

Some functions have two horizontal asymptotes: one to the right and one to the left (see Exercises 59 and 60).

Applications of Asymptotes

There are many examples of asymptotic behavior in real life. For instance, Example 7 describes the asymptotic behavior of an average cost function.

Example 7   Modeling Average Cost

A small business invests $5000 in a new product. In addition to this initial investment, the product will cost $0.50 per unit to produce.

a. Find the average cost per unit when 1000 units are produced.

b. Find the average cost per unit when 10,000 units are produced.

c. Find the average cost per unit when 100,000 units are produced.

d. What is the limit of the average cost as the number of units produced increases?

SOLUTION   From the given information, you can model the total cost C (in dollars) by

$$C = 0.5x + 5000 \qquad \text{Total cost function}$$

where x is the number of units produced. This implies that the average cost function is

$$\overline{C} = \frac{C}{x} = 0.5 + \frac{5000}{x}. \qquad \text{Average cost function}$$

a. When only 1000 units are produced, the average cost per unit is

$$\overline{C} = 0.5 + \frac{5000}{1000} \qquad \text{Substitute 1000 for } x.$$

$$= \$5.50. \qquad \text{Average cost for 1000 units}$$

b. When 10,000 units are produced, the average cost per unit is

$$\overline{C} = 0.5 + \frac{5000}{10,000} \qquad \text{Substitute 10,000 for } x.$$

$$= \$1.00. \qquad \text{Average cost for 10,000 units}$$

c. When 100,000 units are produced, the average cost per unit is

$$\overline{C} = 0.5 + \frac{5000}{100,000} \qquad \text{Substitute 100,000 for } x.$$

$$= \$0.55. \qquad \text{Average cost for 100,000 units}$$

d. As x approaches infinity, the limiting average cost per unit is

$$\lim_{x \to \infty} \left(0.5 + \frac{5000}{x} \right) = \$0.50.$$

As shown in Figure 3.54, this example points out one of the major problems faced by small businesses. That is, it is difficult to have competitively low prices when the production level is low.

Average Cost

$$\overline{C} = \frac{C}{x} = 0.5 + \frac{5000}{x}$$

As $x \to \infty$, the average cost per unit approaches $0.50.

FIGURE 3.54

✓ Checkpoint 7

A small business invests $25,000 in a new product. In addition, the product will cost $0.75 per unit to produce. Find the cost function and the average cost function. What is the limit of the average cost function as the number of units produced increases? ■

In Example 7, suppose that the small business had made an initial investment of $50,000. How would this change the answers to the questions? Would it change the average cost of producing x units? Would it change the limiting average cost per unit?

Example 8 Modeling Smokestack Emission

A manufacturing plant has determined that the cost C (in dollars) of removing $p\%$ of the smokestack pollutants of its main smokestack is modeled by

$$C = \frac{80,000p}{100 - p}, \quad 0 \le p < 100.$$

What is the vertical asymptote of this function? What does the vertical asymptote mean to the plant owners?

SOLUTION   The graph of the cost function is shown in Figure 3.55. From the graph, you can see that $p = 100$ is the vertical asymptote. This means that as the plant attempts to remove higher and higher percents of the pollutants, the cost increases dramatically. For instance, the cost of removing 85% of the pollutants is

$$C = \frac{80,000(85)}{100 - 85} \approx \$453,333 \qquad \text{Cost for 85\% removal}$$

but the cost of removing 90% is

$$C = \frac{80,000(90)}{100 - 90} = \$720,000. \qquad \text{Cost for 90\% removal}$$

Smokestack Emission

(90, 720,000)

(85, 453,333)

$C = \dfrac{80,000p}{100 - p}$

Percent of pollutants removed

FIGURE 3.55

✓ Checkpoint 8

According to the cost function in Example 8, is it possible to remove 100% of the smokestack pollutants? Why or why not?

SUMMARIZE   (Section 3.6)

1. State the definition of vertical asymptote *(page 215)*. For examples of vertical asymptotes, see Examples 1, 2, and 3.

2. State the definition of horizontal asymptote *(page 219)*. For examples of horizontal asymptotes, see Example 6.

3. Describe a real-life example of how asymptotic behavior can be used to analyze the average cost for a new product *(page 221, Example 7)*.

SKILLS WARM UP 3.6   The following warm-up exercises involve skills that were covered in earlier sections. You will use these skills in the exercise set for this section. For additional help, review Sections 1.5, 2.3, and 3.5.

In Exercises 1–8, find the limit.

1. $\lim\limits_{x \to 2} (x + 1)$

2. $\lim\limits_{x \to -1} (3x + 4)$

3. $\lim\limits_{x \to -3} \dfrac{2x^2 + x - 15}{x + 3}$

4. $\lim\limits_{x \to 2} \dfrac{3x^2 - 8x + 4}{x - 2}$

5. $\lim\limits_{x \to 2^+} \dfrac{x^2 - 5x + 6}{x^2 - 4}$

6. $\lim\limits_{x \to 1^-} \dfrac{x^2 - 6x + 5}{x^2 - 1}$

7. $\lim\limits_{x \to 0^+} \sqrt{x}$

8. $\lim\limits_{x \to 1^+} \left(x + \sqrt{x - 1}\right)$

In Exercises 9–12, find the average cost and the marginal cost.

9. $C = 150 + 3x$

10. $C = 1900 + 1.7x + 0.002x^2$

11. $C = 0.005x^2 + 0.5x + 1375$

12. $C = 760 + 0.05x$

Exercises 3.6   See www.CalcChat.com for worked-out solutions to odd-numbered exercises.

Vertical and Horizontal Asymptotes   In Exercises 1–8, find the vertical and horizontal asymptotes.

1. $f(x) = \dfrac{x^2 + 1}{x^2}$

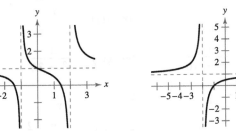

2. $f(x) = \dfrac{4}{(x - 2)^3}$

3. $f(x) = \dfrac{x^2 - 2}{x^2 - x - 2}$

4. $y = \dfrac{x + 1}{x + 2}$

5. $f(x) = \dfrac{3x^2}{2(x^2 + 1)}$

6. $f(x) = \dfrac{-4x}{x^2 + 4}$

7. $f(x) = \dfrac{x^2 - 1}{2x^2 - 8}$

8. $f(x) = \dfrac{x^2 + 1}{x^3 - 8}$

Finding Vertical Asymptotes   In Exercises 9–14, determine all vertical asymptotes of the graph of the function. *See Examples 2 and 3.*

9. $f(x) = \dfrac{x - 3}{x^2 + 3x}$

10. $f(x) = \dfrac{x}{x^2 + 6x}$

11. $f(x) = \dfrac{x^2 - 8x + 15}{x^2 - 9}$

12. $f(x) = \dfrac{x^2 + 2x - 35}{x^2 - 25}$

13. $f(x) = \dfrac{2x^2 - x - 3}{2x^2 - 11x + 12}$

14. $f(x) = \dfrac{x^2 + x - 30}{4x^2 - 17x - 15}$

Determining Infinite Limits   In Exercises 15–20, use a graphing utility to find the limit. *See Example 4.*

15. $\lim\limits_{x \to 6^+} \dfrac{1}{(x - 6)^2}$

16. $\lim\limits_{x \to -2^-} \dfrac{1}{x + 2}$

17. $\lim\limits_{x \to 3^+} \dfrac{x - 4}{x - 3}$

18. $\lim\limits_{x \to 1^+} \dfrac{2 + x}{1 - x}$

19. $\lim\limits_{x \to -1^-} \dfrac{x^2 + 1}{x^2 - 1}$

20. $\lim\limits_{x \to 5^+} \dfrac{2x - 3}{x^2 - 25}$

Finding Limits at Infinity   In Exercises 21–24, find the limit. *See Example 5.*

21. $\lim\limits_{x \to \infty} \left(1 + \dfrac{1}{x}\right)$

22. $\lim\limits_{x \to -\infty} \left(6 - \dfrac{3}{x}\right)$

23. $\lim\limits_{x \to -\infty} \left(7 + \dfrac{4}{x^2}\right)$

24. $\lim\limits_{x \to \infty} \left(10 - \dfrac{8}{x^2}\right)$

Finding Horizontal Asymptotes   In Exercises 25–32, find the horizontal asymptote of the graph of the function. *See Example 6.*

25. $f(x) = \dfrac{4x - 3}{2x + 1}$

26. $f(x) = \dfrac{5x^2 + 1}{10x^3 - 3x^2 + 7}$

27. $f(x) = \dfrac{3x}{4x^2 - 1}$

28. $f(x) = \dfrac{2x^2 - 5x - 12}{1 - 6x - 8x^2}$

29. $f(x) = \dfrac{5x^2}{x + 3}$

30. $f(x) = \dfrac{x^3 - 2x^2 + 3x + 1}{x^2 - 3x + 2}$

31. $f(x) = \dfrac{2x}{x - 1} + \dfrac{3x}{x + 1}$

32. $f(x) = \dfrac{2x^2}{x - 1} + \dfrac{3x}{x + 1}$

Using Horizontal Asymptotes   In Exercises 33–36, match the function with its graph. Use horizontal asymptotes as an aid. [The graphs are labeled (a)–(d).]

(a)

(b)

(c)

(d)

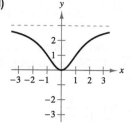

33. $f(x) = \dfrac{3x^2}{x^2 + 2}$

34. $f(x) = \dfrac{x}{x^2 + 2}$

35. $f(x) = 2 + \dfrac{x^2}{x^4 + 1}$

36. $f(x) = 5 - \dfrac{1}{x^2 + 1}$

Finding Limits at Infinity   In Exercises 37 and 38, find $\lim\limits_{x \to 0} h(x)$, if possible.

37. $f(x) = 5x^3 - 3$

    (a) $h(x) = \dfrac{f(x)}{x^2}$ (b) $h(x) = \dfrac{f(x)}{x^3}$ (c) $h(x) = \dfrac{f(x)}{x^4}$

38. $f(x) = 3x^2 + 7$

    (a) $h(x) = \dfrac{f(x)}{x}$ (b) $h(x) = \dfrac{f(x)}{x^2}$ (c) $h(x) = \dfrac{f(x)}{x^3}$

Finding Limits at Infinity   In Exercises 39 and 40, find each limit, if possible.

39. (a) $\lim\limits_{x \to \infty} \dfrac{x^2 + 2}{x^3 - 1}$ (b) $\lim\limits_{x \to \infty} \dfrac{x^2 + 2}{x^2 - 1}$ (c) $\lim\limits_{x \to \infty} \dfrac{x^2 + 2}{x - 1}$

40. (a) $\lim\limits_{x \to \infty} \dfrac{4 - 5x}{2x^3 + 6}$ (b) $\lim\limits_{x \to \infty} \dfrac{4 - 5x}{2x + 6}$ (c) $\lim\limits_{x \to \infty} \dfrac{4 - 5x^2}{2x + 6}$

 Estimating Limits at Infinity   In Exercises 41–44, use a graphing utility or spreadsheet software program to complete the table. Then use the result to estimate the limit of $f(x)$ as x approaches infinity.

x	10^0	10^1	10^2	10^3	10^4	10^5	10^6
$f(x)$							

41. $f(x) = \sqrt{x^3 + 6} - 2x$ **42.** $f(x) = x - \sqrt{x(x - 1)}$

43. $f(x) = \dfrac{x + 1}{x\sqrt{x}}$

44. $f(x) = \dfrac{\sqrt{x}}{x^2 + 3}$

Sketching Graphs   In Exercises 45–60, sketch the graph of the equation. Use intercepts, extrema, and asymptotes as sketching aids.

45. $y = \dfrac{3x}{1 - x}$

46. $y = \dfrac{x - 3}{x - 2}$

47. $f(x) = \dfrac{x^2}{x^2 + 9}$

48. $f(x) = \dfrac{x}{x^2 + 4}$

49. $g(x) = \dfrac{x^2}{x^2 - 16}$

50. $g(x) = \dfrac{x}{x^2 - 36}$

51. $y = 1 - \dfrac{3}{x^2}$

52. $y = 1 + \dfrac{1}{x}$

53. $f(x) = \dfrac{1}{x^2 - x - 2}$

54. $f(x) = \dfrac{x - 2}{x^2 - 4x + 3}$

55. $g(x) = \dfrac{x^2 - x - 2}{x - 2}$

56. $g(x) = \dfrac{x^2 - 9}{x + 3}$

57. $y = \dfrac{2x^2 - 6}{(x - 1)^2}$

58. $y = \dfrac{x}{(x + 1)^2}$

59. $y = \dfrac{x}{\sqrt{x^2 + 1}}$

60. $y = \dfrac{2x}{\sqrt{x^2 + 4}}$

61. Average Cost The cost C (in dollars) of producing x units of a product is $C = 1.15x + 6000$.

(a) Find the average cost function $\overline{C}$.

(b) Find $\overline{C}$ when $x = 600$ and when $x = 6000$.

(c) Determine the limit of the average cost function as x approaches infinity. Interpret the limit in the context of the problem.

62. Average Cost The cost C (in dollars) for a company to recycle x tons of material is $C = 1.25x + 10,500$.

(a) Find the average cost function $\overline{C}$.

(b) Find $\overline{C}$ when $x = 100$ and when $x = 1000$.

(c) Determine the limit of the average cost function as x approaches infinity. Interpret the limit in the context of the problem.

63. Average Profit The cost C and revenue R functions (in dollars) for producing and selling x units of a product are $C = 34.5x + 15,000$ and $R = 69.9x$.

(a) Find the average profit function

$$\overline{P} = \frac{R - C}{x}.$$

(b) Find the average profits when x is 1000, 10,000, and 100,000.

(c) What is the limit of the average profit function as x approaches infinity? Explain your reasoning.

64. HOW DO YOU SEE IT? The graph shows the temperature T (in degrees Fahrenheit) of an apple pie t seconds after it is removed from an oven.

(a) Find $\lim\limits_{t \to 0^+} T$. What does this limit represent?

(b) Find $\lim\limits_{t \to \infty} T$. What does this limit represent?

65. Seizing Drugs The cost C (in millions of dollars) for the federal government to seize $p\%$ of an illegal drug as it enters the country is modeled by

$$C = \frac{528p}{100 - p}, \quad 0 \le p < 100.$$

(a) Find the costs of seizing 25%, 50%, and 75%.

(b) Find the limit of C as $p \to 100^-$. Interpret the limit in the context of the problem. Use a graphing utility to verify your result.

66. Removing Pollutants The cost C (in dollars) of removing $p\%$ of the air pollutants in the stack emission of a utility company that burns coal is modeled by

$$C = \frac{85,000p}{100 - p}, \quad 0 \le p < 100.$$

(a) Find the costs of removing 15%, 50%, and 95%.

(b) Find the limit of C as $p \to 100^-$. Interpret the limit in the context of the problem. Use a graphing utility to verify your result.

67. Learning Curve Psychologists have developed mathematical models to predict performance P (the percent of correct responses in decimal form) as a function of n, the number of times a task is performed. One such model is

$$P = \frac{0.5 + 0.9(n - 1)}{1 + 0.9(n - 1)}, \quad n > 0.$$

(a) Use a spreadsheet software program to complete the table for the model.

n	1	2	3	4	5	6	7	8	9	10
P										

(b) Find the limit as n approaches infinity.

(c) Use a graphing utility to graph this learning curve, and interpret the graph in the context of the problem.

68. Project: Alternative-Fueled Vehicles For a project analyzing the number of alternative-fueled vehicles in use in the United States, visit this text's website at *www.cengagebrain.com*. *(Source: U.S. Energy Information Administration)*

3.7 Curve Sketching: A Summary

■ Analyze the graphs of functions.

■ Recognize the graphs of simple polynomial functions.

Summary of Curve-Sketching Techniques

It would be difficult to overstate the importance of using graphs in mathematics. Descartes's introduction of analytic geometry contributed significantly to the rapid advances in calculus that began during the mid-seventeenth century.

So far, you have studied several concepts that are useful in analyzing the graph of a function.

• *x*-intercepts and *y*-intercepts	(Section 1.2)
• Domain and range	(Section 1.4)
• Continuity	(Section 1.6)
• Differentiability	(Section 2.1)
• Relative extrema	(Section 3.2)
• Concavity	(Section 3.3)
• Points of inflection	(Section 3.3)
• Vertical asymptotes	(Section 3.6)
• Horizontal asymptotes	(Section 3.6)

When you are sketching the graph of a function, either by hand or with a graphing utility, remember that you cannot normally show the *entire* graph. The decision as to which part of the graph to show is crucial. For instance, which of the viewing windows in Figure 3.56 better represents the graph of

$$f(x) = x^3 - 25x^2 + 74x - 20?$$

Figure 3.56(a) gives a more complete view of the graph, but the context of the problem might indicate that Figure 3.56(b) is better.

(a)

(b)

FIGURE 3.56

In Exercise 45 on page 234, you will analyze the graph of the Social Security average monthly benefits to determine whether the model is a good fit for the data.

Guidelines for Analyzing the Graph of a Function

1. Determine the domain and range of the function. When the function models a real-life situation, consider the context.

2. Determine the intercepts and asymptotes of the graph.

3. Locate the *x*-values at which $f'(x)$ and $f''(x)$ are zero or undefined. Use the results to determine where the relative extrema and the points of inflection occur.

Example 1 **Analyzing a Graph**

Analyze the graph of

$$f(x) = x^3 + 3x^2 - 9x + 5.$$

SOLUTION   The y-intercept occurs at $(0, 5)$. Because this function factors as

$$f(x) = (x - 1)^2(x + 5)$$ Factored form

the x-intercepts occur at $(-5, 0)$ and $(1, 0)$. The first derivative is

$$f'(x) = 3x^2 + 6x - 9$$ First derivative
$$= 3(x - 1)(x + 3).$$ Factored form

So, the critical numbers of f are $x = 1$ and $x = -3$. The second derivative of f is

$$f''(x) = 6x + 6$$ Second derivative
$$= 6(x + 1)$$ Factored form

which implies that the second derivative is zero when $x = -1$. By testing the values of $f'(x)$ and $f''(x)$, as shown in the table, you can see that f has one relative minimum, one relative maximum, and one point of inflection. The graph of f is shown in Figure 3.57.

	$f(x)$	$f'(x)$	$f''(x)$	Characteristics of graph
x in $(-\infty, -3)$		+	−	Increasing, concave downward
$x = -3$	32	0	−	Relative maximum
x in $(-3, -1)$		−	−	Decreasing, concave downward
$x = -1$	16	−	0	Point of inflection
x in $(-1, 1)$		−	+	Decreasing, concave upward
$x = 1$	0	0	+	Relative minimum
x in $(1, \infty)$		+	+	Increasing, concave upward

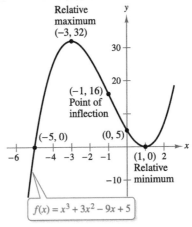

FIGURE 3.57

TECH TUTOR

In Example 1, you are able to find the zeros of f, f', and f'' algebraically (by factoring). When this is not feasible, you can use a graphing utility to find the zeros. For instance, the function

$$g(x) = x^3 + 3x^2 - 9x + 6$$

is similar to the function in the example, but it does not factor with integer coefficients. Using a graphing utility, you can determine that the function has only one x-intercept, $x \approx -5.0275$.

✓**Checkpoint 1**

Analyze the graph of

$$f(x) = -x^3 + 3x^2 + 9x - 27.$$

| Example 2 | **Analyzing a Graph**

Analyze the graph of

$$f(x) = x^4 - 12x^3 + 48x^2 - 64x.$$

SOLUTION   One of the intercepts occurs at $(0, 0)$. Because this function factors as

$$f(x) = x(x^3 - 12x^2 + 48x - 64)$$
$$= x(x - 4)^3 \qquad \text{Factored form}$$

a second x-intercept occurs at $(4, 0)$. The first derivative is

$$f'(x) = 4x^3 - 36x^2 + 96x - 64 \qquad \text{First derivative}$$
$$= 4(x - 1)(x - 4)^2. \qquad \text{Factored form}$$

So, the critical numbers of f are $x = 1$ and $x = 4$. The second derivative of f is

$$f''(x) = 12x^2 - 72x + 96 \qquad \text{Second derivative}$$
$$= 12(x - 4)(x - 2) \qquad \text{Factored form}$$

which implies that the second derivative is zero when $x = 2$ and $x = 4$. By testing the values of $f'(x)$ and $f''(x)$, as shown in the table, you can see that f has one relative minimum and two points of inflection. The graph is shown in Figure 3.58.

	$f(x)$	$f'(x)$	$f''(x)$	Characteristics of graph
x in $(-\infty, 1)$		$-$	$+$	Decreasing, concave upward
$x = 1$	-27	0	$+$	Relative minimum
x in $(1, 2)$		$+$	$+$	Increasing, concave upward
$x = 2$	-16	$+$	0	Point of inflection
x in $(2, 4)$		$+$	$-$	Increasing, concave downward
$x = 4$	0	0	0	Point of inflection
x in $(4, \infty)$		$+$	$+$	Increasing, concave upward

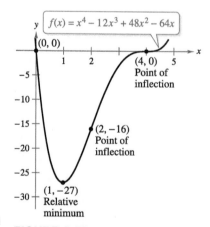

FIGURE 3.58

✓ **Checkpoint 2**

Analyze the graph of

$$f(x) = x^4 - 4x^3 + 5.$$

The fourth-degree polynomial function in Example 2 has one relative minimum and no relative maxima. In general, a polynomial function of degree n can have *at most* $n - 1$ relative extrema, and *at most* $n - 2$ points of inflection. Moreover, polynomial functions of even degree must have at least one relative extremum.

Example 3 Analyzing a Graph

Analyze the graph of

$$f(x) = \frac{x^2 - 2x + 4}{x - 2}.$$

SOLUTION The y-intercept occurs at $(0, -2)$. Using the Quadratic Formula on the numerator, you can see that there are no x-intercepts. Because the denominator is zero when $x = 2$ (and the numerator is not zero when $x = 2$), it follows that $x = 2$ is a vertical asymptote of the graph. There are no horizontal asymptotes because the degree of the numerator is greater than the degree of the denominator. The first derivative is

$$f'(x) = \frac{(x - 2)(2x - 2) - (x^2 - 2x + 4)}{(x - 2)^2}$$ First derivative

$$= \frac{x(x - 4)}{(x - 2)^2}.$$ Factored form

So, the critical numbers of f are $x = 0$ and $x = 4$. The second derivative is

$$f''(x) = \frac{(x - 2)^2(2x - 4) - (x^2 - 4x)(2)(x - 2)}{(x - 2)^4}$$ Second derivative

$$= \frac{(x - 2)(2x^2 - 8x + 8 - 2x^2 + 8x)}{(x - 2)^4}$$

$$= \frac{8}{(x - 2)^3}.$$ Factored form

Because the second derivative has no zeros and because $x = 2$ is not in the domain of the function, you can conclude that the graph has no points of inflection. By testing the values of $f'(x)$ and $f''(x)$, as shown in the table, you can see that f has one relative minimum and one relative maximum. The graph of f is shown in Figure 3.59.

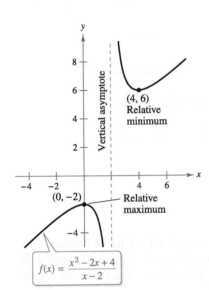

$$f(x) = \frac{x^2 - 2x + 4}{x - 2}$$

FIGURE 3.59

	$f(x)$	$f'(x)$	$f''(x)$	Characteristics of graph
x in $(-\infty, 0)$		$+$	$-$	Increasing, concave downward
$x = 0$	-2	0	$-$	Relative maximum
x in $(0, 2)$		$-$	$-$	Decreasing, concave downward
$x = 2$	Undef.	Undef.	Undef.	Vertical asymptote
x in $(2, 4)$		$-$	$+$	Decreasing, concave upward
$x = 4$	6	0	$+$	Relative minimum
x in $(4, \infty)$		$+$	$+$	Increasing, concave upward

✓ **Checkpoint 3**

Analyze the graph of

$$f(x) = \frac{x^2}{x - 1}.$$

Example 4   Analyzing a Graph

Analyze the graph of

$$f(x) = \frac{2(x^2 - 9)}{x^2 - 4}.$$

SOLUTION   Begin by writing the function in factored form.

$$f(x) = \frac{2(x - 3)(x + 3)}{(x - 2)(x + 2)}$$ Factored form

The y-intercept is $\left(0, \frac{9}{2}\right)$, and the x-intercepts are $(-3, 0)$ and $(3, 0)$. The graph of f has vertical asymptotes at $x = \pm 2$ and a horizontal asymptote at $y = 2$. The first derivative is

$$f'(x) = \frac{2[(x^2 - 4)(2x) - (x^2 - 9)(2x)]}{(x^2 - 4)^2}$$ First derivative

$$= \frac{2(2x^3 - 8x - 2x^3 + 18x)}{(x^2 - 4)^2}$$ Multiply.

$$= \frac{20x}{(x^2 - 4)^2}.$$ Factored form

So, the critical number of f is $x = 0$. The second derivative of f is

$$f''(x) = \frac{(x^2 - 4)^2(20) - (20x)(2)(x^2 - 4)(2x)}{(x^2 - 4)^4}$$ Second derivative

$$= \frac{20(x^2 - 4)(x^2 - 4 - 4x^2)}{(x^2 - 4)^4}$$

$$= -\frac{20(3x^2 + 4)}{(x^2 - 4)^3}.$$ Factored form

Because the second derivative has no zeros and $x = \pm 2$ are not in the domain of the function, you can conclude that the graph has no points of inflection. By testing the values of $f'(x)$ and $f''(x)$, as shown in the table, you can see that f has one relative minimum. The graph of f is shown in Figure 3.60.

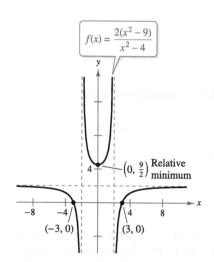

$f(x) = \dfrac{2(x^2 - 9)}{x^2 - 4}$

$\left(0, \frac{9}{2}\right)$ Relative minimum

$(-3, 0)$ $(3, 0)$

FIGURE 3.60

	$f(x)$	$f'(x)$	$f''(x)$	Characteristics of graph
x in $(-\infty, -2)$		$-$	$-$	Decreasing, concave downward
$x = -2$	Undef.	Undef.	Undef.	Vertical asymptote
x in $(-2, 0)$		$-$	$+$	Decreasing, concave upward
$x = 0$	$\frac{9}{2}$	0	$+$	Relative minimum
x in $(0, 2)$		$+$	$+$	Increasing, concave upward
$x = 2$	Undef.	Undef.	Undef.	Vertical asymptote
x in $(2, \infty)$		$+$	$-$	Increasing, concave downward

✓ **Checkpoint 4**

Analyze the graph of

$$f(x) = \frac{x^2 + 1}{x^2 - 1}.$$

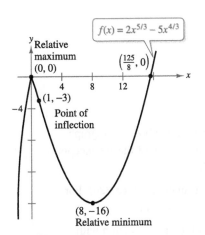

FIGURE 3.61

Example 5 **Analyzing a Graph**

Analyze the graph of

$$f(x) = 2x^{5/3} - 5x^{4/3}.$$

SOLUTION Begin by writing the function in factored form.

$$f(x) = x^{4/3}(2x^{1/3} - 5) \qquad \text{Factored form}$$

One of the intercepts is $(0, 0)$. A second x-intercept occurs when $2x^{1/3} - 5 = 0$.

$$2x^{1/3} - 5 = 0$$
$$2x^{1/3} = 5$$
$$x^{1/3} = \frac{5}{2}$$
$$x = \left(\frac{5}{2}\right)^3$$
$$x = \frac{125}{8}$$

The first derivative is

$$f'(x) = \frac{10}{3}x^{2/3} - \frac{20}{3}x^{1/3} \qquad \text{First derivative}$$

$$= \frac{10}{3}x^{1/3}(x^{1/3} - 2). \qquad \text{Factored form}$$

So, the critical numbers of f are $x = 0$ and $x = 8$. The second derivative is

$$f''(x) = \frac{20}{9}x^{-1/3} - \frac{20}{9}x^{-2/3} \qquad \text{Second derivative}$$

$$= \frac{20}{9}x^{-2/3}(x^{1/3} - 1)$$

$$= \frac{20(x^{1/3} - 1)}{9x^{2/3}}. \qquad \text{Factored form}$$

So, possible points of inflection occur at $x = 1$ and when $x = 0$. By testing the values of $f'(x)$ and $f''(x)$, as shown in the table, you can see that f has one relative maximum, one relative minimum, and one point of inflection. The graph of f is shown in Figure 3.61.

	$f(x)$	$f'(x)$	$f''(x)$	Characteristics of graph
x in $(-\infty, 0)$		$+$	$-$	Increasing, concave downward
$x = 0$	0	0	Undef.	Relative maximum
x in $(0, 1)$		$-$	$-$	Decreasing, concave downward
$x = 1$	-3	$-$	0	Point of inflection
x in $(1, 8)$		$-$	$+$	Decreasing, concave upward
$x = 8$	-16	0	$+$	Relative minimum
x in $(8, \infty)$		$+$	$+$	Increasing, concave upward

✓ **Checkpoint 5**

Analyze the graph of $f(x) = 2x^{3/2} - 6x^{1/2}$.

Summary of Simple Polynomial Graphs

A summary of the graphs of polynomial functions of degrees 0, 1, 2, and 3 is shown in Figure 3.62. Because of their simplicity, lower-degree polynomial functions are commonly used as mathematical models.

Constant function (degree 0): $y = a$

Horizontal line

Linear function (degree 1): $y = ax + b$

Line of slope a

$a < 0$ $a > 0$

Quadratic function (degree 2): $y = ax^2 + bx + c$

Parabola

$a < 0$ $a > 0$

STUDY TIP

The graph of any cubic polynomial has one point of inflection. The slope of the graph at the point of inflection may be zero or nonzero.

Cubic function (degree 3): $y = ax^3 + bx^2 + cx + d$

Cubic curve

$a < 0$ $a > 0$

FIGURE 3.62

SUMMARIZE (Section 3.7)

1. List the concepts you have learned that are useful in analyzing the graph of a function *(page 226)*. For an example that uses some of these concepts to analyze the graph of a function, see Example 1.

2. State the guidelines for analyzing the graph of a function *(page 226)*. For examples that use these guidelines, see Examples 3, 4, and 5.

3. State a general rule relating the degree *n* of a polynomial function with (a) the number of relative extrema and (b) the number of points of inflection *(page 229)*. For an example where this rule can be used to analyze the graph of a polynomial function, see Example 2.

SKILLS WARM UP 3.7   The following warm-up exercises involve skills that were covered in earlier sections. You will use these skills in the exercise set for this section. For additional help, review Sections 3.1 and 3.6.

In Exercises 1–4, find the vertical and horizontal asymptotes of the graph.

1. $f(x) = \dfrac{1}{x^2}$

2. $f(x) = \dfrac{8}{(x - 2)^2}$

3. $f(x) = \dfrac{40x}{x + 3}$

4. $f(x) = \dfrac{x^2 - 3}{x^2 - 4x + 3}$

In Exercises 5–10, determine the open intervals on which the function is increasing or decreasing.

5. $f(x) = x^2 + 4x + 2$

6. $f(x) = -x^2 - 8x + 1$

7. $f(x) = x^3 - 3x + 1$

8. $f(x) = \dfrac{-x^3 + x^2 - 1}{x^2}$

9. $f(x) = \dfrac{x - 2}{x - 1}$

10. $f(x) = -x^3 - 4x^2 + 3x + 2$

Exercises 3.7

See www.CalcChat.com for worked-out solutions to odd-numbered exercises.

Analyzing a Graph In Exercises 1–22, analyze and sketch the graph of the function. Label any intercepts, relative extrema, points of inflection, and asymptotes. *See Examples 1, 2, 3, 4, and 5.*

1. $y = -x^2 - 2x + 3$

2. $y = 2x^2 - 4x + 1$

3. $y = x^3 - 4x^2 + 6$

4. $y = -x^3 + x - 2$

5. $y = 2 - x - x^3$

6. $y = x^3 + 3x^2 + 3x + 2$

7. $y = 3x^4 + 4x^3$

8. $y = x^4 - 2x^2$

9. $y = x^4 - 8x^3 + 18x^2 - 16x + 5$

10. $y = x^4 - 4x^3 + 16x - 16$

11. $y = \dfrac{x^2 + 1}{x}$

12. $y = \dfrac{x + 2}{x}$

13. $y = \dfrac{x^2 - 6x + 12}{x - 4}$

14. $y = \dfrac{x^2 + 4x + 7}{x + 3}$

15. $y = \dfrac{x^2 + 1}{x^2 - 9}$

16. $y = \dfrac{2x}{x^2 - 1}$

17. $y = 3x^{2/3} - x^2$

18. $y = x^{5/3} - 5x^{2/3}$

19. $y = x\sqrt{9 - x}$

20. $y = x\sqrt{4 - x^2}$

21. $y = \begin{cases} x^2 + 1, & x \le 0 \\ 1 - 2x, & x > 0 \end{cases}$

22. $y = \begin{cases} x^2 + 4, & x < 0 \\ 4 - x, & x \ge 0 \end{cases}$

 Graphing a Function In Exercises 23–36, use a graphing utility to graph the function. Choose a window that allows all relative extrema and points of inflection to be identified on the graph.

23. $y = 3x^3 - 9x + 1$

24. $y = -4x^3 + 6x^2$

25. $y = x^5 - 5x$

26. $y = (x - 1)^5$

27. $y = \dfrac{5 - 3x}{x - 2}$

28. $y = \dfrac{x}{x^2 + 1}$

29. $y = 1 - x^{2/3}$

30. $y = (1 - x)^{2/3}$

31. $y = x^{4/3}$

32. $y = x^{-1/3}$

33. $y = \dfrac{x}{\sqrt{x^2 - 4}}$

34. $y = \dfrac{x - 3}{x}$

35. $y = \dfrac{x^3}{x^3 - 1}$

36. $y = \dfrac{x^4}{x^4 - 1}$

Interpreting a Graph In Exercises 37–40, use the graph of f' or f'' to sketch the graph of f. (There are many correct answers.)

37.

38.

39.

40.
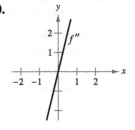

Sketching a Function In Exercises 41 and 42, sketch a graph of a function f having the given characteristics. (There are many correct answers.)

41. $f(-2) = f(0) = 0$
$f'(x) > 0$ if $x < -1$
$f'(x) < 0$ if $-1 < x < 0$
$f'(x) > 0$ if $x > 0$
$f'(-1) = f'(0) = 0$

42. $f(-1) = f(3) = 0$
$f'(1)$ is undefined.
$f'(x) < 0$ if $x < 1$
$f'(x) > 0$ if $x > 1$
$f''(x) < 0, x \neq 1$
$\lim_{x \to \infty} f(x) = 4$

Creating a Function In Exercises 43 and 44, create a function whose graph has the given characteristics. (There are many correct answers.)

43. Vertical asymptote: $x = 5$
Horizontal asymptote: $y = 0$

44. Vertical asymptote: $x = -3$
Horizontal asymptote: None

45. Social Security The table lists the average monthly Social Security benefits B (in dollars) for retired workers aged 62 and over from 2002 through 2009. A model for the data is

$$B = \frac{815.6 + 110.96t}{1 + 0.09t - 0.0033t^2}, \quad 2 \leq t \leq 9$$

where $t = 2$ corresponds to 2002. *(Source: U.S. Social Security Administration)*

t	2	3	4	5	6	7	8	9
B	895	922	955	1002	1044	1079	1153	1164

(a) Use a graphing utility to create a scatter plot of the data and graph the model in the same viewing window. How well does the model fit the data?

(b) Use the model to predict the average monthly benefit in 2014.

(c) Should this model be used to predict the average monthly Social Security benefits in future years? Why or why not?

46. Cost An employee of a delivery company earns $10 per hour driving a delivery van in an area where gasoline costs $2.80 per gallon. When the van is driven at a constant speed s (in miles per hour, with $40 \leq s \leq 65$), the van gets $700/s$ miles per gallon.

(a) Find the cost C as a function of s for a 100-mile trip on an interstate highway.

(b) Use a graphing utility to graph the function found in part (a) and determine the most economical speed.

47. Meteorology The monthly average high temperature T (in degrees Fahrenheit) for Boston, Massachusetts can be modeled by

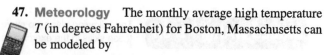

$$T = \frac{30.83 - 2.861t + 0.181t^2}{1 - 0.206t + 0.0139t^2}, \quad 1 \leq t \leq 12$$

where t is the month, with $t = 1$ corresponding to January. Use a graphing utility to graph the model and find all absolute extrema. Interpret the meaning of these values in the context of the problem. *(Source: National Climatic Data Center)*

 48. **HOW DO YOU SEE IT?** The graph shows a company's profits P for the years 1990 through 2010, where t is the year, with $t = 0$ corresponding to 2000.

(a) For which values of t is P' zero? positive? negative? Interpret the meanings of these values in the context of the problem.

(b) For which values of t is P'' zero? positive? negative? Interpret the meanings of these values in the context of the problem.

 Writing In Exercises 49 and 50, use a graphing utility to graph the function. Explain why there is no vertical asymptote when a superficial examination of the function may indicate that there should be one.

49. $h(x) = \dfrac{6 - 2x}{3 - x}$

50. $g(x) = \dfrac{x^2 + x - 2}{x - 1}$

51. Discovery Consider the function

$$f(x) = \frac{x^2 - 2x + 4}{x - 2}.$$

(a) Show that $f(x)$ can be rewritten as

$$f(x) = x + \frac{4}{x - 2}.$$

(b) Use a graphing utility to graph f and the line $y = x$. How do the two graphs compare as you zoom out?

(c) Use the results of part (b) to describe what is meant by a "slant asymptote."

3.8 Differentials and Marginal Analysis

Revenue

■ Find the differentials of functions.
■ Use differentials in economics to approximate changes in revenue, cost, and profit.
■ Find the differential of a function using differentiation formulas.

Differentials

When the derivative was defined in Section 2.1 as the limit of the ratio $\Delta y/\Delta x$, it seemed natural to retain the quotient symbolism for the limit itself. So, the derivative of y with respect to x was denoted by

$$\frac{dy}{dx} = \lim_{\Delta x \to 0} \frac{\Delta y}{\Delta x}$$

even though dy/dx was not interpreted as the quotient of two separate quantities. In this section, you will see that the quantities dy and dx can be assigned meanings in such a way that their quotient, when $dx \neq 0$, is equal to the derivative of y with respect to x.

In Exercise 35 on page 241, you will use differentials to approximate the change in revenue for a one-unit increase in sales of a product.

Definition of Differentials

Let $y = f(x)$ represent a differentiable function. The **differential of x** (denoted by dx) is any nonzero real number. The **differential of y** (denoted by dy) is $dy = f'(x)\, dx$.

In the definition of differentials, dx can have any nonzero value. In most applications, however, dx is chosen to be small, and this choice is denoted by $dx = \Delta x$.

One use of differentials is in approximating the change in $f(x)$ that corresponds to a change in x, as shown in Figure 3.63. This change is denoted by

$$\Delta y = f(x + \Delta x) - f(x). \qquad \text{Change in } y$$

In Figure 3.63, notice that as Δx gets smaller and smaller, the values of dy and Δy get closer and closer. That is, when Δx is small, $dy \approx \Delta y$. This **tangent line approximation** is the basis for most applications of differentials.

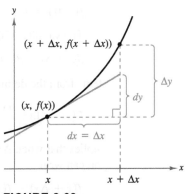

FIGURE 3.63

Note in Figure 3.63 that near the point of tangency, the graph of f is very close to the tangent line. This is the essence of the approximations used in this section. In other words, near the point of tangency, $dy \approx \Delta y$.

Example 1 **Comparing Δy and dy**

Consider the function given by

$$f(x) = x^2.$$

Find the value of dy when $x = 1$ and $dx = 0.01$. Compare this with the value of Δy when $x = 1$ and $\Delta x = 0.01$.

SOLUTION   Begin by finding the derivative of f.

$$f'(x) = 2x \qquad \text{Derivative of } f$$

When $x = 1$ and $dx = 0.01$, the value of the differential dy is

$$
\begin{aligned}
dy &= f'(x)\, dx & &\text{Differential of } y \\
&= f'(1)(0.01) & &\text{Substitute 1 for } x \text{ and 0.01 for } dx. \\
&= 2(1)(0.01) & &\text{Use } f'(x) = 2x. \\
&= 0.02. & &\text{Simplify.}
\end{aligned}
$$

When $x = 1$ and $\Delta x = 0.01$, the value of Δy is

$$
\begin{aligned}
\Delta y &= f(x + \Delta x) - f(x) & &\text{Change in } y \\
&= f(1.01) - f(1) & &\text{Substitute 1 for } x \text{ and 0.01 for } \Delta x. \\
&= (1.01)^2 - (1)^2 & & \\
&= 1.0201 - 1 & & \\
&= 0.0201. & &\text{Simplify.}
\end{aligned}
$$

Note that $dy \approx \Delta y$, as shown in Figure 3.64.

FIGURE 3.64

✓ **Checkpoint 1**

Find the value of dy when $x = 2$ and $dx = 0.01$ for $f(x) = x^4$. Compare this with the value of Δy when $x = 2$ and $\Delta x = 0.01$.

In Example 1, the tangent line to the graph of $f(x) = x^2$ at $x = 1$ is

$$y = 2x - 1 \quad \text{or} \quad g(x) = 2x - 1. \qquad \text{Tangent line to the graph of } f \text{ at } x = 1$$

For x-values near 1, this line is close to the graph of f, as shown in Figure 3.64. For instance,

$$f(1.01) = 1.01^2 = 1.0201 \quad \text{and} \quad g(1.01) = 2(1.01) - 1 = 1.02.$$

The validity of the approximation

$$dy \approx \Delta y, \quad dx \neq 0$$

stems from the definition of the derivative. That is, the existence of the limit

$$f'(x) = \lim_{\Delta x \to 0} \frac{f(x + \Delta x) - f(x)}{\Delta x}$$

implies that when Δx is close to zero, then $f'(x)$ is close to the difference quotient. So, you can write

$$
\begin{aligned}
\frac{f(x + \Delta x) - f(x)}{\Delta x} &\approx f'(x) \\
f(x + \Delta x) - f(x) &\approx f'(x)\, \Delta x \\
\Delta y &\approx f'(x)\, \Delta x.
\end{aligned}
$$

Substituting dx for Δx and dy for $f'(x)\, dx$ produces $\Delta y \approx dy$.

Marginal Analysis

Differentials are used in economics to approximate changes in revenue, cost, and profit. Let $R = f(x)$ be the total revenue for selling x units of a product. When the number of units increases by 1, the change in x is $\Delta x = 1$, and the change in R is

$$\Delta R = f(x + \Delta x) - f(x) \approx dR = \frac{dR}{dx}\, dx.$$

In other words, you can use the differential dR to approximate the change in the revenue that accompanies the sale of one additional unit. Similarly, the differentials dC and dP can be used to approximate the changes in cost and profit that accompany the sale (or production) of one additional unit.

 Example 2 **Using Marginal Analysis**

The demand function for a product is modeled by

$$p = 400 - x, \quad 0 \le x \le 400$$

where p is the price per unit (in dollars) and x is the number of units. Use differentials to approximate the change in revenue as sales increase from 149 units to 150 units. Compare this with the actual change in revenue.

SOLUTION Begin by finding the revenue function. Because the demand is given by $p = 400 - x$, the revenue is

$$R = xp \qquad\qquad\qquad \text{Formula for revenue}$$
$$= x(400 - x) \qquad\quad \text{Use } p = 400 - x.$$
$$= 400x - x^2. \qquad\quad \text{Multiply.}$$

Next, find the marginal revenue, dR/dx.

$$\frac{dR}{dx} = 400 - 2x \qquad\qquad \text{Power Rule}$$

When $x = 149$ and $dx = \Delta x = 1$, the approximate change in the revenue is

$$\Delta R \approx dR$$
$$= \frac{dR}{dx}\, dx$$
$$= (400 - 2x)\, dx$$
$$= [400 - 2(149)](1)$$
$$= \$102.$$

When x increases from 149 to 150 and $R = f(x) = 400x - x^2$, the actual change in revenue is

$$\Delta R = f(x + \Delta x) - f(x)$$
$$= \left[400(150) - 150^2\right] - \left[400(149) - 149^2\right]$$
$$= 37{,}500 - 37{,}399$$
$$= \$101.$$

✓ **Checkpoint 2**

The demand function for a product is modeled by $p = 200 - x, 0 \le x \le 200$, where p is the price per unit (in dollars) and x is the number of units. Use differentials to approximate the change in revenue as sales increase from 89 to 90 units. Compare this with the actual change in revenue.

Example 3   **Using Marginal Analysis**

The profit (in dollars) derived from selling x units of an item is modeled by

$$P = 0.0002x^3 + 10x.$$

Use the differential dP to approximate the change in profit when the production level changes from 50 to 51 units. Compare this with the actual gain in profit obtained by increasing the production level from 50 to 51 units.

SOLUTION   The marginal profit is

$$\frac{dP}{dx} = 0.0006x^2 + 10.$$

When $x = 50$ and $dx = \Delta x = 1$, the approximate change in profit is

$$\begin{aligned}
\Delta P &\approx dP \\
&= \frac{dP}{dx}\,dx \\
&= (0.0006x^2 + 10)\,dx \\
&= [0.0006(50)^2 + 10](1) \\
&= \$11.50.
\end{aligned}$$

When x changes from 50 to 51 units and $P = f(x) = 0.0002x^3 + 10x$, the actual change in profit is

$$\begin{aligned}
\Delta P &= f(x + \Delta x) - f(x) \\
&= [(0.0002)(51)^3 + 10(51)] - [(0.0002)(50)^3 + 10(50)] \\
&\approx 536.53 - 525.00 \\
&= \$11.53.
\end{aligned}$$

These values are shown graphically in Figure 3.65.

STUDY TIP

Example 3 uses differentials to solve the same problem that was solved in Example 5 in Section 2.3. Look back at that solution. Which approach do you prefer?

FIGURE 3.65

✓ **Checkpoint 3**

Use the differential dP to approximate the change in profit for the profit function in Example 3 when the production level changes from 40 to 41 units. Compare this with the actual gain in profit obtained by increasing the production level from 40 to 41 units.

Formulas for Differentials

You can use the definition of differentials to rewrite each differentiation rule in **differential form.**

Differential Forms of Differentiation Rules

Constant Multiple Rule: $\quad d[cu] = c\, du$

Sum or Difference Rule: $\quad d[u \pm v] = du \pm dv$

Product Rule: $\quad d[uv] = u\, dv + v\, du$

Quotient Rule: $\quad d\left[\dfrac{u}{v}\right] = \dfrac{v\, du - u\, dv}{v^2}$

Constant Rule: $\quad d[c] = 0$

Power Rule: $\quad d[x^n] = nx^{n-1}\, dx$

The next example compares the derivatives and differentials of several simple functions.

Example 4 **Finding Differentials**

Function	Derivative	Differential
a. $y = x^2$	$\dfrac{dy}{dx} = 2x$	$dy = 2x\, dx$
b. $y = \dfrac{3x + 2}{5}$	$\dfrac{dy}{dx} = \dfrac{3}{5}$	$dy = \dfrac{3}{5}\, dx$
c. $y = 2x^2 - 3x$	$\dfrac{dy}{dx} = 4x - 3$	$dy = (4x - 3)\, dx$
d. $y = \dfrac{1}{x}$	$\dfrac{dy}{dx} = -\dfrac{1}{x^2}$	$dy = -\dfrac{1}{x^2}\, dx$

✓ **Checkpoint 4**

Find the differential dy of each function.

a. $y = 4x^3$ **b.** $y = \dfrac{2x + 1}{3}$

c. $y = 3x^2 - 2x$ **d.** $y = \dfrac{1}{x^2}$

SUMMARIZE (Section 3.8)

1. State the definition of differentials *(page 235)*. For an example of a differential, see Example 1.

2. Explain what is meant by marginal analysis *(page 237)*. For examples of marginal analysis, see Examples 2 and 3.

3. State the differential forms of the differential rules *(page 239)*. For an example that uses the differential forms of the differential rules, see Example 4.

SKILLS WARM UP 3.8   The following warm-up exercises involve skills that were covered in earlier sections. You will use these skills in the exercise set for this section. For additional help, review Sections 2.2 and 2.4.

In Exercises 1–12, find the derivative.

1. $C = 44 + 0.09x^2$

2. $C = 250 + 0.15x$

3. $R = x(1.25 + 0.02\sqrt{x})$

4. $R = x(15.5 - 1.55x)$

5. $P = -0.03x^{1/3} + 1.4x - 2250$

6. $P = -0.02x^2 + 25x - 1000$

7. $A = \frac{1}{4}\sqrt{3}x^2$

8. $A = 6x^2$

9. $C = 2\pi r$

10. $P = 4w$

11. $S = 4\pi r^2$

12. $P = 2x + \sqrt{2}x$

In Exercises 13–16, write a formula for the quantity.

13. Area A of a circle of radius r

14. Area A of a square of side x

15. Volume V of a cube of edge x

16. Volume V of a sphere of radius r

Exercises 3.8

See www.CalcChat.com for worked-out solutions to odd-numbered exercises.

Comparing Δy and dy   In Exercises 1–6, compare the values of dy and Δy for the function. *See Example 1.*

Function	x-Value	Differential of x
1. $f(x) = 0.5x^3$	$x = 2$	$\Delta x = dx = 0.1$
2. $f(x) = 1 - 2x^2$	$x = 0$	$\Delta x = dx = -0.1$
3. $f(x) = x^4 + 1$	$x = -1$	$\Delta x = dx = 0.01$
4. $f(x) = 2x + 1$	$x = 1$	$\Delta x = dx = 0.01$
5. $f(x) = 3\sqrt{x}$	$x = 4$	$\Delta x = dx = 0.1$
6. $f(x) = 6x^{4/3}$	$x = -1$	$\Delta x = dx = 0.01$

Finding Differentials   In Exercises 7–12, let $x = 2$ and complete the table for the function.

$dx = \Delta x$	dy	Δy	$\Delta y - dy$	$\dfrac{dy}{\Delta y}$
1.000				
0.500				
0.100				
0.010				
0.001				

7. $y = x^2$

8. $y = x^5$

9. $y = \dfrac{1}{x^2}$

10. $y = \dfrac{1}{x}$

11. $y = \sqrt[4]{x}$

12. $y = \sqrt{x}$

Marginal Analysis   In Exercises 13–18, use differentials to approximate the change in cost, revenue, or profit corresponding to an increase in sales of one unit. For instance, in Exercise 13, approximate the change in cost as x increases from 12 units to 13 units. *See Examples 2 and 3.*

Function	x-Value
13. $C = 0.05x^2 + 4x + 10$	$x = 12$
14. $C = 0.025x^2 + 8x + 5$	$x = 10$
15. $R = 30x - 0.15x^2$	$x = 75$
16. $R = 50x - 1.5x^2$	$x = 15$
17. $P = -0.5x^3 + 2500x - 6000$	$x = 50$
18. $P = -x^2 + 60x - 100$	$x = 25$

Finding Differentials   In Exercises 19–28, find the differential dy. *See Example 4.*

19. $y = 6x^4$

20. $y = \dfrac{8 - 4x}{3}$

21. $y = 3x^2 - 4$

22. $y = 3x^{2/3}$

23. $y = (4x - 1)^3$

24. $y = (x^2 + 3)(2x + 4)^2$

25. $y = \dfrac{x + 1}{2x - 1}$

26. $y = \dfrac{x}{x^2 + 1}$

27. $y = \sqrt{9 - x^2}$

28. $y = \sqrt[3]{6x^2}$

Finding an Equation of a Tangent Line In Exercises 29–32, find an equation of the tangent line to the function at the given point. Then find the function values and the tangent line values at $f(x + \Delta x)$ and $y(x + \Delta x)$ for $\Delta x = -0.01$ and 0.01.

Function	Point
29. $f(x) = 2x^3 - x^2 + 1$	$(-2, -19)$
30. $f(x) = 3x^2 - 1$	$(2, 11)$
31. $f(x) = \dfrac{x}{x^2 + 1}$	$(0, 0)$
32. $f(x) = \sqrt{25 - x^2}$	$(3, 4)$

33. Profit The profit P for a company producing x units is

$$P = (500x - x^2) - \left(\frac{1}{2}x^2 - 77x + 3000\right).$$

(a) Use differentials to approximate the change in profit when the production level changes from 115 to 120 units.

(b) Compare this with the actual change in profit.

34. Revenue The revenue R for a company selling x units is $R = 900x - 0.1x^2$.

(a) Use differentials to approximate the change in revenue as the sales increase from 3000 units to 3100 units.

(b) Compare this with the actual change in revenue.

35. Demand The demand function for a product is modeled by $p = 75 - 0.25x$, where p is the price per unit (in dollars) and x is the number of units.

(a) Use differentials to approximate the change in revenue as sales increase from 7 units to 8 units.

(b) Repeat part (a) as sales increase from 70 units to 71 units.

36. HOW DO YOU SEE IT? The graph shows the profit P (in dollars) from selling x units of an item. Use the graph to determine which is greater, the change in profit when the production level changes from 400 to 401 units or the change in profit when the production level changes from 900 to 901 units. Explain your reasoning.

Profit

Number of units

37. Biology: Wildlife Management A state game commission introduces 50 deer into newly acquired state game lands. The population N of the herd can be modeled by

$$N = \frac{10(5 + 3t)}{1 + 0.04t}$$

where t is the time in years. Use differentials to approximate the change in the herd size from $t = 5$ to $t = 6$.

38. Medical Science The concentration C (in milligrams per milliliter) of a drug in a patient's bloodstream t hours after injection into muscle tissue is modeled by

$$C = \frac{3t}{27 + t^3}.$$

Use differentials to approximate the change in the concentration when t changes from $t = 1$ to $t = 1.5$.

39. Marginal Analysis A retailer has determined that the monthly sales x of a watch are 150 units when the price is \$50, but decrease to 120 units when the price is \$60. Assume that the demand is a linear function of the price. Find the revenue R as a function of x and approximate the change in revenue for a one-unit increase in sales when $x = 141$. Make a sketch showing dR and ΔR.

40. Marginal Analysis The demand x for a web camera is 30,000 units per month when the price is \$25 and 40,000 units when the price is \$20. The initial investment is \$275,000 and the cost per unit is \$17. Assume that the demand is a linear function of the price. Find the profit P as a function of x and approximate the change in profit for a one-unit increase in sales when $x = 28,000$. Make a sketch showing dP and ΔP.

Error Propagation In Exercises 41 and 42, use the following information. Given the error in a measurement (Δx), the *propagated error* (Δy) can be approximated by the differential dy. The ratio dy/y is the *relative error*, which corresponds to a *percentage error* of $dy/y \times 100\%$.

41. Area The side of a square measures 6 inches, with a possible error of $\pm\frac{1}{16}$ inch. Estimate the propagated error and the percentage error in computing the area of the square.

42. Volume The radius of a sphere measures 6 inches, with a possible error of ±0.02 inch. Estimate the propagated error and the percentage error in computing the volume of the sphere.

True or False? In Exercises 43 and 44, determine whether the statement is true or false. If it is false, explain why or give an example that shows it is false.

43. If $y = x + c$, then $dy = dx$.

44. If $y = ax + b$, then $\Delta y/\Delta x = dy/dx$.

ALGEBRA TUTOR

Solving Equations

Much of the algebra in Chapter 3 involves simplifying algebraic expressions (see pages 158 and 159) and solving algebraic equations (see page 71). The Algebra Tutor on page 71 illustrates some of the basic techniques for solving equations. On these two pages, you can review some of the more complicated techniques for solving equations.

When solving an equation, remember that your basic goal is to isolate the variable on one side of the equation. To do this, you use inverse operations. For instance, to isolate x in

$$x - 2 = 0$$

you add 2 to each side of the equation, because *addition* is the inverse operation of *subtraction*. To isolate x in

$$\sqrt{x} = 2$$

you square each side of the equation, because *squaring* is the inverse operation of *taking the square root*.

Example 1 Solving Equations

Solve each equation.

a. $\dfrac{36(x^2 - 1)}{(x^2 + 3)^3} = 0$ **b.** $0 = 2x(2x^2 - 3)$ **c.** $\dfrac{dV}{dx} = 0$, where $V = 27x - \dfrac{1}{4}x^3$

SOLUTION

a. $\dfrac{36(x^2 - 1)}{(x^2 + 3)^3} = 0$ Example 2, page 188

$36(x^2 - 1) = 0$ A fraction is equal to zero only when its numerator is zero.

$x^2 - 1 = 0$ Divide each side by 36.

$x^2 = 1$ Add 1 to each side.

$x = \pm 1$ Take the square root of each side.

b. $\quad 0 = 2x(2x^2 - 3)$ Example 2, page 198

$2x = 0 \implies x = 0$ Set first factor equal to zero.

$2x^2 - 3 = 0 \implies x = \pm\sqrt{\dfrac{3}{2}}$ Set second factor equal to zero.

c. $\quad V = 27x - \dfrac{1}{4}x^3$ Example 1, page 196

$\dfrac{dV}{dx} = 27 - \dfrac{3}{4}x^2$ Find derivative of V.

$0 = 27 - \dfrac{3}{4}x^2$ Set derivative equal to 0.

$\dfrac{3}{4}x^2 = 27$ Add $\frac{3}{4}x^2$ to each side.

$x^2 = 36$ Multiply each side by $\frac{4}{3}$.

$x = \pm 6$ Take the square root of each side.

Example 2 **Solving Equations**

Solve each equation.

a. $\dfrac{20(x^{1/3} - 1)}{9x^{2/3}} = 0$ **b.** $\dfrac{25}{\sqrt{x}} - 0.5 = 0$

c. $x^2(4x - 3) = 0$ **d.** $\dfrac{4x}{3(x^2 - 4)^{1/3}} = 0$

e. $g'(x) = 0$, where $g(x) = (x - 2)(x + 1)^2$

SOLUTION

a. $\dfrac{20(x^{1/3} - 1)}{9x^{2/3}} = 0$ Example 5, page 231

$20(x^{1/3} - 1) = 0$ A fraction is equal to zero only when its numerator is zero.

$x^{1/3} - 1 = 0$ Divide each side by 20.

$x^{1/3} = 1$ Add 1 to each side.

$x = 1$ Cube each side.

b. $\dfrac{25}{\sqrt{x}} - 0.5 = 0$ Example 4, page 208

$\dfrac{25}{\sqrt{x}} = 0.5$ Add 0.5 to each side.

$25 = 0.5\sqrt{x}$ Multiply each side by $\sqrt{x}$.

$50 = \sqrt{x}$ Divide each side by 0.5.

$2500 = x$ Square both sides.

c. $x^2(4x - 3) = 0$ Example 2, page 180

$x^2 = 0 \implies x = 0$ Set first factor equal to zero.

$4x - 3 = 0 \implies x = \frac{3}{4}$ Set second factor equal to zero.

d. $\dfrac{4x}{3(x^2 - 4)^{1/3}} = 0$ Example 5, page 172

$4x = 0$ A fraction is equal to zero only when its numerator is zero.

$x = 0$ Divide each side by 4.

e. $g(x) = (x - 2)(x + 1)^2$ Exercise 45, page 194

$g'(x) = (x - 2)(2)(x + 1) + (x + 1)^2(1)$ Find derivative of g.

$(x - 2)(2)(x + 1) + (x + 1)^2(1) = 0$ Set derivative equal to zero.

$(x + 1)[2(x - 2) + (x + 1)] = 0$ Factor.

$(x + 1)(2x - 4 + x + 1) = 0$ Multiply factors.

$(x + 1)(3x - 3) = 0$ Combine like terms.

$x + 1 = 0 \implies x = -1$ Set first factor equal to zero.

$3x - 3 = 0 \implies x = 1$ Set second factor equal to zero.

SUMMARY AND STUDY STRATEGIES

After studying this chapter, you should have acquired the following skills. The exercise numbers are keyed to the Review Exercises that begin on page 246. Answers to odd-numbered Review Exercises are given in the back of the text.*

Section 3.1

	Review Exercises
■ Find the critical numbers of a function.	*1–6*
c is a critical number of f when $f'(c) = 0$ or $f'(c)$ is undefined.	
■ Find the open intervals on which a function is increasing or decreasing.	*7–12*
f is increasing when $f'(x) > 0$.	
f is decreasing when $f'(x) < 0$.	
■ Find intervals on which a real-life model is increasing or decreasing.	*13, 14*

Section 3.2

■ Use the First-Derivative Test to find the relative extrema of a function.	*15–24*
■ Find the absolute extrema of a continuous function on a closed interval.	*25–32*
■ Find minimum and maximum values of a real-life model and interpret the results in context.	*33, 34*

Section 3.3

■ Find the open intervals on which the graph of a function is concave upward or concave downward.	*35–38*
f is concave upward when $f''(x) > 0$.	
f is concave downward when $f''(x) < 0$.	
■ Find the points of inflection of the graph of a function.	*39–42*
■ Use the Second-Derivative Test to find the relative extrema of a function.	*43–48*
■ Find the point of diminishing returns of an input-output model.	*49, 50*

Section 3.4

■ Solve real-life optimization problems.	*51–54*

Section 3.5

■ Solve business and economics optimization problems.	*55–60*
■ Find the price elasticity of demand for a demand function.	*61, 62*

---

* A wide range of valuable study aids are available to help you master the material in this chapter. The *Student Solutions Manual* includes step-by-step solutions to all odd-numbered exercises to help you review and prepare. The student website at *www.cengagebrain.com* offers algebra help and a *Graphing Technology Guide*, which contains step-by-step commands and instructions for a wide variety of graphing calculators.

Section 3.6

Section 3.7

Section 3.8

Study Strategies

■ **Solve Problems Graphically, Analytically, and Numerically**   When analyzing the graph of a function, use a variety of problem-solving strategies. For instance, if you were asked to analyze the graph of

$$f(x) = x^3 - 4x^2 + 5x - 4$$

you could begin *graphically*. That is, you could use a graphing utility to find a viewing window that appears to show the important characteristics of the graph. From the graph shown below, the function appears to have one relative minimum, one relative maximum, and one point of inflection.

Next, you could use calculus to *analyze* the graph. Because the derivative of *f* is

$$f'(x) = 3x^2 - 8x + 5 = (3x - 5)(x - 1)$$

the critical numbers of *f* are $x = \frac{5}{3}$ and $x = 1$. By the First-Derivative Test, you can conclude that $x = \frac{5}{3}$ yields a relative minimum and $x = 1$ yields a relative maximum. Because

$$f''(x) = 6x - 8$$

you can conclude that $x = \frac{4}{3}$ yields a point of inflection. Finally, you could analyze the graph *numerically*. For instance, you could construct a table of values and observe that *f* is increasing on the interval $(-\infty, 1)$, decreasing on the interval $\left(1, \frac{5}{3}\right)$, and increasing on the interval $\left(\frac{5}{3}, \infty\right)$.

■ **Problem-Solving Strategies**   When you get stuck while trying to solve an optimization problem, consider the strategies below.

1. *Draw a Diagram.*   If feasible, draw a diagram that represents the problem. Label all known values and unknown values on the diagram.

2. *Solve a Simpler Problem.*   Simplify the problem, or write several simple examples of the problem. For instance, if you are asked to find the dimensions that will produce a maximum area, try calculating the areas of several examples.

3. *Rewrite the Problem in Your Own Words.*   Rewriting a problem can help you understand it better.

4. *Guess and Check.*   Try guessing the answer, then check your guess in the statement of the original problem. By refining your guesses, you may be able to think of a general strategy for solving the problem.

Review Exercises

See www.CalcChat.com for worked-out solutions to odd-numbered exercises.

Finding Critical Numbers   In Exercises 1–6, find the critical numbers of the function.

1. $f(x) = -x^2 + 2x + 4$

2. $y = 3x^2 + 18x$

3. $y = 4x^3 - 108x$

4. $f(x) = x^4 - 8x^2 + 13$

5. $g(x) = (x - 1)^2(x - 3)$

6. $h(x) = \sqrt{x}(x - 3)$

Intervals on Which f Is Increasing or Decreasing   In Exercises 7–12, find the critical numbers and the open intervals on which the function is increasing or decreasing. Use a graphing utility to verify your results.

7. $f(x) = x^2 + x - 2$

8. $g(x) = (x + 2)^3$

9. $f(x) = -x^3 + 6x^2 - 2$

10. $y = x^3 - 12x^2$

11. $y = (x - 1)^{2/3}$

12. $y = 2x^{1/3} - 3$

13. **Revenue**   The revenue R of Chipotle Mexican Grill (in millions of dollars) from 2004 through 2009 can be modeled by

$$R = 6.268t^2 + 136.07t - 191.3, \quad 4 \le t \le 9$$

where t is the time in years, with $t = 4$ corresponding to 2004. Show that the sales were increasing from 2004 through 2009.   *(Source: Chipotle Mexican Grill, Inc.)*

14. **Revenue**   The revenue R of Cintas (in millions of dollars) from 2000 through 2010 can be modeled by

$$R = -5.5778t^3 + 67.524t^2 + 45.22t + 1969.2$$

for $0 \le t \le 10$, where t is the time in years, with $t = 0$ corresponding to 2000.   *(Source: Cintas Corporation)*

(a) Use a graphing utility to graph the model. Then graphically estimate the years during which the revenue was increasing and the years during which the revenue was decreasing.

(b) Use the test for increasing and decreasing functions to verify the result of part (a).

Finding Relative Extrema   In Exercises 15–24, use the First-Derivative Test to find all relative extrema of the function. Use a graphing utility to verify your result.

15. $f(x) = 4x^3 - 6x^2 - 2$

16. $f(x) = \frac{1}{4}x^4 - 8x$

17. $g(x) = x^2 - 16x + 12$

18. $h(x) = 4 + 10x - x^2$

19. $h(x) = 2x^2 - x^4$

20. $s(x) = x^4 - 8x^2 + 3$

21. $f(x) = \dfrac{6}{x^2 + 1}$

22. $f(x) = \dfrac{2}{x^2 - 1}$

23. $h(x) = \dfrac{x^2}{x - 2}$

24. $g(x) = x - 6\sqrt{x}, \quad x > 0$

Finding Extrema on a Closed Interval   In Exercises 25–32, find the absolute extrema of the function on the closed interval. Use a graphing utility to verify your result.

25. $f(x) = x^2 + 5x + 6; \quad [-3, 0]$

26. $f(x) = x^4 - 2x^3; \quad [0, 2]$

27. $f(x) = x^3 - 12x + 1; \quad [-4, 4]$

28. $f(x) = x^3 + 2x^2 - 3x + 4; \quad [-3, 2]$

29. $f(x) = 2\sqrt{x} - x; \quad [0, 9]$

30. $f(x) = \dfrac{x}{\sqrt{x^2 + 1}}; \quad [0, 2]$

31. $f(x) = \dfrac{2x}{x^2 + 1}; \quad [-1, 2]$

32. $f(x) = \dfrac{8}{x} + x; \quad [1, 4]$

33. **Surface Area**   A right circular cylinder of radius r and height h has a volume of 25 cubic inches (see figure). The total surface area of the cylinder in terms of r is given by

$$S = 2\pi r\left(r + \frac{25}{\pi r^2}\right).$$

Find the radius that will minimize the surface area. Use a graphing utility to verify your result.

34. Profit The profit P (in dollars) made by a company from selling x tablet computers can be modeled by

$$P = 1.64x - \frac{x^2}{15,000} - 2500.$$

Find the number of units sold that will yield a maximum profit. What is the maximum profit?

Applying the Test for Concavity In Exercises 35–38, determine the open intervals on which the graph of the function is concave upward or concave downward.

35. $f(x) = (x - 2)^3$

36. $h(x) = x^5 - 10x^2$

37. $g(x) = \frac{1}{4}(-x^4 + 8x^2 - 12)$

38. $h(x) = x^3 - 6x$

Finding Points of Inflection In Exercises 39–42, discuss the concavity of the graph of the function and find the points of inflection.

39. $f(x) = \frac{1}{2}x^4 - 4x^3$

40. $f(x) = \frac{1}{4}x^4 - 2x^2 - x$

41. $f(x) = x^3(x - 3)^2$

42. $f(x) = (x - 1)^2(x - 3)$

Using the Second-Derivative Test In Exercises 43–48, use the Second-Derivative Test to find all relative extrema of the function.

43. $f(x) = x^3 - 6x^2 + 12x$

44. $f(x) = x^4 - 32x^2 + 12$

45. $f(x) = x^5 - 5x^3$

46. $f(x) = x(x^2 - 3x - 9)$

47. $f(x) = 2x^2(1 - x^2)$

48. $f(x) = x - 4\sqrt{x + 1}$

Point of Diminishing Returns In Exercises 49 and 50, find the point of diminishing returns for the function. For each function, R is the revenue (in thousands of dollars) and x is the amount spent (in thousands of dollars) on advertising. Use a graphing utility to verify your result.

49. $R = \frac{1}{1500}(150x^2 - x^3)$, $0 \le x \le 100$

50. $R = -\frac{2}{3}(x^3 - 12x^2 - 6)$, $0 \le x \le 8$

51. Minimum Perimeter Find the length and width of a rectangle that has an area of 225 square meters and a minimum perimeter.

52. Maximum Volume A rectangular solid with a square base has a surface area of 432 square centimeters.

(a) Determine the dimensions that yield the maximum volume.

(b) Find the maximum volume.

53. Maximum Volume An open box is to be made from a 10-inch by 16-inch rectangular piece of material by cutting equal squares from the corners and turning up the sides (see figure). Find the volume of the largest box that can be made.

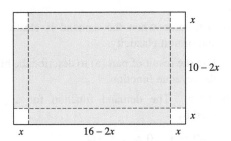

54. Minimum Area A rectangular page is to contain 108 square inches of print. The margins at the top and bottom of the page are to be $\frac{3}{4}$ inch wide. The margins on each side are to be 1 inch wide. Find the dimensions of the page that will minimize the amount of paper used.

Finding the Maximum Revenue In Exercises 55 and 56, find the number of units x that produces a maximum revenue R.

55. $R = 450x - 0.25x^2$

56. $R = 36x^2 - 0.05x^3$

Finding the Minimum Average Cost In Exercises 57 and 58, find the number of units x that produces the minimum average cost per unit $\overline{C}$.

57. $C = 0.2x^2 + 10x + 4500$

58. $C = 0.03x^3 + 30x + 3840$

59. Maximum Profit A commodity has a demand function modeled by

$$p = 36 - 4x$$

and a total cost function modeled by

$$C = 2x^2 + 6$$

where x is the number of units.

(a) What price yields a maximum profit?

(b) When the profit is maximized, what is the average cost per unit?

60. Maximum Profit The profit P (in thousands of dollars) for a company in terms of the amount s spent on advertising (in thousands of dollars) can be modeled by

$$P = -4s^3 + 72s^2 - 240s + 500.$$

Find the amount of advertising that maximizes the profit. Find the point of diminishing returns.

61. Elasticity The demand function for a product is modeled by

$$p = 60 - 0.04x, \quad 0 \le x \le 1500$$

where p is the price (in dollars) and x is the number of units.

(a) Determine when the demand is elastic, inelastic, and of unit elasticity.

(b) Use the result of part (a) to describe the behavior of the revenue function.

62. Elasticity The demand function for a product is modeled by

$$p = 960 - x, \quad 0 \le x \le 960$$

where p is the price (in dollars) and x is the number of units.

(a) Determine when the demand is elastic, inelastic, and of unit elasticity.

(b) Use the result of part (a) to describe the behavior of the revenue function.

Finding Vertical Asymptotes In Exercises 63–66, determine all vertical asymptotes of the graph of the function.

63. $f(x) = \dfrac{x + 4}{x^2 + 7x}$

64. $f(x) = \dfrac{x - 1}{x^2 - 4}$

65. $f(x) = \dfrac{x^2 - 16}{2x^2 + 9x + 4}$

66. $f(x) = \dfrac{x^2 + 6x + 9}{x^2 - 5x - 24}$

 Determining Infinite Limits In Exercises 67–70, use a graphing utility to find the limit.

67. $\lim\limits_{x \to 0^+} \left(x - \dfrac{1}{x^3} \right)$

68. $\lim\limits_{x \to 0^-} \left(3 + \dfrac{1}{x} \right)$

69. $\lim\limits_{x \to -1^+} \dfrac{x^2 - 2x + 1}{x + 1}$

70. $\lim\limits_{x \to 3^-} \dfrac{3x^2 + 1}{x^2 - 9}$

Finding Horizontal Asymptotes In Exercises 71–74, find the horizontal asymptote of the graph of the function.

71. $f(x) = \dfrac{2x^2}{3x^2 + 5}$

72. $f(x) = \dfrac{3x^2 - 2x + 3}{x + 1}$

73. $f(x) = \dfrac{3x}{x^2 + 1}$

74. $f(x) = \dfrac{x}{x - 2} + \dfrac{2x}{x + 2}$

75. Average Cost The cost C (in dollars) of producing x units of a product is

$$C = 0.75x + 4000.$$

(a) Find the average cost function $\overline{C}$.

(b) Find $\overline{C}$ when $x = 100$ and when $x = 1000$.

(c) Determine the limit of the average cost function as x approaches infinity. Interpret the limit in the context of the problem.

76. Average Cost The cost C (in dollars) of producing x units of a product is

$$C = 1.50x + 8000.$$

(a) Find the average cost function $\overline{C}$.

(b) Find $\overline{C}$ when $x = 1000$ and when $x = 10,000$.

(c) Determine the limit of the average cost function as x approaches infinity. Interpret the limit in the context of the problem.

77. Seizing Drugs The cost C (in millions of dollars) for the federal government to seize $p\%$ of an illegal drug as it enters the country is modeled by

$$C = \dfrac{250p}{100 - p}, \quad 0 \le p < 100.$$

(a) Find the costs of seizing 20%, 50%, and 90%.

(b) Find the limit of C as $p \to 100^-$. Interpret the limit in the context of the problem. Use a graphing utility to verify your result.

78. Removing Pollutants The cost C (in dollars) of removing $p\%$ of the air pollutants in the stack emission of a utility company that burns coal is modeled by

$$C = \dfrac{160,000p}{100 - p}, \quad 0 \le p < 100.$$

(a) Find the costs of seizing 25%, 50%, and 75%.

(b) Find the limit of C as $p \to 100^-$. Interpret the limit in the context of the problem. Use a graphing utility to verify your result.

Analyzing a Graph In Exercises 79–90, analyze and sketch the graph of the function. Label any intercepts, relative extrema, points of inflection, and asymptotes.

79. $f(x) = 4x - x^2$

80. $f(x) = 4x^3 - x^4$

81. $f(x) = x^3 - 6x^2 + 3x + 10$

82. $f(x) = -x^3 + 3x^2 + 9x - 2$

83. $f(x) = x^4 - 4x^3 + 16x - 16$

84. $f(x) = x^5 + 1$

85. $f(x) = x\sqrt{16 - x^2}$

86. $f(x) = x^2\sqrt{9 - x^2}$

87. $f(x) = \dfrac{x + 1}{x - 1}$

88. $f(x) = \dfrac{x - 1}{3x^2 + 1}$

89. $f(x) = 3x^{2/3} - 2x$

90. $f(x) = x^{4/5}$

91. Bacteria The data in the table show the number N of bacteria in a culture at time t, where t is measured in days.

t	1	2	3	4	5	6	7	8
N	25	200	804	1756	2296	2434	2467	2473

A model for these data is

$$N = \frac{24{,}670 - 35{,}153t + 13{,}250t^2}{100 - 39t + 7t^2}, \quad 1 \le t \le 8.$$

(a) Use a graphing utility to create a scatter plot of the data and graph the model in the same viewing window. How well does the model fit the data?

(b) Use the model to predict the number of bacteria in the culture after 10 days.

(c) Should this model be used to predict the number of bacteria in the culture after a few months? Why or why not?

92. Meteorology The monthly average high temperatures T (in degrees Fahrenheit) in New York City can be modeled by

$$T = \frac{31.6 - 1.822t + 0.0984t^2}{1 - 0.194t + 0.0131t^2}, \quad 1 \le t \le 12$$

where t is the month, with $t = 1$ corresponding to January. Use a graphing utility to graph the model and find all absolute extrema. Interpret the meaning of these values in the context of the problem. *(Source: National Climatic Data Center)*

Comparing Δy and dy In Exercises 93–96, compare the values of dy and Δy for the function.

Function	x-Value	Differential of x
93. $f(x) = 2x^2$	$x = 2$	$\Delta x = dx = 0.01$
94. $f(x) = x^4 + 3$	$x = 1$	$\Delta x = dx = 0.1$
95. $f(x) = 6x - x^3$	$x = 3$	$\Delta x = dx = 0.1$
96. $f(x) = 5x^{3/2}$	$x = 9$	$\Delta x = dx = 0.01$

Marginal Analysis In Exercises 97–102, use differentials to approximate the change in cost, revenue, or profit corresponding to an increase in sales of one unit. For instance, in Exercise 97, approximate the change in cost as x increases from 10 to 11.

Function	x-Value
97. $C = 40x^2 + 1225$	$x = 10$
98. $C = 1.5\sqrt[3]{x} + 500$	$x = 125$
99. $R = 6.25x + 0.4x^{3/2}$	$x = 225$
100. $R = 80x - 0.35x^2$	$x = 80$
101. $P = 0.003x^2 + 0.019x - 1200$	$x = 750$
102. $P = -0.2x^3 + 3000x - 7500$	$x = 50$

Finding Differentials In Exercises 103–108, find the differential dy.

103. $y = 0.5x^3$

104. $y = 7x^4 + 2x^2$

105. $y = (3x^2 - 2)^3$

106. $y = \sqrt{36 - x^2}$

107. $y = \dfrac{2 - x}{x + 5}$

108. $y = \dfrac{3x^2}{x - 4}$

109. Profit The profit P (in dollars) for a company producing x units is

$$P = -0.8x^2 + 324x - 2000.$$

(a) Use differentials to approximate the change in profit when the production level changes from 100 to 101 units.

(b) Compare this with the actual change in profit.

110. Demand The demand function for a product is

$$p = 108 - 0.2x$$

where p is the price per unit (in dollars) and x is the number of units.

(a) Use differentials to approximate the change in revenue as sales increase from 20 units to 21 units.

(b) Repeat part (a) when sales increase from 40 units to 41 units.

111. Physiology: Body Surface Area The body surface area (BSA) of a 180-centimeter-tall (about six-foot-tall) person is modeled by

$$B = 0.1\sqrt{5w}$$

where B is the BSA (in square meters) and w is the weight (in kilograms). Use differentials to approximate the change in the person's BSA when the person's weight changes from 90 kilograms to 95 kilograms.

TEST YOURSELF

See www.CalcChat.com for worked-out solutions to odd-numbered exercises.

Take this test as you would take a test in class. When you are done, check your work against the answers given in the back of the book.

In Exercises 1–3, find the critical numbers and the open intervals on which the function is increasing or decreasing .

1. $f(x) = 3x^2 - 4$ **2.** $f(x) = x^3 - 12x$ **3.** $f(x) = (x - 5)^4$

In Exercises 4–6, use the First-Derivative Test to find all relative extrema of the function.

4. $f(x) = \dfrac{1}{3}x^3 - 9x + 4$ **5.** $f(x) = 2x^4 - 4x^2 - 5$ **6.** $f(x) = \dfrac{5}{x^2 + 2}$

In Exercises 7–9, find the absolute extrema of the function on the closed interval. Use a graphing utility to verify your result.

7. $f(x) = x^2 + 6x + 8, \ [-4, 0]$ **8.** $f(x) = 12\sqrt{x} - 4x, \ [0, 5]$

9. $f(x) = \dfrac{6}{x} + \dfrac{x}{2}, \ [1, 6]$

In Exercises 10 and 11, determine the open intervals on which the graph of the function is concave upward or concave downward.

10. $f(x) = x^5 - 80x^2$ **11.** $f(x) = \dfrac{20}{3x^2 + 8}$

In Exercises 12 and 13, discuss the concavity of the graph of the function and find the points of inflection.

12. $f(x) = x^4 + 6$ **13.** $f(x) = x^4 - 54x^2 + 230$

In Exercises 14 and 15, use the Second-Derivative Test to find all relative extrema of the function.

14. $f(x) = x^3 - 6x^2 - 36x + 50$ **15.** $f(x) = \dfrac{3}{5}x^5 - 9x^3$

In Exercises 16–18, find the vertical and horizontal asymptotes of the graph of the function.

16. $f(x) = \dfrac{3x + 2}{x - 5}$ **17.** $f(x) = \dfrac{2x^2}{x^2 + 3}$ **18.** $f(x) = \dfrac{2x^2 - 5}{x - 1}$

In Exercises 19–21, analyze and sketch the graph of the function. Label any intercepts, relative extrema, points of inflection, and asymptotes.

19. $y = -x^3 + 3x^2 + 9x - 2$ **20.** $y = x^5 - 5x$ **21.** $y = \dfrac{x}{x^2 - 4}$

In Exercises 22–24, find the differential dy.

22. $y = 5x^2 - 3$ **23.** $y = \dfrac{1 - x}{x + 3}$ **24.** $y = (x + 4)^3$

25. The demand function for a product is modeled by

$$p = 280 - 0.4x, \quad 0 \le x \le 700$$

where p is the price per unit (in dollars) and x is the number of units. Determine when the demand is elastic, inelastic, and of unit elasticity.

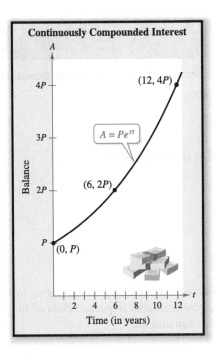

Continuously Compounded Interest

$A = Pe^{rt}$

Points shown: $(0, P)$, $(6, 2P)$, $(12, 4P)$

Balance vs. Time (in years)

Example 3 on page 297 shows how an exponential growth model can be used to find the annual interest rate of an account.

4 Exponential and Logarithmic Functions

251

4.1 Exponential Functions

In Exercise 5 on page 256, you will evaluate an exponential function to find the remaining amount of a radioactive material.

■ Use the properties of exponents to evaluate and simplify exponential expressions.
■ Sketch the graphs of exponential functions.

Exponential Functions

You are already familiar with the behavior of algebraic functions such as

$$f(x) = x^2$$
$$g(x) = \sqrt{x} = x^{1/2}$$

and

$$h(x) = \frac{1}{x} = x^{-1}$$

each of which involves a variable raised to a constant power. By interchanging roles and raising a constant to a variable power, you obtain another important class of functions called **exponential functions.** Some simple examples are

$$f(x) = 2^x$$
$$g(x) = \left(\frac{1}{10}\right)^x = \frac{1}{10^x}$$

and

$$h(x) = 3^{2x} = 9^x.$$

In general, you can use any positive number $a \neq 1$ as the base of an exponential function.

Definition of Exponential Function

If $a > 0$ and $a \neq 1$, then the **exponential function** with base a is given by

$$f(x) = a^x.$$

In the definition of an exponential function, the base $a = 1$ is excluded because it yields

$$f(x) = 1^x = 1.$$

This is a constant function, not an exponential function.

When working with exponential functions, the properties of exponents, shown below, are useful.

Properties of Exponents

Let a and b be positive real numbers.

1. $a^0 = 1$ **2.** $a^x a^y = a^{x+y}$ **3.** $\dfrac{a^x}{a^y} = a^{x-y}$

4. $(a^x)^y = a^{xy}$ **5.** $(ab)^x = a^x b^x$ **6.** $\left(\dfrac{a}{b}\right)^x = \dfrac{a^x}{b^x}$

7. $a^{-x} = \dfrac{1}{a^x}$

Example 1 **Applying Properties of Exponents**

a. $(2^2)(2^3) = 2^{2+3} = 2^5 = 32$ Apply Property 2.

b. $(2^2)(2^{-3}) = 2^{2-3} = 2^{-1} = \dfrac{1}{2}$ Apply Properties 2 and 7.

c. $(3^2)^3 = 3^{2(3)} = 3^6 = 729$ Apply Property 4.

d. $\left(\dfrac{1}{3}\right)^{-2} = \left(\dfrac{3}{1}\right)^2 = \dfrac{3^2}{1^2} = 9$ Apply Properties 7 and 6.

e. $\dfrac{3^2}{3^3} = 3^{2-3} = 3^{-1} = \dfrac{1}{3}$ Apply Properties 3 and 7.

f. $(2^{1/2})(3^{1/2}) = [(2)(3)]^{1/2} = 6^{1/2} = \sqrt{6}$ Apply Property 5.

✓ **Checkpoint 1**

Simplify each expression using the properties of exponents.

a. $(3^2)(3^3)$ **b.** $(3^2)(3^{-1})$ **c.** $(2^3)^2$

d. $(1/2)^{-3}$ **e.** $2^2/2^3$ **f.** $(2^{1/2})(5^{1/2})$

Although Example 1 demonstrates the properties of exponents with integer and rational exponents, it is important to realize that the properties hold for *all* real exponents. With a calculator, you can obtain approximations of a^x for any positive number a and any real number x. Here are some examples.

$$2^{-0.6} \approx 0.660, \qquad \pi^{0.75} \approx 2.360, \qquad (1.56)^{\sqrt{2}} \approx 1.876$$

Example 2 **Dating Organic Material**

In living organic material, the ratio of radioactive carbon isotopes to the total number of carbon atoms is about 1 to 10^{12}. When organic material dies, its radioactive carbon isotopes begin to decay, with a half-life of about 5715 years. This means that after 5715 years, the ratio of isotopes to atoms will have decreased to one-half the original ratio; after a second 5715 years, the ratio will have decreased to one-fourth of the original; and so on. Figure 4.1 shows this decreasing ratio. The formula for the ratio R of carbon isotopes to carbon atoms is $R = (1/10^{12})(1/2)^{t/5715}$, where t is the time in years. Find the value of R for each period of time.

a. 10,000 years   **b.** 20,000 years   **c.** 25,000 years

SOLUTION

a. $R = \left(\dfrac{1}{10^{12}}\right)\left(\dfrac{1}{2}\right)^{10,000/5715} \approx 2.973 \times 10^{-13}$ Ratio for 10,000 years

b. $R = \left(\dfrac{1}{10^{12}}\right)\left(\dfrac{1}{2}\right)^{20,000/5715} \approx 8.842 \times 10^{-14}$ Ratio for 20,000 years

c. $R = \left(\dfrac{1}{10^{12}}\right)\left(\dfrac{1}{2}\right)^{25,000/5715} \approx 4.821 \times 10^{-14}$ Ratio for 25,000 years

Organic Material

FIGURE 4.1

✓ **Checkpoint 2**

Use the formula for the ratio of carbon isotopes to carbon atoms in Example 2 to find the value of R for each period of time.

a. 5000 years   **b.** 15,000 years   **c.** 30,000 years

Graphs of Exponential Functions

The basic nature of the graph of an exponential function can be determined by the point-plotting method or by using a graphing utility.

Example 3   **Graphing Exponential Functions**

Sketch the graph of each exponential function.

a. $f(x) = 2^x$ **b.** $g(x) = \left(\frac{1}{2}\right)^x = 2^{-x}$ **c.** $h(x) = 3^x$

SOLUTION   To sketch these functions by hand, you can begin by constructing a table of values, as shown below.

x	-3	-2	-1	0	1	2	3	4
$f(x) = 2^x$	$\frac{1}{8}$	$\frac{1}{4}$	$\frac{1}{2}$	1	2	4	8	16
$g(x) = 2^{-x}$	8	4	2	1	$\frac{1}{2}$	$\frac{1}{4}$	$\frac{1}{8}$	$\frac{1}{16}$
$h(x) = 3^x$	$\frac{1}{27}$	$\frac{1}{9}$	$\frac{1}{3}$	1	3	9	27	81

The graphs of the three functions are shown in Figure 4.2. Note that the graphs of $f(x) = 2^x$ and $h(x) = 3^x$ are increasing, whereas the graph of $g(x) = 2^{-x}$ is decreasing.

(a)

(b)

(c)

FIGURE 4.2

✓ **Checkpoint 3**

Sketch the graph of

$$f(x) = 5^x.$$

TECH TUTOR

Try graphing the functions

$$f(x) = 2^x \quad \text{and} \quad h(x) = 3^x$$

in the same viewing window, as shown at the right. From the display, you can see that the graph of h is increasing more rapidly than the graph of f.

The forms of the graphs in Figure 4.2 are typical of the graphs of the exponential functions $y = a^{-x}$ and $y = a^x$, where $a > 1$. The basic characteristics of such graphs are summarized in Figure 4.3.

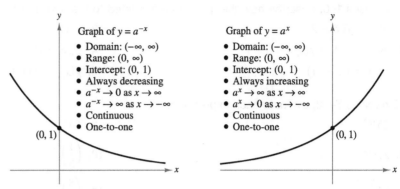

Graph of $y = a^{-x}$
- Domain: $(-\infty, \infty)$
- Range: $(0, \infty)$
- Intercept: $(0, 1)$
- Always decreasing
- $a^{-x} \to 0$ as $x \to \infty$
- $a^{-x} \to \infty$ as $x \to -\infty$
- Continuous
- One-to-one

Graph of $y = a^x$
- Domain: $(-\infty, \infty)$
- Range: $(0, \infty)$
- Intercept: $(0, 1)$
- Always increasing
- $a^x \to \infty$ as $x \to \infty$
- $a^x \to 0$ as $x \to -\infty$
- Continuous
- One-to-one

Characteristics of the Exponential Functions $y = a^{-x}$ and $y = a^x$ $(a > 1)$
FIGURE 4.3

| Example 4 | **Graphing an Exponential Function** |

Sketch the graph of $f(x) = 3^{-x} - 1$.

SOLUTION   Begin by creating a table of values, as shown below.

x	-2	-1	0	1	2
$f(x)$	$3^2 - 1 = 8$	$3^1 - 1 = 2$	$3^0 - 1 = 0$	$3^{-1} - 1 = -\frac{2}{3}$	$3^{-2} - 1 = -\frac{8}{9}$

$f(x) = 3^{-x} - 1$

FIGURE 4.4

From the limit

$$\lim_{x \to \infty} (3^{-x} - 1) = \lim_{x \to \infty} 3^{-x} - \lim_{x \to \infty} 1$$
$$= \lim_{x \to \infty} \frac{1}{3^x} - \lim_{x \to \infty} 1$$
$$= 0 - 1$$
$$= -1$$

you can see that $y = -1$ is a horizontal asymptote of the graph. The graph is shown in Figure 4.4.

✓**Checkpoint 4**

Sketch the graph of $f(x) = 2^{-x} + 1$.

SUMMARIZE   (Section 4.1)

1. State the definition of an exponential function *(page 252)*. For examples of exponential functions, see Example 3.

2. State the properties of exponents *(page 252)*. For examples of the properties of exponents, see Examples 1 and 2.

3. State the basic characteristics of the graphs of the exponential functions $y = a^{-x}$ and $y = a^x$ *(page 255)*. For an example of the graph of an exponential function, see Example 4.

SKILLS WARM UP 4.1 The following warm-up exercises involve skills that were covered in earlier sections. You will use these skills in the exercise set for this section. For additional help, review Section 1.4.

In Exercises 1–6, describe how the graph of g is related to the graph of f.

1. $g(x) = f(x + 2)$

2. $g(x) = -f(x)$

3. $g(x) = -1 + f(x)$

4. $g(x) = f(-x)$

5. $g(x) = f(x - 1)$

6. $g(x) = f(x) + 2$

In Exercises 7–12, evaluate each expression.

7. $25^{3/2}$

8. $64^{3/4}$

9. $27^{2/3}$

10. $\left(\dfrac{1}{5}\right)^3$

11. $\left(\dfrac{1}{8}\right)^{1/3}$

12. $\left(\dfrac{5}{8}\right)^2$

In Exercises 13–18, solve for x.

13. $2x - 6 = 4$

14. $3x + 1 = 5$

15. $(x + 4)^2 = 25$

16. $(x - 2)^2 = 8$

17. $x^2 + 4x - 5 = 0$

18. $2x^2 - 3x + 1 = 0$

Exercises 4.1

See www.CalcChat.com for worked-out solutions to odd-numbered exercises.

Applying Properties of Exponents In Exercises 1–4, use the properties of exponents to simplify the expression. *See Example 1.*

1.
(a) $(5^2)(5^3)$
(b) $(5^2)(5^{-3})$
(c) $(5^2)^2$
(d) 5^{-3}

2.
(a) $\dfrac{5^3}{5^6}$
(b) $\left(\dfrac{1}{5}\right)^{-2}$
(c) $(8^{1/2})(2^{1/2})$
(d) $(32^{3/2})\left(\dfrac{1}{2}\right)^{3/2}$

3.
(a) $\dfrac{5^3}{25^2}$
(b) $(9^{2/3})(3)(3^{2/3})$
(c) $[(25^{1/2})(5^2)]^{1/3}$
(d) $(8^2)(4^3)$

4.
(a) $(4^3)(4^2)$
(b) $\left(\dfrac{1}{4}\right)^2(4^2)$
(c) $(4^6)^{1/2}$
(d) $[(8^{-1})(8^{2/3})]^3$

5. **Radioactive Decay** Beginning with 16 grams of a radioactive element whose half-life is 30 years, the mass y (in grams) remaining after t years is given by

$$y = 16\left(\dfrac{1}{2}\right)^{t/30}, \quad t \geq 0.$$

How much of the initial mass remains after 90 years?

6. **Radioactive Decay** Beginning with 23 grams of a radioactive element whose half-life is 45 years, the mass y (in grams) remaining after t years is given by

$$y = 23\left(\dfrac{1}{2}\right)^{t/45}, \quad t \geq 0.$$

How much of the initial mass remains after 150 years?

Graphing Exponential Functions In Exercises 7–18, sketch the graph of the function. *See Examples 3 and 4.*

7. $f(x) = 6^x$

8. $f(x) = 4^x$

9. $f(x) = \left(\frac{1}{5}\right)^x = 5^{-x}$

10. $f(x) = \left(\frac{1}{4}\right)^x = 4^{-x}$

11. $y = 2^{x-1}$

12. $y = 4^x + 3$

13. $y = -2^x$

14. $y = -5^x$

15. $y = 3^{-x^2}$

16. $y = 2^{-x^2}$

17. $s(t) = \frac{1}{4}(3^{-t})$

18. $s(t) = 2^{-t} + 3$

19. **Population Growth** The resident populations P (in millions) of the United States from 1995 through 2010 can be modeled by the exponential function

$$P(t) = 254.75(1.01)^t$$

where t is the time in years, with $t = 5$ corresponding to 1995. Use the model to estimate the populations in the years (a) 2013 and (b) 2020. *(Source: U.S. Census Bureau)*

20. Sales The sales S (in billions of dollars) for Walgreens from 2000 through 2010 can be modeled by the exponential function

$$S(t) = 22.52(1.125)^t$$

where t is the time in years, with $t = 0$ corresponding to 2000.

(a) Use the model to estimate the sales in 2014.

(b) Use the model to estimate the sales in 2018.

(Source: Walgreen Company)

21. Property Value A piece of property sells for $64,000. The value of the property doubles every 15 years. A model for the value V of the property t years after the date of purchase is

$$V(t) = 64,000(2)^{t/15}.$$

Use the model to approximate the value of the property (a) 5 years and (b) 20 years after it is purchased.

22. HOW DO YOU SEE IT? Match the exponential function with its graph. Explain your reasoning. [The graphs are labeled (i), (ii), (iii), (iv), (v), and (vi).]

(i)

(ii)

(iii)

(iv)

(v)

(vi)

(a) $f(x) = 3^x$
(b) $f(x) = 3^{-x/2}$
(c) $f(x) = -3^x$
(d) $f(x) = 3^{x-2}$
(e) $f(x) = 3^{-x} - 1$
(f) $f(x) = 3^x + 2$

23. Inflation Rate With an annual rate of inflation of 4% over the next 10 years, the approximate cost C of goods or services during any year in the decade is given by

$$C(t) = P(1.04)^t, \ 0 \le t \le 10$$

where t is the time (in years) and P is the present cost. The price of an oil change for a car is presently $24.95. Estimate the price 10 years from now.

24. Inflation Rate Repeat Exercise 23 using an annual rate of inflation of 10% over the next 10 years. The approximate cost C of goods or services is given by

$$C(t) = P(1.10)^t, \ 0 \le t \le 10.$$

25. Depreciation A car sells for $28,000. The car depreciates such that each year it is worth $\frac{3}{4}$ of its value from the previous year. Find a model for the value V of the car after t years. Sketch a graph of the model and determine the value of the car 4 years after it is purchased.

26. Drug Concentration Immediately following an injection, the concentration of a drug in the bloodstream is 300 milligrams per milliliter. After t hours, the concentration is 75% of the level of the previous hour. Find a model for $C(t)$, the concentration of the drug after t hours. Sketch a graph of the model and determine the concentration of the drug after 8 hours.

27. School Nurses For the years 2001 through 2008, the average salaries y (in dollars) of school nurses in the public school system in the United States are shown in the table. *(Source: Educational Research Service)*

Year	2001	2002	2003	2004
Salary	37,188	38,221	39,165	40,201

Year	2005	2006	2007	2008
Salary	40,520	41,746	43,277	46,025

A model for this data is given by

$$y = 35,963(1.0279)^t$$

where t represents the year, with $t = 1$ corresponding to 2001.

(a) Compare the actual salaries with those given by the model. How well does the model fit the data? Explain your reasoning.

(b) Use a graphing utility to graph the model.

(c) Use the *zoom* and *trace* features of a graphing utility to predict the year during which the average salary of school nurses will reach $54,000.

4.2 Natural Exponential Functions

■ Evaluate and graph functions involving the natural exponential function.
■ Solve compound interest problems.
■ Solve present value problems.

Natural Exponential Functions

In Section 4.1, exponential functions were introduced using an unspecified base a. In calculus, the most convenient (or natural) choice for a base is the irrational number e, whose decimal approximation is

$$e \approx 2.71828182846.$$

Although this choice of base may seem unusual, its convenience will become apparent as the rules for differentiating exponential functions are developed in Section 4.3. In that development, you will encounter the limit used in the definition of e.

Limit Definition of e

The irrational number e is defined to be the limit of $(1 + x)^{1/x}$ as $x \to 0$. That is,

$$\lim_{x \to 0} (1 + x)^{1/x} = e.$$

Las Vegas, Nevada

In Exercise 46 on page 266, you will evaluate a natural exponential function to find the population of Las Vegas, Nevada for several years.

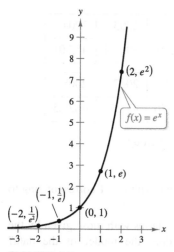

FIGURE 4.5

Example 1 **Graphing the Natural Exponential Function**

Complete the table of values for $f(x) = e^x$. Then sketch the graph of f.

x	-2	-1	0	1	2
$f(x)$					

SOLUTION Begin by completing the table as shown.

x	-2	-1	0	1	2
$f(x)$	$e^{-2} \approx 0.135$	$e^{-1} \approx 0.368$	$e^0 = 1$	$e^1 \approx 2.718$	$e^2 \approx 7.389$

Then use the point-plotting method to sketch the graph of f, as shown in Figure 4.5. Note that e^x is positive for all values of x. Moreover, the graph has the x-axis as a horizontal asymptote to the left. That is,

$$\lim_{x \to -\infty} e^x = 0.$$

✓**Checkpoint 1**

Complete the table of values for $g(x) = e^{-x}$. Then sketch the graph of g.

x	-2	-1	0	1	2
$g(x)$					

Exponential functions are often used to model the growth of a quantity or a population. When the quantity's growth *is not* restricted, an exponential model is often used. When the quantity's growth *is* restricted, the best model is often a **logistic growth model** of the form

$$f(t) = \frac{a}{1 + be^{-kt}}.$$

Graphs of both types of population growth models are shown in Figure 4.6. The graph of a logistic growth model is called a *logistic curve*.

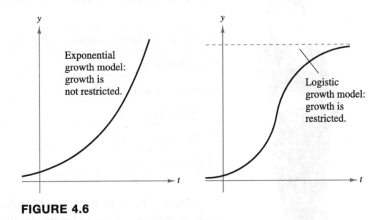

Exponential growth model: growth is not restricted.

Logistic growth model: growth is restricted.

FIGURE 4.6

Example 2 **Modeling a Population**

A bacterial culture is growing according to the logistic growth model

$$y = \frac{1.25}{1 + 0.25e^{-0.4t}}, \quad t \ge 0$$

where y is the culture weight (in grams) and t is the time (in hours). Find the weight of the culture after 0 hours, 1 hour, and 10 hours. What is the limit of the model as t increases without bound?

SOLUTION The graph of the model is shown in Figure 4.7.

$$y = \frac{1.25}{1 + 0.25e^{-0.4(0)}} = 1 \text{ gram} \qquad \text{Weight when } t = 0$$

$$y = \frac{1.25}{1 + 0.25e^{-0.4(1)}} \approx 1.071 \text{ grams} \qquad \text{Weight when } t = 1$$

$$y = \frac{1.25}{1 + 0.25e^{-0.4(10)}} \approx 1.244 \text{ grams} \qquad \text{Weight when } t = 10$$

As t approaches infinity, the limit of y is

$$\lim_{t \to \infty} \frac{1.25}{1 + 0.25e^{-0.4t}} = \lim_{t \to \infty} \frac{1.25}{1 + (0.25/e^{0.4t})} = \frac{1.25}{1 + 0} = 1.25.$$

So, as t increases without bound, the weight of the culture approaches 1.25 grams.

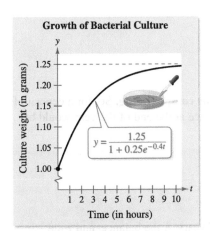

Growth of Bacterial Culture

Culture weight (in grams)

$$y = \frac{1.25}{1 + 0.25e^{-0.4t}}$$

Time (in hours)

When a culture is grown in a dish, the size of the dish and the available food limit the culture's growth.

FIGURE 4.7

✓ Checkpoint 2

A bacterial culture is growing according to the model $y = 1.50/(1 + 0.2e^{-0.5t})$, $t \ge 0$, where y is the culture weight (in grams) and t is the time (in hours). Find the weight of the culture after 0 hours, 1 hour, and 10 hours. What is the limit of the model as t increases without bound?

Extended Application: Compound Interest

An amount of P dollars is deposited in an account at an annual interest rate of r (in decimal form). What is the balance after 1 year? The answer depends on the number of times the interest is compounded, according to the formula

$$A = P\left(1 + \frac{r}{n}\right)^n$$

where n is the number of compoundings per year. The balances for a deposit of $1000 at 8%, for various compounding periods, are shown in the table.

Number of times compounded per year, n	Balance (in dollars), A
Annually, $n = 1$	$A = 1000\left(1 + \frac{0.08}{1}\right)^1 = \$1080.00$
Semiannually, $n = 2$	$A = 1000\left(1 + \frac{0.08}{2}\right)^2 = \$1081.60$
Quarterly, $n = 4$	$A = 1000\left(1 + \frac{0.08}{4}\right)^4 \approx \$1082.43$
Monthly, $n = 12$	$A = 1000\left(1 + \frac{0.08}{12}\right)^{12} \approx \$1083.00$
Daily, $n = 365$	$A = 1000\left(1 + \frac{0.08}{365}\right)^{365} \approx \$1083.28$

You may be surprised to discover that as n increases, the balance A approaches a limit, as indicated in the following development. In this development, let

$$x = \frac{r}{n}.$$

Then $x \to 0$ as $n \to \infty$, and you have

$$A = \lim_{n \to \infty} P\left(1 + \frac{r}{n}\right)^n$$

$$= P \lim_{n \to \infty} \left(1 + \frac{r}{n}\right)^n$$

$$= P \lim_{n \to \infty} \left[\left(1 + \frac{r}{n}\right)^{n/r}\right]^r$$

$$= P\left[\lim_{x \to 0} (1 + x)^{1/x}\right]^r \qquad \text{Substitute } x \text{ for } r/n.$$

$$= Pe^r.$$

This limit is the balance after 1 year of **continuous compounding.** So, for a deposit of $1000 at 8%, compounded continuously, the balance at the end of the year would be

$$A = 1000e^{0.08}$$

$$\approx \$1083.29.$$

Summary of Compound Interest Formulas

Let P be the amount deposited, t the number of years, A the balance, and r the annual interest rate (in decimal form).

1. Compounded n times per year: $A = P\left(1 + \dfrac{r}{n}\right)^{nt}$

2. Compounded continuously: $A = Pe^{rt}$

The average interest rates paid by banks on savings accounts have varied greatly during the past 30 years. At times savings accounts have earned as much as 12% annual interest, and at times they have earned less than 1%. The next example shows how the annual interest rate can affect the balance of an account.

Example 3 Finding Account Balances

You are creating a trust fund for your newborn nephew. You plan to deposit $12,000 in an account, with instructions that the account be turned over to your nephew on his 25th birthday. Compare the balances in the account for each situation. Which account should you choose?

a. 7%, compounded continuously

b. 7%, compounded quarterly

c. 11%, compounded continuously

d. 11%, compounded quarterly

SOLUTION

a. $12{,}000e^{0.07(25)} \approx 69{,}055.23$ 7%, compounded continuously

b. $12{,}000\left(1 + \dfrac{0.07}{4}\right)^{4(25)} \approx 68{,}017.87$ 7%, compounded quarterly

c. $12{,}000e^{0.11(25)} \approx 187{,}711.58$ 11%, compounded continuously

d. $12{,}000\left(1 + \dfrac{0.11}{4}\right)^{4(25)} \approx 180{,}869.07$ 11%, compounded quarterly

The balances in the accounts for parts (a) and (c) are shown in Figure 4.8. Notice the dramatic difference between the balances at 7% and 11%. You should choose the account described in part (c) because it earns more money than the other accounts.

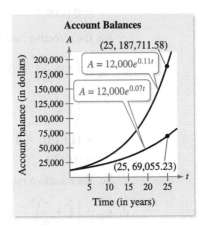

FIGURE 4.8

✓ Checkpoint 3

Find the balance in an account when $2000 is deposited for 10 years at an interest rate of 9%, compounded as follows. Compare the results and make a general statement about compounding.

a. quarterly   **b.** monthly

c. daily   **d.** continuously

In Example 3, note that the interest earned depends on the frequency with which the interest is compounded. The annual percentage rate is called the **stated rate** or **nominal rate.** However, the nominal rate does not reflect the actual rate at which interest is earned, which means that the compounding produced an **effective rate** that is larger than the nominal rate. In general, the effective rate corresponding to a nominal rate of r that is compounded n times per year is

$$\text{Effective rate} = r_{eff} = \left(1 + \frac{r}{n}\right)^n - 1.$$

 Example 4   Finding the Effective Rate of Interest

Find the effective rate of interest corresponding to a nominal rate of 6% per year compounded (a) annually, (b) semiannually, (c) quarterly, and (d) monthly.

SOLUTION

a. $r_{eff} = \left(1 + \dfrac{r}{n}\right)^n - 1$ Formula for effective rate of interest

$\quad\quad = \left(1 + \dfrac{0.06}{1}\right)^1 - 1$ Substitute for r and n.

$\quad\quad = 1.06 - 1$ Simplify.

$\quad\quad = 0.06$

So, the effective rate is 6% per year.

b. $r_{eff} = \left(1 + \dfrac{r}{n}\right)^n - 1$ Formula for effective rate of interest

$\quad\quad = \left(1 + \dfrac{0.06}{2}\right)^2 - 1$ Substitute for r and n.

$\quad\quad = (1.03)^2 - 1$ Simplify.

$\quad\quad = 0.0609$

So, the effective rate is 6.09% per year.

c. $r_{eff} = \left(1 + \dfrac{r}{n}\right)^n - 1$ Formula for effective rate of interest

$\quad\quad = \left(1 + \dfrac{0.06}{4}\right)^4 - 1$ Substitute for r and n.

$\quad\quad = (1.015)^4 - 1$ Simplify.

$\quad\quad \approx 0.0614$

So, the effective rate is about 6.14% per year.

d. $r_{eff} = \left(1 + \dfrac{r}{n}\right)^n - 1$ Formula for effective rate of interest

$\quad\quad = \left(1 + \dfrac{0.06}{12}\right)^{12} - 1$ Substitute for r and n.

$\quad\quad = (1.005)^{12} - 1$ Simplify.

$\quad\quad \approx 0.0617$

So, the effective rate is about 6.17% per year.

✓ **Checkpoint 4**

Repeat Example 4 using a nominal rate of 7%.

Present Value

In planning for the future, this problem often arises: "How much money P should be deposited now, at a fixed rate of interest r, in order to have a balance of A, t years from now?" The answer to this question is given by the **present value** of A.

To find the present value of a future investment, use the formula for compound interest as shown.

$$A = P\left(1 + \frac{r}{n}\right)^{nt} \qquad \text{Formula for compound interest}$$

Solving for P gives a present value of

$$P = \frac{A}{\left(1 + \dfrac{r}{n}\right)^{nt}} \quad \text{or} \quad P = \frac{A}{(1 + i)^N}$$

where $i = r/n$ is the interest rate per compounding period and $N = nt$ is the total number of compounding periods. You will learn another way to find the present value of a future investment in Section 6.1.

 Example 5 **Finding Present Value**

An investor is purchasing a 10-year certificate of deposit that pays an annual percentage rate of 8%, compounded monthly. How much should the person invest in order to obtain a balance of $15,000 at maturity?

SOLUTION Here, $A = 15{,}000$, $r = 0.08$, $n = 12$, and $t = 10$. Using the formula for present value, you obtain

$$P = \frac{15{,}000}{\left(1 + \dfrac{0.08}{12}\right)^{12(10)}} \qquad \text{Substitute for } A, r, n, \text{ and } t.$$

$$\approx 6757.85. \qquad \text{Simplify.}$$

So, the person should invest $6757.85 in the certificate of deposit.

 Checkpoint 5

How much money should be deposited in an account paying 6% interest compounded monthly in order to have a balance of $20,000 after 3 years?

SUMMARIZE (Section 4.2)

1. State the limit definition of e *(page 258)*. For an example of a graph of a natural exponential function, see Example 1.

2. Describe a real-life example of how an exponential function can be used to model a population *(page 259, Example 2)*.

3. State the compound interest formulas for n compoundings per year and for continuous compounding *(page 260)*. For applications of these formulas, see Example 3.

4. State the formula for finding the effective rate of interest *(page 262)*. For an application of this formula, see Example 4.

5. State the formula for present value *(page 263)*. For an application of this formula, see Example 5.

SKILLS WARM UP 4.2   The following warm-up exercises involve skills that were covered in earlier sections. You will use these skills in the exercise set for this section. For additional help, review Sections 1.6 and 3.6.

In Exercises 1–4, discuss the continuity of the function.

1. $f(x) = \dfrac{3x^2 + 2x + 1}{x^2 + 1}$

2. $f(x) = \dfrac{x + 1}{x^2 - 4}$

3. $f(x) = \dfrac{x^2 - 6x + 5}{x^2 - 3}$

4. $g(x) = \dfrac{x^2 - 9x + 20}{x - 4}$

In Exercises 5–12, find the horizontal asymptote of the graph of the function.

5. $f(x) = \dfrac{25}{1 + 4x}$

6. $f(x) = \dfrac{16x}{3 + x^2}$

7. $f(x) = \dfrac{8x^3 + 2}{2x^3 + x}$

8. $f(x) = \dfrac{x}{2x}$

9. $f(x) = \dfrac{3}{2 + (1/x)}$

10. $f(x) = \dfrac{6}{1 + x^{-2}}$

11. $f(x) = 2^{-x}$

12. $f(x) = \dfrac{7}{1 + 5x}$

Exercises 4.2

See www.CalcChat.com for worked-out solutions to odd-numbered exercises.

Applying Properties of Exponents In Exercises 1–4, use the properties of exponents to simplify the expression.

1. (a) $(e^3)(e^4)$ (b) $(e^3)^4$
   (c) $(e^3)^{-2}$ (d) e^0

2. (a) $\left(\dfrac{1}{e}\right)^{-2}$ (b) $\left(\dfrac{e^5}{e^2}\right)^{-1}$

   (c) $\dfrac{e^5}{e^3}$ (d) $\dfrac{1}{e^{-3}}$

3. (a) $(e^2)^{5/2}$ (b) $(e^2)(e^{1/2})$

   (c) $(e^{-2})^{-3}$ (d) $\dfrac{e^5}{e^{-2}}$

4. (a) $(e^{-3})^{2/3}$ (b) $\dfrac{e^4}{e^{-1/2}}$

   (c) $(e^{-2})^{-4}$ (d) $(e^{-4})(e^{-3/2})$

Matching In Exercises 5–10, match the function with its graph. [The graphs are labeled (a)–(f).]

(a)

(b)

(c)   (d)

(e)   (f)

5. $f(x) = e^{2x+1}$ **6.** $f(x) = e^{-x/2}$
7. $f(x) = e^{x^2}$ **8.** $f(x) = e^{-1/x}$
9. $f(x) = e^{\sqrt{x}}$ **10.** $f(x) = -e^x + 1$

Graphing Natural Exponential Functions In Exercises 11–16, sketch the graph of the function. *See Example 1.*

11. $f(x) = e^{-x/3}$ **12.** $f(x) = e^{2x}$
13. $g(x) = e^x - 2$ **14.** $h(x) = e^{-x} + 5$
15. $g(x) = e^{1-x}$ **16.** $j(x) = e^{-x+2}$

Graphing Functions In Exercises 17–24, use a graphing utility to graph the function. Determine whether the function has any horizontal asymptotes and discuss the continuity of the function.

17. $N(t) = 500e^{-0.2t}$

18. $A(t) = 500e^{0.15t}$

19. $g(x) = \dfrac{2}{1 + e^{x^2}}$

20. $g(x) = \dfrac{10}{1 + e^{-x}}$

21. $f(x) = \dfrac{e^x + e^{-x}}{2}$

22. $f(x) = \dfrac{e^x - e^{-x}}{2}$

23. $f(x) = \dfrac{2}{1 + e^{1/x}}$

24. $f(x) = \dfrac{2}{1 + 2e^{-0.2x}}$

25. Graphing Exponential Functions Use a graphing utility to graph $f(x) = e^x$ and the given function in the same viewing window. How are the two graphs related?

(a) $g(x) = e^{x-2}$

(b) $h(x) = -\tfrac{1}{2}e^x$

(c) $q(x) = e^x + 3$

26. Graphing Logistic Growth Functions Use a graphing utility to graph the function. Describe the shape of the graph for very large and very small values of x.

(a) $f(x) = \dfrac{8}{1 + e^{-0.5x}}$

(b) $g(x) = \dfrac{8}{1 + e^{-0.5/x}}$

Finding Account Balances In Exercises 27–30, complete the table to determine the balance A for P dollars invested at rate r for t years, compounded n times per year. *See Example 3.*

n	1	2	4	12	365	Continuous compounding
A						

27. $P = \$1000$, $r = 3\%$, $t = 10$ years

28. $P = \$2500$, $r = 2.5\%$, $t = 20$ years

29. $P = \$1000$, $r = 4\%$, $t = 20$ years

30. $P = \$2500$, $r = 5\%$, $t = 40$ years

Finding Present Value In Exercises 31–34, complete the table to determine the amount of money P that should be invested at rate r to produce a final balance of \$100,000 in t years. *See Example 5.*

t	1	10	20	30	40	50
P						

31. $r = 4\%$, compounded continuously

32. $r = 3\%$, compounded continuously

33. $r = 5\%$, compounded monthly

34. $r = 6\%$, compounded daily

35. Trust Fund On the day of a child's birth, a deposit of \$20,000 is made in a trust fund that pays 8% interest, compounded continuously. Determine the balance in this account on the child's 21st birthday.

36. Trust Fund A deposit of \$10,000 is made in a trust fund that pays 7% interest, compounded continuously. It is specified that the balance will be given to the college from which the donor graduated after the money has earned interest for 50 years. How much will the college receive?

37. Effective Rate Find the effective rate of interest corresponding to a nominal rate of 9% per year compounded (a) annually, (b) semiannually, (c) quarterly, and (d) monthly.

38. Effective Rate Find the effective rate of interest corresponding to a nominal rate of 7.5% per year compounded (a) annually, (b) semiannually, (c) quarterly, and (d) monthly.

39. Present Value How much should be deposited in an account paying 7.2% interest compounded monthly in order to have a balance of \$8000 after 3 years?

40. Present Value How much should be deposited in an account paying 7.8% interest compounded monthly in order to have a balance of \$21,000 after 4 years?

41. Demand The demand function for a product is modeled by

$$p = 5000\left(1 - \dfrac{4}{4 + e^{-0.002x}}\right).$$

Find the price p (in dollars) of the product when the quantity demanded is (a) $x = 100$ units and (b) $x = 500$ units. (c) What is the limit of the price as x increases without bound?

42. Demand The demand function for a product is modeled by

$$p = 10,000\left(1 - \dfrac{3}{3 + e^{-0.001x}}\right).$$

Find the price p (in dollars) of the product when the quantity demanded is (a) $x = 1000$ units and (b) $x = 1500$ units. (c) What is the limit of the price as x increases without bound?

43. Probability The average time between incoming calls at a switchboard is 3 minutes. If a call has just come in, the probability that the next call will come within the next t minutes is $P(t) = 1 - e^{-t/3}$. Find the probability of each situation.

(a) A call comes in within $\tfrac{1}{2}$ minute.

(b) A call comes in within 2 minutes.

(c) A call comes in within 5 minutes.

44. Consumer Awareness An automobile gets 28 miles per gallon at speeds up to and including 50 miles per hour. At speeds greater than 50 miles per hour, the number of miles per gallon drops at the rate of 12% for each 10 miles per hour. If s is the speed (in miles per hour) and y is the number of miles per gallon, then $y = 28e^{0.6 - 0.012s}$, $s > 50$. Use this information and a spreadsheet to create a table showing the miles per gallon for $s = 50$, 55, 60, 65, and 70. What can you conclude?

45. Federal Debt The federal debts D (in billions of dollars) of the United States at the end of each year from 2000 through 2009 are shown in the table. *(Source: U.S. Office of Management and Budget)*

Year	2000	2001	2002	2003	2004
Debt	5629	5770	6198	6760	7355

Year	2005	2006	2007	2008	2009
Debt	7905	8451	8951	9986	11,876

A model for these data is given by $y = 5364.1e^{0.0796t}$, where t represents the year, with $t = 0$ corresponding to 2000.

(a) How well does the model fit the data?

(b) Find a linear model for the data. How well does the linear model fit the data? Which model, exponential or linear, is a better fit?

(c) Use both models to predict the year in which the federal debt will exceed 18,000 billion dollars.

46. Population The populations P (in thousands) of Las Vegas, Nevada from 1960 through 2009 can be modeled by $P = 70.751e^{0.0451t}$, where t is the time in years, with $t = 0$ corresponding to 1960. *(Source: U.S. Census Bureau)*

(a) Find the populations in 1960, 1970, 1980, 1990, 2000, and 2009.

(b) Explain why the change in population from 1960 to 1970 is not the same as the change in population from 1980 to 1990.

(c) Use the model to estimate the population in 2020.

47. Biology The population y of a bacterial culture is modeled by the logistic growth function $y = 925/(1 + e^{-0.3t})$, where t is the time in days.

(a) Use a graphing utility to graph the model.

(b) Does the population have a limit as t increases without bound? Explain your answer.

(c) How would the limit change if the model were $y = 1000/(1 + e^{-0.3t})$? Explain your answer. Draw some conclusions about this type of model.

48. **HOW DO YOU SEE IT?** The figure shows the graphs of $y = 2^x$, $y = e^x$, $y = 10^x$, $y = 2^{-x}$, $y = e^{-x}$, and $y = 10^{-x}$. Match each function with its graph. [The graphs are labeled (a)–(f).] Explain your reasoning.

49. Learning Theory In a learning theory project, the proportion P of correct responses after n trials can be modeled by $P = 0.83/(1 + e^{-0.2n})$.

(a) Find the proportion of correct responses after 3 trials.

(b) Find the proportion of correct responses after 7 trials.

(c) Use a graphing utility to graph the model. Find the number of trials required for the proportion of correct responses to be 0.75.

(d) Does the proportion of correct responses have a limit as n increases without bound? Explain your reasoning.

50. Learning Theory In a typing class, the average number N of words per minute typed after t weeks of lessons can be modeled by $N = 95/(1 + 8.5e^{-0.12t})$.

(a) Find the average number of words per minute typed after 10 weeks.

(b) Find the average number of words per minute typed after 20 weeks.

(c) Use a graphing utility to graph the model. Find the number of weeks required to achieve an average of 70 words per minute.

(d) Does the number of words per minute have a limit as t increases without bound? Explain your reasoning.

51. Certificate of Deposit You want to invest $5000 in a certificate of deposit for 12 months. You are given the options below. Which would you choose? Explain.

(a) $r = 5.25\%$, quarterly compounding

(b) $r = 5\%$, monthly compounding

(c) $r = 4.75\%$, continuous compounding

4.3 Derivatives of Exponential Functions

Average Typing Speed

In Exercise 48 on page 274, you will use the derivative of an exponential function to find the rate of change of the average typing speed after 5, 10, and 30 weeks of lessons.

■ Find the derivatives of natural exponential functions.
■ Use calculus to analyze the graphs of real-life functions that involve the natural exponential function.
■ Explore the normal probability density function.

Derivatives of Exponential Functions

In Section 4.2, it was stated that the most convenient base for exponential functions is the irrational number e. The convenience of this base stems primarily from the fact that the function

$$f(x) = e^x$$

is its own derivative. You will see that this is not true of other exponential functions of the form

$$y = a^x$$

where $a \neq e$. To verify that $f(x) = e^x$ is its own derivative, notice that the limit

$$\lim_{\Delta x \to 0} (1 + \Delta x)^{1/\Delta x} = e$$

implies that for small values of Δx,

$$e \approx (1 + \Delta x)^{1/\Delta x}$$

or

$$e^{\Delta x} \approx 1 + \Delta x.$$

This approximation is used in the following derivation.

$$f'(x) = \lim_{\Delta x \to 0} \frac{f(x + \Delta x) - f(x)}{\Delta x} \qquad \text{Definition of derivative}$$

$$= \lim_{\Delta x \to 0} \frac{e^{x + \Delta x} - e^x}{\Delta x} \qquad \text{Use } f(x) = e^x.$$

$$= \lim_{\Delta x \to 0} \frac{e^x(e^{\Delta x} - 1)}{\Delta x} \qquad \text{Factor numerator.}$$

$$= \lim_{\Delta x \to 0} \frac{e^x[(1 + \Delta x) - 1]}{\Delta x} \qquad \text{Substitute } 1 + \Delta x \text{ for } e^{\Delta x}.$$

$$= \lim_{\Delta x \to 0} \frac{e^x(\Delta x)}{\Delta x} \qquad \text{Divide out common factor.}$$

$$= \lim_{\Delta x \to 0} e^x \qquad \text{Simplify.}$$

$$= e^x \qquad \text{Evaluate limit.}$$

When u is a function of x, you can apply the Chain Rule to obtain the derivative of e^u with respect to x. Both formulas are summarized below.

Derivative of the Natural Exponential Function

Let u be a differentiable function of x.

1. $\dfrac{d}{dx}[e^x] = e^x$ **2.** $\dfrac{d}{dx}[e^u] = e^u \dfrac{du}{dx}$

Example 1   Finding Slopes of Tangent Lines

Find the slopes of the tangent lines to

$$f(x) = e^x$$

at the points $(0, 1)$ and $(1, e)$. What conclusion can you make?

SOLUTION   Because the derivative of f is

$$f'(x) = e^x \qquad \text{Derivative}$$

it follows that the slope of the tangent line to the graph of f is

$$f'(0) = e^0 = 1 \qquad \text{Slope at point } (0, 1)$$

at the point $(0, 1)$ and

$$f'(1) = e^1 = e \qquad \text{Slope at point } (1, e)$$

at the point $(1, e)$, as shown in Figure 4.9. From this pattern, you can see that the slope of the tangent line to the graph of $f(x) = e^x$ at any point (x, e^x) is equal to the y-coordinate of the point.

At the point $(1, e)$, the slope is $e \approx 2.72$.

$f(x) = e^x$

At the point $(0, 1)$, the slope is 1.

FIGURE 4.9

✓ **Checkpoint 1**

Find the slopes of the tangent lines to $f(x) = 2e^x$ at the points $(0, 2)$ and $(1, 2e)$.   ■

Example 2   Differentiating Exponential Functions

Differentiate each function.

a. $f(x) = e^{2x}$ **b.** $f(x) = e^{-3x^2}$

c. $f(x) = 6e^{x^3}$ **d.** $f(x) = e^{-x}$

SOLUTION

a. Let $u = 2x$. Then $du/dx = 2$, and you can apply the Chain Rule.

$$f'(x) = e^u \frac{du}{dx} = e^{2x}(2) = 2e^{2x}$$

b. Let $u = -3x^2$. Then $du/dx = -6x$, and you can apply the Chain Rule.

$$f'(x) = e^u \frac{du}{dx} = e^{-3x^2}(-6x) = -6xe^{-3x^2}$$

c. Let $u = x^3$. Then $du/dx = 3x^2$, and you can apply the Chain Rule.

$$f'(x) = 6e^u \frac{du}{dx} = 6e^{x^3}(3x^2) = 18x^2e^{x^3}$$

d. Let $u = -x$. Then $du/dx = -1$, and you can apply the Chain Rule.

$$f'(x) = e^u \frac{du}{dx} = e^{-x}(-1) = -e^{-x}$$

✓ **Checkpoint 2**

Differentiate each function.

a. $f(x) = e^{3x}$ **b.** $f(x) = e^{-2x^3}$

c. $f(x) = 4e^{x^2}$ **d.** $f(x) = e^{-2x}$ ■

STUDY TIP

In Example 2, notice that when you differentiate an exponential function, the exponent does not change. For instance, the derivative of $f(x) = e^{3x}$ is $f'(x) = 3e^{3x}$. In both f and f', the exponent is $3x$.

The differentiation rules that you studied in Chapter 2 can be used with exponential functions, as shown in Example 3.

Example 3 Differentiating Exponential Functions

Differentiate each function.

a. $f(x) = 4e$ **b.** $f(x) = e^{2x-1}$

c. $f(x) = xe^x$ **d.** $f(x) = \dfrac{e^x - e^{-x}}{2}$

e. $f(x) = \dfrac{e^x}{x}$ **f.** $f(x) = xe^x - e^x$

SOLUTION

a. $f(x) = 4e$ Write original function.

$f'(x) = 0$ Constant Rule

b. $f(x) = e^{2x-1}$ Write original function.

$f'(x) = (e^{2x-1})(2)$ Chain Rule

$= 2e^{2x-1}$ Simplify.

c. $f(x) = xe^x$ Write original function.

$f'(x) = xe^x + e^x(1)$ Product Rule

$= xe^x + e^x$ Simplify.

d. $f(x) = \dfrac{e^x - e^{-x}}{2}$ Write original function.

$= \dfrac{1}{2}(e^x - e^{-x})$ Rewrite.

$f'(x) = \dfrac{1}{2}[e^x - e^{-x}(-1)]$ Constant Multiple and Chain Rules

$= \dfrac{1}{2}(e^x + e^{-x})$ Simplify.

e. $f(x) = \dfrac{e^x}{x}$ Write original function.

$f'(x) = \dfrac{xe^x - e^x(1)}{x^2}$ Quotient Rule

$= \dfrac{e^x(x-1)}{x^2}$ Simplify.

f. $f(x) = xe^x - e^x$ Write original function.

$f'(x) = [xe^x + e^x(1)] - e^x$ Product and Difference Rules

$= xe^x + e^x - e^x$

$= xe^x$ Simplify.

✓ Checkpoint 3

Differentiate each function.

a. $f(x) = 9e$ **b.** $f(x) = e^{3x+1}$ **c.** $f(x) = x^2e^x$

d. $f(x) = \dfrac{e^x + e^{-x}}{2}$ **e.** $f(x) = \dfrac{e^x}{x^2}$ **f.** $f(x) = x^2e^x - e^x$

TECH TUTOR

If you have access to a symbolic differentiation utility, try using it to find the derivatives of the functions in Example 3.

Applications

In Chapter 3, you learned how to use derivatives to analyze the graphs of functions. The next example applies those techniques to a function composed of exponential functions. In the example, notice that

$$e^a = e^b$$

implies that $a = b$.

 Example 4 **Analyzing a Catenary**

When a telephone wire is hung between two poles, the wire forms a U-shaped curve called a **catenary.** For instance, the function

$$y = 30(e^{x/60} + e^{-x/60}), \quad -30 \le x \le 30$$

models the shape of a telephone wire strung between two poles that are 60 feet apart (x and y are measured in feet). Show that the lowest point on the wire is midway between the two poles. How much does the wire sag between the two poles?

SOLUTION   First, find the derivative of the function.

$$y = 30(e^{x/60} + e^{-x/60}) \qquad \text{Write original function.}$$
$$y' = 30\left[e^{x/60}\left(\tfrac{1}{60}\right) + e^{-x/60}\left(-\tfrac{1}{60}\right)\right] \qquad \text{Derivative}$$
$$= 30\left(\tfrac{1}{60}\right)(e^{x/60} - e^{-x/60}) \qquad \text{Factor out } \tfrac{1}{60}.$$
$$= \tfrac{1}{2}(e^{x/60} - e^{-x/60}) \qquad \text{Simplify.}$$

To find the critical numbers, set the derivative equal to zero.

$$\tfrac{1}{2}(e^{x/60} - e^{-x/60}) = 0 \qquad \text{Set derivative equal to 0.}$$
$$e^{x/60} - e^{-x/60} = 0 \qquad \text{Multiply each side by 2.}$$
$$e^{x/60} = e^{-x/60} \qquad \text{Add } e^{-x/60} \text{ to each side.}$$
$$\frac{x}{60} = -\frac{x}{60} \qquad \text{If } e^a = e^b, \text{ then } a = b.$$
$$x = -x \qquad \text{Multiply each side by 60.}$$
$$2x = 0 \qquad \text{Add } x \text{ to each side.}$$
$$x = 0 \qquad \text{Divide each side by 2.}$$

Using the First-Derivative Test, you can determine that the critical number $x = 0$ yields a relative minimum of the function. From the graph in Figure 4.10, you can see that this relative minimum is actually a minimum on the interval

$$[-30, 30].$$

So, you can conclude that the lowest point on the wire lies midway between the two poles. To find how much the wire sags between the two poles, you can compare its height at each pole with its height at the relative minimum.

$$y = 30(e^{-30/60} + e^{-(-30)/60}) \approx 67.7 \text{ feet} \qquad \text{Height at left pole}$$
$$y = 30(e^{0/60} + e^{-(0)/60}) = 60 \text{ feet} \qquad \text{Height at relative minimum}$$
$$y = 30(e^{30/60} + e^{-(30)/60}) \approx 67.7 \text{ feet} \qquad \text{Height at right pole}$$

From this, you can see that the wire sags about 7.7 feet.

FIGURE 4.10

✓**Checkpoint 4**

Use a graphing utility to graph the function in Example 4. Verify the minimum value. Use the information in the example to choose an appropriate viewing window.

Example 5   **Finding a Maximum Revenue**

The demand function for a product is modeled by

$$p = 56e^{-0.000012x}$$ Demand function

where p is the price per unit (in dollars) and x is the number of units. What price will yield a maximum revenue? What is the maximum revenue at this price?

SOLUTION   The revenue function is

$$R = xp = 56xe^{-0.000012x}.$$ Revenue function

To find the maximum revenue *analytically*, you would first find the marginal revenue

$$\frac{dR}{dx} = 56xe^{-0.000012x}(-0.000012) + e^{-0.000012x}(56).$$

You would then set dR/dx equal to zero

$$56xe^{-0.000012x}(-0.000012) + e^{-0.000012x}(56) = 0$$

and solve for x. At this point, you can see that the analytical approach is rather cumbersome. In this problem, it is easier to use a *graphical* approach. After experimenting to find a reasonable viewing window, you can obtain a graph of R that is similar to that shown in Figure 4.11. Using the *maximum* feature, you can conclude that the maximum revenue occurs when x is about 83,333 units. To find the price that corresponds to this production level, substitute $x \approx 83,333$ into the demand function.

$$p \approx 56e^{-0.000012(83,333)} \approx \$20.60.$$

So, a price of about \$20.60 will yield a maximum revenue of

$$R \approx 56(83,333)e^{-0.000012(83,333)}$$

$$\approx \$1,716,771.$$ Maximum revenue

Use the *maximum* feature to approximate the x-value that corresponds to the maximum revenue.

FIGURE 4.11

 Checkpoint 5

The demand function for a product is modeled by

$$p = 50e^{-0.0000125x}$$

where p is the price per unit (in dollars) and x is the number of units. What price will yield a maximum revenue? What is the maximum revenue at this price?

Try solving Example 5 analytically. When you do this, you must solve the equation

$$56xe^{-0.000012x}(-0.000012) + e^{-0.000012x}(56) = 0.$$

Explain how you would solve this equation. What is the solution?

The Normal Probability Density Function

If you take a course in statistics or quantitative business analysis, you will spend quite a bit of time studying the characteristics and use of the **normal probability density function** given by

$$f(x) = \frac{1}{\sigma\sqrt{2\pi}}e^{-(x-\mu)^2/(2\sigma^2)}$$

where σ is the lowercase Greek letter sigma, and μ is the lowercase Greek letter mu. In this formula, σ represents the *standard deviation* of the probability distribution, and μ represents the *mean* of the probability distribution.

Example 6   Exploring a Probability Density Function

Show that the graph of the normal probability density function

$$f(x) = \frac{1}{\sqrt{2\pi}}e^{-x^2/2}$$

has points of inflection at $x = \pm 1$.

Two points of inflection

$$f(x) = \frac{1}{\sqrt{2\pi}}e^{-x^2/2}$$

The graph of the normal probability density function is bell-shaped.

FIGURE 4.12

SOLUTION   Begin by finding the second derivative of the function.

$$f'(x) = \frac{1}{\sqrt{2\pi}}(-x)e^{-x^2/2} \qquad \text{First derivative}$$

$$f''(x) = \frac{1}{\sqrt{2\pi}}[(-x)(-x)e^{-x^2/2} + (-1)e^{-x^2/2}] \qquad \text{Second derivative}$$

$$= \frac{1}{\sqrt{2\pi}}(e^{-x^2/2})(x^2 - 1) \qquad \text{Simplify.}$$

By setting the second derivative equal to 0, you can determine that $x = \pm 1$. By testing the concavity of the graph, you can then conclude that these x-values yield points of inflection, as shown in Figure 4.12.

✓ **Checkpoint 6**

Graph the normal probability density function

$$f(x) = \frac{1}{4\sqrt{2\pi}}e^{-x^2/32}$$

and approximate the points of inflection.

SUMMARIZE   (Section 4.3)

1. State the derivative of the natural exponential function *(page 267)*. For examples of the derivative of the natural exponential function, see Examples 2 and 3.

2. Describe a real-life example of how a natural exponential function can be used to analyze the graph of a catenary *(page 270, Example 4)*.

3. Describe a real-life example of how a natural exponential function can be used to analyze a company's maximum revenue *(page 271, Example 5)*.

4. Describe a use of the natural exponential function in statistics *(page 272)*. For an example of the natural exponential function in statistics, see Example 6.

SKILLS WARM UP 4.3

The following warm-up exercises involve skills that were covered in a previous course or in earlier sections. You will use these skills in the exercise set for this section. For additional help, review Appendix Section A.4, and Sections 2.2, 2.4, and 3.2.

In Exercises 1–4, factor the expression.

1. $x^2 e^x - \frac{1}{2} e^x$ **2.** $(xe^{-x})^{-1} + e^x$ **3.** $xe^x - e^{2x}$ **4.** $e^x - xe^{-x}$

In Exercises 5–8, find the derivative of the function.

5. $f(x) = \dfrac{3}{7x^2}$ **6.** $g(x) = 3x^2 - \dfrac{x}{6}$ **7.** $f(x) = (4x - 3)(x^2 + 9)$ **8.** $f(t) = \dfrac{t - 2}{\sqrt{t}}$

In Exercises 9 and 10, find the relative extrema of the function.

9. $f(x) = \frac{1}{8}x^3 - 2x$ **10.** $f(x) = x^4 - 2x^2 + 5$

Exercises 4.3

See www.CalcChat.com for worked-out solutions to odd-numbered exercises.

Differentiating Exponential Functions In Exercises 1–16, find the derivative of the function. *See Examples 2 and 3.*

1. $f(x) = 3e$ **2.** $f(x) = -5e$

3. $y = e^{5x}$ **4.** $y = e^{1-x}$

5. $y = e^{-x^2}$ **6.** $f(x) = e^{1/x}$

7. $f(x) = e^{-1/x^2}$ **8.** $g(x) = e^{\sqrt{x}}$

9. $f(x) = (x^2 + 1)e^{4x}$ **10.** $y = 4x^3 e^{-x}$

11. $f(x) = \dfrac{2}{(e^x + e^{-x})^3}$ **12.** $f(x) = \dfrac{(e^x + e^{-x})^4}{2}$

13. $f(x) = \dfrac{e^x + 1}{e^x - 1}$ **14.** $f(x) = \dfrac{e^{2x}}{e^{2x} + 1}$

15. $y = xe^x - 4e^{-x}$ **16.** $y = x^2 e^x - 2xe^x + 2e^x$

Finding the Slope of a Tangent Line In Exercises 17–20, find the slope of the tangent line to the exponential function at the point $(0, 1)$.

17. $y = e^{4x}$ **18.** $y = e^{x/2}$

19. $y = e^{-3x}$ **20.** $y = e^{-x/2}$

Finding an Equation of a Tangent Line In Exercises 21–26, find an equation of the tangent line to the graph of the function at the given point.

21. $y = e^{-2x+x^2}$, $(2, 1)$ **22.** $g(x) = e^{x^3}$, $\left(-1, \dfrac{1}{e}\right)$

23. $y = x^2 e^{-x}$, $\left(2, \dfrac{4}{e^2}\right)$ **24.** $y = \dfrac{x}{e^{2x}}$, $\left(1, \dfrac{1}{e^2}\right)$

25. $y = (e^{2x} + 1)^3$, $(0, 8)$ **26.** $y = (e^{4x} - 2)^2$, $(0, 1)$

Finding Derivatives Implicitly In Exercises 27–30, find dy/dx implicitly.

27. $xe^y - 10x + 3y = 0$

28. $x^2 y - e^y - 4 = 0$

29. $x^2 e^{-x} + 2y^2 - xy = 0$

30. $e^{xy} + x^2 - y^2 = 10$

Finding Second Derivatives In Exercises 31–34, find the second derivative.

31. $f(x) = 2e^{3x} + 3e^{-2x}$ **32.** $f(x) = 5e^{-x} - 2e^{-5x}$

33. $f(x) = (1 + 2x)e^{4x}$ **34.** $f(x) = (3 + 2x)e^{-3x}$

Analyzing a Graph In Exercises 35–38, analyze and sketch the graph of the function. Label any relative extrema, points of inflection, and asymptotes.

35. $f(x) = \dfrac{1}{2 - e^{-x}}$ **36.** $f(x) = \dfrac{e^x - e^{-x}}{2}$

37. $f(x) = x^2 e^{-x}$ **38.** $f(x) = xe^{-x}$

Solving Equations In Exercises 39–42, solve the equation for x.

39. $e^{-3x} = e$ **40.** $e^x = 1$

41. $e^{\sqrt{x}} = e^3$ **42.** $e^{-1/x} = e^{1/2}$

Depreciation In Exercises 43 and 44, the value V (in dollars) of an item is a function of the time t (in years).

(a) Sketch the function over the interval $[0, 10]$. Use a graphing utility to verify your graph.

(b) Find the rate of change of V when $t = 1$.

(c) Find the rate of change of V when $t = 5$.

(d) Use the values $(0, V(0))$ and $(10, V(10))$ to find the linear depreciation model for the item.

(e) Compare the exponential function and the model from part (d). What are the advantages of each?

43. $V = 15{,}000e^{-0.6286t}$ **44.** $V = 500{,}000e^{-0.2231t}$

45. Employment From 2000 through 2009, the numbers y (in millions) of employed people in the United States can be modeled by

$$y = 136.855 - 0.5841t + 0.31664t^2 - 0.002166e^t$$

where t represents the year, with $t = 0$ corresponding to 2000. *(Source: U.S. Bureau of Labor Statistics)*

(a) Use a graphing utility to graph the model.

(b) Use the graph to estimate the rates of change in the number of employed people in 2000, 2004, and 2009.

(c) Confirm the results from part (b) analytically.

46. HOW DO YOU SEE IT? The yield y (in pounds per acre) of an orchard at age t (in years) is modeled by

$$y = 7955.6e^{-0.0458/t}.$$

The graph is shown below.

Orchard Yield

(a) What happens to the yield in the long run?

(b) What happens to the rate of change of the yield in the long run?

47. Compound Interest The balance A (in dollars) in a savings account is given by $A = 5000e^{0.08t}$, where t is measured in years. Find the rates at which the balance is changing when (a) $t = 1$ year, (b) $t = 10$ years, and (c) $t = 50$ years.

48. Learning Theory The average typing speed N (in words per minute) after t weeks of lessons is modeled by

$$N = \frac{95}{1 + 8.5e^{-0.12t}}.$$

Find the rates at which the typing speed is changing when (a) $t = 5$ weeks, (b) $t = 10$ weeks, and (c) $t = 30$ weeks.

49. Probability In a recent year, the mean SAT score for college-bound seniors on the mathematics portion was 516, with a standard deviation of 116. *(Source: The College Board)*

(a) Assuming the data can be modeled by a normal probability density function, find a model for these data.

(b) Use a graphing utility to graph the model. Be sure to choose an appropriate viewing window.

(c) Find the derivative of the model.

(d) Show that $f' > 0$ for $x < \mu$ and $f' < 0$ for $x > \mu$.

50. Probability A survey of a college freshman class has determined that the mean height of females in the class is 64 inches, with a standard deviation of 3.2 inches.

(a) Assuming the data can be modeled by a normal probability density function, find a model for these data.

(b) Use a graphing utility to graph the model. Be sure to choose an appropriate viewing window.

(c) Find the derivative of the model.

(d) Show that $f' > 0$ for $x < \mu$ and $f' < 0$ for $x > \mu$.

51. Normal Probability Density Function Use a graphing utility to graph the normal probability density function with $\mu = 0$ and $\sigma = 2, 3$, and 4 in the same viewing window. What effect does the standard deviation σ have on the function? Explain your reasoning.

52. Normal Probability Density Function Use a graphing utility to graph the normal probability density function with

$$\sigma = 1 \quad \text{and} \quad \mu = -2, \ 1, \ \text{and} \ 3$$

in the same viewing window. What effect does the mean μ have on the function? Explain your reasoning.

53. Normal Probability Density Function Use Example 6 as a model to show that the graph of the normal probability density function with $\mu = 0$

$$f(x) = \frac{1}{\sigma\sqrt{2\pi}}e^{-x^2/(2\sigma^2)}$$

has points of inflection at

$$x = \pm\sigma.$$

What is the maximum value of the function? Use a graphing utility to verify your answer by graphing the function for several values of σ.

QUIZ YOURSELF

See www.CalcChat.com for worked-out solutions to odd-numbered exercises.

Take this quiz as you would take a quiz in class. When you are done, check your work against the answers given in the back of the book.

In Exercises 1–8, use properties of exponents to simplify the expression.

1. $4^3(4^2)$

2. $\left(\dfrac{1}{6}\right)^{-3}$

3. $\dfrac{3^8}{3^5}$

4. $(5^{1/2})(3^{1/2})$

5. $(e^2)(e^5)$

6. $(e^{2/3})(e^3)$

7. $\dfrac{e^2}{e^{-4}}$

8. $(e^{-1})^{-3}$

In Exercises 9–14, sketch the graph of the function.

9. $f(x) = 3^x - 2$

10. $f(x) = 5^{-x} + 2$

11. $f(x) = 6^{x-3}$

12. $f(x) = e^{x+2}$

13. $f(x) = e^x + 3$

14. $f(x) = e^{-2x} + 1$

15. After t years, the remaining mass y (in grams) of an initial mass of 35 grams of a radioactive element whose half-life is 80 years is given by

$$y = 35\left(\frac{1}{2}\right)^{t/80}, \quad t \geq 0.$$

How much of the initial mass remains after 50 years?

16. With an annual rate of inflation of 4.5% over the next 10 years, the approximate cost C of goods or services during any year in the decade is given by

$$C(t) = P(1.045)^t, \quad 0 \leq t \leq 10$$

where t is the time (in years) and P is the present cost. The price of a baseball game ticket is presently $20. Estimate the price 10 years from now.

17. For $P = \$3000$, $r = 3.5\%$, and $t = 5$ years, find the balance in an account when interest is compounded (a) quarterly, (b) monthly, and (c) continuously.

18. How much should be deposited in an account paying 6% interest compounded monthly in order to have a balance of $14,000 after 5 years?

In Exercises 19–22, find the derivative of the function.

19. $y = e^{5x}$

20. $y = e^{x-4}$

21. $y = 5e^{x+2}$

22. $y = 3e^x - xe^x$

23. Determine an equation of the tangent line to

$$y = e^{-2x}$$

at the point $(0, 1)$.

24. Analyze and sketch the graph of

$$f(x) = 0.5x^2 e^{-0.5x}.$$

Label any relative extrema, points of inflection, and asymptotes.

4.4 Logarithmic Functions

Orlando, Florida

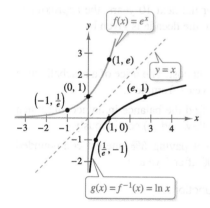

In Exercise 77 on page 283, you will solve a natural exponential equation to predict when the population of Orlando, Florida will reach 300,000.

■ Sketch the graphs of natural logarithmic functions.
■ Use properties of logarithms to simplify, expand, and condense logarithmic expressions.
■ Use inverse properties of exponential and logarithmic functions to solve exponential and logarithmic equations.
■ Use properties of natural logarithms to answer questions about real-life situations.

The Natural Logarithmic Function

From your previous algebra courses, you should be somewhat familiar with logarithms. For instance, the **common logarithm** $\log_{10} x$ is defined as

$$\log_{10} x = b \quad \text{if and only if} \quad 10^b = x.$$

The base of common logarithms is 10. In calculus, the most useful base for logarithms is the number e.

> **Definition of the Natural Logarithmic Function**
>
> The **natural logarithmic function,** denoted by $\ln x$, is defined as
>
> $$\ln x = b \quad \text{if and only if} \quad e^b = x.$$
>
> $\ln x$ is read as "el en of x" or as "the natural log of x."

This definition implies that the natural logarithmic function and the natural exponential function are inverse functions. So, every logarithmic equation can be written in an equivalent exponential form, and every exponential equation can be written in logarithmic form. Here are some examples.

Logarithmic form:	*Exponential form:*
$\ln 1 = 0$	$e^0 = 1$
$\ln e = 1$	$e^1 = e$
$\ln \dfrac{1}{e} = -1$	$e^{-1} = \dfrac{1}{e}$
$\ln 2 \approx 0.693$	$e^{0.693} \approx 2$
$\ln 0.1 \approx -2.303$	$e^{-2.303} \approx 0.1$

Because the functions $f(x) = e^x$ and $g(x) = \ln x$ are inverse functions, their graphs are reflections of each other in the line

$$y = x.$$

This reflective property is illustrated in Figure 4.13. The figure also contains a summary of several properties of the graph of the natural logarithmic function.

Notice that the domain of the natural logarithmic function is the set of *positive real numbers*—be sure you see that $\ln x$ is not defined for zero or for negative numbers. You can test this on your calculator. When you try evaluating

$$\ln(-1) \quad \text{or} \quad \ln 0$$

your calculator should indicate that the value is not a real number.

$g(x) = \ln x$

- Domain: $(0, \infty)$
- Range: $(-\infty, \infty)$
- Intercept: $(1, 0)$
- Always increasing
- $\ln x \to \infty$ as $x \to \infty$
- $\ln x \to -\infty$ as $x \to 0^+$
- Continuous
- One-to-one

FIGURE 4.13

| Example 1 | **Graphing Logarithmic Functions** |

Sketch the graph of each function.

a. $f(x) = \ln(x + 1)$ **b.** $f(x) = 2\ln(x - 2)$

SOLUTION

a. Because the natural logarithmic function is defined only for positive values, the domain of the function is $x + 1 > 0$, or

$x > -1$.   Domain

To sketch the graph, begin by constructing a table of values, as shown below. Then plot the points in the table and connect them with a smooth curve, as shown in Figure 4.14(a).

x	-0.5	0	0.5	1	1.5	2
$\ln(x + 1)$	-0.693	0	0.405	0.693	0.916	1.099

b. The domain of this function is $x - 2 > 0$, or

$x > 2$.   Domain

A table of values for the function is shown below, and its graph is shown in Figure 4.14(b).

x	2.5	3	3.5	4	4.5	5
$2\ln(x - 2)$	-1.386	0	0.811	1.386	1.833	2.197

(a)

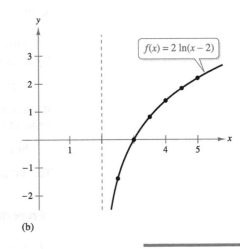

(b)

FIGURE 4.14

✓ **Checkpoint 1**

Complete the table and sketch the graph of

$f(x) = \ln(x + 2)$.

x	-1.5	-1	-0.5	0	0.5	1
$f(x)$						

Properties of Logarithmic Functions

Recall from Section 1.4 that inverse functions have the property that

$$f(f^{-1}(x)) = x \quad \text{and} \quad f^{-1}(f(x)) = x.$$

The properties listed below follow from the fact that the natural logarithmic function and the natural exponential function are inverse functions.

Inverse Properties of Logarithms and Exponents

1. $\ln e^x = x$ 2. $e^{\ln x} = x$

Example 2 **Applying Inverse Properties**

Simplify each expression.

a. $\ln e^{\sqrt{2}}$ **b.** $e^{\ln 3x}$

SOLUTION

a. Because $\ln e^x = x$, it follows that

$$\ln e^{\sqrt{2}} = \sqrt{2}.$$

b. Because $e^{\ln x} = x$, it follows that

$$e^{\ln 3x} = 3x.$$

✓**Checkpoint 2**

Simplify each expression.

a. $\ln e^3$ **b.** $e^{\ln(x+1)}$

Most of the properties of exponential functions can be rewritten in terms of logarithmic functions. For instance, the property

$$e^x e^y = e^{x+y}$$

states that you can multiply two exponential expressions by adding their exponents. In terms of logarithms, this property becomes

$$\ln xy = \ln x + \ln y.$$

This property and two other properties of logarithms are summarized below.

Properties of Logarithms

1. $\ln xy = \ln x + \ln y$ 2. $\ln \dfrac{x}{y} = \ln x - \ln y$ 3. $\ln x^n = n \ln x$

STUDY TIP

There is no general property that can be used to rewrite $\ln(x + y)$. Specifically, $\ln(x + y)$ is not equal to $\ln x + \ln y$.

Rewriting a logarithm of a single quantity as the sum, difference, or multiple of logarithms is called *expanding* the logarithmic expression. The reverse procedure is called *condensing* a logarithmic expression.

Example 3 Expanding Logarithmic Expressions

Use the properties of logarithms to rewrite each expression as a sum, difference, or multiple of logarithms. (Assume $x > 0$ and $y > 0$.)

a. $\ln \dfrac{10}{9}$ **b.** $\ln \sqrt{x^2 + 1}$ **c.** $\ln \dfrac{xy}{5}$ **d.** $\ln[x^2(x + 1)]$

SOLUTION

a. $\ln \dfrac{10}{9} = \ln 10 - \ln 9$ Property 2

b. $\ln \sqrt{x^2 + 1} = \ln(x^2 + 1)^{1/2}$ Rewrite with rational exponent.

$\qquad = \dfrac{1}{2}\ln(x^2 + 1)$ Property 3

c. $\ln \dfrac{xy}{5} = \ln(xy) - \ln 5$ Property 2

$\qquad = \ln x + \ln y - \ln 5$ Property 1

d. $\ln[x^2(x + 1)] = \ln x^2 + \ln(x + 1)$ Property 1

$\qquad = 2 \ln x + \ln(x + 1)$ Property 3

✓ **Checkpoint 3**

Use the properties of logarithms to rewrite each expression as a sum, difference, or multiple of logarithms. (Assume $x > 0$ and $y > 0$.)

a. $\ln \dfrac{2}{5}$ **b.** $\ln \sqrt[3]{x + 2}$ **c.** $\ln \dfrac{x}{5y}$ **d.** $\ln x(x + 1)^2$

Example 4 Condensing Logarithmic Expressions

Use the properties of logarithms to rewrite each expression as the logarithm of a single quantity. (Assume $x > 0$ and $y > 0$.)

a. $\ln x + 2 \ln y$ **b.** $2 \ln(x + 2) - 3 \ln x$

SOLUTION

a. $\ln x + 2 \ln y = \ln x + \ln y^2$ Property 3

$\qquad = \ln xy^2$ Property 1

b. $2 \ln(x + 2) - 3 \ln x = \ln(x + 2)^2 - \ln x^3$ Property 3

$\qquad = \ln \dfrac{(x + 2)^2}{x^3}$ Property 2

✓ **Checkpoint 4**

Use the properties of logarithms to rewrite each expression as the logarithm of a single quantity. (Assume $x > 0$ and $y > 0$.)

a. $4 \ln x + 3 \ln y$ **b.** $\ln(x + 1) - 2 \ln(x + 3)$

TECH TUTOR

Try using a graphing utility to verify the results of Example 3(b). That is, try graphing the functions

$$y = \ln \sqrt{x^2 + 1}$$

and

$$y = \dfrac{1}{2}\ln(x^2 + 1).$$

Because these two functions are equivalent, their graphs should coincide.

Solving Exponential and Logarithmic Equations

To solve an exponential equation, first isolate the exponential expression. Then take the logarithm of each side of the equation and solve for the variable.

Example 5   Solving Exponential Equations

Solve each equation.

a. $e^x = 5$ **b.** $10 + e^{0.1t} = 14$

SOLUTION

a. $e^x = 5$ Write original equation.

$\ln e^x = \ln 5$ Take natural log of each side.

$x = \ln 5$ Inverse property: $\ln e^x = x$

b. $10 + e^{0.1t} = 14$ Write original equation.

$e^{0.1t} = 4$ Subtract 10 from each side.

$\ln e^{0.1t} = \ln 4$ Take natural log of each side.

$0.1t = \ln 4$ Inverse property: $\ln e^{0.1t} = 0.1t$

$t = 10 \ln 4$ Multiply each side by 10.

✓ **Checkpoint 5**

Solve each equation.

a. $e^x = 6$ **b.** $5 + e^{0.2t} = 10$

To solve a logarithmic equation, first isolate the logarithmic expression. Then exponentiate each side of the equation and solve for the variable.

Example 6   Solving Logarithmic Equations

Solve each equation.

a. $\ln x = 5$

b. $3 + 2 \ln x = 7$

SOLUTION

a. $\ln x = 5$ Write original equation.

$e^{\ln x} = e^5$ Exponentiate each side.

$x = e^5$ Inverse property: $e^{\ln x} = x$

b. $3 + 2 \ln x = 7$ Write original equation.

$2 \ln x = 4$ Subtract 3 from each side.

$\ln x = 2$ Divide each side by 2.

$e^{\ln x} = e^2$ Exponentiate each side.

$x = e^2$ Inverse property: $e^{\ln x} = x$

✓ **Checkpoint 6**

Solve each equation.

a. $\ln x = 4$

b. $4 + 5 \ln x = 19$

Application

 Example 7   **Finding Doubling Time**

You deposit P dollars in an account whose annual interest rate is r, compounded continuously. How long will it take for your balance to double?

SOLUTION   The balance in the account after t years is $A = Pe^{rt}$. So, the balance will have doubled when $Pe^{rt} = 2P$. To find the "doubling time," solve this equation for t.

$Pe^{rt} = 2P$	Balance in account has doubled.
$e^{rt} = 2$	Divide each side by P.
$\ln e^{rt} = \ln 2$	Take natural log of each side.
$rt = \ln 2$	Inverse property: $\ln e^{rt} = rt$
$t = \dfrac{1}{r}\ln 2$	Divide each side by r.

From this result, you can see that the time it takes for the balance to double is inversely proportional to the interest rate r. The table shows the doubling times for several interest rates. Notice that the doubling time decreases as the rate increases. The relationship between doubling time and the interest rate is shown graphically in Figure 4.15.

Doubling Account Balances

$t = \dfrac{1}{r}\ln 2$

FIGURE 4.15

r	3%	4%	5%	6%	7%	8%	9%	10%	11%	12%
t	23.1	17.3	13.9	11.6	9.9	8.7	7.7	6.9	6.3	5.8

✓**Checkpoint 7**

Use the equation found in Example 7 to determine the amount of time it would take for your balance to double at an interest rate of 8.75%.

SUMMARIZE   (Section 4.4)

1. State the definition of the natural logarithmic function *(page 276)*. For an example of graphing logarithmic functions, see Example 1.

2. State the inverse properties of logarithms and exponents *(page 278)*. For an example of applying these properties, see Example 2.

3. State the properties of logarithms *(page 278)*. For examples of using these properties to expand and condense logarithmic expressions, see Examples 3 and 4.

4. Identify the properties of logarithms and exponents used to solve the exponential and logarithmic equations in Examples 5 and 6 *(page 280)*.

5. Describe a real-life example of how a logarithm is used to determine how long it will take for an account balance to double *(page 281, Example 7)*.

SKILLS WARM UP 4.4 The following warm-up exercises involve skills that were covered in a previous course or in earlier sections. You will use these skills in the exercise set for this section. For additional help, review Appendix Section A.1, and Sections 1.4 and 4.2.

In Exercises 1–4, find the inverse function of f.

1. $f(x) = 5x$ **2.** $f(x) = x - 6$ **3.** $f(x) = 3x + 2$ **4.** $f(x) = \frac{3}{4}x - 9$

In Exercises 5–8, solve for x.

5. $0 < x + 4$ **6.** $0 < x^2 + 1$
7. $0 < \sqrt{x^2 - 1}$ **8.** $0 < x - 5$

In Exercises 9 and 10, find the balance in the account after 10 years.

9. $P = \$1900$, $r = 6\%$, compounded continuously
10. $P = \$2500$, $r = 3\%$, compounded continuously

Exercises 4.4

See www.CalcChat.com for worked-out solutions to odd-numbered exercises.

Logarithmic and Exponential Forms of Equations In Exercises 1–8, write the logarithmic equation as an exponential equation, or vice versa.

1. $\ln 2 = 0.6931 \ldots$ **2.** $\ln 9 = 2.1972 \ldots$
3. $\ln 0.2 = -1.6094 \ldots$ **4.** $\ln 0.05 = -2.9957 \ldots$
5. $e^0 = 1$ **6.** $e^2 = 7.3891 \ldots$
7. $e^{-3} = 0.0498 \ldots$ **8.** $e^{0.25} = 1.2840 \ldots$

Matching In Exercises 9–12, match the function with its graph. [The graphs are labeled (a)–(d).]

(a)

(b)

(c)

(d)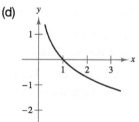

9. $f(x) = 2 + \ln x$
10. $f(x) = -\ln x$
11. $f(x) = \ln(x + 2)$
12. $f(x) = -\ln(x - 1)$

Graphing Logarithmic Functions In Exercises 13–18, sketch the graph of the function. *See Example 1.*

13. $y = \ln(x - 1)$ **14.** $y = \ln|x|$
15. $y = \ln 2x$ **16.** $y = 5 + \ln x$
17. $y = 3 \ln x$ **18.** $y = \frac{1}{4} \ln x$

Applying Inverse Properties In Exercises 19–24, apply the inverse properties of logarithmic and exponential functions to simplify the expression. *See Example 2.*

19. $\ln e^{x^2}$ **20.** $\ln e^{2x-1}$
21. $e^{\ln(5x+2)}$ **22.** $e^{\ln \sqrt{x}}$
23. $-1 + \ln e^{2x}$ **24.** $-8 + e^{\ln x^3}$

Expanding Logarithmic Expressions In Exercises 25–34, use the properties of logarithms to rewrite the expression as a sum, difference, or multiple of logarithms. *See Example 3.*

25. $\ln \frac{2}{3}$ **26.** $\ln \frac{1}{5}$
27. $\ln xyz$ **28.** $\ln \frac{xy}{z}$
29. $\ln \sqrt[3]{2x + 7}$
30. $\ln \sqrt{\frac{x^3}{x + 1}}$
31. $\ln[z(z - 1)^2]$
32. $\ln\left(x \sqrt[3]{x^2 + 1}\right)$
33. $\ln \frac{3x(x + 1)}{(2x + 1)^2}$
34. $\ln \frac{2x}{\sqrt{x^2 - 1}}$

Inverse Functions In Exercises 35–38, analytically show that the functions are inverse functions. Then use a graphing utility to show this graphically.

35. $f(x) = e^{2x}$
  $g(x) = \ln \sqrt{x}$

36. $f(x) = e^x - 1$
  $g(x) = \ln(x + 1)$

37. $f(x) = e^{2x-1}$
  $g(x) = \frac{1}{2} + \ln \sqrt{x}$

38. $f(x) = e^{x/3}$
  $g(x) = \ln x^3$

Using Properties of Logarithms In Exercises 39 and 40, use the properties of logarithms and the fact that $\ln 2 \approx 0.6931$ and $\ln 3 \approx 1.0986$ to approximate the logarithm. Then use a calculator to confirm your approximation.

39. (a) $\ln 6$ (b) $\ln \frac{3}{2}$ (c) $\ln 81$ (d) $\ln \sqrt{3}$
40. (a) $\ln 0.25$ (b) $\ln 24$ (c) $\ln \sqrt[3]{12}$ (d) $\ln \frac{1}{72}$

Condensing Logarithmic Expressions In Exercises 41–50, use the properties of logarithms to rewrite the expression as the logarithm of a single quantity. *See Example 4.*

41. $\ln(x - 2) - \ln(x + 2)$ **42.** $\ln(2x + 1) + \ln(2x - 1)$
43. $3 \ln x + 2 \ln y - 4 \ln z$ **44.** $4 \ln x + 6 \ln y - \ln z$
45. $4 \ln(x - 6) - \frac{1}{2} \ln(3x + 1)$
46. $2 \ln(5x + 3) + \frac{3}{2} \ln(x + 5)$
47. $3[\ln x + \ln(x + 3) - \ln(x + 4)]$
48. $\frac{1}{3}[2 \ln(x + 3) + \ln x - \ln(x^2 - 1)]$
49. $\frac{3}{2}[\ln x(x^2 + 1) - \ln(x + 1)]$
50. $2\left[\ln x + \frac{1}{4} \ln(x + 1)\right]$

Solving Exponential and Logarithmic Equations In Exercises 51–72, solve for x or t. *See Examples 5 and 6.*

51. $e^{\ln x} = 4$ **52.** $e^{\ln x^2} - 9 = 0$
53. $e^{x+1} = 4$ **54.** $e^{-0.5x} = 0.075$
55. $300e^{-0.2t} = 700$ **56.** $400e^{-0.0174t} = 1000$
57. $4e^{2x-1} - 1 = 5$ **58.** $2e^{-x+1} - 5 = 9$
59. $\ln x = 0$ **60.** $2 \ln x = 4$
61. $\ln 2x = 2.4$ **62.** $\ln 4x = 1$
63. $3 + 4 \ln x = 15$ **64.** $6 + 3 \ln x = 8$
65. $\ln x - \ln(x - 6) = 3$ **66.** $\ln x + \ln(x + 2) = 0$
67. $5^{2x} = 15$ **68.** $2^{1-x} = 6$
69. $500(1.07)^t = 1000$ **70.** $400(1.06)^t = 1300$
71. $\left(1 + \frac{0.07}{12}\right)^{12t} = 3$ **72.** $\left(1 + \frac{0.06}{12}\right)^{12t} = 5$

Compound Interest In Exercises 73 and 74, $3000 is invested in an account at interest rate r, compounded continuously. Find the time required for the amount to (a) double and (b) triple.

73. $r = 0.085$ **74.** $r = 0.045$

75. Compound Interest A deposit of $1000 is made in an account that earns interest at an annual rate of 5%. How long will it take for the balance to double when the interest is compounded (a) annually, (b) monthly, (c) daily, and (d) continuously?

76. Compound Interest Complete the table to determine the time t necessary for P dollars to triple when the interest is compounded continuously at rate r.

r	2%	4%	6%	8%	10%	12%	14%
t							

77. Population Growth The population P (in thousands) of Orlando, Florida from 1980 through 2009 can be modeled by $P = 130e^{0.0205t}$, where $t = 0$ corresponds to 1980. *(Source: U.S. Census Bureau)*

(a) What was the population of Orlando in 2009?

(b) In what year will Orlando have a population of 300,000?

78. Population Growth The population P (in thousands) of Phoenix, Arizona from 1980 through 2009 can be modeled by

$P = 788e^{0.0248t}$

where $t = 0$ corresponds to 1980. *(Source: U.S. Census Bureau)*

(a) What was the population of Phoenix in 2009?

(b) In what year will Phoenix have a population of 2,000,000?

Carbon Dating In Exercises 79–82, you are given the ratio of carbon atoms in a fossil. Use the information to estimate the age of the fossil. In living organic material, the ratio of radioactive carbon isotopes to the total number of carbon atoms is about 1 to 10^{12}. (See Example 2 in Section 4.1.) When organic material dies, its radioactive carbon isotopes begin to decay, with a half-life of about 5715 years. So, the ratio R of carbon isotopes to carbon-14 atoms is modeled by $R = 10^{-12}\left(\frac{1}{2}\right)^{t/5715}$, where t is the time (in years) and $t = 0$ represents the time when the organic material died.

79. $R = 0.32 \times 10^{-12}$ **80.** $R = 0.27 \times 10^{-12}$
81. $R = 0.22 \times 10^{-12}$ **82.** $R = 0.13 \times 10^{-12}$

83. Learning Theory Students in a mathematics class were given an exam and then retested monthly with equivalent exams. The average scores S (on a 100-point scale) for the class can be modeled by $S = 80 - 14 \ln(t + 1), 0 \le t \le 12$, where t is the time in months.

(a) What was the average score on the original exam?

(b) What was the average score after 4 months?

(c) After how many months was the average score 46?

84. **HOW DO YOU SEE IT?** The graph shows the percents of American males and females ages 20 and over who are no more than x inches tall. (*Source: National Center for Health Statistics*)

Heights of Americans Age 20 and Over

(a) Use the graph to determine the limit of each function as x approaches infinity. What do they mean?

(b) What is the median height of each sex?

85. Demand The demand function for a product is given by

$$p = 5000\left(1 - \frac{4}{4 + e^{-0.002x}}\right)$$

where p is the price per unit (in dollars) and x is the number of units sold. Find the numbers of units sold for prices of (a) $p = \$200$ and (b) $p = \$800$.

86. Demand The demand function for a product is given by

$$p = 10{,}000\left(1 - \frac{3}{3 + e^{-0.001x}}\right)$$

where p is the price per unit (in dollars) and x is the number of units sold. Find the numbers of units sold for prices of (a) $p = \$500$ and (b) $p = \$1500$.

87. Using a Property of Logarithms Demonstrate that

$$\frac{\ln x}{\ln y} \neq \ln\frac{x}{y} = \ln x - \ln y$$

by using a spreadsheet to complete the table.

x	y	$\dfrac{\ln x}{\ln y}$	$\ln\dfrac{x}{y}$	$\ln x - \ln y$
1	2			
3	4			
10	5			
4	0.5			

88. Finding Limits and Relative Extrema Use a spreadsheet to complete the table using

$$f(x) = \frac{\ln x}{x}.$$

x	1	5	10	10^2	10^4	10^6
$f(x)$						

(a) Use the table to estimate the limit: $\displaystyle\lim_{x\to\infty} f(x)$.

(b) Use a graphing utility to estimate the relative extrema of f.

Verifying Properties of Logarithms In Exercises 89 and 90, use a graphing utility to verify that the functions are equivalent for $x > 0$.

89. $f(x) = \ln\dfrac{x^2}{4}$

$g(x) = 2\ln x - \ln 4$

90. $f(x) = \ln\sqrt{x(x^2 + 1)}$

$g(x) = \frac{1}{2}[\ln x + \ln(x^2 + 1)]$

True or False? In Exercises 91–96, determine whether the statement is true or false given that $f(x) = \ln x$. If it is false, explain why or give an example that shows it is false.

91. $f(0) = 0$

92. $f(ax) = f(a) + f(x)$, $a > 0, x > 0$

93. $f(x - 2) = f(x) - f(2)$, $x > 2$

94. $\sqrt{f(x)} = \frac{1}{2}f(x)$

95. If $f(u) = 2f(v)$, then $v = u^2$.

96. If $f(x) < 0$, then $0 < x < 1$.

97. Finance You are investing P dollars at an annual interest rate of r, compounded continuously, for t years. Which of the following options would you choose to get the highest value of the investment? Explain your reasoning.

(a) Double the amount you invest.

(b) Double your interest rate.

(c) Double the number of years.

98. Think About It Are the times required for the investments in Exercises 75 and 76 to quadruple twice as long as the times for them to double? Give a reason for your answer and verify your answer algebraically.

99. Pursuit Curve Use a graphing utility to graph

$$y = 10\ln\left(\frac{10 + \sqrt{100 - x^2}}{10}\right) - \sqrt{100 - x^2}$$

over the interval $(0, 10]$. This graph is called a *tractrix* or *pursuit curve*. Use your school's library, the Internet, or some other reference source to find information about a tractrix. Explain how such a curve can arise in a real-life setting.

4.5 Derivatives of Logarithmic Functions

■ Find the derivatives of natural logarithmic functions.
■ Find the derivatives of exponential and logarithmic functions involving other bases.

Derivatives of Logarithmic Functions

Implicit differentiation can be used to develop the derivative of the natural logarithmic function.

In Exercise 73 on page 292, you will use the derivative of a logarithmic function to find the rate of change of a demand function.

$$y = \ln x \qquad \text{Natural logarithmic function}$$
$$e^y = x \qquad \text{Write in exponential form.}$$
$$\frac{d}{dx}[e^y] = \frac{d}{dx}[x] \qquad \text{Differentiate with respect to } x.$$
$$e^y \frac{dy}{dx} = 1 \qquad \text{Chain Rule}$$
$$\frac{dy}{dx} = \frac{1}{e^y} \qquad \text{Divide each side by } e^y.$$
$$\frac{dy}{dx} = \frac{1}{x} \qquad \text{Substitute } x \text{ for } e^y.$$

This result and its Chain Rule version are summarized below.

Derivative of the Natural Logarithmic Function

Let u be a differentiable function of x.

1. $\dfrac{d}{dx}[\ln x] = \dfrac{1}{x}$ **2.** $\dfrac{d}{dx}[\ln u] = \dfrac{1}{u}\dfrac{du}{dx}$

Example 1   **Differentiating a Logarithmic Function**

Find the derivative of

$$f(x) = \ln 2x.$$

SOLUTION Let $u = 2x$. Then $du/dx = 2$, and you can apply the Chain Rule as shown.

$$f'(x) = \frac{1}{u}\frac{du}{dx} \qquad \text{Chain Rule}$$
$$= \frac{1}{2x}(2)$$
$$= \frac{1}{x} \qquad \text{Simplify.}$$

✓ **Checkpoint 1**

Find the derivative of

$$f(x) = \ln 5x.$$

Denis Pepin/www.shutterstock.com

Example 2   Differentiating Logarithmic Functions

Find the derivative of each function.

a. $f(x) = \ln(2x^2 + 4)$ **b.** $f(x) = x \ln x$ **c.** $f(x) = \dfrac{\ln x}{x}$

SOLUTION

a. $f'(x) = \dfrac{1}{u}\dfrac{du}{dx}$ Chain Rule

$\quad\quad = \dfrac{1}{2x^2 + 4}(4x)$ $u = 2x^2 + 4,\ du/dx = 4x$

$\quad\quad = \dfrac{2x}{x^2 + 2}$ Simplify.

b. $f'(x) = x\dfrac{d}{dx}[\ln x] + (\ln x)\dfrac{d}{dx}[x]$ Product Rule

$\quad\quad = x\left(\dfrac{1}{x}\right) + (\ln x)(1)$

$\quad\quad = 1 + \ln x$ Simplify.

c. $f'(x) = \dfrac{x\dfrac{d}{dx}[\ln x] - (\ln x)\dfrac{d}{dx}[x]}{x^2}$ Quotient Rule

$\quad\quad = \dfrac{x\left(\dfrac{1}{x}\right) - \ln x}{x^2}$

$\quad\quad = \dfrac{1 - \ln x}{x^2}$ Simplify.

✓ **Checkpoint 2**

Find the derivative of each function.

a. $f(x) = \ln(x^2 - 4)$ **b.** $f(x) = x^2 \ln x$ **c.** $f(x) = -\dfrac{\ln x}{x^2}$

Example 3   Rewriting Before Differentiating

$f(x) = \ln\sqrt{x + 1}$ Original function

$\quad = \ln(x + 1)^{1/2}$ Rewrite with rational exponent.

$\quad = \dfrac{1}{2}\ln(x + 1)$ Property of logarithms

$f'(x) = \dfrac{1}{2}\left(\dfrac{1}{x + 1}\right)$ Differentiate.

$\quad = \dfrac{1}{2(x + 1)}$ Simplify.

✓ **Checkpoint 3**

Find the derivative of

$f(x) = \ln\sqrt[3]{x + 1}.$

STUDY TIP

When you are differentiating logarithmic functions, it is often helpful to use the properties of logarithms to rewrite the function *before* differentiating. To see the advantage of rewriting before differentiating, try using the Chain Rule to differentiate $f(x) = \ln\sqrt{x + 1}$ and compare your work with that shown in Example 3.

Example 4 **Rewriting Before Differentiating**

Find the derivative of $f(x) = \ln[x(x^2 + 1)^2]$.

SOLUTION

$$\begin{aligned}
f(x) &= \ln[x(x^2 + 1)^2] &&\text{Write original function.}\\
&= \ln x + \ln(x^2 + 1)^2 &&\text{Logarithmic properties}\\
&= \ln x + 2\ln(x^2 + 1) &&\text{Logarithmic properties}\\
f'(x) &= \frac{1}{x} + 2\left(\frac{2x}{x^2 + 1}\right) &&\text{Differentiate.}\\
&= \frac{1}{x} + \frac{4x}{x^2 + 1} &&\text{Simplify.}
\end{aligned}$$

✓**Checkpoint 4**

Find the derivative of $f(x) = \ln[x^2\sqrt{x^2 + 1}]$.

Finding the derivative of the function in Example 4 without first rewriting would be a formidable task.

$$f'(x) = \frac{1}{x(x^2 + 1)^2} \frac{d}{dx}[x(x^2 + 1)^2]$$

You might try showing that this yields the same result obtained in Example 4, but be careful—the algebra is messy.

Example 5 **Finding an Equation of a Tangent Line**

Find an equation of the tangent line to the graph of $f(x) = 2 + 3x \ln x$ at the point $(1, 2)$.

SOLUTION Begin by finding the derivative of f.

$$\begin{aligned}
f(x) &= 2 + 3x \ln x &&\text{Write original function.}\\
f'(x) &= 3x\left(\frac{1}{x}\right) + (\ln x)(3) &&\text{Differentiate.}\\
&= 3 + 3\ln x &&\text{Simplify.}
\end{aligned}$$

The slope of the line tangent to the graph of f at $(1, 2)$ is

$$f'(1) = 3 + 3\ln 1 = 3 + 3(0) = 3.$$

Using the point-slope form of a line, you can find the equation of the tangent line to be

$$y = 3x - 1.$$

The graph of the function and the tangent line are shown in Figure 4.16.

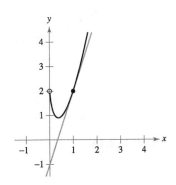

FIGURE 4.16

✓**Checkpoint 5**

Find an equation of the tangent line to the graph of $f(x) = 4 \ln x$ at the point $(1, 0)$.

FIGURE 4.17

Example 6 Analyzing a Graph

Analyze the graph of the function $f(x) = \dfrac{x^2}{2} - \ln x$.

SOLUTION From Figure 4.17, it appears that the function has a minimum at $x = 1$. To find the minimum analytically, find the critical numbers by setting the derivative of f equal to zero and solving for x.

$$f(x) = \frac{x^2}{2} - \ln x \qquad \text{Write original function.}$$

$$f'(x) = x - \frac{1}{x} \qquad \text{Differentiate.}$$

$$x - \frac{1}{x} = 0 \qquad \text{Set derivative equal to 0.}$$

$$x = \frac{1}{x} \qquad \text{Add } 1/x \text{ to each side.}$$

$$x^2 = 1 \qquad \text{Multiply each side by } x.$$

$$x = \pm 1 \qquad \text{Take square root of each side.}$$

Of these two possible critical numbers, only the positive one lies in the domain of f. By applying the First-Derivative Test, you can confirm that the function has a relative minimum at $x = 1$.

✓ **Checkpoint 6**

Determine the relative extrema of the function $f(x) = x - 2 \ln x$.

Example 7 Finding a Rate of Change

A group of 200 college students was tested every 6 months over a four-year period. The group was composed of students who took Spanish during the fall semester of their freshman year and did not take subsequent Spanish courses. The average test score p (in percent) is modeled by

$$p = 91.6 - 15.6 \ln(t + 1), \quad 0 \le t \le 48$$

where t is the time in months, as shown in Figure 4.18. At what rate was the average score changing after 1 year?

SOLUTION The rate of change is

$$\frac{dp}{dt} = -\frac{15.6}{t + 1}.$$

The rate of change when $t = 12$ is

$$\frac{dp}{dt} = -\frac{15.6}{12 + 1} = -\frac{15.6}{13} = -1.2.$$

This means that the average score was decreasing at the rate of 1.2% per month.

Human Memory Model

FIGURE 4.18

✓ **Checkpoint 7**

Suppose the average test score in Example 7 was modeled by

$$p = 92.3 - 16.9 \ln(t + 1), \quad 0 \le t \le 48$$

where t is the time in months. How would the rate at which the average test score was changing after 1 year compare with that of the model in Example 7?

Other Bases

This chapter began with a definition of a general exponential function

$$f(x) = a^x$$

where a is a positive number such that $a \neq 1$. The corresponding **logarithm to the base a** is defined by

$$\log_a x = b \quad \text{if and only if} \quad a^b = x.$$

As with the natural logarithmic function, the domain of the logarithmic function to the base a is the set of positive numbers.

Example 8 Evaluating Logarithms

a. $\log_2 8 = 3$ $2^3 = 8$

b. $\log_{10} 100 = 2$ $10^2 = 100$

c. $\log_{10} \frac{1}{10} = -1$ $10^{-1} = \frac{1}{10}$

d. $\log_3 81 = 4$ $3^4 = 81$

✓ **Checkpoint 8**

Evaluate each logarithm without using a calculator.

a. $\log_2 16$ **b.** $\log_{10} \frac{1}{100}$ **c.** $\log_2 \frac{1}{32}$ **d.** $\log_5 125$

Most calculators have only two logarithm keys—a natural logarithm key denoted by (LN) and a common logarithm key denoted by (LOG). Logarithms to other bases can be evaluated with the following change-of-base formula.

$$\log_a x = \frac{\ln x}{\ln a} \qquad \text{Change-of-base formula}$$

Example 9 Changing Bases to Evaluate Logarithms

Use the change-of-base formula and a calculator to evaluate each logarithm.

a. $\log_2 3$

b. $\log_3 6$

c. $\log_2(-1)$

SOLUTION In each case, use the change-of-base formula and a calculator.

a. $\log_2 3 = \dfrac{\ln 3}{\ln 2} \approx 1.585$ $\qquad \log_a x = \frac{\ln x}{\ln a}$

b. $\log_3 6 = \dfrac{\ln 6}{\ln 3} \approx 1.631$ $\qquad \log_a x = \frac{\ln x}{\ln a}$

c. $\log_2(-1)$ is not defined.

✓ **Checkpoint 9**

Use the change-of-base formula and a calculator to evaluate each logarithm.

a. $\log_2 5$ **b.** $\log_3 18$ **c.** $\log_4 80$ **d.** $\log_{16} 0.25$

To find derivatives of exponential or logarithmic functions to bases other than e, you can either convert to base e or use the differentiation rules shown below.

Other Bases and Differentiation

Let u be a differentiable function of x.

1. $\dfrac{d}{dx}[a^x] = (\ln a)a^x$ 2. $\dfrac{d}{dx}[a^u] = (\ln a)a^u \dfrac{du}{dx}$

3. $\dfrac{d}{dx}[\log_a x] = \left(\dfrac{1}{\ln a}\right)\dfrac{1}{x}$ 4. $\dfrac{d}{dx}[\log_a u] = \left(\dfrac{1}{\ln a}\right)\left(\dfrac{1}{u}\right)\dfrac{du}{dx}$

PROOF By definition, $a^x = e^{(\ln a)x}$. So, you can prove the first rule by letting $u = (\ln a)x$ and differentiating with base e to obtain

$$\frac{d}{dx}[a^x] = \frac{d}{dx}[e^{(\ln a)x}] = e^u \frac{du}{dx} = e^{(\ln a)x}(\ln a) = (\ln a)a^x.$$

 Example 10   **Finding a Rate of Change**

Radioactive carbon isotopes have a half-life of 5715 years. An object contains 1 gram of the isotopes. The amount A (in grams) that will be present after t years is

$$A = \left(\frac{1}{2}\right)^{t/5715}.$$

At what rate is the amount changing when $t = 10{,}000$ years?

SOLUTION The derivative of A with respect to t is

$$\frac{dA}{dt} = \left(\ln\frac{1}{2}\right)\left(\frac{1}{2}\right)^{t/5715}\left(\frac{1}{5715}\right).$$

When $t = 10{,}000$, the rate at which the amount is changing is

$$\left(\ln\frac{1}{2}\right)\left(\frac{1}{2}\right)^{10{,}000/5715}\left(\frac{1}{5715}\right) \approx -0.000036$$

which implies that the amount of isotopes in the object is decreasing at the rate of 0.000036 gram per year.

✓**Checkpoint 10**

Use a graphing utility to graph the model in Example 10. Describe the rate at which the amount is changing as time t increases.

SUMMARIZE   (Section 4.5)

1. State the derivative of the natural logarithmic function *(page 285)*. For examples of the derivative of the natural logarithmic function, see Examples 1, 2, 3, and 4.

2. State the derivative of the logarithmic function to base a *(page 290)*. For an example of a derivative of a logarithmic function to base a, see Example 10.

SKILLS WARM UP 4.5

The following warm-up exercises involve skills that were covered in earlier sections. You will use these skills in the exercise set for this section. For additional help, review Sections 2.6, 2.7, and 4.4.

In Exercises 1–6, expand the logarithmic expression.

1. $\ln(x + 1)^2$

2. $\ln x(x + 1)$

3. $\ln \dfrac{x}{x + 1}$

4. $\ln\left(\dfrac{x}{x - 3}\right)^3$

5. $\ln \dfrac{4x(x - 7)}{x^2}$

6. $\ln x^3(x + 1)$

In Exercises 7 and 8, find dy/dx implicitly.

7. $y^2 + xy = 7$

8. $x^2y - xy^2 = 3x$

In Exercises 9 and 10, find the second derivative of f.

9. $f(x) = x^2(x + 1) - 3x^3$

10. $f(x) = -\dfrac{1}{x^2}$

Exercises 4.5

See www.CalcChat.com for worked-out solutions to odd-numbered exercises.

Differentiating a Logarithmic Function In Exercises 1–22, find the derivative of the function. *See Examples 1, 2, 3, and 4.*

1. $y = \ln x^2$

2. $f(x) = \ln 7x$

3. $y = \ln(x^2 + 3)$

4. $f(x) = \ln(1 - x^2)$

5. $y = \ln\sqrt{x - 4}$

6. $y = \ln(1 - x)^{3/2}$

7. $y = (\ln x)^4$

8. $y = (\ln x^2)^2$

9. $f(x) = 2x \ln x$

10. $y = \dfrac{\ln x}{x^2}$

11. $y = \ln\left(x\sqrt{x^2 - 1}\right)$

12. $y = \ln[x(2x + 3)^2]$

13. $y = \ln\dfrac{x}{x + 1}$

14. $y = \ln\dfrac{x}{x^2 + 1}$

15. $y = \ln\sqrt[3]{\dfrac{x - 1}{x + 1}}$

16. $y = \ln\sqrt{\dfrac{x + 1}{x - 1}}$

17. $y = \ln\dfrac{\sqrt{4 + x^2}}{x}$

18. $y = \ln\dfrac{(6 - x)^{3/2}}{x^{2/3}}$

19. $g(x) = e^{-x} \ln x$

20. $y = e^{x^2} \ln 4x^3$

21. $g(x) = \ln\dfrac{e^x + e^{-x}}{2}$

22. $f(x) = \ln\dfrac{1 + e^x}{1 - e^x}$

Evaluating Logarithms In Exercises 23–28, evaluate the logarithm without using a calculator. *See Example 8.*

23. $\log_5 25$

24. $\log_4 64$

25. $\log_3 \frac{1}{27}$

26. $\log_6 \frac{1}{36}$

27. $\log_7 49$

28. $\log_8 512$

Changing Bases to Evaluate Logarithms In Exercises 29–34, use the change-of-base formula and a calculator to evaluate the logarithm. *See Example 9.*

29. $\log_4 7$

30. $\log_6 10$

31. $\log_2 48$

32. $\log_5 12$

33. $\log_3 \frac{1}{2}$

34. $\log_7 \frac{2}{9}$

Differentiating Functions of Other Bases In Exercises 35–44, find the derivative of the function.

35. $y = 3^x$

36. $y = \left(\frac{1}{4}\right)^x$

37. $f(x) = \log_2 x$

38. $g(x) = \log_5 x$

39. $h(x) = 4^{2x-3}$

40. $f(x) = 10^{x^2}$

41. $y = \log_{10}(x^2 + 6x)$

42. $g(x) = \log_8(2x - 5)$

43. $y = x2^x$

44. $y = x3^{x+1}$

Finding an Equation of a Tangent Line In Exercises 45–52, find an equation of the tangent line to the graph of the function at the given point. *See Example 5.*

45. $y = \ln x^3$; $(1, 0)$

46. $y = \ln x^{5/2}$; $(1, 0)$

47. $y = x \ln x$; (e, e)

48. $y = \dfrac{\ln x}{x}$; $\left(e, \dfrac{1}{e}\right)$

49. $f(x) = \ln\dfrac{5(x + 2)}{x}$; $\left(-\dfrac{5}{2}, 0\right)$

50. $f(x) = \ln\left(x\sqrt{x + 3}\right)$; $\left(\frac{6}{5}, \frac{9}{10}\right)$

51. $y = \log_3 x$; $(27, 3)$

52. $g(x) = \log_{10} 2x$; $(5, 1)$

Finding Derivatives Implicitly In Exercises 53–56, find dy/dx implicitly.

53. $x^2 - 3 \ln y + y^2 = 10$

54. $\ln xy + 5x = 30$

55. $4x^3 + \ln y^2 + 2y = 2x$

56. $4xy + \ln(x^2y) = 7$

Finding an Equation of a Tangent Line In Exercises 57 and 58, use implicit differentiation to find an equation of the tangent line to the graph of the function at the given point.

57. $x + y - 1 = \ln(x^2 + y^2);\ (1, 0)$

58. $y^2 + \ln(xy) = 2;\ (e, 1)$

Finding Higher-Order Derivatives In Exercises 59–64, find the second derivative of the function.

59. $f(x) = x \ln \sqrt{x} + 2x$ **60.** $f(x) = 3 + 2 \ln x$

61. $f(x) = 2 + x^3 \ln x$ **62.** $f(x) = \dfrac{\ln x}{x^3} + x$

63. $f(x) = 5^x$ **64.** $f(x) = \log_{10} x$

65. Sound Intensity The relationship between the number of decibels β and the intensity of a sound I (in watts per square centimeter) is given by

$$\beta = 10 \log_{10}\left(\frac{I}{10^{-16}}\right).$$

Find the rate of change in the number of decibels when the intensity is 10^{-4} watt per square centimeter.

66. Chemistry The temperatures T (in °F) at which water boils at selected pressures p (in pounds per square inch) can be modeled by

$$T = 87.97 + 34.96 \ln p + 7.91\sqrt{p}.$$

Find the rate of change of the temperature when the pressure is 60 pounds per square inch.

Analyzing a Graph In Exercises 67–72, analyze and sketch the graph of the function. Label any relative extrema, points of inflection, and asymptotes. *See Example 6.*

67. $y = x - \ln x$

68. $y = \ln 2x - 2x^2$

69. $y = \dfrac{x}{\ln x}$

70. $y = \dfrac{\ln 5x}{x^2}$

71. $y = x^2 \ln \dfrac{x}{4}$

72. $y = (\ln x)^2$

Demand In Exercises 73 and 74, find dx/dp for the demand function. Interpret this rate of change for a price of $10.

73. $x = \ln \dfrac{1000}{p}$ **74.** $x = \dfrac{500}{\ln(p^2 + 1)}$

75. Demand Solve the demand function in Exercise 73 for p. Use the result to find dp/dx. Then find the rate of change when $p = \$10$. What is the relationship between this derivative and dx/dp?

76. Demand Solve the demand function in Exercise 74 for p. Use the result to find dp/dx. Then find the rate of change when $p = \$10$. What is the relationship between this derivative and dx/dp?

77. Minimum Average Cost The cost of producing x units of a product is modeled by

$$C = 500 + 300x - 300 \ln x, \quad x \ge 1.$$

(a) Find the average cost function $\overline{C}$.

(b) Find the minimum average cost analytically. Use a graphing utility to confirm your result.

78. Minimum Average Cost The cost of producing x units of a product is modeled by

$$C = 100 + 25x - 120 \ln x, \quad x \ge 1.$$

(a) Find the average cost function $\overline{C}$.

(b) Find the minimum average cost analytically. Use a graphing utility to confirm your result.

79. Consumer Trends The numbers of employees E (in thousands) at outpatient care centers from 2004 through 2009 are shown in the table.

Year	2004	2005	2006	2007	2008	2009
Employees	451	473	493	512	533	543

The data can be modeled by $E = 287 + 116.7 \ln t$, where $t = 4$ corresponds to 2004. *(Source: U.S. Bureau of Labor Statistics)*

(a) Use a graphing utility to plot the data and graph E over the interval $[4, 9]$.

(b) At what rate were the numbers of employees changing in 2006?

80. **HOW DO YOU SEE IT?** The graph shows the temperature T (in °C) of an object h hours after it is removed from a furnace.

(a) Find $\lim\limits_{h \to \infty} T$. What does this limit represent?

(b) When is the temperature changing most rapidly?

81. Home Mortgage The term t (in years) of a $200,000 home mortgage at 7.5% interest can be approximated by

$$t = -13.375 \ln \frac{x - 1250}{x}, \quad x > 1250$$

where x is the monthly payment in dollars.

(a) Use a graphing utility to graph the model.

(b) Use the model to approximate the term of a home mortgage for which the monthly payment is $1398.43. What is the total amount paid?

(c) Use the model to approximate the term of a home mortgage for which the monthly payment is $1611.19. What is the total amount paid?

(d) Find the instantaneous rate of change of t with respect to x when $x = \$1398.43$ and $x = \$1611.19$.

(e) Write a short paragraph describing the benefit of the higher monthly payment.

82. Earthquake Intensity On the Richter scale, the magnitude R of an earthquake of intensity I is given by

$$R = \frac{\ln I - \ln I_0}{\ln 10}$$

where I_0 is the minimum intensity used for comparison. Assume $I_0 = 1$.

(a) Find the intensity of the March 11, 2011 earthquake in Japan for which $R = 9.0$.

(b) Find the intensity of the January 12, 2010 earthquake in Haiti for which $R = 7.0$.

(c) Find the factor by which the intensity is increased when the value of R is doubled.

(d) Find dR/dI.

Courtesy of Indochino

83. Learning Theory Students in a learning theory study were given an exam and then retested monthly for 6 months with an equivalent exam. The data obtained in the study are shown in the table, where t is the time in months after the initial exam and s is the average score for the class.

t	1	2	3	4	5	6
s	84.2	78.4	72.1	68.5	67.1	65.3

(a) Use a graphing utility to find a logarithmic model for the average score s in terms of the time t.

(b) Use a graphing utility to plot the data and graph the model. How well does the model fit the data?

(c) Find the rate of change of s with respect to t when $t = 2$. Interpret the meaning of this rate of change in the context of the problem.

Business Capsule

While in college, Heikai Gani had a miserable experience trying to buy a new suit. With his friend Kyle Vucko, he created an online business model to deliver custom-tailored suits for men. With an initial investment of $800,000, Indochino.com was born in 2007. Today the company has seven-digit revenues with over 17,000 customers. Indochino offers a perfect-fit promise; they will pay for alterations at a local tailor or issue a full refund.

84. Research Project Use your school's library, the Internet, or some other reference source to research information about an e-commerce company, such as the one discussed above. Collect data about the company (sales over a 10-year period, for example) and find a mathematical model that represents the data.

4.6 Exponential Growth and Decay

In Exercise 23 on page 300, you will use exponential growth to find the time it takes a population of bacteria to double.

■ Use exponential growth and decay to model real-life situations.

Exponential Growth and Decay

In this section, you will learn to create models of *exponential growth and decay*. Real-life situations that involve exponential growth and decay deal with a substance or population whose *rate of change at any time t is proportional to the amount of the substance present at that time*. For example, the rate of decomposition of a radioactive substance is proportional to the amount of radioactive substance at a given instant. In its simplest form, this relationship is represented by the equation

Rate of change of y ⌐ is ⌐ proportional to y.

$$\frac{dy}{dt} = ky.$$

In this equation, k is a constant and y is a function of t. The solution of this equation is shown below.

Exponential Growth and Decay

If y is a positive quantity whose rate of change with respect to time is proportional to the quantity present at any time t, then y is of the form

$$y = Ce^{kt}$$

where C is the **initial value** and k is the **constant of proportionality. Exponential growth** is indicated by $k > 0$ and **exponential decay** by $k < 0$.

PROOF　Because the rate of change of y is proportional to y, you can write

$$\frac{dy}{dt} = ky.$$

You can see that $y = Ce^{kt}$ is a solution of this equation by differentiating to obtain $dy/dt = kCe^{kt}$ and substituting.

$y = Ce^{kt}$	Original equation
$\dfrac{dy}{dt} = kCe^{kt}$	Differentiate.
$= k(Ce^{kt})$	Rewrite.
$= ky$	Substitute y for Ce^{kt}.

STUDY TIP

In the model $y = Ce^{kt}$, C is called the "initial value" because, when $t = 0$,

$$y = Ce^{k(0)}$$
$$= C(1)$$
$$= C.$$

Radioactive decay is measured in terms of **half-life**, the number of years required for half of the atoms in a sample of radioactive material to decay. The half-lives of some common radioactive isotopes are as shown.

Uranium (^{238}U)	4,470,000,000 years
Plutonium (^{239}Pu)	24,100 years
Carbon (^{14}C)	5,715 years
Radium (^{226}Ra)	1,599 years
Einsteinium (^{254}Es)	276 days
Nobelium (^{257}No)	25 seconds

Example 1   Modeling Radioactive Decay

A sample contains 1 gram of radium. Will more than 0.5 gram of radium remain after 1000 years?

SOLUTION   Let y represent the mass (in grams) of the radium in the sample. Because the rate of decay is proportional to y, you can conclude that y is of the form $y = Ce^{kt}$, where t is the time in years. From the given information, you know that $y = 1$ when $t = 0$. Substituting these values into the model produces

$$1 = Ce^{k(0)} \qquad \text{Substitute 1 for } y \text{ and 0 for } t.$$

which implies that $C = 1$. Because radium has a half-life of 1599 years, you know that $y = \frac{1}{2}$ when $t = 1599$. Substituting these values into the model allows you to solve for k.

$$y = e^{kt} \qquad \text{Exponential decay model}$$
$$\tfrac{1}{2} = e^{k(1599)} \qquad \text{Substitute } \tfrac{1}{2} \text{ for } y \text{ and 1599 for } t.$$
$$\ln \tfrac{1}{2} = 1599k \qquad \text{Take natural log of each side.}$$
$$\tfrac{1}{1599} \ln \tfrac{1}{2} = k \qquad \text{Divide each side by 1599.}$$

So, $k \approx -0.0004335$, and the exponential decay model is

$$y = e^{-0.0004335t}.$$

To find the amount of radium remaining in the sample after 1000 years, substitute $t = 1000$ into the model.

$$y = e^{-0.0004335(1000)} \approx 0.648 \text{ gram}$$

Yes, more than 0.5 gram of radium will remain after 1000 years. The graph of the model is shown in Figure 4.19.

Radioactive Half-Life of Radium

$(0, 1)$

$y = e^{-0.0004335t}$

$y = \frac{1}{2}$

$y = \frac{1}{4}$

$y = \frac{1}{8}$ $y = \frac{1}{16}$

1599 3198 4797 6396

Time (in years)

Mass (in grams)

FIGURE 4.19

✓ Checkpoint 1

Use the model in Example 1 to determine the number of years required for a one-gram sample of radium to decay to 0.4 gram.

Instead of approximating the value of k in Example 1, you could leave the value exact and obtain

$$y = e^{[(1/1599)\ln (1/2)]t}$$
$$= e^{\ln[(1/2)^{(t/1599)}]}$$
$$= \left(\frac{1}{2}\right)^{t/1599}.$$

This version of the model clearly shows the "half-life." When $t = 1599$, the value of y is $\frac{1}{2}$; when $t = 2(1599)$, the value of y is $\frac{1}{4}$; and so on.

Guidelines for Modeling Exponential Growth and Decay

1. Use the given information to write *two* sets of conditions involving y and t.

2. Substitute the given conditions into the model $y = Ce^{kt}$ and use the results to solve for the constants C and k. (When one of the conditions involves $t = 0$, substitute that value first to solve for C.)

3. Use the model $y = Ce^{kt}$ to answer the question.

Example 2 **Modeling Population Growth**

In a research experiment, a population of fruit flies is increasing in accordance with the exponential growth model. After 2 days, there are 100 flies, and after 4 days, there are 300 flies. How many flies will there be after 5 days?

SOLUTION Let y be the number of flies at time t. From the given information, you know that $y = 100$ when $t = 2$ and $y = 300$ when $t = 4$. Substituting this information into the model $y = Ce^{kt}$ produces

$$100 = Ce^{2k} \quad \text{and} \quad 300 = Ce^{4k}.$$

To solve for k, solve for C in the first equation and substitute the result into the second equation.

$300 = Ce^{4k}$	Second equation
$300 = \left(\dfrac{100}{e^{2k}}\right)e^{4k}$	Substitute $100/e^{2k}$ for C.
$\dfrac{300}{100} = e^{2k}$	Divide each side by 100.
$\ln 3 = 2k$	Take natural log of each side.
$\dfrac{1}{2}\ln 3 = k$	Solve for k.

Using $k = \frac{1}{2}\ln 3 \approx 0.5493$, you can determine that

$$C \approx \frac{100}{e^{2(0.5493)}}$$

$$\approx 33.$$

So, the exponential growth model is

$$y = 33e^{0.5493t}$$

as shown in Figure 4.20. This implies that, after 5 days, the population is

$$y = 33e^{0.5493(5)}$$

$$\approx 514 \text{ flies.}$$

ALGEBRA TUTOR *xy*

For help with the algebra in Example 2, see Example 1(c) in the *Chapter 4 Algebra Tutor* on page 302.

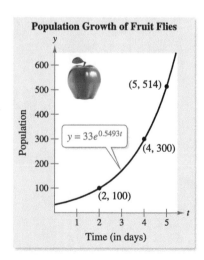

Population Growth of Fruit Flies

$(5, 514)$

$y = 33e^{0.5493t}$

$(4, 300)$

$(2, 100)$

Time (in days)

FIGURE 4.20

✓Checkpoint 2

Find the exponential growth model for a population of fruit flies for which there are 100 flies after 2 days and 400 flies after 4 days.

Example 3   Modeling Compound Interest

Money is deposited in an account for which the interest is compounded continuously. The balance in the account doubles in 6 years. What is the annual interest rate?

SOLUTION   The balance A in an account with continuously compounded interest is given by the exponential growth model

$$A = Pe^{rt} \qquad \text{Exponential growth model}$$

where P is the original deposit, r is the annual interest rate (in decimal form), and t is the time (in years). From the given information, you know that

$$A = 2P$$

when $t = 6$, as shown in Figure 4.21. Use this information to solve for r.

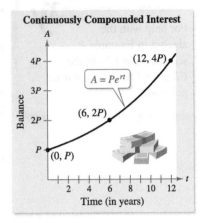

Continuously Compounded Interest

FIGURE 4.21

$$
\begin{array}{ll}
A = Pe^{rt} & \text{Exponential growth model} \\
2P = Pe^{r(6)} & \text{Substitute } 2P \text{ for } A \text{ and } 6 \text{ for } t. \\
2 = e^{6r} & \text{Divide each side by } P. \\
\ln 2 = 6r & \text{Take natural log of each side.} \\
\tfrac{1}{6} \ln 2 = r & \text{Divide each side by } 6.
\end{array}
$$

So, the annual interest rate is

$$r = \tfrac{1}{6} \ln 2$$
$$\approx 0.1155$$

or about 11.55%.

 Checkpoint 3

Find the annual interest rate for an account whose balance doubles in 8 years and for which the interest is compounded continuously.

Each of the examples in this section uses the exponential growth model $y = Ce^{kt}$, in which the base is e. Exponential growth, however, can be modeled with any base. That is, the model

$$y = Ca^{bt}$$

also represents exponential growth. (To see this, note that the model can be written in the form $y = Ce^{(\ln a)bt}$.) In some real-life settings, bases other than e are more convenient. For instance, in Example 1, knowing that the half-life of radium is 1599 years, you can immediately write the exponential decay model as

$$y = \left(\frac{1}{2}\right)^{t/1599}.$$

Using this model, the amount of radium left in the sample after 1000 years is

$$y = \left(\frac{1}{2}\right)^{1000/1599}$$
$$\approx 0.648 \text{ gram}$$

which is the same answer obtained in Example 1.

Example 4   **Modeling Sales**

Four months after discontinuing advertising on national television, a manufacturer notices that sales have dropped from 100,000 MP3 players per month to 80,000. Using an exponential pattern of decline, what will the sales be after another 4 months?

SOLUTION   Let y represent the number of MP3 players, let t represent the time (in months), and consider the exponential decay model

$$y = Ce^{kt}. \qquad \text{Exponential decay model}$$

From the given information, you know that $y = 100,000$ when $t = 0$. Using this information, you have

$$100,000 = Ce^0$$

which implies that $C = 100,000$. To solve for k, use the fact that $y = 80,000$ when $t = 4$.

$y = 100,000e^{kt}$	Exponential decay model
$80,000 = 100,000e^{k(4)}$	Substitute 80,000 for y and 4 for t.
$0.8 = e^{4k}$	Divide each side by 100,000.
$\ln 0.8 = 4k$	Take natural log of each side.
$\frac{1}{4}\ln 0.8 = k$	Divide each side by 4.

So, $k = \frac{1}{4}\ln 0.8 \approx -0.0558$, which means that the model is

$$y = 100,000e^{-0.0558t}.$$

After four more months ($t = 8$), you can expect sales to drop to

$$y = 100,000e^{-0.0558(8)}$$
$$\approx 64,000 \text{ MP3 players}$$

as shown in Figure 4.22.

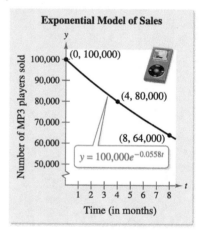

Exponential Model of Sales

FIGURE 4.22

ALGEBRA TUTOR

For help with the algebra in Example 4, see Example 1(b) in the *Chapter 4 Algebra Tutor* on page 302.

✓ **Checkpoint 4**

Use the model in Example 4 to determine when sales will drop to 50,000 MP3 players. ■

SUMMARIZE   (Section 4.6)

1. State the model used for exponential growth and decay *(page 294)*. For examples of the use of this model, see Examples 1, 2, 3, and 4.

2. State the guidelines for modeling exponential growth and decay *(page 296)*. For examples of the use of these guidelines, see Examples 2, 3, and 4.

3. Describe a real-life example of an exponential decay model *(pages 295 and 298, Examples 1 and 4)*.

4. Describe a real-life example of an exponential growth model *(pages 296 and 297, Examples 2 and 3)*.

In Exercises 1–4, solve the equation for k.

1. $12 = 24e^{4k}$

2. $10 = 3e^{5k}$

3. $25 = 16e^{-0.01k}$

4. $22 = 32e^{-0.02k}$

In Exercises 5–8, find the derivative of the function.

5. $y = 32e^{0.23t}$

6. $y = 18e^{0.072t}$

7. $y = 24e^{-1.4t}$

8. $y = 25e^{-0.001t}$

In Exercises 9–12, simplify the expression.

9. $e^{\ln 4}$

10. $4e^{\ln 3}$

11. $e^{\ln(2x+1)}$

12. $e^{\ln(x^2+1)}$

Exercises 4.6

Modeling Exponential Growth and Decay In Exercises 1–6, find the exponential function $y = Ce^{kt}$ that passes through the two given points.

1. $y = Ce^{kt}$

2. $y = Ce^{kt}$

3. $y = Ce^{kt}$

4. $y = Ce^{kt}$

5. $y = Ce^{kt}$

6. $y = Ce^{kt}$

Determining Exponential Growth and Decay In Exercises 7–10, use the given information to write an exponential equation for y. Does the function represent exponential growth or exponential decay?

7. $\dfrac{dy}{dt} = 2y$, $y = 10$ when $t = 0$

8. $\dfrac{dy}{dt} = -\dfrac{2}{3}y$, $y = 20$ when $t = 0$

9. $\dfrac{dy}{dt} = -4y$, $y = 30$ when $t = 0$

10. $\dfrac{dy}{dt} = 5.2y$, $y = 18$ when $t = 0$

Modeling Radioactive Decay In Exercises 11–16, complete the table for each radioactive isotope. *See Example 1.*

	Half-life (in years)	Initial quantity	Amount after 1000 years	Amount after 10,000 years
11. ^{226}Ra	1599	10 grams		
12. ^{226}Ra	1599		1.5 grams	
13. ^{14}C	5715			2 grams
14. ^{14}C	5715	3 grams		
15. ^{239}Pu	24,100		2.1 grams	
16. ^{239}Pu	24,100			0.4 gram

17. Radioactive Decay What percent of a present amount of radioactive radium (^{226}Ra) will remain after 900 years?

18. Radioactive Decay   Find the half-life of a radioactive material for which 99.57% of the initial amount remains after 1 year.

19. Carbon Dating   Carbon-14 (^{14}C) dating assumes that the carbon dioxide on the Earth today has the same radioactive content as it did centuries ago. If this is true, then the amount of ^{14}C absorbed by a tree that grew several centuries ago should be the same as the amount of ^{14}C absorbed by a similar tree today. A piece of ancient charcoal contains only 15% as much of the radioactive carbon as a piece of modern charcoal. How long ago was the tree burned to make the ancient charcoal? (The half-life of ^{14}C is 5715 years.)

20. Carbon Dating   Repeat Exercise 19 for a piece of charcoal that contains 30% as much radioactive carbon as a modern piece.

Finding Exponential Models   In Exercises 21 and 22, find exponential models $y_1 = Ce^{k_1 t}$ and $y_2 = C(2)^{k_2 t}$ that pass through the two given points. Compare the values of k_1 and k_2. Briefly explain your results.

21. $(0, 5)$, $(12, 20)$ **22.** $(0, 8)$, $\left(20, \frac{1}{2}\right)$

23. Population Growth   The number of a certain type of bacteria increases continuously at a rate proportional to the number present. There are 150 bacteria at a given time and 450 bacteria 5 hours later.

(a) How many bacteria will there be 10 hours after the initial time?

(b) How long will it take for the population to double?

(c) Does the answer to part (b) depend on the starting time? Explain your reasoning.

24. **HOW DO YOU SEE IT?**   The graph shows the populations (in thousands) of Cleveland, Ohio and Atlanta, Georgia from 2000 through 2008 using exponential models. *(Source: U.S. Census Bureau)*

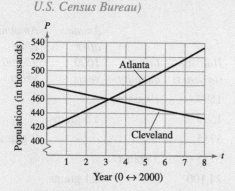

(a) Determine whether the population of each city is modeled by exponential growth or exponential decay. Explain your reasoning.

(b) Estimate the year when the two cities had the same population. What was this population?

Modeling Compound Interest   In Exercises 25–32, complete the table for an account in which interest is compounded continuously. *See Example 3.*

	Initial investment	Annual rate	Time to double	Amount after 10 years	Amount after 25 years
25.	$1000	12%			
26.	$20,000	$10\frac{1}{2}$%			
27.	$750		8 years		
28.	$10,000		10 years		
29.	$500			$1292.85	
30.	$2000				$6008.33
31.		4.5%		$10,000.00	
32.		2%		$2000.00	

Finding Present Value   In Exercises 33 and 34, determine the principal P that must be invested at interest rate r, compounded continuously, so that $1,000,000 will be available for retirement in t years.

33. $r = 7.5\%$, $t = 40$

34. $r = 10\%$, $t = 25$

35. Effective Rate   The effective rate of interest r_{eff} is the annual rate that will produce the same interest per year as the nominal rate r.

(a) For a rate r (in decimal form) that is compounded n times per year, show that the effective rate r_{eff} (in decimal form) is

$$r_{eff} = \left(1 + \frac{r}{n}\right)^n - 1.$$

(b) For a rate r (in decimal form) that is compounded continuously, show that the effective rate r_{eff} (in decimal form) is $r_{eff} = e^r - 1$.

36. Effective Rate   Use the results of Exercise 35 to complete the table showing the effective rates for nominal rates of (a) $r = 5\%$, (b) $r = 6\%$, and (c) $r = 7\frac{1}{2}\%$.

Number of compoundings per year	4	12	365	Continuous
Effective yield				

37. Investment: Rule of 70   Verify that the time necessary for an investment to double in value is approximately $70/r$, where r is the annual interest rate entered as a percent.

38. Investment: Rule of 70   Use the Rule of 70 from Exercise 37 to approximate the times necessary for an investment to double in value when (a) $r = 10\%$ and (b) $r = 7\%$.

39. Depreciation A sports utility vehicle that costs $21,500 new has a book value of $13,600 after 2 years.

(a) Find a linear model for the value of the vehicle.

(b) Find an exponential model for the value of the vehicle.

(c) Find the book values of the vehicle after 1 year and after 4 years using each model.

 (d) Use a graphing utility to graph the two models in the same viewing window. Which model depreciates faster in the first 2 years?

(e) Explain the advantages and disadvantages of using each model to a buyer and to a seller.

40. Population The table shows the populations P (in millions) of the United States from 1960 through 2010. *(Source: U.S. Census Bureau)*

Year	1960	1970	1980	1990	2000	2010
Population, P	181	205	228	250	282	309

(a) Use the 1960 and 1970 data to find an exponential model P_1. Let $t = 0$ represent 1960.

(b) Use a graphing utility to find an exponential model P_2 for all of the data. Let $t = 0$ represent 1960.

(c) Use a graphing utility to plot the data and graph both models in the same viewing window. Compare the actual data with the estimates from the models. Which model is more accurate?

41. Sales The cumulative sales S (in thousands of units) of a new product after it has been on the market for t years are modeled by $S = Ce^{k/t}$. During the first year, 5000 units were sold. The saturation point for the market is 30,000 units. That is, the limit of S as $t \to \infty$ is 30,000.

(a) Solve for C and k in the model.

(b) How many units will be sold after 5 years?

 (c) Use a graphing utility to graph the sales function.

42. Sales The cumulative sales S (in thousands of units) of a new product after it has been on the market for t years are modeled by

$$S = 50(1 - e^{kt}).$$

During the first year, 8000 units were sold.

(a) Solve for k in the model.

(b) What is the saturation point for this product?

(c) How many units will be sold after 5 years?

(d) Use a graphing utility to graph the sales function.

43. Learning Curve The management of a factory finds that the maximum number of units a worker can produce in a day is 30. The learning curve for the number of units N produced per day after a new employee has worked for t days is modeled by

$$N = 30(1 - e^{kt}).$$

After 20 days on the job, a worker is producing 19 units in a day. How many days should pass before this worker is producing 25 units per day?

44. Learning Curve The management in Exercise 43 requires that a new employee be producing at least 20 units per day after 30 days on the job.

(a) Find a learning curve model that describes this minimum requirement.

(b) Find the number of days before a minimal achiever is producing 25 units per day.

45. Revenue A small business assumes that the demand function for one of its new products can be modeled by

$$p = Ce^{kx}.$$

When $p = \$45$, $x = 1000$ units, and when $p = \$40$, $x = 1200$ units.

(a) Solve for C and k in the model.

(b) Find the values of x and p that will maximize the revenue for this product.

46. Revenue Repeat Exercise 45 given that when $p = \$5$, $x = 300$ units, and when $p = \$4$, $x = 400$ units.

47. Project: Cell Phone Subscribers For a project analyzing the numbers of cell phone subscribers from 2000 to 2009, visit this text's website at *www.cengagebrain.com*. *(Source: CTIA-The Wireless Association)*

ALGEBRA TUTOR

xy

Solving Exponential and Logarithmic Equations

To find the extrema or points of inflection of an exponential or logarithmic function, you must know how to solve exponential and logarithmic equations. A few examples are given on page 280. Some additional examples are presented in this Algebra Tutor.

As with all equations, remember that your basic goal is to isolate the variable on one side of the equation. To do this, you use inverse operations. For instance, to isolate x in

$$e^x = 7$$

take the natural log of each side of the equation and use the property $\ln e^x = x$. Similarly, to isolate x in

$$\ln x = 5$$

exponentiate each side of the equation and use the property $e^{\ln x} = x$.

Example 1   Solving Exponential Equations

Solve each exponential equation.

a. $25 = 5e^{7t}$ **b.** $80{,}000 = 100{,}000e^{k(4)}$ **c.** $300 = \left(\dfrac{100}{e^{2k}}\right)e^{4k}$

SOLUTION

a.
$25 = 5e^{7t}$	Write original equation.
$5 = e^{7t}$	Divide each side by 5.
$\ln 5 = \ln e^{7t}$	Take natural log of each side.
$\ln 5 = 7t$	Apply the property $\ln e^a = a$.
$\dfrac{1}{7}\ln 5 = t$	Divide each side by 7.

b.
$80{,}000 = 100{,}000e^{k(4)}$	Example 4, page 298
$0.8 = e^{4k}$	Divide each side by 100,000.
$\ln 0.8 = \ln e^{4k}$	Take natural log of each side.
$\ln 0.8 = 4k$	Apply the property $\ln e^a = a$.
$\dfrac{1}{4}\ln 0.8 = k$	Divide each side by 4.

c.
$300 = \left(\dfrac{100}{e^{2k}}\right)e^{4k}$	Example 2, page 296
$300 = (100)\dfrac{e^{4k}}{e^{2k}}$	Rewrite product.
$300 = 100e^{4k-2k}$	To divide powers, subtract exponents.
$300 = 100e^{2k}$	Simplify.
$3 = e^{2k}$	Divide each side by 100.
$\ln 3 = \ln e^{2k}$	Take natural log of each side.
$\ln 3 = 2k$	Apply the property $\ln e^a = a$.
$\dfrac{1}{2}\ln 3 = k$	Divide each side by 2.

Example 2   Solving Logarithmic Equations

Solve each logarithmic equation.

a. $\ln x = 2$ **b.** $5 + 2 \ln x = 4$

c. $2 \ln 3x = 4$ **d.** $\ln x - \ln(x - 1) = 1$

SOLUTION

a. $\ln x = 2$ Write original equation.

   $e^{\ln x} = e^2$ Exponentiate each side.

    $x = e^2$ Apply the property $e^{\ln a} = a$.

b. $5 + 2 \ln x = 4$ Write original equation.

    $2 \ln x = -1$ Subtract 5 from each side.

    $\ln x = -\dfrac{1}{2}$ Divide each side by 2.

   $e^{\ln x} = e^{-1/2}$ Exponentiate each side.

     $x = e^{-1/2}$ Apply the property $e^{\ln a} = a$.

c. $2 \ln 3x = 4$ Write original equation.

   $\ln 3x = 2$ Divide each side by 2.

   $e^{\ln 3x} = e^2$ Exponentiate each side.

    $3x = e^2$ Apply the property $e^{\ln a} = a$.

    $x = \dfrac{1}{3}e^2$ Divide each side by 3.

d. $\ln x - \ln(x - 1) = 1$ Write original equation.

   $\ln \dfrac{x}{x - 1} = 1$ $\ln m - \ln n = \ln(m/n)$

   $e^{\ln[x/(x-1)]} = e^1$ Exponentiate each side.

   $\dfrac{x}{x - 1} = e^1$ Apply the property $e^{\ln a} = a$.

     $x = ex - e$ Multiply each side by $x - 1$.

   $x - ex = -e$ Subtract ex from each side.

  $x(1 - e) = -e$ Factor.

     $x = \dfrac{-e}{1 - e}$ Divide each side by $1 - e$.

     $x = \dfrac{e}{e - 1}$ Simplify.

STUDY TIP

Because the domain of a logarithmic function generally does not include all real numbers, be sure to check for extraneous solutions.

SUMMARY AND STUDY STRATEGIES

After studying this chapter, you should have acquired the following skills.
The exercise numbers are keyed to the Review Exercises that begin on page 306.
Answers to odd-numbered Review Exercises are given in the back of the text.*

Section 4.1

Review Exercises

- Use the properties of exponents to evaluate and simplify exponential expressions.

  1, 2

$$a^0 = 1, \quad a^x a^y = a^{x+y}, \quad \frac{a^x}{a^y} = a^{x-y}, \quad (a^x)^y = a^{xy}$$

$$(ab)^x = a^x b^x, \quad \left(\frac{a}{b}\right)^x = \frac{a^x}{b^x}, \quad a^{-x} = \frac{1}{a^x}$$

- Sketch the graphs of exponential functions.

  3–8

- Use properties of exponents to answer questions about real-life situations.

  9–12

Section 4.2

- Use the properties of exponents to evaluate and simplify natural exponential expressions.

  13, 14

- Sketch the graphs of natural exponential functions.

  15–18

- Solve compound interest problems.

  19–24

  $$A = P(1 + r/n)^{nt}, \quad A = Pe^{rt}$$

- Solve effective rate of interest problems.

  25, 26

  $$r_{eff} = (1 + r/n)^n - 1$$

- Solve present value problems.

  27, 28

  $$P = \frac{A}{(1 + r/n)^{nt}}$$

- Answer questions involving the natural exponential function as a real-life model.

  29–34

Section 4.3

- Find the derivatives of natural exponential functions.

  35–40

  $$\frac{d}{dx}[e^x] = e^x, \quad \frac{d}{dx}[e^u] = e^u \frac{du}{dx}$$

- Find equations of the tangent lines to the graphs of natural exponential functions.

  41–44

- Use calculus to analyze the graphs of functions that involve the natural exponential function.

  45–48

Section 4.4

- Use the definition of the natural logarithmic function to write exponential equations in logarithmic form, and vice versa.

  49–52

  $$\ln x = b \quad \text{if and only if} \quad e^b = x.$$

---

* A wide range of valuable study aids are available to help you master the material in this chapter. The *Student Solutions Manual* includes step-by-step solutions to all odd-numbered exercises to help you review and prepare. The student website at *www.cengagebrain.com* offers algebra help and a *Graphing Technology Guide,* which contains step-by-step commands and instructions for a wide variety of graphing calculators.

Section 4.4 (continued)

$$\ln xy = \ln x + \ln y, \quad \ln \frac{x}{y} = \ln x - \ln y, \quad \ln x^n = n \ln x$$

$$\ln e^x = x, \quad e^{\ln x} = x$$

Section 4.5

$$\frac{d}{dx}[\ln x] = \frac{1}{x}, \quad \frac{d}{dx}[\ln u] = \frac{1}{u}\frac{du}{dx}$$

$$\log_a x = b \quad \text{if and only if} \quad a^b = x$$

$$\log_a x = \frac{\ln x}{\ln a}$$

$$\frac{d}{dx}[a^x] = (\ln a)a^x, \quad \frac{d}{dx}[a^u] = (\ln a)a^u\frac{du}{dx}$$

$$\frac{d}{dx}[\log_a x] = \left(\frac{1}{\ln a}\right)\frac{1}{x}, \quad \frac{d}{dx}[\log_a u] = \left(\frac{1}{\ln a}\right)\left(\frac{1}{u}\right)\frac{du}{dx}$$

Section 4.6

Study Strategies

■ **Classifying Differentiation Rules**   Differentiation rules fall into two basic classes: (1) general rules that apply to all differentiable functions; and (2) specific rules that apply to special types of functions. At this point in the course, you have studied six general rules: the Constant Rule, the Constant Multiple Rule, the Sum Rule, the Difference Rule, the Product Rule, and the Quotient Rule. Although these rules were introduced in the context of algebraic functions, remember that they also can be used with exponential and logarithmic functions. You have also studied three specific rules: the Power Rule, the derivative of the natural exponential function, and the derivative of the natural logarithmic function. Each of these rules comes in two forms: the "simple" version, such as $D_x[e^x] = e^x$, and the Chain Rule version, such as $D_x[e^u] = e^u(du/dx)$.

■ **To Memorize or Not to Memorize?**   When studying mathematics, you need to memorize some formulas and rules. Much of this will come from practice—the formulas that you use most often will be committed to memory. Some formulas, however, are used only infrequently. With these, it is helpful to be able to *derive* the formula from a *known* formula. For instance, knowing the Log Rule for differentiation and the change-of-base formula, $\log_a x = (\ln x)/(\ln a)$, allows you to derive the formula for the derivative of a logarithmic function to base a.

Review Exercises

See www.CalcChat.com for worked-out solutions to odd-numbered exercises.

Applying Properties of Exponents In Exercises 1 and 2, use the properties of exponents to simplify the expression.

1. (a) $(4^5)(4^2)$ (b) $(7^2)^3$

  (c) 2^{-4} (d) $\dfrac{3^8}{3^4}$

2. (a) $(5^4)(25^2)$ (b) $(9^{1/3})(3^{1/3})$

  (c) $\left(\dfrac{1}{3}\right)^{-3}$ (d) $(6^4)(6^{-5})$

Graphing Exponential Functions In Exercises 3–8, sketch the graph of the function.

3. $f(x) = 9^{x/2}$ 4. $g(x) = 16^{3x/2}$

5. $f(t) = \left(\dfrac{1}{6}\right)^{t}$ 6. $g(t) = \left(\dfrac{1}{3}\right)^{-t}$

7. $f(x) = \left(\dfrac{1}{2}\right)^{2x} + 4$ 8. $g(x) = \left(\dfrac{2}{3}\right)^{2x} + 1$

9. **Population Growth** The resident populations P (in thousands) of Wisconsin from 2000 through 2009 can be modeled by the exponential function

$$P(t) = 5382(1.0057)^t$$

where t is the time in years, with $t = 0$ corresponding to 2000. Use the model to estimate the populations in the years (a) 2016 and (b) 2025. *(Source: U.S. Census Bureau)*

10. **Revenue** The revenues R (in millions of dollars) for Panera Bread Company from 2000 through 2009 can be modeled by the exponential function

$$R(t) = 163.82(1.2924)^t$$

where t is the time in years, with $t = 0$ corresponding to 2000. Use the model to estimate the sales in the years (a) 2014 and (b) 2017. *(Source: Panera Bread Company)*

11. **Property Value** Suppose that the value of a piece of property doubles every 12 years. If you buy the property for $55,000, its value t years after the date of purchase should be

$$V(t) = 55,000(2)^{t/12}.$$

Use the model to approximate the value of the property (a) 4 years and (b) 25 years after it is purchased.

12. **Inflation Rate** Suppose the annual rate of inflation averages 2% over the next 10 years. With this rate of inflation, the approximate cost C of goods or services during any year in the decade will be given by

$$C(t) = P(1.02)^t, \quad 0 \le t \le 10$$

where t is time in years and P is the present cost. If the cost of a graphing calculator is presently $80, estimate the cost 10 years from now.

Applying Properties of Exponents In Exercises 13 and 14, use the properties of exponents to simplify the expression.

13. (a) $(e^5)^2$ (b) $\dfrac{e^3}{e^5}$

  (c) $(e^4)(e^{3/2})$ (d) $(e^2)^{-4}$

14. (a) $(e^6)(e^{-3})$ (b) $(e^{-2})^{-5}$

  (c) $\left(\dfrac{e^6}{e^2}\right)^{-1}$ (d) $(e^3)^{4/3}$

Graphing Natural Exponential Functions In Exercises 15–18, sketch the graph of the function.

15. $f(x) = e^{-x} + 1$

16. $g(x) = e^{2x} - 1$

17. $f(x) = 1 - e^x$

18. $g(x) = 2 + e^{x-1}$

Finding Account Balances In Exercises 19–22, complete the table to determine the balance A for P dollars invested at rate r for t years, compounded n times per year.

n	1	2	4	12	365	Continuous compounding
A						

19. $P = \$1000, r = 4\%, t = 5$ years

20. $P = \$7000, r = 6\%, t = 20$ years

21. $P = \$3000, r = 3.5\%, t = 10$ years

22. $P = \$4500, r = 2\%, t = 25$ years

Comparing Account Balances In Exercises 23 and 24, $2000 is deposited in an account. Decide which account, (a) or (b), will have the greater balance after 10 years.

23. (a) 5%, compounded continuously

  (b) 6%, compounded quarterly

24. (a) $6\frac{1}{2}\%$, compounded monthly

  (b) $6\frac{1}{4}\%$, compounded continuously

25. **Effective Rate** Find the effective rate of interest corresponding to a nominal rate of 6% per year compounded (a) annually, (b) semiannually, (c) quarterly, and (d) monthly.

26. **Effective Rate** Find the effective rate of interest corresponding to a nominal rate of 8.25% per year compounded (a) annually, (b) semiannually, (c) quarterly, and (d) monthly.

27. Present Value How much should be deposited in an account paying 5% interest compounded quarterly in order to have a balance of $12,000 three years from now?

28. Present Value How much should be deposited in an account paying 8% interest compounded monthly in order to have a balance of $20,000 five years from now?

29. Demand The demand function for a product is modeled by

$$p = 12,500 - \frac{10,000}{2 + e^{-0.001x}}.$$

Find the price p (in dollars) of the product when the quantity demanded is (a) $x = 1000$ units and (b) $x = 2500$ units. (c) What is the limit of the price as x increases without bound?

30. Demand The demand function for a product is modeled by

$$p = 8000\left(1 - \frac{5}{5 + e^{-0.002x}}\right).$$

Find the price p (in dollars) of the product when the quantity demanded is (a) $x = 1000$ units and (b) $x = 2500$ units. (c) What is the limit of the price as x increases without bound?

31. Profit The net profits P (in millions of dollars) of Medco Health Solutions from 2000 through 2009 are shown in the table.

Year	2000	2001	2002	2003	2004
Profit	216.8	256.6	361.6	425.8	481.6

Year	2005	2006	2007	2008	2009
Profit	602.0	729.8	912.0	1102.9	1280.3

A model for this data is given by $P = 223.89e^{0.1979t}$, where t represents the year, with $t = 0$ corresponding to 2000. *(Source: Medco Health Solutions, Inc.)*

(a) How well does the model fit the data?

(b) Find a linear model for the data. How well does the linear model fit the data? Which model, exponential or linear, is a better fit?

(c) Use both models to predict the net profit in 2015.

32. Population The populations P (in thousands) of Albuquerque, New Mexico from 2000 through 2009 can be modeled by $P = 450e^{0.019t}$, where t is the time in years, with $t = 0$ corresponding to 2000. *(Source: U.S. Census Bureau)*

(a) Find the populations in 2000, 2005, and 2009.

(b) Use the model to estimate the population in 2020.

33. Biology A lake is stocked with 500 fish, and the fish population P begins to increase according to the logistic growth model

$$P = \frac{10,000}{1 + 19e^{-t/5}}, \quad t \geq 0$$

where t is measured in months.

(a) Find the number of fish in the lake after 4 months.

(b) Use a graphing utility to graph the model. Find the number of months it takes for the population of fish to reach 4000.

(c) Does the population have a limit as t increases without bound? Explain your reasoning.

34. Medicine On a college campus of 5000 students, the spread of a flu virus through the student body is modeled by

$$P = \frac{5000}{1 + 4999e^{-0.8t}}, \quad t \geq 0$$

where P is the total number of infected people and t is the time, measured in days.

(a) Find the number of students infected after 5 days.

(b) Use a graphing utility to graph the model. Find the number of days it takes for 2000 students to become infected with the flu.

(c) According to this model, will all the students on campus become infected with the flu? Explain your reasoning.

Differentiating Exponential Functions In Exercises 35–40, find the derivative of the function.

35. $y = 4e^{x^2}$

36. $y = 4e^{\sqrt{x}}$

37. $y = \dfrac{x}{e^{2x}}$

38. $y = x^2 e^x$

39. $y = \dfrac{5}{1 + e^{2x}}$

40. $y = \dfrac{10}{1 - 2e^x}$

Finding an Equation of a Tangent Line In Exercises 41–44, find an equation of the tangent line to the graph of the function at the given point.

41. $y = e^{2-x}$, $(2, 1)$

42. $y = e^{2x^2}$, $(1, e^2)$

43. $y = x^2 e^{-x}$, $\left(1, \dfrac{1}{e}\right)$

44. $y = xe^x - e^x$, $(1, 0)$

Analyzing a Graph In Exercises 45–48, analyze and sketch the graph of the function. Label any relative extrema, points of inflection, and asymptotes.

45. $f(x) = x^3 e^x$

46. $f(x) = \dfrac{e^x}{x^2}$

47. $f(x) = \dfrac{1}{xe^x}$

48. $f(x) = \dfrac{x^2}{e^x}$

Logarithmic and Exponential Forms of Equations In Exercises 49–52, write the logarithmic equation as an exponential equation, or vice versa.

49. $\ln 12 = 2.4849\ldots$ 50. $\ln 0.6 = -0.5108\ldots$

51. $e^{1.5} = 4.4816\ldots$ 52. $e^{-4} = 0.0183\ldots$

Graphing Logarithmic Expressions In Exercises 53–56, sketch the graph of the function.

53. $y = \ln(4 - x)$ 54. $y = \ln x - 3$

55. $y = \ln \dfrac{x}{3}$ 56. $y = -2 \ln x$

Expanding Logarithmic Expressions In Exercises 57–62, use the properties of logarithms to rewrite the expression as a sum, difference, or multiple of logarithms.

57. $\ln \sqrt{x^2(x - 1)}$

58. $\ln \sqrt[3]{x^2 - 1}$

59. $\ln \dfrac{x^2}{(x + 1)^3}$

60. $\ln \dfrac{x^2}{x^2 + 1}$

61. $\ln\left(\dfrac{1 - x}{3x}\right)^3$

62. $\ln\left(\dfrac{x - 1}{x + 1}\right)^2$

Condensing Logarithmic Expressions In Exercises 63–66, use the properties of logarithms to rewrite the expression as the logarithm of a single quantity.

63. $\ln(2x + 5) + \ln(x - 3)$

64. $\frac{1}{3} \ln(x^2 - 6) - 2 \ln(3x + 2)$

65. $4[\ln(x^3 - 1) + 2 \ln x - \ln(x - 5)]$

66. $\frac{1}{2}[\ln x + 3 \ln(x + 1) - \ln(x - 2)]$

Solving Exponential and Logarithmic Equations In Exercises 67–80, solve for x.

67. $e^{\ln x} = 3$ 68. $e^{\ln(x + 2)} = 5$

69. $\ln x = 3$ 70. $\ln 5x = 2$

71. $\ln 2x - \ln(3x - 1) = 0$

72. $\ln x - \ln(x + 1) = 2$

73. $\ln x + \ln(x - 3) = 0$

74. $2 \ln x + \ln(x - 2) = 0$

75. $e^{-1.386x} = 0.25$

76. $e^{-0.01x} - 5.25 = 0$

77. $e^{2x - 1} - 6 = 0$

78. $4e^{2x - 3} - 5 = 0$

79. $100(1.21)^x = 110$

80. $500(1.075)^{120x} = 100{,}000$

81. **Compound Interest** A deposit of \$400 is made in an account that earns interest at an annual rate of 2.5%. How long will it take for the balance to double when the interest is compounded (a) annually, (b) monthly, (c) daily, and (d) continuously?

82. **Hourly Earnings** The average hourly wages w (in dollars) for private industry employees in the United States from 1990 through 2009 can be modeled by

$$w = 10.2e^{0.0315t}$$

where $t = 0$ corresponds to 1990. *(Source: U.S. Bureau of Labor Statistics)*

   (a) What was the average hourly wage in 2000?

   (b) In what year will the average hourly wage be \$23?

83. **Learning Theory** Students in a psychology experiment were given an exam and then retested monthly with equivalent exams. The average scores S (on a 100-point scale) for the students can be modeled by

$$S = 75 - 6 \ln(t + 1), \quad 0 \le t \le 12$$

where t is the time in months.

   (a) What was the average score on the original exam?

   (b) What was the average score after 4 months?

   (c) After how many months was the average score 60?

84. **Demand** The demand function for a product is given by

$$p = 8000\left(1 - \dfrac{5}{5 + e^{-0.002x}}\right)$$

where p is the price per unit (in dollars) and x is the number of units sold. Find the numbers of units sold for prices of (a) $p = \$200$ and (b) $p = \$800$.

Differentiating a Logarithmic Function In Exercises 85–98, find the derivative of the function.

85. $f(x) = \ln 3x^2$ 86. $y = \ln \sqrt{x}$

87. $y = \ln \dfrac{x(x - 1)}{x - 2}$ 88. $y = \ln \dfrac{x^2}{x + 1}$

89. $f(x) = \ln e^{2x + 1}$ 90. $f(x) = \ln e^{x^2}$

91. $y = \dfrac{\ln x}{x^3}$ 92. $y = \dfrac{x^2}{\ln x}$

93. $y = \ln(x^2 - 2)^{2/3}$

94. $y = \ln \sqrt[3]{x^3 + 1}$

95. $f(x) = \ln\left(x^2 \sqrt{x + 1}\right)$

96. $f(x) = \ln \dfrac{x}{\sqrt{x + 1}}$

97. $y = \ln \dfrac{e^x}{1 + e^x}$

98. $y = \ln\left(e^{2x} \sqrt{e^{2x} - 1}\right)$

Evaluating Logarithms   In Exercises 99–102, evaluate the logarithm without using a calculator.

99. $\log_6 36$

100. $\log_2 32$

101. $\log_{10} 1$

102. $\log_4 \frac{1}{64}$

Changing Bases to Evaluate Logarithms   In Exercises 103–106, use the change-of-base formula and a calculator to evaluate the logarithm.

103. $\log_5 13$

104. $\log_4 18$

105. $\log_{16} 64$

106. $\log_4 125$

Differentiating Functions of Other Bases   In Exercises 107–112, find the derivative of the function.

107. $y = 5^{2x+1}$

108. $y = 8^{x^3}$

109. $y = \log_3(2x - 1)$

110. $y = \log_{16}(x^2 - 3x)$

111. $y = \log_{10} \dfrac{3}{x}$

112. $y = \log_2 \dfrac{1}{x^2}$

Analyzing a Graph   In Exercises 113–116, analyze and sketch the graph of the function. Label any relative extrema, points of inflection, and asymptotes.

113. $y = \ln(x + 3)$

114. $y = \dfrac{8 \ln x}{x^2}$

115. $y = \ln \dfrac{10}{x + 2}$

116. $y = \ln \dfrac{x^2}{9 - x^2}$

117. **Music**   The numbers of download music singles D (in millions) from 2004 through 2009 can be modeled by

$$D = -1671.88 + 1282 \ln t$$

where $t = 4$ corresponds to 2004. Find the rates of change of the number of download music singles in 2005 and 2008. *(Source: Recording Industry Association of America)*

118. **Minimum Average Cost**   The cost of producing x units of a product is modeled by

$$C = 200 + 75x - 300 \ln x, \quad x \geq 1.$$

(a) Find the average cost function $\overline{C}$.

(b) Find the minimum average cost analytically. Use a graphing utility to confirm your result.

Modeling Exponential Growth and Decay   In Exercises 119 and 120, find the exponential function

$$y = Ce^{kt}$$

that passes through the two given points.

119. $(0, 3), (4, 1)$

120. $(1, 1), (5, 5)$

Modeling Radioactive Decay   In Exercises 121–126, complete the table for each radioactive isotope.

	Isotope	Half-life (in years)	Initial quantity	Amount after 1000 years	Amount after 10,000 years
121.	^{226}Ra	1599	8 grams		
122.	^{226}Ra	1599		0.7 gram	
123.	^{14}C	5715			6 grams
124.	^{14}C	5715	5 grams		
125.	^{239}Pu	24,100		2.4 grams	
126.	^{239}Pu	24,100			7.1 grams

Modeling Compound Interest   In Exercises 127–130, complete the table for an account in which interest is compounded continuously.

	Initial investment	Annual rate	Time to double	Amount after 10 years	Amount after 25 years
127.	$600	8%			
128.	$2000		7 years		
129.	$15,000			$18,321.04	
130.		4%			$11,934.60

131. **Medical Science**   Soon after an injection, the concentration D (in milligrams per milliliter) of a drug in a patient's bloodstream is 500 milligrams per milliliter. After 6 hours, 50 milligrams per milliliter of the drug remains in the bloodstream.

(a) Find an exponential model for the concentration D after t hours.

(b) What is the concentration of the drug after 4 hours?

132. **Population Growth**   The number of a certain type of bacteria increases continuously at a rate proportional to the number present. After 2 hours, there are 200 bacteria, and after 4 hours, there are 300 bacteria.

(a) Find an exponential model given the population P after t hours.

(b) How many bacteria will there be after 7 hours?

(c) How long will it take for the population to double?

TEST YOURSELF

See www.CalcChat.com for worked-out solutions to odd-numbered exercises.

Take this test as you would take a test in class. When you are done, check your work against the answers given in the back of the book.

In Exercises 1–4, use the properties of exponents to simplify the expression.

1. $3^2(3^{-2})$

2. $\left(\dfrac{2^3}{2^{-5}}\right)^{-1}$

3. $(e^{1/2})(e^4)$

4. $(e^3)^4$

In Exercises 5–10, sketch the graph of the function.

5. $f(x) = 5^{x-2}$

6. $f(x) = 4^{-x}$

7. $f(x) = e^{x-3}$

8. $f(x) = 8 + \ln x^2$

9. $f(x) = \ln(x - 5)$

10. $f(x) = 0.5 \ln x$

In Exercises 11–13, use the properties of logarithms to rewrite the expression as a sum, difference, or multiple of logarithms.

11. $\ln \dfrac{3}{2}$

12. $\ln \sqrt{x + y}$

13. $\ln \dfrac{x + 1}{y}$

In Exercises 14–16, use the properties of logarithms to rewrite the expression as the logarithm of a single quantity.

14. $\ln y + \ln(x + 1)$

15. $3 \ln x - 2 \ln(x - 1)$

16. $\ln x + 4 \ln y - \frac{1}{2} \ln(z + 4)$

In Exercises 17–19, solve the equation.

17. $e^{x-1} = 9$

18. $10e^{2x+1} = 900$

19. $50(1.06)^x = 1500$

20. A deposit of \$500 is made in an account that earns interest at an annual rate of 4%. How long will it take for the balance to double when the interest is compounded (a) annually, (b) monthly, (c) daily, and (d) continuously?

In Exercises 21–24, find the derivative of the function.

21. $y = e^{-3x} + 5$

22. $y = 7e^{x+2} + 2x$

23. $y = \ln(3 + x^2)$

24. $y = \ln \dfrac{5x}{x + 2}$

25. The revenues R (in millions of dollars) of skiing facilities in the United States from 2000 through 2008 can be modeled by

$$R = 1548e^{0.0617t}$$

where $t = 0$ corresponds to 2000. *(Source: U.S. Census Bureau)*

(a) Use this model to estimate the revenues in 2006.

(b) At what rate were the revenues changing in 2006?

26. What percent of a present amount of radioactive radium (^{226}Ra) will remain after 1200 years? (The half-life of ^{226}Ra is 1599 years.)

27. A population is growing continuously at the rate of 1.75% per year. Find the time necessary for the population to double in size.

5 Integration and Its Applications

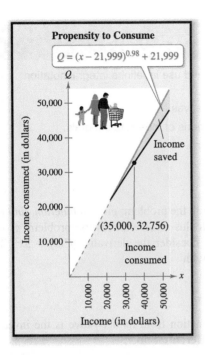

Propensity to Consume

$$Q = (x - 21,999)^{0.98} + 21,999$$

Income saved

(35,000, 32,756)

Income consumed

Income consumed (in dollars)

Income (in dollars)

Example 8 on page 328 shows how integration can be used to analyze the marginal propensity to consume.

5.1 Antiderivatives and Indefinite Integrals

■ Understand the definition of antiderivative and use indefinite integral notation for antiderivatives.
■ Use basic integration rules to find antiderivatives.
■ Use initial conditions to find particular solutions of indefinite integrals.
■ Use antiderivatives to solve real-life problems.

Antiderivatives

In Chapter 2, you were concerned primarily with the problem: *given a function, find its derivative.* Some important applications of calculus involve the inverse problem: *given a derivative, find the function.* For instance, consider the derivative $f'(x) = 3x^2$. To determine the function f, you might come up with

$$f(x) = x^3 \quad \text{because} \quad \frac{d}{dx}[x^3] = 3x^2.$$

This operation of determining the original function from its derivative is the inverse operation of differentiation. It is called **antidifferentiation.**

Horry County, South Carolina

In Exercise 69 on page 321, you will use integration to find a model for the population of a county.

Definition of Antiderivative

A function F is an **antiderivative** of a function f when for every x in the domain of f, it follows that $F'(x) = f(x)$.

If $F(x)$ is an antiderivative of $f(x)$, then $F(x) + C$, where C is any constant, is also an antiderivative of $f(x)$. For example,

$$F(x) = x^3, \quad G(x) = x^3 - 5, \quad \text{and} \quad H(x) = x^3 + 0.3$$

are all antiderivatives of $3x^2$ because the derivative of each is $3x^2$. As it turns out, *all* antiderivatives of $3x^2$ are of the form $x^3 + C$. So, the process of antidifferentiation does not determine a single function, but rather a *family* of functions, each differing from the others by a constant.

The antidifferentiation process is also called **integration** and is denoted by

$$\int \qquad \text{Integral sign}$$

which is called an **integral sign.** The symbol

$$\int f(x)\, dx \qquad \text{Indefinite integral}$$

is the **indefinite integral** of $f(x)$, and it denotes the family of antiderivatives of $f(x)$. That is, if $F'(x) = f(x)$ for all x, then you can write

where $f(x)$ is the **integrand** and C is the **constant of integration.** The differential dx in the indefinite integral identifies the variable of integration. That is, the symbol $\int f(x)\, dx$ denotes the "antiderivative of f with respect to x" just as the symbol dy/dx denotes the "derivative of y with respect to x."

STUDY TIP

In this text, the phrase "$F(x)$ is an antiderivative of $f(x)$" is used synonymously with "F is an antiderivative of f."

Finding Antiderivatives

The inverse relationship between the operations of integration and differentiation can be shown symbolically, as follows.

$$\frac{d}{dx}\left[\int f(x)\, dx\right] = f(x)$$ Differentiation is the inverse of integration.

$$\int f'(x)\, dx = f(x) + C$$ Integration is the inverse of differentiation.

This inverse relationship between integration and differentiation allows you to obtain integration formulas directly from differentiation formulas. The following summary lists the integration formulas that correspond to some of the differentiation formulas you have studied.

Basic Integration Rules

1. $\int k\, dx = kx + C,\quad k$ is a constant.   Constant Rule

2. $\int kf(x)\, dx = k\int f(x)\, dx$ Constant Multiple Rule

3. $\int [f(x) + g(x)]\, dx = \int f(x)\, dx + \int g(x)\, dx$ Sum Rule

4. $\int [f(x) - g(x)]\, dx = \int f(x)\, dx - \int g(x)\, dx$ Difference Rule

5. $\int x^n\, dx = \dfrac{x^{n+1}}{n+1} + C,\quad n \neq -1$ Simple Power Rule

Be sure you see that the Simple Power Rule has the restriction that n cannot be -1. So, you *cannot* use the Simple Power Rule to evaluate the integral

$$\int \frac{1}{x}\, dx.$$

To evaluate this integral, you need the Log Rule, which is described in Section 5.3.

Example 1   Finding Indefinite Integrals

Find each indefinite integral.

a. $\int \dfrac{1}{2}\, dx$ **b.** $\int 1\, dx$ **c.** $\int -5\, dt$

SOLUTION

a. $\int \dfrac{1}{2}\, dx = \dfrac{1}{2}x + C$ **b.** $\int 1\, dx = x + C$ **c.** $\int -5\, dt = -5t + C$

✓ **Checkpoint 1**

Find each indefinite integral.

a. $\int 5\, dx$ **b.** $\int -1\, dr$ **c.** $\int 2\, dt$

Example 2   Finding an Indefinite Integral

$$\int 3x\,dx = 3\int x\,dx \qquad \text{Constant Multiple Rule}$$

$$= 3\int x^1\,dx \qquad \text{Rewrite } x \text{ as } x^1.$$

$$= 3\left(\frac{x^2}{2}\right) + C \qquad \text{Simple Power Rule with } n = 1$$

$$= \frac{3}{2}x^2 + C \qquad \text{Simplify.}$$

✓ Checkpoint 2

Find $\displaystyle\int 5x\,dx$.

In finding indefinite integrals, a strict application of the basic integration rules tends to produce cumbersome constants of integration. For instance, in Example 2, you could have written

$$\int 3x\,dx = 3\int x\,dx = 3\left(\frac{x^2}{2} + C\right) = \frac{3}{2}x^2 + 3C.$$

However, because C represents *any* constant, it is unnecessary to write $3C$ as the constant of integration. You can simply write $\frac{3}{2}x^2 + C$.

In Example 2, note that the general pattern of integration is similar to that of differentiation.

Original Integral: $\displaystyle\int 3x\,dx$	⇒	Rewrite: $3\displaystyle\int x^1\,dx$	⇒	Integrate: $3\left(\dfrac{x^2}{2}\right) + C$	⇒	Simplify: $\dfrac{3}{2}x^2 + C$

Example 3   Rewriting Before Integrating

	Original Integral	Rewrite	Integrate	Simplify
a.	$\displaystyle\int \frac{1}{x^3}\,dx$	$\displaystyle\int x^{-3}\,dx$	$\dfrac{x^{-2}}{-2} + C$	$-\dfrac{1}{2x^2} + C$
b.	$\displaystyle\int \sqrt{x}\,dx$	$\displaystyle\int x^{1/2}\,dx$	$\dfrac{x^{3/2}}{3/2} + C$	$\dfrac{2}{3}x^{3/2} + C$

✓ Checkpoint 3

Find each indefinite integral.

a. $\displaystyle\int \frac{1}{x^2}\,dx$ **b.** $\displaystyle\int \sqrt[3]{x}\,dx$

Remember that you can check your answer to an antidifferentiation problem by differentiating. For instance, in Example 3(b), you can confirm that $\frac{2}{3}x^{3/2} + C$ is the correct antiderivative by differentiating to obtain

$$\frac{d}{dx}\left[\frac{2}{3}x^{3/2} + C\right] = \left(\frac{2}{3}\right)\left(\frac{3}{2}\right)x^{1/2} = \sqrt{x}.$$

With the five basic integration rules, you can integrate *any* polynomial function, as demonstrated in the next example.

Example 4 Integrating Polynomial Functions

Find (a) $\int (x + 2)\, dx$ and (b) $\int (3x^4 - 5x^2 + x)\, dx$.

SOLUTION

a. $\int (x + 2)\, dx = \int x\, dx + \int 2\, dx$ Apply Sum Rule.

$$= \frac{x^2}{2} + C_1 + 2x + C_2 \qquad \text{Apply Simple Power and Constant Rules.}$$

$$= \frac{x^2}{2} + 2x + C \qquad\qquad C = C_1 + C_2$$

The second line in this solution is usually omitted.

b. $\int (3x^4 - 5x^2 + x)\, dx = 3\left(\frac{x^5}{5}\right) - 5\left(\frac{x^3}{3}\right) + \frac{x^2}{2} + C$

$$= \frac{3}{5}x^5 - \frac{5}{3}x^3 + \frac{1}{2}x^2 + C$$

✓ **Checkpoint 4**

Find (a) $\int (x + 4)\, dx$ and (b) $\int (4x^3 - 5x + 2)\, dx$.

STUDY TIP

When integrating quotients, remember *not* to integrate the numerator and denominator separately. For instance, in Example 5, be sure you understand that

$$\int \frac{x - 1}{\sqrt{x}}\, dx = \frac{2}{3}\sqrt{x}(x - 3) + C$$

is not the same as

$$\frac{\int (x - 1)\, dx}{\int \sqrt{x}\, dx} = \frac{\frac{1}{2}x^2 - x + C_1}{\frac{2}{3}x\sqrt{x} + C_2}.$$

ALGEBRA TUTOR *xy*

For help on the algebra in Example 5, see Example 1(a) in the *Chapter 5 Algebra Tutor,* on page 366.

Example 5 Rewriting Before Integrating

Find $\int \frac{x - 1}{\sqrt{x}}\, dx$.

SOLUTION Begin by rewriting the quotient in the integrand as a difference. Then rewrite each term using rational exponents.

$$\int \frac{x - 1}{\sqrt{x}}\, dx = \int \left(\frac{x}{\sqrt{x}} - \frac{1}{\sqrt{x}}\right) dx \qquad \text{Rewrite as a difference.}$$

$$= \int (x^{1/2} - x^{-1/2})\, dx \qquad \text{Rewrite using rational exponents.}$$

$$= \int x^{1/2}\, dx - \int x^{-1/2}\, dx \qquad \text{Apply Difference Rule.}$$

$$= \frac{x^{3/2}}{3/2} - \frac{x^{1/2}}{1/2} + C \qquad \text{Apply Simple Power Rule.}$$

$$= \frac{2}{3}x^{3/2} - 2x^{1/2} + C \qquad \text{Simplify.}$$

$$= \frac{2}{3}\sqrt{x}(x - 3) + C \qquad \text{Factor.}$$

✓ **Checkpoint 5**

Find $\int \frac{x + 2}{\sqrt{x}}\, dx$.

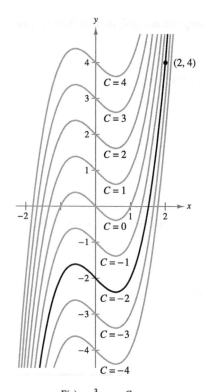

$F(x) = x^3 - x + C$

FIGURE 5.1

Particular Solutions

You have already seen that the equation $y = \int f(x)\, dx$ has many solutions, each differing from the others by a constant. This means that the graphs of any two antiderivatives of f are vertical translations of each other. For example, Figure 5.1 shows the graphs of several antiderivatives of the form

$$y = F(x) = \int (3x^2 - 1)\, dx = x^3 - x + C$$

for various integer values of C. Each of these antiderivatives is a solution of the *differential equation*

$$\frac{dy}{dx} = 3x^2 - 1.$$

A **differential equation** in x and y is an equation that involves x, y, and derivatives of y. The **general solution** of $dy/dx = 3x^2 - 1$ is $F(x) = x^3 - x + C$.

In many applications of integration, you are given enough information to determine a **particular solution.** To do this, you need to know the value of $F(x)$ for only one value of x. (This information is called an **initial condition.**) For example, in Figure 5.1, there is only one curve that passes through the point $(2, 4)$. To find this curve, use the information below.

$$F(x) = x^3 - x + C \qquad \text{General solution}$$
$$F(2) = 4 \qquad \text{Initial condition}$$

By using the initial condition in the general solution, you can determine that $F(2) = 2^3 - 2 + C = 4$, which implies that $C = -2$. So, the particular solution is

$$F(x) = x^3 - x - 2. \qquad \text{Particular solution}$$

Example 6   Finding a Particular Solution

Find the general solution of

$$F'(x) = 2x - 2$$

and find the particular solution that satisfies the initial condition $F(1) = 2$.

SOLUTION   Begin by integrating to find the general solution.

$$F(x) = \int (2x - 2)\, dx \qquad \text{Integrate } F'(x) \text{ to obtain } F(x).$$

$$= x^2 - 2x + C \qquad \text{General solution}$$

Using the initial condition $F(1) = 2$, you can write

$$F(1) = 1^2 - 2(1) + C = 2$$

which implies that $C = 3$. So, the particular solution is

$$F(x) = x^2 - 2x + 3. \qquad \text{Particular solution}$$

This solution is shown graphically in Figure 5.2. Note that each of the gray curves represents a solution of the equation $F'(x) = 2x - 2$. The black curve, however, is the only solution that passes through the point $(1, 2)$, which means that $F(x) = x^2 - 2x + 3$ is the only solution that satisfies the initial condition.

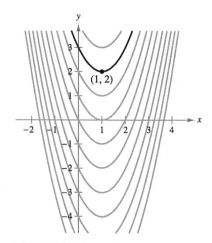

FIGURE 5.2

✓ Checkpoint 6

Find the general solution of $F'(x) = 4x + 2$, and find the particular solution that satisfies the initial condition $F(1) = 8$.

Applications

In Chapter 2, you used the general position function (neglecting air resistance) for a falling object

$$s(t) = -16t^2 + v_0 t + s_0$$

where $s(t)$ is the height (in feet) and t is the time (in seconds). In the next example, integration is used to *derive* this function.

Example 7   Deriving a Position Function

A ball is thrown upward with an initial velocity of 64 feet per second from an initial height of 80 feet, as shown in Figure 5.3. Derive the position function giving the height s (in feet) as a function of the time t (in seconds). Will the ball be in the air for more than 5 seconds?

SOLUTION   Let $t = 0$ represent the initial time. Then the two given conditions can be written as

$$s(0) = 80 \qquad \text{Initial height is 80 feet.}$$
$$s'(0) = 64. \qquad \text{Initial velocity is 64 feet per second.}$$

Because the acceleration due to gravity is -32 feet per second per second, you can integrate the acceleration function to find the velocity function, as shown.

$$s''(t) = -32 \qquad \text{Acceleration due to gravity}$$
$$s'(t) = \int -32 \, dt \qquad \text{Integrate } s''(t) \text{ to obtain } s'(t).$$
$$= -32t + C_1 \qquad \text{Velocity function}$$

Using the initial velocity, you can conclude that $C_1 = 64$. Next, integrate the velocity function to find the position function.

$$s'(t) = -32t + 64 \qquad \text{Velocity function}$$
$$s(t) = \int (-32t + 64) \, dt \qquad \text{Integrate } s'(t) \text{ to obtain } s(t).$$
$$= -16t^2 + 64t + C_2 \qquad \text{Position function}$$

Using the initial height, it follows that $C_2 = 80$. So, the position function is given by

$$s(t) = -16t^2 + 64t + 80. \qquad \text{Position function}$$

To find the time when the ball hits the ground, set the position function equal to 0 and solve for t.

$$-16t^2 + 64t + 80 = 0 \qquad \text{Set } s(t) \text{ equal to zero.}$$
$$-16(t + 1)(t - 5) = 0 \qquad \text{Factor.}$$
$$t = -1, \quad t = 5 \qquad \text{Solve for } t.$$

Because the time must be positive, you can conclude that the ball hits the ground 5 seconds after it is thrown. So, the ball is not in the air for more than 5 seconds.

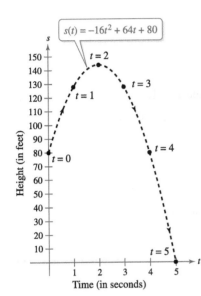

$s(t) = -16t^2 + 64t + 80$

FIGURE 5.3

✓ Checkpoint 7

Derive the position function when a ball is thrown upward with an initial velocity of 32 feet per second from an initial height of 48 feet. When does the ball hit the ground? With what velocity does the ball hit the ground?

Example 8 **Finding a Cost Function**

The marginal cost of producing x units of a product is modeled by

$$\frac{dC}{dx} = 32 - 0.04x.$$ Marginal cost

It costs $50 to produce one unit. Find the total cost of producing 200 units.

SOLUTION   To find the cost function, integrate the marginal cost function.

$$C = \int (32 - 0.04x)\, dx$$ Integrate $\frac{dC}{dx}$ to obtain C.

$$= 32x - 0.04\left(\frac{x^2}{2}\right) + K$$

$$= 32x - 0.02x^2 + K$$ Cost function

To solve for K, use the initial condition $C = 50$ when $x = 1$.

$$50 = 32(1) - 0.02(1)^2 + K$$ Substitute 50 for C and 1 for x.

$$18.02 = K$$ Solve for K.

So, the total cost function is given by

$$C = 32x - 0.02x^2 + 18.02$$ Cost function

which implies that the cost of producing 200 units is

$$C = 32(200) - 0.02(200)^2 + 18.02$$

$$= \$5618.02.$$

✓ Checkpoint 8

The marginal cost function for producing x units of a product is modeled by

$$\frac{dC}{dx} = 28 - 0.02x.$$

It costs $40 to produce one unit. Find the total cost of producing 200 units.

STUDY TIP

In Example 8, note that K is used to represent the constant of integration rather than C. This is done to avoid confusion between the constant C and the cost function

$$C = 32x - 0.02x^2 + 18.02.$$

SUMMARIZE   (Section 5.1)

1. State the definition of antiderivative *(page 312)*. For examples of antiderivatives, see Examples 1, 2, 3, 4, and 5.

2. State the Constant Rule *(page 313)*. For an example of the Constant Rule, see Example 1.

3. State the Constant Multiple Rule *(page 313)*. For an example of the Constant Multiple Rule, see Example 2.

4. State the Sum Rule *(page 313)*. For an example of the Sum Rule, see Example 4.

5. State the Difference Rule *(page 313)*. For an example of the Difference Rule, see Example 5.

6. State the Simple Power Rule *(page 313)*. For examples of the Simple Power Rule, see Examples 2, 3, 4, and 5.

7. Describe a real-life example of how antidifferentiation can be used to find a cost function *(page 318, Example 8)*.

The following warm-up exercises involve skills that were covered in a previous course or in earlier sections. You will use these skills in the exercise set for this section. For additional help, review Appendix Section A.3 and Section 1.2.

In Exercises 1–6, rewrite the expression using rational exponents.

1. $\dfrac{\sqrt{x}}{x}$

2. $\sqrt[3]{2x}(2x)$

3. $\sqrt{5x^3} + \sqrt{x^5}$

4. $\dfrac{1}{\sqrt{x}} + \dfrac{1}{\sqrt[3]{x^2}}$

5. $\dfrac{(x+1)^3}{\sqrt{x+1}}$

6. $\dfrac{\sqrt{x}}{\sqrt[3]{x}}$

In Exercises 7–10, let $(x, y) = (2, 2)$, and solve the equation for C.

7. $y = x^2 + 5x + C$

8. $y = 3x^3 - 6x + C$

9. $y = -16x^2 + 26x + C$

10. $y = -\frac{1}{4}x^4 - 2x^2 + C$

Exercises 5.1

Integration and Differentiation In Exercises 1–6, verify the statement by showing that the derivative of the right side is equal to the integrand on the left side.

1. $\displaystyle\int 4x\,dx = 2x^2 + C$

2. $\displaystyle\int 4x^3\,dx = x^4 + C$

3. $\displaystyle\int \left(-\frac{9}{x^4}\right) dx = \frac{3}{x^3} + C$

4. $\displaystyle\int \frac{4}{\sqrt{x}}\,dx = 8\sqrt{x} + C$

5. $\displaystyle\int \left(4x^3 - \frac{1}{x^2}\right) dx = x^4 + \frac{1}{x} + C$

6. $\displaystyle\int \left(1 - \frac{1}{\sqrt[3]{x^2}}\right) dx = x - 3\sqrt[3]{x} + C$

Finding Indefinite Integrals In Exercises 7–18, find the indefinite integral. Check your result by differentiating. See Examples 1 and 2.

7. $\displaystyle\int du$

8. $\displaystyle\int dr$

9. $\displaystyle\int 6\,dx$

10. $\displaystyle\int -4\,dx$

11. $\displaystyle\int 7x\,dx$

12. $\displaystyle\int 2x\,dx$

13. $\displaystyle\int 5t^2\,dt$

14. $\displaystyle\int 3t^4\,dt$

15. $\displaystyle\int 5x^{-3}\,dx$

16. $\displaystyle\int 4y^{-2}\,dy$

17. $\displaystyle\int y^{3/2}\,dy$

18. $\displaystyle\int v^{-1/2}\,dv$

Rewriting Before Integrating In Exercises 19–24, find the indefinite integral. See Example 3.

Original Integral	Rewrite	Integrate	Simplify
19. $\displaystyle\int \sqrt[3]{x^2}\,dx$			
20. $\displaystyle\int \frac{1}{x^4}\,dx$			
21. $\displaystyle\int \frac{1}{x\sqrt{x}}\,dx$			
22. $\displaystyle\int x(x^2+3)\,dx$			
23. $\displaystyle\int \frac{1}{2x^3}\,dx$			
24. $\displaystyle\int \frac{1}{(3x)^2}\,dx$			

Finding Indefinite Integrals In Exercises 25–36, find the indefinite integral. Check your result by differentiating. See Examples 4 and 5.

25. $\displaystyle\int (x+3)\,dx$

26. $\displaystyle\int (5-x)\,dx$

27. $\displaystyle\int (x^3+2)\,dx$

28. $\displaystyle\int (x^2-7)\,dx$

29. $\displaystyle\int (3x^3 - 6x^2 + 2)\,dx$

30. $\displaystyle\int (x^3 - 4x + 2)\,dx$

31. $\displaystyle\int (x^2 + 5x + 1)\,dx$

32. $\displaystyle\int (2x^4 - x^2 + 3)\,dx$

33. $\displaystyle\int \frac{2x^3 - 1}{x^3}\, dx$

34. $\displaystyle\int \frac{t^2 + 2}{t^2}\, dt$

35. $\displaystyle\int \frac{5x + 4}{\sqrt[3]{x}}\, dx$

36. $\displaystyle\int \frac{2x - 1}{\sqrt{x}}\, dx$

Interpreting a Graph   In Exercises 37–40, the graph of the derivative of a function is given. Sketch the graphs of *two* functions that have the given derivative. (There is more than one correct answer.)

37.

38.

39.

40.

Finding Particular Solutions   In Exercises 41–48, find the particular solution that satisfies the differential equation and the initial condition. *See Example 6.*

41. $f'(x) = 4x$; $f(0) = 6$

42. $f'(x) = 9x^2$; $f(0) = -1$

43. $f'(x) = 2x + 4$; $f(-2) = 3$

44. $f'(x) = \frac{1}{5}x - 2$; $f(10) = -10$

45. $f'(x) = 10x - 12x^3$; $f(3) = 2$

46. $f'(x) = 2\sqrt{x}$; $f(4) = 12$

47. $f'(x) = \dfrac{2 - x}{x^3}$, $x > 0$; $f(2) = \dfrac{3}{4}$

48. $f'(x) = \dfrac{x^2 - 5}{x^2}$, $x > 0$; $f(1) = 2$

Finding Particular Solutions   In Exercises 49–52, find a function f that satisfies the initial conditions.

49. $f''(x) = 2$, $f'(2) = 5$, $f(2) = 10$

50. $f''(x) = x^2$, $f'(0) = 6$, $f(0) = 3$

51. $f''(x) = x^{-2/3}$, $f'(8) = 6$, $f(0) = 0$

52. $f''(x) = x^{-3/2}$, $f'(1) = 2$, $f(9) = -4$

Finding a Cost Function   In Exercises 53–56, find the cost function for the given marginal cost and fixed cost. *See Example 8.*

	Marginal Cost	Fixed Cost ($x = 0$)
53.	$\dfrac{dC}{dx} = 85$	\$5500
54.	$\dfrac{dC}{dx} = \dfrac{1}{50}x + 10$	\$1000
55.	$\dfrac{dC}{dx} = \dfrac{1}{20\sqrt{x}} + 4$	\$750
56.	$\dfrac{dC}{dx} = \dfrac{\sqrt[4]{x}}{10} + 10$	\$2300

Revenue and Demand   In Exercises 57 and 58, find the revenue and demand functions for the given marginal revenue. (Use the fact that $R = 0$ when $x = 0$.)

57. $\dfrac{dR}{dx} = 225 - 3x$ **58.** $\dfrac{dR}{dx} = 310 - 4x$

Profit   In Exercises 59–62, find the profit function for the given marginal profit and initial condition.

	Marginal Profit	Initial Condition
59.	$\dfrac{dP}{dx} = -18x + 1650$	$P(15) = \$22{,}725$
60.	$\dfrac{dP}{dx} = -40x + 250$	$P(5) = \$650$
61.	$\dfrac{dP}{dx} = -24x + 805$	$P(12) = \$8000$
62.	$\dfrac{dP}{dx} = -30x + 920$	$P(8) = \$6500$

Vertical Motion   In Exercises 63–66, use $s''(t) = -32$ feet per second per second as the acceleration due to gravity. *See Example 7.*

63. The Grand Canyon is 6000 feet deep at the deepest part. A rock is dropped from this height. Express the height s (in feet) of the rock as a function of the time t (in seconds). How long will it take the rock to hit the canyon floor?

64. A ball is thrown upward with an initial velocity of 60 feet per second from an initial height of 16 feet. Express the height s (in feet) of the ball as a function of the time t (in seconds). How long will the ball be in the air?

65. With what initial velocity must an object be thrown upward from the ground to reach the height of the Washington Monument (550 feet)?

66. With what initial velocity must an object be thrown upward from a height of 5 feet to reach a maximum height of 230 feet?

67. Cost   A company produces a product for which the marginal cost of producing x units is modeled by $dC/dx = 2x - 12$, and the fixed costs are $125.

(a) Find the total cost function and the average cost function.

(b) Find the total cost of producing 50 units.

(c) In part (b), how much of the total cost is fixed? How much is variable? Give examples of fixed costs associated with the manufacture of a product. Give examples of variable costs.

68. Tree Growth   An evergreen nursery usually sells a certain shrub after 6 years of growth and shaping. The growth rate during those 6 years is approximated by $dh/dt = 1.5t + 5$, where t is the time (in years) and h is the height (in centimeters). The seedlings are 12 centimeters tall when planted ($t = 0$).

(a) Find the height function.

(b) How tall are the shrubs when they are sold?

69. Population Growth   The growth rate of the population of Horry County in South Carolina from 1970 through 2009 can be modeled by

$$\frac{dP}{dt} = 158.80t + 1758.6$$

where t is the time in years, with $t = 0$ corresponding to 1970. The county's population was 263,868 in 2009. (Source: U.S. Census Bureau)

(a) Find the model for Horry County's population.

(b) Use the model to predict the population in 2015. Does your answer seem reasonable? Explain your reasoning.

70.   HOW DO YOU SEE IT?   The graph shows the rate of change of the revenue of a company from 1990 through 2010.

Year (0 ↔ 1990)

(a) Approximate the rate of change of the revenue in 1993. Explain your reasoning.

(b) Approximate the year when the revenue is maximum. Explain your reasoning.

71. Vital Statistics   The rate of increase of the number of married couples M (in thousands) in the United States from 1980 through 2009 can be modeled by

$$\frac{dM}{dt} = -0.105t^2 + 14.02t + 217.8$$

where t is the time in years, with $t = 0$ corresponding to 1980. The number of married couples in 2009 was 60,844 thousand. (Source: U.S. Census Bureau)

(a) Find the model for the number of married couples in the United States.

(b) Use the model to predict the number of married couples in the United States in 2015. Does your answer seem reasonable? Explain your reasoning.

72. Internet Users   The rate of growth of the number of Internet users I (in millions) in the world from 1991 through 2009 can be modeled by

$$\frac{dI}{dt} = 0.0556t^3 - 1.557t^2 + 25.70t - 59.2$$

where t is the time in years, with $t = 1$ corresponding to 1991. The number of Internet users in 2009 was 1833 million. (Source: International Telecommunication Union)

(a) Find the model for the number of Internet users in the world.

(b) Use the model to predict the number of Internet users in the world in 2015. Does your answer seem reasonable? Explain your reasoning.

73. Economics: Marginal Benefits and Costs   The table gives the marginal benefit and marginal cost of producing x units of a product for a given company. (a) Plot the points in each column and use the *regression* feature of a graphing utility to find a linear model for marginal benefit and a quadratic model for marginal cost. (b) Use integration to find the benefit B and cost C equations. Assume $B(0) = 0$ and $C(0) = 425$. (c) Find the intervals in which the benefit exceeds the cost of producing x units. Make a recommendation for how many units the company should produce based on your findings. (Source: Adapted from Taylor, Economics, Fifth Edition)

Number of units	1	2	3	4	5
Marginal benefit	330	320	290	270	250
Marginal cost	150	120	100	110	120

Number of units	6	7	8	9	10
Marginal benefit	230	210	190	170	160
Marginal cost	140	160	190	250	320

5.2 Integration by Substitution and the General Power Rule

In Exercise 49 on page 330, you will use integration to find a model for the cost of producing a product.

Andresr/2010/Used under license from Shutterstock.com

■ Use the General Power Rule to find indefinite integrals.
■ Use substitution to find indefinite integrals.
■ Use the General Power Rule to solve real-life problems.

The General Power Rule

In Section 5.1, you used the Simple Power Rule

$$\int x^n \, dx = \frac{x^{n+1}}{n+1} + C, \quad n \neq -1$$

to find antiderivatives of functions expressed as powers of x alone. In this section, you will study a technique for finding antiderivatives of more complicated functions.

To begin, consider how you might find the antiderivative of

$$2x(x^2 + 1)^3.$$

Because you are hunting for a function whose derivative is $2x(x^2 + 1)^3$, you might discover the antiderivative as shown.

$$\frac{d}{dx}[(x^2 + 1)^4] = 4(x^2 + 1)^3(2x)$$ Use Chain Rule.

$$\frac{d}{dx}\left[\frac{(x^2 + 1)^4}{4}\right] = (x^2 + 1)^3(2x)$$ Divide both sides by 4.

$$\frac{(x^2 + 1)^4}{4} + C = \int 2x(x^2 + 1)^3 \, dx$$ Write in integral form.

The key to this solution is the presence of the factor $2x$ in the integrand. In other words, this solution works because $2x$ is precisely the derivative of $(x^2 + 1)$. Letting $u = x^2 + 1$, you can write

$$\int \overbrace{(x^2 + 1)^3}^{u^3} \underbrace{2x \, dx}_{du} = \int u^3 \, du$$

$$= \frac{u^4}{4} + C.$$

This is an example of the **General Power Rule** for integration.

General Power Rule for Integration

If u is a differentiable function of x, then

$$\int u^n \frac{du}{dx} \, dx = \int u^n \, du$$

$$= \frac{u^{n+1}}{n+1} + C, \quad n \neq -1.$$

When using the General Power Rule, you must first identify a factor u of the integrand that is raised to a power. Then, you must show that its derivative du/dx is also a factor of the integrand. This is demonstrated in Example 1.

Example 1   **Applying the General Power Rule**

Find each indefinite integral.

a. $\int 3(3x - 1)^4 \, dx$ b. $\int (2x + 1)(x^2 + x) \, dx$

c. $\int 3x^2\sqrt{x^3 - 2} \, dx$ d. $\int \dfrac{-4x}{(1 - 2x^2)^2} \, dx$

SOLUTION

a. $\int 3(3x - 1)^4 \, dx = \int \overbrace{(3x - 1)^4}^{u^n}\,\overbrace{(3)}^{\frac{du}{dx}} \, dx$ Let $u = 3x - 1$.

$= \dfrac{(3x - 1)^5}{5} + C$ General Power Rule

STUDY TIP

Example 1(b) illustrates a case of the General Power Rule that is sometimes overlooked—when the power is $n = 1$. In this case, the rule takes the form

$$\int u \, \frac{du}{dx} \, dx = \frac{u^2}{2} + C.$$

b. $\int (2x + 1)(x^2 + x) \, dx = \int \overbrace{(x^2 + x)}^{u^n}\,\overbrace{(2x + 1)}^{\frac{du}{dx}} \, dx$ Let $u = x^2 + x$.

$= \dfrac{(x^2 + x)^2}{2} + C$ General Power Rule

c. $\int 3x^2\sqrt{x^3 - 2} \, dx = \int \overbrace{(x^3 - 2)^{1/2}}^{u^n}\,\overbrace{(3x^2)}^{\frac{du}{dx}} \, dx$ Let $u = x^3 - 2$.

$= \dfrac{(x^3 - 2)^{3/2}}{3/2} + C$ General Power Rule

$= \dfrac{2}{3}(x^3 - 2)^{3/2} + C$ Simplify.

d. $\int \dfrac{-4x}{(1 - 2x^2)^2} \, dx = \int \overbrace{(1 - 2x^2)^{-2}}^{u^n}\,\overbrace{(-4x)}^{\frac{du}{dx}} \, dx$ Let $u = 1 - 2x^2$.

$= \dfrac{(1 - 2x^2)^{-1}}{-1} + C$ General Power Rule

$= -\dfrac{1}{1 - 2x^2} + C$ Simplify.

✓ **Checkpoint 1**

Find each indefinite integral.

a. $\int (3x^2 + 6)(x^3 + 6x)^2 \, dx$ b. $\int 2x\sqrt{x^2 - 2} \, dx$

Remember that you can verify the result of an indefinite integral by differentiating the function. For instance, you can check the answer to Example 1(a) as follows.

$\dfrac{d}{dx}\left[\dfrac{(3x - 1)^5}{5} + C\right] = \left(\dfrac{1}{5}\right)(5)(3x - 1)^4(3)$ Apply Chain Rule.

$= 3(3x - 1)^4$ Simplify.

Many times, part of the derivative du/dx is missing from the integrand, and in *some* cases you can make the necessary adjustments to apply the General Power Rule.

ALGEBRA TUTOR xy

For help on the algebra in Example 2, see Example 1(b) in the *Chapter 5 Algebra Tutor*, on page 366.

STUDY TIP

Try using the Chain Rule to check the result of Example 2. After differentiating

$$-\tfrac{1}{24}(3 - 4x^2)^3 + C$$

and simplifying, you should obtain the original integrand.

Example 2   Multiplying and Dividing by a Constant

Find $\displaystyle\int x(3 - 4x^2)^2 \, dx$.

SOLUTION   Let $u = 3 - 4x^2$. To apply the General Power Rule, you need to create $du/dx = -8x$ as a factor of the integrand. You can accomplish this by multiplying and dividing by the constant -8.

$$\int x(3 - 4x^2)^2 \, dx = \int \left(-\frac{1}{8}\right) \overbrace{(3 - 4x^2)^2}^{u^n} \overbrace{(-8x)}^{\frac{du}{dx}} \, dx \qquad \text{Multiply and divide by } -8.$$

$$= -\frac{1}{8}\int (3 - 4x^2)^2(-8x) \, dx \qquad \text{Factor } -\tfrac{1}{8} \text{ out of integrand.}$$

$$= \left(-\frac{1}{8}\right)\left[\frac{(3 - 4x^2)^3}{3}\right] + C \qquad \text{General Power Rule}$$

$$= -\frac{(3 - 4x^2)^3}{24} + C \qquad \text{Simplify.}$$

✓ **Checkpoint 2**

Find $\displaystyle\int x^3(3x^4 + 1)^2 \, dx$.

Example 3   Multiplying and Dividing by a Constant

Find $\displaystyle\int (x^2 + 2x)^3(x + 1) \, dx$.

SOLUTION   Let $u = x^2 + 2x$. To apply the General Power Rule, you need to create $du/dx = 2x + 2$ as a factor of the integrand. You can accomplish this by multiplying and dividing by the constant 2.

$$\int (x^2 + 2x)^3(x + 1) \, dx = \int \left(\frac{1}{2}\right) \overbrace{(x^2 + 2x)^3}^{u^n} \overbrace{(2)(x + 1)}^{\frac{du}{dx}} \, dx \qquad \text{Multiply and divide by 2.}$$

$$= \frac{1}{2}\int (x^2 + 2x)^3(2x + 2) \, dx \qquad \text{Rewrite integrand.}$$

$$= \frac{1}{2}\left[\frac{(x^2 + 2x)^4}{4}\right] + C \qquad \text{General Power Rule}$$

$$= \frac{1}{8}(x^2 + 2x)^4 + C \qquad \text{Simplify.}$$

✓ **Checkpoint 3**

Find $\displaystyle\int (x^3 - 3x)^2(x^2 - 1) \, dx$.

Example 4   A Failure of the General Power Rule

Find $\int -8(3 - 4x^2)^2 \, dx$.

SOLUTION   Let $u = 3 - 4x^2$. To apply the General Power Rule, you must create $du/dx = -8x$ as a factor of the integrand. In Examples 2 and 3, this was done by multiplying and dividing by a constant, and then factoring that constant out of the integrand. This strategy doesn't work with variables. That is,

$$\int -8(3 - 4x^2)^2 \, dx \neq \frac{1}{x}\int (3 - 4x^2)^2(-8x) \, dx.$$

To find this indefinite integral, you can expand the integrand and use the Simple Power Rule.

$$\int -8(3 - 4x^2)^2 \, dx = \int (-72 + 192x^2 - 128x^4) \, dx$$

$$= -72x + 64x^3 - \frac{128}{5}x^5 + C$$

✓ **Checkpoint 4**

Find $\int 2(3x^4 + 1)^2 \, dx$.

When an integrand contains an extra constant factor that is not needed as part of du/dx, you can simply move the factor outside the integral sign, as shown in the next example.

Example 5   Applying the General Power Rule

Find $\int 7x^2 \sqrt{x^3 + 1} \, dx$.

SOLUTION   Let $u = x^3 + 1$. Then you need to create $du/dx = 3x^2$ by multiplying and dividing by 3. The constant factor $\frac{7}{3}$ is not needed as part of du/dx, and can be moved outside the integral sign.

$$\int 7x^2 \sqrt{x^3 + 1} \, dx = \int 7x^2(x^3 + 1)^{1/2} \, dx \qquad \text{Rewrite with rational exponent.}$$

$$= \int \frac{7}{3}(x^3 + 1)^{1/2}(3x^2) \, dx \qquad \text{Multiply and divide by 3.}$$

$$= \frac{7}{3}\int (x^3 + 1)^{1/2}(3x^2) \, dx \qquad \text{Factor } \tfrac{7}{3} \text{ outside integral.}$$

$$= \frac{7}{3}\left[\frac{(x^3 + 1)^{3/2}}{3/2}\right] + C \qquad \text{General Power Rule}$$

$$= \frac{14}{9}(x^3 + 1)^{3/2} + C \qquad \text{Simplify.}$$

✓ **Checkpoint 5**

Find $\int 5x\sqrt{x^2 - 1} \, dx$.

Substitution

The integration technique used in Examples 1, 2, 3, and 5 depends on your ability to recognize or create an integrand of the form

$$u^n \frac{du}{dx}.$$

With more complicated integrands, it is difficult to recognize the steps needed to fit the integrand to a basic integration formula. When this occurs, an alternative procedure called **substitution** or **change of variables** can be helpful. With this procedure, you completely rewrite the integral in terms of u and du. That is, if $u = f(x)$, then $du = f'(x)\, dx$, and the General Power Rule takes the form

$$\int u^n \frac{du}{dx}\, dx = \int u^n\, du.$$

General Power Rule

Example 6   Integration by Substitution

Find $\displaystyle \int \sqrt{1 - 3x}\, dx$.

SOLUTION   Begin by letting $u = 1 - 3x$. Then, $du/dx = -3$ and $du = -3\, dx$. This implies that

$$dx = -\frac{1}{3}\, du$$

and you can find the indefinite integral as shown.

$$\int \sqrt{1 - 3x}\, dx = \int (1 - 3x)^{1/2}\, dx \qquad \text{Rewrite with rational exponent.}$$

$$= \int u^{1/2}\left(-\frac{1}{3}\, du\right) \qquad \text{Substitute for } x \text{ and } dx.$$

$$= -\frac{1}{3}\int u^{1/2}\, du \qquad \text{Factor } -\tfrac{1}{3} \text{ out of integrand.}$$

$$= \left(-\frac{1}{3}\right)\left(\frac{u^{3/2}}{3/2}\right) + C \qquad \text{Apply Power Rule.}$$

$$= -\frac{2}{9}u^{3/2} + C \qquad \text{Simplify.}$$

$$= -\frac{2}{9}(1 - 3x)^{3/2} + C \qquad \text{Substitute } 1 - 3x \text{ for } u.$$

You can check this result by differentiating.

$$\frac{d}{dx}\left[-\frac{2}{9}(1 - 3x)^{3/2} + C\right] = \left(-\frac{2}{9}\right)\left(\frac{3}{2}\right)(1 - 3x)^{1/2}(-3)$$

$$= \left(-\frac{1}{3}\right)(-3)(1 - 3x)^{1/2}$$

$$= \sqrt{1 - 3x}$$

✓ **Checkpoint 6**

Find $\displaystyle \int \sqrt{1 - 2x}\, dx$ by the method of substitution.

The basic steps for integration by substitution are outlined in the guidelines below.

Guidelines for Integration by Substitution

1. Let u be a function of x (usually part of the integrand).

2. Solve for x and dx in terms of u and du.

3. Convert the entire integral to u-variable form.

4. After integrating, rewrite the antiderivative as a function of x.

5. Check your answer by differentiating.

Example 7 — Integration by Substitution

Find $\displaystyle\int x\sqrt{x^2 - 1}\, dx$.

SOLUTION   Consider the substitution $u = x^2 - 1$, which produces

$$du = 2x\, dx.$$

To create $2x\, dx$ as part of the integral, multiply and divide by 2.

$$\int x\sqrt{x^2 - 1}\, dx = \frac{1}{2}\int \overbrace{(x^2 - 1)^{1/2}}^{u^{1/n}}\overbrace{2x\, dx}^{du} \qquad \text{Multiply and divide by 2.}$$

$$= \frac{1}{2}\int u^{1/2}\, du \qquad \text{Substitute for } x \text{ and } dx.$$

$$= \frac{1}{2}\left(\frac{u^{3/2}}{3/2}\right) + C \qquad \text{Apply Power Rule.}$$

$$= \frac{1}{3}u^{3/2} + C \qquad \text{Simplify.}$$

$$= \frac{1}{3}(x^2 - 1)^{3/2} + C \qquad \text{Substitute for } u.$$

You can check this result by differentiating.

$$\frac{d}{dx}\left[\frac{1}{3}(x^2 - 1)^{3/2} + C\right] = \frac{1}{3}\left(\frac{3}{2}\right)(x^2 - 1)^{1/2}(2x)$$

$$= \frac{1}{2}(2x)(x^2 - 1)^{1/2}$$

$$= x\sqrt{x^2 - 1}$$

✓ **Checkpoint 7**

Find $\displaystyle\int x\sqrt{x^2 + 4}\, dx$ by the method of substitution.

To become efficient at integration, you should learn to use *both* techniques discussed in this section. For simpler integrals, you should use pattern recognition and create du/dx by multiplying and dividing by an appropriate constant. For more complicated integrals, you should use a formal change of variables, as shown in Examples 6 and 7. For the integrals in this section's exercise set, try working several of the problems twice—once with pattern recognition and once using formal substitution.

Extended Application: Propensity to Consume

In 2009, the U.S. poverty level for a family of four was about $22,000. Families at or below the poverty level tend to consume 100% of their income—that is, they use all their income to purchase necessities such as food, clothing, and shelter. As income level increases, the average consumption tends to drop below 100%. For instance, a family earning $25,000 may be able to save $500 and so consume only $24,500 (98%) of their income. As the income increases, the ratio of consumption to savings tends to decrease. The rate of change of consumption with respect to income is called the **marginal propensity to consume.**   *(Source: U.S. Census Bureau)*

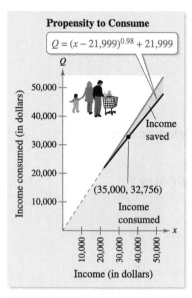

Propensity to Consume

$$Q = (x - 21,999)^{0.98} + 21,999$$

Income consumed (in dollars)

Income saved

(35,000, 32,756)

Income consumed

Income (in dollars)

FIGURE 5.4

Example 8   Analyzing Consumption

For a family of four in 2009, the marginal propensity to consume income x (in dollars) can be modeled by

$$\frac{dQ}{dx} = \frac{0.98}{(x - 21,999)^{0.02}}, \quad x \geq 22,000$$

where Q represents the income consumed (in dollars). Use the model to estimate the amount consumed by a family of four whose 2009 income was $35,000.

SOLUTION   Begin by integrating dQ/dx to find a model for the consumption Q.

$$Q = \int \frac{0.98}{(x - 21,999)^{0.02}} \, dx \qquad \text{Integrate } \frac{dQ}{dx} \text{ to obtain } Q.$$

$$= \int 0.98(x - 21,999)^{-0.02} \, dx \qquad \text{Rewrite.}$$

$$= (x - 21,999)^{0.98} + C \qquad \text{General Power Rule}$$

To solve for C, use the initial condition that $Q = 22,000$ when $x = 22,000$.

$$22,000 = (22,000 - 21,999)^{0.98} + C$$

$$22,000 = 1 + C$$

$$21,999 = C$$

So, you can use the model $Q = (x - 21,999)^{0.98} + 21,999$ to estimate that a family of four with an income of $x = 35,000$ consumed about

$$Q = (35,000 - 21,999)^{0.98} + 21,999 \approx \$32,756.$$

The graph of Q is shown in Figure 5.4.

✓**Checkpoint 8**

According to the model in Example 8, at what income level would a family of four consume $32,000?

SUMMARIZE   (Section 5.2)

1. State the General Power Rule for integration *(page 322)*. For examples of the General Power Rule, see Examples 1, 2, 3, and 5.

2. List the guidelines for integration by substitution *(page 327)*. For examples of integration by substitution, see Examples 6 and 7.

3. Describe a real-life example of how the General Power Rule can be used to analyze the marginal propensity to consume *(page 328, Example 8)*.

SKILLS WARM UP 5.2   The following warm-up exercises involve skills that were covered in earlier sections. You will use these skills in the exercise set for this section. For additional help, review Section 5.1.

In Exercises 1–9, find the indefinite integral.

1. $\int (2x^3 + 1)\, dx$

2. $\int (x^{1/2} + 3x - 4)\, dx$

3. $\int \frac{1}{x^2}\, dx$

4. $\int \frac{1}{3t^3}\, dt$

5. $\int (1 + 2t)t^{3/2}\, dt$

6. $\int \sqrt{x}(2x - 1)\, dx$

7. $\int \frac{5x^3 + 2}{x^2}\, dx$

8. $\int \frac{2x^2 - 5}{x^4}\, dx$

9. $\int \frac{8x^2 + 3}{\sqrt{x}}\, dx$

Exercises 5.2

See www.CalcChat.com for worked-out solutions to odd-numbered exercises.

Finding u and du/dx   In Exercises 1–8, identify u and du/dx for the integral $\int u^n (du/dx)\, dx$.

1. $\int (5x^2 + 1)^2 (10x)\, dx$

2. $\int (3 - 4x^2)^3 (-8x)\, dx$

3. $\int \sqrt{1 - x^2}(-2x)\, dx$

4. $\int 3x^2 \sqrt{x^3 + 1}\, dx$

5. $\int \left(4 + \frac{1}{x^2}\right)^5 \left(\frac{-2}{x^3}\right)\, dx$

6. $\int \frac{1}{(1 + 2x)^2}(2)\, dx$

7. $\int (1 + \sqrt{x})^3 \left(\frac{1}{2\sqrt{x}}\right)\, dx$

8. $\int (4 - \sqrt{x})^2 \left(\frac{-1}{2\sqrt{x}}\right)\, dx$

Applying the General Power Rule   In Exercises 9–34, find the indefinite integral. Check your result by differentiating. *See Examples 1, 2, 3, and 5.*

9. $\int (x - 1)^4\, dx$

10. $\int (x - 3)^{5/2}\, dx$

11. $\int (1 + 2x)^4 (2)\, dx$

12. $\int (x^2 - 1)^3 (2x)\, dx$

13. $\int (x^2 + 3x)(2x + 3)\, dx$

14. $\int (x^3 + 6x)^2 (3x^2 + 6)\, dx$

15. $\int \sqrt{4x^2 - 5}(8x)\, dx$

16. $\int \sqrt[3]{1 - 2x^2}(-4x)\, dx$

17. $\int \frac{6x}{(3x^2 - 5)^4}\, dx$

18. $\int \frac{-12x^2}{(1 - 4x^3)^2}\, dx$

19. $\int x^2 (2x^3 - 1)^4\, dx$

20. $\int x(1 - 2x^2)^3\, dx$

21. $\int t\sqrt{t^2 + 6}\, dt$

22. $\int t^4 \sqrt[3]{t^5 - 9}\, dt$

23. $\int \frac{x^5}{(4 - x^6)^3}\, dx$

24. $\int \frac{x^2}{(x^3 - 1)^2}\, dx$

25. $\int (x^2 - 6x)^4 (x - 3)\, dx$

26. $\int (4x^3 + 8x)^3 (3x^2 + 2)\, dx$

27. $\int \frac{x + 1}{(x^2 + 2x - 3)^2}\, dx$

28. $\int \frac{x - 2}{\sqrt{x^2 - 4x + 3}}\, dx$

29. $\int 5x \sqrt[3]{1 - x^2}\, dx$

30. $\int 9x^3 \sqrt{x^4 + 2}\, dx$

31. $\int \frac{6x}{(1 + x^2)^3}\, dx$

32. $\int \frac{4x + 6}{(x^2 + 3x + 7)^3}\, dx$

33. $\int \frac{-3}{\sqrt{2t + 3}}\, dt$

34. $\int \frac{3x^2}{\sqrt{1 - x^3}}\, dx$

Integration by Substitution   In Exercises 35–42, use formal substitution to find the indefinite integral. Check your result by differentiating. *See Examples 6 and 7.*

35. $\int 12x(6x^2 - 1)^3\, dx$

36. $\int 3x^2 (1 - x^3)^2\, dx$

37. $\int \sqrt[3]{4x + 3}\, dx$

38. $\int t\sqrt{t^2 + 1}\, dt$

39. $\int \frac{x}{\sqrt{x^2 + 25}}\, dx$

40. $\int \frac{3}{\sqrt{2x + 1}}\, dx$

41. $\int \frac{x^2 + 1}{\sqrt{x^3 + 3x + 4}}\, dx$

42. $\int \frac{x^2 + 3}{\sqrt[3]{x^3 + 9x}}\, dx$

Comparing Methods   In Exercises 43–46, (a) perform the integration in two ways: once using the Simple Power Rule and once using the General Power Rule. (b) Explain the difference in the results. (c) Which method do you prefer? Explain your reasoning.

43. $\int (x - 1)^2\, dx$

44. $\int (3 - x)^2\, dx$

45. $\int x(x^2 - 1)^2\, dx$

46. $\int x(2x^2 + 1)^2\, dx$

47. Finding an Equation of a Function Find the equation of the function f whose graph passes through the point $(2, 10)$ and whose derivative is

$$f'(x) = 2x(4x^2 - 10)^2.$$

48. Finding an Equation of a Function Find the equation of the function f whose graph passes through the point $\left(0, \frac{7}{3}\right)$ and whose derivative is

$$f'(x) = x\sqrt{1 - x^2}.$$

49. Cost The marginal cost of a product is modeled by

$$\frac{dC}{dx} = \frac{4}{\sqrt{x + 1}}$$

where x is the number of units. When $x = 15$, $C = 50$.

(a) Find the cost function.

(b) Find the cost of producing 50 units.

50. Cost The marginal cost of a product is modeled by

$$\frac{dC}{dx} = \frac{12}{\sqrt[3]{12x + 1}}$$

where x is the number of units. When $x = 13$, $C = 100$.

(a) Find the cost function.

(b) Find the cost of producing 30 units.

Supply In Exercises 51 and 52, find the supply function $x = f(p)$ that satisfies the initial conditions.

51. $\dfrac{dx}{dp} = p\sqrt{p^2 - 25}$

$x = 600$ when $p = \$13$

52. $\dfrac{dx}{dp} = \dfrac{10}{\sqrt{p - 3}}$

$x = 100$ when $p = \$3$

Demand In Exercises 53 and 54, find the demand function $x = f(p)$ that satisfies the initial conditions.

53. $\dfrac{dx}{dp} = -\dfrac{6000p}{(p^2 - 16)^{3/2}}$

$x = 5000$ when $p = \$5$

54. $\dfrac{dx}{dp} = -\dfrac{400}{(0.02p - 1)^3}$

$x = 10,000$ when $p = \$100$

55. Gardening An evergreen nursery usually sells a type of shrub after 5 years of growth and shaping. The growth rate during those 5 years is approximated by

$$\frac{dh}{dt} = \frac{17.6t}{\sqrt{17.6t^2 + 1}}$$

where t is the time (in years) and h is the height (in inches). The seedlings are 6 inches tall when planted $(t = 0)$.

(a) Find the height function.

(b) How tall are the shrubs when they are sold?

56. **HOW DO YOU SEE IT?** The graph shows the rate of change of the revenue of a company from 1990 through 2010.

(a) Approximate the rate of change of the revenue in 2007. Explain your reasoning.

(b) Is $R(7) - R(6) > 0$? Explain your reasoning.

(c) Approximate the years in which the graph of the revenue is concave upward and the years in which it is concave downward. Approximate the years of any points of inflection.

 Marginal Propensity to Consume In Exercises 57 and 58, (a) use the marginal propensity to consume, dQ/dx, to write Q as a function of x, where x is the income (in dollars) and Q is the income consumed (in dollars). Assume that families who have annual incomes of \$25,000 or less consume 100% of their income. (b) Use the result of part (a) and a spreadsheet to complete the table showing the income consumed and the income saved, $x - Q$, for various incomes. (c) Use a graphing utility to represent graphically the income consumed and saved. See *Example 8*.

x	25,000	50,000	100,000	150,000
Q				
$x - Q$				

57. $\dfrac{dQ}{dx} = \dfrac{0.95}{(x - 24{,}999)^{0.05}}$, $x \geq 25{,}000$

58. $\dfrac{dQ}{dx} = \dfrac{0.93}{(x - 24{,}999)^{0.07}}$, $x \geq 25{,}000$

 Integration Using Technology In Exercises 59 and 60, use a symbolic integration utility to find the indefinite integral. Verify the result by differentiating.

59. $\displaystyle\int \frac{1}{\sqrt{x} + \sqrt{x + 1}}\, dx$

60. $\displaystyle\int \frac{x}{\sqrt{3x + 2}}\, dx$

5.3 Exponential and Logarithmic Integrals

■ Use the Exponential Rule to find indefinite integrals.
■ Use the Log Rule to find indefinite integrals.

Using the Exponential Rule

Each of the differentiation rules for exponential functions has a corresponding integration rule.

Population of Bacteria

In Exercise 51 on page 337, you will use integration to find a model for a population of bacteria.

Integrals of Exponential Functions

Let u be a differentiable function of x.

$$\int e^x \, dx = e^x + C \qquad\qquad \text{Simple Exponential Rule}$$

$$\int e^u \frac{du}{dx} \, dx = \int e^u \, du = e^u + C \qquad \text{General Exponential Rule}$$

Example 1   **Integrating Exponential Functions**

Find each indefinite integral.

a. $\displaystyle\int 2e^x \, dx$ **b.** $\displaystyle\int 2e^{2x} \, dx$ **c.** $\displaystyle\int (e^x + x) \, dx$

SOLUTION

a. $\displaystyle\int 2e^x \, dx = 2 \int e^x \, dx$ Constant Multiple Rule

$\qquad\qquad = 2e^x + C$ Simple Exponential Rule

b. $\displaystyle\int 2e^{2x} \, dx = \int e^{2x}(2) \, dx$ Let $u = 2x$, then $\dfrac{du}{dx} = 2$.

$\qquad\qquad = \displaystyle\int e^u \frac{du}{dx} \, dx$ Substitute u and $\dfrac{du}{dx}$.

$\qquad\qquad = e^u + C$ General Exponential Rule

$\qquad\qquad = e^{2x} + C$ Substitute for u.

c. $\displaystyle\int (e^x + x) \, dx = \int e^x \, dx + \int x \, dx$ Sum Rule

$\qquad\qquad\qquad = e^x + \dfrac{x^2}{2} + C$ Simple Exponential and Power Rules

You can check each of these results by differentiating. For instance, in part (a),

$$\frac{d}{dx}[2e^x + C] = 2e^x.$$

✓ **Checkpoint 1**

Find each indefinite integral.

a. $\displaystyle\int 3e^x \, dx$ **b.** $\displaystyle\int 5e^{5x} \, dx$ **c.** $\displaystyle\int (e^x - x) \, dx$

Example 2   Integrating an Exponential Function

Find $\displaystyle\int e^{3x+1}\,dx$.

SOLUTION   Let $u = 3x + 1$; then $du/dx = 3$. You can introduce the missing factor of 3 in the integrand by multiplying and dividing by 3.

$$\int e^{3x+1}\,dx = \frac{1}{3}\int e^{3x+1}(3)\,dx \qquad\text{Multiply and divide by 3.}$$

$$= \frac{1}{3}\int e^{u}\frac{du}{dx}\,dx \qquad\text{Substitute } u \text{ and } \frac{du}{dx}.$$

$$= \frac{1}{3}e^{u} + C \qquad\text{General Exponential Rule}$$

$$= \frac{1}{3}e^{3x+1} + C \qquad\text{Substitute for } u.$$

✓ **Checkpoint 2**

Find $\displaystyle\int e^{2x+3}\,dx$.

Example 3   Integrating an Exponential Function

Find $\displaystyle\int 5xe^{-x^2}\,dx$.

SOLUTION   Let $u = -x^2$; then $du/dx = -2x$. You can create the factor $-2x$ in the integrand by multiplying and dividing by -2.

$$\int 5xe^{-x^2}\,dx = \int\left(-\frac{5}{2}\right)e^{-x^2}(-2x)\,dx \qquad\text{Multiply and divide by } -2.$$

$$= -\frac{5}{2}\int e^{-x^2}(-2x)\,dx \qquad\text{Factor } -\frac{5}{2} \text{ out of the integrand.}$$

$$= -\frac{5}{2}\int e^{u}\frac{du}{dx}\,dx \qquad\text{Substitute } u \text{ and } \frac{du}{dx}.$$

$$= -\frac{5}{2}e^{u} + C \qquad\text{General Exponential Rule}$$

$$= -\frac{5}{2}e^{-x^2} + C \qquad\text{Substitute for } u.$$

✓ **Checkpoint 3**

Find $\displaystyle\int 4xe^{x^2}\,dx$.

Remember that you cannot introduce a missing *variable* in the integrand. For instance, you cannot find $\int e^{x^2}\,dx$ by multiplying and dividing by $2x$ and then factoring $1/(2x)$ out of the integrand. That is,

$$\int e^{x^2}\,dx \neq \frac{1}{2x}\int e^{x^2}(2x)\,dx.$$

Using the Log Rule

When the Power Rules for integration were introduced in Sections 5.1 and 5.2, you saw that they work for powers other than $n = -1$.

$$\int x^n \, dx = \frac{x^{n+1}}{n+1} + C, \quad n \neq -1 \qquad \text{Simple Power Rule}$$

$$\int u^n \frac{du}{dx} \, dx = \int u^n \, du = \frac{u^{n+1}}{n+1} + C, \quad n \neq -1 \qquad \text{General Power Rule}$$

The Log Rule for integration allows you to integrate functions of the form $\int x^{-1} \, dx$ and $\int u^{-1} \, du$.

Log Rule for Integration

Let u be a differentiable function of x.

$$\int \frac{1}{x} \, dx = \ln|x| + C \qquad\qquad \text{Simple Log Rule}$$

$$\int \frac{du/dx}{u} \, dx = \int \frac{1}{u} \, du = \ln|u| + C \qquad \text{General Log Rule}$$

You can verify each of these rules by differentiating. For instance, to verify that $d/dx[\ln|x|] = 1/x$, notice that

$$\frac{d}{dx}[\ln x] = \frac{1}{x} \quad \text{and} \quad \frac{d}{dx}[\ln(-x)] = \frac{-1}{-x} = \frac{1}{x}.$$

> **STUDY TIP**
>
> Notice the absolute values in the Log Rule. For those special cases in which u or x cannot be negative, you can omit the absolute value. For instance, in Example 4(b), it is not necessary to write the antiderivative as $\ln|x^2| + C$ because x^2 cannot be negative.

Example 4 Using the Log Rule for Integration

Find each indefinite integral.

a. $\displaystyle\int \frac{4}{x} \, dx$ **b.** $\displaystyle\int \frac{2x}{x^2} \, dx$ **c.** $\displaystyle\int \frac{3}{3x+1} \, dx$

SOLUTION

a. $\displaystyle\int \frac{4}{x} \, dx = 4 \int \frac{1}{x} \, dx$ $\qquad$ Constant Multiple Rule

$\qquad\qquad = 4\ln|x| + C$ $\qquad$ Simple Log Rule

b. $\displaystyle\int \frac{2x}{x^2} \, dx = \int \frac{du/dx}{u} \, dx$ $\qquad$ Let $u = x^2$; then $\dfrac{du}{dx} = 2x$.

$\qquad\qquad = \ln|u| + C$ $\qquad$ General Log Rule

$\qquad\qquad = \ln x^2 + C$ $\qquad$ Substitute for u.

c. $\displaystyle\int \frac{3}{3x+1} \, dx = \int \frac{du/dx}{u} \, dx$ $\qquad$ Let $u = 3x + 1$; then $\dfrac{du}{dx} = 3$.

$\qquad\qquad = \ln|u| + C$ $\qquad$ General Log Rule

$\qquad\qquad = \ln|3x + 1| + C$ $\qquad$ Substitute for u.

✓ Checkpoint 4

Find each indefinite integral.

a. $\displaystyle\int \frac{2}{x} \, dx$ **b.** $\displaystyle\int \frac{3x^2}{x^3} \, dx$ **c.** $\displaystyle\int \frac{2}{2x+1} \, dx$

Example 5   Using the Log Rule for Integration

Find $\displaystyle\int \frac{1}{2x-1}\,dx$.

SOLUTION   Let $u = 2x - 1$; then $du/dx = 2$. You can create the necessary factor of 2 in the integrand by multiplying and dividing by 2.

$$\int \frac{1}{2x-1}\,dx = \frac{1}{2}\int \frac{2}{2x-1}\,dx \qquad \text{Multiply and divide by 2.}$$

$$= \frac{1}{2}\int \frac{du/dx}{u}\,dx \qquad \text{Substitute } u \text{ and } \frac{du}{dx}.$$

$$= \frac{1}{2}\ln|u| + C \qquad \text{General Log Rule}$$

$$= \frac{1}{2}\ln|2x-1| + C \qquad \text{Substitute for } u.$$

✓ **Checkpoint 5**

Find $\displaystyle\int \frac{1}{4x+1}\,dx$.

Example 6   Using the Log Rule for Integration

Find $\displaystyle\int \frac{6x}{x^2+1}\,dx$.

SOLUTION   Let $u = x^2 + 1$; then

$$\frac{du}{dx} = 2x.$$

You can create the necessary factor of $2x$ in the integrand by factoring a 3 out of the integrand.

$$\int \frac{6x}{x^2+1}\,dx = 3\int \frac{2x}{x^2+1}\,dx \qquad \text{Factor 3 out of integrand.}$$

$$= 3\int \frac{du/dx}{u}\,dx \qquad \text{Substitute } u \text{ and } \frac{du}{dx}.$$

$$= 3\ln|u| + C \qquad \text{General Log Rule}$$

$$= 3\ln(x^2+1) + C \qquad \text{Substitute for } u.$$

✓ **Checkpoint 6**

Find $\displaystyle\int \frac{3x}{x^2+4}\,dx$.

ALGEBRA TUTOR xy

For help on the algebra at the right, see Example 2(d) in the *Chapter 5 Algebra Tutor*, on page 367.

Integrals to which the Log Rule can be applied are often given in disguised form. For instance, when a rational function has a numerator of degree greater than or equal to that of the denominator, you should use long division to rewrite the integrand. Here is an example.

$$\int \frac{x^2 + 6x + 1}{x^2+1}\,dx = \int \left(1 + \frac{6x}{x^2+1}\right)dx$$

$$= x + 3\ln(x^2+1) + C$$

The next example summarizes some additional situations in which it is helpful to rewrite the integrand in order to recognize the antiderivative.

ALGEBRA TUTOR

For help on the algebra in Example 7, see Example 2(a)–(c) in the *Chapter 5 Algebra Tutor*, on page 367.

Example 7   **Rewriting Before Integrating**

Find each indefinite integral.

a. $\displaystyle\int \frac{3x^2 + 2x - 1}{x^2}\, dx$ **b.** $\displaystyle\int \frac{1}{1 + e^{-x}}\, dx$ **c.** $\displaystyle\int \frac{x^2 + x + 1}{x - 1}\, dx$

SOLUTION

a. Begin by rewriting the integrand as the sum of three fractions.

$$\int \frac{3x^2 + 2x - 1}{x^2}\, dx = \int \left(\frac{3x^2}{x^2} + \frac{2x}{x^2} - \frac{1}{x^2}\right) dx$$

$$= \int \left(3 + \frac{2}{x} - \frac{1}{x^2}\right) dx$$

$$= 3x + 2\ln|x| + \frac{1}{x} + C$$

b. Begin by rewriting the integrand by multiplying and dividing by e^x.

$$\int \frac{1}{1 + e^{-x}}\, dx = \int \left(\frac{e^x}{e^x}\right)\frac{1}{1 + e^{-x}}\, dx$$

$$= \int \frac{e^x}{e^x + 1}\, dx$$

$$= \ln(e^x + 1) + C$$

c. Begin by dividing the numerator by the denominator.

$$\int \frac{x^2 + x + 1}{x - 1}\, dx = \int \left(x + 2 + \frac{3}{x - 1}\right) dx$$

$$= \frac{x^2}{2} + 2x + 3\ln|x - 1| + C$$

✓**Checkpoint 7**

Find each indefinite integral.

a. $\displaystyle\int \frac{4x^2 - 3x + 2}{x^2}\, dx$ **b.** $\displaystyle\int \frac{2}{e^{-x} + 1}\, dx$ **c.** $\displaystyle\int \frac{x^2 + 2x + 4}{x + 1}\, dx$

SUMMARIZE   (Section 5.3)

1. State the Simple Exponential Rule *(page 331)*. For an example of the Simple Exponential Rule, see Example 1.

2. State the General Exponential Rule *(page 331)*. For examples of the General Exponential Rule, see Examples 2 and 3.

3. State the Simple Log Rule *(page 333)*. For an example of the Simple Log Rule, see Example 4.

4. State the General Log Rule *(page 333)*. For examples of the General Log Rule, see Examples 5 and 6.

In Exercises 1–4, use long division to rewrite the quotient.

1. $\dfrac{x^2 + 4x + 2}{x + 2}$

2. $\dfrac{x^2 - 6x + 9}{x - 4}$

3. $\dfrac{x^3 + 4x^2 - 30x - 4}{x^2 - 4x}$

4. $\dfrac{x^4 - x^3 + x^2 + 15x + 2}{x^2 + 5}$

In Exercises 5–8, find the indefinite integral.

5. $\displaystyle\int \left(x^3 + \frac{1}{x^2} \right) dx$

6. $\displaystyle\int \frac{x^2 + 2x}{x} \, dx$

7. $\displaystyle\int \frac{x^3 + 4}{x^2} \, dx$

8. $\displaystyle\int \frac{x + 3}{x^3} \, dx$

Exercises 5.3

Integrating Exponential Functions In Exercises 1–12, use the Exponential Rule to find the indefinite integral. *See Examples 1, 2, and 3.*

1. $\displaystyle\int 2e^{2x} \, dx$

2. $\displaystyle\int -3e^{-3x} \, dx$

3. $\displaystyle\int e^{4x} \, dx$

4. $\displaystyle\int e^{-0.25x} \, dx$

5. $\displaystyle\int e^{5x-3} \, dx$

6. $\displaystyle\int e^{-x-1} \, dx$

7. $\displaystyle\int 9xe^{-x^2} \, dx$

8. $\displaystyle\int 3xe^{0.5x^2} \, dx$

9. $\displaystyle\int 5x^2 e^{x^3} \, dx$

10. $\displaystyle\int -3x^3 e^{-2x^4} \, dx$

11. $\displaystyle\int (2x + 1)e^{x^2+x} \, dx$

12. $\displaystyle\int (x - 4)e^{x^2-8x} \, dx$

Using the Log Rule for Integration In Exercises 13–30, use the Log Rule to find the indefinite integral. *See Examples 4, 5, and 6.*

13. $\displaystyle\int \frac{1}{x + 1} \, dx$

14. $\displaystyle\int \frac{1}{x - 5} \, dx$

15. $\displaystyle\int \frac{5}{5x + 2} \, dx$

16. $\displaystyle\int \frac{4}{4x - 7} \, dx$

17. $\displaystyle\int \frac{1}{3 - 2x} \, dx$

18. $\displaystyle\int \frac{1}{6x - 5} \, dx$

19. $\displaystyle\int \frac{2}{3x + 5} \, dx$

20. $\displaystyle\int \frac{5}{2x - 1} \, dx$

21. $\displaystyle\int \frac{x}{x^2 + 1} \, dx$

22. $\displaystyle\int \frac{x^2}{3 - x^3} \, dx$

23. $\displaystyle\int \frac{x^2}{x^3 + 1} \, dx$

24. $\displaystyle\int \frac{x}{x^2 + 4} \, dx$

25. $\displaystyle\int \frac{x + 3}{x^2 + 6x + 7} \, dx$

26. $\displaystyle\int \frac{x^2 + 2x + 3}{x^3 + 3x^2 + 9x + 1} \, dx$

27. $\displaystyle\int \frac{1}{x \ln x} \, dx$

28. $\displaystyle\int \frac{1}{x(\ln x)^2} \, dx$

29. $\displaystyle\int \frac{e^{-x}}{1 - e^{-x}} \, dx$

30. $\displaystyle\int \frac{e^x}{1 + e^x} \, dx$

Finding Indefinite Integrals In Exercises 31–46, use any basic integration formula or formulas to find the indefinite integral. State which integration formula(s) you used to find the integral.

31. $\displaystyle\int \frac{x^3 - 8x}{2x^2} \, dx$

32. $\displaystyle\int \frac{x - 1}{4x} \, dx$

33. $\displaystyle\int \frac{8x^3 + 3x^2 + 6}{x^3} \, dx$

34. $\displaystyle\int \frac{2x^3 - 6x^2 - 5x}{x^2} \, dx$

35. $\displaystyle\int \frac{e^{2x} + 2e^x + 1}{e^x} \, dx$

36. $\displaystyle\int \frac{e^{5x} - 3e^{3x} + e^x}{e^{3x}} \, dx$

37. $\displaystyle\int e^x \sqrt{1 - e^x} \, dx$

38. $\displaystyle\int (6x + e^x) \sqrt{3x^2 + e^x} \, dx$

39. $\displaystyle\int \frac{1 + e^{-x}}{1 + xe^{-x}} \, dx$

40. $\displaystyle\int \frac{2(e^x - e^{-x})}{(e^x + e^{-x})^2} \, dx$

41. $\displaystyle\int \frac{5}{e^{-5x} + 7} \, dx$

42. $\displaystyle\int \frac{3}{1 + e^{-3x}} \, dx$

43. $\int \dfrac{x^2 + 2x + 5}{x - 1}\, dx$ **44.** $\int \dfrac{x^3 - 36x + 3}{x + 6}\, dx$

45. $\int \dfrac{x - 3}{x + 3}\, dx$ **46.** $\int \dfrac{x^2 + x + 1}{x^2 + 1}\, dx$

Finding an Equation of a Function In Exercises 47–50, find the equation of the function f whose graph passes through the given point.

47. $f'(x) = \dfrac{1}{x^2} e^{2/x}; \ (4, 6)$

48. $f'(x) = \dfrac{2}{1 + e^{-x}}; \ (0, 3)$

49. $f'(x) = \dfrac{x^2 + 4x + 3}{x - 1}; \ (2, 4)$

50. $f'(x) = \dfrac{x^3 - 4x^2 + 3}{x - 3}; \ (4, -1)$

51. Biology A population P of bacteria is growing at the rate of

$$\frac{dP}{dt} = \frac{3000}{1 + 0.25t}$$

where t is the time (in days). When $t = 0$, the population is 1000.

(a) Find a model for the population.

(b) What is the population after 3 days?

(c) After how many days will the population be 12,000?

52. Biology Because of an insufficient oxygen supply, the trout population P in a lake is dying. The population's rate of change can be modeled by

$$\frac{dP}{dt} = -125e^{-t/20}$$

where t is the time (in days). When $t = 0$, the population is 2500.

(a) Find a model for the population.

(b) What is the population after 15 days?

(c) How long will it take for the entire trout population to die?

53. Demand The marginal price for the demand of a product can be modeled by

$$\frac{dp}{dx} = 0.1e^{-x/500}$$

where x is the quantity demanded. When the demand is 600 units, the price p is \$30.

(a) Find the demand function.

(b) Use a graphing utility to graph the demand function. Does price increase or decrease as demand increases?

(c) Use the *zoom* and *trace* features of the graphing utility to find the quantity demanded when the price is \$22.

54. **HOW DO YOU SEE IT?** The graph shows the rate of change of the revenue of a company from 1990 through 2010.

Year (0 ↔ 1990)

(a) Approximate the rate of change of the revenue in 2009. Explain your reasoning.

(b) Approximate the year when the rate of change of the revenue is the greatest. Explain your reasoning.

(c) Approximate the year when the revenue is maximum. Explain your reasoning.

55. Revenue The rate of change in revenue for Cablevision from 2002 through 2009 can be modeled by

$$\frac{dR}{dt} = 320.1e^{0.0993t}$$

where R is the revenue (in millions of dollars) and t is the time (in years), with $t = 2$ corresponding to 2002. In 2007, the revenue for Cablevision was \$6484.5 million. *(Source: Cablevision Systems Corporation)*

(a) Find a model for the revenue of Cablevision.

(b) Find Cablevision's revenue in 2009.

56. Revenue The rate of change in revenue for Under Armour from 2004 through 2009 can be modeled by

$$\frac{dR}{dt} = 13.897t + \frac{284.653}{t}$$

where R is the revenue (in millions of dollars) and t is the time (in years), with $t = 4$ corresponding to 2004. In 2008, the revenue for Under Armour was \$725.2 million. *(Source: Under Armour, Inc.)*

(a) Find a model for the revenue of Under Armour.

(b) Find Under Armour's revenue in 2006.

True or False In Exercises 57 and 58, determine whether the statement is true or false. If it is false, explain why or give an example that shows it is false.

57. $(\ln x)^{1/2} = \frac{1}{2}(\ln x)$

58. $\int \dfrac{1}{x}\, dx = \ln|ax| + C, \ a \neq 0$

QUIZ YOURSELF

See www.CalcChat.com for worked-out solutions to odd-numbered exercises.

Take this quiz as you would take a quiz in class. When you are done, check your work against the answers given in the back of the book.

In Exercises 1–9, find the indefinite integral. Check your result by differentiation.

1. $\int 3\,dx$

2. $\int 10x\,dx$

3. $\int \frac{1}{x^5}\,dx$

4. $\int (x^2 - 2x + 15)\,dx$

5. $\int (6x + 1)^3(6)\,dx$

6. $\int x(5x^2 - 2)^4\,dx$

7. $\int (x^2 - 5x)(2x - 5)\,dx$

8. $\int \frac{3x^2}{(x^3 + 3)^3}\,dx$

9. $\int \sqrt{5x + 2}\,dx$

In Exercises 10 and 11, find the particular solution that satisfies the differential equation and initial condition.

10. $f'(x) = 16x; f(0) = 1$

11. $f'(x) = 9x^2 + 4; f(1) = 5$

12. The marginal cost function for producing x units of a product is modeled by

$$\frac{dC}{dx} = 16 - 0.06x.$$

It costs \$25 to produce one unit. Find (a) the cost function C (in dollars), (b) the fixed cost (when $x = 0$), and (c) the total cost of producing 500 units.

13. Find the equation of the function f whose graph passes through the point $(0, 1)$ and whose derivative is

$$f'(x) = 2x^2 + 1.$$

14. The number of bolts B produced by a foundry changes according to the model

$$\frac{dB}{dt} = \frac{250t}{\sqrt{t^2 + 36}}, \quad 0 \le t \le 40$$

where t is the time (in hours). Find the number of bolts produced in (a) 8 hours and (b) 40 hours.

In Exercises 15–17, use the Exponential Rule to find the indefinite integral.

15. $\int 5e^{5x+4}\,dx$

16. $\int 3x^2 e^{x^3}\,dx$

17. $\int (x - 3)e^{x^2 - 6x}\,dx$

In Exercises 18–20, use the Log Rule to find the indefinite integral.

18. $\int \frac{2}{2x - 1}\,dx$

19. $\int \frac{1}{3 - 8x}\,dx$

20. $\int \frac{x}{3x^2 + 4}\,dx$

21. The rate of change in sales for Advance Auto Parts from 2001 through 2009 can be modeled by

$$\frac{dS}{dt} = 26.32t + \frac{848.99}{t}$$

where S is the sales (in millions) and t is the time (in years), with $t = 1$ corresponding to 2001. In 2001, the sales for Advance Auto Parts were \$2517.6 million. *(Source: Advance Auto Parts, Inc.)*

(a) Find a model for the sales of Advance Auto Parts.

(b) Find the sales for Advance Auto Parts in 2008.

5.4 Area and the Fundamental Theorem of Calculus

■ Understand the relationship between area and definite integrals.
■ Evaluate definite integrals using the Fundamental Theorem of Calculus.
■ Use definite integrals to solve marginal analysis problems.
■ Find the average values of functions over closed intervals.
■ Use properties of even and odd functions to help evaluate definite integrals.
■ Find the amounts of annuities.

One- to Four-Family Homes

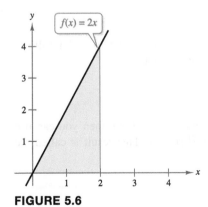

In Exercise 79 on page 350, you will use integration to find a model for the mortgage debt outstanding for one- to four-family homes.

Area and Definite Integrals

From your study of geometry, you know that area is a number that defines the size of a bounded region. For simple regions, such as rectangles, triangles, and circles, area can be found using geometric formulas.

In this section, you will learn how to use calculus to find the areas of nonstandard regions, such as the region R shown in Figure 5.5.

$$\int_a^b f(x)\, dx = \text{Area}$$

FIGURE 5.5

Definition of a Definite Integral

Let f be nonnegative and continuous on the closed interval $[a, b]$. The area of the region bounded by the graph of f, the x-axis, and the lines $x = a$ and $x = b$ is denoted by

$$\text{Area} = \int_a^b f(x)\, dx.$$

The expression $\int_a^b f(x)\, dx$ is called the **definite integral** from a to b, where a is the **lower limit of integration** and b is the **upper limit of integration.**

FIGURE 5.6

Example 1 Evaluating a Definite Integral Using a Geometric Formula

The definite integral

$$\int_0^2 2x\, dx$$

represents the area of the region bounded by the graph of $f(x) = 2x$, the x-axis, and the line $x = 2$, as shown in Figure 5.6. The region is triangular, with a height of 4 units and a base of 2 units. Using the formula for the area of a triangle, you have

$$\int_0^2 2x\, dx = \frac{1}{2}(\text{base})(\text{height}) = \frac{1}{2}(2)(4) = 4.$$

✓**Checkpoint 1**

Evaluate the definite integral using a geometric formula. Illustrate your answer with an appropriate sketch.

$$\int_0^3 4x\, dx$$

The Fundamental Theorem of Calculus

Consider the function A, which denotes the area of the region shown in Figure 5.7.

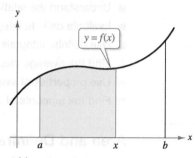

$A(x) = $ Area from a to x

FIGURE 5.7

To discover the relationship between A and f, let x increase by an amount Δx. This increases the area by ΔA. Let $f(m)$ and $f(M)$ denote the minimum and maximum values of f on the interval $[x, x + \Delta x]$.

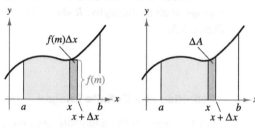

FIGURE 5.8

As indicated in Figure 5.8, you can write the inequality below.

$$f(m)\,\Delta x \leq \quad \Delta A \quad \leq f(M)\,\Delta x \qquad \text{See Figure 5.8.}$$

$$f(m) \leq \quad \frac{\Delta A}{\Delta x} \quad \leq f(M) \qquad \text{Divide each term by } \Delta x.$$

$$\lim_{\Delta x \to 0} f(m) \leq \lim_{\Delta x \to 0} \frac{\Delta A}{\Delta x} \leq \lim_{\Delta x \to 0} f(M) \qquad \text{Take limit of each term.}$$

$$f(x) \leq \quad A'(x) \quad \leq f(x) \qquad \text{Definition of derivative of } A(x)$$

So, $f(x) = A'(x)$, and $A(x) = F(x) + C$, where $F'(x) = f(x)$. Because $A(a) = 0$, it follows that $C = -F(a)$. So, $A(x) = F(x) - F(a)$, which implies that

$$A(b) = \int_a^b f(x)\,dx = F(b) - F(a).$$

This equation tells you that *if you can find an antiderivative for* f, then you can use the antiderivative to evaluate the definite integral $\int_a^b f(x)\,dx$. This result is called the **Fundamental Theorem of Calculus.**

The Fundamental Theorem of Calculus

If f is nonnegative and continuous on the closed interval $[a, b]$, then

$$\int_a^b f(x)\,dx = F(b) - F(a)$$

where F is any function such that $F'(x) = f(x)$ for all x in $[a, b]$.

Guidelines for Using the Fundamental Theorem of Calculus

1. The Fundamental Theorem of Calculus describes a way of *evaluating* a definite integral, not a procedure for finding antiderivatives.

2. In applying the Fundamental Theorem, it is helpful to use the notation

$$\int_a^b f(x)\ dx = F(x)\bigg]_a^b = F(b) - F(a).$$

For instance, to evaluate $\int_1^3 x^3\ dx$, you can write

$$\int_1^3 x^3\ dx = \frac{x^4}{4}\bigg]_1^3$$
$$= \frac{3^4}{4} - \frac{1^4}{4}$$
$$= 20.$$

3. The constant of integration C can be dropped because

$$\int_a^b f(x)\ dx = \bigg[F(x) + C\bigg]_a^b$$
$$= [F(b) + C] - [F(a) + C]$$
$$= F(b) - F(a) + C - C$$
$$= F(b) - F(a).$$

In the development of the Fundamental Theorem of Calculus, f was assumed to be nonnegative on the closed interval $[a, b]$. As such, the definite integral was defined as an area. Now, with the Fundamental Theorem, the definition can be extended to include functions that are negative on all or part of the closed interval $[a, b]$. Specifically, if f is *any* function that is continuous on a closed interval $[a, b]$, then the **definite integral** of $f(x)$ from a to b is defined to be

$$\int_a^b f(x)\ dx = F(b) - F(a)$$

where F is an antiderivative of f. Remember that definite integrals do not necessarily represent areas and can be negative, zero, or positive.

STUDY TIP

Be sure you see the distinction between indefinite and definite integrals. The *indefinite integral*

$$\int f(x)\ dx$$

denotes a *family of functions*, each of which is an antiderivative of f, whereas the *definite integral*

$$\int_a^b f(x)\ dx$$

is a *number*.

Properties of Definite Integrals

Let f and g be continuous on the closed interval $[a, b]$.

1. $\displaystyle\int_a^b kf(x)\ dx = k\int_a^b f(x)\ dx,$ k is a constant.

2. $\displaystyle\int_a^b [f(x) \pm g(x)]\ dx = \int_a^b f(x)\ dx \pm \int_a^b g(x)\ dx$

3. $\displaystyle\int_a^b f(x)\ dx = \int_a^c f(x)\ dx + \int_c^b f(x)\ dx,$ $a < c < b$

4. $\displaystyle\int_a^a f(x)\ dx = 0$

5. $\displaystyle\int_a^b f(x)\ dx = -\int_b^a f(x)\ dx$

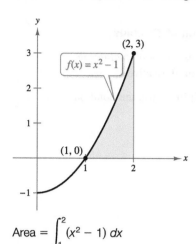

Area $= \int_1^2 (x^2 - 1)\, dx$

FIGURE 5.9

Example 2   **Finding Area by the Fundamental Theorem**

Find the area of the region bounded by the x-axis and the graph of

$$f(x) = x^2 - 1, \quad 1 \le x \le 2.$$

SOLUTION   Note that $f(x) \ge 0$ on the interval $1 \le x \le 2$, as shown in Figure 5.9. So,
you can represent the area of the region by a definite integral. To find the area, use the
Fundamental Theorem of Calculus.

$$\text{Area} = \int_1^2 (x^2 - 1)\, dx \qquad \text{Definition of definite integral}$$

$$= \left[\frac{x^3}{3} - x \right]_1^2 \qquad \text{Find antiderivative.}$$

$$= \left(\frac{2^3}{3} - 2 \right) - \left(\frac{1^3}{3} - 1 \right) \qquad \text{Apply Fundamental Theorem.}$$

$$= \frac{2}{3} - \left(-\frac{2}{3} \right)$$

$$= \frac{4}{3} \qquad \text{Simplify.}$$

So, the area of the region is $\frac{4}{3}$ square units.

✓**Checkpoint 2**

Find the area of the region bounded by the x-axis and the graph of

$$f(x) = x^2 + 1, \quad 2 \le x \le 3.$$

Example 3   **Evaluating a Definite Integral**

Evaluate the definite integral

$$\int_0^1 (4t + 1)^2\, dt$$

and sketch the region whose area is represented by the integral.

SOLUTION

$$\int_0^1 (4t + 1)^2\, dt = \frac{1}{4} \int_0^1 (4t + 1)^2 (4)\, dt \qquad \text{Multiply and divide by 4.}$$

$$= \frac{1}{4} \left[\frac{(4t + 1)^3}{3} \right]_0^1 \qquad \text{Find antiderivative.}$$

$$= \frac{1}{4} \left[\left(\frac{5^3}{3} \right) - \left(\frac{1}{3} \right) \right] \qquad \text{Apply Fundamental Theorem.}$$

$$= \frac{1}{4} \left(\frac{124}{3} \right)$$

$$= \frac{31}{3} \qquad \text{Simplify.}$$

The region is shown in Figure 5.10.

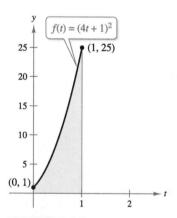

FIGURE 5.10

✓**Checkpoint 3**

Evaluate $\int_0^1 (2t + 3)^3\, dt.$

Example 4   Evaluating Definite Integrals

Evaluate each definite integral.

a. $\displaystyle\int_0^3 e^{2x}\,dx$ **b.** $\displaystyle\int_1^2 \frac{1}{x}\,dx$ **c.** $\displaystyle\int_1^4 -3\sqrt{x}\,dx$

SOLUTION

a. $\displaystyle\int_0^3 e^{2x}\,dx = \frac{1}{2}e^{2x}\Big]_0^3 = \frac{1}{2}(e^6 - e^0) \approx 201.21$

b. $\displaystyle\int_1^2 \frac{1}{x}\,dx = \ln x\Big]_1^2 = \ln 2 - \ln 1 = \ln 2 \approx 0.69$

c. $\displaystyle\int_1^4 -3\sqrt{x}\,dx = -3\int_1^4 x^{1/2}\,dx$ Rewrite with rational exponent.

$\displaystyle\qquad\qquad\qquad = -3\left[\frac{x^{3/2}}{3/2}\right]_1^4$ Find antiderivative.

$\displaystyle\qquad\qquad\qquad = -2x^{3/2}\Big]_1^4$

$\displaystyle\qquad\qquad\qquad = -2(4^{3/2} - 1^{3/2})$ Apply Fundamental Theorem.

$\displaystyle\qquad\qquad\qquad = -2(8 - 1)$

$\displaystyle\qquad\qquad\qquad = -14$ Simplify.

STUDY TIP

In Example 4(c), note that the value of a definite integral can be negative.

✓ **Checkpoint 4**

Evaluate each definite integral.

a. $\displaystyle\int_0^1 e^{4x}\,dx$ **b.** $\displaystyle\int_2^5 -\frac{1}{x}\,dx$

Example 5   Interpreting Absolute Value

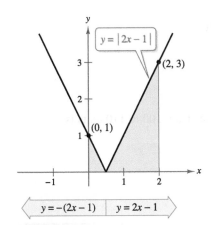

$y = |2x - 1|$

(2, 3)

(0, 1)

$y = -(2x - 1)$ $y = 2x - 1$

FIGURE 5.11

Evaluate $\displaystyle\int_0^2 |2x - 1|\,dx$.

SOLUTION   The region represented by the definite integral is shown in Figure 5.11. From the definition of absolute value, you can write

$$|2x - 1| = \begin{cases} -(2x - 1), & x < \frac{1}{2} \\ 2x - 1, & x \geq \frac{1}{2} \end{cases}.$$

Using Property 3 of definite integrals, rewrite the integral as two definite integrals.

$\displaystyle\int_0^2 |2x - 1|\,dx = \int_0^{1/2} -(2x - 1)\,dx + \int_{1/2}^2 (2x - 1)\,dx$

$\displaystyle\qquad\qquad\qquad = \left[-x^2 + x\right]_0^{1/2} + \left[x^2 - x\right]_{1/2}^2$

$\displaystyle\qquad\qquad\qquad = \left(-\frac{1}{4} + \frac{1}{2}\right) - (0 + 0) + (4 - 2) - \left(\frac{1}{4} - \frac{1}{2}\right)$

$\displaystyle\qquad\qquad\qquad = \frac{5}{2}$

✓ **Checkpoint 5**

Evaluate $\displaystyle\int_0^5 |x - 2|\,dx$.

Marginal Analysis

You have already studied *marginal analysis* in the context of derivatives and differentials (Sections 2.3 and 3.8). There, you were given a cost, revenue, or profit function, and you used the derivative to approximate the additional cost, revenue, or profit obtained by selling one additional unit. In this section, you will examine the reverse process. That is, you will be given the marginal cost, marginal revenue, or marginal profit and you will use a definite integral to find the exact increase or decrease in cost, revenue, or profit obtained by selling one or several additional units.

For instance, you are asked to find the additional revenue obtained by increasing sales from x_1 to x_2 units. When you know the revenue function R, you can find the additional revenue by subtracting $R(x_1)$ from $R(x_2)$. When you don't know R, you can use the marginal revenue function dR/dx to find the additional revenue by using a definite integral.

$$\int_{x_1}^{x_2} \frac{dR}{dx}\, dx = R(x_2) - R(x_1)$$

 Example 6   Analyzing a Profit Function

The marginal profit for a product is modeled by

$$\frac{dP}{dx} = -0.0005x + 12.2.$$

a. Find the change in profit when sales increase from 100 to 101 units.

b. Find the change in profit when sales increase from 100 to 110 units.

SOLUTION

a. The change in profit obtained by increasing sales from 100 to 101 units is

$$\int_{100}^{101} \frac{dP}{dx}\, dx = \int_{100}^{101} (-0.0005x + 12.2)\, dx$$
$$= \left[-0.00025x^2 + 12.2x \right]_{100}^{101}$$
$$\approx \$12.15.$$

b. The change in profit obtained by increasing sales from 100 to 110 units is

$$\int_{100}^{110} \frac{dP}{dx}\, dx = \int_{100}^{110} (-0.0005x + 12.2)\, dx$$
$$= \left[-0.00025x^2 + 12.2x \right]_{100}^{110}$$
$$\approx \$121.48.$$

✓**Checkpoint 6**

The marginal profit for a product is modeled by

$$\frac{dP}{dx} = -0.0002x + 14.2.$$

a. Find the change in profit when sales increase from 100 to 101 units.

b. Find the change in profit when sales increase from 100 to 110 units.

Average Value

The *average value* of a function on a closed interval is defined below.

Definition of the Average Value of a Function

If f is continuous on $[a, b]$, then the **average value** of f on $[a, b]$ is

$$\text{Average value of } f \text{ on } [a, b] = \frac{1}{b - a} \int_a^b f(x) \, dx.$$

In Section 3.5, you studied the effects of production levels on cost using an average cost function. In the next example, you will study the effects of time on cost by using integration to find the average cost.

Average Cost

$c = 0.005t^2 + 0.01t + 13.15$

Average cost = $14.23

Cost per unit (in dollars)

Time (in months)

FIGURE 5.12

Example 7 Finding the Average Cost

The cost per unit c of producing MP3 players over a two-year period is modeled by

$$c = 0.005t^2 + 0.01t + 13.15, \quad 0 \le t \le 24$$

where t is the time (in months). Approximate the average cost per unit over the two-year period.

SOLUTION The average cost can be found by integrating c over the interval $[0, 24]$.

$$\text{Average cost per unit} = \frac{1}{24} \int_0^{24} (0.005t^2 + 0.01t + 13.15) \, dt$$

$$= \frac{1}{24} \left[\frac{0.005t^3}{3} + \frac{0.01t^2}{2} + 13.15t \right]_0^{24}$$

$$= \frac{1}{24}(341.52)$$

$$= \$14.23 \qquad \text{(See Figure 5.12.)}$$

✓**Checkpoint 7**

Find the average cost per unit over a two-year period when the cost per unit c of inline skates is given by

$$c = 0.005t^2 + 0.02t + 12.5, \quad 0 \le t \le 24$$

where t is the time (in months).

You can use a spreadsheet, as shown at the left, to check the reasonableness of the average value found in Example 7. The spreadsheet assumes that one unit is produced each month, beginning with $t = 0$ and ending with $t = 24$. So, when $t = 0$, the cost is

$$c = 0.005(0)^2 + 0.01(0) + 13.15$$

$$= \$13.15$$

and when $t = 1$ the cost is

$$c = 0.005(1)^2 + 0.01(1) + 13.15$$

$$= \$13.165$$

and so on. Note in the spreadsheet that the cost increases each month, and the average of the 25 costs is $14.25. So, you can conclude that the result of Example 7 is reasonable.

	A	B
1	t	$c = 0.005t^2 + 0.01t + 13.15$
2	0	13.15
3	1	13.165
4	2	13.19
5	3	13.225
6	4	13.27
7	5	13.325
8	6	13.39
9	7	13.465
10	8	13.55
11	9	13.645
12	10	13.75
13	11	13.865
14	12	13.99
15	13	14.125
16	14	14.27
17	15	14.425
18	16	14.59
19	17	14.765
20	18	14.95
21	19	15.145
22	20	15.35
23	21	15.565
24	22	15.79
25	23	16.025
26	24	16.27
27		
28	**Sum**	356.25
29	**Average**	14.25

Even and Odd Functions

Several common functions have graphs that are symmetric with respect to the y-axis or the origin, as shown in Figure 5.13. If the graph of f is symmetric with respect to the y-axis, as in Figure 5.13(a), then

$$f(-x) = f(x) \qquad \text{Even function}$$

and f is called an **even** function. If the graph of f is symmetric with respect to the origin, as in Figure 5.13(b), then

$$f(-x) = -f(x) \qquad \text{Odd function}$$

and f is called an **odd** function.

(a) y-axis symmetry   (b) Origin symmetry

FIGURE 5.13

Integration of Even and Odd Functions

1. If f is an *even* function, then $\displaystyle\int_{-a}^{a} f(x)\, dx = 2\int_{0}^{a} f(x)\, dx$.

2. If f is an *odd* function, then $\displaystyle\int_{-a}^{a} f(x)\, dx = 0$.

Example 8   Integrating Even and Odd Functions

Evaluate each definite integral.

a. $\displaystyle\int_{-2}^{2} x^2\, dx$ **b.** $\displaystyle\int_{-2}^{2} x^3\, dx$

SOLUTION

a. Because $f(x) = x^2$ is an even function,

$$\int_{-2}^{2} x^2\, dx = 2\int_{0}^{2} x^2\, dx = 2\left[\frac{x^3}{3}\right]_{0}^{2} = 2\left(\frac{8}{3} - 0\right) = \frac{16}{3}.$$

b. Because $f(x) = x^3$ is an odd function,

$$\int_{-2}^{2} x^3\, dx = 0.$$

✓ **Checkpoint 8**

Evaluate each definite integral.

a. $\displaystyle\int_{-1}^{1} x^4\, dx$ **b.** $\displaystyle\int_{-1}^{1} x^5\, dx$

Annuity

A sequence of equal payments made at regular time intervals over a period of time is called an **annuity.** Some examples of annuities are payroll savings plans, monthly home mortgage payments, and individual retirement accounts. The **amount of an annuity** is the sum of the payments plus the interest earned.

Amount of an Annuity

If c represents a continuous income function in dollars per year (where t is the time in years), r represents the interest rate compounded continuously, and T represents the term of the annuity in years, then the **amount of an annuity** is

$$\text{Amount of an annuity} = e^{rT} \int_0^T c(t)e^{-rt}\, dt.$$

 Example 9 **Finding the Amount of an Annuity**

You deposit $2000 each year for 15 years in an individual retirement account (IRA) paying 5% interest. How much will you have in your IRA after 15 years?

SOLUTION The income function for your deposit is

$$c(t) = 2000.$$

So, the amount of the annuity after 15 years will be

$$
\begin{aligned}
\text{Amount of an annuity} &= e^{rT} \int_0^T c(t)e^{-rt}\, dt \\
&= e^{(0.05)(15)} \int_0^{15} 2000e^{-0.05t}\, dt \\
&= 2000e^{0.75}\left[-\frac{e^{-0.05t}}{0.05} \right]_0^{15} \\
&\approx \$44{,}680.00.
\end{aligned}
$$

✓**Checkpoint 9**

You deposit $1000 each year in a savings account paying 4% interest. How much will be in the account after 10 years?

SUMMARIZE (Section 5.4)

1. State the definition of a definite integral *(page 339)*. For an example of a definite integral, see Example 1.

2. State the Fundamental Theorem of Calculus *(page 340)*. For examples of the Fundamental Theorem of Calculus, see Examples 2 and 3.

3. State the properties of definite integrals *(page 341)*. For examples of the properties, see Examples 4 and 5.

4. State the definition of the average value of a function *(page 345)*. For an example of finding the average value of a function, see Example 7.

5. State the rules for integrating even and odd functions *(page 346)*. For an example of integrating even and odd functions, see Example 8.

SKILLS WARM UP 5.4   The following warm-up exercises involve skills that were covered in earlier sections. You will use these skills in the exercise set for this section. For additional help, review Sections 5.1–5.3.

In Exercises 1–4, find the indefinite integral.

1. $\int (3x + 7)\, dx$

2. $\int \left(x^{3/2} + 2\sqrt{x}\right) dx$

3. $\int \frac{1}{5x}\, dx$

4. $\int e^{-6x}\, dx$

In Exercises 5–8, integrate the marginal function.

5. $\dfrac{dC}{dx} = 0.02x^{3/2} + 29{,}500$

6. $\dfrac{dR}{dx} = 9000 + 2x$

7. $\dfrac{dP}{dx} = 25{,}000 - 0.01x$

8. $\dfrac{dC}{dx} = 0.03x^2 + 4600$

Exercises 5.4

See www.CalcChat.com for worked-out solutions to odd-numbered exercises.

Evaluating a Definite Integral Using a Geometric Formula In Exercises 1–6, sketch the region whose area is represented by the definite integral. Then use a geometric formula to evaluate the integral. *See Example 1.*

1. $\int_0^2 3\, dx$

2. $\int_0^3 4\, dx$

3. $\int_0^4 x\, dx$

4. $\int_0^3 \frac{x}{3}\, dx$

5. $\int_{-3}^3 \sqrt{9 - x^2}\, dx$

6. $\int_0^2 \sqrt{4 - x^2}\, dx$

Using Properties of Definite Integrals In Exercises 7 and 8, use the values $\int_0^5 f(x)\, dx = 6$ and $\int_0^5 g(x)\, dx = 2$ to evaluate the definite integral.

7. (a) $\int_0^5 [f(x) + g(x)]\, dx$ (b) $\int_0^5 [f(x) - g(x)]\, dx$

    (c) $\int_0^5 -4f(x)\, dx$ (d) $\int_0^5 [f(x) - 3g(x)]\, dx$

8. (a) $\int_0^5 2g(x)\, dx$ (b) $\int_5^0 f(x)\, dx$

    (c) $\int_5^5 f(x)\, dx$ (d) $\int_0^5 [f(x) - f(x)]\, dx$

Finding Area by the Fundamental Theorem In Exercises 9–16, find the area of the region. *See Example 2.*

9. $y = x - x^2$

10. $y = 1 - x^4$

11. $y = \dfrac{1}{x^2}$

12. $y = \dfrac{2}{\sqrt{x}}$

13. $y = 3e^{-x/2}$

14. $y = 2e^{x/4}$

15. $y = \dfrac{x^2 + 4}{x}$

16. $y = \dfrac{x - 2}{x}$

Evaluating a Definite Integral In Exercises 17–38, evaluate the definite integral. *See Examples 3 and 4.*

17. $\int_0^1 2x\, dx$

18. $\int_2^7 3v\, dv$

19. $\int_{-1}^0 (x - 2)\, dx$

20. $\int_2^5 (-3x + 4)\, dx$

21. $\int_{-1}^1 (3t + 4)^2\, dt$

22. $\int_0^1 (1 - 2x)^2\, dx$

23. $\int_0^3 (x-2)^3 \, dx$

24. $\int_1^3 (x-3)^4 \, dx$

25. $\int_{-1}^1 \left(\sqrt[3]{t} - 2 \right) dt$

26. $\int_1^4 \left(\sqrt{x} + x \right) dx$

27. $\int_{-1}^0 (t^{1/3} - t^{2/3}) \, dt$

28. $\int_0^4 (x^{1/2} + x^{1/4}) \, dx$

29. $\int_2^8 \frac{3}{x} \, dx$

30. $\int_1^4 -\frac{4}{x} \, dx$

31. $\int_0^4 \frac{1}{\sqrt{2x+1}} \, dx$

32. $\int_0^2 \frac{x}{\sqrt{1+2x^2}} \, dx$

33. $\int_1^2 e^{1-x} \, dx$

34. $\int_{-1}^1 (e^x - e^{-x}) \, dx$

35. $\int_0^1 e^{2x}\sqrt{e^{2x}+1} \, dx$

36. $\int_0^1 \frac{e^{-x}}{\sqrt{e^{-x}+1}} \, dx$

37. $\int_0^2 \frac{x}{1+4x^2} \, dx$

38. $\int_0^1 \frac{e^{2x}}{e^{2x}+1} \, dx$

Interpreting Absolute Value In Exercises 39–42, evaluate the definite integral. *See Example 5.*

39. $\int_{-2}^1 |4x| \, dx$

40. $\int_{-1}^3 \left| \frac{x}{3} \right| dx$

41. $\int_2^8 |3x-9| \, dx$

42. $\int_0^3 |2x-3| \, dx$

Area of a Region In Exercises 43–46, find the area of the region bounded by the graphs of the equations. Use a graphing utility to verify your results.

43. $y = 3x^2 + 1$, $y = 0$, $x = 0$, and $x = 2$

44. $y = 1 + \sqrt{x}$, $y = 0$, $x = 0$, and $x = 4$

45. $y = 4/x$, $y = 0$, $x = 1$, and $x = 3$

46. $y = e^x$, $y = 0$, $x = 0$, and $x = 2$

Marginal Analysis In Exercises 47–52, find the change in cost C, revenue R, or profit P, for the given marginal. In each case, assume that the number of units x increases by 3 from the specified value of x. *See Example 6.*

Marginal	*Number of Units, x*
47. $\dfrac{dC}{dx} = 2.25$	$x = 100$
48. $\dfrac{dC}{dx} = \dfrac{20{,}000}{x^2}$	$x = 10$
49. $\dfrac{dR}{dx} = 48 - 3x$	$x = 12$
50. $\dfrac{dR}{dx} = 75\left(20 + \dfrac{900}{x}\right)$	$x = 500$
51. $\dfrac{dP}{dx} = \dfrac{400 - x}{150}$	$x = 200$
52. $\dfrac{dP}{dx} = 12.5\left(40 - 3\sqrt{x}\right)$	$x = 125$

Average Value of a Function In Exercises 53–60, find the average value of the function on the interval. Then find all x-values in the interval for which the function is equal to its average value.

53. $f(x) = 6x$; $[1, 3]$

54. $f(x) = x^3$; $[0, 2]$

55. $f(x) = 4 - x^2$; $[-2, 2]$

56. $f(x) = x - 2\sqrt{x}$; $[0, 4]$

57. $f(x) = 2e^x$; $[-1, 1]$

58. $f(x) = e^{x/4}$; $[0, 4]$

59. $f(x) = \dfrac{3}{x+2}$; $[1, 5]$

60. $f(x) = \dfrac{1}{(x-3)^2}$; $[0, 2]$

Integrating Even and Odd Functions In Exercises 61–64, evaluate the definite integral using the properties of even and odd functions. *See Example 8.*

61. $\int_{-1}^1 3x^4 \, dx$

62. $\int_{-2}^2 (x^3 - 4x) \, dx$

63. $\int_{-1}^1 (2t^5 - 2t) \, dt$

64. $\int_{-2}^2 \left(\frac{1}{2}t^4 + 1 \right) dt$

65. Using Properties of Definite Integrals Use the value $\int_0^1 x^2 \, dx = \frac{1}{3}$ to evaluate each definite integral. Explain your reasoning.

(a) $\int_{-1}^0 x^2 \, dx$

(b) $\int_{-1}^1 x^2 \, dx$

(c) $\int_0^1 -x^2 \, dx$

66. Using Properties of Definite Integrals Use the value $\int_0^4 x^3 \, dx = 64$ to evaluate each definite integral. Explain your reasoning.

(a) $\int_{-4}^0 x^3 \, dx$

(b) $\int_{-4}^4 x^3 \, dx$

(c) $\int_0^4 2x^3 \, dx$

Finding the Amount of an Annuity In Exercises 67–70, find the amount of an annuity with income function $c(t)$, interest rate r, and term T. *See Example 9.*

67. $c(t) = \$250$, $r = 8\%$, $T = 6$ years

68. $c(t) = \$500$, $r = 7\%$, $T = 4$ years

69. $c(t) = \$1500$, $r = 2\%$, $T = 10$ years

70. $c(t) = \$2000$, $r = 3\%$, $T = 15$ years

Capital Accumulation   In Exercises 71–74, you are given the rate of investment dI/dt. Find the capital accumulation over a five-year period by evaluating the definite integral

$$\text{Capital accumulation} = \int_0^5 \frac{dI}{dt}\, dt$$

where t is the time (in years).

71. $\dfrac{dI}{dt} = 500$ **72.** $\dfrac{dI}{dt} = 100t$

73. $\dfrac{dI}{dt} = 500\sqrt{t + 1}$

74. $\dfrac{dI}{dt} = \dfrac{12{,}000t}{\left(t^2 + 2\right)^2}$

75. Cost   The total cost of purchasing a piece of equipment and maintaining it for x years can be modeled by

$$C = 5000\left(25 + 3\int_0^x t^{1/4}\, dt\right).$$

Find the total cost after (a) 1 year, (b) 5 years, and (c) 10 years.

76. Depreciation   A company purchases a new machine for which the rate of depreciation can be modeled by

$$\frac{dV}{dt} = 10{,}000(t - 6), \quad 0 \le t \le 5$$

where V is the value of the machine after t years. Set up and evaluate the definite integral that yields the total loss of value of the machine over the first 3 years.

77. Compound Interest   A deposit of $2250 is made in a savings account at an annual interest rate of 6%, compounded continuously. Find the average balance in the account during the first 5 years.

78. HOW DO YOU SEE IT?   A college graduate has two job offers. The starting salary for each is $32,000, and after 8 years of service each will pay $54,000. The salary increase for each offer is shown in the figure. From a strictly monetary viewpoint, which is the better offer? Explain your reasoning.

79. Mortgage Debt   The rate of change of mortgage debt outstanding for one- to four-family homes in the United States from 2000 through 2009 can be modeled by

$$\frac{dM}{dt} = 547.56t - 69.459t^2 + 331.258e^{-t}$$

where M is the mortgage debt outstanding (in billions of dollars) and t is the year, with $t = 0$ corresponding to 2000. In 2000, the mortgage debt outstanding in the United States was $5107 billion.   *(Source: Board of Governors of the Federal Reserve System)*

(a) Write a model for the debt as a function of t.

(b) What was the average mortgage debt outstanding for 2000 through 2009?

Business Capsule

After losing her job as an account executive in 1985, Avis Yates Rivers used $2500 to start a word processing business from the basement of her home. In 1996, as a spin-off, Ms. Yates Rivers established Technology Concepts Group. Today, this Somerset, New Jersey-based firm provides a wide range of information technology solutions. Revenues in 2010 were about $3 million, and the company projects revenues of $30 million in 2011 with the acquisition of equipment leasing expertise. Ms. Yates Rivers has become a nationally recognized leader, speaker, and advocate for minority- and women-owned small businesses.

80. Research Project   Use your school's library, the Internet, or some other reference source to research a small company similar to the one described above. Describe the impact of different factors, such as start-up capital and market conditions, on a company's revenue.

5.5 The Area of a Region Bounded by Two Graphs

■ Find the areas of regions bounded by two graphs.
■ Find consumer and producer surpluses.
■ Use the areas of regions bounded by two graphs to solve real-life problems.

Area of a Region Bounded by Two Graphs

With a few modifications, you can extend the use of definite integrals from finding the area of a region *under a graph* to finding the area of a region *bounded by two graphs*. To see how this is done, consider the region bounded by the graphs of

$$f, \quad g, \quad x = a, \quad \text{and} \quad x = b$$

as shown in Figure 5.14. If the graphs of both f and g lie above the x-axis, then you can interpret the area of the region between the graphs as the area of the region under the graph of g subtracted from the area of the region under the graph of f, as shown in Figure 5.14.

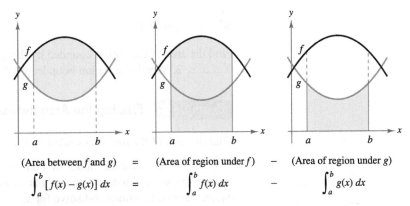

(Area between f and g)   =   (Area of region under f)   −   (Area of region under g)

$$\int_a^b [f(x) - g(x)]\, dx \quad = \quad \int_a^b f(x)\, dx \quad - \quad \int_a^b g(x)\, dx$$

FIGURE 5.14

Although Figure 5.14 depicts the graphs of f and g lying above the x-axis, this is not necessary, and the same integrand

$$[f(x) - g(x)]$$

can be used as long as both functions are continuous and $g(x) \le f(x)$ on the interval $[a, b]$.

Area of a Region Bounded by Two Graphs

If f and g are continuous on $[a, b]$ and $g(x) \le f(x)$ for all x in $[a, b]$, then the area of the region bounded by the graphs of

$$f, \quad g, \quad x = a, \quad \text{and} \quad x = b$$

(see Figure 5.15) is given by

$$A = \int_a^b [f(x) - g(x)]\, dx.$$

FIGURE 5.15

Airplane Engines

Fuel cost (in millions of dollars)

In Exercise 49 on page 358, you will use integration to find the amount saved on fuel costs by switching to more efficient airplane engines.

Example 1   Finding the Area Bounded by Two Graphs

Find the area of the region bounded by the graphs of $y = x^2 + 2$ and $y = x$ for $0 \le x \le 1$.

SOLUTION   Begin by sketching the graphs of both functions, as shown in Figure 5.16. From the figure, you can see that $x \le x^2 + 2$ for all x in $[0, 1]$. So, you can let $f(x) = x^2 + 2$ and $g(x) = x$. Then find the area as shown.

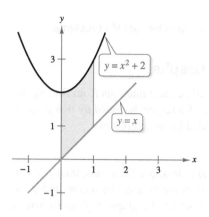

$$\text{Area} = \int_a^b [f(x) - g(x)]\, dx \qquad \text{Area between } f \text{ and } g$$

$$= \int_0^1 [(x^2 + 2) - (x)]\, dx \qquad \text{Substitute for } f \text{ and } g.$$

$$= \int_0^1 (x^2 - x + 2)\, dx$$

$$= \left[\frac{x^3}{3} - \frac{x^2}{2} + 2x \right]_0^1 \qquad \text{Find antiderivative.}$$

$$= \frac{11}{6} \text{ square units} \qquad \text{Apply Fundamental Theorem.}$$

FIGURE 5.16

✓ **Checkpoint 1**

Find the area of the region bounded by the graphs of $y = x^2 + 1$ and $y = x$ for $0 \le x \le 2$. Sketch the region bounded by the graphs. ■

Example 2   Finding the Area Between Intersecting Graphs

Find the area of the region bounded by the graphs of $y = 2 - x^2$ and $y = x$.

SOLUTION   Because the values of a and b are not given, you must determine them by finding the x-coordinates of the points of intersection of the two graphs. To do this, equate the two functions and solve for x.

$$2 - x^2 = x \qquad \text{Equate functions.}$$

$$-x^2 - x + 2 = 0 \qquad \text{Write in general form.}$$

$$-(x + 2)(x - 1) = 0 \qquad \text{Factor.}$$

$$x = -2, \, x = 1 \qquad \text{Solve for } x.$$

So, $a = -2$ and $b = 1$. In Figure 5.17, you can see that the graph of $f(x) = 2 - x^2$ lies above the graph of $g(x) = x$ for all x in the interval $[-2, 1]$.

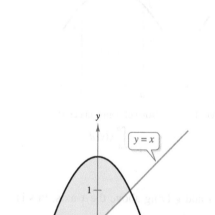

$$\text{Area} = \int_a^b [f(x) - g(x)]\, dx \qquad \text{Area between } f \text{ and } g$$

$$= \int_{-2}^1 [(2 - x^2) - (x)]\, dx \qquad \text{Substitute for } f \text{ and } g.$$

$$= \int_{-2}^1 (-x^2 - x + 2)\, dx$$

$$= \left[-\frac{x^3}{3} - \frac{x^2}{2} + 2x \right]_{-2}^1 \qquad \text{Find antiderivative.}$$

$$= \frac{9}{2} \text{ square units} \qquad \text{Apply Fundamental Theorem.}$$

FIGURE 5.17

✓ **Checkpoint 2**

Find the area of the region bounded by the graphs of $y = 3 - x^2$ and $y = 2x$. ■

Example 3   **Finding an Area Below the x-Axis**

Find the area of the region bounded by the graph of

$$y = x^2 - 3x - 4$$

and the x-axis.

SOLUTION   Begin by finding the x-intercepts of the graph. To do this, set the function equal to zero and solve for x.

$$x^2 - 3x - 4 = 0$$ Set function equal to 0.

$$(x - 4)(x + 1) = 0$$ Factor.

$$x = 4, x = -1$$ Solve for x.

From Figure 5.18, you can see that $x^2 - 3x - 4 \le 0$ for all x in the interval $[-1, 4]$.

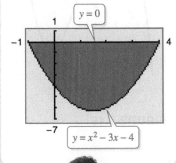

TECH TUTOR

Most graphing utilities can display regions that are bounded by two graphs. For instance, to graph the region in Example 3, set the viewing window to $-1 \le x \le 4$ and $-7 \le y \le 1$. Consult your user's manual for specific keystrokes on how to shade the graph. You should obtain the graph below.

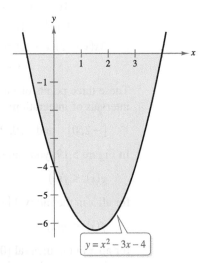

FIGURE 5.18

So, you can let

$$f(x) = 0 \quad \text{and} \quad g(x) = x^2 - 3x - 4$$

and find the area as shown.

$$\text{Area} = \int_a^b \left[f(x) - g(x) \right] dx$$ Area between f and g

$$= \int_{-1}^4 \left[(0) - (x^2 - 3x - 4) \right] dx$$ Substitute for f and g.

$$= \int_{-1}^4 (-x^2 + 3x + 4)\, dx$$

$$= \left[-\frac{x^3}{3} + \frac{3x^2}{2} + 4x \right]_{-1}^4$$ Find antiderivative.

$$= \frac{125}{6} \text{ square units}$$ Apply Fundamental Theorem.

✓**Checkpoint 3**

Find the area of the region bounded by the graph of

$$y = x^2 - x - 2$$

and the x-axis.

Sometimes two graphs intersect at more than two points. To determine the area of the region bounded by two such graphs, you must find *all* points of intersection and check to see which graph is above the other in each interval determined by the points.

Example 4 **Using Multiple Points of Intersection**

Find the area of the region bounded by the graphs of

$$f(x) = 3x^3 - x^2 - 10x \quad \text{and} \quad g(x) = -x^2 + 2x.$$

SOLUTION To find the points of intersection of the two graphs, set the functions equal to each other and solve for x.

$f(x) = g(x)$	Set $f(x)$ equal to $g(x)$.
$3x^3 - x^2 - 10x = -x^2 + 2x$	Substitute for $f(x)$ and $g(x)$.
$3x^3 - 12x = 0$	Write in general form.
$3x(x^2 - 4) = 0$	
$3x(x - 2)(x + 2) = 0$	Factor.
$x = 0, x = 2, x = -2$	Solve for x.

These three points of intersection determine two intervals of integration:

$$[-2, 0] \quad \text{and} \quad [0, 2].$$

In Figure 5.19, you can see that

$$g(x) \leq f(x)$$

for all x in the interval $[-2, 0]$, and that

$$f(x) \leq g(x)$$

for all x in the interval $[0, 2]$. So, you must use two integrals to determine the area of the region bounded by the graphs of f and g: one for the interval $[-2, 0]$ and one for the interval $[0, 2]$.

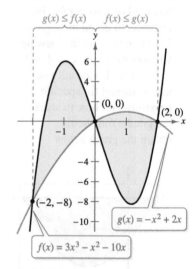

FIGURE 5.19

$$\text{Area} = \int_{-2}^{0} [f(x) - g(x)] \, dx + \int_{0}^{2} [g(x) - f(x)] \, dx$$

$$= \int_{-2}^{0} (3x^3 - 12x) \, dx + \int_{0}^{2} (-3x^3 + 12x) \, dx$$

$$= \left[\frac{3x^4}{4} - 6x^2 \right]_{-2}^{0} + \left[-\frac{3x^4}{4} + 6x^2 \right]_{0}^{2}$$

$$= (0 - 0) - (12 - 24) + (-12 + 24) - (0 + 0)$$

$$= 24$$

So, the region has an area of 24 square units.

✓ **Checkpoint 4**

Find the area of the region bounded by the graphs of

$$f(x) = x^3 + 2x^2 - 3x \quad \text{and} \quad g(x) = x^2 + 3x.$$

Sketch a graph of the region.

Consumer Surplus and Producer Surplus

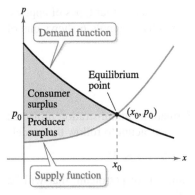

FIGURE 5.20

In Section 1.2, you learned that a demand function relates the price of a product to the consumer demand. You also learned that a supply function relates the price of a product to producers' willingness to supply the product. The point (x_0, p_0) at which a demand function $p = D(x)$ and a supply function $p = S(x)$ intersect is the equilibrium point.

Economists call the area of the region bounded by the graph of the demand function, the horizontal line $p = p_0$, and the vertical line $x = 0$ the **consumer surplus,** as shown in Figure 5.20. Consumer surplus is the difference between the amount consumers would be willing to pay and the actual amount paid for a product. The area of the region bounded by the graph of the supply function, the horizontal line $p = p_0$, and the vertical line $x = 0$ is called the **producer surplus,** as shown in Figure 5.20. Producer surplus is the difference between the amount a producer receives for selling a product and the minimum price needed to get the producer to supply the product.

Example 5 Finding Surpluses

The demand and supply functions for a product are modeled by

$$\text{Demand: } p = -0.36x + 9 \quad \text{and} \quad \text{Supply: } p = 0.14x + 2$$

where p is the price (in dollars) and x is the number of units (in millions). Find the consumer and producer surpluses for this product.

SOLUTION By equating the demand and supply functions, you can determine that the point of equilibrium occurs when $x = 14$ (million) and the price is \$3.96 per unit.

$$\begin{aligned}
\text{Consumer surplus} &= \int_0^{14} (\text{demand function} - \text{price})\, dx \\
&= \int_0^{14} [(-0.36x + 9) - 3.96]\, dx \\
&= \left[-0.18x^2 + 5.04x \right]_0^{14} \\
&= 35.28
\end{aligned}$$

The consumer surplus is \$35.28.

$$\begin{aligned}
\text{Producer surplus} &= \int_0^{14} (\text{price} - \text{supply function})\, dx \\
&= \int_0^{14} [3.96 - (0.14x + 2)]\, dx \\
&= \left[-0.07x^2 + 1.96x \right]_0^{14} \\
&= 13.72
\end{aligned}$$

The producer surplus is \$13.72. The consumer surplus and producer surplus are shown in Figure 5.21.

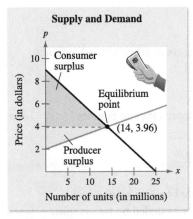

FIGURE 5.21

✓ Checkpoint 5

The demand and supply functions for a product are modeled by

$$\text{Demand: } p = -0.2x + 8 \quad \text{and} \quad \text{Supply: } p = 0.1x + 2$$

where p is the price (in dollars) and x is the number of units (in millions). Find the consumer and producer surpluses for this product.

Application

In addition to consumer and producer surpluses, there are many other types of applications involving the area of a region bounded by two graphs. Example 6 shows one of these applications.

 Example 6   Petroleum Consumption

In the *Annual Energy Outlook*, the U.S. Energy Information Administration projected the consumption C (in quadrillions of Btu per year) of petroleum to follow the model

$$C_1 = 0.00078t^3 - 0.0445t^2 + 0.917t + 35.49, \quad 15 \le t \le 35$$

where $t = 15$ corresponds to 2015. Determine the amount of petroleum that will be saved when the actual consumption follows the model

$$C_2 = 0.0067t^2 - 0.211t + 40.95, \quad 15 \le t \le 35.$$

SOLUTION   The petroleum saved can be represented as the area of the region between the graphs of C_1 and C_2, as shown in Figure 5.22.

$$\begin{aligned}
\text{Petroleum saved} &= \int_{15}^{35} (C_1 - C_2) \, dt \\
&= \int_{15}^{35} (0.00078t^3 - 0.0512t^2 + 1.128t - 5.46) \, dt \\
&= \left[\frac{0.00078}{4}t^4 - \frac{0.0512}{3}t^3 + \frac{1.128}{2}t^2 - 5.46t \right]_{15}^{35} \\
&\approx 63.42
\end{aligned}$$

So, about 63.42 quadrillion Btu of petroleum would be saved.

FIGURE 5.22

✓**Checkpoint 6**

The projected fuel cost C (in millions of dollars per year) for a trucking company from 2012 through 2024 is

$$C_1 = 2.21t + 5.6, \quad 12 \le t \le 24$$

where $t = 12$ corresponds to 2012. After purchasing more efficient truck engines, the company expects fuels costs to follow the model

$$C_2 = 2.04t + 4.7, \quad 12 \le t \le 24.$$

How much money will the company save with the more efficient engines?

SUMMARIZE   (Section 5.5)

1. State the definition of the area of a region bounded by two graphs *(page 351)*. For examples of finding the area of a region bounded by two graphs, see Examples 1, 2, 3, and 4.

2. Describe a real-life example of how finding the area of a region bounded by two graphs can be used to find the consumer and producer surpluses for a product *(page 355, Example 5)*.

3. Describe a real-life example of how finding the area of a region bounded by two graphs can be used to analyze petroleum consumption *(page 356, Example 6)*.

SKILLS WARM UP 5.5

The following warm-up exercises involve skills that were covered in earlier sections. You will use these skills in the exercise set for this section. For additional help, review Section 1.2.

In Exercises 1–4, simplify the expression.

1. $(-x^2 + 4x + 3) - (x + 1)$

2. $(-2x^2 + 3x + 9) - (-x + 5)$

3. $(-x^3 + 3x^2 - 1) - (x^2 - 4x + 4)$

4. $(3x + 1) - (-x^3 + 9x + 2)$

In Exercises 5–8, find the points of intersection of the graphs.

5. $f(x) = x^2 - 4x + 4$, $g(x) = 4$

6. $f(x) = -3x^2$, $g(x) = 6 - 9x$

7. $f(x) = x^2$, $g(x) = -x + 6$

8. $f(x) = \frac{1}{2}x^3$, $g(x) = 2x$

Exercises 5.5

See www.CalcChat.com for worked-out solutions to odd-numbered exercises.

Finding the Area Bounded by Two Graphs In Exercises 1–8, find the area of the region. *See Examples 1, 2, 3, and 4.*

1. $f(x) = x^2 - 6x$
   $g(x) = 0$

2. $f(x) = x^2 + 2x + 1$
   $g(x) = 2x + 5$

3. $f(x) = x^2 - 4x + 3$
   $g(x) = -x^2 + 2x + 3$

4. $f(x) = x^2$
   $g(x) = x^3$

5. $f(x) = e^x - 1$
   $g(x) = 0$

6. $f(x) = -x + 3$
   $g(x) = \dfrac{2}{x}$

7. $f(x) = 3(x^3 - x)$
   $g(x) = 0$

8. $f(x) = (x - 1)^3$
   $g(x) = x - 1$

Finding the Region In Exercises 9–12, the integrand of the definite integral is a difference of two functions. Sketch the graph of each function and shade the region whose area is represented by the integral.

9. $\displaystyle\int_0^4 \left[(x + 1) - \tfrac{1}{2}x\right] dx$

10. $\displaystyle\int_{-1}^1 \left[(1 - x^2) - (x^2 - 1)\right] dx$

11. $\displaystyle\int_{-2}^2 \left[2x^2 - (x^4 - 2x^2)\right] dx$

12. $\displaystyle\int_{-4}^0 \left[(x - 6) - (x^2 + 5x - 6)\right] dx$

Think About It In Exercises 13 and 14, determine which value best approximates the area of the region bounded by the graphs of f and g. Make your selection based on a sketch of the region and not by performing any calculations.

13. $f(x) = x + 1$, $g(x) = (x - 1)^2$

(a) -2 (b) 2   (c) 10   (d) 4   (e) 8

14. $f(x) = 2 - \dfrac{1}{2}x$, $g(x) = 2 - \sqrt{x}$

(a) 1   (b) 6   (c) -3 (d) 3   (e) 4

Finding the Area Bounded by Two Graphs In Exercises 15–30, sketch the region bounded by the graphs of the functions and find the area of the region. *See Examples 1, 2, 3, and 4.*

15. $y = \dfrac{1}{x^2}, y = 0, x = 1, x = 5$

16. $y = 2x - 3, y = x^2 + 2x + 1, x = -2, x = 1$

17. $y = x^2 - 4x + 3, y = 3 + 4x - x^2$

18. $y = 4 - x^2, y = x^2$

19. $y = x^2 - 1, y = -x + 2, x = 0, x = 1$

20. $y = -x^3 + 3, y = x, x = -1, x = 1$

21. $f(x) = \sqrt[3]{x}, g(x) = x$

22. $f(x) = \sqrt{3x} + 1, g(x) = x + 1$

23. $f(x) = x^3 + 4x^2, g(x) = x + 4$

24. $f(x) = 1 - x, g(x) = x^4 - x$

25. $y = xe^{-x^2}, y = 0, x = 0, x = 1$

26. $y = \dfrac{e^{1/x}}{x^2}, y = 0, x = 1, x = 3$

27. $f(x) = e^{0.5x}, g(x) = -\dfrac{1}{x}, x = 1, x = 2$

28. $f(x) = \dfrac{1}{x}, g(x) = -e^x, x = \dfrac{1}{2}, x = 1$

29. $y = \dfrac{8}{x}, y = x^2, y = 0, x = 1, x = 4$

30. $y = x^2 - 2x + 1, y = x^2 - 10x + 25, y = 0$

 Writing Integrals In Exercises 31–34, use a graphing utility to graph the region bounded by the graphs of the functions. Write the definite integral that represents the area of the region. (*Hint:* Multiple integrals may be necessary.)

31. $f(x) = 2x, g(x) = 4 - 2x, h(x) = 0$

32. $f(x) = x(x^2 - 3x + 3), g(x) = x^2$

33. $y = \dfrac{4}{x}, y = x, x = 1, x = 4$

34. $y = x^3 - 4x^2 + 1, y = x - 3$

 Finding Area In Exercises 35–38, use a graphing utility to graph the region bounded by the graphs of the functions. Find the area of the region by hand.

35. $f(x) = x^2 - 4x, g(x) = 0$

36. $f(x) = 3 - 2x - x^2, g(x) = 0$

37. $f(x) = x^2 + 2x + 1, g(x) = x + 1$

38. $f(x) = -x^2 + 4x + 2, g(x) = x + 2$

Area of a Region In Exercises 39 and 40, use integration to find the area of the triangular region having the given vertices.

39. $(0, 0), (4, 0), (4, 4)$

40. $(0, 0), (4, 0), (6, 4)$

Consumer and Producer Surpluses In Exercises 41–46, find the consumer and producer surpluses by using the demand and supply functions, where p is the price (in dollars) and x is the number of units (in millions). *See Example 5.*

Demand Function	Supply Function
41. $p = 50 - 0.5x$	$p = 0.125x$
42. $p = 300 - x$	$p = 100 + x$
43. $p = 200 - 0.4x$	$p = 100 + 1.6x$
44. $p = 975 - 23x$	$p = 42x$
45. $p = 42 - 0.015x^2$	$p = 0.01x^2 + 2$
46. $p = 62 - 0.3x$	$p = 0.002x^2 + 12$

Revenue In Exercises 47 and 48, two models, R_1 and R_2, are given for revenue (in billions of dollars) for a large corporation. Both models are estimates of revenues for 2015 through 2020, where $t = 15$ corresponds to 2015. Which model projects the greater revenue? How much more total revenue does that model project over the six-year period?

47. $R_1 = 7.21 + 0.58t, R_2 = 7.21 + 0.45t$

48. $R_1 = 7.21 + 0.26t + 0.02t^2, R_2 = 7.21 + 0.1t + 0.01t^2$

49. Fuel Cost The projected fuel cost C (in millions of dollars) for an airline from 2015 through 2025 is

$$C_1 = 568.5 + 7.15t$$

where $t = 15$ corresponds to 2015. If the airline purchases more efficient airplane engines, then fuel cost is expected to decrease and to follow the model

$$C_2 = 525.6 + 6.43t.$$

How much can the airline save with the more efficient engines? Explain your reasoning.

50. Health An epidemic was spreading such that t weeks after its outbreak it had infected

$$N_1(t) = 0.1t^2 + 0.5t + 150, \quad 0 \le t \le 50$$

people. Twenty-five weeks after the outbreak, a vaccine was developed and administered to the public. At that point, the number of people infected was governed by the model

$$N_2(t) = -0.2t^2 + 6t + 200.$$

Approximate the number of people that the vaccine prevented from becoming ill during the epidemic.

51. Consumer Trends For the years 1998 through 2008, the per capita consumption C of all fruit (in pounds) in the United States can be modeled by

$$C(t) = \begin{cases} -0.443t^2 + 5.02t + 277.7, & 8 \le t \le 12 \\ -0.775t^2 + 18.73t + 170.5, & 12 < t \le 18 \end{cases}$$

where t is the year, with $t = 8$ corresponding to 1998. *(Source: U.S. Department of Agriculture)*

(a) Use a graphing utility to graph this model.

(b) Suppose the fruit consumption from 2003 through 2008 had continued to follow the model for 1998 through 2002. How many more or fewer pounds of fruit would have been consumed from 2003 through 2008?

52. **HOW DO YOU SEE IT?** A state legislature is debating two proposals for eliminating the annual budget deficits by the year 2020. The rate of decrease of the deficits for each proposal is shown in the figure.

(a) What does the area between the two graphs represent?

(b) From the viewpoint of minimizing the cumulative state deficit, which is the better proposal? Explain your reasoning.

53. Cost, Revenue, and Profit The revenue from a manufacturing process (in millions of dollars) is projected to follow the model $R = 100$ for 10 years. Over the same period of time, the cost (in millions of dollars) is projected to follow the model $C = 60 + 0.2t^2$, where t is the time (in years). Approximate the profit over the 10-year period.

54. Cost, Revenue, and Profit Repeat Exercise 53 for revenue and cost models given by $R = 100 + 0.08t$ and $C = 60 + 0.2t^2$. Did the profit increase or decrease? Explain why.

55. Consumer and Producer Surpluses Factory orders for an air conditioner are about 6000 units per week when the price is $331 and about 8000 units per week when the price is $303. The supply function is given by $p = 0.0275x$. Find the consumer and producer surpluses. (Assume the demand function is linear.)

56. Consumer and Producer Surpluses Repeat Exercise 55 with a demand of about 6000 units per week when the price is $325 and about 8000 units per week when the price is $300. Find the consumer and producer surpluses. (Assume the demand function is linear.)

57. Lorenz Curve Economists use *Lorenz curves* to illustrate the distribution of income in a country. Letting x represent the percent of families in a country and y the percent of total income, the model $y = x$ would represent a country in which each family had the same income. The Lorenz curve, $y = f(x)$, represents the actual income distribution. The area between these two models, for $0 \le x \le 100$, indicates the "income inequality" of a country. In 2009, the Lorenz curve for the United States could be modeled by

$$y = (0.00061x^2 + 0.0224x + 1.666)^2, \quad 0 \le x \le 100$$

where x is measured from the poorest to the wealthiest families. Find the income inequality for the United States in 2009. *(Source: U.S. Census Bureau)*

58. Income Distribution Using the Lorenz curve in Exercise 57 and a spreadsheet, complete the table, which lists the percent of total income earned by each quintile in the United States in 2009.

Quintile	Lowest	2nd	3rd	4th	Highest
Percent					

59. Project: Social Security For a project analyzing the receipts and expenditures for the Old-Age and Survivors Insurance Trust Fund (Social Security Trust Fund) from 1990 through 2009, visit this text's website at *www.cengagebrain.com*. *(Source: Social Security Administration)*

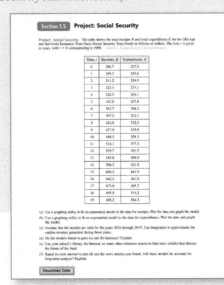

5.6 The Definite Integral as the Limit of a Sum

■ Use the Midpoint Rule to approximate definite integrals.
■ Understand the definite integral as the limit of a sum.

The Midpoint Rule

In Section 5.4, you learned that you cannot use the Fundamental Theorem of Calculus to evaluate a definite integral unless you can find an antiderivative of the integrand. When you cannot find an antiderivative of an integrand, you can use an approximation technique. One such technique, the **Midpoint Rule,** is demonstrated in Example 1.

In Exercise 28 on page 365, you will use the Midpoint Rule to estimate the surface area of a golf green.

Example 1   **Approximating the Area of a Plane Region**

Use the five rectangles in Figure 5.23 to approximate the area of the region bounded by the graph of $f(x) = -x^2 + 5$, the x-axis, and the lines $x = 0$ and $x = 2$.

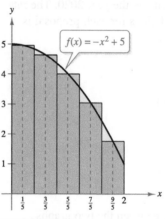

FIGURE 5.23

SOLUTION   You can find the heights of the five rectangles by evaluating f at the midpoint of each of the following intervals.

$$\left[0, \frac{2}{5}\right], \quad \left[\frac{2}{5}, \frac{4}{5}\right], \quad \left[\frac{4}{5}, \frac{6}{5}\right], \quad \left[\frac{6}{5}, \frac{8}{5}\right], \quad \left[\frac{8}{5}, \frac{10}{5}\right]$$

The width of each rectangle is $\frac{2}{5}$. So, the sum of the five areas is

$$\begin{aligned}
\text{Area} &\approx \frac{2}{5}f\left(\frac{1}{5}\right) + \frac{2}{5}f\left(\frac{3}{5}\right) + \frac{2}{5}f\left(\frac{5}{5}\right) + \frac{2}{5}f\left(\frac{7}{5}\right) + \frac{2}{5}f\left(\frac{9}{5}\right) \\
&= \frac{2}{5}\left[f\left(\frac{1}{5}\right) + f\left(\frac{3}{5}\right) + f\left(\frac{5}{5}\right) + f\left(\frac{7}{5}\right) + f\left(\frac{9}{5}\right)\right] \\
&= \frac{2}{5}\left(\frac{124}{25} + \frac{116}{25} + \frac{100}{25} + \frac{76}{25} + \frac{44}{25}\right) \\
&= \frac{920}{125} \\
&= 7.36.
\end{aligned}$$

✓**Checkpoint 1**

Use four rectangles to approximate the area of the region bounded by the graph of $f(x) = x^2 + 1$, the x-axis, $x = 0$, and $x = 2$.

For the region in Example 1, you can find the exact area with a definite integral. That is,

$$\text{Area} = \int_0^2 (-x^2 + 5)\, dx = \frac{22}{3} \approx 7.33.$$

The approximation procedure used in Example 1 is the **Midpoint Rule.** You can use the Midpoint Rule to approximate *any* definite integral—not just those representing areas. The basic steps are summarized below.

Guidelines for Using the Midpoint Rule

To approximate the definite integral $\int_a^b f(x)\, dx$ with the Midpoint Rule, use the steps below.

1. Divide the interval $[a, b]$ into n subintervals, each of width

$$\Delta x = \frac{b - a}{n}.$$

2. Find the midpoint of each subinterval.

$$\text{Midpoints} = \{x_1, x_2, x_3, \ldots, x_n\}$$

3. Evaluate f at each midpoint and form the sum as shown.

$$\int_a^b f(x)\, dx \approx \frac{b - a}{n}[f(x_1) + f(x_2) + f(x_3) + \cdots + f(x_n)]$$

An important characteristic of the Midpoint Rule is that the approximation tends to improve as n increases. The table below shows the approximations for the area of the region described in Example 1 for various values of n. For example, when $n = 10$, the Midpoint Rule yields

$$\int_0^2 (-x^2 + 5)\, dx \approx \frac{2}{10}\left[f\left(\frac{1}{10}\right) + f\left(\frac{3}{10}\right) + \cdots + f\left(\frac{19}{10}\right)\right]$$

$$= 7.34.$$

n	5	10	15	20	25	30
Approximation	7.3600	7.3400	7.3363	7.3350	7.3344	7.3341

Note that as n increases, the approximation gets closer and closer to the exact value of the integral, which was found to be

$$\frac{22}{3} \approx 7.3333.$$

STUDY TIP

In Example 1, the Midpoint Rule is used to approximate an integral whose exact value can be found with the Fundamental Theorem of Calculus. This was done to illustrate the accuracy of the rule. In practice, of course, you would use the Midpoint Rule to approximate the values of definite integrals for which you cannot find an antiderivative. Examples 2 and 3 illustrate such integrals.

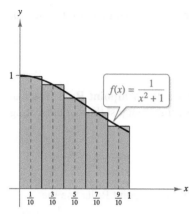

FIGURE 5.24

Example 2 **Using the Midpoint Rule**

Use the Midpoint Rule with $n = 5$ to approximate the area of the region bounded by the graph of

$$f(x) = \frac{1}{x^2 + 1}$$

the x-axis, and the lines $x = 0$ and $x = 1$.

SOLUTION The region is shown in Figure 5.24. With $n = 5$, the interval $[0, 1]$ is divided into five subintervals.

$$\left[0, \frac{1}{5}\right], \quad \left[\frac{1}{5}, \frac{2}{5}\right], \quad \left[\frac{2}{5}, \frac{3}{5}\right], \quad \left[\frac{3}{5}, \frac{4}{5}\right], \quad \left[\frac{4}{5}, 1\right]$$

The midpoints of these intervals are $\frac{1}{10}, \frac{3}{10}, \frac{5}{10}, \frac{7}{10}$, and $\frac{9}{10}$. Because each subinterval has a width of $\Delta x = (1 - 0)/5 = \frac{1}{5}$, you can approximate the value of the definite integral as shown.

$$\int_0^1 \frac{1}{x^2 + 1}\, dx \approx \frac{1}{5}\left(\frac{1}{1.01} + \frac{1}{1.09} + \frac{1}{1.25} + \frac{1}{1.49} + \frac{1}{1.81}\right)$$

$$\approx 0.786$$

The actual area of this region is $\pi/4 \approx 0.785$. So, the approximation is off by about 0.001.

✓ **Checkpoint 2**

Use the Midpoint Rule with $n = 4$ to approximate the area of the region bounded by the graph of $f(x) = 1/(x^2 + 2)$, the x-axis, and the lines $x = 0$ and $x = 1$.

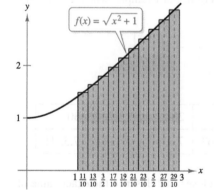

FIGURE 5.25

Example 3 **Using the Midpoint Rule**

Use the Midpoint Rule with $n = 10$ to approximate the area of the region bounded by the graph of $f(x) = \sqrt{x^2 + 1}$, the x-axis, and the lines $x = 1$ and $x = 3$.

SOLUTION The region is shown in Figure 5.25. After dividing the interval $[1, 3]$ into 10 subintervals, you can determine that the midpoints of these intervals are

$$\frac{11}{10}, \quad \frac{13}{10}, \quad \frac{3}{2}, \quad \frac{17}{10}, \quad \frac{19}{10}, \quad \frac{21}{10}, \quad \frac{23}{10}, \quad \frac{5}{2}, \quad \frac{27}{10}, \quad \text{and} \quad \frac{29}{10}.$$

Because each subinterval has a width of $\Delta x = (3 - 1)/10 = \frac{1}{5}$, you can approximate the value of the definite integral as shown.

$$\int_1^3 \sqrt{x^2 + 1}\, dx \approx \frac{1}{5}\left[\sqrt{(1.1)^2 + 1} + \sqrt{(1.3)^2 + 1} + \cdots + \sqrt{(2.9)^2 + 1}\right]$$

$$\approx 4.504$$

It can be shown that the actual area is

$$\frac{1}{2}\left[3\sqrt{10} + \ln\left(3 + \sqrt{10}\right) - \sqrt{2} - \ln\left(1 + \sqrt{2}\right)\right] \approx 4.505.$$

So, the approximation is off by about 0.001.

STUDY TIP

The Midpoint Rule is necessary for solving certain real-life problems, such as measuring irregular areas like bodies of water (see Exercise 27).

✓ **Checkpoint 3**

Use the Midpoint Rule with $n = 4$ to approximate the area of the region bounded by the graph of $f(x) = \sqrt{x^2 - 1}$, the x-axis, and the lines $x = 2$ and $x = 4$.

The Definite Integral as the Limit of a Sum

Consider the closed interval $[a, b]$, divided into n subintervals whose midpoints are x_i and whose widths are $\Delta x = (b - a)/n$. In this section, you have seen that the midpoint approximation

$$\int_a^b f(x)\, dx \approx f(x_1)\, \Delta x + f(x_2)\, \Delta x + f(x_3)\, \Delta x + \cdots + f(x_n)\, \Delta x$$

$$= [f(x_1) + f(x_2) + f(x_3) + \cdots + f(x_n)]\, \Delta x$$

becomes better and better as n increases. In fact, the limit of this sum as n approaches infinity is exactly equal to the definite integral. That is,

$$\int_a^b f(x)\, dx = \lim_{n \to \infty} [f(x_1) + f(x_2) + f(x_3) + \cdots + f(x_n)]\, \Delta x.$$

It can be shown that this limit is valid as long as x_i is *any* point in the ith interval.

FIGURE 5.26

Example 4 **Approximating a Definite Integral**

Use the Midpoint Rule program in Appendix E or a symbolic integration utility to approximate the definite integral

$$\int_0^1 e^{-x^2}\, dx.$$

SOLUTION Using the Midpoint Rule program (see Figure 5.26), you can complete the following table.

n	10	20	30	40	50
Approximation	0.7471	0.7469	0.7469	0.7468	0.7468

From the table, it appears that

$$\int_0^1 e^{-x^2}\, dx \approx 0.7468.$$

Using a symbolic integration utility, the value of the integral is approximately 0.7468241328.

✓**Checkpoint 4**

Use the Midpoint Rule program in Appendix E or a symbolic integration utility to approximate the definite integral

$$\int_0^1 e^{x^2}\, dx.$$

SUMMARIZE   (Section 5.6)

1. Describe how to approximate the area of a region using rectangles (*page 360, Example 1*).

2. State the guidelines for using the Midpoint Rule (*page 361*). For examples of using these guidelines, see Examples 2 and 3.

3. State the definite integral as the limit of a sum (*page 363*).

In Exercises 1–6, find the midpoint of the interval.

1. $\left[0, \frac{1}{3}\right]$

2. $\left[\frac{1}{10}, \frac{2}{10}\right]$

3. $\left[\frac{3}{20}, \frac{4}{20}\right]$

4. $\left[1, \frac{7}{6}\right]$

5. $\left[2, \frac{31}{15}\right]$

6. $\left[\frac{26}{9}, 3\right]$

In Exercises 7–10, find the limit.

7. $\lim\limits_{x \to \infty} \dfrac{2x^2 + 4x - 1}{3x^2 - 2x}$

8. $\lim\limits_{x \to \infty} \dfrac{4x + 5}{7x - 5}$

9. $\lim\limits_{x \to \infty} \dfrac{x - 7}{x^2 + 1}$

10. $\lim\limits_{x \to \infty} \dfrac{5x^3 + 1}{x^3 + x^2 + 4}$

Exercises 5.6

Approximating the Area of a Plane Region In Exercises 1–6, use the rectangles to approximate the area of the region. Compare your result with the exact area obtained using a definite integral. *See Example 1.*

1. $f(x) = -2x + 3, [0, 1]$ **2.** $f(x) = \dfrac{1}{x}, [1, 5]$

3. $f(x) = \sqrt{x}, [0, 1]$ **4.** $f(x) = 1 - x^2, [-1, 1]$

5. $f(x) = x^3 + 1, [0, 1]$ **6.** $f(x) = e^{-x/2}, [0, 3]$

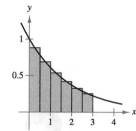

Using the Midpoint Rule In Exercises 7–12, use the Midpoint Rule with $n = 5$ to approximate the area of the region bounded by the graph of f and the x-axis over the interval. Sketch the region. *See Examples 2 and 3.*

Function	Interval
7. $f(x) = x^2$	$[1, 6]$
8. $f(x) = 4 - x^2$	$[-1, 0]$
9. $f(x) = x\sqrt{x + 4}$	$[0, 1]$
10. $f(x) = (x^2 + 1)^{2/3}$	$[0, 5]$
11. $f(x) = \dfrac{8}{x^2 + 1}$	$[-5, 5]$
12. $f(x) = \dfrac{5x}{x + 1}$	$[0, 2]$

Using the Midpoint Rule In Exercises 13–18, use the Midpoint Rule with $n = 4$ to approximate the area of the region bounded by the graph of f and the x-axis over the interval. Sketch the region. *See Examples 2 and 3.*

Function	Interval
13. $f(x) = 2x^2$	$[1, 3]$
14. $f(x) = x^2 - x^3$	$[0, 1]$
15. $f(x) = (x^2 - 4)^2$	$[-2, 2]$
16. $f(x) = \sqrt{x^2 + 3}$	$[-1, 1]$
17. $f(x) = \dfrac{1}{(x^2 + 1)^2}$	$[-1, 3]$
18. $f(x) = \dfrac{2}{x^2 + 1}$	$[0, 2]$

Approximating a Definite Integral In Exercises 19–22, use the Midpoint Rule program in Appendix E or a symbolic integration utility to approximate the definite integral. If you use a Midpoint Rule program, complete the table. *See Example 4.*

n	10	20	30	40	50
Approximation					

19. $\displaystyle\int_0^4 \sqrt{2 + 3x^2}\,dx$ **20.** $\displaystyle\int_0^2 \frac{5}{x^3 + 1}\,dx$

21. $\displaystyle\int_1^3 x\sqrt[3]{x + 1}\,dx$ **22.** $\displaystyle\int_1^6 \frac{4}{\sqrt{1 + x^2}}\,dx$

Making a Closer Approximation In Exercises 23–26, use the Midpoint Rule program in Appendix E to approximate the definite integral. How large must n be to obtain an approximation that is correct to within 0.01?

23. $\displaystyle\int_0^4 (2x^2 + 3)\,dx$ **24.** $\displaystyle\int_1^2 (x^3 - 1)\,dx$

25. $\displaystyle\int_1^4 \frac{1}{x + 1}\,dx$ **26.** $\displaystyle\int_1^2 \sqrt{x + 2}\,dx$

27. Surface Area Use the Midpoint Rule to estimate the surface area of the pond shown in the figure.

28. Surface Area Use the Midpoint Rule to estimate the surface area of the golf green shown in the figure.

29. Surface Area Use the Midpoint Rule to estimate the surface area of the oil spill shown in the figure.

30. HOW DO YOU SEE IT? The graph shows three areas representing awake time, REM (rapid eye movement) sleep time, and non-REM sleep time, over a typical individual's lifetime. *(Source: Adapted from Bernstein/Clarke-Stewart/Roy/Wickens, Psychology, Seventh Edition)*

(a) Make generalizations about the amount of total sleep time (REM and non-REM) an individual gets as he or she gets older.

(b) How would you use the Midpoint Rule to estimate the amount of REM sleep time an individual gets between birth and age 10?

31. Numerical Approximation Use the Midpoint Rule with $n = 4$ to approximate π, where

$$\pi = \int_0^1 \frac{4}{1 + x^2}\,dx.$$

Then use a graphing utility to evaluate the definite integral. Compare your results.

ALGEBRA TUTOR

xy

"Unsimplifying" an Algebraic Expression

In algebra it is often helpful to write an expression in its simplest form. In this chapter, you have seen that the reverse is often true in integration. That is, to fit an integrand to an integration formula, it often helps to "unsimplify" the expression. To do this, you use the same algebraic rules, but your goal is different. Here are some examples.

Example 1   Rewriting Algebraic Expressions

Rewrite each algebraic expression as indicated in the example.

a. $\dfrac{x - 1}{\sqrt{x}}$

b. $x(3 - 4x^2)^2$

c. $7x^2\sqrt{x^3 + 1}$

d. $5xe^{-x^2}$

SOLUTION

a. $\dfrac{x - 1}{\sqrt{x}} = \dfrac{x}{\sqrt{x}} - \dfrac{1}{\sqrt{x}}$
    Example 5, page 315
    Rewrite as two fractions.

$\qquad = \dfrac{x^1}{x^{1/2}} - \dfrac{1}{x^{1/2}}$
    Rewrite with rational exponents.

$\qquad = x^{1-1/2} - x^{-1/2}$
    Properties of exponents

$\qquad = x^{1/2} - x^{-1/2}$
    Simplify exponent.

b. $x(3 - 4x^2)^2 = \dfrac{-8}{-8}x(3 - 4x^2)^2$
    Example 2, page 324
    Multiply and divide by -8.

$\qquad = \left(-\dfrac{1}{8}\right)(-8)x(3 - 4x^2)^2$
    Regroup.

$\qquad = \left(-\dfrac{1}{8}\right)(3 - 4x^2)^2(-8x)$
    Regroup.

c. $7x^2\sqrt{x^3 + 1} = 7x^2(x^3 + 1)^{1/2}$
    Example 5, page 325
    Rewrite with rational exponent.

$\qquad = \dfrac{3}{3}(7x^2)(x^3 + 1)^{1/2}$
    Multiply and divide by 3.

$\qquad = \dfrac{7}{3}(3x^2)(x^3 + 1)^{1/2}$
    Regroup.

$\qquad = \dfrac{7}{3}(x^3 + 1)^{1/2}(3x^2)$
    Regroup.

d. $5xe^{-x^2} = \dfrac{-2}{-2}(5x)e^{-x^2}$
    Example 3, page 332
    Multiply and divide by -2.

$\qquad = \left(-\dfrac{5}{2}\right)(-2x)e^{-x^2}$
    Regroup.

$\qquad = \left(-\dfrac{5}{2}\right)e^{-x^2}(-2x)$
    Regroup.

Example 2 **Rewriting Algebraic Expressions**

Rewrite each algebraic expression.

a. $\dfrac{3x^2 + 2x - 1}{x^2}$

b. $\dfrac{1}{1 + e^{-x}}$

c. $\dfrac{x^2 + x + 1}{x - 1}$

d. $\dfrac{x^2 + 6x + 1}{x^2 + 1}$

SOLUTION

a. $\dfrac{3x^2 + 2x - 1}{x^2} = \dfrac{3x^2}{x^2} + \dfrac{2x}{x^2} - \dfrac{1}{x^2}$

        Example 7(a), page 335
        Rewrite as separate fractions.

$= 3 + \dfrac{2}{x} - x^{-2}$

        Properties of exponents

$= 3 + 2\left(\dfrac{1}{x}\right) - x^{-2}$

        Regroup.

b. $\dfrac{1}{1 + e^{-x}} = \left(\dfrac{e^x}{e^x}\right)\dfrac{1}{1 + e^{-x}}$

        Example 7(b), page 335
        Multiply and divide by e^x.

$= \dfrac{e^x}{e^x + e^x(e^{-x})}$

        Multiply.

$= \dfrac{e^x}{e^x + e^{x-x}}$

        Property of exponents

$= \dfrac{e^x}{e^x + e^0}$

        Simplify exponent.

$= \dfrac{e^x}{e^x + 1}$

        $e^0 = 1$

c. $\dfrac{x^2 + x + 1}{x - 1} = x + 2 + \dfrac{3}{x - 1}$

        Example 7(c), page 335
        Use long division as shown below.

$$
\begin{array}{r}
x + 2 \\
x - 1 \overline{)\, x^2 + x + 1} \\
\underline{x^2 - x} \\
2x + 1 \\
\underline{2x - 2} \\
3
\end{array}
$$

d. $\dfrac{x^2 + 6x + 1}{x^2 + 1} = 1 + \dfrac{6x}{x^2 + 1}$

        Bottom of page 334
        Use long division as shown below.

$$
\begin{array}{r}
1 \\
x^2 + 1 \overline{)\, x^2 + 6x + 1} \\
\underline{x^2 + 1} \\
6x
\end{array}
$$

SUMMARY AND STUDY STRATEGIES

After studying this chapter, you should have acquired the following skills.
The exercise numbers are keyed to the Review Exercises that begin on page 370.
Answers to odd-numbered Review Exercises are given in the back of the text.*

Section 5.1

Review Exercises

■ Use basic integration rules to find indefinite integrals.   *1–14*

$$\int k\,dx = kx + C$$

$$\int kf(x)\,dx = k\int f(x)\,dx$$

$$\int [f(x) + g(x)]\,dx = \int f(x)\,dx + \int g(x)\,dx$$

$$\int [f(x) - g(x)]\,dx = \int f(x)\,dx - \int g(x)\,dx$$

$$\int x^n\,dx = \frac{x^{n+1}}{n+1} + C, \quad n \neq -1$$

■ Use initial conditions to find particular solutions of indefinite integrals.   *15–18*
■ Use antiderivatives to solve real-life problems.   *19, 20*

Section 5.2

■ Use the General Power Rule or integration by substitution to find indefinite integrals.   *21–32*

$$\int u^n \frac{du}{dx}\,dx = \int u^n\,du = \frac{u^{n+1}}{n+1} + C, \quad n \neq -1$$

■ Use the General Power Rule or integration by substitution to solve real-life problems.   *33, 34*

Section 5.3

■ Use the Exponential and Log Rules to find indefinite integrals.   *35–46*

$$\int e^x\,dx = e^x + C \qquad\qquad \int \frac{1}{x}\,dx = \ln|x| + C$$

$$\int e^u \frac{du}{dx}\,dx = \int e^u\,du = e^u + C \qquad \int \frac{du/dx}{u}\,dx = \int \frac{1}{u}\,du = \ln|u| + C$$

Section 5.4

■ Find the areas of regions using a geometric formula.   *47–50*
■ Use properties of definite integrals.   *51, 52*
■ Find the areas of regions bounded by the graph of a function and the *x*-axis.   *53–58*

---

* A wide range of valuable study aids are available to help you master the material in this chapter.
The *Student Solutions Manual* includes step-by-step solutions to all odd-numbered exercises to
help you review and prepare. The student website at *www.cengagebrain.com* offers algebra help
and a *Graphing Technology Guide*, which contains step-by-step commands and instructions for a
wide variety of graphing calculators.

Section 5.4 (continued)

■ Use the Fundamental Theorem of Calculus to evaluate definite integrals.

$$\int_a^b f(x)\,dx = F(x)\Big]_a^b = F(b) - F(a), \quad \text{where} \quad F'(x) = f(x)$$

■ Find average values of functions over closed intervals.

$$\text{Average value} = \frac{1}{b-a}\int_a^b f(x)\,dx$$

■ Use properties of even and odd functions to help evaluate definite integrals.

Even function: $f(-x) = f(x)$

If f is an *even* function, then $\displaystyle\int_{-a}^a f(x)\,dx = 2\int_0^a f(x)\,dx$.

Odd function: $f(-x) = -f(x)$

If f is an *odd* function, then $\displaystyle\int_{-a}^a f(x)\,dx = 0$.

■ Find amounts of annuities.
■ Use definite integrals to solve marginal analysis problems.
■ Use average values to solve real-life problems.

Section 5.5

■ Find areas of regions bounded by two graphs.

$$A = \int_a^b [f(x) - g(x)]\,dx$$

■ Find consumer and producer surpluses.
■ Use the areas of regions bounded by two graphs to solve real-life problems.

Section 5.6

■ Use the Midpoint Rule to approximate values of definite integrals.

$$\int_a^b f(x)\,dx \approx \frac{b-a}{n}[f(x_1) + f(x_2) + f(x_3) + \cdots + f(x_n)]$$

■ Use the Midpoint Rule to solve real-life problems.

Study Strategies

■ **Indefinite and Definite Integrals**   When evaluating integrals, remember that an indefinite integral is a *family of antiderivatives*, each differing by a constant C, whereas a definite integral is a *number*.

■ **Checking Antiderivatives by Differentiating**   When finding an antiderivative, remember that you can check your result by differentiating. For example, you can confirm that the antiderivative

$$\int (3x^3 - 4x)\,dx = \frac{3}{4}x^4 - 2x^2 + C \quad \text{is correct by differentiating to obtain} \quad \frac{d}{dx}\left[\frac{3}{4}x^4 - 2x^2 + C\right] = 3x^3 - 4x.$$

Because the derivative is equal to the original integrand, you know that the antiderivative is correct.

■ **Grouping Symbols and the Fundamental Theorem**   When using the Fundamental Theorem of Calculus to evaluate a definite integral, you can avoid sign errors by using grouping symbols. Here is an example.

$$\int_1^3 (x^3 - 9x)\,dx = \left[\frac{x^4}{4} - \frac{9x^2}{2}\right]_1^3 = \left[\frac{3^4}{4} - \frac{9(3^2)}{2}\right] - \left[\frac{1^4}{4} - \frac{9(1^2)}{2}\right] = \frac{81}{4} - \frac{81}{2} - \frac{1}{4} + \frac{9}{2} = -16$$

Review Exercises

See www.CalcChat.com for worked-out solutions to odd-numbered exercises.

Finding Indefinite Integrals In Exercises 1–14, find the indefinite integral. Check your result by differentiation.

1. $\displaystyle\int 16\,dx$

2. $\displaystyle\int -9\,dx$

3. $\displaystyle\int \frac{3}{5}x\,dx$

4. $\displaystyle\int 6x\,dx$

5. $\displaystyle\int 3x^2\,dx$

6. $\displaystyle\int 8x^3\,dx$

7. $\displaystyle\int (2x^2 + 5x)\,dx$

8. $\displaystyle\int (5 - 6x^2)\,dx$

9. $\displaystyle\int \frac{2}{3\sqrt[3]{x}}\,dx$

10. $\displaystyle\int 6x^{5/2}\,dx$

11. $\displaystyle\int \left(\sqrt[3]{x^4} + 3x\right)dx$

12. $\displaystyle\int \left(\frac{4}{\sqrt{x}} + \sqrt{x}\right)dx$

13. $\displaystyle\int \frac{2x^4 - 1}{\sqrt{x}}\,dx$

14. $\displaystyle\int \frac{1 - 3x}{x^2}\,dx$

Finding Particular Solutions In Exercises 15–18, find the particular solution that satisfies the differential equation and the initial condition.

15. $f'(x) = 12x;\ f(0) = -3$

16. $f'(x) = 3x + 1;\ f(2) = 6$

17. $f'(x) = 3x^2 - 8x;\ f(1) = 12$

18. $f'(x) = \sqrt{x};\ f(9) = 4$

19. **Vertical Motion** An object is projected upward from the ground with an initial velocity of 80 feet per second. Express the height s (in feet) of the object as a function of the time t (in seconds). How long will the object be in the air? (Use $s''(t) = -32$ feet per second per second as the acceleration due to gravity.)

20. **Revenue** A company produces a new product for which the rate of change of the revenue can be modeled by

$$\frac{dR}{dt} = 0.675t^{3/2}, \quad 0 \le t \le 225$$

where t is the time (in weeks). When $t = 0$, $R = 0$.
(a) Find a model for the revenue function.
(b) What is the revenue after 20 weeks?
(c) When will the weekly revenue be $27,000?

Applying the General Power Rule In Exercises 21–32, find the indefinite integral. Check your result by differentiation.

21. $\displaystyle\int (x + 4)^3\,dx$

22. $\displaystyle\int (x - 6)^{4/3}\,dx$

23. $\displaystyle\int (5x + 1)^4(5)\,dx$

24. $\displaystyle\int (x^3 + 1)^2(3x^2)\,dx$

25. $\displaystyle\int (1 + 5x)^2\,dx$

26. $\displaystyle\int (6x - 2)^4\,dx$

27. $\displaystyle\int x^2(3x^3 + 1)^2\,dx$

28. $\displaystyle\int x(1 - 4x^2)^3\,dx$

29. $\displaystyle\int \frac{x^2}{(2x^3 - 5)^3}\,dx$

30. $\displaystyle\int \frac{x^2}{(x^3 - 4)^2}\,dx$

31. $\displaystyle\int \frac{1}{\sqrt{5x - 1}}\,dx$

32. $\displaystyle\int \frac{4x}{\sqrt{1 - 3x^2}}\,dx$

33. **Production** The rate of change of the output of a small sawmill is modeled by

$$\frac{dP}{dt} = 2t(0.001t^2 + 0.5)^{1/4}, \quad 0 \le t \le 40$$

where t is the time (in hours) and P is the output (in board-feet). Find the numbers of board-feet produced in (a) 6 hours and (b) 12 hours.

34. Cost The marginal cost for a catering service to cater to x people can be modeled by

$$\frac{dC}{dx} = \frac{5x}{\sqrt{x^2 + 1000}}.$$

When $x = 225$, the cost C (in dollars) is \$1136.06. Find the costs of catering to (a) 500 people and (b) 1000 people.

Using the Exponential and Log Rules In Exercises 35–46, use the Exponential Rule or the Log Rule to find the indefinite integral.

35. $\displaystyle\int 4e^{4x}\, dx$

36. $\displaystyle\int 3e^{-3x}\, dx$

37. $\displaystyle\int e^{-5x}\, dx$

38. $\displaystyle\int e^{6x}\, dx$

39. $\displaystyle\int 7xe^{3x^2}\, dx$

40. $\displaystyle\int (2t - 1)e^{t^2 - t}\, dt$

41. $\displaystyle\int \frac{1}{x - 6}\, dx$

42. $\displaystyle\int \frac{1}{1 - 4x}\, dx$

43. $\displaystyle\int \frac{4}{6x - 1}\, dx$

44. $\displaystyle\int \frac{5}{2x + 3}\, dx$

45. $\displaystyle\int \frac{x^2}{1 - x^3}\, dx$

46. $\displaystyle\int \frac{x - 4}{x^2 - 8x}\, dx$

Evaluating a Definite Integral Using a Geometric Formula In Exercises 47–50, sketch the region whose area is given by the definite integral. Then use a geometric formula to evaluate the integral.

47. $\displaystyle\int_0^3 2\, dx$

48. $\displaystyle\int_0^6 \frac{x}{2}\, dx$

49. $\displaystyle\int_0^4 (4 - x)\, dx$

50. $\displaystyle\int_{-4}^4 \sqrt{16 - x^2}\, dx$

51. Using Properties of Definite Integrals Given

$$\int_2^6 f(x)\, dx = 10 \quad \text{and} \quad \int_2^6 g(x)\, dx = 3$$

evaluate the definite integral.

(a) $\displaystyle\int_2^6 [f(x) + g(x)]\, dx$ (b) $\displaystyle\int_2^6 [f(x) - g(x)]\, dx$

(c) $\displaystyle\int_2^6 [2f(x) - 3g(x)]\, dx$ (d) $\displaystyle\int_2^6 5f(x)\, dx$

52. Using Properties of Definite Integrals Given

$$\int_0^3 f(x)\, dx = 4 \quad \text{and} \quad \int_3^6 f(x)\, dx = -1$$

evaluate the definite integral.

(a) $\displaystyle\int_0^6 f(x)\, dx$ (b) $\displaystyle\int_6^3 f(x)\, dx$

(c) $\displaystyle\int_4^4 f(x)\, dx$ (d) $\displaystyle\int_3^6 -10f(x)\, dx$

Finding Area by the Fundamental Theorem In Exercises 53–58, find the area of the region.

53. $f(x) = 4 - x^2$ **54.** $f(x) = 9 - x^2$

     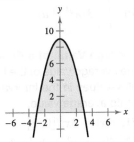

55. $f(x) = \dfrac{2}{x + 1}$ **56.** $f(x) = \dfrac{4}{\sqrt{x}}$

57. $f(x) = 2e^{x/2}$ **58.** $f(x) = \dfrac{x - 1}{x}$

Evaluating a Definite Integral In Exercises 59–70, use the Fundamental Theorem of Calculus to evaluate the definite integral.

59. $\displaystyle\int_0^4 (2 + x)\, dx$

60. $\displaystyle\int_{-1}^1 (t^2 + 2)\, dt$

61. $\displaystyle\int_{-1}^1 (4t^3 - 2t)\, dt$

62. $\displaystyle\int_{-2}^2 (x^4 + 2x^2 - 5)\, dx$

63. $\displaystyle\int_{-2}^0 (x + 2)^3\, dx$

64. $\displaystyle\int_2^4 (2x - 3)^2\, dx$

65. $\displaystyle\int_0^3 \frac{1}{\sqrt{1 + x}}\, dx$

66. $\displaystyle\int_3^6 \frac{x}{3\sqrt{x^2 - 8}}\, dx$

67. $\displaystyle\int_3^9 \frac{5}{x}\, dx$

68. $\displaystyle\int_1^2 \left(\frac{1}{x^2} - \frac{1}{x^3}\right) dx$

69. $\displaystyle\int_0^{\ln 5} e^{x/5}\, dx$

70. $\displaystyle\int_{-1}^1 3xe^{x^2 - 1}\, dx$

Average Value of a Function In Exercises 71–76, find the average value of the function on the interval. Then find all x-values in the interval for which the function is equal to its average value.

71. $f(x) = 3x;\ [0, 2]$

72. $f(x) = x^2 + 2;\ [-3, 3]$

73. $f(x) = -2e^x;\ [0, 3]$

74. $f(x) = e^{5-x};\ [2, 5]$

75. $f(x) = \dfrac{1}{\sqrt{x}};\ [4, 9]$

76. $f(x) = \dfrac{1}{(x + 5)^2};\ [-1, 6]$

Integrating Even and Odd Functions In Exercises 77–80, evaluate the definite integral by using the properties of even and odd functions.

77. $\displaystyle\int_{-2}^2 6x^5\, dx$

78. $\displaystyle\int_{-4}^4 3x^4\, dx$

79. $\displaystyle\int_{-3}^3 (x^4 + x^2)\, dx$

80. $\displaystyle\int_{-1}^1 (x^3 - x)\, dx$

Finding the Amount of an Annuity In Exercises 81 and 82, find the amount of an annuity with income function $c(t)$, interest rate r, and term T.

81. $c(t) = \$3000,\ r = 6\%,\ T = 5$ years

82. $c(t) = \$1200,\ r = 7\%,\ T = 8$ years

83. Cost The marginal cost of serving an additional typical client at a law firm can be modeled by

$$\frac{dC}{dx} = 675 + 0.5x$$

where x is the number of clients. Find the change in cost C (in dollars) when x increases from 50 to 51 clients.

84. Profit The marginal profit obtained by selling x dollars of automobile insurance can be modeled by

$$\frac{dP}{dx} = 0.4\left(1 - \frac{5000}{x}\right), \quad x \ge 5000.$$

Find the change in the profit P (in dollars) when x increases from \$75,000 to \$100,000.

85. Compound Interest A deposit of \$500 is made in a savings account at an annual interest rate of 4%, compounded continuously. Find the average balance in the account during the first 2 years.

86. Revenue The rate of change in revenue for Texas Roadhouse from 2003 through 2009 can be modeled by

$$\frac{dR}{dt} = -11.5000t^2 + 142.140t - 294.91$$

where R is the revenue (in millions of dollars) and t is the time in years, with $t = 3$ corresponding to 2003. In 2006, the revenue for Texas Roadhouse was \$597.1 million. *(Source: Texas Roadhouse, Inc.)*

(a) Find the model for the revenue of Texas Roadhouse.

(b) What was the average revenue of Texas Roadhouse for 2003 through 2009?

Finding the Area Bounded by Two Graphs In Exercises 87–94, sketch the region bounded by the graphs of the functions and find the area of the region.

87. $y = \dfrac{1}{x^3},\ y = 0,\ x = 1,\ x = 3$

88. $y = x^2 + 4x - 5,\ y = 4x - 1$

89. $y = (x - 3)^2,\ y = 8 - (x - 3)^2$

90. $y = 4 - x,\ y = x^2 - 5x + 8,\ x = 0$

91. $y = \dfrac{4}{\sqrt{x + 1}},\ y = 0,\ x = 0,\ x = 8$

92. $y = \sqrt{x}(1 - x),\ y = 0$

93. $y = x,\ y = x^3$

94. $y = x^3 - 4x,\ y = -x^2 - 2x$

Consumer and Producer Surpluses In Exercises 95–98, find the consumer and producer surpluses by using the demand and supply functions, where p is the price (in dollars) and x is the number of units (in millions).

Demand Function	Supply Function
95. $p = 36 - 0.35x$	$p = 0.05x$
96. $p = 200 - 0.2x$	$p = 50 + 1.3x$
97. $p = 250 - x$	$p = 150 + x$
98. $p = 500 - x$	$p = 1.25x + 162.5$

99. Revenue For the years 2015 through 2020, two models, R_1 and R_2, used to project the revenue (in millions of dollars) for a company are

$$R_1 = 24.3 + 8.24t$$

and

$$R_2 = 21.6 + 9.36t$$

where $t = 15$ corresponds to 2015. Which model projects the greater revenue? How much more total revenue does that model project over the six-year period?

100. Sales For the years 2000 through 2009, the sales (in millions of dollars) for Men's Wearhouse can be modeled by

$$R = \begin{cases} 23.596t^2 - 41.55t + 1310.5, & 0 \le t \le 6 \\ 38.7t^2 - 720.7t + 5261.2, & 6 < t \le 9 \end{cases}$$

where t is the year, with $t = 0$ corresponding to 2000. *(Source: Men's Wearhouse, Inc.)*

(a) Use a graphing utility to graph this model.

(b) Suppose the sales from 2007 through 2009 had continued to follow the model for 2000 through 2006. How much more or less would the sales have been for Men's Wearhouse?

101. Cost, Revenue, and Profit The revenue from a manufacturing process (in millions of dollars) is projected to follow the model

$$R = 70$$

for 10 years. Over the same period of time, the cost (in millions of dollars) is projected to follow the model

$$C = 30 + 0.3t^2$$

where t is the time (in years). Approximate the profit over the 10-year period.

102. Cost, Revenue, and Profit Repeat Exercise 101 for revenue and cost models given by

$$R = 70 + 0.1t$$

and

$$C = 30 + 0.3t^2.$$

Did the profit increase or decrease? Explain why.

Approximating the Area of a Plane Region In Exercises 103 and 104, use the rectangles to approximate the area of the region. Compare your result with the exact area obtained using a definite integral.

103. $f(x) = \dfrac{x}{3}$, $[0, 3]$

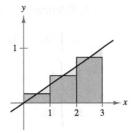

104. $f(x) = x^2 + 1$, $[0, 1]$

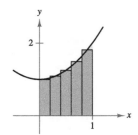

Using the Midpoint Rule In Exercises 105–108, use the Midpoint Rule with $n = 4$ to approximate the area of the region bounded by the graph of f and the x-axis over the interval. Sketch the region.

Function	Interval
105. $f(x) = x^2$	$[0, 2]$
106. $f(x) = 2x - x^3$	$[0, 1]$
107. $f(x) = (x^2 - 1)^2$	$[-1, 1]$
108. $f(x) = \dfrac{3x}{x + 2}$	$[0, 4]$

Using the Midpoint Rule In Exercises 109–112, use the Midpoint Rule with $n = 6$ to approximate the area of the region bounded by the graph of f and the x-axis over the interval. Sketch the region.

Function	Interval
109. $f(x) = x + 3$	$[0, 3]$
110. $f(x) = 9 - x^2$	$[-3, 3]$
111. $f(x) = x\sqrt{x + 1}$	$[0, 2]$
112. $f(x) = \dfrac{3}{x^2 + 1}$	$[-6, 6]$

113. Surface Area Use the Midpoint Rule to estimate the surface area of the swamp shown in the figure.

TEST YOURSELF

See www.CalcChat.com for worked-out solutions to odd-numbered exercises.

Take this test as you would take a test in class. When you are done, check your work against the answers given in the back of the book.

In Exercises 1–6, find the indefinite integral.

1. $\displaystyle\int (9x^2 - 4x + 13)\, dx$

2. $\displaystyle\int (x + 1)^2\, dx$

3. $\displaystyle\int 4x^3\sqrt{x^4 - 7}\, dx$

4. $\displaystyle\int \frac{5x - 6}{\sqrt{x}}\, dx$

5. $\displaystyle\int 15e^{3x}\, dx$

6. $\displaystyle\int \frac{3}{4x - 1}\, dx$

In Exercises 7 and 8, find the particular solution that satisfies the differential equation and initial condition.

7. $f'(x) = 6x - 5; f(-1) = 6$

8. $f'(x) = e^x + 1; f(0) = 1$

In Exercises 9–14, evaluate the definite integral.

9. $\displaystyle\int_0^1 16x\, dx$

10. $\displaystyle\int_{-3}^3 (3 - 2x)\, dx$

11. $\displaystyle\int_{-1}^1 (x^3 + x^2)\, dx$

12. $\displaystyle\int_{-1}^2 \frac{2x}{\sqrt{x^2 + 1}}\, dx$

13. $\displaystyle\int_0^3 e^{4x}\, dx$

14. $\displaystyle\int_{-2}^3 \frac{1}{x + 3}\, dx$

15. The rate of change in sales of PetSmart from 2000 through 2009 can be modeled by

$$\frac{dS}{dt} = 226.912e^{0.1013t}$$

where S is the sales (in millions of dollars) and t is the time (in years), with $t = 0$ corresponding to 2000. In 2004, the sales of PetSmart were $3363.5 million. (*Source: PetSmart, Inc.*)

(a) Find the model for the sales of PetSmart.

(b) What were the average sales for 2000 through 2009?

In Exercises 16 and 17, sketch the region bounded by the graphs of the functions and find the area of the region.

16. $f(x) = 6,\ g(x) = x^2 - x - 6$

17. $f(x) = \sqrt[3]{x},\ g(x) = x^2$

18. The demand and supply functions for a product are modeled by

Demand: $p = -0.625x + 10$ and   *Supply:* $p = 0.25x + 3$

where p is the price (in dollars) and x is the number of units (in millions). Find the consumer and producer surpluses for this product.

In Exercises 19 and 20, use the Midpoint Rule with $n = 4$ to approximate the area of the region bounded by the graph of f and the x-axis over the interval. Compare your result with the exact area. Sketch the region.

19. $f(x) = 3x^2,\quad [0, 1]$

20. $f(x) = x^2 + 1,\quad [-1, 1]$

Appendices

Appendices D and E are located on the website that accompanies this text at *www.cengagebrain.com*.

A

Precalculus Review

A.1 The Real Number Line and Order

■ Represent, classify, and order real numbers.
■ Use inequalities to represent sets of real numbers.
■ Solve inequalities.
■ Use inequalities to model and solve real-life problems.

The Real Number Line

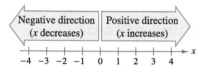

The Real Number Line

FIGURE A.1

Real numbers can be represented with a coordinate system called the **real number line** (or x-axis), as shown in Figure A.1. The **positive direction** (to the right) is denoted by an arrowhead and indicates the direction of increasing values of x. The real number corresponding to a particular point on the real number line is called the **coordinate** of the point. As shown in Figure A.1, it is customary to label those points whose coordinates are integers.

The point on the real number line corresponding to zero is called the **origin.** Numbers to the right of the origin are **positive,** and numbers to the left of the origin are **negative.** The term **nonnegative** describes a number that is either positive or zero.

The importance of the real number line is that it provides you with a conceptually perfect picture of the real numbers. That is, each point on the real number line corresponds to one and only one real number, and each real number corresponds to one and only one point on the real number line. This type of relationship is called a **one-to-one correspondence** and is illustrated in Figure A.2.

Every point on the real number line corresponds to one and only one real number.

Every real number corresponds to one and only one point on the real number line.

FIGURE A.2

Each of the four points in Figure A.2 corresponds to a real number that can be expressed as the ratio of two integers.

$$-2.6 = -\frac{13}{5} \qquad \frac{5}{4} \qquad -\frac{7}{3} \qquad 1.85 = \frac{37}{20}$$

Such numbers are called **rational.** Rational numbers have either terminating or infinitely repeating decimal representations.

Terminating Decimals

$$\frac{2}{5} = 0.4$$

$$\frac{7}{8} = 0.875$$

Infinitely Repeating Decimals

$$\frac{1}{3} = 0.333 \ldots = 0.\overline{3}*$$

$$\frac{12}{7} = 1.714285714285 \ldots = 1.\overline{714285}$$

Real numbers that are not rational are called **irrational,** and they cannot be represented as the ratio of two integers (or as terminating or infinitely repeating decimals). So, a decimal approximation is used to represent an irrational number. Some irrational numbers occur so frequently in applications that mathematicians have invented special symbols to represent them. For example, the symbols $\sqrt{2}$, π, and e represent irrational numbers whose decimal approximations are as shown. (See Figure A.3.)

$$\sqrt{2} \approx 1.4142135623$$

$$\pi \approx 3.1415926535$$

$$e \approx 2.7182818284$$

FIGURE A.3

---

*The bar indicates which digit or digits repeat infinitely.

Order and Intervals on the Real Number Line

One important property of the real numbers is that they are **ordered:** 0 is less than 1, -3 is less than -2.5, π is less than $\frac{22}{7}$, and so on. You can visualize this property on the real number line by observing that a is less than b if and only if a lies to the left of b on the real number line. Symbolically, "a is less than b" is denoted by the inequality $a < b$. For example, the inequality

$$\tfrac{3}{4} < 1$$

follows from the fact that $\frac{3}{4}$ lies to the left of 1 on the real number line, as shown in Figure A.4.

$\frac{3}{4}$ lies to the left of 1, so $\frac{3}{4} < 1$.

FIGURE A.4

When three real numbers a, x, and b are ordered such that $a < x$ and $x < b$, we say that x is **between** a and b and write

$a < x < b.$ x is between a and b.

The set of *all* real numbers between a and b is called the **open interval** between a and b and is denoted by (a, b). An interval of the form (a, b) does not contain the "endpoints" a and b. Intervals that include their endpoints are called **closed** and are denoted by $[a, b]$. Intervals of the form $[a, b)$ and $(a, b]$ are neither open nor closed. Figure A.5 shows the nine types of intervals on the real number line.

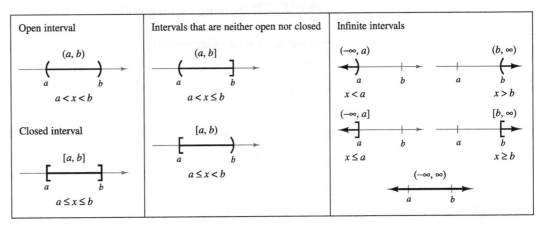

Intervals on the Real Number Line

FIGURE A.5

Note that a square bracket is used to denote "less than or equal to" ($\leq$) or "greater than or equal to" ($\geq$). Furthermore, the symbols

∞ Positive infinity

and

$-\infty$ Negative infinity

denote **positive** and **negative infinity,** respectively. These symbols do not denote real numbers; they merely let you describe unbounded conditions more concisely. For instance, the interval $[b, \infty)$ is unbounded to the right because it includes *all* real numbers that are greater than or equal to b.

Solving Inequalities

In calculus, you are frequently required to "solve inequalities" involving variable expressions such as $3x - 4 < 5$. The number a is a **solution** of an inequality if the inequality is true when a is substituted for x. The set of all values of x that satisfy an inequality is called the **solution set** of the inequality. The following properties are useful for solving inequalities. (Similar properties are obtained when $<$ is replaced by $\le$ and $>$ is replaced by $\ge$.)

Properties of Inequalities

Let a, b, c, and d be real numbers.

1. Transitive property: $a < b$ and $b < c$ $\implies$ $a < c$
2. Adding inequalities: $a < b$ and $c < d$ $\implies$ $a + c < b + d$
3. Multiplying by a (positive) constant: $a < b$ $\implies$ $ac < bc, \quad c > 0$
4. Multiplying by a (negative) constant: $a < b$ $\implies$ $ac > bc, \quad c < 0$
5. Adding a constant: $a < b$ $\implies$ $a + c < b + c$
6. Subtracting a constant: $a < b$ $\implies$ $a - c < b - c$

Note that you *reverse the inequality* when you multiply by a negative number. For example, if $x < 3$, then $-4x > -12$. This principle also applies to division by a negative number. So, if $-2x > 4$, then $x < -2$.

Example 1   **Solving an Inequality**

Find the solution set of the inequality

$$3x - 4 < 5.$$

SOLUTION

$3x - 4 < 5$	Write original inequality.
$3x - 4 + 4 < 5 + 4$	Add 4 to each side.
$3x < 9$	Simplify.
$\dfrac{1}{3}(3x) < \dfrac{1}{3}(9)$	Multiply each side by $\frac{1}{3}$.
$x < 3$	Simplify.

So, the solution set is the interval $(-\infty, 3)$, as shown in Figure A.6. Once you have solved an inequality, it is a good idea to check some x-values in your solution set to see whether they satisfy the original inequality. You should also check some values outside your solution set to verify that they do *not* satisfy the inequality. For instance, Figure A.6 shows that when $x = 0$ or $x = 2$, the inequality is satisfied, but when $x = 4$, the inequality is not satisfied.

For $x = 0$, $3(0) - 4 = -4$.
For $x = 2$, $3(2) - 4 = 2$.
For $x = 4$, $3(4) - 4 = 8$.

Solution set for
$3x - 4 < 5$

FIGURE A.6

✓ **Checkpoint 1**

Find the solution set of the inequality

$$2x - 3 < 7.$$

In Example 1, all five inequalities listed as steps in the solution have the same solution set, and they are called **equivalent inequalities**.

The inequality in Example 1 involves a first-degree polynomial. To solve inequalities involving polynomials of higher degree, you can use the fact that a polynomial can change signs *only* at its real zeros (the real numbers that make the polynomial zero). Between two consecutive real zeros, a polynomial must be entirely positive or entirely negative. This means that when the real zeros of a polynomial are put in order, they divide the real number line into **test intervals** in which the polynomial has no sign changes. That is, if a polynomial has the factored form

$$(x - r_1)(x - r_2), \ldots, (x - r_n), \qquad r_1 < r_2 < r_3 < \cdots < r_{n-1} < r_n$$

then the test intervals are

$$(-\infty, r_1), \quad (r_1, r_2), \quad \ldots, \quad (r_{n-1}, r_n), \quad \text{and} \quad (r_n, \infty).$$

For example, the polynomial

$$x^2 - x - 6 = (x - 3)(x + 2)$$

can change signs only at $x = -2$ and $x = 3$. To determine the sign of the polynomial in the intervals $(-\infty, -2)$, $(-2, 3)$, and $(3, \infty)$, you need to test only *one value* in each interval.

Example 2   Solving a Polynomial Inequality

$$\begin{array}{ll} x^2 < x + 6 & \text{Original inequality} \\ x^2 - x - 6 < 0 & \text{Polynomial form} \\ (x - 3)(x + 2) < 0 & \text{Factor.} \end{array}$$

So, the polynomial $x^2 - x - 6$ has $x = -2$ and $x = 3$ as its zeros. You can solve the inequality by testing the sign of the polynomial in each of the intervals $(-\infty, -2)$, $(-2, 3)$, and $(3, \infty)$. In each interval, choose a representative x-value and evaluate the polynomial.

Interval	x-Value	Polynomial Value	Conclusion
$(-\infty, -2)$	$x = -3$	$(-3)^2 - (-3) - 6 = 6$	Positive
$(-2, 3)$	$x = 0$	$(0)^2 - (0) - 6 = -6$	Negative
$(3, \infty)$	$x = 4$	$(4)^2 - (4) - 6 = 6$	Positive

From this you can conclude that the inequality is satisfied for all x-values in $(-2, 3)$. This implies that the solution of the inequality $x^2 < x + 6$ is the interval $(-2, 3)$, as shown in Figure A.7. Note that the original inequality contains a "less than" symbol. This means that the solution set does not contain the endpoints of the test interval $(-2, 3)$.

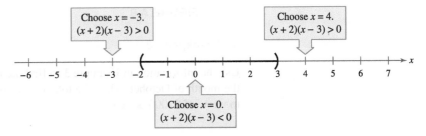

FIGURE A.7

✓ **Checkpoint 2**

Find the solution set of the inequality

$$x^2 > 3x + 10.$$

Application

Inequalities are frequently used to describe conditions that occur in business and science. For instance, the inequality

$$8.8 \leq W \leq 26.4$$

describes the typical weights W (in pounds) of adult rhesus monkeys. Example 3 shows how an inequality can be used to describe the production levels in a manufacturing plant.

 Example 3   **Production Levels**

In addition to fixed overhead costs of $500 per day, the cost of producing x units of an item is $2.50 per unit. During the month of August, the total cost of production varied from a high of $1325 to a low of $1200 per day. Find the high and low *production levels* during the month.

SOLUTION   Because it costs $2.50 to produce one unit, it costs $2.5x$ to produce x units. Furthermore, because the fixed cost per day is $500, the total daily cost C (in dollars) of producing x units is

$$C = 2.5x + 500.$$

Now, because the cost ranged from $1200 to $1325, you can write the following.

$$1200 \leq \quad 2.5x + 500 \quad \leq 1325 \qquad \text{Write original inequality.}$$
$$1200 - 500 \leq 2.5x + 500 - 500 \leq 1325 - 500 \qquad \text{Subtract 500 from each part.}$$
$$700 \leq \quad 2.5x \quad \leq 825 \qquad \text{Simplify.}$$
$$\frac{700}{2.5} \leq \quad \frac{2.5x}{2.5} \quad \leq \frac{825}{2.5} \qquad \text{Divide each part by 2.5.}$$
$$280 \leq \quad x \quad \leq 330 \qquad \text{Simplify.}$$

So, the daily production levels during the month of August varied from a low of 280 units to a high of 330 units, as shown in Figure A.8.

Each day's production during the month fell in this interval.

Low daily production

High daily production

FIGURE A.8

✓ **Checkpoint 3**

Use the information in Example 3 to find the high and low production levels during the month of October, when the total cost of production varied from a high of $1500 to a low of $1000 per day.

Exercises A.1

See www.CalcChat.com for worked-out solutions to odd-numbered exercises.

Classifying Real Numbers In Exercises 1–10, determine whether the real number is rational or irrational.

1. 0.25

2. -3678

3. $\dfrac{3\pi}{2}$

4. $3\sqrt{2} - 1$

5. $4.3\overline{451}$

6. $\dfrac{22}{7}$

7. $\sqrt[3]{64}$

8. $0.\overline{8177}$

9. $\sqrt[3]{60}$

10. $2e$

Checking Solutions In Exercises 11–14, determine whether each given value of x satisfies the inequality.

11. $5x - 12 > 0$

   (a) $x = 3$ (b) $x = -3$ (c) $x = \frac{5}{2}$

12. $x + 1 < \dfrac{x}{3}$

   (a) $x = 0$ (b) $x = 4$ (c) $x = -4$

13. $0 < \dfrac{x-2}{4} < 2$

   (a) $x = 4$ (b) $x = 10$ (c) $x = 0$

14. $-1 < \dfrac{3-x}{2} \le 1$

   (a) $x = 0$ (b) $x = 1$ (c) $x = 5$

Solving an Inequality In Exercises 15–28, solve the inequality. Then graph the solution set on the real number line. *See Examples 1 and 2.*

15. $x - 5 \ge 7$

16. $2x > 3$

17. $4x + 1 < 2x$

18. $2x + 7 < 3$

19. $4 - 2x < 3x - 1$

20. $x - 4 \le 2x + 1$

21. $-4 < 2x - 3 < 4$

22. $0 \le x + 3 < 5$

23. $\dfrac{3}{4} > x + 1 > \dfrac{1}{4}$

24. $-1 < -\dfrac{x}{3} < 1$

25. $\dfrac{x}{2} + \dfrac{x}{3} > 5$

26. $\dfrac{x}{2} - \dfrac{x}{3} > 5$

27. $2x^2 - x < 6$

28. $2x^2 + 1 < 9x - 3$

Writing Inequalities In Exercises 29–32, use inequality notation to describe the subset of real numbers.

29. **Earnings Per Share** A company expects its earnings per share E for the next quarter to be no less than $4.10 and no more than $4.25.

30. **Production** The estimated daily oil production p at a refinery is greater than 2 million barrels but less than 2.4 million barrels.

31. **Survey** According to a survey, the percent p of Americans who now conduct most of their banking transactions online is no more than 40%.

32. **Income** The net income I of a company is expected to be no less than $239 million.

33. **Physiology** The maximum heart rate of a person in normal health is related to the person's age by the equation

$$r = 220 - A$$

where r is the maximum heart rate (in beats per minute) and A is the person's age (in years). Some physiologists recommend that during physical activity, a sedentary person should strive to increase his or her heart rate to at least 60% of the maximum heart rate, and a highly fit person should strive to increase his or her heart rate to at most 90% of the maximum heart rate. Use inequality notation to express the range of the target heart rate for physical activity for a 20-year-old.

34. **Annual Operating Costs** A utility company has a fleet of vans. The annual operating cost C (in dollars) of each van is estimated to be

$$C = 0.35m + 2500$$

where m is the number of miles driven. What number of miles will yield an annual operating cost that is less than $13,000?

35. **Profit** The revenue for selling x units of a product is

$$R = 115.95x$$

and the cost of producing x units is

$$C = 95x + 750.$$

To obtain a profit, the revenue must be *greater than* the cost. For what values of x will this product return a profit?

36. **Sales** A doughnut shop sells a dozen doughnuts for $4.50. Beyond the fixed cost of $220 per day, it costs $2.75 for enough materials and labor to produce each dozen doughnuts. During the month of January, the daily profit varies between $60 and $270. Between what levels (in dozens) do the daily sales vary?

True or False? In Exercises 37 and 38, determine whether each statement is true or false, given $a < b$.

37. (a) $-2a < -2b$

   (b) $a + 2 < b + 2$

   (c) $6a < 6b$

   (d) $\dfrac{1}{a} < \dfrac{1}{b}$

38. (a) $a - 4 < b - 4$

   (b) $4 - a < 4 - b$

   (c) $-3b < -3a$

   (d) $\dfrac{a}{4} < \dfrac{b}{4}$

A.2 Absolute Value and Distance on the Real Number Line

- Find the absolute values of real numbers and understand the properties of absolute value.
- Find the distance between two numbers on the real number line.
- Define intervals on the real number line.
- Use intervals to model and solve real-life problems and find the midpoint of an interval.

Absolute Value of a Real Number

TECH TUTOR

Absolute value expressions can be evaluated on a graphing utility. When an expression such as $|3 - 8|$ is evaluated, parentheses should surround the expression, as in abs$(3 - 8)$.

Definition of Absolute Value

The **absolute value** of a real number a is

$$|a| = \begin{cases} a, & \text{if } a \geq 0 \\ -a, & \text{if } a < 0. \end{cases}$$

At first glance, it may appear from this definition that the absolute value of a real number can be negative, but this is not possible. For example, let $a = -3$. Then, because $-3 < 0$, you have

$$|a| = |-3| = -(-3) = 3.$$

The following properties are useful for working with absolute values.

Properties of Absolute Value

1. Multiplication: $|ab| = |a||b|$

2. Division: $\left|\dfrac{a}{b}\right| = \dfrac{|a|}{|b|}, \quad b \neq 0$

3. Power: $|a^n| = |a|^n$

4. Square root: $\sqrt{a^2} = |a|$

Be sure you understand the fourth property in this list. A common error in algebra is to imagine that by squaring a number and then taking the square root, you come back to the original number. But this is true only if the original number is nonnegative. For instance, if $a = 2$, then

$$\sqrt{2^2} = \sqrt{4} = 2$$

but if $a = -2$, then

$$\sqrt{(-2)^2} = \sqrt{4} = 2.$$

The reason for this is that (by definition) the square root symbol

$$\sqrt{}$$

denotes only the nonnegative root.

Distance on the Real Number Line

Directed distance
from a to b:

$b - a$

Directed distance
from b to a:

$a - b$

Distance between
a and b:

$|a - b|$ or $|b - a|$

FIGURE A.9

Consider two distinct points on the real number line, as shown in Figure A.9.

1. The **directed distance from a to b** is

   $b - a$.

2. The **directed distance from b to a** is

   $a - b$.

3. The **distance between a and b** is

   $|a - b|$ or $|b - a|$.

   In Figure A.9, note that because b is to the right of a, the directed distance from a to b (moving to the right) is positive. Moreover, because a is to the left of b, the directed distance from b to a (moving to the left) is negative. The distance *between* two points on the real number line can never be negative.

Distance Between Two Points on the Real Number Line

The distance d between points x_1 and x_2 on the real number line is given by

$$d = |x_2 - x_1| = \sqrt{(x_2 - x_1)^2}.$$

Note that the order of subtraction with x_1 and x_2 does not matter because

$$|x_2 - x_1| = |x_1 - x_2| \quad \text{and} \quad (x_2 - x_1)^2 = (x_1 - x_2)^2.$$

Example 1 Finding Distance on the Real Number Line

Determine the distance between -3 and 4 on the real number line. What is the directed distance from -3 to 4? What is the directed distance from 4 to -3?

SOLUTION   The distance between -3 and 4 is given by

$$|-3 - 4| = |-7| = 7 \qquad |a - b|$$

or

$$|4 - (-3)| = |7| = 7 \qquad |b - a|$$

as shown in Figure A.10.

FIGURE A.10

The directed distance from -3 to 4 is

$$4 - (-3) = 7. \qquad b - a$$

The directed distance from 4 to -3 is

$$-3 - 4 = -7. \qquad a - b$$

✓ **Checkpoint 1**

Determine the distance between -2 and 6 on the real number line. What is the directed distance from -2 to 6? What is the directed distance from 6 to -2?

Intervals Defined by Absolute Value

Example 2   Defining an Interval on the Real Number Line

Find the interval on the real number line that contains all numbers that lie no more than two units from 3.

SOLUTION   Let x be any point in this interval. You need to find all x such that the distance between x and 3 is less than or equal to 2. This implies that

$$|x - 3| \leq 2.$$

Requiring the absolute value of $x - 3$ to be less than or equal to 2 means that $x - 3$ must lie between -2 and 2. So, you can write

$$-2 \leq x - 3 \leq 2.$$

Solving this pair of inequalities, you have

$$-2 + 3 \leq x - 3 + 3 \leq 2 + 3$$
$$1 \leq \quad x \quad \leq 5. \qquad \text{Solution set}$$

So, the interval is $[1, 5]$, as shown in Figure A.11.

FIGURE A.11

✓ Checkpoint 2

Find the interval on the real number line that contains all numbers that lie no more than four units from 6.

Two Basic Types of Inequalities Involving Absolute Value

Let a and d be real numbers, where $d > 0$.

$|x - a| \leq d$ if and only if $a - d \leq x \leq a + d$.

$|x - a| \geq d$ if and only if $x \leq a - d$ or $a + d \leq x$.

Inequality	Interpretation	Graph
$|x - a| \leq d$	All numbers x whose distance from a is less than or equal to d.	
$|x - a| \geq d$	All numbers x whose distance from a is greater than or equal to d.	

Be sure you see that inequalities of the form $|x - a| \geq d$ have solution sets consisting of two intervals. To describe the two intervals without using absolute values, you must use *two* separate inequalities, connected by an "or" to indicate union.

Application

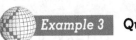 Example 3 **Quality Control**

A large manufacturer hired a quality control firm to determine the reliability of a product. Using statistical methods, the firm determined that the manufacturer could expect 0.35% ± 0.17% of the units to be defective. The manufacturer offers a money-back guarantee on this product. How much should be budgeted to cover the refunds on 100,000 units? (Assume that the retail price is $8.95.) Will the manufacturer have to establish a refund budget greater than $5000?

SOLUTION   Let r represent the percent of defective units (in decimal form). You know that r will differ from 0.0035 by at most 0.0017.

$$0.0035 - 0.0017 \le r \le 0.0035 + 0.0017$$
$$0.0018 \le r \le 0.0052 \qquad \text{Figure A.12(a)}$$

Now, letting x be the number of defective units out of 100,000, it follows that $x = 100,000r$ and you have

$$0.0018(100,000) \le 100,000r \le 0.0052(100,000)$$
$$180 \le \quad x \quad \le 520. \qquad \text{Figure A.12(b)}$$

Finally, letting C be the cost of refunds, you have $C = 8.95x$. So, the total cost of refunds for 100,000 units should fall within the interval given by

$$180(8.95) \le 8.95x \le 520(8.95)$$
$$\$1611 \le \quad C \quad \le \$4654. \qquad \text{Figure A.12(c)}$$

The manufacturer will *not* have to establish a refund budget greater than $5000.

(a) Percent of defective units

(b) Number of defective units

(c) Cost of refunds

FIGURE A.12

✓**Checkpoint 3**

Use the information in Example 3 to determine how much should be budgeted to cover refunds on 250,000 units.

In Example 3, the manufacturer should expect to spend between $1611 and $4654 for refunds. Of course, the safer budget figure for refunds would be the higher of these estimates. From a statistical point of view, however, the most representative estimate would be the average of these two extremes. Graphically, the average of two numbers is the **midpoint** of the interval with the two numbers as endpoints, as shown in Figure A.13.

FIGURE A.13

Midpoint of an Interval

The **midpoint** of the interval with endpoints a and b is found by taking the average of the endpoints.

$$\text{Midpoint} = \frac{a + b}{2}$$

Exercises A.2

Finding Distance on the Real Number Line In Exercises 1–6, determine (a) the distance between a and b, (b) the directed distance from a to b, and (c) the directed distance from b to a. *See Example 1.*

1. $a = 126, b = 75$
2. $a = -126, b = -75$
3. $a = 9.34, b = -5.65$
4. $a = -2.05, b = 4.25$
5. $a = \frac{16}{5}, b = \frac{112}{75}$
6. $a = -\frac{18}{5}, b = \frac{61}{15}$

Describing Intervals Using Absolute Value In Exercises 7–18, use absolute values to describe the given interval (or pair of intervals) on the real number line.

7. $[-2, 2]$
8. $(-3, 3)$
9. $(-\infty, -2) \cup (2, \infty)$
10. $(-\infty, -3] \cup [3, \infty)$
11. $[2, 8]$
12. $(-7, -1)$
13. $(-\infty, 0) \cup (4, \infty)$
14. $(-\infty, 20) \cup (24, \infty)$
15. All numbers *less than* three units from 5
16. All numbers *more than* five units from 2
17. y is at most *two units* from a.
18. y is *less than h* units from c.

Solving an Inequality In Exercises 19–34, solve the inequality. Then graph the solution set on the real number line. *See Example 2.*

19. $|x| < 4$
20. $|2x| < 6$
21. $\left|\frac{x}{2}\right| > 3$
22. $|3x| > 12$
23. $|x - 5| < 2$
24. $|3x + 1| \geq 4$
25. $\left|\frac{x-3}{2}\right| \geq 5$
26. $|2x + 1| < 5$
27. $|10 - x| > 4$
28. $|25 - x| \geq 20$
29. $|9 - 2x| < 1$
30. $\left|1 - \frac{2x}{3}\right| < 1$
31. $|x - a| \leq b, \ b > 0$
32. $|2x - a| \geq b, \ b > 0$
33. $\left|\frac{3x-a}{4}\right| < 2b, \ b > 0$
34. $\left|a - \frac{5x}{2}\right| > b, \ b > 0$

Finding a Midpoint In Exercises 35–40, find the midpoint of the given interval.

35. $[8, 24]$
36. $[7.3, 12.7]$
37. $[-6.85, 9.35]$
38. $[-4.6, -1.3]$
39. $\left[-\frac{1}{2}, \frac{3}{4}\right]$
40. $\left[\frac{5}{6}, \frac{5}{2}\right]$

41. **Stock Price** A stock market analyst predicts that over the next year, the price p of a stock will not change from its current price of $33.15 by more than $2. Use absolute values to write this prediction as an inequality.

42. **Production** The estimated daily production x at a refinery is given by

$$|x - 200{,}000| \leq 25{,}000$$

where x is measured in barrels of oil. Determine the high and low production levels.

43. **Manufacturing** The acceptable weights for a 20-ounce cereal box are given by

$$|x - 20| \leq 0.75$$

where x is measured in ounces. Determine the high and low weights for the cereal box.

44. **Weight** The American Kennel Club has developed guidelines for judging the features of various breeds of dogs. To not receive a penalty, the guidelines specify that the weights for male collies must satisfy the inequality

$$\left|\frac{w - 67.5}{7.5}\right| \leq 1$$

where w is the weight (in pounds). Determine the interval on the real number line in which these weights lie. *(Source: The American Kennel Club, Inc.)*

Budget Variance In Exercises 45–48, (a) use absolute value notation to represent the two intervals in which expenses must lie if they are to be within $500 and within 5% of the specified budget amount and (b) using the more stringent constraint, determine whether the given expense is at variance with the budget restriction.

Item	Budget	Expense
45. Utilities	$4750.00	$5116.37
46. Insurance	$15,000.00	$14,695.00
47. Maintenance	$20,000.00	$22,718.35
48. Taxes	$7500.00	$8691.00

49. **Quality Control** In determining the reliability of a product, a manufacturer determines that it should expect $0.05\% \pm 0.01\%$ of the units to be defective. The manufacturer offers a money-back guarantee on this product. How much should be budgeted to cover the refunds on 150,000 units? (Assume that the retail price is $195.99.)

A.3 Exponents and Radicals

■ Evaluate expressions involving exponents or radicals.
■ Simplify expressions with exponents.
■ Find the domains of algebraic expressions.

Expressions Involving Exponents or Radicals

Properties of Exponents

1. Whole-number exponents: $x^n = \underbrace{x \cdot x \cdot x \cdots x}_{n \text{ factors}}$

2. Zero exponent: $x^0 = 1, \quad x \neq 0$

3. Negative exponents: $x^{-n} = \dfrac{1}{x^n}, \quad x \neq 0$

4. Radicals (principal nth root): $\sqrt[n]{x} = a \implies x = a^n$

5. Rational exponents $(1/n)$: $x^{1/n} = \sqrt[n]{x}$

6. Rational exponents (m/n): $x^{m/n} = \left(x^{1/n}\right)^m = \left(\sqrt[n]{x}\right)^m$

   $x^{m/n} = (x^m)^{1/n} = \sqrt[n]{x^m}$

7. Special convention (square root): $\sqrt[2]{x} = \sqrt{x}$

STUDY TIP

If n is even, then the principal nth root is positive. For example, $\sqrt{4} = +2$ and $\sqrt[4]{81} = +3$.

Example 1 Evaluating Expressions

	Expression	*x-Value*	*Substitution*
a.	$y = -2x^2$	$x = 4$	$y = -2(4^2) = -2(16) = -32$
b.	$y = 3x^{-3}$	$x = -1$	$y = 3(-1)^{-3} = \dfrac{3}{(-1)^3} = \dfrac{3}{-1} = -3$
c.	$y = (-x)^2$	$x = \dfrac{1}{2}$	$y = \left(-\dfrac{1}{2}\right)^2 = \dfrac{1}{4}$
d.	$y = \dfrac{2}{x^{-2}}$	$x = 3$	$y = \dfrac{2}{3^{-2}} = 2(3^2) = 18$

✓ **Checkpoint 1**

Evaluate $y = 4x^{-2}$ for $x = 3$.

Example 2 Evaluating Expressions

	Expression	*x-Value*	*Substitution*
a.	$y = 2x^{1/2}$	$x = 4$	$y = 2\sqrt{4} = 2(2) = 4$
b.	$y = \sqrt[3]{x^2}$	$x = 8$	$y = 8^{2/3} = (8^{1/3})^2 = 2^2 = 4$

✓ **Checkpoint 2**

Evaluate $y = 4x^{1/3}$ for $x = 8$.

Operations with Exponents

TECH TUTOR

Graphing utilities perform the established order of operations when evaluating an expression. To see this, try entering the expressions

$$1200\left(1 + \frac{0.09}{12}\right)^{12\cdot6}$$

and

$$1200 \times 1 + \left(\frac{0.09}{12}\right)^{12\cdot6}$$

into your graphing utility to see that the expressions result in different values.

Operations with Exponents

1. Multiplying like bases: $x^n x^m = x^{n+m}$ Add exponents.

2. Dividing like bases: $\dfrac{x^n}{x^m} = x^{n-m}$ Subtract exponents.

3. Removing parentheses: $(xy)^n = x^n y^n$

$$\left(\frac{x}{y}\right)^n = \frac{x^n}{y^n}$$

$$(x^n)^m = x^{nm}$$

4. Special conventions: $-x^n = -(x^n), \quad -x^n \neq (-x)^n$

$$cx^n = c(x^n), \quad cx^n \neq (cx)^n$$

$$x^{n^m} = x^{(n^m)}, \quad x^{n^m} \neq (x^n)^m$$

Example 3   Simplifying Expressions with Exponents

Simplify each expression.

a. $2x^2(x^3)$ b. $(3x)^2 \sqrt[3]{x}$ c. $\dfrac{3x^2}{(x^{1/2})^3}$

d. $\dfrac{5x^4}{(x^2)^3}$ e. $x^{-1}(2x^2)$ f. $\dfrac{-\sqrt{x}}{5x^{-1}}$

SOLUTION

a. $2x^2(x^3) = 2x^{2+3} = 2x^5$ $x^n x^m = x^{n+m}$

b. $(3x)^2 \sqrt[3]{x} = 9x^2 x^{1/3} = 9x^{2+(1/3)} = 9x^{7/3}$ $x^n x^m = x^{n+m}$

c. $\dfrac{3x^2}{(x^{1/2})^3} = 3\left(\dfrac{x^2}{x^{3/2}}\right) = 3x^{2-(3/2)} = 3x^{1/2}$ $(x^n)^m = x^{nm}, \ \dfrac{x^n}{x^m} = x^{n-m}$

d. $\dfrac{5x^4}{(x^2)^3} = \dfrac{5x^4}{x^6} = 5x^{4-6} = 5x^{-2} = \dfrac{5}{x^2}$ $(x^n)^m = x^{nm}, \ \dfrac{x^n}{x^m} = x^{n-m}$

e. $x^{-1}(2x^2) = 2x^{-1}x^2 = 2x^{-1+2} = 2x$ $x^n x^m = x^{n+m}$

f. $\dfrac{-\sqrt{x}}{5x^{-1}} = -\dfrac{1}{5}\left(\dfrac{x^{1/2}}{x^{-1}}\right) = -\dfrac{1}{5}x^{(1/2)+1} = -\dfrac{1}{5}x^{3/2}$ $\dfrac{x^n}{x^m} = x^{n-m}$

✓ **Checkpoint 3**

Simplify each expression.

a. $3x^2(x^4)$

b. $(2x)^3 \sqrt{x}$

c. $\dfrac{4x^2}{(x^{1/3})^2}$

Note in Example 3 that one characteristic of simplified expressions is the absence of negative exponents. Another characteristic of simplified expressions is that sums and differences are written in *factored form*. To do this, you can use the **Distributive Property.**

$$abx^n + acx^{n+m} = ax^n(b + cx^m)$$

Study the next example carefully to be sure that you understand the concepts involved in the factoring process.

Example 4   Simplifying by Factoring

Simplify each expression by factoring.

a. $2x^2 - x^3$ **b.** $2x^3 + x^2$ **c.** $2x^{1/2} + 4x^{5/2}$ **d.** $2x^{-1/2} + 3x^{5/2}$

SOLUTION

a. $2x^2 - x^3 = x^2(2 - x)$

b. $2x^3 + x^2 = x^2(2x + 1)$

c. $2x^{1/2} + 4x^{5/2} = 2x^{1/2}(1 + 2x^2)$

d. $2x^{-1/2} + 3x^{5/2} = x^{-1/2}(2 + 3x^3) = \dfrac{2 + 3x^3}{\sqrt{x}}$

✓ **Checkpoint 4**

Simplify each expression by factoring.

a. $x^3 - 2x$

b. $2x^{1/2} + 8x^{3/2}$

> **STUDY TIP**
>
> To check that a simplified expression is equivalent to the original expression, try substituting values for x into each expression.

Many algebraic expressions obtained in calculus occur in unsimplified form. For instance, the two expressions shown in the following example are the result of an operation in calculus called *differentiation*. [The first is the derivative of $2(x + 1)^{3/2}(2x - 3)^{5/2}$, and the second is the derivative of $2(x + 1)^{1/2}(2x - 3)^{5/2}$.]

Example 5   Simplifying by Factoring

a. $3(x + 1)^{1/2}(2x - 3)^{5/2} + 10(x + 1)^{3/2}(2x - 3)^{3/2}$

$$= (x + 1)^{1/2}(2x - 3)^{3/2}[3(2x - 3) + 10(x + 1)]$$
$$= (x + 1)^{1/2}(2x - 3)^{3/2}(6x - 9 + 10x + 10)$$
$$= (x + 1)^{1/2}(2x - 3)^{3/2}(16x + 1)$$

b. $(x + 1)^{-1/2}(2x - 3)^{5/2} + 10(x + 1)^{1/2}(2x - 3)^{3/2}$

$$= (x + 1)^{-1/2}(2x - 3)^{3/2}[(2x - 3) + 10(x + 1)]$$
$$= (x + 1)^{-1/2}(2x - 3)^{3/2}(2x - 3 + 10x + 10)$$
$$= (x + 1)^{-1/2}(2x - 3)^{3/2}(12x + 7)$$
$$= \dfrac{(2x - 3)^{3/2}(12x + 7)}{(x + 1)^{1/2}}$$

✓ **Checkpoint 5**

Simplify the expression by factoring.

$$(x + 2)^{1/2}(3x - 1)^{3/2} + 4(x + 2)^{-1/2}(3x - 1)^{5/2}$$

Example 6 shows some additional types of expressions that can occur in calculus. [The expression in Example 6(d) is an antiderivative of $(x + 1)^{2/3}(2x + 3)$, and the expression in Example 6(e) is the derivative of $(x + 2)^3/(x - 1)^3$.]

Example 6   Factors Involving Quotients

Simplify each expression by factoring.

a. $\dfrac{3x^2 + x^4}{2x}$

b. $\dfrac{\sqrt{x} + x^{3/2}}{x}$

c. $(9x + 2)^{-1/3} + 18(9x + 2)$

d. $\dfrac{3}{5}(x + 1)^{5/3} + \dfrac{3}{4}(x + 1)^{8/3}$

e. $\dfrac{3(x + 2)^2(x - 1)^3 - 3(x + 2)^3(x - 1)^2}{[(x - 1)^3]^2}$

SOLUTION

a. $\dfrac{3x^2 + x^4}{2x} = \dfrac{x^2(3 + x^2)}{2x} = \dfrac{x^{2-1}(3 + x^2)}{2} = \dfrac{x(3 + x^2)}{2}$

b. $\dfrac{\sqrt{x} + x^{3/2}}{x} = \dfrac{x^{1/2}(1 + x)}{x} = \dfrac{1 + x}{x^{1-(1/2)}} = \dfrac{1 + x}{\sqrt{x}}$

c. $(9x + 2)^{-1/3} + 18(9x + 2) = (9x + 2)^{-1/3}[1 + 18(9x + 2)^{4/3}]$

$= \dfrac{1 + 18(9x + 2)^{4/3}}{\sqrt[3]{9x + 2}}$

d. $\dfrac{3}{5}(x + 1)^{5/3} + \dfrac{3}{4}(x + 1)^{8/3} = \dfrac{12}{20}(x + 1)^{5/3} + \dfrac{15}{20}(x + 1)^{8/3}$

$= \dfrac{3}{20}(x + 1)^{5/3}[4 + 5(x + 1)]$

$= \dfrac{3}{20}(x + 1)^{5/3}(4 + 5x + 5)$

$= \dfrac{3}{20}(x + 1)^{5/3}(5x + 9)$

e. $\dfrac{3(x + 2)^2(x - 1)^3 - 3(x + 2)^3(x - 1)^2}{[(x - 1)^3]^2}$

$= \dfrac{3(x + 2)^2(x - 1)^2[(x - 1) - (x + 2)]}{(x - 1)^6}$

$= \dfrac{3(x + 2)^2(x - 1 - x - 2)}{(x - 1)^{6-2}}$

$= \dfrac{-9(x + 2)^2}{(x - 1)^4}$

✓ **Checkpoint 6**

Simplify the expression by factoring.

$\dfrac{5x^3 + x^6}{3x}$

TECH TUTOR

A graphing utility offers several ways to calculate rational exponents and radicals. You should be familiar with the *x*-squared key (x²). This key squares the value of an expression.

For rational exponents or exponents other than 2, use the (∧) key.

For radical expressions, you can use the square root key (√), the cube root key (³√), or the *x*th root key (ˣ√). Consult your graphing utility user's guide for specific keystrokes you can use to evaluate rational exponents and radical expressions.

Domain of an Algebraic Expression

When working with algebraic expressions involving x, you face the potential difficulty of substituting a value of x for which the expression is not defined (does not produce a real number). For example, the expression $\sqrt{2x + 3}$ is *not defined* when $x = -2$ because

$$\sqrt{2(-2) + 3} = \sqrt{-1}$$

is not a real number.

The set of all values for which an expression is defined is called its **domain.** So, the domain of $\sqrt{2x + 3}$ is the set of all values of x such that $\sqrt{2x + 3}$ is a real number. In order for $\sqrt{2x + 3}$ to represent a real number, it is necessary that

$2x + 3 \geq 0.$ Expression must be nonnegative.

In other words, $\sqrt{2x + 3}$ is defined only for those values of x that lie in the interval $\left[-\frac{3}{2}, \infty\right)$, as shown in Figure A.14.

FIGURE A.14

Example 7   **Finding the Domain of an Expression**

Find the domain of each expression.

a. $\sqrt{3x - 2}$

b. $\dfrac{1}{\sqrt{3x - 2}}$

c. $\sqrt[3]{9x + 1}$

SOLUTION

a. The domain of $\sqrt{3x - 2}$ consists of all x such that

$3x - 2 \geq 0$ Expression must be nonnegative.

which implies that $x \geq \frac{2}{3}$. So, the domain is $\left[\frac{2}{3}, \infty\right)$.

b. The domain of $1/\sqrt{3x - 2}$ is the same as the domain of $\sqrt{3x - 2}$, except that $1/\sqrt{3x - 2}$ is not defined when $3x - 2 = 0$. Because this occurs when $x = \frac{2}{3}$, the domain is $\left(\frac{2}{3}, \infty\right)$.

c. Because $\sqrt[3]{9x + 1}$ is defined for all real numbers, its domain is $(-\infty, \infty)$.

✓Checkpoint 7

Find the domain of each expression.

a. $\sqrt{x - 2}$

b. $\dfrac{1}{\sqrt{x - 2}}$

c. $\sqrt[3]{x - 2}$

Exercises A.3

See www.CalcChat.com for worked-out solutions to odd-numbered exercises.

Evaluating Expressions In Exercises 1–20, evaluate the expression for the given value of *x*. *See Examples 1 and 2.*

Expression	x-Value	Expression	x-Value
1. $-2x^3$	$x = 3$	**2.** $\dfrac{x^2}{3}$	$x = 6$
3. $4x^{-3}$	$x = 2$	**4.** $7x^{-2}$	$x = 5$
5. $\dfrac{1 + x^{-1}}{x^{-1}}$	$x = 3$	**6.** $x - 4x^{-2}$	$x = 3$
7. $3x^2 - 4x^3$	$x = -2$	**8.** $5(-x)^3$	$x = 3$
9. $6x^0 - (6x)^0$	$x = 10$	**10.** $\dfrac{1}{(-x)^{-3}}$	$x = 4$
11. $\sqrt[3]{x^2}$	$x = 27$	**12.** $\sqrt{x^3}$	$x = \frac{1}{9}$
13. $x^{-1/2}$	$x = 4$	**14.** $x^{-3/4}$	$x = 16$
15. $x^{-2/5}$	$x = -32$	**16.** $(x^{2/3})^3$	$x = 10$
17. $500x^{60}$	$x = 1.01$	**18.** $\dfrac{10{,}000}{x^{120}}$	$x = 1.1$
19. $\sqrt[3]{x}$	$x = -54$	**20.** $\sqrt[6]{x}$	$x = 325$

Simplifying Expressions with Exponents In Exercises 21–30, simplify the expression. *See Example 3.*

21. $6y^{-2}(2y^4)^{-3}$

22. $z^{-3}(3z^4)$

23. $10(x^2)^2$

24. $(4x^3)^2$

25. $\dfrac{7x^2}{x^{-3}}$

26. $\dfrac{x^{-3}}{\sqrt{x}}$

27. $\dfrac{10(x + y)^3}{4(x + y)^{-2}}$

28. $\left(\dfrac{12s^2}{9s}\right)^3$

29. $\dfrac{3x\sqrt{x}}{x^{1/2}}$

30. $\left(\sqrt[3]{x^2}\right)^3$

Simplifying Radicals In Exercises 31–36, simplify by removing all possible factors from the radical.

31. $\sqrt{8}$

32. $\sqrt[3]{\frac{16}{27}}$

33. $\sqrt[3]{54x^5}$

34. $\sqrt[4]{(3x^2y^3)^4}$

35. $\sqrt[3]{144x^9y^{-4}z^5}$

36. $\sqrt[4]{32xy^5z^{-8}}$

Simplifying by Factoring In Exercises 37–44, simplify each expression by factoring. *See Examples 4, 5, and 6.*

37. $3x^3 - 12x$

38. $8x^4 - 6x^2$

39. $2x^{5/2} + x^{-1/2}$

40. $5x^{3/2} - x^{-3/2}$

41. $3x(x + 1)^{3/2} - 6(x + 1)^{1/2}$

42. $2x(x - 1)^{5/2} - 4(x - 1)^{3/2}$

43. $\dfrac{5x^6 + x^3}{3x^2}$

44. $\dfrac{(x + 1)(x - 1)^2 - (x - 1)^3}{(x + 1)^2}$

Finding the Domain of an Expression In Exercises 45–52, find the domain of the expression. *See Example 7.*

45. $\sqrt{x - 4}$

46. $\sqrt{5 - 2x}$

47. $\sqrt{x^2 + 3}$

48. $\sqrt{4x^2 + 1}$

49. $\dfrac{1}{\sqrt[3]{x - 4}}$

50. $\dfrac{1}{\sqrt[3]{x + 4}}$

51. $\dfrac{\sqrt{x + 2}}{1 - x}$

52. $\dfrac{1}{\sqrt{2x + 3}} + \sqrt{6 - 4x}$

 Compound Interest In Exercises 53–56, a certificate of deposit has a principal of *P* dollars and an annual percentage rate of *r* (expressed as a decimal) compounded *n* times per year. The balance *A* in the account is given by

$$A = P\left(1 + \frac{r}{n}\right)^N$$

where *N* is the number of compoundings. Use a graphing utility to find the balance in the account.

53. $P = \$10{,}000,\quad r = 6.5\%,\quad n = 12,\quad N = 120$

54. $P = \$7000,\quad r = 5\%,\quad n = 365,\quad N = 1000$

55. $P = \$5000,\quad r = 5.5\%,\quad n = 4,\quad N = 60$

56. $P = \$8000,\quad r = 7\%,\quad n = 6,\quad N = 90$

57. Period of a Pendulum The period of a pendulum is

$$T = 2\pi\sqrt{\frac{L}{32}}$$

where *T* is the period (in seconds) and *L* is the length (in feet) of the pendulum. Find the period of a pendulum whose length is 4 feet.

58. Annuity After *n* annual payments of *P* dollars have been made into an annuity earning an annual percentage rate of *r* compounded annually, the balance *A* is given by

$$A = P(1 + r) + P(1 + r)^2 + \cdots + P(1 + r)^n.$$

Rewrite this formula by completing the following factorization.

$$A = P(1 + r)(\qquad)$$

A.4 Factoring Polynomials

■ Use special products and factorization techniques to factor polynomials.
■ Use synthetic division to factor polynomials of degree three or more.
■ Use the Rational Zero Theorem to find the real zeros of polynomials.

Factorization Techniques

The **Fundamental Theorem of Algebra** states that every nth-degree polynomial

$$a_n x^n + a_{n-1} x^{n-1} + \cdots + a_1 x + a_0, \quad a_n \neq 0$$

has precisely n **zeros.** (The zeros may be repeated or imaginary.) The zeros of a polynomial in x are the values of x that make the polynomial zero. The problem of finding the zeros of a polynomial is equivalent to the problem of factoring the polynomial into linear factors.

Special Products and Factorization Techniques

Quadratic Formula

$$ax^2 + bx + c = 0 \implies x = \frac{-b \pm \sqrt{b^2 - 4ac}}{2a}$$

Example

$$x^2 + 3x - 1 = 0 \implies x = \frac{-3 \pm \sqrt{13}}{2}$$

Special Products

$$x^2 - a^2 = (x - a)(x + a)$$
$$x^3 - a^3 = (x - a)(x^2 + ax + a^2)$$
$$x^3 + a^3 = (x + a)(x^2 - ax + a^2)$$
$$x^4 - a^4 = (x - a)(x + a)(x^2 + a^2)$$

Examples

$$x^2 - 9 = (x - 3)(x + 3)$$
$$x^3 - 8 = (x - 2)(x^2 + 2x + 4)$$
$$x^3 + 64 = (x + 4)(x^2 - 4x + 16)$$
$$x^4 - 16 = (x - 2)(x + 2)(x^2 + 4)$$

Binomial Theorem

$$(x + a)^2 = x^2 + 2ax + a^2$$
$$(x - a)^2 = x^2 - 2ax + a^2$$
$$(x + a)^3 = x^3 + 3ax^2 + 3a^2x + a^3$$
$$(x - a)^3 = x^3 - 3ax^2 + 3a^2x - a^3$$
$$(x + a)^4 = x^4 + 4ax^3 + 6a^2x^2 + 4a^3x + a^4$$
$$(x - a)^4 = x^4 - 4ax^3 + 6a^2x^2 - 4a^3x + a^4$$

Examples

$$(x + 3)^2 = x^2 + 6x + 9$$
$$(x^2 - 5)^2 = x^4 - 10x^2 + 25$$
$$(x + 2)^3 = x^3 + 6x^2 + 12x + 8$$
$$(x - 1)^3 = x^3 - 3x^2 + 3x - 1$$
$$(x + 2)^4 = x^4 + 8x^3 + 24x^2 + 32x + 16$$
$$(x - 4)^4 = x^4 - 16x^3 + 96x^2 - 256x + 256$$

$$(x + a)^n = x^n + nax^{n-1} + \frac{n(n-1)}{2!}a^2x^{n-2} + \frac{n(n-1)(n-2)}{3!}a^3x^{n-3} + \cdots + na^{n-1}x + a^{n*}$$

$$(x - a)^n = x^n - nax^{n-1} + \frac{n(n-1)}{2!}a^2x^{n-2} - \frac{n(n-1)(n-2)}{3!}a^3x^{n-3} + \cdots \pm na^{n-1}x \mp a^n$$

Factoring by Grouping

$$acx^3 + adx^2 + bcx + bd = ax^2(cx + d) + b(cx + d)$$
$$= (ax^2 + b)(cx + d)$$

Example

$$3x^3 - 2x^2 - 6x + 4 = x^2(3x - 2) - 2(3x - 2)$$
$$= (x^2 - 2)(3x - 2)$$

---

* The factorial symbol ! is defined as follows: $0! = 1$, $1! = 1$, $2! = 2 \cdot 1 = 2$, $3! = 3 \cdot 2 \cdot 1 = 6$, $4! = 4 \cdot 3 \cdot 2 \cdot 1 = 24$, and so on.

Example 1   **Applying the Quadratic Formula**

Use the Quadratic Formula to find all real zeros of each polynomial.

a. $4x^2 + 6x + 1$

b. $x^2 + 6x + 9$

c. $2x^2 - 6x + 5$

SOLUTION

a. Using $a = 4$, $b = 6$, and $c = 1$, you can write

$$
\begin{aligned}
x &= \frac{-b \pm \sqrt{b^2 - 4ac}}{2a} = \frac{-6 \pm \sqrt{6^2 - 4(4)(1)}}{2(4)} \\
&= \frac{-6 \pm \sqrt{36 - 16}}{8} \\
&= \frac{-6 \pm \sqrt{20}}{8} \\
&= \frac{-6 \pm 2\sqrt{5}}{8} \\
&= \frac{2(-3 \pm \sqrt{5})}{2(4)} \\
&= \frac{-3 \pm \sqrt{5}}{4}.
\end{aligned}
$$

So, there are two real zeros:

$$
x = \frac{-3 - \sqrt{5}}{4} \approx -1.309 \quad \text{and} \quad x = \frac{-3 + \sqrt{5}}{4} \approx -0.191.
$$

b. In this case, $a = 1$, $b = 6$, and $c = 9$, and the Quadratic Formula yields

$$
x = \frac{-b \pm \sqrt{b^2 - 4ac}}{2a} = \frac{-6 \pm \sqrt{36 - 36}}{2} = -\frac{6}{2} = -3.
$$

So, there is one (repeated) real zero: $x = -3$.

c. For this quadratic equation, $a = 2$, $b = -6$, and $c = 5$. So,

$$
x = \frac{-b \pm \sqrt{b^2 - 4ac}}{2a} = \frac{6 \pm \sqrt{36 - 40}}{4} = \frac{6 \pm \sqrt{-4}}{4}.
$$

Because $\sqrt{-4}$ is imaginary, there are no real zeros.

✓ **Checkpoint 1**

Use the Quadratic Formula to find all real zeros of each polynomial.

a. $2x^2 + 4x + 1$

b. $x^2 - 8x + 16$

c. $2x^2 - x + 5$

The zeros in Example 1(a) are irrational, and the zeros in Example 1(c) are imaginary. In both of these cases the quadratic is said to be **irreducible** because it cannot be factored into linear factors with rational coefficients. The next example shows how to find the zeros associated with *reducible* quadratics. In this example, factoring is used to find the zeros of each quadratic. Try using the Quadratic Formula to obtain the same zeros.

Recall that the zeros of a polynomial in x are the values of x that make the polynomial zero. To find the zeros, factor the polynomial into linear factors and set each factor equal to zero. For instance, the zeros of $(x - 2)(x - 3)$ occur when $x - 2 = 0$ and $x - 3 = 0$.

Example 2   Finding Real Zeros by Factoring

Find all the real zeros of each quadratic polynomial.

a. $x^2 - 5x + 6$ **b.** $x^2 - 6x + 9$ **c.** $2x^2 + 5x - 3$

SOLUTION

a. Because

$$x^2 - 5x + 6 = (x - 2)(x - 3)$$

the zeros are $x = 2$ and $x = 3$.

b. Because

$$x^2 - 6x + 9 = (x - 3)^2$$

the only zero is $x = 3$.

c. Because

$$2x^2 + 5x - 3 = (2x - 1)(x + 3)$$

the zeros are $x = \frac{1}{2}$ and $x = -3$.

✓ **Checkpoint 2**

Find all the real zeros of each quadratic polynomial.

a. $x^2 - 2x - 15$ **b.** $x^2 + 2x + 1$ **c.** $2x^2 - 7x + 6$

Example 3   Finding the Domain of a Radical Expression

Find the domain of $\sqrt{x^2 - 3x + 2}$.

SOLUTION Because

$$x^2 - 3x + 2 = (x - 1)(x - 2)$$

you know that the zeros of the quadratic are $x = 1$ and $x = 2$. So, you need to test the sign of the quadratic in the three intervals $(-\infty, 1)$, $(1, 2)$, and $(2, \infty)$, as shown in Figure A.15. After testing each of these intervals, you can see that the quadratic is negative in the center interval and positive in the outer two intervals. Moreover, because the quadratic is zero when $x = 1$ and $x = 2$, you can conclude that the domain of $\sqrt{x^2 - 3x + 2}$ is

$$(-\infty, 1] \cup [2, \infty). \qquad \text{Domain}$$

Values of $\sqrt{x^2 - 3x + 2}$

x	$\sqrt{x^2 - 3x + 2}$
0	$\sqrt{2}$
1	0
1.5	Undefined
2	0
3	$\sqrt{2}$

FIGURE A.15

✓ **Checkpoint 3**

Find the domain of

$$\sqrt{x^2 + x - 2}.$$

Factoring Polynomials of Degree Three or More

It can be difficult to find the zeros of polynomials of degree three or more. However, if one of the zeros of a polynomial is known, then you can use that zero to reduce the degree of the polynomial. For example, if you know that $x = 2$ is a zero of

$$x^3 - 4x^2 + 5x - 2$$

then you know that $(x - 2)$ is a factor, and you can use long division to factor the polynomial as shown.

$$\begin{aligned} x^3 - 4x^2 + 5x - 2 &= (x - 2)(x^2 - 2x + 1) \\ &= (x - 2)(x - 1)(x - 1) \end{aligned}$$

As an alternative to long division, many people prefer to use **synthetic division** to reduce the degree of a polynomial.

Synthetic Division for a Cubic Polynomial

Given: $x = x_1$ is a zero of $ax^3 + bx^2 + cx + d$.

| | a | b | c | d |

Vertical pattern:
Add terms.

Diagonal pattern:
Multiply by x_1.

Coefficients for quadratic factor

Performing synthetic division on the polynomial

$$x^3 - 4x^2 + 5x - 2$$

using the given zero, $x = 2$, produces the following.

$$\begin{array}{c|cccc} 2 & 1 & -4 & 5 & -2 \\ & & 2 & -4 & 2 \\ \hline & 1 & -2 & 1 & 0 \end{array}$$

$(x - 2)(x^2 - 2x + 1) = x^3 - 4x^2 + 5x - 2$

When you use synthetic division, remember to take *all* coefficients into account—*even when some of them are zero.* For instance, when you know that $x = -2$ is a zero of $x^3 + 3x + 14$, you can apply synthetic division as shown.

$$\begin{array}{c|cccc} -2 & 1 & 0 & 3 & 14 \\ & & -2 & 4 & -14 \\ \hline & 1 & -2 & 7 & 0 \end{array}$$

$(x + 2)(x^2 - 2x + 7) = x^3 + 3x + 14$

STUDY TIP

The algorithm for synthetic division given above works *only* for divisors of the form $x - x_1$. Remember that $x + x_1 = x - (-x_1)$.

The Rational Zero Theorem

There is a systematic way to find the *rational* zeros of a polynomial. You can use the **Rational Zero Theorem** (also called the Rational Root Theorem).

Rational Zero Theorem

If a polynomial

$$a_n x^n + a_{n-1} x^{n-1} + \cdots + a_1 x + a_0$$

has integer coefficients, then every *rational* zero is of the form

$$x = \frac{p}{q}$$

where p is a factor of a_0, and q is a factor of a_n.

Example 4   **Using the Rational Zero Theorem**

Find all real zeros of the polynomial.

$$2x^3 + 3x^2 - 8x + 3$$

SOLUTION

$$2x^3 + 3x^2 - 8x + 3$$

Factors of constant term: $\pm 1, \pm 3$

Factors of leading coefficient: $\pm 1, \pm 2$

The possible rational zeros are the factors of the constant term divided by the factors of the leading coefficient.

$$1, -1, 3, -3, \frac{1}{2}, -\frac{1}{2}, \frac{3}{2}, -\frac{3}{2}$$

By testing these possible zeros, you can see that $x = 1$ works.

$$2(1)^3 + 3(1)^2 - 8(1) + 3 = 2 + 3 - 8 + 3 = 0$$

Now, by synthetic division you have the following.

$$
\begin{array}{r|rrrr}
1 & 2 & 3 & -8 & 3 \\
  &   & 2 & 5 & -3 \\
\hline
  & 2 & 5 & -3 & 0 \\
\end{array}
$$

$$(x - 1)(2x^2 + 5x - 3) = 2x^3 + 3x^2 - 8x + 3$$

Finally, by factoring the quadratic

$$2x^2 + 5x - 3 = (2x - 1)(x + 3)$$

you have

$$2x^3 + 3x^2 - 8x + 3 = (x - 1)(2x - 1)(x + 3)$$

and you can conclude that the zeros are $x = 1$, $x = \frac{1}{2}$, and $x = -3$.

STUDY TIP

In Example 4, you can check that the zeros are correct by substituting into the original polynomial.

Check that $x = 1$ is a zero.
$$2(1)^3 + 3(1)^2 - 8(1) + 3$$
$$= 2 + 3 - 8 + 3$$
$$= 0$$

Check that $x = \frac{1}{2}$ is a zero.
$$2\left(\frac{1}{2}\right)^3 + 3\left(\frac{1}{2}\right)^2 - 8\left(\frac{1}{2}\right) + 3$$
$$= \frac{1}{4} + \frac{3}{4} - 4 + 3$$
$$= 0$$

Check that $x = -3$ is a zero.
$$2(-3)^3 + 3(-3)^2 - 8(-3) + 3$$
$$= -54 + 27 + 24 + 3$$
$$= 0$$

✓ **Checkpoint 4**

Find all real zeros of the polynomial.

$$2x^3 - 3x^2 - 3x + 2$$

Exercises A.4

See www.CalcChat.com for worked-out solutions to odd-numbered exercises.

Applying the Quadratic Formula In Exercises 1–8, use the Quadratic Formula to find all real zeros of the second-degree polynomial. *See Example 1.*

1. $6x^2 - 7x + 1$
2. $8x^2 - 2x - 1$
3. $4x^2 - 12x + 9$
4. $9x^2 + 12x + 4$
5. $y^2 + 4y + 1$
6. $y^2 + 5y - 2$
7. $2x^2 + 3x - 4$
8. $3x^2 - 8x - 4$

Factoring Polynomials In Exercises 9–18, write the second-degree polynomial as the product of two linear factors.

9. $x^2 - 4x + 4$
10. $x^2 + 10x + 25$
11. $4x^2 + 4x + 1$
12. $9x^2 - 12x + 4$
13. $3x^2 - 4x + 1$
14. $2x^2 - x - 1$
15. $3x^2 - 5x + 2$
16. $4x^2 + 19x + 12$
17. $x^2 - 4xy + 4y^2$
18. $x^2 - xy - 2y^2$

Factoring Polynomials In Exercises 19–34, completely factor the polynomial.

19. $81 - y^4$
20. $x^4 - 16$
21. $x^3 - 8$
22. $y^3 - 64$
23. $y^3 + 64$
24. $z^3 + 125$
25. $x^3 - y^3$
26. $(x - a)^3 + b^3$
27. $x^3 - 4x^2 - x + 4$
28. $x^3 - x^2 - x + 1$
29. $2x^3 - 3x^2 + 4x - 6$
30. $x^3 - 5x^2 - 5x + 25$
31. $2x^3 - 4x^2 - x + 2$
32. $x^3 - 7x^2 - 4x + 28$
33. $x^4 - 15x^2 - 16$
34. $2x^4 - 49x^2 - 25$

Finding Real Zeros by Factoring In Exercises 35–54, find all real zeros of the polynomial. *See Example 2.*

35. $x^2 - 5x$
36. $2x^2 - 3x$
37. $x^2 - 9$
38. $x^2 - 25$
39. $x^2 - 3$
40. $x^2 - 8$
41. $(x - 3)^2 - 9$
42. $(x + 1)^2 - 36$
43. $x^2 + x - 2$
44. $x^2 + 5x + 6$
45. $x^2 - 5x - 6$
46. $x^2 + x - 20$
47. $3x^2 + 5x + 2$
48. $2x^2 - x - 1$
49. $x^3 + 64$
50. $x^3 - 216$
51. $x^4 - 16$
52. $x^4 - 625$
53. $x^3 - x^2 - 4x + 4$
54. $2x^3 + x^2 + 6x + 3$

Finding the Domain of a Radical Expression In Exercises 55–60, find the domain of the expression. *See Example 3.*

55. $\sqrt{x^2 - 4}$
56. $\sqrt{4 - x^2}$
57. $\sqrt{x^2 - 7x + 12}$
58. $\sqrt{x^2 - 8x + 15}$
59. $\sqrt{5x^2 + 6x + 1}$
60. $\sqrt{3x^2 - 10x + 3}$

Using Synthetic Division In Exercises 61–64, use synthetic division to complete the indicated factorization.

61. $x^3 - 3x^2 - 6x - 2 = (x + 1)(\quad)$
62. $x^3 - 2x^2 - x + 2 = (x - 2)(\quad)$
63. $2x^3 - x^2 - 2x + 1 = (x + 1)(\quad)$
64. $x^4 - 16x^3 + 96x^2 - 256x + 256 = (x - 4)(\quad)$

Using the Rational Zero Theorem In Exercises 65–74, use the Rational Zero Theorem to find all real zeros of the polynomial. *See Example 4.*

65. $x^3 - x^2 - 10x - 8$
66. $x^3 - 7x - 6$
67. $x^3 - 6x^2 + 11x - 6$
68. $x^3 + 2x^2 - 5x - 6$
69. $6x^3 - 11x^2 - 19x - 6$
70. $18x^3 - 9x^2 - 8x + 4$
71. $x^3 - 3x^2 - 3x - 4$
72. $2x^3 - x^2 - 13x - 6$
73. $4x^3 + 11x^2 + 5x - 2$
74. $3x^3 + 4x^2 - 13x + 6$

75. **Production Level** The minimum average cost of producing x units of a product occurs when the production level is set at the (positive) solution of

$$0.0003x^2 - 1200 = 0.$$

How many solutions does this equation have? Find and interpret the solution(s) in the context of the problem. What production level will minimize the average cost?

76. **Profit** The profit P (in dollars) from sales is given by

$$P = -200x^2 + 2000x - 3800$$

where x is the number of units sold per day (in hundreds). Determine the interval for x such that the profit will be greater than $1000.

A.5 Fractions and Rationalization

- Simplify rational expressions.
- Add and subtract rational expressions.
- Simplify rational expressions involving radicals.
- Rationalize numerators and denominators of rational expressions.

Simplifying Rational Expressions

In this section, you will review operations involving fractional expressions such as

$$\frac{2}{x}, \quad \frac{x^2 + 2x - 4}{x + 6}, \quad \text{and} \quad \frac{1}{\sqrt{x^2 + 1}}.$$

The first two expressions have polynomials as both numerator and denominator and are called **rational expressions.** A rational expression is **proper** when the degree of the numerator is less than the degree of the denominator. For example,

$$\frac{x}{x^2 + 1}$$

is proper. If the degree of the numerator is greater than or equal to the degree of the denominator, then the rational expression is **improper.** For example,

$$\frac{x^2}{x^2 + 1} \quad \text{and} \quad \frac{x^3 + 2x + 1}{x + 1}$$

are both improper.

A fraction is in simplest form when its numerator and denominator have no factors in common aside from ± 1. To write a fraction in simplest form, divide out common factors.

$$\frac{a \cdot c}{b \cdot c} = \frac{a}{b}, \quad c \neq 0$$

The key to success in simplifying rational expressions lies in your ability to factor polynomials. When simplifying rational expressions, be sure to factor each polynomial completely before concluding that the numerator and denominator have no common factors.

Example 1   Simplifying a Rational Expression

Write $\dfrac{12 + x - x^2}{2x^2 - 9x + 4}$ in simplest form.

SOLUTION

$$\frac{12 + x - x^2}{2x^2 - 9x + 4} = \frac{(4 - x)(3 + x)}{(2x - 1)(x - 4)} \qquad \text{Factor completely.}$$

$$= \frac{-(x - 4)(3 + x)}{(2x - 1)(x - 4)} \qquad (4 - x) = -(x - 4)$$

$$= -\frac{3 + x}{2x - 1}, \quad x \neq 4 \qquad \text{Divide out common factors.}$$

STUDY TIP

To simplify a rational expression, it may be necessary to change the sign of a factor by factoring out (-1), as shown in Example 1.

✓ **Checkpoint 1**

Write $\dfrac{x^2 + 8x - 20}{x^2 + 11x + 10}$ in simplest form.

Operations with Fractions

Operations with Fractions

1. Add fractions (find a common denominator):

$$\frac{a}{b} + \frac{c}{d} = \frac{a}{b}\left(\frac{d}{d}\right) + \frac{c}{d}\left(\frac{b}{b}\right) = \frac{ad}{bd} + \frac{bc}{bd} = \frac{ad + bc}{bd}, \quad b \neq 0, d \neq 0$$

2. Subtract fractions (find a common denominator):

$$\frac{a}{b} - \frac{c}{d} = \frac{a}{b}\left(\frac{d}{d}\right) - \frac{c}{d}\left(\frac{b}{b}\right) = \frac{ad}{bd} - \frac{bc}{bd} = \frac{ad - bc}{bd}, \quad b \neq 0, d \neq 0$$

3. Multiply fractions:

$$\left(\frac{a}{b}\right)\left(\frac{c}{d}\right) = \frac{ac}{bd}, \quad b \neq 0, d \neq 0$$

4. Divide fractions (invert and multiply):

$$\frac{a/b}{c/d} = \left(\frac{a}{b}\right)\left(\frac{d}{c}\right) = \frac{ad}{bc}, \quad b \neq 0, c \neq 0, d \neq 0$$

$$\frac{a/b}{c} = \frac{a/b}{c/1} = \left(\frac{a}{b}\right)\left(\frac{1}{c}\right) = \frac{a}{bc}, \quad b \neq 0, c \neq 0$$

5. Divide out common factors:

$$\frac{ab}{ac} = \frac{b}{c}, \quad a \neq 0, c \neq 0$$

$$\frac{ab + ac}{ad} = \frac{a(b + c)}{ad} = \frac{b + c}{d}, \quad a \neq 0, d \neq 0$$

Example 2   Adding and Subtracting Rational Expressions

Perform each indicated operation and simplify.

a. $x + \dfrac{1}{x}$ **b.** $\dfrac{1}{x + 1} - \dfrac{2}{2x - 1}$

SOLUTION

a. $x + \dfrac{1}{x} = \dfrac{x^2}{x} + \dfrac{1}{x}$ Write with common denominator.

$\qquad = \dfrac{x^2 + 1}{x}$ Add fractions.

b. $\dfrac{1}{x + 1} - \dfrac{2}{2x - 1} = \dfrac{(2x - 1)}{(x + 1)(2x - 1)} - \dfrac{2(x + 1)}{(x + 1)(2x - 1)}$

$\qquad = \dfrac{2x - 1 - 2x - 2}{2x^2 + x - 1}$

$\qquad = \dfrac{-3}{2x^2 + x - 1}$

✓ **Checkpoint 2**

Perform each indicated operation and simplify.

a. $x + \dfrac{2}{x}$ **b.** $\dfrac{2}{x + 1} - \dfrac{1}{2x + 1}$

In adding (or subtracting) fractions whose denominators have no common factors, it is convenient to use the following pattern.

$$\frac{a}{b} + \frac{c}{d} = \frac{a}{b} \diagup + \diagup \frac{c}{d} = \frac{ad + bc}{bd}$$

For instance, in Example 2(b), you could have used this pattern as shown.

$$\frac{1}{x + 1} - \frac{2}{2x - 1} = \frac{(2x - 1) - 2(x + 1)}{(x + 1)(2x - 1)}$$

$$= \frac{2x - 1 - 2x - 2}{(x + 1)(2x - 1)}$$

$$= \frac{-3}{2x^2 + x - 1}$$

In Example 2, the denominators of the rational expressions have no common factors. When the denominators do have common factors, it is best to find the least common denominator before adding or subtracting. For instance, when adding

$$\frac{1}{x} \quad \text{and} \quad \frac{2}{x^2}$$

you can recognize that the least common denominator is x^2 and write

$$\frac{1}{x} + \frac{2}{x^2} = \frac{x}{x^2} + \frac{2}{x^2}$$ Write with common denominator.

$$= \frac{x + 2}{x^2}.$$ Add fractions.

This is further demonstrated in Example 3.

Example 3   Adding Rational Expressions

Add the rational expressions.

$$\frac{x}{x^2 - 1} + \frac{3}{x + 1}$$

SOLUTION   Because $x^2 - 1 = (x + 1)(x - 1)$, the least common denominator is $x^2 - 1$.

$$\frac{x}{x^2 - 1} + \frac{3}{x + 1} = \frac{x}{(x - 1)(x + 1)} + \frac{3}{x + 1}$$ Factor.

$$= \frac{x}{(x - 1)(x + 1)} + \frac{3(x - 1)}{(x - 1)(x + 1)}$$ Write with common denominator.

$$= \frac{x + 3(x - 1)}{(x - 1)(x + 1)}$$ Add fractions.

$$= \frac{x + 3x - 3}{(x - 1)(x + 1)}$$ Multiply.

$$= \frac{4x - 3}{x^2 - 1}$$ Simplify.

✓ **Checkpoint 3**

Add the rational expressions.

$$\frac{x}{x^2 - 4} + \frac{2}{x - 2}$$

Example 4 **Subtracting Rational Expressions**

Subtract the rational expressions.

$$\frac{1}{2(x^2 + 2x)} - \frac{1}{4x}$$

SOLUTION In this case, the least common denominator is $4x(x + 2)$.

$$\frac{1}{2(x^2 + 2x)} - \frac{1}{4x} = \frac{1}{2x(x + 2)} - \frac{1}{2(2x)} \qquad \text{Factor.}$$

$$= \frac{2}{2(2x)(x + 2)} - \frac{x + 2}{2(2x)(x + 2)} \qquad \begin{array}{l}\text{Write with common}\\ \text{denominator.}\end{array}$$

$$= \frac{2 - (x + 2)}{4x(x + 2)} \qquad \text{Subtract fractions.}$$

$$= \frac{2 - x - 2}{4x(x + 2)} \qquad \text{Remove parentheses.}$$

$$= \frac{-x}{4x(x + 2)} \qquad \begin{array}{l}\text{Divide out}\\ \text{common factor.}\end{array}$$

$$= \frac{-1}{4(x + 2)}, \quad x \neq 0 \qquad \text{Simplify.}$$

✓**Checkpoint 4**

Subtract the rational expressions.

$$\frac{1}{3(x^2 + 2x)} - \frac{1}{3x}$$

Example 5 **Combining Three Rational Expressions**

Perform the operations and simplify.

$$\frac{3}{x - 1} - \frac{2}{x} + \frac{x + 3}{x^2 - 1}$$

SOLUTION Using the factored denominators $(x - 1)$, x, and $(x + 1)(x - 1)$, you can see that the least common denominator is $x(x + 1)(x - 1)$.

$$\frac{3}{x - 1} - \frac{2}{x} + \frac{x + 3}{x^2 - 1} = \frac{3(x)(x + 1)}{x(x + 1)(x - 1)} - \frac{2(x + 1)(x - 1)}{x(x + 1)(x - 1)} + \frac{(x + 3)(x)}{x(x + 1)(x - 1)}$$

$$= \frac{3(x)(x + 1) - 2(x + 1)(x - 1) + (x + 3)(x)}{x(x + 1)(x - 1)}$$

$$= \frac{3x^2 + 3x - 2x^2 + 2 + x^2 + 3x}{x(x + 1)(x - 1)}$$

$$= \frac{2x^2 + 6x + 2}{x(x + 1)(x - 1)}$$

$$= \frac{2(x^2 + 3x + 1)}{x(x + 1)(x - 1)}$$

✓**Checkpoint 5**

Perform the operations and simplify.

$$\frac{4}{x} - \frac{2}{x^2} + \frac{4}{x + 3}$$

Expressions Involving Radicals

In calculus, the operation of differentiation tends to produce "messy" expressions when applied to fractional expressions. This is especially true when the fractional expressions involve radicals. When differentiation is used, it is important to be able to simplify these expressions in order to obtain more manageable forms. The expressions in Example 6 are the results of differentiation. In each case, note how much *simpler* the simplified form is than the original form.

Example 6   Simplifying an Expression with Radicals

Simplify each expression.

a. $\dfrac{\sqrt{x+1} - \dfrac{x}{2\sqrt{x+1}}}{x+1}$

b. $\left(\dfrac{1}{x + \sqrt{x^2+1}}\right)\left(1 + \dfrac{2x}{2\sqrt{x^2+1}}\right)$

SOLUTION

a. $\dfrac{\sqrt{x+1} - \dfrac{x}{2\sqrt{x+1}}}{x+1} = \dfrac{\dfrac{2(x+1)}{2\sqrt{x+1}} - \dfrac{x}{2\sqrt{x+1}}}{x+1}$ Write with common denominator.

$= \dfrac{\dfrac{2x+2-x}{2\sqrt{x+1}}}{\dfrac{x+1}{1}}$ Subtract fractions.

$= \dfrac{x+2}{2\sqrt{x+1}}\left(\dfrac{1}{x+1}\right)$ To divide, invert and multiply.

$= \dfrac{x+2}{2(x+1)^{3/2}}$ Multiply.

b. $\left(\dfrac{1}{x + \sqrt{x^2+1}}\right)\left(1 + \dfrac{2x}{2\sqrt{x^2+1}}\right) = \left(\dfrac{1}{x + \sqrt{x^2+1}}\right)\left(1 + \dfrac{x}{\sqrt{x^2+1}}\right)$

$= \left(\dfrac{1}{x + \sqrt{x^2+1}}\right)\left(\dfrac{\sqrt{x^2+1}}{\sqrt{x^2+1}} + \dfrac{x}{\sqrt{x^2+1}}\right)$

$= \left(\dfrac{1}{x + \sqrt{x^2+1}}\right)\left(\dfrac{x + \sqrt{x^2+1}}{\sqrt{x^2+1}}\right)$

$= \dfrac{1}{\sqrt{x^2+1}}$

✓ **Checkpoint 6**

Simplify each expression.

a. $\dfrac{\sqrt{x+2} - \dfrac{x}{4\sqrt{x+2}}}{x+2}$

b. $\left(\dfrac{1}{x + \sqrt{x^2+4}}\right)\left(1 + \dfrac{x}{\sqrt{x^2+4}}\right)$

Rationalization Techniques

In working with quotients involving radicals, it is often convenient to move the radical expression from the denominator to the numerator, or vice versa. For example, you can move $\sqrt{2}$ from the denominator to the numerator in the following quotient by multiplying by $\sqrt{2}/\sqrt{2}$.

Radical in Denominator	*Rationalize*	*Radical in Numerator*
$\dfrac{1}{\sqrt{2}}$	$\dfrac{1}{\sqrt{2}}\left(\dfrac{\sqrt{2}}{\sqrt{2}}\right)$	$\dfrac{\sqrt{2}}{2}$

This process is called **rationalizing the denominator.** A similar process is used to **rationalize the numerator.**

STUDY TIP

The success of the second and third rationalizing techniques stems from the following.

$$(\sqrt{a} - \sqrt{b})(\sqrt{a} + \sqrt{b})$$
$$= a - b$$

Rationalizing Techniques

1. When the denominator is $\sqrt{a}$, multiply by $\dfrac{\sqrt{a}}{\sqrt{a}}$.

2. When the denominator is $\sqrt{a} - \sqrt{b}$, multiply by $\dfrac{\sqrt{a} + \sqrt{b}}{\sqrt{a} + \sqrt{b}}$.

3. When the denominator is $\sqrt{a} + \sqrt{b}$, multiply by $\dfrac{\sqrt{a} - \sqrt{b}}{\sqrt{a} - \sqrt{b}}$.

The same guidelines apply to rationalizing numerators.

Example 7   Rationalizing Denominators and Numerators

Rationalize the denominator or numerator.

a. $\dfrac{3}{\sqrt{12}}$ **b.** $\dfrac{\sqrt{x + 1}}{2}$ **c.** $\dfrac{1}{\sqrt{5} + \sqrt{2}}$ **d.** $\dfrac{1}{\sqrt{x} - \sqrt{x + 1}}$

SOLUTION

a. $\dfrac{3}{\sqrt{12}} = \dfrac{3}{2\sqrt{3}} = \dfrac{3}{2\sqrt{3}}\left(\dfrac{\sqrt{3}}{\sqrt{3}}\right) = \dfrac{3\sqrt{3}}{2(3)} = \dfrac{\sqrt{3}}{2}$

b. $\dfrac{\sqrt{x + 1}}{2} = \dfrac{\sqrt{x + 1}}{2}\left(\dfrac{\sqrt{x + 1}}{\sqrt{x + 1}}\right) = \dfrac{x + 1}{2\sqrt{x + 1}}$

c. $\dfrac{1}{\sqrt{5} + \sqrt{2}} = \dfrac{1}{\sqrt{5} + \sqrt{2}}\left(\dfrac{\sqrt{5} - \sqrt{2}}{\sqrt{5} - \sqrt{2}}\right) = \dfrac{\sqrt{5} - \sqrt{2}}{5 - 2} = \dfrac{\sqrt{5} - \sqrt{2}}{3}$

d. $\dfrac{1}{\sqrt{x} - \sqrt{x + 1}} = \dfrac{1}{\sqrt{x} - \sqrt{x + 1}}\left(\dfrac{\sqrt{x} + \sqrt{x + 1}}{\sqrt{x} + \sqrt{x + 1}}\right)$

$$= \dfrac{\sqrt{x} + \sqrt{x + 1}}{x - (x + 1)}$$

$$= -\sqrt{x} - \sqrt{x + 1}$$

✓ Checkpoint 7

Rationalize the denominator or numerator.

a. $\dfrac{5}{\sqrt{8}}$ **b.** $\dfrac{\sqrt{x + 2}}{4}$ **c.** $\dfrac{1}{\sqrt{6} - \sqrt{3}}$ **d.** $\dfrac{1}{\sqrt{x} + \sqrt{x + 2}}$

Exercises A.5

See www.CalcChat.com for worked-out solutions to odd-numbered exercises.

Simplifying a Rational Expression In Exercises 1–4, write the rational expression in simplest form. *See Example 1.*

1. $\dfrac{x^2 - 7x + 12}{x^2 + 3x - 18}$

2. $\dfrac{x^2 - 5x - 6}{x^2 + 11x + 10}$

3. $\dfrac{x^2 + 3x - 10}{2x^2 - x - 6}$

4. $\dfrac{3x^2 + 13x + 12}{x^2 - 4x - 21}$

Adding and Subtracting Rational Expressions In Exercises 5–16, perform the indicated operations and simplify. *See Examples 2, 3, 4, and 5.*

5. $\dfrac{x}{x - 2} + \dfrac{3}{x - 2}$

6. $\dfrac{5x + 10}{2x - 1} - \dfrac{2x + 10}{2x - 1}$

7. $x - \dfrac{3}{x}$

8. $3x + \dfrac{2}{x^2}$

9. $\dfrac{2}{x - 3} + \dfrac{5x}{3x + 4}$

10. $\dfrac{3}{3x - 1} - \dfrac{1}{x + 2}$

11. $\dfrac{2}{x^2 - 4} - \dfrac{1}{x - 2}$

12. $\dfrac{5}{x^2 - 9} + \dfrac{x}{x + 3}$

13. $\dfrac{x}{x^2 + x - 2} - \dfrac{1}{x + 2}$

14. $\dfrac{2}{x + 1} + \dfrac{3x - 2}{x^2 - 2x - 3}$

15. $\dfrac{2}{x^2 + 1} - \dfrac{1}{x} + \dfrac{1}{x^3 + x}$

16. $\dfrac{3}{x + 2} + \dfrac{3}{x - 2} + \dfrac{1}{x^2 - 4}$

Simplifying an Expression with Radicals In Exercises 17–28, simplify the expression. *See Example 6.*

17. $\dfrac{-x}{(x + 1)^{3/2}} + \dfrac{2}{(x + 1)^{1/2}}$

18. $2\sqrt{x}(x - 2) + \dfrac{(x - 2)^2}{2\sqrt{x}}$

19. $\dfrac{2 - t}{2\sqrt{1 + t}} - \sqrt{1 + t}$

20. $-\dfrac{\sqrt{x^2 + 1}}{x^2} + \dfrac{1}{\sqrt{x^2 + 1}}$

21. $\left(2x\sqrt{x^2 + 1} - \dfrac{x^3}{\sqrt{x^2 + 1}}\right) \div (x^2 + 1)$

22. $\left(\sqrt{x^3 + 1} - \dfrac{3x^3}{2\sqrt{x^3 + 1}}\right) \div (x^3 + 1)$

23. $\dfrac{(x^2 + 2)^{1/2} - x^2(x^2 + 2)^{-1/2}}{x^2}$

24. $\dfrac{x(x + 1)^{-1/2} - (x + 1)^{1/2}}{x^2}$

25. $\dfrac{\dfrac{\sqrt{x + 1}}{\sqrt{x}} - \dfrac{\sqrt{x}}{\sqrt{x + 1}}}{2(x + 1)}$

26. $\dfrac{\dfrac{2x^2}{3(x^2 - 1)^{2/3}} - (x^2 - 1)^{1/3}}{x^2}$

27. $\dfrac{-x^2}{(2x + 3)^{3/2}} + \dfrac{2x}{(2x + 3)^{1/2}}$

28. $\dfrac{-x}{2(3 + x^2)^{3/2}} + \dfrac{3}{(3 + x^2)^{1/2}}$

Rationalizing Denominators and Numerators In Exercises 29–42, rationalize the denominator or numerator and simplify. *See Example 7.*

29. $\dfrac{2}{\sqrt{10}}$

30. $\dfrac{3}{\sqrt{21}}$

31. $\dfrac{4x}{\sqrt{x - 1}}$

32. $\dfrac{5y}{\sqrt{y + 7}}$

33. $\dfrac{49(x - 3)}{\sqrt{x^2 - 9}}$

34. $\dfrac{10(x + 2)}{\sqrt{x^2 - x - 6}}$

35. $\dfrac{5}{\sqrt{14} - 2}$

36. $\dfrac{13}{6 + \sqrt{10}}$

37. $\dfrac{1}{\sqrt{6} + \sqrt{5}}$

38. $\dfrac{x}{\sqrt{2} + \sqrt{3}}$

39. $\dfrac{2}{\sqrt{x} + \sqrt{x - 2}}$

40. $\dfrac{10}{\sqrt{x} + \sqrt{x + 5}}$

41. $\dfrac{\sqrt{x + 2} - \sqrt{2}}{x}$

42. $\dfrac{\sqrt{x + 1} - 1}{x}$

43. Installment Loan The monthly payment M (in dollars) for an installment loan is given by the formula

$$M = P\left[\dfrac{r/12}{1 - \left(\dfrac{1}{(r/12) + 1}\right)^N}\right]$$

where P is the amount of the loan (in dollars), r is the annual percentage rate (in decimal form), and N is the number of monthly payments. Enter the formula into a graphing utility, and use it to find the monthly payment for a loan of $10,000 at an annual percentage rate of 7.5% ($r = 0.075$) for 5 years ($N = 60$ monthly payments).

44. Inventory A retailer has determined that the cost C (in dollars) of ordering and storing x units of a product is

$$C = 6x + \dfrac{900,000}{x}.$$

(a) Write the expression for cost as a single fraction.

(b) Which order size should the retailer place: 240 units, 387 units, or 480 units? Explain your reasoning.

B Alternative Introduction to the Fundamental Theorem of Calculus

In this appendix, a summation process is used to provide an alternative development of the definite integral. It is intended that this supplement follow Section 5.3 in the text. If used, this appendix should replace the material preceding Example 2 in Section 5.4. Example 1 below shows how the area of a region in the plane can be approximated by the use of rectangles.

Example 1   Using Rectangles to Approximate the Area of a Region

Use the four rectangles shown in Figure B.1 to approximate the area of the region lying between the graph of

$$f(x) = \frac{x^2}{2}$$

and the x-axis, between $x = 0$ and $x = 4$.

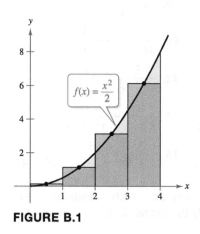

FIGURE B.1

SOLUTION   You can find the heights of the rectangles by evaluating the function f at each of the midpoints of the subintervals

$$[0, 1], \quad [1, 2], \quad [2, 3], \quad [3, 4].$$

Because the width of each rectangle is 1, the sum of the areas of the four rectangles is

$$S = \overbrace{(1)}^{\text{width}} \overbrace{f\left(\frac{1}{2}\right)}^{\text{height}} + \overbrace{(1)}^{\text{width}} \overbrace{f\left(\frac{3}{2}\right)}^{\text{height}} + \overbrace{(1)}^{\text{width}} \overbrace{f\left(\frac{5}{2}\right)}^{\text{height}} + \overbrace{(1)}^{\text{width}} \overbrace{f\left(\frac{7}{2}\right)}^{\text{height}}$$

$$= \frac{1}{8} + \frac{9}{8} + \frac{25}{8} + \frac{49}{8}$$

$$= \frac{84}{8}$$

$$= 10.5.$$

So, you can approximate the area of the region to be 10.5 square units.

STUDY TIP

The approximation technique used in Example 1 is called the *Midpoint Rule*. The Midpoint Rule is discussed further in Section 5.6.

The procedure shown in Example 1 can be generalized. Let f be a continuous function defined on the closed interval $[a, b]$. To begin, partition the interval into n subintervals, each of width

$$\Delta x = \frac{b - a}{n}$$

as shown.

$$a = x_0 < x_1 < x_2 < \cdots < x_{n-1} < x_n = b$$

In each subinterval $[x_{i-1}, x_i]$, choose an arbitrary point c_i and form the sum

$$S = f(c_1)\,\Delta x + f(c_2)\,\Delta x + \cdots + f(c_{n-1})\,\Delta x + f(c_n)\,\Delta x.$$

This type of summation is called a **Riemann sum** and is often written using summation notation, as shown below.

$$S = \sum_{i=1}^{n} f(c_i)\,\Delta x, \quad x_{i-1} \le c_i \le x_i$$

For the Riemann sum in Example 1, the interval is $[a, b] = [0, 4]$, the number of subintervals is $n = 4$, the width of each subinterval is $\Delta x = 1$, and the point c_i in each subinterval is its midpoint. So, you can write the approximation in Example 1 as

$$S = \sum_{i=1}^{n} f(c_i)\,\Delta x$$
$$= \sum_{i=1}^{4} f(c_i)(1)$$
$$= \frac{1}{8} + \frac{9}{8} + \frac{25}{8} + \frac{49}{8}$$
$$= \frac{84}{8}.$$

Example 2   Using a Riemann Sum to Approximate Area

Use a Riemann sum to approximate the area of the region bounded by the graph of

$$f(x) = -x^2 + 2x$$

and the x-axis, for $0 \le x \le 2$. In the Riemann sum, let $n = 6$ and choose c_i to be the left endpoint of each subinterval.

SOLUTION   Subdivide the interval $[0, 2]$ into six subintervals, each of width

$$\Delta x = \frac{2 - 0}{6}$$
$$= \frac{1}{3}$$

as shown in Figure B.2. Because c_i is the left endpoint of each subinterval, the Riemann sum is given by

$$S = \sum_{i=1}^{n} f(c_i)\,\Delta x$$
$$= \left[f(0) + f\left(\frac{1}{3}\right) + f\left(\frac{2}{3}\right) + f(1) + f\left(\frac{4}{3}\right) + f\left(\frac{5}{3}\right) \right]\left(\frac{1}{3}\right)$$
$$= \left[0 + \frac{5}{9} + \frac{8}{9} + 1 + \frac{8}{9} + \frac{5}{9} \right]\left(\frac{1}{3}\right)$$
$$= \frac{35}{27} \text{ square units.}$$

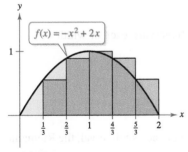

$f(x) = -x^2 + 2x$

FIGURE B.2

Example 2 illustrates an important point. If a function f is continuous and nonnegative over the interval $[a, b]$, then the Riemann sum

$$S = \sum_{i=1}^{n} f(c_i)\,\Delta x$$

can be used to approximate the area of the region bounded by the graph of f and the x-axis, between $x = a$ and $x = b$. Moreover, for a given interval, as the number of subintervals increases, the approximation to the actual area will improve. This is illustrated in the next two examples by using Riemann sums to approximate the area of a triangle.

Example 3   Approximating the Area of a Triangle

Use a Riemann sum to approximate the area of the triangular region bounded by the graph of

$$f(x) = 2x$$

and the x-axis, $0 \le x \le 3$. Use a partition of six subintervals and choose c_i to be the left endpoint of each subinterval.

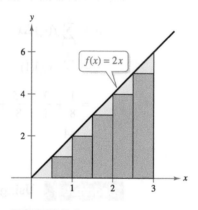

FIGURE B.3

SOLUTION   Subdivide the interval $[0, 3]$ into six subintervals, each of width

$$\Delta x = \frac{3 - 0}{6}$$

$$= \frac{1}{2}$$

as shown in Figure B.3. Because c_i is the left endpoint of each subinterval, the Riemann sum is given by

$$S = \sum_{i=1}^{n} f(c_i)\,\Delta x$$

$$= \left[f(0) + f\!\left(\frac{1}{2}\right) + f(1) + f\!\left(\frac{3}{2}\right) + f(2) + f\!\left(\frac{5}{2}\right) \right]\!\left(\frac{1}{2}\right)$$

$$= [0 + 1 + 2 + 3 + 4 + 5]\!\left(\frac{1}{2}\right)$$

$$= \frac{15}{2} \text{ square units.}$$

The approximations in Examples 2 and 3 are called **left Riemann sums,** because c_i was chosen to be the left endpoint of each subinterval. Using the right endpoints in Example 3, the **right Riemann sum** is $\frac{21}{2}$. Note that the exact area of the triangular region in Example 3 is

$$\text{Area} = \frac{1}{2}(\text{base})(\text{height})$$

$$= \frac{1}{2}(3)(6)$$

$$= 9 \text{ square units.}$$

So, the left Riemann sum gives an approximation that is less than the actual area, and the right Riemann sum gives an approximation that is greater than the actual area.

In Example 4, you will see that the approximation improves as the number of subintervals increases.

TECH TUTOR

Most graphing utilities are able to sum the first n terms of a sequence. Try using a graphing utility to verify the right Riemann sum in Example 3.

Example 4   Increasing the Number of Subintervals

Let $f(x) = 2x$, $0 \le x \le 3$. Use a graphing utility to determine the left and right Riemann sums for $n = 10$, $n = 100$, and $n = 1000$ subintervals.

SOLUTION   A graphing utility program for this problem is shown in Figure B.4. [Note that the function $f(x) = 2x$ is entered as Y1.]

```
PROGRAM:RIEMANN
:Input ("ENTER V
ALUE OF N",N)
:Input ("ENTER V
ALUE OF A",A)
:Input ("ENTER V
ALUE OF B",B)
:(B-A)/N→D
```
```
PROGRAM:RIEMANN
:0→R
:0→L
:A→X
:For(I,1,N)
:L+Y1→L
:A+ID→X
:R+Y1→R
```
```
PROGRAM:RIEMANN
:End
:LD→L
:RD→R
:Disp "LEFT SUM"
,L
:Disp "RIGHT SUM
",R
```

FIGURE B.4

Running this program for $n = 10$, $n = 100$, and $n = 1000$ gives the results shown in the table.

n	Left Reimann sum	Right Reimann sum
10	8.100	9.900
100	8.910	9.090
1000	8.991	9.009

From the results of Example 4, it appears that the Riemann sums are approaching the limit 9 as n approaches infinity. It is this observation that motivates the definition of a **definite integral.** In this definition, consider the partition of $[a, b]$ into n subintervals of equal width $\Delta x = (b - a)/n$, as shown.

$$a = x_0 < x_1 < x_2 < \cdots < x_{n-1} < x_n = b$$

Moreover, consider c_i to be an arbitrary point in the ith subinterval $[x_{i-1}, x_i]$. To say that the number of subintervals n approaches infinity is equivalent to saying that the width, Δx, of the subintervals approaches zero.

Definition of Definite Integral

If f is a continuous function defined on the closed interval $[a, b]$, then the **definite integral of f on $[a, b]$** is

$$\int_a^b f(x)\, dx = \lim_{\Delta x \to 0} \sum_{i=1}^n f(c_i)\, \Delta x$$

$$= \lim_{n \to \infty} \sum_{i=1}^n f(c_i)\, \Delta x.$$

If f is continuous and nonnegative on the interval $[a, b]$, then the definite integral of f on $[a, b]$ gives the area of the region bounded by the graph of f, the x-axis, and the vertical lines $x = a$ and $x = b$.

Evaluation of a definite integral by its limit definition can be difficult. However, there are times when a definite integral can be solved by recognizing that it represents the area of a common type of geometric figure.

(a) $\int_1^3 4\, dx$

Rectangle

(b) $\int_0^3 (x + 2)\, dx$

Trapezoid

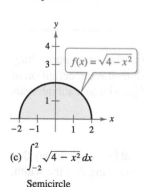

(c) $\int_{-2}^2 \sqrt{4 - x^2}\, dx$

Semicircle

FIGURE B.5

Example 5   The Areas of Common Geometric Figures

Sketch the region corresponding to each of the definite integrals. Then evaluate each definite integral using a geometric formula.

a. $\displaystyle\int_1^3 4\, dx$

b. $\displaystyle\int_0^3 (x + 2)\, dx$

c. $\displaystyle\int_{-2}^2 \sqrt{4 - x^2}\, dx$

SOLUTION   A sketch of each region is shown in Figure B.5.

a. The region associated with this definite integral is a rectangle of height 4 and width 2. Moreover, because the function $f(x) = 4$ is continuous and nonnegative on the interval $[1, 3]$, you can conclude that the area of the rectangle is given by the definite integral. So, the value of the definite integral is

$$\int_1^3 4\, dx = 4(2) = 8 \text{ square units.}$$

b. The region associated with this definite integral is a trapezoid with an altitude of 3 and parallel bases of lengths 2 and 5. The formula for the area of a trapezoid is $\frac{1}{2}h(b_1 + b_2)$, and so you have

$$\int_0^3 (x + 2)\, dx = \frac{1}{2}(3)(2 + 5)$$

$$= \frac{21}{2} \text{ square units.}$$

c. The region associated with this definite integral is a semicircle of radius 2. The formula for the area of a semicircle is $\frac{1}{2}\pi r^2$, and so you have

$$\int_{-2}^2 \sqrt{4 - x^2}\, dx = \frac{1}{2}\pi(2^2)$$

$$= 2\pi \text{ square units.}$$

For some simple functions, it is possible to evaluate definite integrals by the Riemann sum definition. In the next example, you will use the fact that the sum of the first n integers is given by the formula

$$1 + 2 + \cdots + n = \sum_{i=1}^{n} i = \frac{n(n+1)}{2} \qquad \text{See Exercise 29.}$$

to compute the area of the triangular region in Examples 3 and 4.

Example 6   Evaluating a Definite Integral by Its Definition

Evaluate $\displaystyle\int_{0}^{3} 2x\, dx$.

SOLUTION   Let

$$\Delta x = \frac{b - a}{n} = \frac{3}{n}$$

and choose c_i to be the right endpoint of each subinterval,

$$c_i = \frac{3i}{n}.$$

Then you have

$$\int_{0}^{3} 2x\, dx = \lim_{\Delta x \to 0} \sum_{i=1}^{n} f(c_i)\Delta x$$

$$= \lim_{n \to \infty} \sum_{i=1}^{n} 2\left(i\frac{3}{n}\right)\left(\frac{3}{n}\right)$$

$$= \lim_{n \to \infty} \frac{18}{n^2} \sum_{i=1}^{n} i$$

$$= \lim_{n \to \infty} \left(\frac{18}{n^2}\right)\left(\frac{n(n+1)}{2}\right)$$

$$= \lim_{n \to \infty} \left(9 + \frac{9}{n}\right).$$

This limit can be evaluated in the same way that you calculated horizontal asymptotes in Section 3.6. In particular, as n approaches infinity, you see that $9/n$ approaches 0, and the limit above is 9. So, you can conclude that

$$\int_{0}^{3} 2x\, dx = 9.$$

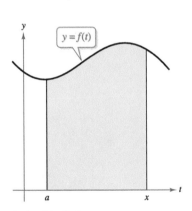

FIGURE B.6

From Example 6, you can see that it can be difficult to evaluate the definite integral of even a simple function by using Riemann sums. A computer can help in calculating these sums for large values of n, but this procedure would give only an approximation of the definite integral. Fortunately, the **Fundamental Theorem of Calculus** provides a technique for evaluating definite integrals using antiderivatives, and for this reason it is often thought to be the most important theorem in calculus. In the remainder of this appendix, you will see how derivatives and integrals are related via the Fundamental Theorem of Calculus.

To simplify the discussion, assume that f is a continuous nonnegative function defined on the interval $[a, b]$. Let $A(x)$ be the area of the region under the graph of f from a to x, as indicated in Figure B.6. The area under the shaded region in Figure B.7 is

$$A(x + \Delta x) - A(x).$$

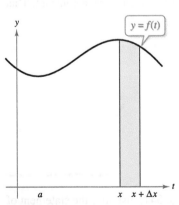

FIGURE B.7

If Δx is small, then this area is approximated by the area of the rectangle of height $f(x)$ and width Δx. So, you have

$$A(x + \Delta x) - A(x) \approx f(x)\, \Delta x.$$

Dividing by Δx produces

$$f(x) \approx \frac{A(x + \Delta x) - A(x)}{\Delta x}.$$

By taking the limit as Δx approaches 0, you can see that

$$f(x) = \lim_{\Delta x \to 0} \frac{A(x + \Delta x) - A(x)}{\Delta x}$$

$$= A'(x)$$

and you can establish the fact that the area function $A(x)$ is an antiderivative of f. Although it was assumed that f is continuous and nonnegative, this development is valid when the function f is simply continuous on the closed interval $[a, b]$. This result is used in the proof of the Fundamental Theorem of Calculus.

Fundamental Theorem of Calculus

If f is a continuous function on the closed interval $[a, b]$, then

$$\int_a^b f(x)\,dx = F(b) - F(a)$$

where F is any function such that $F'(x) = f(x)$.

PROOF   From the discussion above, you know that

$$\int_a^x f(x)\, dx = A(x)$$

and in particular,

$$A(a) = \int_a^a f(x)\, dx = 0$$

and

$$A(b) = \int_a^b f(x)\, dx.$$

If F is *any* antiderivative of f, then you know that F differs from A by a constant. That is,

$$A(x) = F(x) + C.$$

So,

$$\int_a^b f(x)\, dx = A(b) - A(a)$$

$$= [F(b) + C] - [F(a) + C]$$

$$= F(b) + C - F(a) - C$$

$$= F(b) - F(a).$$

You are now ready to continue Section 5.4, on page 341, just after the statement of the Fundamental Theorem of Calculus.

Exercises B

See www.CalcChat.com for worked-out solutions to odd-numbered exercises.

Using Rectangles to Approximate the Area of a Region In Exercises 1 and 2, use the rectangles to approximate the area of the region. *See Example 1.*

1. $y = x + 1$

2. $y = 4 - x^2$

Using a Riemann Sum to Approximate Area In Exercises 3–8, use the left Riemann sum and the right Riemann sum to approximate the area of the region using the indicated number of subintervals. *See Examples 2 and 3.*

3. $y = \sqrt{x}$

4. $y = \sqrt{x} + 1$

5. $y = \dfrac{1}{x}$

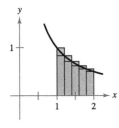

6. $y = \dfrac{1}{x - 2}$

7. $y = \sqrt{1 - x^2}$

8. $y = \sqrt{x} + 1$

9. Comparing Riemann Sums Consider a triangle of area 2 bounded by the graphs of $y = x$, $y = 0$, and $x = 2$.

(a) Sketch the graph of the region.

(b) Divide the interval $[0, 2]$ into n equal subintervals and show that the endpoints of the subintervals are

$$0 < 1\left(\frac{2}{n}\right) < \cdots < (n - 1)\left(\frac{2}{n}\right) < n\left(\frac{2}{n}\right).$$

(c) Show that the left Riemann sum is

$$S_L = \sum_{i=1}^{n} \left[(i - 1)\left(\frac{2}{n}\right)\right]\left(\frac{2}{n}\right).$$

(d) Show that the right Riemann sum is

$$S_R = \sum_{i=1}^{n} \left[i\left(\frac{2}{n}\right)\right]\left(\frac{2}{n}\right).$$

(e) Complete the table below.

n	5	10	50	100
Left sum, S_L				
Right sum, S_R				

(f) Show that $\lim\limits_{n \to \infty} S_L = \lim\limits_{n \to \infty} S_R = 2$.

10. Comparing Riemann Sums Consider a trapezoid of area 4 bounded by the graphs of $y = x$, $y = 0$, $x = 1$, and $x = 3$.

(a) Sketch the graph of the region.

(b) Divide the interval $[1, 3]$ into n equal subintervals and show that the endpoints of the subintervals are

$$1 < 1 + 1\left(\frac{2}{n}\right) < \cdots < 1 + (n - 1)\left(\frac{2}{n}\right) < 1 + n\left(\frac{2}{n}\right).$$

(c) Show that the left Riemann sum is

$$S_L = \sum_{i=1}^{n} \left[1 + (i - 1)\left(\frac{2}{n}\right)\right]\left(\frac{2}{n}\right).$$

(d) Show that the right Riemann sum is

$$S_R = \sum_{i=1}^{n} \left[1 + i\left(\frac{2}{n}\right)\right]\left(\frac{2}{n}\right).$$

(e) Complete the table below.

n	5	10	50	100
Left sum, S_L				
Right sum, S_R				

(f) Show that $\lim\limits_{n \to \infty} S_L = \lim\limits_{n \to \infty} S_R = 4$.

Writing a Definite Integral   In Exercises 11–18, set up a definite integral that yields the area of the region. (Do not evaluate the integral.)

11. $f(x) = 3$

12. $f(x) = 4 - 2x$

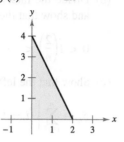

13. $f(x) = 4 - |x|$

14. $f(x) = x^2$

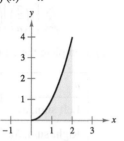

15. $f(x) = 4 - x^2$

16. $f(x) = \dfrac{1}{x^2 + 1}$

17. $f(x) = \sqrt{x + 1}$

18. $f(x) = (x^2 + 1)^2$

Finding Areas of Common Geometric Figures   In Exercises 19–28, sketch the region whose area is given by the definite integral. Then use a geometric formula to evaluate the integral ($a > 0, r > 0$). *See Example 5.*

19. $\displaystyle\int_0^3 4\, dx$

20. $\displaystyle\int_{-a}^{a} 4\, dx$

21. $\displaystyle\int_0^4 x\, dx$

22. $\displaystyle\int_0^4 \frac{x}{2}\, dx$

23. $\displaystyle\int_0^2 (2x + 5)\, dx$

24. $\displaystyle\int_0^5 (5 - x)\, dx$

25. $\displaystyle\int_{-1}^{1} \left(1 - |x|\right) dx$

26. $\displaystyle\int_{-a}^{a} \left(a - |x|\right) dx$

27. $\displaystyle\int_{-3}^{3} \sqrt{9 - x^2}\, dx$

28. $\displaystyle\int_{-r}^{r} \sqrt{r^2 - x^2}\, dx$

29. Proving a Sum   Show that $\displaystyle\sum_{i=1}^{n} i = \frac{n(n+1)}{2}$.
(*Hint:* Add the two sums below.)
$$S = 1 + 2 + 3 + \cdots + (n - 2) + (n - 1) + n$$
$$S = n + (n - 1) + (n - 2) + \cdots + 3 + 2 + 1$$

30. Evaluating a Definite Integral by Its Definition   Use the Riemann sum definition and the result of Exercise 29 to evaluate the definite integrals.

(a) $\displaystyle\int_1^2 x\, dx$ (b) $\displaystyle\int_0^4 3x\, dx$

Comparing a Sum with an Integral   In Exercises 31 and 32, use the figure to fill in the blank with the symbol <, >, or =.

31. The interval $[1, 5]$ is partitioned into n subintervals of equal width Δx, and x_i is the left endpoint of the ith subinterval.

$$\sum_{i=1}^{n} f(x_i)\, \Delta x \quad\underline{\quad\quad}\quad \int_1^5 f(x)\, dx$$

32. The interval $[1, 5]$ is partitioned into n subintervals of equal width Δx, and x_i is the right endpoint of the ith subinterval.

$$\sum_{i=1}^{n} f(x_i)\, \Delta x \quad\underline{\quad\quad}\quad \int_1^5 f(x)\, dx$$

C Formulas

C.1 Differentiation and Integration Formulas

■ Use differentiation and integration tables to supplement differentiation and integration techniques.

Differentiation Formulas

1. $\dfrac{d}{dx}[cu] = cu'$

2. $\dfrac{d}{dx}[u \pm v] = u' \pm v'$

3. $\dfrac{d}{dx}[uv] = uv' + vu'$

4. $\dfrac{d}{dx}\left[\dfrac{u}{v}\right] = \dfrac{vu' - uv'}{v^2}$

5. $\dfrac{d}{dx}[c] = 0$

6. $\dfrac{d}{dx}[u^n] = nu^{n-1}u'$

7. $\dfrac{d}{dx}[x] = 1$

8. $\dfrac{d}{dx}[\ln u] = \dfrac{u'}{u}$

9. $\dfrac{d}{dx}[e^u] = e^u u'$

10. $\dfrac{d}{dx}[\sin u] = (\cos u)u'$

11. $\dfrac{d}{dx}[\cos u] = -(\sin u)u'$

12. $\dfrac{d}{dx}[\tan u] = (\sec^2 u)u'$

13. $\dfrac{d}{dx}[\cot u] = -(\csc^2 u)u'$

14. $\dfrac{d}{dx}[\sec u] = (\sec u \tan u)u'$

15. $\dfrac{d}{dx}[\csc u] = -(\csc u \cot u)u'$

Integration Formulas

Forms Involving u^n

1. $\displaystyle\int u^n \, du = \dfrac{u^{n+1}}{n+1} + C, \quad n \neq -1$

2. $\displaystyle\int \dfrac{1}{u} \, du = \ln|u| + C$

Forms Involving $a + bu$

3. $\displaystyle\int \dfrac{u}{a + bu} \, du = \dfrac{1}{b^2}(bu - a\ln|a + bu|) + C$

4. $\displaystyle\int \dfrac{u}{(a + bu)^2} \, du = \dfrac{1}{b^2}\left(\dfrac{a}{a + bu} + \ln|a + bu|\right) + C$

5. $\displaystyle\int \dfrac{u}{(a + bu)^n} \, du = \dfrac{1}{b^2}\left[\dfrac{-1}{(n-2)(a+bu)^{n-2}} + \dfrac{a}{(n-1)(a+bu)^{n-1}}\right] + C, \quad n \neq 1, 2$

6. $\displaystyle\int \dfrac{u^2}{a + bu} \, du = \dfrac{1}{b^3}\left[-\dfrac{bu}{2}(2a - bu) + a^2\ln|a + bu|\right] + C$

7. $\displaystyle\int \dfrac{u^2}{(a + bu)^2} \, du = \dfrac{1}{b^3}\left(bu - \dfrac{a^2}{a + bu} - 2a\ln|a + bu|\right) + C$

8. $\displaystyle\int \dfrac{u^2}{(a + bu)^3} \, du = \dfrac{1}{b^3}\left[\dfrac{2a}{a + bu} - \dfrac{a^2}{2(a + bu)^2} + \ln|a + bu|\right] + C$

9. $\displaystyle\int \dfrac{u^2}{(a + bu)^n} \, du = \dfrac{1}{b^3}\left[\dfrac{-1}{(n-3)(a+bu)^{n-3}} + \dfrac{2a}{(n-2)(a+bu)^{n-2}} - \dfrac{a^2}{(n-1)(a+bu)^{n-1}}\right] + C, \quad n \neq 1, 2, 3$

10. $\displaystyle\int \dfrac{1}{u(a + bu)} \, du = \dfrac{1}{a}\ln\left|\dfrac{u}{a + bu}\right| + C$

Integration Formulas   (continued)

11. $\displaystyle\int \frac{1}{u(a+bu)^2}\,du = \frac{1}{a}\left(\frac{1}{a+bu} + \frac{1}{a}\ln\left|\frac{u}{a+bu}\right|\right) + C$

12. $\displaystyle\int \frac{1}{u^2(a+bu)}\,du = -\frac{1}{a}\left(\frac{1}{u} + \frac{b}{a}\ln\left|\frac{u}{a+bu}\right|\right) + C$

13. $\displaystyle\int \frac{1}{u^2(a+bu)^2}\,du = -\frac{1}{a^2}\left[\frac{a+2bu}{u(a+bu)} + \frac{2b}{a}\ln\left|\frac{u}{a+bu}\right|\right] + C$

Forms Involving $\sqrt{a+bu}$

14. $\displaystyle\int u^n\sqrt{a+bu}\,du = \frac{2}{b(2n+3)}\left[u^n(a+bu)^{3/2} - na\int u^{n-1}\sqrt{a+bu}\,du\right]$

15. $\displaystyle\int \frac{1}{u\sqrt{a+bu}}\,du = \frac{1}{\sqrt{a}}\ln\left|\frac{\sqrt{a+bu}-\sqrt{a}}{\sqrt{a+bu}+\sqrt{a}}\right| + C,\quad a > 0$

16. $\displaystyle\int \frac{1}{u^n\sqrt{a+bu}}\,du = \frac{-1}{a(n-1)}\left[\frac{\sqrt{a+bu}}{u^{n-1}} + \frac{(2n-3)b}{2}\int\frac{1}{u^{n-1}\sqrt{a+bu}}\,du\right],\quad n \neq 1$

17. $\displaystyle\int \frac{\sqrt{a+bu}}{u}\,du = 2\sqrt{a+bu} + a\int\frac{1}{u\sqrt{a+bu}}\,du$

18. $\displaystyle\int \frac{\sqrt{a+bu}}{u^n}\,du = \frac{-1}{a(n-1)}\left[\frac{(a+bu)^{3/2}}{u^{n-1}} + \frac{(2n-5)b}{2}\int\frac{\sqrt{a+bu}}{u^{n-1}}\,du\right],\quad n \neq 1$

19. $\displaystyle\int \frac{u}{\sqrt{a+bu}}\,du = -\frac{2(2a-bu)}{3b^2}\sqrt{a+bu} + C$

20. $\displaystyle\int \frac{u^n}{\sqrt{a+bu}}\,du = \frac{2}{(2n+1)b}\left(u^n\sqrt{a+bu} - na\int\frac{u^{n-1}}{\sqrt{a+bu}}\,du\right)$

Forms Involving $u^2 - a^2$, $a > 0$

21. $\displaystyle\int \frac{1}{u^2-a^2}\,du = -\int\frac{1}{a^2-u^2}\,du = \frac{1}{2a}\ln\left|\frac{u-a}{u+a}\right| + C$

22. $\displaystyle\int \frac{1}{(u^2-a^2)^n}\,du = \frac{-1}{2a^2(n-1)}\left[\frac{u}{(u^2-a^2)^{n-1}} + (2n-3)\int\frac{1}{(u^2-a^2)^{n-1}}\,du\right],\quad n \neq 1$

Forms Involving $\sqrt{u^2 \pm a^2}$, $a > 0$

23. $\displaystyle\int \sqrt{u^2 \pm a^2}\,du = \frac{1}{2}\left(u\sqrt{u^2 \pm a^2} \pm a^2\ln\left|u + \sqrt{u^2 \pm a^2}\right|\right) + C$

24. $\displaystyle\int u^2\sqrt{u^2 \pm a^2}\,du = \frac{1}{8}\left[u(2u^2 \pm a^2)\sqrt{u^2 \pm a^2} - a^4\ln\left|u + \sqrt{u^2 \pm a^2}\right|\right] + C$

25. $\displaystyle\int \frac{\sqrt{u^2 + a^2}}{u}\,du = \sqrt{u^2 + a^2} - a\ln\left|\frac{a + \sqrt{u^2 + a^2}}{u}\right| + C$

26. $\displaystyle\int \frac{\sqrt{u^2 \pm a^2}}{u^2}\,du = \frac{-\sqrt{u^2 \pm a^2}}{u} + \ln\left|u + \sqrt{u^2 \pm a^2}\right| + C$

27. $\displaystyle\int \frac{1}{\sqrt{u^2 \pm a^2}}\,du = \ln\left|u + \sqrt{u^2 \pm a^2}\right| + C$

28. $\displaystyle\int \frac{1}{u\sqrt{u^2 + a^2}}\,du = \frac{-1}{a}\ln\left|\frac{a + \sqrt{u^2 + a^2}}{u}\right| + C$

29. $\displaystyle\int \frac{u^2}{\sqrt{u^2 \pm a^2}}\, du = \frac{1}{2}\left(u\sqrt{u^2 \pm a^2} \mp a^2 \ln|u + \sqrt{u^2 \pm a^2}|\right) + C$

30. $\displaystyle\int \frac{1}{u^2\sqrt{u^2 \pm a^2}}\, du = \mp \frac{\sqrt{u^2 \pm a^2}}{a^2 u} + C$

31. $\displaystyle\int \frac{1}{(u^2 \pm a^2)^{3/2}}\, du = \frac{\pm u}{a^2\sqrt{u^2 \pm a^2}} + C$

Forms Involving $\sqrt{a^2 - u^2}$, $a > 0$

32. $\displaystyle\int \frac{\sqrt{a^2 - u^2}}{u}\, du = \sqrt{a^2 - u^2} - a \ln\left|\frac{a + \sqrt{a^2 - u^2}}{u}\right| + C$

33. $\displaystyle\int \frac{1}{u\sqrt{a^2 - u^2}}\, du = \frac{-1}{a} \ln\left|\frac{a + \sqrt{a^2 - u^2}}{u}\right| + C$

34. $\displaystyle\int \frac{1}{u^2\sqrt{a^2 - u^2}}\, du = \frac{-\sqrt{a^2 - u^2}}{a^2 u} + C$

35. $\displaystyle\int \frac{1}{(a^2 - u^2)^{3/2}}\, du = \frac{u}{a^2\sqrt{a^2 - u^2}} + C$

Forms Involving e^u

36. $\displaystyle\int e^u\, du = e^u + C$

37. $\displaystyle\int u e^u\, du = (u - 1)e^u + C$

38. $\displaystyle\int u^n e^u\, du = u^n e^u - n \int u^{n-1} e^u\, du$

39. $\displaystyle\int \frac{1}{1 + e^u}\, du = u - \ln(1 + e^u) + C$

40. $\displaystyle\int \frac{1}{1 + e^{nu}}\, du = u - \frac{1}{n} \ln(1 + e^{nu}) + C$

Forms Involving ln u

41. $\displaystyle\int \ln u\, du = u(-1 + \ln u) + C$

42. $\displaystyle\int u \ln u\, du = \frac{u^2}{4}(-1 + 2 \ln u) + C$

43. $\displaystyle\int u^n \ln u\, du = \frac{u^{n+1}}{(n+1)^2}[-1 + (n+1) \ln u] + C, \quad n \neq -1$

44. $\displaystyle\int (\ln u)^2\, du = u[2 - 2 \ln u + (\ln u)^2] + C$

45. $\displaystyle\int (\ln u)^n\, du = u(\ln u)^n - n \int (\ln u)^{n-1}\, du$

Forms Involving sin u or cos u

46. $\displaystyle\int \sin u\, du = -\cos u + C$

47. $\displaystyle\int \cos u\, du = \sin u + C$

48. $\displaystyle\int \sin^2 u\, du = \frac{1}{2}(u - \sin u \cos u) + C$

49. $\displaystyle\int \cos^2 u\, du = \frac{1}{2}(u + \sin u \cos u) + C$

50. $\displaystyle\int \sin^n u\, du = -\frac{\sin^{n-1} u \cos u}{n} + \frac{n-1}{n} \int \sin^{n-2} u\, du$

51. $\displaystyle\int \cos^n u\, du = \frac{\cos^{n-1} u \sin u}{n} + \frac{n-1}{n} \int \cos^{n-2} u\, du$

52. $\displaystyle\int u \sin u\, du = \sin u - u \cos u + C$

53. $\displaystyle\int u \cos u\, du = \cos u + u \sin u + C$

54. $\displaystyle\int u^n \sin u\, du = -u^n \cos u + n \int u^{n-1} \cos u\, du$

Integration Formulas   (continued)

55. $\displaystyle\int u^n \cos u \, du = u^n \sin u - n\int u^{n-1} \sin u \, du$

56. $\displaystyle\int \frac{1}{1 \pm \sin u} \, du = \tan u \mp \sec u + C$

57. $\displaystyle\int \frac{1}{1 \pm \cos u} \, du = -\cot u \pm \csc u + C$

58. $\displaystyle\int \frac{1}{\sin u \cos u} \, du = \ln|\tan u| + C$

Forms Involving tan u, cot u, sec u, or csc u

59. $\displaystyle\int \tan u \, du = -\ln|\cos u| + C$

60. $\displaystyle\int \cot u \, du = \ln|\sin u| + C$

61. $\displaystyle\int \sec u \, du = \ln|\sec u + \tan u| + C$

62. $\displaystyle\int \csc u \, du = \ln|\csc u - \cot u| + C$

63. $\displaystyle\int \tan^2 u \, du = -u + \tan u + C$

64. $\displaystyle\int \cot^2 u \, du = -u - \cot u + C$

65. $\displaystyle\int \sec^2 u \, du = \tan u + C$

66. $\displaystyle\int \csc^2 u \, du = -\cot u + C$

67. $\displaystyle\int \tan^n u \, du = \frac{\tan^{n-1} u}{n-1} - \int \tan^{n-2} u \, du, \quad n \neq 1$

68. $\displaystyle\int \cot^n u \, du = -\frac{\cot^{n-1} u}{n-1} - \int \cot^{n-2} u \, du, \quad n \neq 1$

69. $\displaystyle\int \sec^n u \, du = \frac{\sec^{n-2} u \tan u}{n-1} + \frac{n-2}{n-1} \int \sec^{n-2} u \, du, \quad n \neq 1$

70. $\displaystyle\int \csc^n u \, du = -\frac{\csc^{n-2} u \cot u}{n-1} + \frac{n-2}{n-1} \int \csc^{n-2} u \, du, \quad n \neq 1$

71. $\displaystyle\int \frac{1}{1 \pm \tan u} \, du = \frac{1}{2}(u \pm \ln|\cos u \pm \sin u|) + C$

72. $\displaystyle\int \frac{1}{1 \pm \cot u} \, du = \frac{1}{2}(u \mp \ln|\sin u \pm \cos u|) + C$

73. $\displaystyle\int \frac{1}{1 \pm \sec u} \, du = u + \cot u \mp \csc u + C$

74. $\displaystyle\int \frac{1}{1 \pm \csc u} \, du = u - \tan u \pm \sec u + C$

C.2 Formulas from Business and Finance

■ Summary of business and finance formulas

Formulas from Business

Basic Terms

x = number of units produced (or sold)

p = price per unit

R = total revenue from selling x units

C = total cost of producing x units

$\overline{C}$ = average cost per unit

P = total profit from selling x units

Basic Equations

$$R = xp \qquad \overline{C} = \frac{C}{x} \qquad P = R - C$$

Typical Graphs of Supply and Demand Curves

Supply curves increase as price increases and demand curves decrease as price increases. The equilibrium point occurs when the supply and demand curves intersect.

Demand Function: $p = f(x)$ = price required to sell x units

$$\eta = \frac{p/x}{dp/dx} = \text{price elasticity of demand}$$

(When $|\eta| < 1$, the demand is inelastic. When $|\eta| > 1$, the demand is elastic.)

Typical Graphs of Revenue, Cost, and Profit Functions

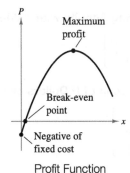

Revenue Function

The low prices required to sell more units eventually result in a decreasing revenue.

Cost Function

The total cost to produce x units includes the fixed cost.

Profit Function

The break-even point occurs when $R = C$.

Formulas from Business   (continued)

Marginals

$\dfrac{dR}{dx}$ = marginal revenue ≈ the *extra* revenue from selling one additional unit

$\dfrac{dC}{dx}$ = marginal cost ≈ the *extra* cost of producing one additional unit

$\dfrac{dP}{dx}$ = marginal profit ≈ the *extra* profit from selling one additional unit

}Marginal revenue

1 unit

Extra revenue for one unit

Revenue Function

Formulas from Finance

Basic Terms

P = amount of deposit r = interest rate

n = number of times interest is compounded per year

t = number of years A = balance after t years

Compound Interest Formulas

1. Balance when interest is compounded n times per year: $A = P\left(1 + \dfrac{r}{n}\right)^{nt}$

2. Balance when interest is compounded continuously: $A = Pe^{rt}$

Effective Rate of Interest

$$r_{eff} = \left(1 + \frac{r}{n}\right)^{n} - 1$$

Present Value of a Future Investment

$$P = \frac{A}{\left(1 + \dfrac{r}{n}\right)^{nt}}$$

Balance of an Increasing Annuity After n Deposits of P per Year for t Years

$$A = P\left[\left(1 + \frac{r}{n}\right)^{nt} - 1\right]\left(1 + \frac{n}{r}\right)$$

Initial Deposit for a Decreasing Annuity with n Withdrawals of W per Year for t Years

$$P = W\left(\frac{n}{r}\right)\left\{1 - \left[\frac{1}{1 + (r/n)}\right]^{nt}\right\}$$

Monthly Installment M for a Loan of P Dollars over t Years at $r\%$ Interest

$$M = P\left\{\frac{r/12}{1 - \left[\dfrac{1}{1 + (r/12)}\right]^{12t}}\right\}$$

Amount of an Annuity

$$e^{rT}\int_{0}^{T} c(t)e^{-rt}\, dt$$

$c(t)$ is the continuous income function in dollars per year and T is the term of the annuity in years.

Answers to Selected Exercises

Chapter 1

Section 1.1   *(page 8)*

Skills Warm Up   *(page 8)*

1. $3\sqrt{5}$ **2.** $2\sqrt{5}$ **3.** $\frac{1}{2}$ **4.** -2 **5.** $5\sqrt{3}$
6. $-\sqrt{2}$ **7.** $x = -3, x = 9$
8. $y = -8, y = 4$ **9.** $x = 19$ **10.** $y = 1$

1.

3. (a)

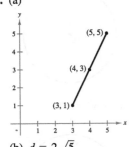

(b) $d = 2\sqrt{5}$
(c) Midpoint: $(4, 3)$

5. (a)

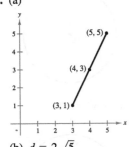

(b) $d = 2\sqrt{10}$
(c) Midpoint: $\left(-\frac{1}{2}, -2\right)$

7. (a)

(b) $d = 2\sqrt{37}$
(c) Midpoint: $(3, 8)$

9. (a)

(b) $d = 13$
(c) Midpoint: $\left(1, \frac{1}{2}\right)$

11. (a)

(b) $d = \sqrt{116.89}$ (c) Midpoint: $(0.25, 0.6)$
13. (a) $a = 4, b = 3, c = 5$
(b) $4^2 + 3^2 = 5^2$
15. (a) $a = 10, b = 3, c = \sqrt{109}$
(b) $10^2 + 3^2 = \left(\sqrt{109}\right)^2$

17. $d_1 = \sqrt{45}, d_2 = \sqrt{20},$
$d_3 = \sqrt{65}$
$d_1^2 + d_2^2 = d_3^2$

19. $d_1 = d_2 = d_3 = d_4$
$= \sqrt{5}$

21. $x = 4, -2$ **23.** $y = \pm\sqrt{55}$ **25.** About 45 yards
27.

The number of cable high-speed Internet customers increases each year.
29. (a) 7600; 9200; 10,500   (b) 8.2% decrease
31. (a) Revenue: $434.3 million
Profit: $25.2 million
(b) Actual 2008 revenue: $422.4 million
Actual 2008 profit: $24.4 million
(c) Yes, the actual amounts were very close to those predicted by the Midpoint Formula.
(d) Expenses for 2007: $310 million
Expenses for 2008: $398 million
Expenses for 2009: $508.2 million
(e) Answers will vary.
33. (a)

(b) The larger the clinic, the more patients a doctor can treat.

35. $(-6, -6), (-4, -7), (-3, -5)$

37. $\left(\dfrac{3x_1 + x_2}{4}, \dfrac{3y_1 + y_2}{4}\right), \left(\dfrac{x_1 + x_2}{2}, \dfrac{y_1 + y_2}{2}\right),$
$\left(\dfrac{x_1 + 3x_2}{4}, \dfrac{y_1 + 3y_2}{4}\right)$

39. $x_1 + \left(\dfrac{x_2 - x_1}{3}\right) = \dfrac{3x_1 + x_2 - x_1}{3} = \dfrac{1}{3}(2x_1 + x_2)$

$y_1 + \left(\dfrac{y_2 - y_1}{3}\right) = \dfrac{3y_1 + y_2 - y_1}{3} = \dfrac{1}{3}(2y_1 + y_2)$

So, $\left(\dfrac{1}{3}[2x_1 + x_2], \dfrac{1}{3}[2y_1 + y_2]\right)$ is a point of trisection.

$\left(\dfrac{\frac{2}{3}x_1 + \frac{1}{3}x_2 + x_2}{2}, \dfrac{\frac{2}{3}y_1 + \frac{1}{3}y_2 + y_2}{2}\right)$

$= \left(\dfrac{\frac{2}{3}x_1 + \frac{4}{3}x_2}{2}, \dfrac{\frac{2}{3}y_1 + \frac{4}{3}y_2}{2}\right)$

$= \left(\dfrac{1}{3}x_1 + \dfrac{2}{3}x_2, \dfrac{1}{3}y_1 + \dfrac{2}{3}y_2\right)$

$= \left(\dfrac{1}{3}[x_1 + 2x_2], \dfrac{1}{3}[y_1 + 2y_2]\right)$

Section 1.2   *(page 19)*

1. e   **2.** b   **3.** c   **4.** f   **5.** a   **6.** d

7.

9.

11.

13.

15.

17.

19.

21.

23. $(0, -3), \left(\frac{3}{2}, 0\right)$ **25.** $(0, -2), (-2, 0), (1, 0)$
27. $(-2, 0), (0, 2), (2, 0)$ **29.** $(-2, 0), (0, 2)$ **31.** $(0, 0)$
33. $x^2 + y^2 = 16$ **35.** $(x - 2)^2 + (y + 1)^2 = 9$

37. $(x + 1)^2 + (y - 1)^2 = 16$ **39.** $x^2 + y^2 = 100$

41. $(1, 1)$ **43.** $(1, 14), (-4, -1)$
45. $(0, 0), \left(\sqrt{2}, 2\sqrt{2}\right), \left(-\sqrt{2}, -2\sqrt{2}\right)$
47. $(-1, 0), (0, 1), (1, 0)$
49. 50,000 units   **51.** 193 units   **53.** 1250 units
55. (a) $C = 11.8x + 15,000; R = 19.3x$
        (b) 2000 units
        (c) 2134 units
57. $(15, 180)$
59. (a)

Year	2004	2005	2006	2007	2008	2009
Amount	30	44	54	67	113	313
Model	26	55	48	56	126	308

The model fits the data well.
Answers will vary.

(b) $4605 million

61. (a)

Year	2004	2005	2006
Degrees	667.4	692	713.6

Year	2007	2008	2012
Degrees	732.2	747.8	780.2

(b) Answers will vary.

(c) 764.6; No; the number of associate's degrees should keep increasing over time.

63.

The greater the value of c, the steeper the line.

65.

$(0, 5.36)$

67.

$(1.4780, 0), (12.8553, 0), (0, 2.3875)$

69.

$(0, 0.4167)$

71. Answers will vary.

Section 1.3 *(page 31)*

Skills Warm Up *(page 31)*

1. -1 **2.** 1 **3.** $\frac{1}{3}$ **4.** $-\frac{7}{6}$

5. $y = 4x + 7$ **6.** $y = 3x - 7$

7. $y = 3x - 10$ **8.** $y = -x - 7$

9. $y = 7x - 17$ **10.** $y = \frac{2}{3}x + \frac{5}{3}$

---

1. 1 **3.** 0 **5.** $m = 1, (0, 7)$ **7.** $m = -5, (0, 20)$

9. $m = -\frac{7}{6}, (0, 5)$ **11.** $m = 3, (0, -15)$

13. m is undefined; no y-intercept.   **15.** $m = 0, (0, 4)$

17.

19.

21.

23.

25.

27.

$m = \frac{1}{3}$

29.

$m = 3$

31.

$m = -4$

33.

m is undefined.

35.

$m = -\frac{2}{3}$

37.

$m = -\frac{24}{5}$

39.

$m = 8$

41. $(0, 1), (1, 1), (3, 1)$ **43.** $(0, 10), (2, 4), (3, 1)$

45. $(3, -6), (9, -2), (12, 0)$ **47.** $(-8, 0), (-8, 2), (-8, 3)$

49. The points are not collinear. Explanations will vary.
51. The points are collinear. Explanations will vary.
53. $3x - 4y + 12 = 0$ **55.** $x + 1 = 0$

57. $y - 7 = 0$ **59.** $4x + y + 2 = 0$

61. $9x - 12y + 8 = 0$ **63.** $y = 2x - 5$

65. $3x + y = 0$ **67.** $x - 2 = 0$

69. $y + 1 = 0$ **71.** $3x - 6y + 7 = 0$

73. $4x - y + 6 = 0$

75. $x - 3 = 0$ **77.** $y + 10 = 0$
79. (a) $x + y + 1 = 0$ (b) $x - y + 5 = 0$

81. (a) $6x + 8y - 3 = 0$ (b) $96x - 72y + 127 = 0$

83. (a) $y = 0$ (b) $x + 1 = 0$

85. (a) $x - 1 = 0$ (b) $y - 1 = 0$

87. (a) The average salary increased the most from 2006 to 2008 and increased the least from 2002 to 2004.
    (b) $m = 2350.75$
    (c) The average salary increased $2350.75 per year over the 12 years between 1996 and 2008.
89. $F = \frac{9}{5}C + 32$ or $C = \frac{5}{9}F - \frac{160}{9}$
91. (a) $y = 28.8t + 5395.8$; The slope $m = 28.8$ indicates that the population increases by 28.8 thousand each year.
    (b) 5568.6 thousand (5,568,600)
    (c) 5572 thousand (5,572,000); The estimate was very close to the actual population.
    (d) The model could possibly be used to predict the population in 2015 if the population continues to grow at the same linear rate.
93. (a) $y = 447.6t + 8146.6$ (b) $10,832.2 billion
    (c) $13,070.2 billion   (d) Answers will vary.
95. (a) $C = 50x + 350,000$; $R = 120x$
    (b) $P = 70x - 350,000$ (c) $560,000 profit

Quiz Yourself *(page 34)*

1. (a)

(b) $d = 3\sqrt{5}$
(c) Midpoint: $(0, -0.5)$

2. (a)

(b) $d = \sqrt{12.3125}$
(c) Midpoint: $\left(\frac{3}{8}, \frac{1}{4}\right)$

3. (a)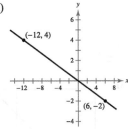

(b) $d = 6\sqrt{10}$
(c) Midpoint: $(-3, 1)$

4. $d_1 = \sqrt{5}$
$d_2 = \sqrt{45}$
$d_3 = \sqrt{50}$
$d_1{}^2 + d_2{}^2 = d_3{}^2$

5. 9681.5 thousand

6.

7.

8.

9. $x^2 + y^2 = 81$

10. $(x + 1)^2 + y^2 = 36$

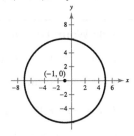

11. $(x - 2)^2 + (y + 2)^2 = 25$ **12.** 4735 units

13. $y = \frac{1}{2}x - 3$

14. $y = 2x - 1$

15. $y = -\frac{1}{3}x + 7$

16. $y = -1.2x + 0.2$

17. $x = -2$

18. $y = 2$

19. (a) $y = -0.25x - 4.25$ (b) $y = 4x - 17$
20. 2015: \$2,270,000; 2018: \$2,622,500
21. $C = 0.55x + 175$
22. (a) $S = 1600t + 20,200$ (b) \$44,200

CHAPTER 1

Section 1.4   *(page 44)*

Skills Warm Up   *(page 44)*

1. 20   **2.** 10   **3.** $x^2 + x - 6$

4. $x^3 + 9x^2 + 26x + 30$ **5.** $\dfrac{1}{x}$ **6.** $\dfrac{2x - 1}{x}$

7. $y = -2x + 17$ **8.** $y = \frac{6}{5}x^2 + \frac{1}{5}$

9. $y = 3 \pm \sqrt{5 + (x + 1)^2}$ **10.** $y = \pm\sqrt{4x^2 + 2}$

11. $y = 2x + \dfrac{1}{2}$ **12.** $y = \dfrac{x^3}{2} + \dfrac{1}{2}$

---

1. y is not a function of x.   **3.** y is a function of x.
5. y is a function of x.   **7.** y is a function of x.
9. y is not a function of x.   **11.** y is a function of x.
13. Domain: $(-\infty, \infty)$ **15.** Domain: $(-\infty, \infty)$
Range: $(-\infty, \infty)$ Range: $(-\infty, 4]$

17.   **19.**

Domain: $(-\infty, \infty)$ Domain: $(-\infty, 0) \cup (0, \infty)$
Range: $[-2.125, \infty)$ Range: $y = -1$ or $y = 1$

21.   **23.**

Domain: $(4, \infty)$ Domain:
Range: $[4, \infty)$ $(-\infty, -4) \cup (-4, \infty)$
    Range: $(-\infty, 1) \cup (1, \infty)$

25. (a) -2 (b) 13   (c) $3x - 5$

27. (a) 4   (b) $-\dfrac{1}{4}$ (c) $\dfrac{1}{x + 4}$

29. $\Delta x + 2x - 5, \ \Delta x \neq 0$

31. $\dfrac{1}{\sqrt{x + \Delta x + 1} + \sqrt{x + 1}}, \ \Delta x \neq 0$

33. $-\dfrac{1}{(x + \Delta x - 2)(x - 2)}, \ \Delta x \neq 0$

35. (a) $2x$ (b) $2x - 10$ (c) $10x - 25$ (d) $\dfrac{2x - 5}{5}$
(e) 5   (f) 5

37. (a) $x^2 + x$ (b) $x^2 - x + 2$
(c) $(x^2 + 1)(x - 1) = x^3 - x^2 + x - 1$
(d) $\dfrac{x^2 + 1}{x - 1}$ (e) $x^2 - 2x + 2$ (f) x^2

39. (a) 0   (b) 0   (c) -1 (d) $\sqrt{15}$
(e) $\sqrt{x^2 - 1}$ (f) $x - 1, x \geq 0$

41. $f^{-1}(x) = \frac{1}{4}x$
$f(f^{-1}(x)) = 4(\frac{1}{4}x) = x$
$f^{-1}(f(x)) = \frac{1}{4}(4x) = x$

43. $f^{-1}(x) = x - 12$
$f(f^{-1}(x)) = (x - 12) + 12 = x$
$f^{-1}(f(x)) = (x + 12) - 12 = x$

45. $f^{-1}(x) = \dfrac{x + 3}{2}$ **47.** $f^{-1}(x) = \frac{2}{3}(x - 1)$

49. $f^{-1}(x) = \sqrt[5]{x}$ **51.** $f^{-1}(x) = \dfrac{1}{x}$

53. $f^{-1}(x) = \sqrt{9 - x^2}, \ 0 \leq x \leq 3$

55. $f^{-1}(x) = x^{3/2}, \ x \geq 0$

57.

$f(x)$ is one-to-one. $f^{-1}(x) = \dfrac{3 - x}{7}$

59.   **61.**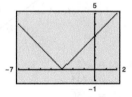

$f(x)$ is not one-to-one. $f(x)$ is not one-to-one.

63. (a)   (b)

(c)   (d)

(e)   (f)

65. (a) $y = (x + 3)^2$ (b) $y = -(x + 6)^2 - 3$

67. (a) 2000: \$120 billion
   2003: \$170 billion
   2007: \$225 billion
   (b) 2000: \$121.3 billion
   2003: \$173.8 billion
   2007: \$225.6 billion
   The model fits the data well.

69. $R_T = R_1 + R_2 = -0.8t^2 - 7.22t + 1148$
   $t = 5, 6, \ldots, 11$

71. (a) $C(x) = 1.95x + 6000$
   (b) $C = 1.95 + \dfrac{6000}{x}$
   (c) More than 2000 units

73. (a) $C(x(t)) = 2800t + 500$
   This function gives the production cost for t hours.
   (b) \$11,700
   (c) 6.25 hours

75. (a) $C(x) = 12.30x + 98,000$
   (b) $R(x) = 17.98x$
   (c) $P(x) = 5.68x - 98,000$

77.   **79.**

Zeros: $x = 0, \frac{9}{4}$ Zero: $t = -3$
$f(x)$ is not one-to-one. $g(t)$ is one-to-one.

81.

Zeros: ± 2
$g(x)$ is not one-to-one.

83. Answers will vary.

Section 1.5   *(page 57)*

Skills Warm Up   *(page 57)*

1. $\frac{1}{3}x^2 + \frac{1}{6}x$ **2.** $x^2(x + 9)$ **3.** $x + 4$ **4.** $x + 6$
5. (a) 7   (b) $c^2 - 3c + 3$
   (c) $x^2 + 2xh + h^2 - 3x - 3h + 3$
6. (a) -4 (b) 10   (c) $3t^2 + 4$ **7.** h **8.** 4

---

9. Domain: $(-\infty, 0) \cup (0, \infty)$
   Range: $(-\infty, 0) \cup (0, \infty)$

10. Domain: $[-5, 5]$ **11.** Domain: $(-\infty, \infty)$
   Range: $[0, 5]$ Range: $[0, \infty)$

   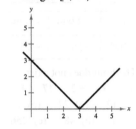

12. Domain: **13.** y is not a function of x.
   $(-\infty, 0) \cup (0, \infty)$ **14.** y is a function of x.
   Range: $-1, 1$

1. (a) 1   (b) 3   **3.** (a) 1   (b) 3

5.

x	1.9	1.99	1.999	2
$f(x)$	8.8	8.98	8.998	?

x	2.001	2.01	2.1
$f(x)$	9.002	9.02	9.2

$\lim\limits_{x \to 2}(2x + 5) = 9$

7.

x	1.9	1.99	1.999	2
$f(x)$	0.2564	0.2506	0.2501	?

x	2.001	2.01	2.1
$f(x)$	0.2499	0.2494	0.2439

$\lim\limits_{x \to 2} \dfrac{x - 2}{x^2 - 4} = \dfrac{1}{4}$

CHAPTER 1

9.

x	−0.1	−0.01	−0.001	0
f(x)	0.5132	0.5013	0.5001	?

x	0.001	0.01	0.1
f(x)	0.4999	0.4988	0.4881

$$\lim_{x \to 0}\frac{\sqrt{x+1}-1}{x} = 0.5$$

11.

x	−4.1	−4.01	−4.001	−4
f(x)	2.5	25	250	?

x	−3.999	−3.99	−3.9
f(x)	−250	−25	−2.5

The limit does not exist.

13. 6   **15.** −2   **17.** 49   **19.** 4
21. (a) 12   (b) 27   (c) $\frac{1}{3}$
23. (a) 4   (b) 48   (c) 256
25. −1   **27.** 0   **29.** 3   **31.** −2   **33.** $-\frac{3}{4}$ **35.** 2
37. −6   **39.** $-\frac{1}{4}$ **41.** 12   **43.** 2   **45.** $2t - 5$
47. $\frac{1}{6}$ **49.** $\frac{1}{2\sqrt{5}}$ **51.** 2   **53.** −1
55. Limit does not exist.   **57.** Limit does not exist.
59. $\lim\limits_{x \to -3^-}\dfrac{|x+3|}{x+3} = -1$, $\lim\limits_{x \to -3^+}\dfrac{|x+3|}{x+3} = 1$

61.

x	0	0.5	0.9	0.99
f(x)	−2	−2.67	−10.53	−100.5

x	0.999	0.9999	1
f(x)	−1000.5	−10,000.5	Undefined

$-\infty$

63.

x	−3	−2.5	−2.1	−2.01
f(x)	−1	−2	−10	−100

x	−2.001	−2.0001	−2
f(x)	−1000	−10,000	Undefined

$-\infty$

65. (a) 1   (b) 1   (c) 1
67. (a) 0   (b) 0   (c) 0
69. (a) 3   (b) −3   (c) Limit does not exist.
71.

Limit does not exist.
73.

$-\frac{17}{9} \approx -1.8889$
75. (a) $25 thousand   (b) 80%
(c) ∞; The cost function increases without bound as x approaches 100 from the left. Therefore, according to the model, it is not possible to remove 100% of the pollutants.
77. (a)

(b) For $x = 0.25$, $A \approx$ $2685.06.
For $x = \frac{1}{365}$, $A \approx$ $2717.91.
(c) $\lim\limits_{x \to 0^+} 1000(1 + 0.1x)^{10/x} = 1000e \approx$ $2718.28; continuous compounding

Section 1.6   *(page 67)*

Skills Warm Up   *(page 67)*

1. $\dfrac{x+4}{x-8}$ **2.** $\dfrac{x+1}{x-3}$ **3.** $\dfrac{x+2}{2(x-3)}$ **4.** $\dfrac{x-4}{x-2}$

5. $x = 0, -7$ **6.** $x = -5, 1$ **7.** $x = -\frac{2}{3}, -2$
8. $x = 0, 3, -8$ **9.** 13   **10.** −1

---

1. Continuous; The function is a polynomial.
3. Not continuous ($x \neq \pm 4$)
5. Continuous; The rational function's domain is the set of real numbers.
7. Not continuous ($x \neq 3$ and $x \neq 5$)
9. Not continuous ($x \neq \pm 2$)
11. $(-\infty, 0)$ and $(0, \infty)$; Explanations will vary. There is a discontinuity at $x = 0$, because $f(0)$ is not defined.
13. $(-\infty, -1)$ and $(-1, \infty)$; Explanations will vary. There is a discontinuity at $x = -1$, because $f(-1)$ is not defined.
15. $(-\infty, \infty)$; Explanations will vary.
17. $(-\infty, -1)$, $(-1, 1)$, and $(1, \infty)$; Explanations will vary. There are discontinuities at $x = \pm 1$, because $f(\pm 1)$ is not defined.

19. $(-\infty, \infty)$; Explanations will vary.

21. $(-\infty, 4)$, $(4, 5)$, and $(5, \infty)$; Explanations will vary. There are discontinuities at $x = 4$ and $x = 5$, because $f(4)$ and $f(5)$ are not defined.

23. $(-\infty, 4]$; Explanations will vary.

25. $[0, \infty)$; Explanations will vary.

27. $[-1, 3]$; Explanations will vary.

29. $(-\infty, \infty)$; Explanations will vary.

31. $(-\infty, -1)$ and $(-1, \infty)$; Explanations will vary. There is a discontinuity at $x = -1$, because $f(-1)$ is not defined.

33. $[-3, \infty)$; Explanations will vary.

35. Continuous on all intervals $\left(\dfrac{c}{2}, \dfrac{c}{2} + \dfrac{1}{2}\right)$, where c is an integer. Explanations will vary. There are discontinuities at $x = \dfrac{c}{2}$, where c is an integer, because $\lim\limits_{x \to c} f\left(\dfrac{c}{2}\right)$ does not exist.

37. Continuous on all intervals $(c, c + 1)$, where c is an integer. Explanations will vary. There are discontinuities at $x = c$, where c is an integer, because $\lim\limits_{x \to c} f(c)$ does not exist.

39. $(1, \infty)$; Explanations will vary.

41.

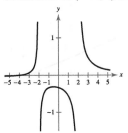

Continuous on $(-\infty, 4)$ and $(4, \infty)$

43.

Continuous on $(-\infty, -2)$, $(-2, 2)$, and $(2, \infty)$

45.

Continuous on $(-\infty, 0)$ and $(0, \infty)$

47. Continuous   **49.** Nonremovable discontinuity at $x = 2$

51.

Not continuous at $x = 2$ and $x = -1$, because $f(-1)$ and $f(2)$ are not defined.

53.

Not continuous at $x = 3$, because $\lim\limits_{x \to 3} f(3)$ does not exist.

55.

Not continuous at all integers c, because $\lim\limits_{x \to c} f(c)$ does not exist.

57. $a = 2$

59.

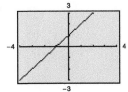

The graph of $f(x) = \dfrac{x^2 + x}{x}$ appears to be continuous on $[-4, 4]$, but f is not continuous at $x = 0$. Explanations will vary.

61. (a) $[0, 100)$; Explanations will vary.

(b)

Continuous; Explanations will vary.

(c) $6 million

63.

There are nonremovable discontinuities at $t = 1, 2, 3, 4, 5,$ and 6.

65. (a)

Discontinuities at $x = 1$, $x = 2$, $x = 3$
Explanations will vary.

(b) $0.84

67. (a) The graph has nonremovable discontinuities at
$t = \frac{1}{4}, \frac{1}{2}, \frac{3}{4}, 1, \frac{5}{4}, \ldots$

(b) \$8448.69

(c) \$11,379.17

69. (a)

Nonremovable discontinuities at $t = 2, 4, 6, 8, \ldots$;
N is not continuous at $t = 2, 4, 6, 8, \ldots$.

(b) The company must replenish its inventory every two months.

Review Exercises for Chapter 1   *(page 74)*

1.

3. $\sqrt{29}$ **5.** $3\sqrt{2}$ **7.** $\dfrac{\sqrt{17}}{2}$ **9.** $(7, 4)$

11. $(-8, 6)$ **13.** $\left(\dfrac{5}{2}, \dfrac{2}{5}\right)$

15. $P = R - C$; The difference in the heights of the bars that represent revenue and cost is equal to the height of the bar that represents profit.

17. $(-2, 7), (-1, 8), (1, 5)$

19.   **21.**

23.   **25.**

27.

29. $\left(-\frac{3}{4}, 0\right), (0, -3)$ **31.** $(-4, 0), (2, 0), (0, -8)$

33. $x^2 + y^2 = 64$ **35.** $x^2 + y^2 = 9$

37. $(-2, 9)$ **39.** $(-1, -1), (0, 0), (1, 1)$

41. (a) $C = 10x + 200$ **43.** $p = \$46.40$
    $R = 14x$ $x = 5000$ units

(b) 50 shirts

45. Slope: -1 **47.** Slope: -3
    y-intercept: $(0, 12)$ y-intercept: $(0, -2)$

49. Slope: 0 (horizontal line)   **51.** Slope: $-\frac{2}{5}$
    y-intercept: $\left(0, -\frac{5}{3}\right)$ y-intercept: $(0, -1)$

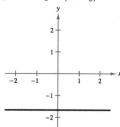

53. $\dfrac{6}{7}$ **55.** $\dfrac{20}{21}$

57. $y = -2x + 5$ **59.** $y = -4$

61. $y = 2x - 9$ **63.** $x = 5$

65. (a) $7x - 8y + 69 = 0$ (b) $2x + y = 0$
(c) $2x + y = 0$ (d) $2x + 3y - 12 = 0$

67. (a) $x = -10p + 1070$ (b) 725 units   (c) 650 units

69. y is a function of x.   **71.** y is not a function of x.

73. Domain: $(-\infty, \infty)$ **75.** Domain: $[-1, \infty)$
Range: $(-\infty, \infty)$ Range: $[0, \infty)$

77. Domain: $(-\infty, -4) \cup (-4, 3) \cup (3, \infty)$
Range: $(-\infty, 0) \cup \left(0, \frac{1}{7}\right) \cup \left(\frac{1}{7}, \infty\right)$

79. (a) 7 (b) -11 (c) $3x + 7$

81. (a) $x^2 + 2x$ (b) $x^2 - 2x + 2$ (c) $2x^3 - x^2 + 2x - 1$
(d) $\dfrac{1 + x^2}{2x - 1}$ (e) $4x^2 - 4x + 2$ (f) $2x^2 + 1$

83.

$f(x)$ is one-to-one.
$f^{-1}(x) = \frac{1}{4}(x + 3)$

85.

$f(x)$ does not have an
inverse function.

87.

$f(x)$ does not have an
inverse function.

89.

x	0.9	0.99	0.999	1	1.001	1.01	1.1
$f(x)$	0.6	0.96	0.996	?	1.004	1.04	1.4

$\lim\limits_{x \to 1} (4x - 3) = 1$

91.

x	-0.1	-0.01	-0.001	0
$f(x)$	35.71	355.26	3550.71	?

x	0.001	0.01	0.1
$f(x)$	-3550.31	-354.85	-35.30

$\lim\limits_{x \to 0} \dfrac{\sqrt{x + 6} - 6}{x}$ does not exist.

93. 8 **95.** 7 **97.** $-\frac{2}{5}$ **99.** Limit does not exist.

101. $-\frac{1}{4}$ **103.** $-\infty$ **105.** Limit does not exist.

107. 5 **109.** $3x^2 - 1$

111. $(-\infty, \infty)$; For any c on the real number line, $F(c)$ is defined,
$\lim\limits_{x \to c} f(x)$ exists, and $\lim\limits_{x \to c} f(x) = f(c)$.

113. $(-\infty, -4)$ and $(-4, \infty)$; $f(-4)$ is undefined.

115. $(-\infty, -1)$ and $(-1, \infty)$; $f(-1)$ is undefined.

117. Continuous on all intervals $(c, c + 1)$, where c is an integer;
$\lim\limits_{x \to c} f(c)$ does not exist.

119. $(-\infty, 0)$ and $(0, \infty)$; $\lim\limits_{x \to 0} f(x)$ does not exist.

121. $a = 2$

123. (a)

Explanations will vary. The function is defined for all values
of x greater than zero. The function is discontinuous when
$x = 5, x = 10$, and $x = 15$.

(b) $\$49.90$

125. (a) $C(t) = \begin{cases} 1 + 0.1[\![t]\!], & t > 0,\ t \text{ not an integer} \\ 1 + 0.1[\![t - 1]\!], & t > 0,\ t \text{ an integer} \end{cases}$

(b)

C is not continuous at $t = 1, 2, 3, \ldots$

Chapter Test   *(page 78)*

1. (a) $d = 5\sqrt{2}$ (b) Midpoint: $(-1.5, 1.5)$
(c) $m = -1$ (d) $y = -x$
(e)

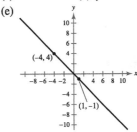

2. (a) $d = 2.5$ (b) Midpoint: $(1.25, 2)$
(c) $m = 0$ (d) $y = 2$
(e)

3. (a) $d = 2\sqrt{10}$ (b) Midpoint: $(-1, 2)$
(c) $m = \frac{1}{3}$ (d) $y = \frac{1}{3}x + \frac{7}{3}$
(e)

4. $(5.5, 53.45)$

5. $m = \frac{1}{5}$; $(0, -2)$

6. m is undefined; no y-intercept

7. $m = -2.5$; $(0, 6.25)$

8. $y = -\frac{1}{4}x - \frac{29}{4}$ **9.** $y = \frac{5}{2}x - 4$

10. (a)

(b) Domain: $(-\infty, \infty)$
   Range: $(-\infty, \infty)$
(c) $f(-3) = -1$; $f(-2) = 1$; $f(3) = 11$
(d) The function is one-to-one.

11. (a)

(b) Domain: $(-\infty, \infty)$
   Range: $(-2.25, \infty)$
(c) $f(-3) = 10$; $f(-2) = 4$; $f(3) = 4$
(d) The function is not one-to-one.

12. (a)

(b) Domain: $[-5, \infty)$
   Range: $[0, \infty)$
(c) $f(-3) = \sqrt{2}$; $f(-2) = \sqrt{3}$; $f(3) = 2\sqrt{2}$
(d) The function is one-to-one.

13. $f^{-1}(x) = \frac{1}{4}x - \frac{3}{2}$ **14.** $f^{-1}(x) = -\frac{1}{3}x^3 + \frac{8}{3}$

15. -1 **16.** Limit does not exist.   **17.** 2   **18.** $\frac{1}{6}$

19. $(-\infty, 4)$ and $(4, \infty)$; Explanations will vary. There is a discontinuity at $x = 4$, because $f(4)$ is not defined.

20. $(-\infty, 5]$; Explanations will vary.

21. $(-\infty, \infty)$; Explanations will vary.

22. (a) The model fits the data well. Explanations will vary.
   (b) 128,087.392 thousand (128,087,392)

Chapter 2

Section 2.1   *(page 88)*

Skills Warm Up   *(page 88)*

1. $x = 2$ **2.** $y = 2$ **3.** $y = -x + 2$

4. $y = 3x - 4$ **5.** $2x$ **6.** $3x^2$ **7.** $\dfrac{1}{x^2}$

8. $2x$ **9.** $(-\infty, \infty)$ **10.** $(-\infty, 1) \cup (1, \infty)$

11. $(-\infty, \infty)$ **12.** $(-\infty, 0) \cup (0, \infty)$

1.

3.

5.

7. $m = 1$ **9.** $m = 0$ **11.** $m = -\frac{1}{3}$

13. 2005: $m \approx 119$
   2007: $m \approx 161$
   The slope is the rate of change of revenue at the given point in time.

15. $t = 3$: $m \approx 9$
$t = 7$: $m \approx 0$
$t = 10$: $m \approx -10$
The slope is the rate of change of the average temperature at the given point in time.

17. $f'(x) = 0$
$f'(0) = 0$

19. $f'(x) = -3$
$f'(2) = -3$

21. $f'(x) = 4x$
$f'(2) = 8$

23. $f'(x) = 3x^2 - 1$
$f'(2) = 11$

25. $f'(x) = \dfrac{1}{\sqrt{x}}$
$f'(4) = \dfrac{1}{2}$

27. $f(x) = 3$
$f(x + \Delta x) = 3$
$f(x + \Delta x) - f(x) = 0$
$\dfrac{f(x + \Delta x) - f(x)}{\Delta x} = 0$
$\lim\limits_{\Delta x \to 0} \dfrac{f(x + \Delta x) - f(x)}{\Delta x} = 0$

29. $f(x) = -5x$
$f(x + \Delta x) = -5x - 5\Delta x$
$f(x + \Delta x) - f(x) = -5\Delta x$
$\dfrac{f(x + \Delta x) - f(x)}{\Delta x} = -5$
$\lim\limits_{\Delta x \to 0} \dfrac{f(x + \Delta x) - f(x)}{\Delta x} = -5$

31. $g(s) = \dfrac{1}{3}s + 2$
$g(s + \Delta s) = \dfrac{1}{3}s + \dfrac{1}{3}\Delta s + 2$
$g(s + \Delta s) - g(s) = \dfrac{1}{3}\Delta s$
$\dfrac{g(s + \Delta s) - g(s)}{\Delta s} = \dfrac{1}{3}$
$\lim\limits_{\Delta s \to 0} \dfrac{g(s + \Delta s) - g(s)}{\Delta s} = \dfrac{1}{3}$

33. $f(x) = 4x^2 - 5x$
$f(x + \Delta x) = 4x^2 + 8x\Delta x + 4(\Delta x)^2 - 5x - 5\Delta x$
$f(x + \Delta x) - f(x) = 8x\Delta x + 4(\Delta x)^2 - 5\Delta x$
$\dfrac{f(x + \Delta x) - f(x)}{\Delta x} = 8x + 4\Delta x - 5$
$\lim\limits_{\Delta x \to 0} \dfrac{f(x + \Delta x) - f(x)}{\Delta x} = 8x - 5$

35. $h(t) = \sqrt{t - 1}$
$h(t + \Delta t) = \sqrt{t + \Delta t - 1}$
$h(t + \Delta t) - h(t) = \sqrt{t + \Delta t - 1} - \sqrt{t - 1}$
$\dfrac{h(t + \Delta t) - h(t)}{\Delta t} = \dfrac{1}{\sqrt{t + \Delta t - 1} + \sqrt{t - 1}}$
$\lim\limits_{\Delta t \to 0} \dfrac{h(t + \Delta t) - h(t)}{\Delta t} = \dfrac{1}{2\sqrt{t - 1}}$

37. $f(t) = t^3 - 12t$
$f(t + \Delta t) = t^3 + 3t^2\Delta t + 3t(\Delta t)^2 + (\Delta t)^3 - 12t - 12\Delta t$
$f(t + \Delta t) - f(t) = 3t^2\Delta t + 3t(\Delta t)^2 + (\Delta t)^3 - 12\Delta t$
$\dfrac{f(t + \Delta t) - f(t)}{\Delta t} = 3t^2 + 3t\Delta t + (\Delta t)^2 - 12$
$\lim\limits_{\Delta t \to 0} \dfrac{f(t + \Delta t) - f(t)}{\Delta t} = 3t^2 - 12$

39. $f(x) = \dfrac{1}{x + 2}$
$f(x + \Delta x) = \dfrac{1}{x + \Delta x + 2}$
$f(x + \Delta x) - f(x) = \dfrac{-\Delta x}{(x + \Delta x + 2)(x + 2)}$
$\dfrac{f(x + \Delta x) - f(x)}{\Delta x} = \dfrac{-1}{(x + \Delta x + 2)(x + 2)}$
$\lim\limits_{\Delta x \to 0} \dfrac{f(x + \Delta x) - f(x)}{\Delta x} = -\dfrac{1}{(x + 2)^2}$

41. $y = 2x - 2$

43. $y = -6x - 3$

45. $y = \dfrac{x}{4} + 2$

47. $y = -x + 2$

49. $y = -x + 1$ **51.** $y = -9x + 18$, $y = -9x - 18$

53. y is differentiable for all $x \neq -3$.
At $(-3, 0)$ the graph has a node.

55. y is differentiable for all $x \neq 3$.
At $(3, 0)$ the graph has a cusp.

57. y is differentiable for all $x = \pm 2$.
The function is not defined at $x = \pm 2$.

59. $f(x) = -3x + 2$

61.

$f'(x) = \frac{3}{4}x^2$

x	-2	$-\frac{3}{2}$	-1	$-\frac{1}{2}$
$f(x)$	-2	-0.8438	-0.25	-0.0313
$f'(x)$	3	1.6875	0.75	0.1875

x	0	$\frac{1}{2}$	1	$\frac{3}{2}$	2
$f(x)$	0	0.0313	0.25	0.8438	2
$f'(x)$	0	0.1875	0.75	1.6875	3

63.

$f'(x) = -\frac{3}{2}x^2$

x	-2	$-\frac{3}{2}$	-1	$-\frac{1}{2}$
$f(x)$	4	1.6875	0.5	0.0625
$f'(x)$	-6	-3.375	-1.5	-0.375

x	0	$\frac{1}{2}$	1	$\frac{3}{2}$	2
$f(x)$	0	-0.0625	-0.5	-1.6875	-4
$f'(x)$	0	-0.375	-1.5	-3.375	-6

65. $f'(x) = 2x - 4$

The x-intercept of the derivative indicates a point of horizontal tangency for f.

67. $f'(x) = 3x^2 - 3$

The x-intercepts of the derivative indicate points of horizontal tangency for f.

69. True   **71.** True

73.

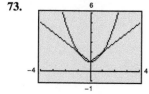

The graph of f is smooth at $(0, 1)$, but the graph of g has a sharp point at $(0, 1)$. The function f is differentiable at $x = 0$.

Section 2.2   *(page 100)*

Skills Warm Up   *(page 100)*

1. (a) 8   (b) 16   (c) $\frac{1}{2}$

2. (a) $\frac{1}{36}$ (b) $\frac{1}{32}$ (c) $\frac{1}{64}$

3. $4x(3x^2 + 1)$ **4.** $\frac{3}{2}x^{1/2}(x^{3/2} - 1)$ **5.** $\frac{1}{4x^{3/4}}$

6. $x^2 - \frac{1}{x^{1/2}} + \frac{1}{3x^{2/3}}$ **7.** $0, -\frac{2}{3}$

8. $0, \pm 1$ **9.** $-10, 2$ **10.** $-2, 12$

1. 0   **3.** $5x^4$ **5.** $9x^2$ **7.** $2x^2$ **9.** 4   **11.** $-3x^2$

13. $8x - 3$ **15.** $-6t + 2$ **17.** $3t^2 - 2$ **19.** $\frac{2}{3\sqrt[3]{x}}$

21. $\frac{16}{3}t^{1/3}$ **23.** $-\frac{8}{x^3} + 4x$

25. Function: $y = \frac{2}{7x^4}$

Rewrite: $y = \frac{2}{7}x^{-4}$

Differentiate: $y' = -\frac{8}{7}x^{-5}$

Simplify: $y' = -\frac{8}{7x^5}$

27. Function: $y = \frac{1}{(4x)^3}$

Rewrite: $y = \frac{1}{64}x^{-3}$

Differentiate: $y' = -\frac{3}{64}x^{-4}$

Simplify: $y' = -\frac{3}{64x^4}$

29. Function: $y = \frac{4}{(2x)^{-5}}$

Rewrite: $y = 128x^5$

Differentiate: $y' = 128(5)x^4$

Simplify: $y' = 640x^4$

31. Function: $y = 6\sqrt{x}$

Rewrite: $y = 6x^{1/2}$

Differentiate: $y' = 6\left(\frac{1}{2}\right)x^{-1/2}$

Simplify: $y' = \frac{3}{\sqrt{x}}$

33. Function: $y = \frac{1}{5\sqrt[5]{x}}$

Rewrite: $y = \frac{1}{5}x^{-1/5}$

Differentiate: $y' = \frac{1}{5}\left(-\frac{1}{5}\right)x^{-6/5}$

Simplify: $y' = -\frac{1}{25\sqrt[5]{x^6}}$

35. Function: $y = \sqrt{3x}$

Rewrite: $y = (3x)^{1/2}$

Differentiate: $y' = \left(\frac{1}{2}\right)(3x)^{-1/2}(3)$

Simplify: $y' = \frac{3}{2\sqrt{3x}}$

37. $\frac{3}{2}$ **39.** 8   **41.** -11 **43.** -2

45. (a) $y = 2x - 2$ **47.** (a) $y = \frac{8}{15}x + \frac{22}{15}$

(b) and (c)   (b) and (c)

49. (a) $y = 36x - 54$

(b) and (c)

51. $2x + \dfrac{4}{x^2} + \dfrac{6}{x^3}$ **53.** $2x - 2 + \dfrac{8}{x^5}$ **55.** $\dfrac{4}{5x^{1/5}} + 1$

57. $3x^2 + 1$ **59.** $\dfrac{2x^3 - 6}{x^3}$ **61.** $\dfrac{4x^3 - 2x - 10}{x^3}$

63. $(0, -1), \left(-\dfrac{\sqrt{6}}{2}, \dfrac{5}{4}\right), \left(\dfrac{\sqrt{6}}{2}, \dfrac{5}{4}\right)$ **65.** $(-5, -12.5)$

67. (a)   (b) $f'(1) = g'(1) = 3$

(c)   (d) $f' = g' = 3x^2$ for every
value of x.

69. $f'(x) = g'(x)$ **71.** $-5f'(x) = g'(x)$

73. (a) 2005: $m \approx 119.2$; 2007: $m \approx 161$

(b) These results are close to the estimates in Exercise 13 in Section 2.1.

(c) The slope of the graph at time t is the rate at which sales are increasing in millions of dollars per year.

75. (a) The men and women who seem to suffer most from migraines are those between 30 and 40 years old. More females than males suffer from migraines. Fewer people whose incomes are greater than or equal to $30,000 suffer from migraines than people whose incomes are less than $10,000.

(b) The derivatives are positive up to approximately 37 years old and negative after about 37 years of age. The percent of adults suffering from migraines increases up to about 37 years old, then decreases. The units of the derivative are percents of adults suffering from migraines per year.

77. $C = 7.75x + 500$

$C' = 7.75$, which equals the marginal cost.

79. $(0.11, 0.14), (1.84, -10.49)$

81. False. Let $f(x) = x$ and $g(x) = x + 1$.

Section 2.3   *(page 113)*

Skills Warm Up   *(page 113)*

1. 3   **2.** -7 **3.** -3 **4.** 2.4

5. $y' = 8x - 2$ **6.** $y' = -9t^2 + 4t$

7. $s' = -32t + 24$ **8.** $y' = -32x + 54$

9. $A' = -\frac{3}{5}r^2 + \frac{3}{5}r + \frac{1}{2}$ **10.** $y' = 2x^2 - 4x + 7$

11. $y' = 12 - \dfrac{x}{2500}$ **12.** $y' = 74 - \dfrac{3x^2}{10,000}$

1. (a) $10.4 billion/yr   (b) $7.4 billion/yr

(c) $6.4 billion/yr   (d) $16.6 billion/yr

(e) $11 billion/yr   (f) $11.96 billion/yr

(g) $13.67 billion/yr   (h) $16.38 billion/yr

3.   **5.**

Average rate: 3   Average rate: -4

Instantaneous rates: Instantaneous rates:

$f'(1) = f'(2) = 3$ $h'(-2) = -8, h'(2) = 0$

7.   **9.**

Average rate: $\frac{45}{7}$ Average rate: $-\frac{1}{4}$

Instantaneous rates: Instantaneous rates:

$f'(1) = 4, f'(8) = 8$ $f'(1) = -1, f'(4) = -\frac{1}{16}$

11.   Average rate: 36

Instantaneous rates:

$g'(1) = 2, g'(3) = 102$

13. (a) -450

The number of visitors to the park is decreasing at an average rate of 450 thousand people per month from September to December.

(b) Answers will vary. The instantaneous rate of change at $t = 8$ is approximately 0.

15. (a) Average rate: 14 ft/sec

Instantaneous rates: $s'(0) = 30$ ft/sec

$s'(1) = -2$ ft/sec

(b) Average rate: -18 ft/sec

Instantaneous rates: $s'(1) = -2$ ft/sec

$s'(2) = -34$ ft/sec

(c) Average rate: -50 ft/sec

Instantaneous rates: $s'(2) = -34$ ft/sec

$s'(3) = -66$ ft/sec

(d) Average rate: -82 ft/sec

Instantaneous rates: $s'(3) = -66$ ft/sec

$s'(4) = -98$ ft/sec

17. (a) -80 ft/sec

(b) $s'(2) = -64$ ft/sec,

$s'(3) = -96$ ft/sec

(c) $\dfrac{\sqrt{555}}{4} \approx 5.89$ sec

(d) $-8\sqrt{555} \approx -188.5$ ft/sec

19. 9800 dollars   **21.** $470 - 0.5x$ dollars, $0 \le x \le 940$

23. $50 - x$ dollars   **25.** $-18x^2 + 16x + 200$ dollars

27. $-4x + 72$ dollars   **29.** $0.0039x^2 + 12$ dollars

31. (a) \$0.58   (b) \$0.60

(c) The results are nearly the same.

33. (a) \$12.96   (b) \$13.00

(c) The results are nearly the same.

35. (a) $P(0) = 117{,}001{,}000$ people

$P(5) = 120{,}622{,}500$ people

$P(10) = 123{,}466{,}000$ people

$P(15) = 125{,}531{,}500$ people

$P(20) = 126{,}819{,}000$ people

$P(25) = 127{,}328{,}500$ people

$P(30) = 127{,}060{,}000$ people

The population is growing from 1980 to 2005. It then begins to decline.

(b) $\dfrac{dP}{dt} = -31.12t + 802.1$

(c) $P'(0) = 802{,}100$ people per year

$P'(5) = 646{,}500$ people per year

$P'(10) = 490{,}900$ people per year

$P'(15) = 335{,}300$ people per year

$P'(20) = 179{,}700$ people per year

$P'(25) = 24{,}100$ people per year

$P'(30) = -131{,}500$ people per year

The rate of growth is decreasing.

37. (a) $TR = -10Q^2 + 160Q$

(b) $(TR)' = MR = -20Q + 160$

(c)

Q	0	2	4	6	8	10
Model	160	120	80	40	0	-40
Table	$-$	130	90	50	10	-30

Answers will vary.

39. (a) $P = -0.0025x^2 + 2.65x - 25$

(b)

When $x = 300$, slope is positive.

When $x = 700$, slope is negative.

(c) $P'(300) = 1.15$

$P'(700) = -0.85$

41. (a) $C = \dfrac{44{,}250}{x}$

(b) $\dfrac{dC}{dx} = \dfrac{-44{,}250}{x^2}$

This is the rate of change of fuel cost.

(c)

x	10	15	20	25
C	4425.00	2950.00	2212.50	1770.00
dC/dx	-442.5	-196.67	-110.63	-70.80

x	30	35	40
C	1475.00	1264.29	1106.25
dC/dx	-49.17	-36.12	-27.66

(d) The driver who gets 15 mi/gal; Explanations will vary.

43. (a) Average rate of change from 1995 to 2009:

$\dfrac{\Delta p}{\Delta t} = \dfrac{10{,}428.05 - 5117.12}{19 - 5} \approx 379.35$ dollars per year

(b) Average rate of change from 1996 to 2000:

$\dfrac{\Delta p}{\Delta t} = \dfrac{10{,}786.85 - 6448.26}{10 - 6} \approx \$1084.65$

(c) Average rate of change from 1997 to 1999:

$\dfrac{\Delta p}{\Delta t} = \dfrac{11{,}497.12 - 7908.24}{9 - 7} \approx \$1794.44$

(d) The average rate of change from 1997 to 1999 is a better estimate because the data are closer to the year in question.

Section 2.4   (page 124)

Skills Warm Up   (page 124)

1. $2(3x^2 + 7x + 1)$ **2.** $4x^2(6 - 5x^2)$

3. $8x^2(x^2 + 2)^3 + (x^2 + 4)$

4. $(2x)(2x + 1)[2x + (2x + 1)^3]$

5. $\dfrac{23}{(2x + 7)^2}$ **6.** $-\dfrac{x^2 + 8x + 4}{(x^2 - 4)^2}$

7. $-\dfrac{2(x^2 + x - 1)}{(x^2 + 1)^2}$ **8.** $\dfrac{4(3x^4 - x^3 + 1)}{(1 - x^4)^2}$

9. $\dfrac{4x^3 - 3x^2 + 3}{x^2}$ **10.** $\dfrac{x^2 - 2x + 4}{(x - 1)^2}$

11. 11 **12.** 0 **13.** $-\frac{1}{4}$ **14.** $\frac{17}{4}$

1. $f'(x) = (2x - 3)(-5) + (2)(1 - 5x) = -20x + 17$

3. $f'(x) = (6x - x^2)(3) + (6 - 2x)(4 + 3x)$

$= -9x^2 + 28x + 24$

5. $f'(x) = x(2x) + 1(x^2 + 3) = 3x^2 + 3$

7. $h'(x) = \left(\dfrac{2}{x} - 3\right)(2x) + \left(-\dfrac{2}{x^2}\right)(x^2 + 7) = -\dfrac{14}{x^2} - 6x + 2$

9. $g'(x) = (x^2 - 4x + 3)(1) + (2x - 4)(x - 2)$
$= 3x^2 - 12x + 11$

11. $h'(x) = \dfrac{(x - 5)(1) - (x)(1)}{(x - 5)^2} = -\dfrac{5}{(x - 5)^2}$

13. $f'(t) = \dfrac{(3t + 1)(4t) - (2t^2 - 3)3}{(3t + 1)^2} = \dfrac{6t^2 + 4t + 9}{(3t + 1)^2}$

15. $f'(t) = \dfrac{(t + 4)(2t) - (t^2 - 1)(1)}{(t + 4)^2} = \dfrac{t^2 + 8t + 1}{(t + 4)^2}$

17. $f'(x) = \dfrac{(2x - 1)(2x + 6) - (x^2 + 6x + 5)(2)}{(2x - 1)^2}$
$= \dfrac{2x^2 - 2x - 16}{(2x - 1)^2}$

19. $f'(x) = \dfrac{(3x - 1)\left(-\dfrac{2}{x^2}\right) - \left(6 + \dfrac{2}{x}\right)(3)}{(3x - 1)^2}$
$= \dfrac{-18x^2 - 12x + 2}{x^2(3x - 1)^2}$

21. Function: $f(x) = \dfrac{x^3 + 6x}{3}$

Rewrite: $f(x) = \dfrac{x^3}{3} + 2x$

Differentiate: $f'(x) = x^2 + 2$
Simplify: $f'(x) = x^2 + 2$

23. Function: $y = \dfrac{x^2 + 2x}{3}$

Rewrite: $y = \dfrac{1}{3}(x^2 + 2x)$

Differentiate: $y' = \dfrac{1}{3}(2x + 2)$

Simplify: $y' = \dfrac{2}{3}(x + 1)$

25. Function: $y = \dfrac{7}{3x^3}$

Rewrite: $y = \dfrac{7}{3}x^{-3}$

Differentiate: $y' = -7x^{-4}$

Simplify: $y' = -\dfrac{7}{x^4}$

27. Function: $y = \dfrac{4x^2 - 3x}{8\sqrt{x}}$

Rewrite: $y = \dfrac{1}{2}x^{3/2} - \dfrac{3}{8}x^{1/2}, \ x \neq 0$

Differentiate: $y' = \dfrac{3}{4}x^{1/2} - \dfrac{3}{16}x^{-1/2}$

Simplify: $y' = \dfrac{3}{4}\sqrt{x} - \dfrac{3}{16\sqrt{x}}$

29. Function: $y = \dfrac{x^2 - 4x + 3}{2(x - 1)}$

Rewrite: $y = \dfrac{1}{2}(x - 3), \ x \neq 1$

Differentiate: $y' = \dfrac{1}{2}(1), \ x \neq 1$

Simplify: $y' = \dfrac{1}{2}, \ x \neq 1$

31. $10x^4 + 12x^3 - 3x^2 - 18x - 15$; Product Rule

33. $\dfrac{x^4 - 6x^2 - 4x - 3}{(x^2 - 1)^2}$; Quotient Rule   **35.** 1; Power Rule

37. $12t^2(2t^3 - 1)$; Product Rule

39. $\dfrac{3s^2 - 2s - 5}{2s^{3/2}}$; Quotient Rule

41. $\dfrac{12x^2 + 12x - 2}{(4x + 2)^2}$; Quotient Rule

43. $\dfrac{2x^3 + 11x^2 - 8x - 17}{(x + 4)^2}$; Quotient Rule

45. $y = 3x + 3$ **47.** $y = -7x + 4$

49. $y = \dfrac{3}{4}x - \dfrac{5}{4}$ **51.** $y = \dfrac{31}{5}x + \dfrac{26}{5}$

53. $(0, 0), (2, 4)$ **55.** $(0, 0), \left(\sqrt[3]{-4}, -2.117\right)$

57.   **59.**

61. $-\$1.87$/unit   **63.** 31.55 bacteria/hr

65. (a) -0.480/wk   (b) 0.120/wk   (c) 0.015/wk
Each rate in parts (a), (b), and (c) is the rate at which the level of oxygen in the pond is changing at that particular time.

67. (a)

(b) At $x = 6.683$, $\dfrac{C}{x} = \dfrac{dC}{dx} \approx 20.50$.

So, the point of intersection is $(6.683, 20.50)$. At this point the average cost is at a minimum.

69. (a) -38.125 (b) -10.37 (c) -3.80
Increasing the order size reduces the cost per item; Choices and explanations will vary.

71. $f'(2) = 0$ **73.** $f'(2) = 14$ **75.** Answers will vary.

Quiz Yourself   *(page 127)*

1. $f(x) = 5x + 3$

$f(x + \Delta x) = 5x + 5\Delta x + 3$

$f(x + \Delta x) - f(x) = 5\Delta x$

$\dfrac{f(x + \Delta x) - f(x)}{\Delta x} = 5$

$\lim\limits_{\Delta x \to 0} \dfrac{f(x + \Delta x) - f(x)}{\Delta x} = 5$

$f'(x) = 5$

$f'(-2) = 5$

2. $f(x) = \sqrt{x + 3}$

$f(x + \Delta x) = \sqrt{x + \Delta x + 3}$

$f(x + \Delta x) - f(x) = \sqrt{x + \Delta x + 3} - \sqrt{x + 3}$

$\dfrac{f(x + \Delta x) - f(x)}{\Delta x} = \dfrac{1}{\sqrt{x + \Delta x + 3} + \sqrt{x + 3}}$

$\lim\limits_{\Delta x \to 0} \dfrac{f(x + \Delta x) - f(x)}{\Delta x} = \dfrac{1}{2\sqrt{x + 3}}$

$f'(x) = \dfrac{1}{2\sqrt{x + 3}}$

$f'(1) = \dfrac{1}{4}$

3. $f(x) = x^2 - 2x$

$f(x + \Delta x) = x^2 + 2x\Delta x + (\Delta x)^2 - 2x - 2\Delta x$

$f(x + \Delta x) - f(x) = 2x\Delta x + (\Delta x)^2 - 2\Delta x$

$\dfrac{f(x + \Delta x) - f(x)}{\Delta x} = 2x + \Delta x - 2$

$\lim\limits_{\Delta x \to 0} \dfrac{f(x + \Delta x) - f(x)}{\Delta x} = 2x - 2$

$f'(x) = 2x - 2$

$f'(3) = 4$

4. $f'(x) = 0$ **5.** $f'(x) = 19$ **6.** $f'(x) = -6x$

7. $f'(x) = \dfrac{3}{x^{3/4}}$ **8.** $f'(x) = -\dfrac{8}{x^3}$ **9.** $f'(x) = \dfrac{1}{\sqrt{x}}$

10. $f'(x) = -\dfrac{5}{(3x + 2)^2}$ **11.** $f'(x) = -6x^2 + 8x - 2$

12. $f'(x) = 15x^2 + 26x + 14$ **13.** $f'(x) = \dfrac{-4(x^2 - 3)}{(x^2 + 3)^2}$

14.

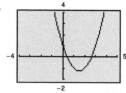

Average rate: 0

Instantaneous rates: $f'(0) = -3, f'(3) = 3$

15.

Average rate: 1

Instantaneous rates: $f'(-1) = 3, f'(1) = 7$

16.

Average rate: $-\dfrac{1}{20}$

Instantaneous rates: $f'(2) = -\dfrac{1}{8}, f'(5) = -\dfrac{1}{50}$

17.

Average rate: $\dfrac{1}{19}$

Instantaneous rates: $f'(8) = \dfrac{1}{12}, f'(27) = \dfrac{1}{27}$

18. (a) \$11.61   (b) \$11.63

(c) The results are approximately equal.

19. $y = -4x - 6$ **20.** $y = 10x - 8$

21. (a) $\dfrac{dS}{dt} = -0.40668t^2 + 3.7364t - 4.351$

(b) 2004: \$4.08772/yr

2007: \$1.87648/yr

2008: $-\$0.48732$/yr

Section 2.5   *(page 135)*

Skills Warm Up   *(page 135)*

1. $(1 - 5x)^{2/5}$ **2.** $(2x - 1)^{3/4}$

3. $(4x^2 + 1)^{-1/2}$ **4.** $(x - 6)^{-1/3}$

5. $x^{1/2}(1 - 2x)^{-1/3}$ **6.** $(2x)^{-1}(3 - 7x)^{3/2}$

7. $(x - 2)(3x^2 + 5)$ **8.** $(x - 1)(5\sqrt{x} - 1)$

9. $(x^2 + 1)^2(4 - x - x^3)$

10. $(3 - x^2)(x - 1)(x^2 + x + 1)$

$y = f(g(x))$	$u = g(x)$	$y = f(u)$
1. $y = (6x - 5)^4$	$u = 6x - 5$	$y = u^4$
3. $y = \sqrt{5x - 2}$	$u = 5x - 2$	$y = \sqrt{u}$
5. $y = (3x + 1)^{-1}$	$u = 3x + 1$	$y = u^{-1}$

7. $\dfrac{dy}{du} = 2u$ **9.** $\dfrac{dy}{du} = \dfrac{1}{2\sqrt{u}}$

$\dfrac{du}{dx} = 4$ $\dfrac{du}{dx} = -2x$

$\dfrac{dy}{dx} = 32x + 56$ $\dfrac{dy}{dx} = -\dfrac{x}{\sqrt{3 - x^2}}$

11. $\dfrac{dy}{du} = \dfrac{2}{3u^{1/3}}$

$\dfrac{du}{dx} = 20x^3 - 2$

$\dfrac{dy}{dx} = \dfrac{40x^3 - 4}{3\sqrt[3]{5x^4 - 2x}}$

13. c   **15.** b   **17.** a   **19.** c   **21.** $6(2x - 7)^2$

23. $\dfrac{3\sqrt{5x - x^2}\,(5 - 2x)}{2}$ **25.** $6x(6 - x^2)(2 - x^2)$

27. $\dfrac{1}{2\sqrt{t + 1}}$ **29.** $\dfrac{4t + 5}{2\sqrt{2t^2 + 5t + 2}}$ **31.** $\dfrac{6x}{(9x^2 + 4)^{2/3}}$

33. $\dfrac{54}{(2 - 9x)^4}$ **35.** $\dfrac{-x}{(25 + x^2)^{3/2}}$

37. $y = 216x - 378$ **39.** $y = \dfrac{8}{3}x - \dfrac{7}{3}$

41. $y = x - 1$

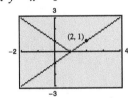

43. $f'(x) = \dfrac{1 - 3x^2 - 4x^{3/2}}{2\sqrt{x}(x^2 + 1)^2}$

The zero of $f'(x)$ corresponds to the point on the graph of $f(x)$ where the tangent line is horizontal.

45. $f'(x) = -\dfrac{\sqrt{(x + 1)/x}}{2x(x + 1)}$

$f'(x)$ has no zeros.

In Exercises 47–61, the differentiation rule(s) used may vary. A sample answer is provided.

47. $\dfrac{2x}{(4 - x^2)^2}$; Chain Rule   **49.** $\dfrac{8}{(t + 2)^3}$; Chain Rule

51. $-6(3x^2 - x - 3)$; Product Rule

53. $-\dfrac{1}{2(x + 2)^{3/2}}$; Power Rule

55. $27(x - 3)^2(4x - 3)$; Product Rule and Chain Rule

57. $\dfrac{3(x + 1)}{\sqrt{2x + 3}}$; Product Rule and Chain Rule

59. $\dfrac{t(5t - 8)}{2\sqrt{t - 2}}$; Product Rule and Chain Rule

61. $\dfrac{2(6 - 5x)(5x^2 - 12x + 5)}{(x^2 - 1)^3}$; Chain Rule and Quotient Rule

63. $y = \dfrac{8}{3}t + 4$ **65.** $y = \dfrac{1}{2}x + 1$

67. $y = -6t - 14$ **69.** $y = -2x + 7$

71. (a) $74.00 per 1\%

(b) $81.59 per 1\%

(c) $89.94 per 1\%

73. (a) $V = \dfrac{10{,}000}{\sqrt{t + 1}}$

(b) About $-$1767.77 per year

(c) $-$625.00 per year

75. (a) $r'(t) = \dfrac{11.4228t^3 - 218.376t^2 + 1352.28t - 2706}{2\sqrt{2.8557t^4 - 72.792t^3 + 676.14t^2 - 2706t + 4096}}$;

Chain Rule

(b)

(c) $t = 3$ (d) $t \approx 4.52, t \approx 6.36, t \approx 8.24$

Section 2.6   *(page 142)*

Skills Warm Up   *(page 142)*

1. $t = 0, \dfrac{3}{2}$ **2.** $t = -2, 7$ **3.** $t = -2, 10$

4. $t = \dfrac{9 \pm 3\sqrt{10{,}249}}{32}$ **5.** $\dfrac{dy}{dx} = 6x^2 + 14x$

6. $\dfrac{dy}{dx} = 8x^3 + 18x^2 - 10x - 15$

7. $\dfrac{dy}{dx} = \dfrac{2x(x + 7)}{(2x + 7)^2}$ **8.** $\dfrac{dy}{dx} = -\dfrac{6x^2 + 10x + 15}{(2x^2 - 5)^2}$

9. Domain: $(-\infty, \infty)$ **10.** Domain: $[7, \infty)$

Range: $[-4, \infty)$ Range: $[0, \infty)$

CHAPTER 2

1. 0   **3.** 2   **5.** $2t - 8$ **7.** $\dfrac{9}{2t^4}$

9. $18(2 - x^2)(5x^2 - 2)$ **11.** $\dfrac{4}{(x - 1)^3}$ **13.** $60x^2 - 72x$

15. $120x + 360$ **17.** $-\dfrac{9}{2x^5}$ **19.** 260   **21.** $-\dfrac{1}{648}$

23. 12   **25.** $4x$ **27.** $\dfrac{1}{\sqrt{x - 1}}$ **29.** $12x^2 + 4$

31. $f''(x) = 6(x - 3) = 0$ at $x = 3$.

33. $f''(x) = \dfrac{x(2x^2 - 3)}{(x^2 - 1)^{3/2}} = 0$ at $x = \pm\dfrac{\sqrt{6}}{2}$.

35. (a) $s(t) = -16t^2 + 144t$
   $v(t) = -32t + 144$
   $a(t) = -32$
   (b) $s(3) = 288$ ft
   $v(3) = 48$ ft/sec
   $a(3) = -32$ ft/sec^2
   (c) 4.5 sec; 324 ft
   (d) $v(9) = -144$ ft/sec, which is the same speed as the initial velocity

37.

t	0	10	20	30	40	50	60
$\dfrac{ds}{dt}$	0	45	60	67.5	72	75	77.1
$\dfrac{d^2s}{dt^2}$	9	2.25	1	0.56	0.36	0.25	0.18

As time increases, velocity increases and acceleration decreases.

39. (a)

   (b) The degree decreases by 1 for each successive derivative.
   (c)

   (d) The degree decreases by 1 for each successive derivative.

41. (a) $y = -68.991t^3 + 1208.34t^2 - 5445.4t + 10,145$
   (b) $y'(t) = -206.973t^2 + 2416.68t - 5445.4$
   $y''(t) = -413.946t + 2416.68$
   (c) $y'(t) > 0$ on $[5, 8]$
   (d) 2005 ($t \approx 5.84$)

43. False. The Product Rule is
   $[f(x)g(x)]' = f(x)g'(x) + g(x)f'(x)$.

45. Answers will vary.

Section 2.7   *(page 149)*

Skills Warm Up   *(page 149)*

1. $y = x^2 - 2x$ **2.** $y = \dfrac{x - 3}{4}$

3. $y = 1, x \neq -6$ **4.** $y = -4, x \neq \pm\sqrt{3}$

5. $y = \pm\sqrt{5 - x^2}$ **6.** $y = \pm\sqrt{6 - x^2}$ **7.** $\frac{8}{3}$

8. $-\frac{1}{2}$ **9.** $\frac{5}{7}$

---

1. $-\dfrac{y}{x}$ **3.** $-\dfrac{x}{y}$ **5.** $\dfrac{1 - xy^2}{x^2y}$ **7.** $\dfrac{y}{8y - x}$ **9.** 0

11. $-\dfrac{1}{10y - 2}$ **13.** 0   **15.** $-\dfrac{1}{4}$ **17.** $\dfrac{1}{2}$ **19.** -1

21. $-\dfrac{5}{4}$ **23.** $\dfrac{1}{4}$ **25.** $\dfrac{1}{3}$ **27.** 3   **29.** 0   **31.** 2

33. $\dfrac{1}{2y}, -\dfrac{1}{2}$

35. At $(8, 6)$: $y = -\frac{4}{3}x + \frac{50}{3}$
   At $(-6, 8)$: $y = \frac{3}{4}x + \frac{25}{2}$

37. At $(1, \sqrt{5})$: $15x - 2\sqrt{5}y - 5 = 0$
   At $(1, -\sqrt{5})$: $15x + 2\sqrt{5}y - 5 = 0$
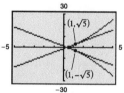

39. At $(0, 2)$: $y = 2$
   At $(2, 0)$: $x = 2$

41. At $(-2, 1)$: $y = \frac{1}{2}x + 2$
   At $(6, \frac{1}{5})$: $y = -0.06x + 0.56$

43. $-\dfrac{2}{p^2(0.00003x^2 + 0.1)}$ **45.** $-\dfrac{4xp}{2p^2 + 1}$

47. (a) -2

(b)

As more labor is used, less capital is available.

As more capital is used, less labor is available.

49. (a)

The number of cases of HIV/AIDS decreases from 2004 through 2007, then begins to increase.

(b) 2005

(c)

t	4	5	6	7	8
y	44.11	41.06	38.46	37.46	39.21
y'	-2.95	-3.00	-2.01	0.22	3.38

2005

Section 2.8   *(page 156)*

Skills Warm Up   *(page 156)*

1. $A = \pi r^2$ **2.** $V = \frac{4}{3}\pi r^3$ **3.** $S = 6s^2$

4. $V = s^3$ **5.** $V = \frac{1}{3}\pi r^2 h$ **6.** $A = \frac{1}{2}bh$

7. $-\dfrac{x}{y}$ **8.** $\dfrac{2x - 3y}{3x}$ **9.** $-\dfrac{2x + y}{x + 2}$

10. $-\dfrac{y^2 - y + 1}{2xy - 2y - x}$

1. (a) $\frac{3}{4}$ (b) 20   **3.** (a) $-\frac{5}{8}$ (b) $\frac{3}{2}$

5. (a) 36π in.^{2}/min   (b) 144π in.^{2}/min

7. If $\dfrac{dr}{dt}$ is constant, $\dfrac{dA}{dt} = 2\pi r \dfrac{dr}{dt}$ and so is proportional to r.

9. (a) $\dfrac{5}{2\pi}$ ft/min   (b) $\dfrac{5}{8\pi}$ ft/min

11. (a) 112.5 dollars/wk

(b) 7500 dollars/wk

(c) 7387.5 dollars/wk

13. (a) 9 cm^3/sec   (b) 900 cm^3/sec

15. (a) -18 in./sec   (b) 0 in./sec

(c) 6 in./sec   (d) 18 in./sec

17. -10.4 ft/sec; As $x \to 0$, $\dfrac{dx}{dt}$ increases.   **19.** 300 mi/h

21. (a) -750 mi/h   (b) 20 min

23. About 37.7 ft^3/min   **25.** 4 units/wk

Review Exercises for Chapter 2   *(page 162)*

1. -2 **3.** 0

5. Answers will vary. Sample answer:

$t = 4$: slope $\approx$ \$290 million/yr; Sales were increasing by about \$290 million/yr in 2004.

$t = 7$: slope $\approx$ \$320 million/yr; Sales were increasing by about \$320 million/yr in 2007.

7. Answers will vary. Sample answer:

$t = 1$: slope $\approx$ 65 thousand visitors/month; The number of visitors to the national park is increasing at about 65,000 visitors per month in January.

$t = 8$: slope $\approx$ 0 visitors/month; The number of visitors to the national park is neither increasing nor decreasing in August.

$t = 12$: slope ≈ -1000 thousand visitors/month; The number of visitors to the national park is decreasing at about 1,000,000 visitors per month in December.

9. -3 **11.** -2 **13.** $\frac{1}{4}$ **15.** -1 **17.** 9

19. $-x + 2$ **21.** $\dfrac{1}{2\sqrt{x - 5}}$ **23.** $-\dfrac{5}{x^2}$

25. All values except $x = 1$; The function is not defined at $x = 1$.

27. All values except $x = 0$; A function is not differentiable at a discontinuity.

29. 0   **31.** $3x^2$ **33.** $8x$ **35.** $\dfrac{8x^3}{5}$ **37.** $8x^3 + 6x$

39. $2x + 6$ **41.** -0.125 **43.** 5

45. (a) $y = 5x - 7$

(b) and (c)

47. (a) $y = x - 1$

(b) and (c)

49. (a) 2004: $m \approx 290$

2007: $m \approx 320$

(b) Results should be similar.

(c) The slope shows the rate at which sales were increasing or decreasing in a particular year.

51.

Average rate of change: 4

Instantaneous rate of change at $t = -3$: 4

Instantaneous rate of change at $t = 1$: 4

53.

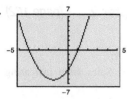

Average rate of change: 4

Instantaneous rate of change at $x = 0$: 3

Instantaneous rate of change at $x = 1$: 5

55. (a) -24 ft/sec   (b) $t = 1$: -8 ft/sec

$t = 3$: -72 ft/sec

(c) 5.14 sec

(d) -140.5 ft/sec

57. $\dfrac{dC}{dx} = 320$ **59.** $\dfrac{dC}{dx} = \dfrac{1.275}{\sqrt{x}}$

61. $\dfrac{dR}{dx} = -1.2x + 150$ **63.** $\dfrac{dR}{dx} = -12x^2 + 4x + 100$

65. $\dfrac{dP}{dx} = -0.0006x^2 + 12x - 1$

67. (a) \$9.95   (b) \$10

(c) Parts (a) and (b) differ by only \$0.05.

In Exercises 69–89, the differentiation rule(s) used may vary. A sample answer is provided.

69. $15x^2(1 - x^2)$; Power Rule

71. $16x^3 - 33x^2 + 12x$; Product Rule

73. $\dfrac{3}{(x + 3)^2}$; Quotient Rule

75. $\dfrac{2(3 + 5x - 3x^2)}{(x^2 + 1)^2}$; Quotient Rule

77. $30x(5x^2 + 2)^2$; Chain Rule

79. $-\dfrac{1}{(x + 1)^{3/2}}$; Quotient Rule   **81.** $\dfrac{2x^2 + 1}{\sqrt{x^2 + 1}}$; Product Rule

83. $80x^4 - 24x^2 + 1$; Product Rule

85. $18x^5(x + 1)(2x + 3)^2$; Chain Rule

87. $x(x - 1)^4(7x - 2)$; Product Rule

89. $\dfrac{3(9t + 5)}{2\sqrt{3t + 1}(1 - 3t)^3}$; Quotient Rule

91. (a) $t = 1$: -6.63 $t = 3$: -6.5

$t = 5$: -4.33 $t = 10$: -1.36

(b)

The rate of decrease is approaching zero.

93. 6   **95.** $-\dfrac{120}{x^6}$ **97.** $\dfrac{35x^{3/2}}{2}$ **99.** $\dfrac{2}{x^{2/3}}$

101. (a) $s(t) = -16t^2 + 5t + 30$ (b) About 1.534 sec

(c) About -44.09 ft/sec   (d) -32 ft/sec^2

103. $-\dfrac{2x + 3y}{3(x + y^2)}$ **105.** $\dfrac{2x - 8}{2y - 9}$ **107.** $y = \dfrac{1}{3}x + \dfrac{1}{3}$

109. $y = \dfrac{4}{3}x + \dfrac{2}{3}$

111. (a) 12π square inches per minute

(b) 40π square inches per minute

113. $\dfrac{1}{64}$ ft/min

Test Yourself   *(page 166)*

1. $f(x) = x^2 + 1$

$f(x + \Delta x) = x^2 + 2x\Delta x + \Delta x^2 + 1$

$f(x + \Delta x) - f(x) = 2x\Delta x + \Delta x^2$

$\dfrac{f(x + \Delta x) - f(x)}{\Delta x} = 2x + \Delta x$

$\lim\limits_{\Delta x \to 0} \dfrac{f(x + \Delta x) - f(x)}{\Delta x} = 2x$

$f'(x) = 2x$

$f'(2) = 4$

2. $f(x) = \sqrt{x} - 2$

$f(x + \Delta x) = \sqrt{x + \Delta x} - 2$

$f(x + \Delta x) - f(x) = \sqrt{x + \Delta x} - \sqrt{x}$

$\dfrac{f(x + \Delta x) - f(x)}{\Delta x} = \dfrac{1}{\sqrt{x + \Delta x} + \sqrt{x}}$

$\lim\limits_{\Delta x \to 0} \dfrac{f(x + \Delta x) - f(x)}{\Delta x} = \dfrac{1}{2\sqrt{x}}$

$f'(x) = \dfrac{1}{2\sqrt{x}}$

$f'(4) = \dfrac{1}{4}$

3. $f'(t) = 3t^2 + 2$ **4.** $f'(x) = 8x - 8$ **5.** $f'(x) = \dfrac{3\sqrt{x}}{2}$

6. $f'(x) = 3x^2 + 10x + 6$ **7.** $f'(x) = \dfrac{9}{x^4}$

8. $f'(x) = \dfrac{5 + x}{2\sqrt{x}} + \sqrt{x}$ **9.** $f'(x) = 36x^3 + 48x$

10. $f'(x) = -\dfrac{1}{\sqrt{1 - 2x}}$

11. $f'(x) = \dfrac{(10x + 1)(5x - 1)^2}{x^2} = 250x - 75 + \dfrac{1}{x^2}$

12. $y = 2x - 2$

13. (a) \$18.69 billion/yr

(b) 2005: \$10.50 billion/yr

2008: \$14.95 billion/yr

(c) The annual sales of CVS Caremark from 2005 to 2008 increased on average by about \$18.69 billion/yr, and the instantaneous rates of change for 2005 and 2008 are \$10.50 billion/yr and \$14.95 billion/yr, respectively.

14. (a) $P = -0.016x^2 + 1460x - 715,000$ (b) \$1437.60

15. 0   **16.** $-\dfrac{3}{8(3 - x)^{5/2}}$ **17.** $-\dfrac{96}{(2x - 1)^4}$

18. $s(t) = -16t^2 + 30t + 75$ $s(2) = 71$ ft

$v(t) = -32t + 30$ $v(2) = -34$ ft/sec

$a(t) = -32$ $a(2) = -32$ ft/sec^2

19. $\dfrac{dy}{dx} = -\dfrac{1 + y}{x}$ **20.** $\dfrac{dy}{dx} = -\dfrac{1}{y - 1}$ **21.** $\dfrac{dy}{dx} = \dfrac{x}{2y}$

22. (a) 3.75π cm^3/min   (b) 15π cm^3/min

Chapter 3

Section 3.1   *(page 175)*

1. Increasing on $(-\infty, -1)$
Decreasing on $(-1, \infty)$
3. Increasing on $(-1, 0)$ and $(1, \infty)$
Decreasing on $(-\infty, -1)$ and $(0, 1)$
5. $x = \frac{3}{4}$ **7.** $x = 0, x = -3$ **9.** $x = \pm 2$
11. No critical numbers
Increasing on $(-\infty, \infty)$

13. Critical number: $x = 3$
Decreasing on $(-\infty, 3)$
Increasing on $(3, \infty)$

15. Critical number: $x = 1$
Increasing on $(-\infty, 1)$
Decreasing on $(1, \infty)$

17. Critical numbers:
  $x = -1, x = -\frac{5}{3}$
Increasing on $\left(-\infty, -\frac{5}{3}\right)$
  and $(-1, \infty)$
Decreasing on $\left(-\frac{5}{3}, -1\right)$

19. Critical numbers:
  $x = 0, x = \frac{3}{2}$
Decreasing on $\left(-\infty, \frac{3}{2}\right)$
Increasing on $\left(\frac{3}{2}, \infty\right)$

21. Critical number: $x = -2$
Decreasing on $(-\infty, -2)$
Increasing on $(-2, \infty)$

23. Critical number: $x = 1$
Increasing on $(-\infty, 1)$
Decreasing on $(1, \infty)$

25. Critical number: $x = 0$
Increasing on $(-\infty, 0)$
  and $(0, \infty)$

27. Critical numbers:
  $x = -1, x = 1$
Decreasing on $(-\infty, -1)$
Increasing on $(1, \infty)$

29. Critical number: $x = -2$
Increasing on $(-\infty, -2)$
  and $(-2, \infty)$

31. Critical numbers:
  $x = -1, x = -\frac{2}{3}$
Decreasing on $\left(-1, -\frac{2}{3}\right)$
Increasing on $\left(-\frac{2}{3}, \infty\right)$

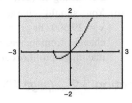

33. Critical numbers:
  $x = -3, x = 3$
Decreasing on $(-\infty, -3)$
  and $(3, \infty)$
Increasing on $(-3, 3)$

35. No critical numbers
Discontinuity: $x = 5$
Decreasing on $(-\infty, 5)$
  and $(5, \infty)$

37. No critical numbers
Discontinuities: $x = \pm 4$
Increasing on $(-\infty, -4)$,
  $(-4, 4)$, and $(4, \infty)$

CHAPTER 3

39. Critical number: $x = 0$
Discontinuity: $x = 0$
Increasing on $(-\infty, 0)$
Decreasing on $(0, \infty)$

41. Critical numbers: $x = -1, 0$
Increasing on $(-\infty, -1)$
and $(0, \infty)$
Decreasing on $(-1, 0)$

43. No critical numbers
$s'(t) = -3.196t + 45.61$
Increasing on $(3, 9)$

45. (a)

Increasing from 1970 to late 1987 and from late 2000 to 2008
Decreasing from late 1987 to late 2000

(b) $y' = 2.076t^2 - 100.22t + 1119.7$
Critical numbers: $t = 17.6, t = 30.7$
Therefore, the model is increasing from 1970 to late 1987 and from late 2000 to 2008 and decreasing from late 1987 to late 2000.

47. (a) Critical number: $x = 29,500$
Increasing on $(0, 29,500)$
Decreasing on $(29,500, 50,000)$

(b) You should charge the price that yields sales of $x = 29,500$ bags of popcorn. Because the function changes from increasing to decreasing at $x = 29,500$, the maximum profit occurs at this value.

Section 3.2   *(page 184)*

Skills Warm Up   *(page 184)*

1. $0, \pm\frac{1}{2}$ **2.** $-2, 5$ **3.** 1   **4.** $0, 125$
5. $-4 \pm \sqrt{17}$ **6.** $1 \pm \sqrt{5}$
7. Negative   **8.** Positive   **9.** Positive
10. Negative   **11.** Increasing   **12.** Decreasing

---

1. Relative maximum: $(1, 5)$ **3.** Relative minimum: $(3, -9)$
5. Relative minimum: $(9, -2187)$ **7.** No relative extrema
9. Relative maximum: $(0, 15)$
Relative minimum: $(4, -17)$
11. Relative maximum: $(-1, 2)$; Relative minimum: $(0, 0)$
13.

Relative maximum: $(0, 0)$
Relative minimum: $(8, -8)$

15.

Relative maximum: $\left(-1, -\frac{3}{2}\right)$

17.
No relative extrema

19. Minimum: $(2, 2)$
Maximum: $(-1, 8)$

21. Maximum: $(0, 5)$
Minimum: $(3, -13)$

23. Minima: $(-1, -4), (2, -4)$
Maxima: $(0, 0), (3, 0)$

25. Maximum: $(2, 1)$
Minimum: $\left(0, \frac{1}{3}\right)$

27. Maxima: $\left(-1, \frac{1}{4}\right), \left(1, \frac{1}{4}\right)$
Minimum: $(0, 0)$

29. Maximum: $(-7, 4)$
Minimum: $(1, 0)$

31. 2, absolute maximum (and relative maximum)

33. 1, absolute maximum (and relative maximum);
2, absolute minimum (and relative minimum);
3, absolute maximum (and relative maximum)

35. Maximum: $(5, 7)$
Minimum: $(2.69, -5.55)$

37. Maximum: $(2, 2.\overline{6})$
Minima: $(0, 0), (3, 0)$

39. No relative maximum
Minimum: $(2, 12)$

41. Maximum: $\left(2, \frac{1}{2}\right)$
Minimum: $(0, 0)$

43. Answers will vary. Sample answer:

45. (a) Population tends to increase each year, so the minimum population occurred in 1790 and the maximum population occurred in 2010.

(b) Maximum population: 310.07 million
Minimum population: 3.69 million

(c) The minimum population was about 3.69 million in 1790 and the maximum population was about 310.07 million in 2010.

47. 82 units   **49.** 3500 units, $2.25

Section 3.3   *(page 193)*

Skills Warm Up   *(page 193)*

1. $f''(x) = 48x^2 - 54x$ **2.** $g''(s) = 12s^2 - 18s + 2$
3. $g''(x) = 56x^6 + 120x^4 + 72x^2 + 8$
4. $f''(x) = \dfrac{4}{9(x-3)^{2/3}}$ **5.** $h''(x) = \dfrac{190}{(5x-1)^3}$
6. $f''(x) = -\dfrac{42}{(3x+2)^3}$ **7.** $x = \pm\dfrac{\sqrt{3}}{3}$
8. $x = 0, 3$ **9.** $t = \pm4$ **10.** $x = 0, \pm5$

---

1. Sign of $f'(x)$ on $(0, 2)$ is positive.
Sign of $f''(x)$ on $(0, 2)$ is positive.

3. Sign of $f'(x)$ on $(0, 2)$ is negative.
　Sign of $f''(x)$ on $(0, 2)$ is negative.

5. Concave downward on $(-\infty, \infty)$

7. Concave upward on $(-\infty, 1)$
　Concave downward on $(1, \infty)$

9. Concave upward on $\left(-\infty, -\frac{1}{2}\right)$
　Concave downward on $\left(-\frac{1}{2}, \infty\right)$

11. Concave upward on $(-\infty, -2)$ and $(2, \infty)$
　Concave downward on $(-2, 2)$

13. Concave downward on $(-\infty, 3)$
　Concave upward on $(3, \infty)$
　Point of inflection: $(3, 0)$

15. Concave downward on $\left(-\infty, \frac{1}{2}\right)$
　Concave upward on $\left(\frac{1}{2}, \infty\right)$
　Point of inflection: $\left(\frac{1}{2}, -\frac{3}{2}\right)$

17. Concave upward on $(-\infty, \infty)$
　No inflection points

19. Concave downward on $(-\infty, 4)$
　Concave upward on $(4, \infty)$
　Inflection point: $(4, 16)$

21. Relative maximum: $(3, 9)$

23. Relative maximum: $(1, 3)$
　Relative minimum: $\left(\frac{7}{3}, \frac{49}{27}\right)$

25. Relative minimum: $(0, -3)$

27. Relative minimum: $(0, 1)$

29. Relative maximum: $(0, 3)$

31. Relative maximum: $(0, 4)$

33. No relative extrema

35. Relative maximum: $(2, 9)$
　Relative minimum: $(0, 5)$

37. Relative maximum: $(0, 0)$
　Relative minima: $(-0.5, -0.052)$, $(1, -0.\overline{3})$

39. Relative maximum: $(-2, 16)$
　Relative minimum: $(2, -16)$
　Point of inflection: $(0, 0)$

41. No relative maximum
　Relative minimum: $(4, 4)$
　Point of inflection:
$$\left(12, \frac{8\sqrt{3}}{3}\right)$$

43. Relative maximum: $(0, 0)$
　Relative minima: $(\pm 2, -4)$
　Points of inflection:
$$\left(\pm \frac{2\sqrt{3}}{3}, -\frac{20}{9}\right)$$

45. Relative maximum: $(-1, 0)$
　Relative minimum: $(1, -4)$
　Point of inflection: $(0, -2)$

47. Relative minimum: $(-2, -2)$
　No inflection points

49. Relative maximum: $(0, 4)$
　Points of inflection:
$$\left(\pm\frac{\sqrt{3}}{3}, 3\right)$$

51.

53.

55.

(a) f': Positive on $(-\infty, 0)$
　　f: Increasing on $(-\infty, 0)$
(b) f': Negative on $(0, \infty)$
　　f: Decreasing on $(0, \infty)$
(c) f': Not increasing
　　f: Not concave upward
(d) f': Decreasing on $(-\infty, \infty)$
　　f: Concave downward on $(-\infty, \infty)$

57. (a) f': Increasing on $(-\infty, \infty)$
　　(b) f: Concave upward on $(-\infty, \infty)$
　　(c) Relative minimum: $x = -2.5$
　　　　No inflection points

59. (a) f': Increasing on $(-\infty, 1)$
Decreasing on $(1, \infty)$
(b) f: Concave upward on $(-\infty, 1)$
Concave downward on $(1, \infty)$
(c) No relative extrema
Point of inflection: $x = 1$

61. $(200, 320)$ **63.** 8:30 P.M.

65.
Relative minimum: $(0, -5)$
Relative maximum: $(3, 8.5)$
Point of inflection:
$\left(\frac{2}{3}, -3.2963\right)$

When f' is positive, f is increasing. When f' is negative, f is decreasing. When f'' is positive, f is concave upward. When f'' is negative, f is concave downward.

67.
Relative maximum: $(0, 2)$
Points of inflection:
$(0.58, 1.5), (-0.58, 1.5)$

When f' is positive, f is increasing. When f' is negative, f is decreasing. When f'' is positive, f is concave upward. When f'' is negative, f is concave downward.

69. 120 units

71. (a)

(b) 1995
(c) 2007
(d) Greatest: 2003
Least: 2009

73. (a)

(b) Concave downward on $(5, 6.6517)$
Concave upward on $(6.6517, 16.4123)$
Concave downward on $(16.4123, 18)$
(c) Points of inflection: $(6.6517, 3291.0160)$ and $(16.4123, 3638.4227)$
(d) The first inflection point is where the change in the number of veterans receiving benefits starts to increase after it has been decreasing. The second inflection point is where the change in the number of veterans receiving benefits starts to decrease again.

75. Answers will vary.

Section 3.4   *(page 201)*

Skills Warm Up   *(page 201)*

1. $x + \frac{1}{2}y = 12$ **2.** $2xy = 24$ **3.** $xy = 24$
4. $\sqrt{(x_2 - x_1)^2 + (y_2 - y_1)^2} = 10$
5. $x = -3$ **6.** $x = -\frac{2}{3}, 1$ **7.** $x = \pm 5$
8. $x = 4$ **9.** $x = \pm 1$ **10.** $x = \pm 3$

1. $l = w = 25$ m   **3.** $l = w = 8$ ft
5. $x = 25$ ft, $y = \frac{100}{3}$ ft
7. (a) Proof
(b) $V_1 = 99$ in.^{3}
$V_2 = 125$ in.^{3}
$V_3 = 117$ in.^{3}
(c) 5 in. $\times$ 5 in. $\times$ 5 in.
9. (a) $l = w = h = 20$ in.
(b) 2400 in.^{2}
11. Width of rectangle: $\dfrac{100}{\pi} \approx 31.8$ m
Length of rectangle: 50 m
13. $l = w = 2\sqrt[3]{5} \approx 3.42$
$h = 4\sqrt[3]{5} \approx 6.84$
15. $V = 16$ in.^{3} **17.** 9 in. by 9 in.
19. Length: 3 units
Width: 1.5 units
21. Length: $5\sqrt{2}$ units
Width: $\dfrac{5\sqrt{2}}{2}$ units
23. Radius: about 1.51 in.
Height: about 3.02 in.
25. $(1, 1)$ **27.** $\left(3.5, \dfrac{\sqrt{14}}{2}\right)$ **29.** 18 in. $\times$ 18 in. $\times$ 36 in.
31. Radius: $\sqrt[3]{\dfrac{562.5}{\pi}} \approx 5.636$ ft
Height: about 22.545 ft
33. Radius of circle: $\dfrac{8}{\pi + 4}$
Side of square: $\dfrac{16}{\pi + 4}$
35. (a) $A(x) = \left(1 + \dfrac{4}{\pi}\right)x^2 - \dfrac{8}{\pi}x + \dfrac{4}{\pi}$
(b) $0 \le x \le 1$
(c)

(d) The total area is minimum when 2.24 feet is used for the square and 1.76 feet is used for the circle.
The total area is maximum when all 4 feet is used for the circle.
37. 4.75 weeks; 135 bushels; $3645

Quiz Yourself   *(page 204)*

1. Critical number: $x = 3$
Increasing on $(3, \infty)$
Decreasing on $(-\infty, 3)$

2. Critical numbers:
$x = -4, x = 0$
Increasing on
$(-\infty, -4)$ and $(0, \infty)$
Decreasing on $(-4, 0)$

3. Critical numbers: $x = 5$,
$x = -5$
Increasing on $(-5, 5)$
Decreasing on $(-\infty, -5)$
and $(5, \infty)$

4. Relative minimum: $(0, -5)$
Relative maximum: $(-2, -1)$
5. Relative minima: $(2, -13), (-2, -13)$
Relative maximum: $(0, 3)$
6. Relative minimum: $(0, 0)$
7. Minimum: $(-1, -9)$ **8.** Minimum: $(3, -54)$
Maximum: $(1, -5)$ Maximum: $(-3, 54)$

9. Minimum: $(0, 0)$
Maximum: $(1, 0.5)$

10. Point of inflection: $(2, -2)$
Concave downward on $(-\infty, 2)$
Concave upward on $(2, \infty)$
11. Points of inflection: $(-2, -80)$ and $(2, -80)$
Concave downward on $(-2, 2)$
Concave upward on $(-\infty, -2)$ and $(2, \infty)$
12. Relative minimum: $(1, 9)$
Relative maximum: $(-2, 36)$
13. Relative minimum: $(3, 12)$
Relative maximum: $(-3, -12)$
14. $120,000 (x = 120)$ **15.** 50 ft by 100 ft
16. (a) Increasing from 2000 to early 2008
Decreasing from early 2008 to 2009
(b) Early 2008; 2000

Section 3.5   *(page 212)*

> ### Skills Warm Up   *(page 212)*
>
> **1.** 1   **2.** $\frac{6}{5}$ **3.** 2   **4.** $\frac{1}{2}$
>
> **5.** $\dfrac{dC}{dx} = 1.2 + 0.006x$ **6.** $\dfrac{dP}{dx} = 0.02x + 11$
>
> **7.** $\dfrac{dP}{dx} = -1.4x + 7$ **8.** $\dfrac{dC}{dx} = 4.2 + 0.003x^2$
>
> **9.** $\dfrac{dR}{dx} = 14 - \dfrac{x}{1000}$ **10.** $\dfrac{dR}{dx} = 3.4 - \dfrac{x}{750}$

1. 2000 units   **3.** 200 units   **5.** 200 units
7. 50 units   **9.** $60   **11.** $40
13. 3 units

$$\overline{C}(3) = 17; \frac{dC}{dx} = 4x + 5; \text{ when } x = 3, \frac{dC}{dx} = 17$$

15. (a) $55   (b) $30.32
17. The maximum profit occurs when $s = 10$ (or $10,000$).
The point of diminishing returns occurs at $s = \frac{35}{6}$ (or 5833.33).
19. 350 players   **21.** $50
23. C = cost under water + cost on land
$= 25(5280)\sqrt{x^2 + 0.25} + 18(5280)(6 - x)$
$= 132,000\sqrt{x^2 + 0.25} + 570,240 - 95,040x$

The line should run from the power station to a point across the
river approximately 0.52 mile downstream.

$$\left(\text{Exact: } x = \frac{9\sqrt{301}}{301} \text{ mi}\right)$$

25. $v = 60$ mi/h
27. -1, unit elastic

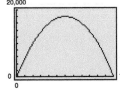

Elastic: $(0, 60)$
Inelastic: $(60, 120)$

29. $-\frac{2}{3}$, inelastic

Elastic: $\left(0, 83\frac{1}{3}\right)$
Inelastic: $\left(83\frac{1}{3}, 166\frac{2}{3}\right)$

CHAPTER 3

31. $-\frac{25}{23}$, elastic

Elastic: $(0, \infty)$

33. (a) Elastic: $[0, 500)$
  Unit elastic: $x = 500$
  Inelastic: $(500, 1000]$
(b) The revenue function increases on the interval $[0, 500)$, then is flat at 500, and decreases on the interval $(500, 1000]$.

35. 500 units $(x = 5)$

37. No; when $p = 8$, $x = 540$ and $\eta = -\frac{2}{3}$.
  Because $|\eta| = \frac{2}{3} < 1$, demand is inelastic.

39. (a) 2007
(b) 2001
(c) 2007: \$237.55 million/yr
   2001: \$17.78 million/yr
(d)

41. Proof   **43.** Answers will vary.

Section 3.6   *(page 223)*

Skills Warm Up   *(page 223)*

1. 3   **2.** 1   **3.** -11 **4.** 4   **5.** $-\frac{1}{4}$
6. -2 **7.** 0   **8.** 1
9. $\overline{C} = \dfrac{150}{x} + 3$ **10.** $\overline{C} = \dfrac{1900}{x} + 1.7 + 0.002x$

$\dfrac{dC}{dx} = 3$ $\dfrac{dC}{dx} = 1.7 + 0.004x$

11. $\overline{C} = 0.005x + 0.5 + \dfrac{1375}{x}$ **12.** $\overline{C} = \dfrac{760}{x} + 0.05$

$\dfrac{dC}{dx} = 0.01x + 0.5$ $\dfrac{dC}{dx} = 0.05$

1. Vertical asymptote: $x = 0$
  Horizontal asymptote: $y = 1$
3. Vertical asymptotes: $x = -1, x = 2$
  Horizontal asymptote: $y = 1$
5. Vertical asymptote: none
  Horizontal asymptote: $y = \frac{3}{2}$
7. Vertical asymptotes: $x = \pm 2$
  Horizontal asymptote: $y = \frac{1}{2}$
9. $x = 0, x = -3$ **11.** $x = -3$ **13.** $x = 4$ **15.** ∞
17. $-\infty$ **19.** ∞ **21.** 1   **23.** 7   **25.** $y = 2$
27. $y = 0$ **29.** No horizontal asymptote   **31.** $y = 5$

33. d   **34.** b   **35.** a   **36.** c
37. (a) ∞ (b) 5   (c) 0
39. (a) 0   (b) 1   (c) ∞

41.

x	10^0	10^1	10^2	10^3
$f(x)$	0.646	11.718	800.003	29,622.777

x	10^4	10^5	10^6
$f(x)$	980,000	31,422,776.6	998,000,000

$\displaystyle\lim_{x \to \infty} \sqrt{x^3 + 6} - 2x = \infty$

43.

x	10^0	10^1	10^2	10^3
$f(x)$	2.000	0.348	0.101	0.032

x	10^4	10^5	10^6
$f(x)$	0.010	0.003	0.001

$\displaystyle\lim_{x \to \infty} \frac{x + 1}{x\sqrt{x}} = 0$

45.   **47.**

49.   **51.**

53.   **55.**

57.   **59.**

61. (a) $\overline{C} = 1.15 + \dfrac{6000}{x}$

(b) $\overline{C}(600) = 11.15$; $\overline{C}(6000) = 2.15$

(c) \$1.15; The cost approaches \$1.15 as the number of units produced increases.

63. (a) $\overline{P} = 35.4 - \dfrac{15,000}{x}$

(b) $\overline{P}(1000) = \$20.40$; $\overline{P}(10,000) = \$33.90$;
$\overline{P}(100,000) = \$35.25$

(c) \$35.40; Explanations will vary.

65. (a) 25%: \$176 million; 50%: \$528 million;
75%: \$1584 million

(b) ∞; The limit does not exist, which means the cost increases without bound as the government approaches 100% seizure of the illegal drug entering the country.

67. (a)

n	1	2	3	4	5
P	0.5	0.74	0.82	0.86	0.89

n	6	7	8	9	10
P	0.91	0.92	0.93	0.94	0.95

(b) 1

(c)

The percent of correct responses approaches 100% as the number of times the task is performed increases.

Section 3.7   *(page 233)*

Skills Warm Up   *(page 233)*

1. Vertical asymptote: $x = 0$
Horizontal asymptote: $y = 0$

2. Vertical asymptote: $x = 2$
Horizontal asymptote: $y = 0$

3. Vertical asymptote: $x = -3$
Horizontal asymptote: $y = 40$

4. Vertical asymptotes: $x = 1, x = 3$
Horizontal asymptote: $y = 1$

5. Decreasing on $(-\infty, -2)$
Increasing on $(-2, \infty)$

6. Increasing on $(-\infty, -4)$
Decreasing on $(-4, \infty)$

7. Increasing on $(-\infty, -1)$ and $(1, \infty)$
Decreasing on $(-1, 1)$

8. Decreasing on $(-\infty, 0)$ and $\left(\sqrt[3]{2}, \infty\right)$
Increasing on $\left(0, \sqrt[3]{2}\right)$

9. Increasing on $(-\infty, 1)$ and $(1, \infty)$

10. Decreasing on $(-\infty, -3)$ and $\left(\frac{1}{3}, \infty\right)$
Increasing on $\left(-3, \frac{1}{3}\right)$

1.

3.

5.

7.

9.

11.

13.

15.

17.

19.

21.

23.

25.

27.

29.

31.

49.

33.

35.

37. Answers will vary.
Sample answer:

39. Answers will vary.
Sample answer:

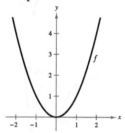

41. Answers will vary. Sample answer:

43. Answers will vary. Sample answer: $y = \dfrac{1}{x - 5}$

45. (a)

The model fits the data well.

(b) $1468.54

(c) No, because the benefits increase without bound as time approaches the year 2035 ($x = 35$), and the benefits are negative for the years past 2035.

47.

Absolute maximum: $(7, 82.28)$
Absolute minimum: $(1, 34.84)$
The maximum temperature of 82.28°F occurs in July.
The minimum temperature of 34.84°F occurs in January.

The rational function has the common factor $3 - x$ in the numerator and denominator. At $x = 3$, there is a hole in the graph, not a vertical asymptote.

51. (a) $f(x) = \dfrac{x^2 - 2x + 4}{x - 2} = \dfrac{x^2 - 2x}{x - 2} + \dfrac{4}{x - 2}$

$= \dfrac{x(x - 2)}{x - 2} + \dfrac{4}{x - 2} = x + \dfrac{4}{x - 2}$

(b)

The graphs become almost identical as you zoom out.

(c) A slant asymptote is neither horizontal nor vertical. It is diagonal, following $y = x$.

Section 3.8   (page 240)

Skills Warm Up   (page 240)

1. $\dfrac{dC}{dx} = 0.18x$ **2.** $\dfrac{dC}{dx} = 0.15$

3. $\dfrac{dR}{dx} = 1.25 + 0.03\sqrt{x}$ **4.** $\dfrac{dR}{dx} = 15.5 - 3.1x$

5. $\dfrac{dP}{dx} = -\dfrac{0.01}{\sqrt[3]{x^2}} + 1.4$ **6.** $\dfrac{dP}{dx} = -0.04x + 25$

7. $\dfrac{dA}{dx} = \dfrac{\sqrt{3}}{2}x$ **8.** $\dfrac{dA}{dx} = 12x$ **9.** $\dfrac{dC}{dr} = 2\pi$

10. $\dfrac{dP}{dw} = 4$ **11.** $\dfrac{dS}{dr} = 8\pi r$ **12.** $\dfrac{dP}{dx} = 2 + \sqrt{2}$

13. $A = \pi r^2$ **14.** $A = x^2$

15. $V = x^3$ **16.** $V = \frac{4}{3}\pi r^3$

1. $dy = 0.6$ **3.** $dy = -0.04$ **5.** $dy = 0.075$
$\Delta y = 0.6305$ $\Delta y \approx -0.0394$ $\Delta y \approx 0.0745$

7.

$dx = \Delta x$	dy	Δy	$\Delta y - dy$	$\dfrac{dy}{\Delta y}$
1.000	4.000	5.000	1.0000	0.8000
0.500	2.000	2.2500	0.2500	0.8889
0.100	0.400	0.4100	0.0100	0.9756
0.010	0.040	0.0401	0.0001	0.9975
0.001	0.004	0.0040	0.0000	1.0000

9.

$dx = \Delta x$	dy	Δy	$\Delta y - dy$	$\dfrac{dy}{\Delta y}$
1.000	-0.25000	-0.13889	0.11111	1.79999
0.500	-0.12500	-0.09000	0.03500	1.38889
0.100	-0.02500	-0.02324	0.00176	1.07573
0.010	-0.00250	-0.00248	0.00002	1.00806
0.001	-0.00025	-0.00025	0.00000	1.00000

11.

$dx = \Delta x$	dy	Δy	$\Delta y - dy$	$\dfrac{dy}{\Delta y}$
1.000	0.14865	0.12687	-0.02178	1.17167
0.500	0.07433	0.06823	-0.00610	1.08940
0.100	0.01487	0.01459	-0.00028	1.01919
0.010	0.00149	0.00148	-0.00001	1.00676
0.001	0.00015	0.00015	0.00000	1.00000

13. $5.20   **15.** $7.50   **17.** $-$1250   **19.** $dy = 24x^3\,dx$

21. $dy = 6x\,dx$ **23.** $dy = 12(4x - 1)^2\,dx$

25. $dy = -\dfrac{3}{(2x - 1)^2}\,dx$ **27.** $dy = \dfrac{-x}{\sqrt{9 - x^2}}\,dx$

29. $y = 28x + 37$
For $\Delta x = -0.01, f(x + \Delta x) = -19.281302$ and
$y(x + \Delta x) = -19.28$
For $\Delta x = 0.01, f(x + \Delta x) = -18.721298$ and
$y(x + \Delta x) = -18.72$

31. $y = x$
For $\Delta x = -0.01, f(x + \Delta x) = -0.009999$ and
$y(x + \Delta x) = -0.01$
For $\Delta x = 0.01, f(x + \Delta x) = 0.009999$ and
$y(x + \Delta x) = 0.01$

33. (a) $dP = \$1160$ (b) Actual: $1122.50

35. (a) $71.50   (b) $40.00

37. Approximately 19 deer

39. $R = -\frac{1}{3}x^2 + 100x$; $6

41. $\pm\frac{3}{4}$ in.^{2} **43.** True
2.08%

Review Exercises for Chapter 3   *(page 246)*

1. $x = 1$ **3.** $x = -3, x = 3$ **5.** $x = 1, x = \frac{7}{3}$

7. Critical number: $x = -\frac{1}{2}$
Increasing on $\left(-\frac{1}{2}, \infty\right)$
Decreasing on $\left(-\infty, -\frac{1}{2}\right)$

9. Critical numbers: $x = 0, x = 4$
Increasing on $(0, 4)$
Decreasing on $(-\infty, 0)$ and $(4, \infty)$

11. Critical number: $x = 1$
Increasing on $(1, \infty)$
Decreasing on $(-\infty, 1)$

13. The only critical number is $t \approx -10.85$. Any $t > -10.85$ produces a positive dR/dt, so the sales were increasing from 2004 to 2009.

15. Relative maximum: $(0, -2)$
Relative minimum: $(1, -4)$

17. Relative minimum: $(8, -52)$

19. Relative maxima: $(-1, 1), (1, 1)$
Relative minimum: $(0, 0)$

21. Relative maximum: $(0, 6)$

23. Relative maximum: $(0, 0)$
Relative minimum: $(4, 8)$

25. Maximum: $(0, 6)$
Minimum: $\left(-\frac{5}{2}, -\frac{1}{4}\right)$

27. Maxima: $(-2, 17), (4, 17)$
Minima: $(-4, -15), (2, -15)$

29. Maximum: $(1, 1)$
Minimum: $(9, -3)$

31. Maximum: $(1, 1)$
Minimum: $(-1, -1)$

33. $r \approx 1.58$ in.

35. Concave upward on $(2, \infty)$
Concave downward on $(-\infty, 2)$

37. Concave upward on $\left(-\dfrac{2\sqrt{3}}{3}, \dfrac{2\sqrt{3}}{3}\right)$
Concave downward on $\left(-\infty, -\dfrac{2\sqrt{3}}{3}\right)$ and $\left(\dfrac{2\sqrt{3}}{3}, \infty\right)$

39. $(0, 0), (4, -128)$

41. $(0, 0), (1.0652, 4.5244), (2.5348, 3.5246)$

43. No relative extrema

45. Relative maximum: $\left(-\sqrt{3}, 6\sqrt{3}\right)$
Relative minimum: $\left(\sqrt{3}, -6\sqrt{3}\right)$

47. Relative maxima: $\left(-\dfrac{\sqrt{2}}{2}, \dfrac{1}{2}\right), \left(\dfrac{\sqrt{2}}{2}, \dfrac{1}{2}\right)$
Relative minimum: $(0, 0)$

49. $\left(50, 166\frac{2}{3}\right)$ **51.** $l = w = 15$ m   **53.** 144 in.^{3}

55. $x = 900$ **57.** $x = 150$ **59.** (a) $24   (b) $8

61. (a) For $0 < x < 750, |\eta| > 1$ and the demand is elastic.
For $750 < x < 1500, |\eta| < 1$ and the demand is inelastic.
For $x = 750$, the demand has unit elasticity.
(b) From 0 to 750 units, revenue is increasing.
From 750 to 1500 units, revenue does not increase.

63. $x = -7, x = 0$ **65.** $x = -\frac{1}{2}$ **67.** $-\infty$

69. ∞ **71.** $y = \frac{2}{3}$ **73.** $y = 0$

75. (a) $\overline{C} = 0.75 + \dfrac{4000}{x}$

(b) $\overline{C}(100) = 40.75$

$\overline{C}(1000) = 4.75$

(c) The limit is 0.75. As more and more units are produced, the average cost per unit will approach $0.75.

77. (a) 20%: $62.5 million

50%: $250 million

90%: $2250 million

(b) The limit is ∞, meaning that as the percent gets very close to 100, the cost grows without bound.

79.

81.

83.

85.

87.

89.

91. (a)

The model fits the data well.

(b) ≈ 2434 bacteria

(c) Answers will vary.

93. $dy = 0.08, \Delta y = 0.0802$ **95.** $dy = -2.1, \Delta y = -2.191$

97. $800   **99.** $15.25   **101.** $\approx$ $4.52

103. $dy = 1.5x^2\, dx$ **105.** $dy = 18x(3x^2 - 2)^2\, dx$

107. $dy = -\dfrac{7}{(x + 5)^2}\, dx$

109. (a) $164

(b) $163.2, a difference of $0.80.

111. $B = 0.1\sqrt{5w}$

$\dfrac{dB}{dw} = \dfrac{0.05\sqrt{5}}{\sqrt{w}}$

$\Delta B \approx dB = \dfrac{0.05\sqrt{5}}{\sqrt{w}}\, dw$

$= \dfrac{0.05\sqrt{5}}{\sqrt{90}}(5)$

$\approx 0.059\ \text{m}^2$

Test Yourself   *(page 250)*

1. Critical number: $x = 0$

Increasing on $(0, \infty)$

Decreasing on $(-\infty, 0)$

2. Critical numbers: $x = -2, x = 2$

Increasing on $(-\infty, -2)$ and $(2, \infty)$

Decreasing on $(-2, 2)$

3. Critical number: $x = 5$

Increasing on $(5, \infty)$

Decreasing on $(-\infty, 5)$

4. Relative minimum: $(3, -14)$

Relative maximum: $(-3, 22)$

5. Relative minima: $(-1, -7)$ and $(1, -7)$

Relative maximum: $(0, -5)$

6. Relative maximum: $(0, 2.5)$

7. Minimum: $(-3, -1)$ **8.** Minimum: $(0, 0)$

Maximum: $(0, 8)$ Maximum: $(2.25, 9)$

9. Minimum: $\left(2\sqrt{3}, 2\sqrt{3}\right)$

Maximum: $(1, 6.5)$

10. Concave upward: $(2, \infty)$

Concave downward: $(-\infty, 2)$

11. Concave upward: $\left(-\infty, -\dfrac{2\sqrt{2}}{3}\right)$ and $\left(\dfrac{2\sqrt{2}}{3}, \infty\right)$

Concave downward: $\left(-\dfrac{2\sqrt{2}}{3}, \dfrac{2\sqrt{2}}{3}\right)$

12. No point of inflection

The graph is concave upward on its entire domain.

13. Concave upward: $(-\infty, -3)$ and $(3, \infty)$

Concave downward: $(-3, 3)$

Points of inflection: $(-3, -175)$ and $(3, -175)$

14. Relative minimum: $(6, -166)$

Relative maximum: $(-2, 90)$

15. Relative minimum: $(3, -97.2)$

Relative maximum: $(-3, 97.2)$

16. Vertical asymptote: $x = 5$

Horizontal asymptote: $y = 3$

17. Horizontal asymptote: $y = 2$

18. Vertical asymptote: $x = 1$

19.

20.

21.

22. $dy = 10x \, dx$

23. $dy = \dfrac{-4}{(x+3)^2} \, dx$ **24.** $dy = 3(x+4)^2 \, dx$

25. For $0 \le x < 350$, $|\eta| > 1$ and the demand is elastic.

For $350 < x \le 700$, $|\eta| < 1$ and the demand is inelastic.

For $x = 350$, the demand has unit elasticity.

Chapter 4

Section 4.1   *(page 256)*

Skills Warm Up   *(page 256)*

1. Horizontal shift to the left two units

2. Reflection about the x-axis

3. Vertical shift down one unit

4. Reflection about the y-axis

5. Horizontal shift to the right one unit

6. Vertical shift up two units

7. 125   **8.** 22.63   **9.** 9   **10.** $\frac{1}{125}$

11. $\frac{1}{2}$ **12.** $\frac{25}{64}$ **13.** 5   **14.** $\frac{4}{3}$ **15.** $-9, 1$

16. $2 \pm 2\sqrt{2}$ **17.** $1, -5$ **18.** $\frac{1}{2}, 1$

1. (a) 3125   (b) $\frac{1}{5}$ (c) 625   (d) $\frac{1}{125}$

3. (a) $\frac{1}{5}$ (b) 27   (c) 5   (d) 4096

5. 2 g

7.

9.

11.

13.

15.

17.

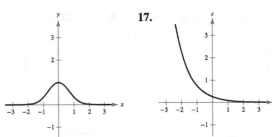

19. (a) $P(23) \approx 320.26$ million

(b) $P(30) \approx 343.36$ million

21. (a) $V(5) \approx \$80,634.95$ (b) $V(20) \approx \$161,269.89$

23. \$36.93

25. $V(t) = 28,000\left(\frac{3}{4}\right)^t$

$V(4) = 28,000\left(\frac{3}{4}\right)^4 \approx 8859.38$

27. (a)

Year	2001	2002	2003	2004
Actual	37,188	38,221	39,165	40,201
Model	36,966	37,998	39,058	40,148

Year	2005	2006	2007	2008
Actual	40,520	41,746	43,277	46,025
Model	41,268	42,419	43,603	44,819

The model fits the data well. Explanations will vary.

(b)

(c) 2014

Section 4.2   *(page 264)*

Skills Warm Up   *(page 264)*

1. Continuous on $(-\infty, \infty)$

2. Discontinuous at $x = \pm 2$

3. Discontinuous at $x = \pm\sqrt{3}$

4. Removable discontinuity at $x = 4$

5. $y = 0$ **6.** $y = 0$ **7.** $y = 4$ **8.** $y = \frac{1}{2}$

9. $y = \frac{3}{2}$ **10.** $y = 6$ **11.** $y = 0$ **12.** $y = 0$

1. (a) e^7 (b) e^{12} (c) $\dfrac{1}{e^6}$ (d) 1

3. (a) e^5 (b) $e^{5/2}$ (c) e^6 (d) e^7

5. f   **6.** e   **7.** d   **8.** b   **9.** c   **10.** a

11.

13.

15.

17.

Horizontal asymptote: $N = 0$
Continuous on the entire
real number line

19.

Horizontal asymptote: $g = 0$
Continuous on the entire
real number line

21.

No horizontal asymptotes
Continuous on the entire
real number line

23.

Horizontal asymptote: $y = 1$
Discontinuous at $x = 0$

25. (a)

The graph of $g(x) = e^{x-2}$ is
shifted horizontally two units
to the right.

(b)

The graph of $h(x) = -\frac{1}{2}e^x$
decreases at a rate slower
than the rate at which the
graph of $f(x) = e^x$ increases.

(c)

The graph of $q(x) = e^x + 3$
is shifted vertically three
units upward.

27.

n	1	2	4	12
A	1343.92	1346.86	1348.35	1349.35

n	365	Continuous compounding
A	1349.84	1349.86

29.

n	1	2	4	12
A	2191.12	2208.04	2216.72	2222.58

n	365	Continuous compounding
A	2225.44	2225.54

31.

t	1	10	20
P	96,078.94	67,032.00	44,932.90

t	30	40	50
P	30,119.42	20,189.65	13,533.53

33.

t	1	10	20
P	95,132.82	60,716.10	36,864.45

t	30	40	50
P	22,382.66	13,589.88	8251.24

35. $107,311.12
37. (a) 9%   (b) 9.20%   (c) 9.31%   (d) 9.38%
39. $6450.04
41. (a) $849.53   (b) $421.12   (c) $\lim\limits_{x\to\infty} p = 0$
43. (a) 0.1535   (b) 0.4866   (c) 0.8111
45. (a) The model fits the data well.
(b) $y = 637.11x + 5021.1$; The linear model fits the data
well, but the exponential model fits the data better.
(c) Exponential model: 2016
Linear model: 2021
47. (a)

(b) Yes, $\lim\limits_{t\to\infty} \dfrac{925}{1 + e^{-0.3t}} = 925$

(c) $\lim\limits_{t\to\infty} \dfrac{1000}{1 + e^{-0.3t}} = 1000$

Models similar to this logistic growth model, where
$y = \dfrac{a}{1 + be^{-ct}}$ have a limit of a as $t \to \infty$.

49. (a) 0.536   (b) 0.666

(c)   11

(d) Yes, $\lim\limits_{n\to\infty} \dfrac{0.83}{1 + e^{-0.2n}} = 0.83$

51. Amounts earned:

(a) \$5267.71   (b) \$5255.81   (c) \$5243.23

You should choose the certificate of deposit in part (a) because it earns more money than the others.

Section 4.3   *(page 273)*

Skills Warm Up   *(page 273)*

1. $\dfrac{1}{2}e^x(2x^2 - 1)$ **2.** $\dfrac{e^x(x + 1)}{x}$ **3.** $e^x(x - e^x)$

4. $e^{-x}(e^{2x} - x)$ **5.** $-\dfrac{6}{7x^3}$ **6.** $6x - \dfrac{1}{6}$

7. $6(2x^2 - x + 6)$ **8.** $\dfrac{t + 2}{2t^{3/2}}$

9. Relative maximum: $\left(-\dfrac{4\sqrt{3}}{3}, \dfrac{16\sqrt{3}}{9}\right)$

Relative minimum: $\left(\dfrac{4\sqrt{3}}{3}, -\dfrac{16\sqrt{3}}{9}\right)$

10. Relative maximum: $(0, 5)$

Relative minima: $(-1, 4), (1, 4)$

---

1. 0   **3.** $5e^{5x}$ **5.** $-2xe^{-x^2}$ **7.** $\dfrac{2}{x^3}e^{-1/x^2}$

9. $e^{4x}(4x^2 + 2x + 4)$ **11.** $-\dfrac{6(e^x - e^{-x})}{(e^x + e^{-x})^4}$

13. $-\dfrac{2e^x}{(e^x - 1)^2}$ **15.** $xe^x + e^x + 4e^{-x}$ **17.** 4   **19.** -3

21. $y = 2x - 3$ **23.** $y = \dfrac{4}{e^2}$ **25.** $y = 24x + 8$

27. $\dfrac{dy}{dx} = \dfrac{10 - e^y}{xe^y + 3}$ **29.** $\dfrac{dy}{dx} = \dfrac{e^{-x}(x^2 - 2x) + y}{4y - x}$

31. $6(3e^{3x} + 2e^{-2x})$ **33.** $32e^{4x}(x + 1)$

35.

No relative extrema

No points of inflection

Horizontal asymptote to the right: $y = \dfrac{1}{2}$

Horizontal asymptote to the left: $y = 0$

Vertical asymptote: $x \approx -0.693$

37.

Relative minimum: $(0, 0)$

Relative maximum: $\left(2, \dfrac{4}{e^2}\right)$

Points of inflection:

$\left(2 - \sqrt{2}, 0.191\right)$,

$\left(2 + \sqrt{2}, 0.384\right)$

Horizontal asymptote to the right: $y = 0$

39. $x = -\dfrac{1}{3}$ **41.** $x = 9$

43. (a)

(b) $-\$5028.84/\text{yr}$

(c) $-\$406.89/\text{yr}$

(d) $V = -1497.2t + 15,000$

(e) In the exponential function, the initial rate of depreciation is greater than in the linear model. The linear model has a constant rate of depreciation.

45. (a)

(b and c) 2000: -0.59 million people/yr

2004: 1.83 million people/yr

2009: -12.44 million people/yr

47. (a) \$433.31 per year

(b) \$890.22 per year

(c) \$21,839.26 per year

49. (a) $f(x) = \dfrac{1}{116\sqrt{2\pi}}e^{-(x - 516)^2/26,912}$

(b)

(c) $f'(x) = \dfrac{-1}{1,560,896\sqrt{2\pi}}(x - 516)e^{-(x - 516)^2/26,912}$

(d) Answers will vary.

51.

As σ increases, the graph becomes flatter.

53. Proof; maximum: $\left(0, \dfrac{1}{\sigma\sqrt{2\pi}}\right)$; answers will vary.

Sample answer:

Quiz Yourself   *(page 275)*

1. 1024   **2.** 216   **3.** 27   **4.** $\sqrt{15}$
5. e^7 **6.** $e^{11/3}$ **7.** e^6 **8.** e^3
9.   **10.**

11.   **12.**

13.   **14.**

15. 22.69 grams   **16.** $31.06
17. (a) $3571.02   (b) $3572.83   (c) $3573.74
18. $10,379.21   **19.** $5e^{5x}$ **20.** e^{x-4} **21.** $5e^{x+2}$
22. $e^x(2 - x)$ **23.** $y = -2x + 1$
24.

Relative maximum: $(4, 8e^{-2})$
Relative minimum: $(0, 0)$
Points of inflection:
$(4 - 2\sqrt{2}, 0.382)$,
$(4 + 2\sqrt{2}, 0.767)$
Horizontal asymptote to the right: $y = 0$

Section 4.4   *(page 282)*

Skills Warm Up   *(page 282)*

1. $f^{-1}(x) = \frac{1}{5}x$ **2.** $f^{-1}(x) = x + 6$
3. $f^{-1}(x) = \frac{x - 2}{3}$ **4.** $f^{-1}(x) = \frac{4}{3}(x + 9)$
5. $x > -4$ **6.** Any real number x
7. $x < -1$ or $x > 1$ **8.** $x > 5$
9. $3462.03   **10.** $3374.65

1. $e^{0.6931\ldots} = 2$ **3.** $e^{-1.6094\ldots} = 0.2$ **5.** $\ln 1 = 0$
7. $\ln(0.0498\ldots) = -3$ **9.** c   **10.** d
11. b   **12.** a
13.   **15.**

17.

19. x^2 **21.** $5x + 2$ **23.** $2x - 1$
25. $\ln 2 - \ln 3$ **27.** $\ln x + \ln y + \ln z$
29. $\frac{1}{3}\ln(2x + 7)$ **31.** $\ln z + 2\ln(z - 1)$
33. $\ln 3 + \ln x + \ln(x + 1) - 2\ln(2x + 1)$
35. Answers will vary.   **37.** Answers will vary.

39. (a) 1.7917   (b) 0.4055   (c) 4.3944   (d) 0.5493
41. $\ln \dfrac{x - 2}{x + 2}$ **43.** $\ln \dfrac{x^3 y^2}{z^4}$ **45.** $\dfrac{\ln(x - 6)^4}{\sqrt{3x + 1}}$
47. $\ln\left[\dfrac{x(x + 3)}{x + 4}\right]^3$ **49.** $\ln\left[\dfrac{x(x^2 + 1)}{x + 1}\right]^{3/2}$
51. $x = 4$ **53.** $x = \ln 4 - 1 \approx 0.3863$
55. $t = \dfrac{\ln 7 - \ln 3}{-0.2} \approx -4.2365$
57. $x = \frac{1}{2}\left(1 + \ln\frac{3}{2}\right) \approx 0.7027$ **59.** $x = 1$
61. $x = \dfrac{e^{2.4}}{2} \approx 5.5116$ **63.** $x = e^3 \approx 20.0855$
65. $x = \dfrac{6e^3}{e^3 - 1} \approx 6.314$ **67.** $x = \dfrac{\ln 15}{2 \ln 5} \approx 0.8413$
69. $t = \dfrac{\ln 2}{\ln 1.07} \approx 10.2448$
71. $t = \dfrac{\ln 3}{12 \ln[1 + (0.07/12)]} \approx 15.7402$
73. (a) 8.15 yr   (b) 12.92 yr
75. (a) 14.21 yr   (b) 13.89 yr   (c) 13.86 yr   (d) 13.86 yr
77. (a) $P(29) \approx 235{,}576$ (b) 2020
79. 9395 yr   **81.** 12,484 yr
83. (a) 80   (b) 57.5   (c) 10 mo
85. (a) ≈ 896 units   (b) ≈ 136 units

87.

x	y	$\dfrac{\ln x}{\ln y}$	$\ln \dfrac{x}{y}$	$\ln x - \ln y$
1	2	0	-0.6931	-0.6931
3	4	0.7925	-0.2877	-0.2877
10	5	1.4307	0.6931	0.6931
4	0.5	-2	2.0794	2.0794

89.

91. False. $f(x) = \ln x$ is undefined for $x \le 0$.

93. False. $f\left(\dfrac{x}{2}\right) = f(x) - f(2)$ **95.** False. $u = v^2$

97. Options (b) and (c) will give you the same amount, but it makes more sense to double the rate, not the time. So option (b) is better than option (c). If you are looking for a long-term investment, choose option (a).

99.

Answers will vary.

Section 4.5   (page 291)

Skills Warm Up   (page 291)

1. $2\ln(x + 1)$ **2.** $\ln x + \ln(x + 1)$

3. $\ln x - \ln(x + 1)$ **4.** $3[\ln x - \ln(x - 3)]$

5. $\ln 4 + \ln x + \ln(x - 7) - 2\ln x$

6. $3\ln x + \ln(x + 1)$

7. $-\dfrac{y}{x + 2y}$ **8.** $\dfrac{3 - 2xy + y^2}{x(x - 2y)}$

9. $-12x + 2$ **10.** $-\dfrac{6}{x^4}$

---

1. $\dfrac{2}{x}$ **3.** $\dfrac{2x}{x^2 + 3}$ **5.** $\dfrac{1}{2(x - 4)}$ **7.** $\dfrac{4}{x}(\ln x)^3$

9. $2\ln x + 2$ **11.** $\dfrac{2x^2 - 1}{x(x^2 - 1)}$ **13.** $\dfrac{1}{x(x + 1)}$

15. $\dfrac{2}{3(x^2 - 1)}$ **17.** $-\dfrac{4}{x(4 + x^2)}$ **19.** $e^{-x}\left(\dfrac{1}{x} - \ln x\right)$

21. $\dfrac{e^x - e^{-x}}{e^x + e^{-x}}$ **23.** 2   **25.** -3 **27.** 2   **29.** 1.404

31. 5.585   **33.** -0.631 **35.** $(\ln 3)3^x$ **37.** $\dfrac{1}{x \ln 2}$

39. $(2\ln 4)4^{2x-3}$ **41.** $\dfrac{2x + 6}{(x^2 + 6x)\ln 10}$ **43.** $2^x(1 + x \ln 2)$

45. $y = 3x - 3 = 3(x - 1)$ **47.** $y = 2x - e$

49. $y = -\dfrac{8}{5}x - 4$ **51.** $y = \dfrac{1}{27\ln 3}x - \dfrac{1}{\ln 3} + 3$

53. $\dfrac{2xy}{3 - 2y^2}$ **55.** $\dfrac{y(1 - 6x^2)}{1 + y}$ **57.** $y = x - 1$

59. $\dfrac{1}{2x}$ **61.** $x(6\ln x + 5)$ **63.** $(\ln 5)^2\, 5^x$

65. $\dfrac{d\beta}{dI} = \dfrac{10}{(\ln 10)I}$, so for $I = 10^{-4}$, the rate of change is about 43,429.4 db/W/cm^2.

67.

Relative minimum: $(1, 1)$

69.

Discontinuity: $x = 1$
Relative minimum: (e, e)
Point of inflection: $\left(e^2, \dfrac{e^2}{2}\right)$

71.

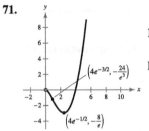

Relative minimum: $\left(4e^{-1/2}, \dfrac{-8}{e}\right)$

Point of inflection: $\left(4e^{-3/2}, \dfrac{-24}{e^3}\right)$

73. $-\dfrac{1}{p}, -\dfrac{1}{10}$

75. $p = 1000e^{-x}$

$\dfrac{dp}{dx} = -1000e^{-x}$

At $p = 10$, rate of change $= -10$.

$\dfrac{dp}{dx}$ and $\dfrac{dx}{dp}$ are reciprocals of each other.

77. (a) $\overline{C} = \dfrac{500 + 300x - 300\ln x}{x}$

(b) Minimum of 279.15 at $e^{8/3}$

79. (a)

(b) 19.45 (thousand) per year

81. (a)

(b) $t \approx 30$; \$503,434.80   (c) $t \approx 20$; \$386,685.60

(d) ≈ -0.081; ≈ -0.029

(e) For a higher monthly payment, the term is shorter, and the total amount paid is smaller.

CHAPTER 4

83. (a) $s(t) = 84.66 - 11.00 \ln t$

(b)

The model fits the data well.

(c) -5.5; The average score is decreasing at a rate of 5.5 points per month after 2 months.

Section 4.6   *(page 299)*

Skills Warm Up   *(page 299)*

1. $-\dfrac{1}{4} \ln 2$ **2.** $\dfrac{1}{5} \ln \dfrac{10}{3}$ **3.** $-\dfrac{\ln(25/16)}{0.01}$

4. $-\dfrac{\ln(11/16)}{0.02}$ **5.** $7.36e^{0.23t}$ **6.** $1.296e^{0.072t}$

7. $-33.6e^{-1.4t}$ **8.** $-0.025e^{-0.001t}$ **9.** 4

10. 12 **11.** $2x + 1$ **12.** $x^2 + 1$

---

1. $y = 2e^{0.1014t}$ **3.** $y = 4e^{-0.4159t}$

5. $y = 4\sqrt[3]{2}e^{((\ln 0.5)/3)t}$ **7.** $y = 10e^{2t}$, exponential growth

9. $y = 30e^{-4t}$, exponential decay

11. *Amount after 1000 years:* 6.48 g
Amount after 10,000 years: 0.13 g

13. *Initial quantity:* 6.73 g
Amount after 1000 years: 5.96 g

15. *Initial quantity:* 2.16 g
Amount after 10,000 years: 1.62 g

17. 68%   **19.** 15,642 yr

21. $k_1 = \dfrac{\ln 4}{12} \approx 0.1155$, so $y_1 = 5e^{0.1155t}$.

$k_2 = \dfrac{1}{6}$, so $y_2 = 5(2)^{t/6}$.

Explanations will vary.

23. (a) 1350   (b) $\dfrac{5 \ln 2}{\ln 3} \approx 3.15$ hr

(c) No. Answers will vary.

25. *Time to double:* 5.78 yr
Amount after 10 years: $3320.12
Amount after 25 years: $20,085.54

27. *Annual rate:* 8.66%
Amount after 10 years: $1783.04
Amount after 25 years: $6535.95

29. *Annual rate:* 9.50%
Time to double: 7.30 yr
Amount after 25 years: $5375.51

31. *Initial investment:* $6376.28
Time to double: 15.40 yr
Amount after 25 years: $19,640.33

33. $49,787.07

35. (a) Answers will vary.   (b) Answers will vary.

37. Answers will vary.

39. (a) $y = 21{,}500 - 3950x$

(b) $y = 21{,}500e^{-0.229x}$

(c) Linear Model:
after 1 year: $17,550
after 4 years: $5700
Exponential Model:
after 1 year: $17,099.56
after 4 years: $8602.50

(d)

The exponential model depreciates slightly faster.

(e) After the second year, a buyer would gain an advantage by using the linear model, because it yields a lower value for the vehicle. A seller would want to use the exponential model, because it yields a higher value for the vehicle.

41. (a) $C = 30$
$k = \ln\left(\dfrac{1}{6}\right) \approx -1.7918$

(b) $30e^{-0.35836} = 20.9646$ thousand, or 20,965 units

(c)

43. About 36 days

45. (a) $C \approx 81.090$, $k = \dfrac{\ln(45/40)}{-200} \approx -0.0005889$

(b) $x = 1/0.0005889 \approx 1698$ units, $p \approx \$29.83$

47. Answers will vary.

Review Exercises for Chapter 4   *(page 306)*

1. (a) 16,384   (b) 117,649   (c) 0.0625   (d) 81

3.

5.

7.

9. (a) 5894.39 (thousand)   (b) 6203.76 (thousand)

11. (a) $69,295.66   (b) $233,081.88

13. (a) e^{10} (b) $\dfrac{1}{e^2}$ (c) $e^{11/2}$ (d) $\dfrac{1}{e^8}$

15. 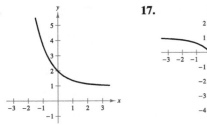 **17.**

19.

n	1	2	4	12
A	\$1216.65	\$1218.99	\$1220.19	\$1221.00

n	365	Continuous compounding
A	\$1221.39	\$1221.40

21.

n	1	2	4	12
A	4231.80	4244.33	4250.73	4255.03

n	365	Continuous compounding
A	4257.13	4257.20

23. b   **25.** (a) 6%   (b) 6.09%   (c) 6.14%   (d) 6.17%
27. \$10,338.10
29. (a) \$8276.81   (b) \$7697.12   (c) \$7500
31. (a) The model fits the data very well.
(b) $y = 116.85x + 111.1$
The linear model fits the data moderately well.
The exponential model is a better fit.
(c) Exponential: \$4357.50 (million)
Linear: \$1863.85 (million)
33. (a) $P \approx 1049$ fish
(b) 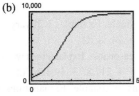   13 months
(c) Yes, P approaches 10,000 fish as t approaches ∞.
35. $8xe^{x^2}$ **37.** $\dfrac{1 - 2x}{e^{2x}}$ **39.** $-\dfrac{10e^{2x}}{(1 + e^{2x})^2}$
41. $y = 3 - x$ **43.** $y = \dfrac{x}{e}$
45.
Relative minimum: $(-3, -1.344)$
Inflection points: $(0, 0)$, $(-3 + \sqrt{3}, -0.574)$,
and $(-3 - \sqrt{3}, -0.933)$
Horizontal asymptote: $y = 0$

47.   Relative maximum: $(-1, -2.718)$
Horizontal asymptote: $y = 0$
Vertical asymptote: $x = 0$

49. $e^{2.4849} \approx 12$ **51.** $\ln 4.4816 \approx 1.5$
53.   **55.**
57. $\ln x + \frac{1}{2}\ln(x - 1)$ **59.** $2\ln x - 3\ln(x + 1)$
61. $3[\ln(1 - x) - \ln 3 - \ln x]$
63. $\ln(2x^2 - x - 15)$ **65.** $4\ln\left(\dfrac{x^5 - x^2}{x - 5}\right)$
67. 3   **69.** $e^3 \approx 20.09$ **71.** 1
73. $\dfrac{3 + \sqrt{13}}{2} \approx 3.3028$ **75.** $-\dfrac{\ln(0.25)}{1.386} \approx 1.0002$
77. $\frac{1}{2}(\ln 6 + 1) \approx 1.3959$ **79.** $\dfrac{\ln 1.1}{\ln 1.21} = 0.5$
81. (a) ≈ 28.07 years   (b) ≈ 27.75 years
(c) ≈ 27.73 years   (d) ≈ 27.73 years
83. (a) 75   (b) 65.34   (c) ≈ 11 months
85. $\dfrac{2}{x}$ **87.** $\dfrac{1}{x} + \dfrac{1}{x - 1} - \dfrac{1}{x - 2} = \dfrac{x^2 - 4x + 2}{x(x - 2)(x - 1)}$
89. 2   **91.** $\dfrac{1 - 3\ln x}{x^4}$ **93.** $\dfrac{4x}{3(x^2 - 2)}$
95. $\dfrac{2}{x} + \dfrac{1}{2(x + 1)}$ **97.** $\dfrac{1}{1 + e^x}$ **99.** 2   **101.** 0
103. 1.594   **105.** 1.500   **107.** $(2\ln 5)5^{2x+1}$
109. $\dfrac{2}{(2x - 1)\ln 3}$ **111.** $\dfrac{-1}{\ln 10} \cdot \dfrac{1}{x} = -\dfrac{1}{x\ln 10}$
113.   **115.**
No relative extrema   No relative extrema
No points of inflection   No points of inflection
117. 2005: 256.4 (million)
2008: 160.25 (million)
119. $y = 3e^{-0.27465t}$ **121.** 5.19 g; 0.10 g
123. 20.18 g; 17.88 g   **125.** 2.47 g; 1.85 g
127. 8.66 yr, \$1335.32, \$4433.43
129. 2%, 34.66 yr, \$24,730.82
131. (a) $D = 500e^{-0.38376t}$
(b) 107.72 milligrams per milliliter

CHAPTER 4

Test Yourself   *(page 310)*

1. 1   **2.** $\frac{1}{256}$ **3.** $e^{9/2}$ **4.** e^{12}

5.

6.

7.

8.

9.

10.

11. $\ln 3 - \ln 2$ **12.** $\frac{1}{2}\ln(x + y)$ **13.** $\ln(x + 1) - \ln y$

14. $\ln[y(x + 1)]$ **15.** $\ln\dfrac{x^3}{(x - 1)^2}$ **16.** $\ln\dfrac{xy^4}{\sqrt{(z + 4)}}$

17. $x \approx 3.197$ **18.** $x \approx 1.750$ **19.** $x \approx 58.371$

20. (a) 17.67 yr   (b) 17.36 yr   (c) 17.33 yr   (d) 17.33 yr

21. $-3e^{-3x}$ **22.** $7e^{x+2} + 2$

23. $\dfrac{2x}{3 + x^2}$ **24.** $\dfrac{2}{x(x + 2)}$

25. (a) \$2241.54 million   (b) \$138.30 million/yr

26. 59.4%   **27.** 39.61 yr

Chapter 5

Section 5.1   *(page 319)*

Skills Warm Up   *(page 319)*

1. $x^{-1/2}$ **2.** $(2x)^{4/3}$ **3.** $5^{1/2}x^{3/2} + x^{5/2}$

4. $x^{-1/2} + x^{-2/3}$ **5.** $(x + 1)^{5/2}$ **6.** $x^{1/6}$

7. -12 **8.** -10 **9.** 14   **10.** 14

1–5. Answers will vary.   **7.** $u + C$ **9.** $6x + C$

11. $\frac{7}{2}x^2 + C$ **13.** $\frac{5}{3}t^3 + C$

15. $-\dfrac{5}{2x^2} + C$ **17.** $\frac{2}{5}y^{5/2} + C$

	Rewrite	*Integrate*	*Simplify*
19.	$\displaystyle\int x^{2/3}\,dx$	$\dfrac{x^{5/3}}{5/3} + C$	$\dfrac{3}{5}x^{5/3} + C$
21.	$\displaystyle\int x^{-3/2}\,dx$	$\dfrac{x^{-1/2}}{-1/2} + C$	$-\dfrac{2}{\sqrt{x}} + C$
23.	$\dfrac{1}{2}\displaystyle\int x^{-3}\,dx$	$\dfrac{1}{2}\left(\dfrac{x^{-2}}{-2}\right) + C$	$-\dfrac{1}{4x^2} + C$

25. $\dfrac{x^2}{2} + 3x + C$ **27.** $\frac{1}{4}x^4 + 2x + C$

29. $\frac{3}{4}x^4 - 2x^3 + 2x + C$ **31.** $\frac{1}{3}x^3 + \frac{5}{2}x^2 + x + C$

33. $2x + \dfrac{1}{2x^2} + C$ **35.** $3x^{2/3}(x + 2) + C$

37.

39.

41. $f(x) = 2x^2 + 6$ **43.** $f(x) = x^2 + 4x + 7$

45. $f(x) = 5x^2 - 3x^4 + 200$ **47.** $f(x) = -\dfrac{1}{x^2} + \dfrac{1}{x} + \dfrac{1}{2}$

49. $f(x) = x^2 + x + 4$ **51.** $f(x) = \frac{9}{4}x^{4/3}$

53. $C = 85x + 5500$ **55.** $C = \frac{1}{10}\sqrt{x} + 4x + 750$

57. $R = 225x - \frac{3}{2}x^2,\ p = 225 - \frac{3}{2}x$

59. $P = -9x^2 + 1650x$ **61.** $P = -12x^2 + 805x + 68$

63. $s(t) = -16t^2 + 6000$; about 19.36 sec

65. $v_0 = 40\sqrt{22} \approx 187.62$ ft/sec

67. (a) $C = x^2 - 12x + 125$ (b) \$2025

$\quad \overline{C} = x - 12 + \dfrac{125}{x}$

(c) \$125 is fixed. \$1900 is variable. Examples will vary.

69. (a) $P(t) = 79.4t^2 + 1758.6t + 74{,}515.2$

(b) 314,437.2; Yes, this seems reasonable. Explanations will vary.

71. (a) $M(t) = -0.035t^3 + 7.01t^2 + 217.8t + 49{,}486.005$

(b) 64,195.63; Yes, this seems reasonable. Explanations will vary.

73. (a)

$\dfrac{dB}{dx} = -19.9x + 351$

$\dfrac{dC}{dx} = 5.38x^2 - 40.6x + 182$

(b) $B(x) = -9.95x^2 + 351x$;
$C(x) = 1.79x^3 - 20.3x^2 + 182x + 425$

(c) Graphing the benefit and cost equations together, you see that benefit exceeds cost on the interval (2.32, 12.00).

The company should produce from 3 to 11 units.

Section 5.2   *(page 329)*

Skills Warm Up   *(page 329)*

1. $\frac{1}{2}x^4 + x + C$ **2.** $\frac{3}{2}x^2 + \frac{2}{3}x^{3/2} - 4x + C$

3. $-\dfrac{1}{x} + C$ **4.** $-\dfrac{1}{6t^2} + C$ **5.** $\frac{4}{7}t^{7/2} + \frac{2}{5}t^{5/2} + C$

6. $\frac{4}{5}x^{5/2} - \frac{2}{3}x^{3/2} + C$ **7.** $\dfrac{5x^3 - 4}{2x} + C$

8. $\dfrac{-6x^2 + 5}{3x^3} + C$ **9.** $\frac{2}{5}\sqrt{x}(8x^2 + 15) + C$

$\displaystyle\int u^n \dfrac{du}{dx}\, dx$	u	$\dfrac{du}{dx}$
1. $\displaystyle\int (5x^2 + 1)^2(10x)\, dx$	$5x^2 + 1$	$10x$
3. $\displaystyle\int \sqrt{1 - x^2}\,(-2x)\, dx$	$1 - x^2$	$-2x$
5. $\displaystyle\int \left(4 + \dfrac{1}{x^2}\right)^5\!\left(\dfrac{-2}{x^3}\right) dx$	$4 + \dfrac{1}{x^2}$	$-\dfrac{2}{x^3}$
7. $\displaystyle\int (1 + \sqrt{x})^3\!\left(\dfrac{1}{2\sqrt{x}}\right) dx$	$1 + \sqrt{x}$	$\dfrac{1}{2\sqrt{x}}$

9. $\frac{1}{5}(x - 1)^5 + C$ **11.** $\frac{1}{5}(1 + 2x)^5 + C$

13. $\frac{1}{2}(x^2 + 3x)^2 + C$ **15.** $\frac{2}{3}(4x^2 - 5)^{3/2} + C$

17. $\dfrac{1}{3(5 - 3x^2)^3} + C$ **19.** $\dfrac{(2x^3 - 1)^5}{30} + C$

21. $\frac{1}{3}(t^2 + 6)^{3/2} + C$ **23.** $\dfrac{1}{12(x^6 - 4)^2} + C$

25. $\dfrac{1}{10}(x^2 - 6x)^5 + C$ **27.** $-\dfrac{1}{2(x^2 + 2x - 3)} + C$

29. $-\dfrac{15}{8}(1 - x^2)^{4/3} + C$ **31.** $-\dfrac{3}{2(1 + x^2)} + C$

33. $-3\sqrt{2t + 3} + C$ **35.** $\frac{1}{4}(6x^2 - 1)^4 + C$

37. $\frac{3}{16}(4x + 3)^{4/3} + C$ **39.** $\sqrt{x^2 + 25} + C$

41. $\frac{2}{3}\sqrt{x^3 + 3x + 4} + C$

43. (a) $\frac{1}{3}x^3 - x^2 + x + C_1 = \frac{1}{3}(x - 1)^3 + C_2$

  (b) Answers differ by a constant: $C_1 = C_2 - \frac{1}{3}$

  (c) Answers will vary.

45. (a) $\dfrac{1}{6}x^6 - \dfrac{1}{2}x^4 + \dfrac{1}{2}x^2 + C_1 = \dfrac{(x^2 - 1)^3}{6} + C_2$

  (b) Answers differ by a constant: $C_1 = C_2 - \frac{1}{6}$

  (c) Answers will vary.

47. $f(x) = \frac{1}{12}(4x^2 - 10)^3 - 8$

49. (a) $C = 8\sqrt{x + 1} + 18$ (b) $\$75.13$

51. $x = \dfrac{1}{3}(p^2 - 25)^{3/2} + 24$ **53.** $x = \dfrac{6000}{\sqrt{p^2 - 16}} + 3000$

55. (a) $h = \sqrt{17.6t^2 + 1} + 5$ (b) 26 in.

57. (a) $Q = (x - 24{,}999)^{0.95} + 24{,}999$

  (b)

x	25,000	50,000	100,000	150,000
Q	25,000	40,067.14	67,786.18	94,512.29
$x - Q$	0	9932.86	32,213.82	55,487.71

  (c)

59. $-\frac{2}{3}x^{3/2} + \frac{2}{3}(x + 1)^{3/2} + C$

Section 5.3   *(page 336)*

Skills Warm Up   *(page 336)*

1. $x + 2 - \dfrac{2}{x + 2}$ **2.** $x - 2 + \dfrac{1}{x - 4}$

3. $x + 8 + \dfrac{2x - 4}{x^2 - 4x}$ **4.** $x^2 - x - 4 + \dfrac{20x + 22}{x^2 + 5}$

5. $\dfrac{1}{4}x^4 - \dfrac{1}{x} + C$ **6.** $\dfrac{1}{2}x^2 + 2x + C$

7. $\dfrac{1}{2}x^2 - \dfrac{4}{x} + C$ **8.** $-\dfrac{1}{x} - \dfrac{3}{2x^2} + C$

1. $e^{2x} + C$ **3.** $\frac{1}{4}e^{4x} + C$ **5.** $\frac{1}{5}e^{5x-3} + C$

7. $-\frac{9}{2}e^{-x^2} + C$ **9.** $\frac{5}{3}e^{x^3} + C$ **11.** $e^{x^2+x} + C$

13. $\ln|x + 1| + C$ **15.** $\ln|5x + 2| + C$

17. $-\frac{1}{2}\ln|3 - 2x| + C$ **19.** $\frac{2}{3}\ln|3x + 5| + C$

21. $\ln\sqrt{x^2 + 1} + C$ **23.** $\frac{1}{3}\ln|x^3 + 1| + C$

25. $\frac{1}{2}\ln|x^2 + 6x + 7| + C$ **27.** $\ln|\ln x| + C$

29. $\ln|1 - e^{-x}| + C$

31. $\frac{1}{4}x^2 - 4\ln|x| + C$; General Power Rule and Log Rule

33. $8x + 3\ln|x| - \dfrac{3}{x^2} + C$; General Power Rule and Log Rule

35. $e^x + 2x - e^{-x} + C$;
Exponential Rule and General Power Rule

37. $-\frac{2}{3}(1 - e^x)^{3/2} + C$; Exponential Rule

39. $\ln|e^x + x| + C$; Log Rule

41. $\frac{1}{7}\ln(7e^{5x} + 1) + C$; Log Rule

43. $\frac{1}{2}x^2 + 3x + 8\ln|x - 1| + C$;
General Power Rule and Log Rule

45. $x - 6\ln|x + 3| + C$;
General Power Rule, General Log Rule

47. $f(x) = \dfrac{-e^{2/x}}{2} + \dfrac{e^{1/2}}{2} + 6$

49. $f(x) = \frac{1}{2}x^2 + 5x + 8\ln|x - 1| - 8$

51. (a) $P(t) = 1000[1 + \ln(1 + 0.25t)^{12}]$

  (b) $P(3) \approx 7715$ bacteria   (c) $t \approx 6$ days

53. (a) $p = -50e^{-x/500} + 45.06$

(b)

The price increases as the demand increases.

(c) 387

55. (a) $R(t) = 3223.56e^{0.0993t} + 24.78$

(b) $R(9) \approx \$7903.66$

57. False. $\ln x^{1/2} = \frac{1}{2}\ln x$

Quiz Yourself   *(page 338)*

1. $3x + C$ **2.** $5x^2 + C$ **3.** $-\dfrac{1}{4x^4} + C$

4. $\dfrac{x^3}{3} - x^2 + 15x + C$ **5.** $\dfrac{(6x+1)^4}{4} + C$

6. $\dfrac{1}{50}(5x^2 - 2)^5 + C$ **7.** $\dfrac{(x^2 - 5x)^2}{2} + C$

8. $-\dfrac{1}{2(x^3 + 3)^2} + C$ **9.** $\dfrac{2}{15}(5x + 2)^{3/2} + C$

10. $f(x) = 8x^2 + 1$ **11.** $f(x) = 3x^3 + 4x - 2$

12. (a) $C = -0.03x^2 + 16x + 9.03$ (b) $\$9.03$ (c) $\$509.03$

13. $f(x) = \dfrac{2}{3}x^3 + x + 1$

14. (a) 1000 bolts   (b) About 8612 bolts

15. $e^{5x+4} + C$ **16.** $e^{x^3} + C$

17. $\frac{1}{2}e^{(x^2 - 6x)} + C$ **18.** $\ln|2x - 1| + C$

19. $-\frac{1}{8}\ln|3 - 8x| + C$ **20.** $\frac{1}{6}\ln(3x^2 + 4) + C$

21. (a) $S(t) = 13.16t^2 + 848.99\ln(t) + 2504.44$

(b) $\$5112.11$ million

Section 5.4   *(page 348)*

Skills Warm Up   *(page 348)*

1. $\frac{3}{2}x^2 + 7x + C$ **2.** $\frac{2}{5}x^{5/2} + \frac{4}{3}x^{3/2} + C$

3. $\dfrac{1}{5}\ln|x| + C$ **4.** $-\dfrac{1}{6e^{6x}} + C$

5. $C = 0.008x^{5/2} + 29,500x + C$

6. $R = x^2 + 9000x + C$

7. $P = 25,000x - 0.005x^2 + C$

8. $C = 0.01x^3 + 4600x + C$

1.

Area = 6

3.

Area = 8

5.

$\text{Area} = \dfrac{9\pi}{2}$

7. (a) 8   (b) 4   (c) -24 (d) 0

9. $\dfrac{1}{6}$ **11.** $\dfrac{1}{2}$ **13.** $6\left(1 - \dfrac{1}{e^2}\right)$ **15.** $8\ln 2 + \dfrac{15}{2}$

17. 1   **19.** $-\frac{5}{2}$ **21.** 38   **23.** $-\frac{15}{4}$ **25.** -4

27. $-\frac{27}{20}$ **29.** $6\ln 2 \approx 4.16$ **31.** 2

33. $-e^{-1} + 1 \approx 0.63$ **35.** $\frac{1}{3}\left[(e^2 + 1)^{3/2} - 2\sqrt{2}\right] \approx 7.157$

37. $\frac{1}{8}\ln 17 \approx 0.354$ **39.** 10   **41.** 39   **43.** 10

45. $4\ln 3 \approx 4.394$ **47.** $\$6.75$ **49.** $\$22.50$ **51.** $\$3.97$

53. Average = 12

$x = 2$

55. Average = $\dfrac{8}{3}$

$x = \pm\dfrac{2\sqrt{3}}{3} \approx \pm 1.155$

57. Average = $e - e^{-1} \approx 2.3504$

$x = \ln\left(\dfrac{e - e^{-1}}{2}\right) \approx 0.1614$

59. Average = $\frac{3}{4}\ln\frac{7}{3} \approx 0.6355$ **61.** $\frac{6}{5}$ **63.** 0

$x = 4/\ln(7/3) - 2 \approx 2.721$

65. (a) $\frac{1}{3}$ (b) $\frac{2}{3}$ (c) $-\frac{1}{3}$

Explanations will vary.

67. $\$1925.23$ **69.** $\$16,605.21$

71. $\$2500$ **73.** $\$4565.65$

75. (a) $\$137,000$ (b) $\$214,720.93$ (c) $\$338,393.53$

77. $\$2623.94$

79. (a) $M(t) = 273.78t^2 - 23.153t^3 - 331.258e^{-t} + 5438.258$

(b) $\$8573.88$ billion

Section 5.5   *(page 357)*

Skills Warm Up   *(page 357)*

1. $-x^2 + 3x + 2$ **2.** $-2x^2 + 4x + 4$

3. $-x^3 + 2x^2 + 4x - 5$ **4.** $x^3 - 6x - 1$

5. $(0, 4), (4, 4)$ **6.** $(1, -3), (2, -12)$

7. $(-3, 9), (2, 4)$ **8.** $(-2, -4), (0, 0), (2, 4)$

---

1. 36   **3.** 9   **5.** $e - 2$ **7.** $\frac{3}{2}$

9.

11.

13. d

15.

Area $= \frac{4}{5}$

17.

Area $= \frac{64}{3}$

19.

Area $= 2\frac{1}{6}$

21.

Area $= \frac{1}{2}$

23.

Area $= 21\frac{1}{12}$

25.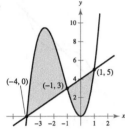

Area $= -\frac{1}{2}e^{-1} + \frac{1}{2}$

27.

Area $= (2e + \ln 2) - 2e^{1/2}$

29.

Area $= \frac{7}{3} + 8\ln 2$

31.

Area $= \int_0^1 2x\,dx + \int_1^2 (4 - 2x)\,dx$

33.

Area $= \int_1^2 \left(\frac{4}{x} - x\right)dx + \int_2^4 \left(x - \frac{4}{x}\right)dx$

35.

Area $= \frac{32}{3}$

37.

Area $= \frac{1}{6}$

39. 8

41. Consumer surplus $= 1600$
Producer surplus $= 400$

43. Consumer surplus $= 500$
Producer surplus $= 2000$

45. Consumer surplus $= 640.00$
Producer surplus ≈ 426.67

47. R_1; \$11.375 billion

49. \$573 million; Explanations will vary.

51. (a)   (b) 124.25 fewer pounds

53. \$333.33 million

55. $CS = \$700{,}000$
$PS = \$1{,}375{,}000$

57. 2077.10   **59.** Answers will vary.

Section 5.6   *(page 364)*

> **Skills Warm Up**   *(page 364)*
>
> **1.** $\frac{1}{6}$ **2.** $\frac{3}{20}$ **3.** $\frac{7}{40}$ **4.** $\frac{13}{12}$ **5.** $\frac{61}{30}$ **6.** $\frac{53}{18}$
>
> **7.** $\frac{2}{3}$ **8.** $\frac{4}{7}$ **9.** 0   **10.** 5

1. Approximation: 2
Exact area: 2

3. Approximation: 0.6730
Exact area: $\frac{2}{3} \approx 0.6667$

5. Approximation: 1.245
Exact area: $\frac{5}{4} = 1.25$

7. 71.25

9. 1.079

11. 24.28

13. 17.25

15. 34.25   **17.** 1.39

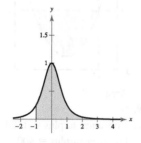

19.

n	10	20	30
Approximation	15.4543	15.4628	15.4644

n	40	50
Approximation	15.4650	15.4652

21.

n	10	20	30
Approximation	5.8520	5.8526	5.8528

n	40	50
Approximation	5.8528	5.8528

23. Area ≈ 54.6667,   **25.** Area ≈ 0.9163,
      $n = 33$ $n = 3$

27. 9920 ft^2 **29.** 381.6 mi^2

31. Midpoint Rule: 3.1468
      Graphing utility: 3.141593

Review Exercises for Chapter 5   *(page 370)*

1. $16x + C$ **3.** $\frac{3}{10}x^2 + C$ **5.** $x^3 + C$

7. $\frac{2}{3}x^3 + \frac{5}{2}x^2 + C$ **9.** $x^{2/3} + C$ **11.** $\frac{3}{7}x^{7/3} + \frac{3}{2}x^2 + C$

13. $\frac{4}{9}x^{9/2} - 2\sqrt{x} + C$ **15.** $6x^2 - 3$ **17.** $x^3 - 4x^2 + 15$

19. $s(t) = -16t^2 + 80t$
      5 seconds

21. $\frac{1}{4}(x + 4)^4 + C$ **23.** $\frac{1}{5}(5x + 1)^5 + C$

25. $x + 5x^2 + \frac{25}{3}x^3 + C$ or $\frac{1}{15}(1 + 5x)^3 + C_1$

27. $\dfrac{(3x^3 + 1)^3}{27} + C$ **29.** $\dfrac{-1}{12(2x^3 - 5)^2} + C$

31. $\frac{2}{5}\sqrt{5x - 1} + C$

33. (a) 30.54 board-feet   (b) 125.2 board-feet

35. $e^{4x} + C$ **37.** $-\frac{1}{5}e^{-5x} + C$

39. $\dfrac{7e^{3x^2}}{6} + C$ **41.** $\ln|x - 6| + C$

43. $\frac{2}{3}\ln|6x - 1| + C$ **45.** $-\frac{1}{3}\ln|1 - x^3| + C$

47.   **49.**

Area $= 6$ Area $= 8$

51. (a) 13   (b) 7   (c) 11   (d) 50

53. $\frac{32}{3}$ **55.** 2 ln 2   **57.** $4e^{1/2} - 4$ **59.** 16

61. 0   **63.** 4   **65.** 2   **67.** 5 ln 3 ≈ 5.49

69. 1.899   **71.** Average value $= 3$; $x = 1$

73. Average value $= \frac{2}{3}(1 - e^3) \approx -12.724$;
      $x = \ln\left[-\frac{1}{3}(1 - e^3)\right] \approx 1.850$

75. Average value $= \frac{2}{5}$; $x = \frac{25}{4}$ **77.** 0   **79.** 115.2

81. $17,492.94   **83.** Increases by $700.25   **85.** $520.54

87.   **89.**

          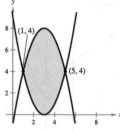

Area $= \frac{4}{9}$ Area $= \frac{64}{3}$

91.   **93.**

Area $= 16$ Area $= \frac{1}{2}$

95. Consumer surplus $= 1417.5$
      Producer surplus $= 202.5$

97. Consumer surplus $= 1250$
      Producer surplus $= 1250$

99. R_2; $84.5 million

101. $300 million

103. Approximation: 1.5
       Actual area: 1.5

105. 2.625   **107.** 1.070

109. 13.5   **111.** 3.032

113. 9840 ft^2

Test Yourself   *(page 374)*

1. $3x^3 - 2x^2 + 13x + C$ **2.** $\dfrac{(x + 1)^3}{3} + C$

3. $\dfrac{2(x^4 - 7)^{3/2}}{3} + C$ **4.** $\dfrac{10x^{3/2}}{3} - 12x^{1/2} + C$

5. $5e^{3x} + C$ **6.** $\frac{3}{4}\ln|4x - 1| + C$

7. $f(x) = 3x^2 - 5x - 2$ **8.** $f(x) = e^x + x$

9. 8   **10.** 18   **11.** $\frac{2}{3}$

12. $2\sqrt{5} - 2\sqrt{2} \approx 1.644$ **13.** $\frac{1}{4}(e^{12} - 1) \approx 40{,}688.4$

14. $\ln 6 \approx 1.792$

15. (a) $S(t) = 2240e^{0.1013t} + 4.3906, \ 0 \le t \le 9$
   (b) \$3661.68 million

16.   **17.**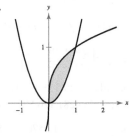

Area $= \frac{343}{6} \approx 57.167$ Area $= \frac{5}{12}$

18. Consumer surplus = 20 million
Producer surplus = 8 million

19. Midpoint Rule: $\frac{63}{64} \approx 0.9844$ **20.** Midpoint Rule: $\frac{21}{8} = 2.625$

Exact area: 1   Exact area: $\frac{8}{3} = 2.\overline{6}$

21. $-4e^{-x/4}(x + 4) + C$

23. $\frac{1}{2}t^2 \ln(t + 1) - \frac{1}{2}\ln(t + 1) - \frac{1}{4}t^2 + \frac{1}{2}t + C$

25. $-e^{1/t} + C$ **27.** $\frac{1}{2}x^2(\ln x)^2 - \frac{1}{2}x^2 \ln x + \frac{1}{4}x^2 + C$

29. $\frac{1}{3}(\ln x)^3 + C$ **31.** $-\dfrac{1}{x}(\ln x + 1) + C$

33. $\frac{2}{3}x(x - 1)^{3/2} - \frac{4}{15}(x - 1)^{5/2} + C$

35. $\frac{1}{4}x^4 + \frac{2}{3}x^3 + \frac{1}{2}x^2 + C$ **37.** $\dfrac{e^{2x}}{4(2x + 1)} + C$

39. $\frac{5}{36}e^6 + \frac{1}{36} \approx 56.060$ **41.** $\frac{3}{2}\ln 3 - 1 \approx 0.648$

43. $\frac{1192}{15} \approx 79.467$ **45.** $e(2e - 1) \approx 12.060$

47. Area $= 2e^2 + 6 \approx 20.778$

49. Area $= \dfrac{e - 2}{e}$ **51.** Area $= \dfrac{1}{9}(2e^3 + 1)$

     ≈ 0.2642 ≈ 4.575

    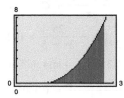

53. Proof   **55.** $\dfrac{e^{5x}}{125}(25x^2 - 10x + 2) + C$

57. $-\dfrac{1}{9x^3}(1 + 3\ln x) + C$ **59.** $\dfrac{3}{128} - \dfrac{379}{128}e^{-8} \approx 0.022$

61. $\dfrac{1{,}171{,}875}{256}\pi \approx 14{,}381.070$

63.
   (a) Increase
   (b) 113,212 units
   (c) 11,321 units/yr

65. (a) $3.2 \ln 2 - 0.2 \approx 2.018$
   (b) $12.8 \ln 4 - 7.2 \ln 3 - 1.8 \approx 8.035$

67. \$18,482.03   **69.** \$931,265.10   **71.** \$4103.07

73. \$1,055,267   **75.** (a) \$1,200,000   (b) \$1,094,142.27

77. (a) \$18,000,000   (b) \$16,133,084   **79.** \$45,957.78

81. (a) \$17,378.62   (b) \$3681.26   **83.** ≈ 4.254

Chapter 6

Section 6.1   *(page 383)*

Skills Warm Up   *(page 383)*

1. $\dfrac{1}{x + 1}$ **2.** $\dfrac{2x}{x^2 - 1}$ **3.** $3x^2 e^{x^3}$

4. $-2xe^{-x^2}$ **5.** $e^x(x^2 + 2x)$ **6.** $e^{-2x}(1 - 2x)$

7. $\frac{64}{3}$ **8.** $\frac{4}{3}$ **9.** 36   **10.** 8

---

1. $u = x; \ dv = e^{3x}\,dx$ **3.** $u = \ln 2x; \ dv = x\,dx$

5. $\frac{1}{3}xe^{3x} - \frac{1}{9}e^{3x} + C$ **7.** $\dfrac{x^4}{16}(4\ln x - 1) + C$

9. $x\ln 2x - x + C$ **11.** $-x^2 e^{-x} - 2xe^{-x} - 2e^{-x} + C$

13. $\frac{2}{3}x^{3/2}\left(\ln x - \frac{2}{3}\right) + C$ **15.** $2x^2 e^x - 4e^x x + 4e^x + C$

17. $\frac{1}{4}e^{4x} + C$ **19.** $\frac{1}{4}xe^{4x} - \frac{1}{16}e^{4x} + C$

Section 6.2   *(page 391)*

Skills Warm Up   *(page 391)*

1. $x^2 + 8x + 16$ **2.** $x^2 - 2x + 1$

3. $x^2 + x + \frac{1}{4}$ **4.** $x^2 - \frac{2}{3}x + \frac{1}{9}$

5. $2e^x(x - 1) + C$ **6.** $x^3 \ln x - \dfrac{x^3}{3} + C$

CHAPTER 6

1. $\frac{1}{9}\left(\frac{2}{2+3x} + \ln|2+3x|\right) + C$

3. $\frac{2(3x-4)}{27}\sqrt{2+3x} + C$ **5.** $\ln\left(x^2 + \sqrt{x^4-9}\right) + C$

7. $\frac{1}{2}(x^2-1)e^{x^2} + C$ **9.** $\ln\left|\frac{x}{1+x}\right| + C$

11. $-\frac{1}{3}\ln\left|\frac{3+\sqrt{x^2+9}}{x}\right| + C$

13. $-\frac{1}{2}\ln\left|\frac{2+\sqrt{4-x^2}}{x}\right| + C$ **15.** $\frac{3}{4}x^2[-1+2\ln(3x)] + C$

17. $3x^2 - \ln(1+e^{3x^2}) + C$

19. $\frac{2}{35}(x+3)^{3/2}(5x^2 - 12x + 24) + C$

21. $\frac{1}{27}\left[\frac{4}{2+3t} - \frac{2}{(2+3t)^2} + \ln|2+3t|\right] + C$

23. $\frac{1}{\sqrt{3}}\ln\left|\frac{\sqrt{3+4x}-\sqrt{3}}{\sqrt{3+4x}+\sqrt{3}}\right| + C$

25. $-\frac{1}{2}x(2-x) + \ln|x+1| + C$

27. $\frac{1}{8}\left[\frac{-1}{2(3+2x)^2} + \frac{2}{(3+2x)^3} - \frac{9}{4(3+2x)^4}\right] + C$

29. $-\frac{\sqrt{1-x^2}}{x} + C$ **31.** $\frac{4}{9}x^3(3\ln 2x - 1) + C$

33. $\frac{1}{27}\left(3x - \frac{25}{3x-5} + 10\ln|3x-5|\right) + C$

35. $\frac{1}{9}(3\ln x - 4\ln|4+3\ln x|) + C$

37. $\frac{-2\sqrt{2}+4}{3} \approx 0.3905$ **39.** $-\frac{5}{9} + \ln\frac{9}{4} \approx 0.2554$

41. $12\left(2 + \ln\left|\frac{2}{1+e^2}\right|\right) \approx 6.7946$ **43.** $8\ln 2 - \frac{15}{8} \approx 3.6702$

45. Area $= \frac{1}{8\sqrt{3}} \approx 0.0722$ **47.** Area $= \frac{3\ln\frac{4}{5}+1}{36} \approx 0.0092$

49. Area $= \frac{1}{4}\left[21\sqrt{5} - 8\ln\left(\sqrt{5}+3\right) + 8\ln 2\right] \approx 9.8145$

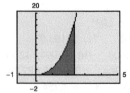

51. $x\left(\ln\frac{x}{3} - 1\right) + C$ **53.** $\frac{2}{147}(7x+6)\sqrt{7x-3} + C$

55. (a) 0.483   (b) 0.283

57.

Average value: 401.40

59. $1138.43

61. Consumer surplus: ≈ 17.92
Producer surplus: 24

Quiz Yourself   *(page 393)*

1. $\frac{1}{5}xe^{5x} - \frac{1}{25}e^{5x} + C$ **2.** $3x\ln x - 3x + C$

3. $\frac{1}{2}x^2\ln x + x\ln x - \frac{1}{4}x^2 - x + C$

4. $\frac{2}{3}x(x+3)^{3/2} - \frac{4}{15}(x+3)^{5/2} + C$

5. $\frac{x^2}{4}\ln x - \frac{x^2}{8} + C$ **6.** $-\frac{1}{2}e^{-2x}\left(x^2 + x + \frac{1}{2}\right) + C$

7. (a) 282,016 units   (b) 56,403 units

8. (a) $784,000   (b) $673,108.31

9. $\frac{1}{4}(2x - \ln|1 + 2x|) + C$ **10.** $10\ln\left|\frac{x}{0.1 + 0.2x}\right| + C$

11. $\ln\left|x + \sqrt{x^2-16}\right| - \frac{\sqrt{x^2-16}}{x} + C$

12. $\frac{1}{2}\ln\left|\frac{\sqrt{4+9x}-2}{\sqrt{4+9x}+2}\right| + C$

13. $\frac{1}{4}[4x^2 - \ln(1+e^{4x^2})] + C$ **14.** $x^2e^{x^2+1} + C$

15. (a) $84,281,126.52   (b) $257,392,429.72

16. $\frac{8}{e} - 4 \approx -1.0570$ **17.** $10\ln 2 - \frac{15}{4} \approx 3.1815$

18. $\frac{64}{3}\left(\sqrt{2}-1\right) \approx 8.8366$ **19.** $e - 2 \approx 0.7183$

20. $\frac{\sqrt{5}}{18} \approx 0.1242$ **21.** $\frac{1}{4}\left(\ln\frac{17}{19} - \ln\frac{7}{9}\right) \approx 0.0350$

Section 6.3   *(page 400)*

Skills Warm Up   *(page 400)*

1. $\frac{2}{x^3}$ **2.** $-\frac{96}{(2x+1)^4}$ **3.** $-\frac{12}{x^4}$ **4.** $6x - 4$

5. $16e^{2x}$ **6.** $e^{x^2}(4x^2 + 2)$ **7.** $(3, 18)$

8. $(1, 8)$ **9.** $n < -5\sqrt{10},\ n > 5\sqrt{10}$

10. $n < -5, n > 5$

	Trapezoidal Rule	Simpson's Rule	Exact Value
1.	2.7500	2.6667	2.6667
3.	0.2704	0.2512	0.2499
5.	0.6941	0.6932	0.6931
7.	5.2650	5.3046	5.3333
9.	3.8643	3.3022	3.1809

11. (a) 0.783   (b) 0.785   **13.** (a) 2.540   (b) 2.541

15. (a) 3.283   (b) 3.240   **17.** (a) 1.470   (b) 1.463

19. (a) 1.879   (b) 1.888   **21.** $21,831.20; $21,836.98

23. $678.36   **25.** $0.3413 = 34.13\%$

27. $0.5000 = 50.00\%$ **29.** 89,500 ft²

31. (a) $|E| \le \frac{1}{12} \approx 0.0833$ (b) $|E| \le 0$

33. (a) $|E| \le \frac{5e}{64} \approx 0.212$ (b) $|E| \le \frac{13e}{1024} \approx 0.035$

35. (a) $n = 566$ (b) $n = 16$

37. (a) $n = 3280$ (b) $n = 60$ **39.** 19.5215   **41.** 3.6558

43. (a) 36.2 years   (b) 36.2 years
(c) The results are the same.

45. 58.912 mg   **47.** 1878 subscribers

49. Answers will vary.

Section 6.4   *(page 410)*

Skills Warm Up   *(page 410)*

1. 9   **2.** 3   **3.** $-\frac{1}{8}$ **4.** Limit does not exist.

5. Limit does not exist.   **6.** -4

7. (a) $\frac{32}{3}b^3 - 16b^2 + 8b - \frac{4}{3}$ (b) $-\frac{4}{3}$

8. (a) $\dfrac{b^2 - b - 11}{(b-2)^2(b-5)}$ (b) $\dfrac{11}{20}$

9. (a) $\ln\!\left(\dfrac{5 - 3b^2}{b+1}\right)$ (b) $\ln 5 \approx 1.609$

10. (a) $e^{-3b^2}(e^{6b^2} + 1)$ (b) 2

1. Improper; The integrand has an infinite discontinuity when $x = \frac{2}{3}$, and $0 \le \frac{2}{3} \le 1$.

3. Not improper; continuous on $[0, 1]$

5. Not improper; continuous on $[0, 5]$

7. Converges; 1   **9.** Diverges   **11.** Diverges

13. Diverges   **15.** Diverges   **17.** Converges; 0

19. Converges; $\dfrac{1}{2\,(\ln 4)^2}$ **21.** 1   **23.** $\dfrac{1}{2}$ **25.** ∞

27. (a) 0.9026   (b) 0.0738   (c) 0.00235

29. (a) $\displaystyle\int_{35.5}^{\infty} f(x)\,dx \approx 0.9938$ (b) $\displaystyle\int_{35.9}^{\infty} f(x)\,dx \approx 0.6915$

31. $66,666.67   **33.** Yes, $360,000 < $400,000.

35. (a) $4,637,228   (b) $5,555,556

37. (a) $748,367.34   (b) $808,030.14   (c) $900,000.00

39. (a) $453,901.30   (b) $807,922.43   (c) $4,466,666.67

Review Exercises for Chapter 6   *(page 416)*

1. $2\sqrt{x}\ln x - 4\sqrt{x} + C$ **3.** $xe^x + C$

5. $\frac{2}{15}(x-5)^{3/2}(3x+10) + C$ **7.** $x^2e^{2x} - xe^{2x} + \frac{1}{2}e^{2x} + C$

9. $3e^2 - \dfrac{3(e^2 - 1)}{2} \approx 12.584$ **11.** $16 - 20e^{-1/4} \approx 0.4240$

13. $90,634.62   **15.** $865,958.50

17. (a) $1,200,000   (b) $1,052,649.52

19. $\frac{1}{54}(9x^2 - 12x + 8\ln|3x+2|) + C$

21. $\dfrac{x}{2}\sqrt{x^2-16} - 8\ln\!\left(\sqrt{x^2-16} + x\right) + C$

23. $\dfrac{1}{9}\!\left(\dfrac{2}{2+3x} + \ln|2+3x|\right) + C$

25. $\sqrt{x^2+25} - 5\ln\left|\dfrac{5 + \sqrt{x^2+25}}{x}\right| + C$

27. $\dfrac{1}{4}\ln\left|\dfrac{x-2}{x+2}\right| + C$ **29.** $\frac{2}{3}(x-2)\sqrt{1+x} + C$

31. $2\sqrt{1+x} + \ln\left|\dfrac{\sqrt{1+x}-1}{\sqrt{1+x}+1}\right| + C$

33. (a) 0.675   (b) 0.290

35. Exact: $\frac{2}{3} \approx 0.6667$ **37.** Exact: $\frac{3}{8} = 0.375$

Trapezoidal: 0.7050   Trapezoidal: 0.3786

Simpson's: 0.6715   Simpson's: 0.3751

39. Exact: $2 - 2e^{-2} \approx 1.7293$ **41.** (a) 0.741   (b) 0.737

Trapezoidal: 1.7652

Simpson's: 1.7299

43. (a) 0.305   (b) 0.289   **45.** (a) 2.961   (b) 2.936

47. (a) $|E| \le \dfrac{e^4}{6} \approx 9.0997$ (b) $|E| \le \dfrac{e^4}{90} \approx 0.6066$

49. (a) $n = 214$ (b) $n = 2$

51. Converges, $-\frac{1}{4}$ **53.** Diverges   **55.** Diverges

57. $A \approx 4$ **59.** $A = 1$ **61.** $266,666.67   **63.** No

Test Yourself   *(page 418)*

1. $xe^{x+1} - e^{x+1} + C$ **2.** $3x^3\ln x - x^3 + C$

3. $-3x^2e^{-x/3} - 18xe^{-x/3} - 54e^{-x/3} + C$

4. (a) $\approx$$6494.47 million   (b) $\approx$$811.81 million

5. $\dfrac{1}{4}\!\left(\dfrac{7}{7+2x} + \ln|7+2x|\right) + C$ **6.** $x^3 - \ln(1 + e^{x^3}) + C$

7. $-\frac{2}{75}(2 - 5x^2)\sqrt{1+5x^2} + C$ **8.** $-1 + \frac{3}{2}\ln 3 \approx 0.6479$

9. $8\frac{2}{3}$ **10.** $4\ln\!\left[3\left(\sqrt{17} - 4\right)\right] + \sqrt{17} - 5 \approx -4.8613$

11. Exact: 18.0

Trapezoidal: 18.28

12. Simpson's Rule: 41.3606; Exact: 41.1711

13. Converges; $\frac{1}{3}$ **14.** Converges; 12   **15.** Diverges

16. (a) $498.75   (b) Plan B, because $149 < $498.75.

Chapter 7

Section 7.1   *(page 425)*

Skills Warm Up   *(page 425)*

1. $2\sqrt{5}$ **2.** 5   **3.** 8   **4.** 8   **5.** $(4, 7)$

6. $(1, 0)$ **7.** $(0, 3)$ **8.** $(-1, 1)$

9. $(x-2)^2 + (y-3)^2 = 4$

10. $(x-1)^2 + (y-4)^2 = 25$

1.   **3.**

5. $(-3, 4, 5)$ **7.** $(10, 0, 0)$ **9.** 0   **11.** $3\sqrt{2}$

13. $\sqrt{206}$ **15.** $\left(2, -\frac{3}{2}, \frac{5}{2}\right)$ **17.** $\left(\frac{1}{2}, \frac{1}{2}, -1\right)$

19. $(6, -3, 5)$ **21.** $(1, 2, 1)$ **23.** $3, 3\sqrt{5}, 6$; right triangle

25. $\sqrt{41}, \sqrt{14}, \sqrt{41}$; isosceles triangle

27. $(0, 0, -5), (2, 2, -4), (2, -4, -1)$

29. $x^2 + (y-2)^2 + (z-2)^2 = 4$

31. $\left(x - \frac{3}{2}\right)^2 + (y-2)^2 + (z-1)^2 = \frac{21}{4}$

33. $(x-3)^2 + (y+2)^2 + (z+3)^2 = 16$

35. $(x-1)^2 + (y-3)^2 + z^2 = 10$

37. $(x+4)^2 + (y-3)^2 + (z-2)^2 = 4$

39. Center: $\left(\frac{5}{2}, 0, 0\right)$ **41.** Center: $(-2, 1, -4)$

Radius: $\frac{5}{2}$ Radius: 5

43. Center: $(1, 3, 2)$

Radius: $\dfrac{5\sqrt{2}}{2}$

45.

47.

9.

11.

49.

51.

13. Perpendicular   **15.** Parallel   **17.** Parallel
19. Neither parallel nor perpendicular   **21.** Perpendicular
23. c; Ellipsoid   **24.** e; Hyperboloid of two sheets
25. f; Hyperboloid of one sheet   **26.** b; Elliptic cone
27. d; Elliptic paraboloid   **28.** a; Hyperbolic paraboloid
29. (a) $x = \pm y$; Lines
     (b) $z = 9 - y^2$; Parabola
     (c) $z = x^2$; Parabola
     Hyperbolic parabola

53. (a)

(b)

31. (a) $\dfrac{x^2}{4} + y^2 = 1$; Ellipse   (b) $\dfrac{x^2}{4} + z^2 = 1$; Ellipse
     (c) $y^2 + z^2 = 1$; Circle
     Ellipsoid

33. (a) $z^2 - \dfrac{x^2}{9} = 1$; Hyperbola

     (b) $\dfrac{9}{13}z^2 - \dfrac{9}{208}y^2 = 1$; Hyperbola

     (c) $\dfrac{x^2}{135} + \dfrac{y^2}{240} = 1$; Ellipse
     Hyperboloid of two sheets

55. (a)

(b)

35. Ellipsoid   **37.** Hyperboloid of one sheet
39. Hyperbolic paraboloid   **41.** Elliptic paraboloid
43. Elliptic cone   **45.** Hyperboloid of two sheets
47. Hyperbolic paraboloid

57. $x^2 + y^2 + z^2 = 6806.25$

49. $\dfrac{x^2}{3963^2} + \dfrac{y^2}{3963^2} + \dfrac{z^2}{3950^2} = 1$

Section 7.2   *(page 434)*

51. (a)

Year	2004	2005	2006
x	33.1	34.9	37.4
y	13.2	13.8	14.9
z (actual)	15.5	16.3	17.8
z (approximated)	15.5	16.4	17.5

Year	2007	2008	2009
x	40.6	43.0	41.8
y	15.0	15.4	14.5
z (actual)	19.5	20.5	20.7
z (approximated)	19.4	20.7	20.4

The approximated values of z are very close to the actual values.

(b) According to the model, increases in expenditures of recreation types y and z will correspond to an increase in expenditures of recreation type x.

Skills Warm Up   *(page 434)*

1. $(4, 0), (0, 3)$ **2.** $\left(-\frac{4}{3}, 0\right), (0, -8)$
3. $(1, 0), (0, -2)$ **4.** $(-5, 0), (0, -5)$
5. $x^2 + y^2 + z^2 = \frac{1}{4}$ **6.** $x^2 + y^2 + z^2 = 4$

1.

3.

5.

7.

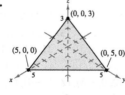

Section 7.3   *(page 441)*

Skills Warm Up   *(page 441)*

1. 11   **2.** -16 **3.** 7   **4.** 4   **5.** $(-\infty, \infty)$
6. $(-\infty, -3) \cup (-3, 0) \cup (0, \infty)$
7. $[5, \infty)$ **8.** $\left(-\infty, -\sqrt{5}\,\right] \cup \left[\sqrt{5}, \infty\right)$
9. 55.0104   **10.** 6.9165

---

1. (a) $\dfrac{3}{2}$ (b) $-\dfrac{1}{4}$ (c) 6 (d) $\dfrac{5}{y}$ (e) $\dfrac{x}{2}$ (f) $\dfrac{5}{t}$

3. (a) 5 (b) $3e^2$ (c) $2e^{-1}$ (d) $5e^y$ (e) xe^2 (f) te^t

5. (a) $\frac{2}{3}$ (b) 0   **7.** (a) 90π (b) 50π

9. (a) \$20,655.20 (b) \$1,397,672.67   **11.** (a) 0 (b) 6

13. (a) $x^2 + 2x\,\Delta x + (\Delta x)^2 - 2y$ (b) $-2, \Delta y \ne 0$

15. Domain: all points (x, y) **17.** Domain: all points (x, y)
inside and on the circle   Range: $[0, \infty)$
$$x^2 + y^2 = 16$$
Range: $[0, 4]$

19. Domain: all points (x, y) **21.** Domain: the half-plane
such that $y \ne 0$ below the line $y = -x + 4$
Range: $(0, \infty)$ Range: $(-\infty, \infty)$

23. Domain: all points (x, y) **25.** Domain: all points (x, y)
inside and on the ellipse   such that $x \ne 0$
$$3x^2 + y^2 = 9$$ Range: $(-\infty, \infty)$
Range: $[0, 3]$

27. Domain: all points (x, y) **29.** Domain: all points (x, y)
such that $x \ne 0$ and $y \ne 0$ such that $y \ge 0$
Range: $(-\infty, 0)$ and $(0, \infty)$ Range: $(-\infty, \infty)$

31. b   **32.** d   **33.** a   **34.** c

35. The level curves are   **37.** The level curves are
parallel lines.   circles.

39. The level curves are   **41.** The level curves are
hyperbolas.   circles.

43. 135,540 units

45. (a) \$15,250   (b) \$18,425   (c) \$30,025

47.

$\dfrac{I}{R}$	0	0.03	0.05
0	\$5187.48	\$3859.98	\$3184.67
0.28	\$4008.46	\$2982.67	\$2460.85
0.35	\$3754.27	\$2793.53	\$2304.80

49. (a) C   (b) A   (c) B

51. (a) \$2.78 earnings per share
(b) x; Explanations will vary. Sample answer: The x-variable has a greater influence on the earnings per share because the absolute value of its coefficient is larger than the absolute value of the coefficient of the y-term.

53. Option (a): \$1003.73, \$240,895.20;
Option (b): \$798.36, \$287,409.60;
Option (c): \$1078.59, \$194,146.20;
Answers will vary.

Section 7.4   *(page 452)*

Skills Warm Up   *(page 452)*

1. $\dfrac{x}{\sqrt{x^2 + 3}}$ **2.** $-6x(3 - x^2)^2$ **3.** $e^{2t+1}(2t + 1)$

4. $\dfrac{e^{2x}(2 - 3e^{2x})}{\sqrt{1 - e^{2x}}}$ **5.** $-\dfrac{2}{3 - 2x}$ **6.** $\dfrac{3(t^2 - 2)}{2t(t^2 - 6)}$

7. $-\dfrac{10x}{(4x - 1)^3}$ **8.** $-\dfrac{(x + 2)^2(x^2 + 8x + 27)}{(x^2 - 9)^3}$

9. $f'(2) = 8$ **10.** $g'(2) = \frac{7}{2}$

---

1. $\dfrac{\partial z}{\partial x} = 3$; $\dfrac{\partial z}{\partial y} = 5$ **3.** $f_x(x, y) = 3$; $f_y(x, y) = -12y$

5. $f_x(x, y) = \dfrac{1}{y}$; $f_y(x, y) = -\dfrac{x}{y^2}$

7. $f_x(x, y) = \dfrac{x}{\sqrt{x^2 + y^2}}$; $f_y(x, y) = \dfrac{y}{\sqrt{x^2 + y^2}}$

9. $\dfrac{\partial z}{\partial x} = 2xe^{2y}$; $\dfrac{\partial z}{\partial y} = 2x^2 e^{2y}$

11. $h_x(x, y) = -2xe^{-(x^2+y^2)}$; $h_y(x, y) = -2ye^{-(x^2+y^2)}$

13. $\dfrac{\partial z}{\partial x} = -\dfrac{2y}{x^2 - y^2}$; $\dfrac{\partial z}{\partial y} = \dfrac{2x}{x^2 - y^2}$

15. $f_x(x, y) = 6x + y$, 13; $f_y(x, y) = x - 2y$, 0

17. $f_x(x, y) = 3ye^{3xy}$, 12; $f_y(x, y) = 3xe^{3xy}$, 0

19. $f_x(x, y) = -\dfrac{y^2}{(x - y)^2}$, $-\dfrac{1}{4}$; $f_y(x, y) = \dfrac{x^2}{(x - y)^2}$, $\dfrac{1}{4}$

21. $f_x(x, y) = \dfrac{3}{3x + 5y}$, 1; $f_y(x, y) = \dfrac{5}{3x + 5y}$, $\dfrac{5}{3}$

23. (a) 2   (b) 1   **25.** (a) -2 (b) -2

27. $w_x = y^2 z^4$
$w_y = 2xyz^4$
$w_z = 4xy^2 z^3$

29. $w_x = -\dfrac{2z}{(x + y)^2}$

$w_y = -\dfrac{2z}{(x + y)^2}$

$w_z = \dfrac{2}{x + y}$

CHAPTER 7

31. $w_x = 2z^2 + 3yz,\ 2$
$w_y = 3xz - 12yz,\ 30$
$w_z = 4xz + 3xy - 6y^2,\ -1$

33. $w_x = \dfrac{x}{\sqrt{x^2 + y^2 + z^2}},\ \dfrac{2}{3}$

$w_y = \dfrac{y}{\sqrt{x^2 + y^2 + z^2}},\ -\dfrac{1}{3}$

$w_z = \dfrac{z}{\sqrt{x^2 + y^2 + z^2}},\ \dfrac{2}{3}$

35. $w_x = 4xy^3z^2e^{2x^2},\ -8\sqrt{e}$
$w_y = 3y^2z^2e^{2x^2},\ 12\sqrt{e}$
$w_z = 2y^3ze^{2x^2},\ -4\sqrt{e}$

37. $w_x = \dfrac{5}{5x + 2y^3 - 3z},\ \dfrac{1}{5}$

$w_y = \dfrac{6y^2}{5x + 2y^3 - 3z},\ \dfrac{6}{25}$

$w_z = -\dfrac{3}{5x + 2y^3 - 3z},\ -\dfrac{3}{25}$

39. $(-6, 4)$ **41.** $(1, 1)$

43. $\dfrac{\partial^2 z}{\partial x^2} = 6x$

$\dfrac{\partial^2 z}{\partial y^2} = -8$

$\dfrac{\partial^2 z}{\partial y \partial x} = \dfrac{\partial^2 z}{\partial x \partial y} = 0$

45. $\dfrac{\partial^2 z}{\partial x^2} = 2$

$\dfrac{\partial^2 z}{\partial x \partial y} = \dfrac{\partial^2 z}{\partial y \partial x} = -2$

$\dfrac{\partial^2 z}{\partial y^2} = 6$

47. $\dfrac{\partial^2 z}{\partial x^2} = 108x^2(3x^4 - 2y^3)(11x^4 - 2y^3)$

$\dfrac{\partial^2 z}{\partial y^2} = 36y(2y^3 - 3x^4)(3x^4 - 8y^3)$

$\dfrac{\partial^2 z}{\partial x \partial y} = \dfrac{\partial^2 z}{\partial y \partial x} = 432x^3y^2(2y^3 - 3x^4)$

49. $\dfrac{\partial^2 z}{\partial x^2} = -\dfrac{y}{x^3}$

$\dfrac{\partial^2 z}{\partial x \partial y} = -\dfrac{x^2 - y^2}{2x^2y^2}$

$\dfrac{\partial^2 z}{\partial y \partial x} = -\dfrac{x^2 - y^2}{2x^2y^2}$

$\dfrac{\partial^2 z}{\partial y^2} = \dfrac{x}{y^3}$

51. $f_{xx}(x, y) = 12x^2 - 6y^2,\ 12$
$f_{xy}(x, y) = -12xy,\ 0$
$f_{yy}(x, y) = -6x^2 + 2,\ -4$
$f_{yx}(x, y) = -12xy,\ 0$

53. $f_{xx}(x, y) = e^{x^2}(4x^2y^3 + 2y^3),\ -6e$
$f_{xy}(x, y) = f_{yx}(x, y) = 6xy^2e^{x^2},\ 6e$
$f_{yy}(x, y) = 6ye^{x^2},\ -6e$

55. $f_{xx}(x, y, z) = 2$
$f_{xy}(x, y, z) = f_{yx}(x, y, z) = -3$
$f_{xz}(x, y, z) = f_{yy}(x, y, z) = f_{zz}(x, y, z) = 0$
$f_{yz}(x, y, z) = f_{zy}(x, y, z) = 4$
$f_{zz}(x, y, z) = 6z$

57. $f_{xx}(x, y, z) = -\dfrac{8yz}{(x + y)^3}$

$f_{xy}(x, y, z) = \dfrac{4z(x - y)}{(x + y)^3}$

$f_{xz}(x, y, z) = \dfrac{4y}{(x + y)^2}$

$f_{yy}(x, y, z) = \dfrac{8xz}{(x + y)^3}$

$f_{yx}(x, y, z) = \dfrac{4z(x - y)}{(x + y)^3}$

$f_{yz}(x, y, z) = -\dfrac{4x}{(x + y)^2}$

$f_{zz}(x, y, z) = 0$

$f_{zx}(x, y, z) = \dfrac{4y}{(x + y)^2}$

$f_{zy}(x, y, z) = -\dfrac{4x}{(x + y)^2}$

59. (a) At $(120, 160)$, $\dfrac{\partial C}{\partial x} \approx 154.77$; At $(120, 160)$, $\dfrac{\partial C}{\partial y} \approx 193.33$

(b) Racing bikes; Explanations will vary. Sample answer: The absolute value of dC/dy is greater than the absolute value of dC/dx at $(120, 160)$.

61. (a) About 113.72   (b) About 97.47

63. Complementary

65. (a) $\dfrac{\partial z}{\partial x} = 0.62$; $\dfrac{\partial z}{\partial y} = -0.41$

(b) For every increase of 1 billion dollars in expenditures on amusement parks and campgrounds, the expenditures for spectator sports will increase by 0.62 billion dollars. For every increase of 1 billion dollars in expenditures on live entertainment (excluding sports), the expenditures for spectator sports will decrease by 0.41 billion dollars.

67. $IQ_M(M, C) = \dfrac{100}{C}$, $IQ_M(12, 10) = 10$; For a child who has a current mental age of 12 years and a chronological age of 10 years, the IQ is increasing at a rate of 10 IQ points for every increase of 1 year in the child's mental age.

$IQ_C(M, C) = \dfrac{-100M}{C^2}$, $IQ_C(12, 10) = -12$; For a child who has a current mental age of 12 years and a chronological age of 10 years, the IQ is decreasing at a rate of 12 IQ points for every increase of 1 year in the child's chronological age.

69. $V_I(0.03, 0.28) \approx -14{,}478.99$
$V_R(0.03, 0.28) \approx -1391.17$
The rate of inflation has the greater negative influence on the growth of the investment because $|-14{,}478.99| > |-1391.17|$.

71. (a) $U_x = -10x + y$ (b) $U_y = x - 6y$
(c) When $x = 2$ and $y = 3$, $U_x = -17$ and $U_y = -16$. The person should consume one more unit of product y, because the rate of decrease of satisfaction is less for y.
(d)

The slope of U in the x-direction is 0 when $y = 10x$ and negative when $y < 10x$. The slope of U in the y-direction is 0 when $x = 6y$ and negative when $x < 6y$.

Section 7.5   *(page 461)*

Skills Warm Up   *(page 461)*

1. $(3, 2)$ **2.** $(11, 6)$ **3.** $(1, 4)$ **4.** $(4, 4)$
5. $(5, 2)$ **6.** $(3, -2)$ **7.** $(0, 0), (-1, 0)$
8. $(-2, 0), (2, -2)$

9. $\dfrac{\partial z}{\partial x} = 12x^2$ $\dfrac{\partial^2 z}{\partial y^2} = -6$

$\dfrac{\partial z}{\partial y} = -6y$ $\dfrac{\partial^2 z}{\partial x \partial y} = 0$

$\dfrac{\partial^2 z}{\partial x^2} = 24x$ $\dfrac{\partial^2 z}{\partial y \partial x} = 0$

10. $\dfrac{\partial z}{\partial x} = 10x^4$ $\dfrac{\partial^2 z}{\partial y^2} = -6y$

$\dfrac{\partial z}{\partial y} = -3y^2$ $\dfrac{\partial^2 z}{\partial x \partial y} = 0$

$\dfrac{\partial^2 z}{\partial x^2} = 40x^3$ $\dfrac{\partial^2 z}{\partial y \partial x} = 0$

11. $\dfrac{\partial z}{\partial x} = 4x^3 - \dfrac{\sqrt{xy}}{2x}$ $\dfrac{\partial^2 z}{\partial y^2} = \dfrac{\sqrt{xy}}{4y^2}$

$\dfrac{\partial z}{\partial y} = -\dfrac{\sqrt{xy}}{2y} + 2$ $\dfrac{\partial^2 z}{\partial x \partial y} = -\dfrac{\sqrt{xy}}{4xy}$

$\dfrac{\partial^2 z}{\partial x^2} = 12x^2 + \dfrac{\sqrt{xy}}{4x^2}$ $\dfrac{\partial^2 z}{\partial y \partial x} = -\dfrac{\sqrt{xy}}{4xy}$

12. $\dfrac{\partial z}{\partial x} = 4x - 3y$ $\dfrac{\partial^2 z}{\partial y^2} = 2$

$\dfrac{\partial z}{\partial y} = 2y - 3x$ $\dfrac{\partial^2 z}{\partial x \partial y} = -3$

$\dfrac{\partial^2 z}{\partial x^2} = 4$ $\dfrac{\partial^2 z}{\partial y \partial x} = -3$

13. $\dfrac{\partial z}{\partial x} = y^3 e^{xy^2}$ $\dfrac{\partial^2 z}{\partial y^2} = 4x^2 y^3 e^{xy^2} + 6xye^{xy^2}$

$\dfrac{\partial z}{\partial y} = 2xy^2 e^{xy^2} + e^{xy^2}$ $\dfrac{\partial^2 z}{\partial x \partial y} = 2xy^4 e^{xy^2} + 3y^2 e^{xy^2}$

$\dfrac{\partial^2 z}{\partial x^2} = y^5 e^{xy^2}$ $\dfrac{\partial^2 z}{\partial y \partial x} = 2xy^4 e^{xy^2} + 3y^2 e^{xy^2}$

14. $\dfrac{\partial z}{\partial x} = e^{xy}(xy + 1)$ $\dfrac{\partial^2 z}{\partial y^2} = x^3 e^{xy}$

$\dfrac{\partial z}{\partial y} = x^2 e^{xy}$ $\dfrac{\partial^2 z}{\partial x \partial y} = xe^{xy}(xy + 2)$

$\dfrac{\partial^2 z}{\partial x^2} = ye^{xy}(xy + 2)$ $\dfrac{\partial^2 z}{\partial y \partial x} = xe^{xy}(xy + 2)$

1. Critical point: $(-2, -4)$
No relative extrema
$(-2, -4, 1)$ is a saddle point.
3. Critical point: $(0, 0)$
Relative minimum: $(0, 0, 1)$
5. Critical point: $(1, 3)$
Relative minimum: $(1, 3, 0)$
7. Critical point: $(-1, 1)$
Relative minimum: $(-1, 1, -4)$
9. Critical point: $(8, 16)$
Relative maximum: $(8, 16, 74)$

11. Critical point: $(1, 1)$
Relative minimum: $(1, 1, 11)$
13. Critical points: $(0, 0), \left(\frac{4}{3}, \frac{4}{3}\right)$
Saddle point: $(0, 0, 1)$
Relative maximum: $\left(\frac{4}{3}, \frac{4}{3}, \frac{59}{27}\right)$
15. Critical point: $(0, 0)$
Saddle point: $(0, 0, 0)$
17. Critical points: $\left(\frac{1}{2}, \frac{1}{2}\right), \left(-\frac{1}{2}, -\frac{1}{2}\right)$
Relative maximum: $\left(\frac{1}{2}, \frac{1}{2}, e^{1/2}\right)$
Relative minimum: $\left(-\frac{1}{2}, -\frac{1}{2}, -e^{1/2}\right)$
19. Insufficient information   **21.** $f(x_0, y_0)$ is a saddle point.
23. $f(x_0, y_0)$ is a relative minimum.
25. Relative minima: $(a, 0, 0), (0, b, 0)$
Second-Partials Test fails at $(a, 0)$ and $(0, b)$.
27. Saddle point: $(0, 0, 0)$
Second-Partials Test fails at $(0, 0)$.
29. Relative minimum: $(0, 0, 0)$
Second-Partials Test fails at $(0, 0)$.
31. Relative minimum: $(1, -3, 0)$
33. 15, 15, 15   **35.** 20, 20, 20   **37.** $x_1 = 3, x_2 = 6$
39. $p_1 = 2500, p_2 = 3000$ **41.** $x_1 \approx 94, x_2 \approx 157$
43. 32 in. $\times$ 16 in. $\times$ 16 in.
45. Base dimensions: 3 ft $\times$ 3 ft
Height: 2 ft; Minimum cost: $5.40
47. $x = 1.25, y = 2.5$; $4.625 million
49. 500 smallmouth bass; 200 largemouth bass
51. Proof   **53.** True

Quiz Yourself   *(page 464)*

1. (a)

2. (a)

(b) 3   (c) $\left(0, \frac{5}{2}, 1\right)$ (b) $2\sqrt{35}$ (c) $(2, 2, -1)$

3. (a)

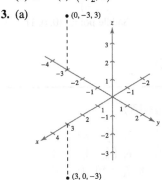

(b) $3\sqrt{6}$ (c) $\left(\frac{3}{2}, -\frac{3}{2}, 0\right)$
4. $(x - 2)^2 + (y + 1)^2 + (z - 3)^2 = 16$
5. $(x - 1)^2 + (y - 4)^2 + (z + 2)^2 = 11$
6. Center: $(4, 1, 3)$; radius: 7

7.

8.

9.

10. Ellipsoid

11. Hyperboloid of two sheets   **12.** Elliptic paraboloid

13. $f(1, 0) = 1$
$f(4, -1) = -5$

14. $f(1, 0) = 2$
$f(4, -1) = 3\sqrt{7}$

15. $f(1, 0) = 0$
$f(4, -1) = \ln 6 \approx 1.79$

16. (a) Between 30° and 50°   (b) Between 40° and 80°
(c) Between 70° and 90°

17. $f_x = 2x - 3$; $f_x(-2, 3) = -7$
$f_y = 4y - 1$; $f_y(-2, 3) = 11$

18. $f_x = \dfrac{y(3 + y)}{(x + y)^2}$; $f_x(-2, 3) = 18$

$f_y = \dfrac{-2xy - y^2 - 3x}{(x + y)^2}$; $f_y(-2, 3) = 9$

19. $f_x = 3x^2 e^{2y}$; $f_x(-2, 3) = 12e^6 \approx 4841.15$
$f_y = 2x^3 e^{2y}$; $f_y(-2, 3) = -16e^6 \approx -6454.86$

20. $f_x = \dfrac{2}{2x + 7y}$; $f_x(-2, 3) = \dfrac{2}{17} \approx 0.118$

$f_y = \dfrac{7}{2x + 7y}$; $f_y(-2, 3) = \dfrac{7}{17} \approx 0.412$

21. Critical point: $(1, 0)$
Relative minimum:
$(1, 0, -3)$

22. Critical points: $(0, 0)$, $\left(\frac{4}{3}, \frac{4}{3}\right)$
Relative maximum:
$\left(\frac{4}{3}, \frac{4}{3}, \frac{59}{27}\right)$
Saddle point: $(0, 0, 1)$

23. $x = 80$, $y = 20$; \$20,000

Section 7.6   *(page 470)*

Skills Warm Up   *(page 470)*

1. $\left(\frac{7}{8}, \frac{1}{12}\right)$ **2.** $\left(-\frac{1}{24}, -\frac{7}{8}\right)$ **3.** $\left(\frac{55}{12}, -\frac{25}{12}\right)$
4. $\left(\frac{22}{23}, -\frac{3}{23}\right)$ **5.** $\left(\frac{5}{3}, \frac{1}{3}, 0\right)$ **6.** $\left(\frac{14}{19}, -\frac{10}{19}, -\frac{32}{57}\right)$
7. $f_x = 2xy + y^2$ **8.** $f_x = 50y^2(x + y)$
    $f_y = x^2 + 2xy$ $f_y = 50y(x + y)(x + 2y)$
9. $f_x = 3x^2 - 4xy + yz$ **10.** $f_x = yz + z^2$
    $f_y = -2x^2 + xz$ $f_y = xz + z^2$
    $f_z = xy$ $f_z = xy + 2xz + 2yz$

1. $f(5, 5) = 25$ **3.** $f(4, 4) = 32$ **5.** $f(\sqrt{2}, 1) = 1$
7. $f(25, 50) = 2600$ **9.** $f(1, 1) = 2$
11. $f(2, 2) = e^4$ **13.** $f(9, 6, 9) = 432$

15. $f\left(\frac{1}{3}, \frac{1}{3}, \frac{1}{3}\right) = \frac{1}{3}$ **17.** $f\left(\frac{\sqrt{3}}{3}, \frac{\sqrt{3}}{3}, \frac{\sqrt{3}}{3}\right) = \sqrt{3}$

19. 20, 20, 20   **21.** 40, 40, 40   **23.** $3\sqrt{2}$ **25.** $\sqrt{3}$
27. 15 units × 10 units × 6 units   **29.** 12 ft × 12 ft × 18 ft
31. $x_1 = 145$ units, $x_2 = 855$ units

33. (a) $f\left(\frac{3125}{6}, \frac{6250}{3}\right) \approx 147{,}314$ (b) 1.473
(c) 184,142 units   (d) 515,599 units

35. (a) $x \approx 317$ units, $y \approx 68$ units   (b) Answers will vary.
37. (a) 50 ft × 120 ft   (b) \$2400
39. $x = \sqrt[3]{0.065} \approx 0.402$ L
$y = \frac{1}{2}\sqrt[3]{0.065} \approx 0.201$ L
$z = \frac{1}{3}\sqrt[3]{0.065} \approx 0.134$ L

41. About 190.7 g
43. (a) Cable television: \$1200
    Newspaper: \$600
    Radio: \$900
(b) About 3718 responses

Section 7.7   *(page 478)*

Skills Warm Up   *(page 478)*

1. 5.0225   **2.** 0.0189
3. $S_a = 2a - 4 - 4b$ **4.** $S_a = 8a - 6 - 2b$
    $S_b = 12b - 8 - 4a$ $S_b = 18b - 4 - 2a$
5. 15   **6.** 42   **7.** $\frac{25}{12}$ **8.** 14   **9.** 31   **10.** 95

1. $S = 1.6$; $S = 0.8259$ **3.** $S = 6.46$; $S = 0.125$
5. $y = x + \frac{2}{3}$ **7.** $y = -2.3x - 0.9$

9. $y = 0.8x + 2$ **11.** $y = -1.1824x + 6.385$
13. (a) $y = 4.13t + 11.6$ (b) About \$69.4 billion   (c) 2018
15. (a) $y = 0.138x + 22.1$ (b) 44.18 bushels/acre

17.

19.

Positive correlation,
$r \approx 0.9981$

No correlation, $r = 0$

21.

No correlation, $r \approx 0.0750$

23. False; The data modeled by $y = 3.29x - 4.17$ have a positive correlation.

25. True   **27.** True   **29.** Answers will vary.

Section 7.8   *(page 486)*

> ### Skills Warm Up   *(page 486)*
>
> **1.** 1   **2.** 6   **3.** 42   **4.** $\frac{1}{2}$ **5.** $\frac{19}{4}$
> **6.** $\frac{16}{3}$ **7.** $\frac{1}{7}$ **8.** 4   **9.** $\ln 5$ **10.** $\ln(e - 1)$
> **11.** $\frac{e}{2}(e^4 - 1)$ **12.** $\frac{1}{2}\left(1 - \frac{1}{e^2}\right)$
>
> **13.**
>
> **14.**
>
> **15.**
>
> **16.**

1. $\frac{3x^2}{2}$ **3.** $\frac{x}{2}(x^2 - 1)$ **5.** $2y^4 + y^3 - 2y^2 - 16y$

7. $x^2\sqrt{x} + x^{3/2} - x^5 - x^9$ **9.** $\frac{y^3}{2}$ **11.** 3   **13.** 36

15. 64   **17.** $\frac{1}{2}$ **19.** $\frac{21}{2}$ **21.** $\frac{1}{3}$ **23.** 4   **25.** 24

27. 8   **29.** $\frac{16}{3}$ **31.** 36   **33.** 5   **35.** 2

37.

$$\int_0^1 \int_0^2 dy\, dx = \int_0^2 \int_0^1 dx\, dy = 2$$

39.

$$\int_0^1 \int_{2y}^2 dx\, dy = \int_0^2 \int_0^{x/2} dy\, dx = 1$$

41.

$$\int_0^2 \int_{x/2}^1 dy\, dx = \int_0^1 \int_0^{2y} dx\, dy = 1$$

43.

$$\int_0^1 \int_{y^2}^{\sqrt[3]{y}} dx\, dy = \int_0^1 \int_{x^3}^{\sqrt{x}} dy\, dx = \frac{5}{12}$$

45. (a) Answers will vary; $\frac{1}{2}(e^9 - 1) \approx 4051.042$
   (b) Answers will vary; $\frac{1}{2}(1 - e^{-4}) \approx 0.491$

47. 0.6588   **49.** 8.1747   **51.** 0.4521

53. 1.1190   **55.** True

Section 7.9   *(page 494)*

> ### Skills Warm Up   *(page 494)*
>
> **1.**
>
> **2.**
>
> **3.**
>
> **4.**
>
>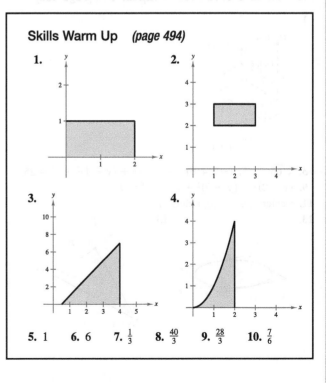
>
> **5.** 1   **6.** 6   **7.** $\frac{1}{3}$ **8.** $\frac{40}{3}$ **9.** $\frac{28}{3}$ **10.** $\frac{7}{6}$

1.

3.

10

$\frac{2}{15}$

5.

7.

πa^2

$\frac{3}{35}$

9. $\displaystyle\int_0^3 \int_0^5 xy \, dy \, dx = \int_0^5 \int_0^3 xy \, dx \, dy = \frac{225}{4}$

11. $\displaystyle\int_0^2 \int_x^{2x} \frac{y}{x^2+y^2} \, dy \, dx = \int_0^2 \int_{y/2}^y \frac{y}{x^2+y^2} \, dx \, dy$

$+ \displaystyle\int_2^4 \int_{y/2}^2 \frac{y}{x^2+y^2} \, dx \, dy = \ln \frac{5}{2}$

13. 4   **15.** 12   **17.** 4   **19.** $\frac{40}{3}$ **21.** $\frac{81}{2}$
23. $\frac{134}{3}$ **25.** 10,000   **27.** $\frac{3}{2}$ **29.** $\frac{8}{3}$
31. \$13,400   **33.** \$75,125   **35.** 25,645.24

Review Exercises for Chapter 7   *(page 500)*

1.

3. $\sqrt{65}$ **5.** $(-1, 4, 6)$ **7.** $x^2 + (y-1)^2 + z^2 = 25$
9. $(x-2)^2 + (y+2)^2 + (z+3)^2 = 9$
11. Center: $(4, -2, 3)$; radius: 7
13.

15.

17.

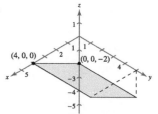

19. Sphere   **21.** Ellipsoid   **23.** Elliptic paraboloid
25. Top half of a circular cone
27. (a) 18   (b) 0   (c) -245 (d) -32
29. Domain: all points (x, y) inside or on the circle $x^2 + y^2 = 1$
Range: $[0, 1]$
31. Domain: all points (x, y)
Range: $(0, \infty)$
33. The level curves are lines of slope $-\frac{2}{5}$.

35. The level curves are hyperbolas.

37. (a) No; the precipitation increments are 7.99 in., 9.99 in., 9.99 in., 9.99 in., and 19.99 in.
(b) Increase the number of level curves to correspond to smaller increments of precipitation.
39. (a) \$2.49
(b) Because $\dfrac{\partial z}{\partial y} = 0.060 > \dfrac{\partial z}{\partial x} = 0.046$, y has the greater influence.
41. $f_x = 2xy + 3y + 2$
$f_y = x^2 + 3x - 5$
43. $z_x = \dfrac{2x}{y^2}$

$z_y = \dfrac{-2x^2}{y^3}$

45. $f_x = \dfrac{5}{5x + 4y}$

$f_y = \dfrac{4}{5x + 4y}$

47. $f_x = ye^x + e^y$
$f_y = xe^y + e^x$
49. $w_x = yz^2$
$w_y = xz^2$
$w_z = 2xyz$
51. (a) -9 (b) -6 **53.** (a) -2 (b) -2
55. $f_{xx} = 6$
$f_{yy} = 12y$
$f_{xy} = f_{yx} = -1$
57. $f_{xx} = f_{yy} = f_{xy} = f_{yx} = \dfrac{-1}{4(1 + x + y)^{3/2}}$
59. $f_{xx} = 10yz^3$ $f_{yx} = 1 + 10xz^3$ $f_{zx} = 30xyz^2$
$f_{xy} = 1 + 10xz^3$ $f_{yy} = -18yz$ $f_{zy} = 15x^2z^2 - 9y^2$
$f_{xz} = 30xyz^2$ $f_{yz} = 15x^2z^2 - 9y^2$ $f_{zz} = 30x^2yz$
61. (a) $C_x(500, 250) = 99.50$
$C_y(500, 250) = 140$
(b) Downhill skis; this is determined by comparing the marginal costs for the two models of skis at the production level (500, 250).

63. Critical point: $(0,0)$
Relative minimum: $(0,0,0)$
65. Critical point: $(-2,3)$
Saddle point: $(-2,3,1)$
67. Critical points: $(0,0), \left(\frac{1}{6},\frac{1}{12}\right)$
Relative minimum: $\left(\frac{1}{6},\frac{1}{12},-\frac{1}{432}\right)$
Saddle point: $(0,0,0)$
69. Critical points: $(1,1),(-1,-1).(1,-1),(-1,1)$
Relative minimum: $(1,1,-2)$
Relative maximum: $(-1,-1,6)$
Saddle points: $(1,-1,2),(-1,1,2)$
71. $x_1=50, x_2=200$
73. At $(3,6)$, the relative maximum is 36.
75. At $(2,2)$, the relative minimum is 8.
77. At $\left(\frac{4}{3},\frac{2}{3},\frac{4}{3}\right)$, the relative maximum is $\frac{32}{27}$.
79. $x_1=378$ units; $x_2=623$ units
81. $y=\frac{60}{59}x-\frac{15}{59}$
83. (a) $y=-2.6x+347$
(b) 126 cameras
(c) About \$56.54

85. 1   **87.** $\frac{7}{4}$ **89.** $\frac{32}{3}$ **91.** $\frac{9}{2}$ **93.** 20   **95.** 8
97. $\frac{4096}{9}$ **99.** 3   **101.** \$5700   **103.** About \$155.69/ft²

Test Yourself   *(page 504)*

1. (a)

(b) $2\sqrt{2}$
(c) $(2,-2,0)$
2. (a)
(b) 3
(c) $(-3,1,2.5)$
3. (a)

(b) $14\sqrt{2}$
(c) $(4,2,-2)$
4. Center: $(10,-5,5)$; radius: 5

5. Hyperboloid of one sheet
6. Elliptic cone   **7.** Hyperbolic paraboloid
8. $f(3,3)=19$ **9.** $f(3,3)=\frac{3}{2}$
$f(1,4)=6$ $f(1,4)=-9$
10. $f(3,3)=0$
$f(1,4)=4\ln\frac{1}{4}\approx-5.5$
11. $f_x=6x+9y^2;\ f_x(10,-1)=69$
$f_y=18xy;\ f_y(10,-1)=-180$
12. $f_x=(x+y)^{1/2}+\frac{x}{2(x+y)^{1/2}};\ f_x(10,-1)=\frac{14}{3}$
$f_y=\frac{x}{2(x+y)^{1/2}};\ f_y(10,-1)=\frac{5}{3}$
13. Critical point: $(1,-2)$; Relative minimum: $(1,-2,-23)$
14. Critical points: $(0,0),(1,1),(-1,-1)$
Saddle point: $(0,0,0)$
Relative maxima: $(1,1,2),(-1,-1,2)$
15. About 128,613 units   **16.** $y=0.52x+1.4$
17. $\frac{3}{2}$ **18.** 1   **19.** $\frac{4}{3}$ units²   **20.** 48   **21.** $\frac{11}{6}$

Chapter 8

Section 8.1   *(page 511)*

Skills Warm Up   *(page 511)*

1. 35 cm²   **2.** 12 in.²   **3.** $c=13$ **4.** $b=4$
5. $b=15$ **6.** $a=6$ **7.** Equilateral triangle
8. Isosceles triangle   **9.** Right triangle
10. Isosceles triangle and right triangle

1. $405°, -315°$ **3.** $240°, -480°$ **5.** $300°, -60°$
7. $\frac{19\pi}{9}, -\frac{17\pi}{9}$ **9.** $\frac{28\pi}{15}, -\frac{32\pi}{15}$ **11.** $\frac{\pi}{6}$ **13.** $\frac{3\pi}{2}$
15. $\frac{15\pi}{4}$ **17.** $-\frac{2\pi}{15}$ **19.** $-\frac{4\pi}{5}$ **21.** $\frac{11\pi}{6}$
23. $450°$ **25.** $420°$ **27.** $-15°$ **29.** $48°$
31. $570°$ **33.** $c=10, \theta=60°$ **35.** $a=4\sqrt{3}, \theta=30°$
37. $\theta=40°$ **39.** $s=\sqrt{3}, \theta=60°$ **41.** $4\sqrt{3}$ in.²
43. $\frac{25\sqrt{3}}{4}$ ft²   **45.** 18 ft
47.

r	8 ft	15 in.	85 cm	24 in.	$\frac{12{,}963}{\pi}$ mi
s	12 ft	24 in.	200.28 cm	96 in.	8642 mi
θ	1.5	1.6	$\frac{3\pi}{4}$	4	$\frac{2\pi}{3}$

49. $\frac{35\pi}{12}\approx9.16$ inches
51. (a) About 500 revolutions per minute
(b) About 20 minutes
53. $\frac{4900\pi}{3}$ ft²
55. False. An obtuse angle is between 90° and 180°.
57. True   **59.** Answers will vary.

Section 8.2 *(page 522)*

Skills Warm Up *(page 522)*

1. $\dfrac{7\pi}{4}$ 2. $-\dfrac{5\pi}{3}$ 3. $-\dfrac{5\pi}{4}$ 4. $\dfrac{13\pi}{6}$

5. $x = 0, 1$ 6. $x = 0, -\frac{1}{2}$ 7. $x = -1, 3$

8. $x = 2, 3$ 9. $t = 10$ 10. $t = \frac{7}{2}$

11. $t = \frac{445}{8}$ 12. $t = 7$

---

1. $\sin\theta = \frac{3}{5}$, $\csc\theta = \frac{5}{3}$
$\cos\theta = \frac{4}{5}$, $\sec\theta = \frac{5}{4}$
$\tan\theta = \frac{3}{4}$, $\cot\theta = \frac{4}{3}$

3. $\sin\theta = -\frac{5}{13}$, $\csc\theta = -\frac{13}{5}$
$\cos\theta = -\frac{12}{13}$, $\sec\theta = -\frac{13}{12}$
$\tan\theta = \frac{5}{12}$, $\cot\theta = \frac{12}{5}$

5. $\sin\theta = \dfrac{2\sqrt{5}}{5}$, $\csc\theta = \dfrac{\sqrt{5}}{2}$

$\cos\theta = -\dfrac{\sqrt{5}}{5}$, $\sec\theta = -\sqrt{5}$

$\tan\theta = -2$, $\cot\theta = -\dfrac{1}{2}$

7.

$\csc\theta = 3$
$\cos\theta = \dfrac{2\sqrt{2}}{3}$, $\sec\theta = \dfrac{3\sqrt{2}}{4}$
$\tan\theta = \dfrac{\sqrt{2}}{4}$, $\cot\theta = 2\sqrt{2}$

9.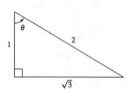

$\sin\theta = \dfrac{\sqrt{3}}{2}$, $\csc\theta = \dfrac{2\sqrt{3}}{3}$
$\cos\theta = \dfrac{1}{2}$
$\tan\theta = \sqrt{3}$, $\cot\theta = \dfrac{\sqrt{3}}{3}$

11.

$\sin\theta = \dfrac{3\sqrt{10}}{10}$, $\csc\theta = \dfrac{\sqrt{10}}{3}$
$\cos\theta = \dfrac{\sqrt{10}}{10}$, $\sec\theta = \sqrt{10}$
$\cot\theta = \dfrac{1}{3}$

13. Quadrant IV   15. Quadrant I   17. Quadrant II

19. $\sin 60° = \dfrac{\sqrt{3}}{2}$, $\csc 60° = \dfrac{2\sqrt{3}}{3}$

$\cos 60° = \dfrac{1}{2}$, $\sec 60° = 2$

$\tan 60° = \sqrt{3}$, $\cot 60° = \dfrac{\sqrt{3}}{3}$

21. $\sin\dfrac{\pi}{4} = \dfrac{\sqrt{2}}{2}$, $\csc\dfrac{\pi}{4} = \sqrt{2}$

$\cos\dfrac{\pi}{4} = \dfrac{\sqrt{2}}{2}$, $\sec\dfrac{\pi}{4} = \sqrt{2}$

$\tan\dfrac{\pi}{4} = 1$, $\cot\dfrac{\pi}{4} = 1$

23. $\sin\left(-\dfrac{\pi}{2}\right) = -1$, $\csc\left(-\dfrac{\pi}{2}\right) = -1$

$\cos\left(-\dfrac{\pi}{2}\right) = 0$, $\sec\left(-\dfrac{\pi}{2}\right) = $ undefined

$\tan\left(-\dfrac{\pi}{2}\right) = $ undefined, $\cot\left(-\dfrac{\pi}{2}\right) = 0$

25. $\sin 225° = -\dfrac{\sqrt{2}}{2}$, $\csc 225° = -\sqrt{2}$

$\cos 225° = -\dfrac{\sqrt{2}}{2}$, $\sec 225° = -\sqrt{2}$

$\tan 225° = 1$, $\cot 225° = 1$

27. $\sin 300° = -\dfrac{\sqrt{3}}{2}$, $\csc 300° = -\dfrac{2\sqrt{3}}{3}$

$\cos 300° = \dfrac{1}{2}$, $\sec 300° = 2$

$\tan 300° = -\sqrt{3}$, $\cot 300° = -\dfrac{\sqrt{3}}{3}$

29. $\sin 750° = \dfrac{1}{2}$, $\csc 750° = 2$

$\cos 750° = \dfrac{\sqrt{3}}{2}$, $\sec 750° = \dfrac{2\sqrt{3}}{3}$

$\tan 750° = \dfrac{\sqrt{3}}{3}$, $\cot 750° = \sqrt{3}$

31. $\sin\dfrac{10\pi}{3} = -\dfrac{\sqrt{3}}{2}$, $\csc\dfrac{10\pi}{3} = -\dfrac{2\sqrt{3}}{3}$

$\cos\dfrac{10\pi}{3} = -\dfrac{1}{2}$, $\sec\dfrac{10\pi}{3} = -2$

$\tan\dfrac{10\pi}{3} = \sqrt{3}$, $\cot\dfrac{10\pi}{3} = \dfrac{\sqrt{3}}{3}$

33. 0.1736   35. 0.3640   37. -0.3420 39. 1.7321

41. -0.6052 43. $\dfrac{100\sqrt{3}}{3}$ 45. $\dfrac{25\sqrt{3}}{3}$ 47. 15.5572

49. $\dfrac{\pi}{6}, \dfrac{5\pi}{6}$ 51. $\dfrac{\pi}{3}, \dfrac{4\pi}{3}$ 53. $\dfrac{\pi}{3}, \dfrac{2\pi}{3}$ 55. $\dfrac{\pi}{3}, \dfrac{5\pi}{3}$

57. $\dfrac{5\pi}{4}, \dfrac{7\pi}{4}$ 59. $\dfrac{\pi}{3}, \dfrac{2\pi}{3}$ 61. $\dfrac{\pi}{4}, \dfrac{3\pi}{4}, \dfrac{5\pi}{4}, \dfrac{7\pi}{4}$

63. $0, \dfrac{\pi}{4}, \pi, \dfrac{5\pi}{4}, 2\pi$ 65. $\dfrac{\pi}{6}, \dfrac{\pi}{2}, \dfrac{5\pi}{6}, \dfrac{3\pi}{2}$ 67. $\dfrac{\pi}{4}, \dfrac{5\pi}{4}$

69. $0, \dfrac{\pi}{2}, \pi, 2\pi$ 71. About 19.3 ft

73. (a) 12 mi   (b) About 6.9 mi   (c) 6 mi

75. About 443.2 m; about 323.3 m

77. About 11.5370°   79. About 1.3 mi

81. (a) 102.6°F   (b) 102.1°F   (c) 100.6°F

(d) At 4 P.M. the following afternoon, the patient's temperature should return to normal. This is determined by setting the function equal to 98.6 and solving for t.

83.

x	0	2	4	6	8	10
$f(x)$	0	2.7021	2.7756	1.2244	1.2979	4

85. True

87. False. Because $\sin 45° = \cos 45°$, $\sin^2 45° - \cos^2 45° = 0$.

Section 8.3 *(page 531)*

Skills Warm Up *(page 531)*

1. 14 **2.** 10 **3.** 0 **4.** 0 **5.** 1

6. $-\dfrac{\sqrt{3}}{3}$ **7.** $-\dfrac{1}{2}$ **8.** $-\dfrac{\sqrt{3}}{2}$ **9.** $\dfrac{1}{2}$

10. $-\dfrac{\sqrt{3}}{2}$ **11.** 0.9659 **12.** -0.6428

13. -0.9962 **14.** 0.6428 **15.** 0.9744

16. 0.3090 **17.** -0.6494 **18.** -0.8391

1. Period: π **3.** Period: 4π **5.** Period: 2
  Amplitude: 2   Amplitude: $\frac{3}{2}$ Amplitude: $\frac{1}{2}$

7. Period: $\dfrac{2\pi}{3}$ **9.** Period: $\dfrac{\pi}{3}$
  Amplitude: 1   Amplitude: $\dfrac{3}{2}$

11. Period: 3π **13.** Period: $\frac{1}{2}$
  Amplitude: $\frac{1}{2}$ Amplitude: 3

15. π **17.** $\dfrac{2\pi}{5}$ **19.** 6 **21.** c; π **22.** e; π

23. f; 2 **24.** a; 2π **25.** b; 4π **26.** d; 2π

27.

29.

31.

33.

35.

37.

39.

41.

43.

45.

47.

49.

51.

x	-0.1	-0.01	-0.001
$f(x)$	1.9471	1.9995	2.0000

x	0.001	0.01	0.1
$f(x)$	2.0000	1.9995	1.9471

$$\lim_{x\to 0}\frac{\sin 4x}{2x}=2$$

53.

x	-0.1	-0.01	-0.001
$f(x)$	0.7316	0.7498	0.75

x	0.001	0.01	0.1
$f(x)$	0.75	0.7498	0.7316

$$\lim_{x\to 0}\frac{\tan 3x}{\tan 4x}=0.75$$

55.

x	-0.1	-0.01	-0.001
$f(x)$	-0.1499	-0.0150	-0.0015

x	0.001	0.01	0.1
$f(x)$	0.0015	0.0150	0.1499

$$\lim_{x \to 0} \frac{3(1 - \cos x)}{x} = 0$$

57.

x	-0.1	-0.01	-0.001
$f(x)$	2.0271	2.0003	2.0000

x	0.001	0.01	0.1
$f(x)$	2.0000	2.0003	2.0271

$$\lim_{x \to 0} \frac{\tan 2x}{x} = 2$$

59.

x	-0.1	-0.01	-0.001
$f(x)$	-0.0997	-0.0100	-0.0010

x	0.001	0.01	0.1
$f(x)$	0.0010	0.0100	0.0997

$$\lim_{x \to 0} \frac{\sin^2 x}{x} = 0$$

61. $a = 2, d = 1$ **63.** $a = -4, d = 4$
65. b   **66.** d   **67.** a   **68.** c
69. (a)

(b) As the population of the prey increases, the population of the predator increases as well. At some point, the predator eliminates the prey faster than the prey can reproduce, and the prey population decreases rapidly. As the prey becomes scarce, the predator population decreases, releasing the prey from predator pressure, and the cycle begins again.

71. $P(8930) \approx 0.9977$
$E(8930) \approx -0.4339$
$I(8930) \approx -0.6182$

73. (a) 6 sec (b) 10
(c)

75. (a) $\frac{1}{440}$ (b) 440
(c)

77. (a)

(b) Yes; May, June, July, August, September, and October

79. (a) A   (b) B   (c) B
(d) The frequency is the inverse of the period.

81. (a)

(b) $\dfrac{\pi}{6} < x < \dfrac{5\pi}{6}$

(c) As x approaches π, $f(x) = 2 \sin x$ approaches 0. Because $g(x) = \dfrac{1}{f(x)}$, $g(x) = 0.5 \csc x$ approaches infinity as x approaches π.

83. False. The amplitude is $|-3| = 3$.   **85.** True

Quiz Yourself   *(page 535)*

1. $\dfrac{\pi}{12}$ **2.** $\dfrac{7\pi}{12}$ **3.** $-\dfrac{4\pi}{9}$ **4.** $\dfrac{7\pi}{36}$ **5.** $120°$

6. $48°$ **7.** $-240°$ **8.** $165°$ **9.** $-\dfrac{\sqrt{2}}{2}$

10. $-\dfrac{1}{2}$ **11.** $-\dfrac{\sqrt{3}}{3}$ **12.** 1 **13.** 2 **14.** -1

15. $\dfrac{\pi}{4}, \dfrac{5\pi}{4}$ **16.** $0, 2\pi$ **17.** $\dfrac{\pi}{3}, \dfrac{2\pi}{3}, \dfrac{4\pi}{3}, \dfrac{5\pi}{3}$

18. $\theta = 30°; a = 5\sqrt{3}$ **19.** $\theta = 40°; a \approx 10.285$

20. $\theta = 65°; a \approx 5.5957$ **21.** $d \approx 286.8$ ft

22. (a)

23. (a)

(b) $\dfrac{8\pi}{3}$ (b) $\dfrac{\pi}{2}$

24. (a)

(b) 3

25. (a)

(b) Maximum: December
Minimum: June

Section 8.4   *(page 542)*

Skills Warm Up   *(page 542)*

1. $f'(x) = 9x^2 - 4x + 4$ **2.** $g'(x) = 12x^2(x^3 + 4)^3$

3. $f'(x) = 3x^2 + 2x + 1$ **4.** $g'(x) = \dfrac{2(5 - x^2)}{(x^2 + 5)^2}$

5. Relative minimum: $(-2, -3)$

6. Relative maximum: $\left(-2, \dfrac{22}{3}\right)$
Relative minimum: $\left(2, -\dfrac{10}{3}\right)$

7. $x = \dfrac{\pi}{3}, x = \dfrac{2\pi}{3}$ **8.** $x = \dfrac{2\pi}{3}, x = \dfrac{4\pi}{3}$

9. $x = \pi$ **10.** No solution

---

1. $\dfrac{1}{3} \cos \dfrac{x}{3}$ **3.** $12x^2 \sec^2 4x^3$ **5.** $5 \sec^2 5t$

7. $2 \sin x \cos x$ **9.** $\pi \tan \pi x \sec \pi x$

11. $-2 \csc^2(2x + 1)$ **13.** $\dfrac{\sec^2 2x}{\sqrt{\tan 2x}}$

15. $-t^2 \sin t + 2t \cos t$ **17.** $-\dfrac{t \sin t + \cos t}{t^2}$

19. $e^{x^2} \sec x(\tan x + 2x)$ **21.** $-3 \sin 3x + 2 \sin x \cos x$

23. $\sin \dfrac{1}{x} - \dfrac{1}{x} \cos \dfrac{1}{x}$ **25.** $16 \sec^2 4x \tan 4x$

27. $2e^{2x}(\cos 2x + \sin 2x)$ **29.** $-2 \cos x \sin x = -\sin 2x$

31. $-4 \cos x \sin x = -2 \sin 2x$

33. $2 \sin 2x + 2 \sin x \cos x = 3 \sin 2x$

35. $\sec^2 x - 1 = \tan^2 x$

37. $\sin^2 x \cos x - \sin^4 x \cos x = \sin^2 x \cos^3 x$

39. $\dfrac{2 \cos x}{\sin x} = 2 \cot x$ **41.** $y = 2x + \dfrac{\pi}{2} - 1$

43. $y = 4x - 4\pi$ **45.** $y = -2x + \dfrac{3}{2}\pi - 1$

47. $y = 0$ **49.** $\dfrac{\cos x}{2 \sin 2y}; 0$ **51.** $\dfrac{5}{4}$; one complete cycle

53. 2; two complete cycles   **55.** 1; one complete cycle

57. Relative maximum: $(4, 1)$
Relative minima: $(2, -1), (6, -1)$

59. Relative maximum: $(\pi, 1)$
Relative minima: $\left(\dfrac{\pi}{2}, 0\right), \left(\dfrac{3\pi}{2}, 0\right)$

61. Relative maximum: $\left(\dfrac{\pi}{3}, \dfrac{3\sqrt{3}}{2}\right)$

Relative minimum: $\left(\dfrac{5\pi}{3}, -\dfrac{3\sqrt{3}}{2}\right)$

63. Relative maximum: $\left(\dfrac{\pi}{4}, 1.5509\right)$

Relative minimum: $\left(\dfrac{5\pi}{4}, -35.8885\right)$

65. Relative maximum: $\left(\dfrac{5\pi}{3}, \dfrac{5\pi}{3} + \sqrt{3}\right)$

Relative minimum: $\left(\dfrac{\pi}{3}, \dfrac{\pi}{3} - \sqrt{3}\right)$

67. $-x \sin x + 2 \cos x$ **69.** $-4x^2 \cos x^2 - 2 \sin x^2$

71. (a) $h'(t)$ is a maximum when $t = 0$, or at midnight.
(b) $h'(t)$ is a minimum when $t = \dfrac{1}{2}$, or at noon.

73. August; about 5836 thousand, or 5,836,000, workers

75. June; about 14 hr   **77.** (a)–(d) Proofs

79. (a)

(b) 2.2889, 5.0870
(c) $f' > 0$ on $(0, 2.2889), (5.0870, 2\pi)$
$f' < 0$ on $(2.2889, 5.0870)$
(d) Relative maximum: $(2.2889, 3.9453)$
Relative minimum: $(5.0870, -24.0830)$

81. (a)

(b) $0.5236, \pi/2, 2.6180$
(c) $f' > 0$ on $(0, 0.5236), (0.5236, \pi/2)$
$f' < 0$ on $(\pi/2, 2.6180), (2.6180, \pi)$
(d) Relative maximum: $\left(\dfrac{\pi}{2}, 1.5333\right)$

CHAPTER 8

83. (a)

(b) 1.8366, 4.8158

(c) $f' > 0$ on $(0, 1.8366)$, $(4.8158, 2\pi)$

$f' < 0$ on $(1.8366, 4.8158)$

(d) Relative maximum: $(1.8366, 1.8493)$

Relative minimum: $(4.8158, -3.0869)$

85. False. $y' = \frac{1}{2} \sin x (1 - \cos x)^{-1/2}$

87. False. $y' = x \sin 2x + \sin^2 x$ **89.** Answers will vary.

Section 8.5   *(page 551)*

Skills Warm Up   *(page 551)*

1. $-\dfrac{\sqrt{2}}{2}$ **2.** $-\dfrac{1}{2}$ **3.** $-\dfrac{\sqrt{3}}{2}$ **4.** $\dfrac{\sqrt{3}}{2}$

5. $-\dfrac{\sqrt{3}}{3}$ **6.** $-\dfrac{\sqrt{3}}{3}$ **7.** -1 **8.** 0

9. $\tan x$ **10.** $\cot x$ **11.** $\sin^2 x$ **12.** $\cos^2 x$

13. 1 **14.** $\cos x$ **15.** $\csc x$ **16.** $\cos x \sin x$

17. $\frac{88}{3}$ **18.** $\frac{4}{3}$ **19.** 4 **20.** $\frac{17}{4}$

---

1. $-4 \cos x + C$ **3.** $-\frac{1}{2} \cos 2x + C$ **5.** $\sin x^4 + C$

7. $5 \tan \dfrac{x}{5} + C$ **9.** $\frac{1}{2} \sec 2x + C$ **11.** $\frac{1}{4} \tan^4 x + C$

13. $\ln|\tan x| + C$ **15.** $\ln|\sec x - 1| + C$

17. $-\ln|1 + \cos x| + C$ **19.** $\dfrac{1}{\pi} \ln|\sin \pi x| + C$

21. $\frac{1}{2} \ln|\csc 2x - \cot 2x| + C$ **23.** $\dfrac{2}{3} \sec^6 \dfrac{x}{4} + C$

25. $\frac{1}{2} \tan^2 x + C$ **27.** $-\cos e^x + C$ **29.** $\dfrac{1}{\pi} e^{\sin \pi x} + C$

31. $-\cos^2 x + x + C$ or $\sin^2 x + x + C$

33. $\frac{1}{2} x \sin 2x + \frac{1}{4} \cos 2x + C$ **35.** $6x \tan x + 6 \ln|\cos x| + C$

37. $-\dfrac{t}{3} \csc 3t + \dfrac{1}{9} \ln|\csc 3t - \cot 3t| + C$

39. $\dfrac{3\sqrt{3}}{8} \approx 0.6495$ **41.** $2(\sqrt{3} - 1) \approx 1.4641$

43. $\frac{1}{2}$ **45.** $-\ln(\cos 1) \approx 0.6156$ **47.** 4

49. $\dfrac{\pi^2}{2} + 2 \approx 6.9348$ **51.** 2

53.

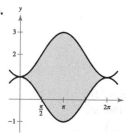

$4\pi \approx 12.566$ square units

55.

$1 - \ln 2 \approx 0.3069$ square unit

57. 17.69 in.

59. (a) About 1061.8 trillion Btu

(b) About 576.9 trillion Btu

(c) About 579.6 trillion Btu

61. (a) $C \approx \$27.50$ (b) $C \approx \$18.08$

63. 182,427 lb/day   **65.** 0.9777   **67.** True

Review Exercises for Chapter 8   *(page 558)*

1. $30°, -330°$ **3.** $315°, -45°$ **5.** $\dfrac{17\pi}{9}$

7. $-\dfrac{\pi}{3}$ **9.** $-\dfrac{8\pi}{3}$ **11.** $\dfrac{11\pi}{18}$

13. $240°$ **15.** $-120°$ **17.** $b = 4\sqrt{3}, \theta = 60°$

19. $a = \dfrac{5\sqrt{3}}{2}, c = 5, \theta = 60°$ **21.** About 15.38 ft

23. $\sin \theta = \dfrac{\sqrt{2}}{2}$, $\csc \theta = \sqrt{2}$

$\cos \theta = -\dfrac{\sqrt{2}}{2}$, $\sec \theta = -\sqrt{2}$

$\tan \theta = -1$, $\cot \theta = -1$

25. $\sin(-45°) = -\dfrac{\sqrt{2}}{2}$, $\csc(-45°) = -\sqrt{2}$

$\cos(-45°) = \dfrac{\sqrt{2}}{2}$, $\sec(-45°) = \sqrt{2}$

$\tan(-45°) = -1$, $\cot(-45°) = -1$

27. $\sin \dfrac{5\pi}{3} = -\dfrac{\sqrt{3}}{2}$, $\csc \dfrac{5\pi}{3} = -\dfrac{2\sqrt{3}}{3}$

$\cos \dfrac{5\pi}{3} = \dfrac{1}{2}$, $\sec \dfrac{5\pi}{3} = 2$

$\tan \dfrac{5\pi}{3} = -\sqrt{3}$, $\cot \dfrac{5\pi}{3} = -\dfrac{\sqrt{3}}{3}$

29. $\sin(-225°) = \dfrac{\sqrt{2}}{2}$, $\csc(-225°) = \sqrt{2}$

$\cos(-225°) = -\dfrac{\sqrt{2}}{2}$, $\sec(-225°) = -\sqrt{2}$

$\tan(-225°) = -1$, $\cot(-225°) = -1$

31. $\sin\left(-\dfrac{11\pi}{6}\right) = \dfrac{1}{2}$, $\csc\left(-\dfrac{11\pi}{6}\right) = 2$

$\cos\left(-\dfrac{11\pi}{6}\right) = \dfrac{\sqrt{3}}{2}$, $\sec\left(-\dfrac{11\pi}{6}\right) = \dfrac{2\sqrt{3}}{3}$

$\tan\left(-\dfrac{11\pi}{6}\right) = \dfrac{\sqrt{3}}{3}$, $\cot\left(-\dfrac{11\pi}{6}\right) = \sqrt{3}$

33. 0.6494   **35.** 3.2361   **37.** -0.3420

39. -0.2588 **41.** $r \approx 146.19$ **43.** $x \approx 68.69$

45. $\dfrac{2\pi}{3}, \dfrac{4\pi}{3}$ **47.** $\dfrac{7\pi}{6}, \dfrac{3\pi}{2}, \dfrac{11\pi}{6}$ **49.** $\dfrac{\pi}{3}, \pi, \dfrac{5\pi}{3}$

51. About 81.18 ft

53. Period: $\dfrac{\pi}{2}$ **55.** Period: $\dfrac{4\pi}{3}$

Amplitude: 2   Amplitude: 2

57.

59.

61.

63.

65. (a)

(b) Yes; May and June

67. $5\pi \cos 5\pi x$ **69.** $9x^2 \sec^2 3x^3$ **71.** $-\dfrac{6x}{5} \csc^2 \dfrac{3x^2}{5}$

73. $-\dfrac{\pi \sin 2\pi x}{\sqrt{\cos 2\pi x}}$ **75.** $-x \sec^2 x - \tan x$

77. $-\dfrac{x \sin x + 2 \cos x}{x^3}$ **79.** $2 \sin x \cos x + 1 = \sin 2x + 1$

81. $-4 \cot x \csc^4 x$ **83.** $e^x(\cot x - \csc^2 x)$

85. $y = -2x + \dfrac{\pi}{2}$ **87.** $y = -1$ **89.** $y = \dfrac{1}{2}$

91. Relative maximum: $(2, 1)$
Relative minimum: $(6, -1)$

93. Relative maximum: $\left(\dfrac{\pi}{6}, \dfrac{\pi + 6\sqrt{3}}{12}\right)$

Relative minimum: $\left(\dfrac{5\pi}{6}, \dfrac{5\pi - 6\sqrt{3}}{12}\right)$

95. Relative maxima: $\left(\dfrac{\pi}{2}, 2\right), \left(\dfrac{3\pi}{2}, 0\right)$

Relative minima: $\left(\dfrac{7\pi}{6}, -\dfrac{1}{4}\right), \left(\dfrac{11\pi}{6}, -\dfrac{1}{4}\right)$

97. June; 114 units   **99.** $-\dfrac{1}{3} \cos 3x + C$

101. $-\dfrac{1}{5} \csc 5x + C$ **103.** $-\dfrac{1}{2} \cot x^2 + C$

105. $\dfrac{1}{2} \ln|\tan 2x| + C$ **107.** $-\dfrac{1}{3} \ln|\cos 3x| + C$

109. $\dfrac{1}{4} \sin^4 x + C$ **111.** $\pi + 2$ **113.** $\dfrac{2\sqrt{3}}{3}$

115. 0   **117.** 2   **119.** $\dfrac{2}{3}$ **121.** $\dfrac{5}{3}$

123. About 22.3 in.   **125.** About \$37 billion

Test Yourself   *(page 562)*

Function	θ (deg)	θ (rad)	Function Value
1. sin	67.5°	$\dfrac{3\pi}{8}$	0.9239
2. cos	36°	$\dfrac{\pi}{5}$	0.8090
3. tan	15°	$\dfrac{\pi}{12}$	0.2679
4. cot	$-30°$	$-\dfrac{\pi}{6}$	$-\sqrt{3}$
5. sec	$-40°$	$-\dfrac{2\pi}{9}$	1.3054
6. csc	$-225°$	$-\dfrac{5\pi}{4}$	$\sqrt{2}$

7. About 27.37 in.

8. $\dfrac{\pi}{4}, \dfrac{3\pi}{4}$ **9.** $\dfrac{\pi}{4}, \dfrac{3\pi}{4}, \dfrac{5\pi}{4}, \dfrac{7\pi}{4}$ **10.** $\dfrac{\pi}{6}, \dfrac{7\pi}{6}$

11.

12.

13.

14. (a) $y' = \sin 2x - \sin x$

(b) Relative maxima: $\left(\dfrac{\pi}{3}, \dfrac{1}{4}\right), \left(\dfrac{5\pi}{3}, \dfrac{1}{4}\right)$

Relative minimum: $(\pi, -2)$

15. (a) $y' = \sec\left(x - \dfrac{\pi}{4}\right) \tan\left(x - \dfrac{\pi}{4}\right)$

(b) Relative maximum: $\left(\dfrac{5\pi}{4}, -1\right)$

Relative minimum: $\left(\dfrac{\pi}{4}, 1\right)$

16. (a) $y' = \dfrac{\cos(x + \pi)}{[3 - \sin(x + \pi)]^2}$

(b) Relative maximum: $\left(\dfrac{3\pi}{2}, \dfrac{1}{2}\right)$

Relative minimum: $\left(\dfrac{\pi}{2}, \dfrac{1}{4}\right)$

17. $-\dfrac{1}{5} \cos 5x + C$ **18.** $4 \tan \dfrac{x}{4} + C$

19. $-\dfrac{1}{2} \ln|\csc x^2 + \cot x^2| + C$ **20.** $\dfrac{2 - \sqrt{2}}{2\pi}$

21. $\dfrac{9}{2}$ **22.** $\dfrac{\sqrt{3}}{3} - \dfrac{1}{2} \approx 0.077$ **23.** $\dfrac{1}{8}$

24. (a) \$243.6 thousand   (b) \$29.06 thousand

Chapter 9

Section 9.1   *(page 570)*

1. (a) $S = \{HHH, HHT, HTH, HTT, THH,$
$THT, TTH, TTT\}$
(b) $A = \{HHH, HHT, HTH, THH\}$
(c) $B = \{HTT, THT, TTH, TTT\}$

3. (a) $S = \{III, IIO, IIU, IOI, IOO, IOU, IUI, IUO, IUU,$
$OII, OIO, OIU, OOI, OOO, OOU, OUI, OUO,$
$OUU, UII, UIO, UIU, UOI, UOO, UOU, UUI,$
$UUO, UUU\}$

(b) $A = \{III, IIO, IIU, IOI, IUI, OII, UII\}$

(c) $B = \{III, IIO, IIU, IOI, IOU, IUI, IUO, IUU, OII,$
$OIU, OUI, OUU, UII, UIO, UIU, UOI, UOU,$
$UUI, UUO, UUU\}$

5. (a)

Random variable	0	1	2	3	4
Frequency	1	4	6	4	1

(b)

Random variable, x	0	1	2	3	4
Probability, $P(x)$	$\frac{1}{16}$	$\frac{4}{16}$	$\frac{6}{16}$	$\frac{4}{16}$	$\frac{1}{16}$

7. (a) $\frac{7}{24}$ (b) $\frac{17}{24}$ (c) $\frac{4}{9}$ 9. $P(3) = 0.25$

11.

The table represents a probability distribution.

13. The table does not represent a probability distribution because the sum of the probabilities does not equal 1 and $P(4) < 0$.

15.   17.

(a) $\frac{3}{4}$ (b) $\frac{4}{5}$ (a) 0.803   (b) 0.197

19. (a)

(b) 0.715   (c) 0.536   (d) 0.202

21. (a) $S = \{gggg, gggb, ggbg, gbgg, bggg, ggbb,$
$gbgb, gbbg, bgbg, bbgg, bggb, gbbb,$
$bgbb, bbgb, bbbg, bbbb\}$

(b)

x	0	1	2	3	4
$P(x)$	$\frac{1}{16}$	$\frac{4}{16}$	$\frac{6}{16}$	$\frac{4}{16}$	$\frac{1}{16}$

(c)

(d) $\frac{15}{16}$

23. $E(x) = 3$ 25. $E(x) = 0.8$
    $V(x) = 0.875$ $V(x) = 8.16$
    $\sigma \approx 0.9354$ $\sigma \approx 2.8566$

27. (a) Mean: 2.5   29. (a) $E(x) = 18.5$
    Variance: 1.25 $\sigma \approx 8.0777$
    $\sigma \approx 1.1180$
(b) Mean: 5   (b) $91,575
    Variance: 2.5
    $\sigma \approx 1.5811$

31. $201

33. (a)

x	0	1	2	3	4
$P(x)$	$\frac{40}{160}$	$\frac{61}{160}$	$\frac{40}{160}$	$\frac{17}{160}$	$\frac{2}{160}$

(b)

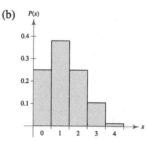

(c) $\frac{59}{80}$

(d) $E(x) = \frac{5}{4}$; $V(x) = \frac{39}{40}$; $\sigma = \frac{\sqrt{390}}{20}$

On average, you can expect the player to get 1.25 hits per game. The variance and standard deviation are measures of how spread out the data are.

35. $\approx -0.0526   37. City 1   39. Answers will vary.

Section 9.2   (page 578)

1.

$f(x)$ is a probability density function.

$$\int_0^8 \frac{1}{8}\, dx = \left[\frac{1}{8}x\right]_0^8 = 1$$

3.

$f(x)$ is a probability density function.

$$\int_0^4 \frac{4-x}{8}\,dx = \left[\frac{1}{2}x - \frac{1}{16}x^2\right]_0^4 = 1$$

5.   0.2

$f(x)$ is not a probability density function because

$$\int_0^3 \frac{1}{7}e^{-x/7}\,dx = \left[-e^{-x/7}\right]_0^3 \approx 0.349 \neq 1.$$

7.   5

$f(x)$ is not a probability density function because

$$\int_0^2 2\sqrt{4-x}\,dx = \left[-\frac{4}{3}(4-x)^{3/2}\right]_0^2 \approx 6.90 \neq 1.$$

9.

f is a probability density function.

$$\int_0^3 \left(\frac{2}{3}x - \frac{2}{9}x^2\right)dx = \left[\frac{x^2}{3} - \frac{2x^3}{27}\right]_0^3 = 1$$

11. $\frac{2}{15}$ **13.** $\frac{3}{32}$ **15.** $\frac{1}{2}$

17.

(a) $\frac{2}{3}$ (b) $\frac{1}{3}$
(c) $\frac{2}{3}$ (d) 0

19.

(a) $\frac{9}{25}$ (b) $\frac{1}{5}$
(c) $\frac{9}{25}$ (d) $\frac{24}{25}$

21.

(a) $\frac{\sqrt{2}}{4} \approx 0.354$

(b) $1 - \frac{\sqrt{2}}{4} \approx 0.646$

(c) $\frac{1}{8}(3\sqrt{3} - 1) \approx 0.525$

(d) $\frac{3\sqrt{3}}{8} \approx 0.650$

23.

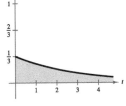

(a) $1 - e^{-2/3} \approx 0.4866$
(b) $e^{-2/3} \approx 0.5134$
(c) $e^{-1/3} - e^{-4/3} \approx 0.4529$
(d) 0

25. (a) $\frac{1}{6}$ (b) $\frac{2}{5}$

27. (a) $1 - \frac{1}{3}\sqrt{6} \approx 0.1835$ (b) $\frac{25}{81}\sqrt{5} - \frac{7}{81} \approx 0.6037$

29. (a) $1 - e^{-2/3} \approx 0.487$ **31.** (a) $1 - e^{-6/5} \approx 0.699$
(b) $e^{-2/3} - e^{-4/3} \approx 0.250$ (b) $e^{-2/5} - e^{-6/5} = 0.369$
(c) $e^{-2/3} \approx 0.513$ (c) $e^{-8/5} \approx 0.202$

33. (a) 0.75. There is a 75% probability that the community will receive up to 10 inches of rain.
(b) 0.25. There is a 25% probability that the community will receive 10 to 15 inches of rain.
(c) 0.25. There is a 25% probability that the community will receive up to 5 inches of rain.
(d) About 0.095. There is a probability of approximately 9.5% that the community will receive 12 to 15 inches of rain.

35. About 23.34 tons

Section 9.3   *(page 587)*

Skills Warm Up   *(page 587)*

1. 8   **2.** $3\ln 2$ **3.** $\frac{4}{3}$ **4.** $\frac{4}{3}$

5. (a) $\frac{1}{4}$ (b) $\frac{1}{2}$ **6.** (a) $\frac{1}{2}$ (b) $\frac{11}{16}$

1. (a) $\frac{3}{2}$ (b) $\frac{3}{4}$ (c) $\frac{\sqrt{3}}{2}$
(d)

3. (a) 4   (b) 2   (c) $\sqrt{2}$
(d)

5. (a) $\frac{4}{3}\ln 4 \approx 1.848$ (b) $4 - \frac{16}{9}(\ln 4)^2 \approx 0.583$
(c) $\sqrt{0.583} \approx 0.76$
(d)

7. (a) $\frac{2}{3}$ (b) $\frac{2}{9}$ (c) $\frac{\sqrt{2}}{3}$

(d)

9. (a) $\frac{1}{2}$ (b) $\frac{1}{20}$ (c) $\frac{\sqrt{5}}{10}$

(d)

11. (a) $\frac{8}{5}$ (b) $\frac{192}{175}$ (c) $\frac{8\sqrt{21}}{35}$

(d)

13. Mean: $\frac{11}{2}$ = median

15. Mean: $\frac{1}{6}$

Median: $\frac{2 - \sqrt{2}}{4} \approx 0.1464$

17. Mean: 9; Median: $9 \ln 2 \approx 6.238$

19. Uniform probability density function

Mean: 5

Variance: $\frac{25}{3}$

Standard deviation: $\frac{5\sqrt{3}}{3} \approx 2.887$

21. Exponential probability density function

Mean: 8

Variance: 64

Standard deviation: 8

23. Normal probability density function

Mean: 100

Variance: 121

Standard deviation: 11

25. Mean: 0

Standard deviation: 1

$P(0 \le x \le 0.85) \approx 0.3023$

27. Mean: 6

Standard deviation: 6

$P(x \ge 2.23) \approx 0.6896$

29. Mean: 8

Standard deviation: 2

$P(3 \le x \le 13) \approx 0.9876$

31. (a) About 0.309   (b) About 0.159

(c) About 0.841   (d) About 0.669

33. (a) $f(t) = \frac{1}{10}$, $[0, 10]$

(b) Mean: 10:05 A.M.

Standard deviation: $\frac{5\sqrt{3}}{3} \approx 2.9$ minutes

(c) $\frac{3}{10}$

35. (a) $f(t) = \frac{1}{2}e^{-t/2}$ (b) $1 - e^{-1/2} \approx 0.3935$

37. (a) $f(t) = \frac{1}{5}e^{-t/5}$ (b) $1 - e^{-2} \approx 0.8647$

39. (a) Mean: $\frac{7}{2}$

Standard deviation: $\frac{7\sqrt{5}}{10}$

(b) $\frac{7}{2}$ (c) About 0.6260

41. $\frac{15}{8}$

43. (a) Mean: 6

Standard deviation: $3\sqrt{2} \approx 4.243$

(b) About 0.6151

45. (a) -2.5 (b) 0.9938

47. (a) 0.6827   (b) No

49. (a)

(b) 0.757 or 75.7%

(c) 0.191 or 19.1%

51. (a)

(b) 0.184 or 18.4%

(c) 0.296 or 29.6%

Review Exercises for Chapter 9   *(page 593)*

1. (a) $S = \{1, 2, 3, 4, 5, 6, 7, 8, 9, 10, 11, 12\}$

(b) $A = \{9, 10, 11, 12\}$

(c) $B = \{1, 3, 5, 7, 9, 11\}$

3. (a) $S = \{000, 001, 002, 003, \ldots, 997, 998, 999\}$

The sample space consists of all distinct orders of three digits from 0 to 9.

(b) $A = \{100, 101, 102, 103, \ldots, 198, 199\}$

(c) $B = \{050, 100, 150, 200, 250, 300, 350, \ldots, 900, 950\}$

5.

x	0	1	2	3
$n(x)$	1	3	3	1

7.

x	0	1	2	3
$P(x)$	$\frac{1}{8}$	$\frac{3}{8}$	$\frac{3}{8}$	$\frac{1}{8}$

9. The table does not represent a probability distribution because the sum of the probabilities does not equal 1.

11.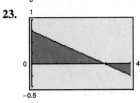
(a) $\frac{5}{6}$ (b) $\frac{5}{9}$

13. $E(x) = 2$; $V(x) = \frac{7}{5}$; $\sigma = \frac{\sqrt{35}}{5}$

15. $E(x) = 1.888$; $V(x) = 0.391456$; $\sigma \approx 0.626$

17. (a) $E(x) = 20.5$; $\sigma \approx 7.05$ (b) \$80,975

19. $E(x) = 1.83$; $V(x) \approx 1.1611$; $\sigma \approx 1.0775$

21.
$f(x)$ is a probability density function.

$$\int_0^{12} \frac{1}{12}\, dx = \left[\frac{x}{12}\right]_0^{12} = 1$$

23.

Although $\int_0^4 \frac{1}{4}(3-x)\, dx = \left[\frac{3}{4}x - \frac{x^2}{8}\right]_0^4 = 1$, $f(x)$ is not a probability density function because $f(x) < 0$ over the interval $(3, 4]$.

25.
$f(x)$ is a probability density function.

$$\int_1^9 \frac{1}{4\sqrt{x}}\, dx = \frac{1}{4}\left[2\sqrt{x}\right]_1^9 = 1$$

27.
0.15

$f(x)$ is not a probability density function because

$$\int_0^8 \frac{1}{8}e^{-x/8}\, dx = \left[-e^{-x/8}\right]_0^8 \approx 0.632 \neq 1.$$

29.

31.

(a) $\frac{5}{16}$ (b) $\frac{1}{16}$
(c) $\frac{11}{16}$ (d) $\frac{1}{4}$

(a) $\frac{9}{25}$ (b) $\frac{9}{100}$
(c) $\frac{3}{4}$ (d) $\frac{3}{100}$

33.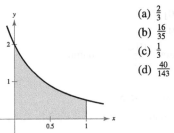
(a) $\frac{2}{3}$
(b) $\frac{16}{35}$
(c) $\frac{1}{3}$
(d) $\frac{40}{143}$

35. (a) $1 - e^{-5/12} \approx 0.341$ (b) $e^{-3/4} - e^{-1} \approx 0.104$

37. (a) $\frac{7}{2}$ (b) $\frac{49}{12}$ (c) $\frac{7\sqrt{3}}{6}$

(d)

39. (a) $\frac{3}{2}\ln 3 \approx 1.648$ (b) $3 - \left(\frac{3}{2}\ln 3\right)^2 \approx 0.284$

(c) $\sqrt{3 - \left(\frac{3}{2}\ln 3\right)^2} \approx 0.533$

(d)

41. (a) $\frac{3}{2}$ (b) $\frac{9}{20}$ (c) $\frac{3\sqrt{5}}{10}$

(d)

43. 7   **45.** $4\ln 2 \approx 2.7726$

47. Uniform probability density function
Mean: 1
Variance: $\frac{1}{3}$
Standard deviation: $\frac{\sqrt{3}}{3}$

49. Exponential probability density function
Mean: 6
Variance: 36
Standard deviation: 6

51. Normal probability density function
Mean: 16
Variance: 9
Standard deviation: 3

53. (a) $f(t) = \frac{1}{20}$, $[0, 20]$

(b) Mean: 7:10 A.M.

Standard deviation: $\dfrac{10\sqrt{3}}{3} \approx 5.8$ min

(c) $\frac{1}{5}$

55. (a) $f(t) = \frac{1}{15}e^{-t/15}$, $0 \le t < \infty$

(b) $1 - e^{-2/3} \approx 0.4866$

57. (a) Mean: 4

Standard deviation: $\dfrac{4\sqrt{5}}{5}$

(b) 4

(c) About 0.626, or 62.6%

59. (a)

(b) About 0.006, or 0.6%

(c) About 0.973, or 97.3%

Test Yourself   (page 596)

1. (a) $S = \{TTTT, TTTF, TTFT, TTFF, TFTT, TFTF,$
$TFFT, TFFF, FTTT, FTTF, FTFT, FTFF,$
$FFTT, FFTF, FFFT, FFFF\}$

(b)

Random variable, x	0	1	2	3	4
Frequency of x, $n(x)$	1	4	6	4	1

(c)

Random variable, x	0	1	2	3	4
Probability, $P(x)$	$\frac{1}{16}$	$\frac{4}{16}$	$\frac{6}{16}$	$\frac{4}{16}$	$\frac{1}{16}$

2. $P(\text{red non-face card}) = \frac{5}{13}$

3.

4.

(a) $\frac{5}{8}$ (b) $\frac{3}{8}$

(a) 0.95   (b) 0.66

5. $E(x) = 1.8$
$V(x) = 1.16$
$\sigma \approx 1.0770$

6. $E(x) = -0.056$
$V(x) \approx 1.8649$
$\sigma \approx 1.3656$

7.

$f(x)$ is not a probability density function because

$$\int_0^8 \frac{1}{16} \, dx = \left[\frac{1}{16}x\right]_0^8 = \frac{1}{2} \neq 1.$$

8.

$f(x)$ is a probability density function.

$$\int_{-1}^1 \frac{3 - x}{6} \, dx = \left[-\frac{x}{12}(x - 6)\right]_{-1}^1 = 1$$

9.

$f(x)$ is a probability density function.

$$\int_0^\infty \frac{3}{4}e^{-3x/4} \, dx = \left[-e^{-3x/4}\right]_0^\infty = 1$$

10. (a) $\frac{1}{9}$ (b) $\frac{5}{9}$ **11.** (a) $\frac{7}{16}$ (b) $\frac{225}{256}$

12. (a) 0.6321   (b) 0.3679

13. $\mu = 7$
$V(x) = \frac{49}{3}$
$\sigma \approx 4.041$

14. $\mu = \frac{5}{8}$
$V(x) \approx 0.0594$
$\sigma \approx 0.2437$

15. $\mu = 1$
$V(x) = 1$
$\sigma = 1$

16. $P(100 \le x \le 120) \approx 0.683$

Chapter 10

Section 10.1   (page 604)

Skills Warm Up   (page 604)

1. 0   **2.** 2   **3.** ∞ **4.** 0

5. $\dfrac{n - 2}{n}$, $n \neq -2$ **6.** $\dfrac{n - 3}{n - 4}$, $n \neq -4$

7. $\dfrac{3n^2 + 1}{n^3}$ **8.** $\dfrac{2n + 1}{(n - 1)(n + 2)}$, $n \geq 2$

---

1. 1, 3, 5, 7, 9   **3.** 3, 9, 27, 81, 243   **5.** $\frac{1}{2}, \frac{2}{3}, \frac{3}{4}, \frac{4}{5}, \frac{5}{6}$

7. $3, \frac{9}{2}, \frac{27}{6}, \frac{81}{24}, \frac{243}{120}$ **9.** $-1, \frac{1}{4}, -\frac{1}{9}, \frac{1}{16}, -\frac{1}{25}$

11. 0; converges   **13.** 3; converges   **15.** 0; converges

17. 1; converges   **19.** $\frac{1}{2}$; converges   **21.** ∞; diverges

23. 0; converges   **25.** ∞; diverges   **27.** ∞; diverges

29. Limit does not exist; diverges   **31.** Diverges

33. $3n - 2$ **35.** $5n - 6$ **37.** $\dfrac{n + 1}{n + 2}$

39. $\dfrac{(-1)^{n-1}}{2^{n-2}}$ **41.** $\dfrac{n + 1}{n}$ **43.** $2(-1)^n$ **45.** $\dfrac{4n}{n!}$

47. 2, 5, 8, 11, 14, 17, . . . ; Pattern: each term is 1 less than 3 times n.

49. $1, \frac{5}{3}, \frac{7}{3}, 3, \frac{11}{3}, \frac{13}{3}$, . . . ; Pattern: each term is $\frac{1}{3}$ more than $\frac{2}{3}$ times n.

51. $3, -\frac{3}{2}, \frac{3}{4}, -\frac{3}{8}, \frac{3}{16}, -\frac{3}{32}, \ldots$; Pattern: each term is 3 times the quantity $\left(-\frac{1}{2}\right)$ raised to the $(n-1)$ power.

53. $2, 6, 18, 54, 162, 486, \ldots$; Pattern: each term is 3 raised to the n power times $\frac{2}{3}$.

55. Geometric, $20\left(\frac{1}{2}\right)^{n-1}$ **57.** Arithmetic, $\frac{2}{3}n + 2$

59. $\dfrac{3n+1}{4n}$

61. $9045.00, \$9090.23, \$9135.68, \$9181.35, \$9227.26,$
$9273.40, \$9319.76, \$9366.36, \$9413.20, \$9460.26$

63. (a)

Year	1	2	3
Balance	$2200	$4620	$7282

Year	4	5	6
Balance	$10,210.20	$13,431.22	$16,974.34

(b) $126,005.00 (c) $973,703.62

65. (a) $a_n = 1.7n + 337$ **67.** (a) $a_n = 72.6n + 333$

(b) 405 parts per million   (b) About 1495 stores

69. (a) $a_n = -0.01394n^3 + 0.2648n^2 - 0.573n + 9.52$

(b) About $13.46 billion

71. (a) $h_n = 12\left(\frac{2}{3}\right)^n$

(b) 8 ft   (c) This sequence converges because
$\frac{16}{3} \approx 5.3$ ft $\lim\limits_{n\to\infty} 12\left(\frac{2}{3}\right)^n = 0.$
$\frac{32}{9} \approx 3.6$ ft
$\frac{64}{27} \approx 2.4$ ft
$\frac{128}{81} \approx 1.6$ ft
$\frac{256}{243} \approx 1.1$ ft

73. (a) $37,970.10
(b) The sequence diverges because
$\lim\limits_{n\to\infty} 32,800(1.05)^{n-1} = \infty.$

75. Answers will vary.

Section 10.2   (page 616)

Skills Warm Up   (page 616)

1. $\frac{77}{60}$ **2.** $\frac{73}{24}$ **3.** $\frac{31}{16}$ **4.** $\frac{40}{9}$ **5.** $\frac{21}{8}$
6. $\frac{31}{32}$ **7.** $\frac{3}{4}$ **8.** 0   **9.** 1   **10.** $\frac{1}{2}$

1. $\sum\limits_{n=1}^{5} 2n$ **3.** $\sum\limits_{n=1}^{7} \dfrac{1}{2n-1}$

5. $S_1 = 1$ **7.** $S_1 = 3$
$S_2 = \frac{5}{4} = 1.25$ $S_2 = -\frac{3}{2} = -1.5$
$S_3 = \frac{49}{36} \approx 1.361$ $S_3 = \frac{21}{4} = 5.25$
$S_4 = \frac{205}{144} \approx 1.424$ $S_4 = -\frac{39}{8} = -4.875$
$S_5 = \frac{5269}{3600} \approx 1.464$ $S_5 = \frac{165}{16} = 10.3125$

9. Geometric series: $|r| = \frac{5}{2} > 1$

11. Geometric series: $|r| = 1.055 > 1$

13. nth-Term Test: $\lim\limits_{n\to\infty} \dfrac{n}{n+1} = 1 \neq 0$

15. nth-Term Test: $\lim\limits_{n\to\infty} \dfrac{n^2}{n^2+1} = 1 \neq 0$ **17.** $|r| = \frac{3}{4} < 1$

19. $|r| = 0.9 < 1$ **21.** $\frac{21}{2}$ **23.** 8   **25.** $\frac{1}{2}$ **27.** $\frac{40}{3}$

29. $S_4 = \frac{3}{7}\left[8 - \left(\frac{1}{8}\right)^4\right] \approx 3.428$ **31.** $S_5 = \frac{5}{3}\left[2 - \left(\frac{1}{2}\right)^5\right] \approx 3.281$
$S_6 = \frac{3}{7}\left[8 - \left(\frac{1}{8}\right)^6\right] \approx 3.429$ $S_7 = \frac{5}{3}\left[2 - \left(\frac{1}{2}\right)^7\right] \approx 3.320$
$S_{10} = \frac{3}{7}\left[8 - \left(\frac{1}{8}\right)^{10}\right] \approx 3.429$ $S_{10} = \frac{5}{3}\left[2 + \left(\frac{1}{2}\right)^{10}\right] \approx 3.335$

33. $\lim\limits_{n\to\infty} \dfrac{n+10}{10n+1} = \dfrac{1}{10} \neq 0$; diverges

35. $\lim\limits_{n\to\infty} \dfrac{n!+1}{n!} = 1 \neq 0$; diverges

37. $\lim\limits_{n\to\infty} \dfrac{3n-1}{2n+1} = \dfrac{3}{2} \neq 0$; diverges

39. Geometric series: $|r| = 1.075 > 1$; diverges

41. Geometric series: $|r| = \frac{1}{5} < 1$; converges   **43.** $\frac{4}{9}$ **45.** $\frac{9}{11}$

47. (a) $80,000(1 - 0.9^n)$ (b) 80,000   **49.** About 152.42 ft

51. (a) $\sum\limits_{n=1}^{60} 100\left(1 + \dfrac{0.09}{12}\right)^n$ (b) $7598.98   **53.** Proof

55. $\sum\limits_{n=0}^{\infty} 500(0.75)^n = \$2000$ million

57. $V = 225,000(0.7)^n$; $37,815.75   **59.** $3,801,020.63

61. $\sum\limits_{n=1}^{\infty} \left(\frac{1}{2}\right)^n = -1 + \sum\limits_{n=0}^{\infty} \left(\frac{1}{2}\right)^n = -1 + \dfrac{1}{1-\frac{1}{2}} = 1$

63. $P(2) = \dfrac{1}{8}$; $\sum\limits_{n=0}^{\infty} \dfrac{1}{2}\left(\dfrac{1}{2}\right)^n = \dfrac{\frac{1}{2}}{1-\frac{1}{2}} = 1$

65. $(0.85)^{12}\,500 \approx 71.12$ ppm   **67.** 6   **69.** About 0.5431

71. False. $\lim\limits_{n\to\infty} \dfrac{1}{n} = 0$, but $\sum\limits_{n=1}^{\infty} \dfrac{1}{n}$ diverges.

Section 10.3   (page 624)

Skills Warm Up   (page 624)

1. $\dfrac{1}{n+1}$ **2.** $n+1$ **3.** $\dfrac{3n}{n+1}$ **4.** $\dfrac{n+1}{n^2}$
5. 1   **6.** 5   **7.** 1   **8.** $\frac{1}{3}$
9. Geometric series   **10.** Not a geometric series

1. p-series   **3.** Not a p-series   **5.** Not a p-series
7. p-series   **9.** Converges   **11.** Diverges
13. Converges   **15.** Diverges   **17.** Diverges
19. Converges   **21.** Converges   **23.** Converges
25. Diverges   **27.** Converges   **29.** Diverges

31. Converges

33. $\lim\limits_{n\to\infty}\left|\dfrac{a_{n+1}}{a_n}\right| = \lim\limits_{n\to\infty}\dfrac{1/[(n+1)^{3/2}]}{1/(n^{3/2})}$

$\qquad = \lim\limits_{n\to\infty}\left(\dfrac{n}{n+1}\right)^{3/2} = 1$

35. $\lim\limits_{n\to\infty}\left|\dfrac{a_{n+1}}{a_n}\right| = \lim\limits_{n\to\infty}\dfrac{1/(n+1)^3}{1/n^3}$

$\qquad = \lim\limits_{n\to\infty}\left(\dfrac{n}{n+1}\right)^3 = 1$

37. About 1.1777; maximum error $\le \frac{1}{32}$.

39. About 1.1256; maximum error $\le \dfrac{\sqrt{10}}{2500} \approx 0.0013$.

41. a; diverges: $p = \frac{3}{4} < 1$

42. d; diverges: $p = 1$, harmonic series

43. e; converges: $p = \frac{5}{2} > 1$ **44.** b; diverges: $p = \frac{2}{5} < 1$

45. f; converges: $p = \frac{3}{2} > 1$ **46.** c; converges: $p = 2 > 1$

47. Diverges; nth-Term Test

49. Converges; p-Series Test; about 18.38

51. Converges; Geometric Series Test; $-\frac{3}{7} \approx -0.43$

53. Converges; Geometric Series Test; $\frac{3}{5}$

55. Converges; p-Series Test; about 0.4429

57. Diverges; Geometric Series Test

59. Diverges; Ratio Test   **61.** Diverges; nth-Term Test

63. Converges; Geometric Series Test; $\frac{10}{3}$

65. No; although the terms approach zero, the series diverges because the partial sums approach infinity.

Quiz Yourself   (page 626)

1. $-\frac{1}{4}, \frac{1}{16}, -\frac{1}{64}, \frac{1}{256}, -\frac{1}{1024}$ **2.** $\frac{1}{2}, \frac{3}{5}, \frac{2}{3}, \frac{5}{7}, \frac{3}{4}$

3. $-5, 5, -5, 5, -5$ **4.** $-1, 0, \frac{1}{6}, \frac{1}{12}, \frac{1}{40}$

5. 0; converges   **6.** $\frac{1}{2}$; converges   **7.** 0; converges

8. Does not exist; diverges   **9.** $\dfrac{n-1}{n^2}$

10. $(-1)^n \cdot 3^{1/n}$ **11.** $2^{(-1)^n}$

12. $S_1 = 0$ **13.** $S_1 = 1$

$\quad S_2 = \frac{1}{2} = 0.5$ $\quad S_2 = 0$

$\quad S_3 = \frac{5}{6} = 0.8\overline{3}$ $\quad S_3 = \frac{3}{4} = 0.75$

$\quad S_4 = \frac{23}{24} = 0.958\overline{3}$ $\quad S_4 = \frac{1}{4} = 0.25$

$\quad S_5 = \frac{119}{120} = 0.991\overline{6}$ $\quad S_5 = \frac{9}{16} = 0.5625$

14. 12   **15.** 1   **16.** $\frac{50}{9}$

17. Diverges by the nth-Term Test because

$\quad \lim\limits_{n\to\infty}\dfrac{2n^2 - 1}{n^2 + 1} = 2 \ne 0$.

18. Converges by the Geometric Series Test because

$\quad |r| = \left|\frac{1}{2}\right| < 1$.

19. Diverges by the Geometric Series Test because

$\quad |r| = \left|\frac{5}{3}\right| > 1$.

20. Converges by the p-Series Test because $p = \frac{5}{3} > 1$.

21. Converges by the Ratio Test because

$\quad \lim\limits_{n\to\infty}\left|\dfrac{a_{n+1}}{a_n}\right| = \lim\limits_{n\to\infty}\dfrac{n+1}{n^2} = 0 < 1$.

22. Diverges by the Ratio Test because

$\quad \lim\limits_{n\to\infty}\left|\dfrac{a_{n+1}}{a_n}\right| = \lim\limits_{n\to\infty}\dfrac{2(n+1)}{3} = \infty$.

23. (a) $\sum\limits_{n=1}^{36} 200(1.005)^n$ (b) \$7906.56

Section 10.4   (page 635)

Skills Warm Up   (page 635)

1. $f(g(x)) = (x-1)^2$ **2.** $f(g(x)) = 6x + 3$
$\quad g(f(x)) = x^2 - 1$ $\qquad g(f(x)) = 6x + 1$

3. $f(g(x)) = \sqrt{x^2 + 4}$
$\quad g(f(x)) = x + 4, \; x \ge -4$

4. $f(g(x)) = e^{x^2}$ **5.** $\quad f'(x) = 5e^x$
$\quad g(f(x)) = e^{2x}$ $\qquad f''(x) = 5e^x$
$\qquad\qquad\qquad\qquad f'''(x) = 5e^x$
$\qquad\qquad\qquad\qquad f^{(4)}(x) = 5e^x$

6. $\quad f'(x) = \dfrac{1}{x}$ **7.** $\quad f'(x) = 6e^{2x}$

$\qquad f''(x) = -\dfrac{1}{x^2}$ $\qquad f''(x) = 12e^{2x}$

$\qquad f'''(x) = \dfrac{2}{x^3}$ $\qquad f'''(x) = 24e^{2x}$

$\qquad f^{(4)}(x) = -\dfrac{6}{x^4}$ $\qquad f^{(4)}(x) = 48e^{2x}$

8. $\quad f'(x) = \dfrac{1}{x}$ **9.** $\dfrac{n+1}{3}$ **10.** $\dfrac{n+3}{n+1}$

$\qquad f''(x) = -\dfrac{1}{x^2}$

$\qquad f'''(x) = \dfrac{2}{x^3}$

$\qquad f^{(4)}(x) = -\dfrac{6}{x^4}$

1. $c = 0; 1, \dfrac{x}{4}, \left(\dfrac{x}{4}\right)^2, \left(\dfrac{x}{4}\right)^3, \left(\dfrac{x}{4}\right)^4$

3. $c = -1; -1, (x+1), -\dfrac{(x+1)^2}{2}, \dfrac{(x+1)^3}{6}, -\dfrac{(x+1)^4}{24}$

5. 2   **7.** 1   **9.** ∞ **11.** 0   **13.** 4

15. 5   **17.** 1   **19.** 3   **21.** $\frac{1}{2}$ **23.** ∞

25. $e\sum\limits_{n=0}^{\infty}\dfrac{(x-1)^n}{n!}, \quad R = \infty$ **27.** $\sum\limits_{n=0}^{\infty}\dfrac{(3x)^n}{n!}, \quad R = \infty$

29. $\sum\limits_{n=0}^{\infty}(-1)^n x^n, \quad R = 1$

31. $1 + \dfrac{1}{2}(x-1) + \sum\limits_{n=2}^{\infty}\dfrac{(-1)^{n+1}\, 1 \cdot 3 \cdot 5 \cdots (2n-3)(x-1)^n}{2^n \cdot n!}$,

$\quad R = 1$

33. $\sum\limits_{n=0}^{\infty}(-1)^n (n+1)x^n, \quad R = 1$

35. $\sum\limits_{n=0}^{\infty}\dfrac{(-1)^n(n+2)(n+1)x^n}{2}, \quad R = 1$

37. (a)–(d) $R = 2$ **39.** (a)–(d) $R = 1$

41. $\sum\limits_{n=0}^{\infty}\dfrac{x^{3n}}{n!}$ **43.** $3\sum\limits_{n=0}^{\infty}\dfrac{x^{3n+2}}{n!}$ **45.** $\sum\limits_{n=0}^{\infty}(-1)^n x^{4n}$

47. $\displaystyle\sum_{n=0}^{\infty} (-1)^n 3x^{2n+1}$ **49.** $\displaystyle\sum_{n=0}^{\infty} \frac{(-1)^n(x-1)^{n+1}}{n+1}$

51. $\displaystyle\sum_{n=1}^{\infty} (-1)^{n+1}n(x-1)^{n-1}$

53. (a) $\frac{8}{3}$ (b) $\frac{8}{13}$

(c) In part (a), the rate of convergence is slower but all of the partial sums approach the line from below. In part (b), the partial sums approach the sum more quickly, but they oscillate above and below the line.

Section 10.5   *(page 642)*

Skills Warm Up   *(page 642)*

1. $\displaystyle\sum_{n=0}^{\infty} \frac{3^n x^n}{n!}$ **2.** $\displaystyle\sum_{n=0}^{\infty} \frac{(-1)^n 3^n x^n}{n!}$

3. $4\displaystyle\sum_{n=0}^{\infty} (-1)^n (x-1)^n$ **4.** $\ln 5 + \displaystyle\sum_{n=1}^{\infty} \frac{(-1)^{n-1}(x-1)^n}{n}$

5. $1 + \dfrac{x}{4} - \dfrac{3x^2}{4^2 2!} + \dfrac{3\cdot 7x^3}{4^3 3!} - \dfrac{3\cdot 7\cdot 11x^4}{4^4 4!} + \cdots$

6. $1 + \dfrac{x}{2} - \dfrac{x^2}{2^2 2!} + \dfrac{1\cdot 3x^3}{2^3 3!} - \dfrac{1\cdot 3\cdot 5x^4}{2^4 4!} + \cdots$

7. $\frac{47}{60}$ **8.** $\frac{311}{576}$ **9.** $\frac{5}{12}$ **10.** $\frac{77}{192}$

1.

x	0	$\frac{1}{4}$	$\frac{1}{2}$	$\frac{3}{4}$	1
$f(x)$	1.0000	1.1331	1.2840	1.4550	1.6487
$S_1(x)$	1.0000	1.1250	1.2500	1.3750	1.5000
$S_2(x)$	1.0000	1.1328	1.2813	1.4453	1.6250
$S_3(x)$	1.0000	1.1331	1.2839	1.4541	1.6458
$S_4(x)$	1.0000	1.1331	1.2840	1.4549	1.6484

3. (a) $S_1(x) = 1 + x$ (b) $S_2(x) = 1 + x + \dfrac{x^2}{2}$

(c) $S_3(x) = 1 + x + \dfrac{x^2}{2} + \dfrac{x^3}{6}$

(d) $S_4(x) = 1 + x + \dfrac{x^2}{2} + \dfrac{x^3}{6} + \dfrac{x^4}{24}$

5. (a) $S_1(x) = 1 + 2x$ (b) $S_2(x) = 1 + 2x + 2x^2$

(c) $S_3(x) = 1 + 2x + 2x^2 + \dfrac{4x^3}{3}$

(d) $S_4(x) = 1 + 2x + 2x^2 + \dfrac{4x^3}{3} + \dfrac{2x^4}{3}$

7. (a) $S_1(x) = x$ (b) $S_2(x) = x - \dfrac{x^2}{2}$

(c) $S_3(x) = x - \dfrac{x^2}{2} + \dfrac{x^3}{3}$ (d) $S_4(x) = x - \dfrac{x^2}{2} + \dfrac{x^3}{3} - \dfrac{x^4}{4}$

9. (a) $S_1(x) = 1 + \dfrac{x}{2}$ (b) $S_2(x) = 1 + \dfrac{x}{2} - \dfrac{x^2}{8}$

(c) $S_3(x) = 1 + \dfrac{x}{2} - \dfrac{x^2}{8} + \dfrac{x^3}{16}$

(d) $S_4(x) = 1 + \dfrac{x}{2} - \dfrac{x^2}{8} + \dfrac{x^3}{16} - \dfrac{5x^4}{128}$

11. (a) $S_1(x) = 1 - 2x$ (b) $S_2(x) = 1 - 2x + 3x^2$
(c) $S_3(x) = 1 - 2x + 3x^2 - 4x^3$
(d) $S_4(x) = 1 - 2x + 3x^2 - 4x^3 + 5x^4$

13. (a) $S_1(x) = x$ (b) $S_2(x) = x - x^2$
(c) $S_3(x) = x - x^2 + x^3$ (d) $S_4(x) = x - x^2 + x^3 - x^4$

15. (a) $S_2(x) = 1 - x^2$ (b) $S_4(x) = 1 - x^2 + x^4$
(c) $S_6(x) = 1 - x^2 + x^4 - x^6$
(d) $S_8(x) = 1 - x^2 + x^4 - x^6 + x^8$

17. $S_4(x) = 1 - \dfrac{x}{3} + \dfrac{2x^2}{9} - \dfrac{14x^3}{81} + \dfrac{35x^4}{243}$ **19.** d

20. c   **21.** a   **22.** b   **23.** 0.607; 0.00000155

25. 0.4055; 0.0000087   **27.** $\dfrac{1}{6!} \approx 0.00139$ **29.** 7

31. About 0.82143   **33.** 0.481

35. (a) $P_4(x) \approx 1 + x + \dfrac{x^2}{2} + \dfrac{x^3}{6} + \dfrac{x^4}{24}$

$Q_5(x) \approx x + x^2 + \dfrac{x^3}{2} + \dfrac{x^4}{6} + \dfrac{x^5}{24}$

$Q_5(x) = xP_4(x)$

(b) $P_6(x) \approx x^2 + x^3 + \dfrac{x^4}{2} + \dfrac{x^5}{6} + \dfrac{x^6}{24}$; degree 6

(c) $P_3(x) \approx \dfrac{1}{x} + 1 + \dfrac{x}{2} + \dfrac{x^2}{6} + \dfrac{x^3}{24}$; degree 3

Section 10.6   *(page 649)*

Skills Warm Up   *(page 649)*

1. $f(2.4) = -0.04$ **2.** $f(-0.6) = 0.064$
$f'(2.4) = 2.8$ $f'(-0.6) = 3.48$
3. $f(0.35) = 0.01$ **4.** $f(1.4) = 0.30$
$f'(0.35) = 4.03$ $f'(1.4) = 12.88$
5. $4.9 \le x \le 5.1$ **6.** $0.798 \le x \le 0.802$
7. $5.97 \le x \le 6.03$ **8.** $-3.505 \le x \le -3.495$

9. $\left(\dfrac{3+\sqrt{13}}{2}, 2+\sqrt{13}\right)\left(\dfrac{3-\sqrt{13}}{2}, 2-\sqrt{13}\right)$

10. $\left(\dfrac{1-\sqrt{5}}{2}, \dfrac{3-\sqrt{5}}{2}\right), \left(\dfrac{1+\sqrt{5}}{2}, \dfrac{3+\sqrt{5}}{2}\right)$

---

1. $x_2 = 2.25, x_3 \approx 2.2361$
3. Newton's Method: 0.682, graphing utility: 0.682
5. Newton's Method: 1.25, graphing utility: 1.25
7. Newton's Method: 0.567, graphing utility: 0.567
9. Newton's Method: $-1.597, 1.118$
Graphing utility: $-1.597, 1.118$
11. Newton's Method: $-1.380, 0.819$
Graphing utility: $-1.380, 0.819$
13. 2.893   **15.** 0.567

17. 11.8033

19. $-0.8937, 2.0720$

21. $0.9, 1.1, 1.9$

23. $1.1459, 7.8541$

25. $-1.999, 0.542$

27. 2.208

29. 0.8655

31. Newton's Method fails because $f'(x_1) = 0$.

33. Newton's Method fails because $1 = x_1 = x_3 = \ldots$;
$0 = x_2 = x_4 = \ldots$. So, the limit does not exist.

35. $x_{n+1} = \dfrac{x_n^2 + a}{2x_n}$ **37.** 2.646 **39.** 1.565

41. $f(x) = \dfrac{1}{x} - a$

$f'(x) = -\dfrac{1}{x^2}$

Newton's Method: $x_{n+1} = x_n - \dfrac{f(x_n)}{f'(x_n)}$

$$x_{n+1} = x_n - \dfrac{\dfrac{1}{x_n} - a}{-\dfrac{1}{x_n^2}}$$

$$= x_n(2 - ax_n)$$

43. $(1.939, 0.240)$ **45.** $x \approx 1.563$ miles down the coast

47. 131 units   **49.** $x \approx 40.45$ (about 4045 units of product)

51. False. Let $f(x) = \dfrac{x^2 - 1}{x - 1}$.

Review Exercises for Chapter 10   *(page 656)*

1. $7, 10, 13, 16, 19$ **3.** $\frac{3}{2}, \frac{9}{4}, \frac{27}{8}, \frac{81}{16}, \frac{243}{32}$ **5.** $4, 8, \frac{32}{3}, \frac{32}{3}, \frac{128}{15}$

7. 0; converges   **9.** ∞; diverges   **11.** 5; converges

13. 0; converges   **15.** ∞; diverges

17. $2n + 5, n = 1, 2, 3, \ldots$ **19.** $\dfrac{1}{n!}, \quad n = 1, 2, 3, \ldots$

21. $(-1)^n \dfrac{2^n}{3^{n+1}}, \quad n = 0, 1, 2, \ldots$

23. \$1002.50, \$1005.01, \$1007.52, \$1010.04, \$1012.56, \$1015.09, \$1017.63, \$1020.18, \$1022.73, \$1025.28

25. (a) $16\left(\frac{3}{4}\right)^n$

(b) 12 ft
9 ft
$\frac{27}{4} = 6.75$ ft
$\frac{81}{16} \approx 5.06$ ft
$\frac{243}{64} \approx 3.80$ ft

(c) Converges; 0

27. $S_1 = \frac{3}{2}$

$S_2 = \frac{15}{4} = 3.75$

$S_3 = \frac{57}{8} = 7.125$

$S_4 = \frac{195}{16} \approx 12.188$

$S_5 = \frac{633}{32} \approx 19.781$

29. $S_1 = \frac{1}{2} = 0.5$

$S_2 = \frac{11}{24} \approx 0.4583$

$S_3 = \frac{331}{720} \approx 0.4597$

$S_4 = \frac{18,535}{40,320} \approx 0.4597$

$S_5 = \frac{1,668,151}{3,628,800} \approx 0.4597$

31. Diverges   **33.** Converges

35. $\lim\limits_{n\to\infty} \dfrac{2n}{n + 5} = 2 \neq 0$ **37.** $\lim\limits_{n\to\infty} \dfrac{n^2}{n^2 + 1} = 1 \neq 0$

39. $S_3 = \frac{130}{27} \approx 4.8148$

$S_5 = \frac{1330}{243} \approx 5.4733$

$S_{10} = \frac{350,198}{59,049} \approx 5.9306$

41. Diverges   **43.** Diverges   **45.** Converges to $\frac{13}{4}$

47. (a) $60{,}000[1 - (0.85)^n]$ units   (b) 60,000 units

49. \$2000   **51.** \$2181.82

53. (a) $V_n = 120{,}000(0.7)^n$ (b) \$20,168.40

55. Converges   **57.** Converges

59. Converges   **61.** Diverges   **63.** Converges

65. b; diverges: $p = \frac{1}{2} < 1$ **66.** d; converges: $p = \frac{4}{3} > 1$

67. a; diverges: $p = 1$, harmonic series

68. c; converges: $p = \frac{3}{2} > 1$

69. $c = 2; \frac{1}{2}(x - 2), \frac{1}{4}(x - 2)^2, \frac{1}{8}(x - 2)^3, \frac{1}{16}(x - 2)^4, \frac{1}{32}(x - 2)^5$

71. $c = 0; -\dfrac{x}{3}, \dfrac{x^2}{9}, -\dfrac{x^3}{27}, \dfrac{x^4}{81}, -\dfrac{x^5}{243}$ **73.** $R = 10$

75. $R = \infty$ **77.** $R = \frac{1}{3}$ **79.** $R = 2$

81. $\displaystyle\sum_{n=0}^{\infty} \left(-\frac{1}{2}\right)^n \dfrac{x^n}{n!}; R = \infty$

83. $1 + \displaystyle\sum_{n=1}^{\infty} (-1)^n \left[\dfrac{1 \cdot 3 \cdot 5 \ldots (2n - 1)}{2^n \, n!}\right](x - 1)^n, R = 1$

85. $1 + \displaystyle\sum_{n=1}^{\infty} (-1)^{n-1} \left[\dfrac{1 \cdot 3 \cdot 7 \ldots (4n - 5)}{4^n \, n!}\right]x^n, R = 1$

87. $\ln 2 + \displaystyle\sum_{n=1}^{\infty} (-1)^{n+1} \dfrac{(x/2)^n}{n}$ **89.** $1 + 2x^2 + x^4$

91. $x^2 \displaystyle\sum_{n=0}^{\infty} \dfrac{x^n}{n!} = \sum_{n=0}^{\infty} \dfrac{x^{n+2}}{n!}$

93. $x^2 \displaystyle\sum_{n=0}^{\infty} (-1)^n x^n = \sum_{n=0}^{\infty} (-1)^n x^{n+2}$

95. (a) $S_1(x) = 1 - 4x$

(b) $S_2(x) = 1 - 4x + 8x^2$

(c) $S_3(x) = 1 - 4x + 8x^2 - \dfrac{32x^3}{3}$

(d) $S_4(x) = 1 - 4x + 8x^2 - \dfrac{32x^3}{3} + \dfrac{32x^4}{3}$

97. (a) $S_1(x) = \ln(2) + \dfrac{x}{2}$

(b) $S_2(x) = \ln(2) + \dfrac{x}{2} - \dfrac{x^2}{8}$

(c) $S_3(x) = \ln(2) + \dfrac{x}{2} - \dfrac{x^2}{8} + \dfrac{x^3}{24}$

(d) $S_4(x) = \ln(2) + \dfrac{x}{2} - \dfrac{x^2}{8} + \dfrac{x^3}{24} - \dfrac{x^4}{64}$

99. (a) $S_1(x) = \dfrac{1}{9} - \dfrac{2x}{27}$

(b) $S_2(x) = \dfrac{1}{9} - \dfrac{2x}{27} + \dfrac{x^2}{27}$

(c) $S_3(x) = \dfrac{1}{9} - \dfrac{2x}{27} + \dfrac{x^2}{27} - \dfrac{4x^3}{243}$

(d) $S_4(x) = \dfrac{1}{9} - \dfrac{2x}{27} + \dfrac{x^2}{27} - \dfrac{4x^3}{243} + \dfrac{5x^4}{729}$

101. 1.5169; 0.00000066   **103.** 0.9163; 0.0000087

105. 0.301   **107.** 0.1233

109. Newton's Method: 0.322, graphing utility: 0.322

111. Newton's Method: -1.562, graphing utility: -1.562

113. Newton's Method: -1.453, 1.164

Graphing utility: -1.453, 1.164

115. 1.341   **117.** 0.773

119. -2.926

Test Yourself   (page 660)

1. 2, 6, 10, 14, 18   **2.** 2, 4, 8, 16, 32   **3.** $4, \frac{5}{2}, 2, \frac{7}{4}, \frac{8}{5}$

4. $-1, \frac{1}{2}, -\frac{1}{6}, \frac{1}{24}, -\frac{1}{120}$ **5.** 0; converges

6. $\frac{1}{3}$; converges   **7.** Limit does not exist; diverges

8. 0; converges   **9.** $\dfrac{(-1)^{n+1} n}{n^2 + 1}$

10. Converges by the Ratio Test because

$$\lim_{n \to \infty} \left| \frac{a_{n+1}}{a_n} \right| = \lim_{n \to \infty} \frac{4}{n+1} = 0 < 1.$$

11. Diverges by the nth-Term Test because $\displaystyle\lim_{n \to \infty} \frac{n+1}{n-3} = 1 \neq 0.$

12. Converges by the Geometric Series Test because

$$|r| = \left| \frac{1}{5} \right| < 1.$$

13. Diverges by the p-Series Test because $p = \frac{1}{6} < 1.$

14. Diverges by the Geometric Series Test because

$$|r| = \left| \frac{5}{3} \right| > 1.$$

15. Converges by the p-Series Test because $p = \frac{5}{4} > 1.$

16. Converges by the Geometric Series Test because

$$|r| = \left| -\frac{1}{6} \right| < 1.$$

17. Diverges by the Ratio Test because

$$\lim_{n \to \infty} \left| \frac{a_{n+1}}{a_n} \right| = \lim_{n \to \infty} \frac{n+2}{5} = \infty.$$

18. $\frac{7}{3}$

19. (a) $c = 0$ (c) $R = 3$

(b) $S_0 = -1$

$S_1 = -1 + \dfrac{x}{3}$

$S_2 = -1 + \dfrac{x}{3} - \dfrac{x^2}{9}$

$S_3 = -1 + \dfrac{x}{3} - \dfrac{x^2}{9} + \dfrac{x^3}{27}$

$S_4 = -1 + \dfrac{x}{3} - \dfrac{x^2}{9} + \dfrac{x^3}{27} - \dfrac{x^4}{81}$

20. (a) $c = 0$ (c) $R = \infty$

(b) $S_0 = 1$

$S_1 = 1 + \dfrac{x}{2}$

$S_2 = 1 + \dfrac{x}{2} + \dfrac{x^2}{6}$

$S_3 = 1 + \dfrac{x}{2} + \dfrac{x^2}{6} + \dfrac{x^3}{24}$

$S_4 = 1 + \dfrac{x}{2} + \dfrac{x^2}{6} + \dfrac{x^3}{24} + \dfrac{x^4}{120}$

21. (a) $c = 3$ (c) $R = 1$

(b) $S_0 = \dfrac{1}{16}$

$S_1 = \dfrac{1}{16} - \dfrac{(x-3)}{25}$

$S_2 = \dfrac{1}{16} - \dfrac{(x-3)}{25} + \dfrac{(x-3)^2}{36}$

$S_3 = \dfrac{1}{16} - \dfrac{(x-3)}{25} + \dfrac{(x-3)^2}{36} - \dfrac{(x-3)^3}{49}$

$S_4 = \dfrac{1}{16} - \dfrac{(x-3)}{25} + \dfrac{(x-3)^2}{36} - \dfrac{(x-3)^3}{49} + \dfrac{(x-3)^4}{64}$

22. $e \displaystyle\sum_{n=0}^{\infty} \dfrac{3^n x^n}{n!}$ **23.** $1 + \dfrac{2x}{3} - \dfrac{x^2}{9} + \dfrac{4x^3}{81} - \dfrac{7x^4}{243} + \cdots$

24. (a) $S_1(x) = 1 + \dfrac{x}{2}$ (b) $S_2(x) = 1 + \dfrac{x}{2} + \dfrac{x^2}{8}$

(c) $S_3(x) = 1 + \dfrac{x}{2} + \dfrac{x^2}{8} + \dfrac{x^3}{48}$

(d) $S_4(x) = 1 + \dfrac{x}{2} + \dfrac{x^2}{8} + \dfrac{x^3}{48} + \dfrac{x^4}{384}$

25. (a) $S_1(x) = 1 - \dfrac{x}{2}$ (b) $S_2(x) = 1 - \dfrac{x}{2} + \dfrac{x^2}{4}$

(c) $S_3(x) = 1 - \dfrac{x}{2} + \dfrac{x^2}{4} - \dfrac{x^3}{8}$

(d) $S_4(x) = 1 - \dfrac{x}{2} + \dfrac{x^2}{4} - \dfrac{x^3}{8} + \dfrac{x^4}{16}$

26. (a) $S_1(x) = \dfrac{1}{16} - \dfrac{x}{32}$ (b) $S_2(x) = \dfrac{1}{16} - \dfrac{x}{32} + \dfrac{3x^2}{256}$

(c) $S_3(x) = \dfrac{1}{16} - \dfrac{x}{32} + \dfrac{3x^2}{256} - \dfrac{x^3}{256}$

(d) $S_4(x) = \dfrac{1}{16} - \dfrac{x}{32} + \dfrac{3x^2}{256} - \dfrac{x^3}{256} + \dfrac{5x^4}{4096}$

27. (a) $a_n = 2.7n + 283$ (b) 337 million

28. Newton's Method: 1.213, graphing utility: 1.213

Chapter 11

Section 11.1   *(page 666)*

1. $y' = 4Ce^{4x} = 4y$

3. $y' = 6x^2$ and $y' - \dfrac{3}{x}y = 6x^2 - \dfrac{3}{x}(2x^3) = 0$

5. $y' = 2Cx - 3$ and
   $xy' - 3x - 2y = x(2Cx - 3) - 3x - 2(Cx^2 - 3x) = 0$

7. $y' = \ln x + 1 + C$ and
   $x(y' - 1) - (y - 4) = x(\ln x + 1 + C - 1)$
   $\qquad - (x\ln x + Cx + 4 - 4) = 0$

9. $y'' = 2$ and $x^2y'' - 2y = x^2(2) - 2(x^2) = 0$

11. $y'' = -C_1 \sin x + C_2 \cos x$ and
   $y'' + y = -C_1 \sin x + C_2 \cos x + C_1 \sin x - C_2 \cos x = 0$

13. Solution   **15.** Not a solution   **17.** Not a solution

19. Solution   **21.** $y' = -2Ce^{-2x}$, so $y' + 2y = 0$; $y = 3e^{-2x}$.

23. $y' = C_2(1/x)$ and $y'' = -C_2(1/x^2)$,
   so $xy'' + y' = 0$; $y = 5 + \frac{1}{2}\ln|x|$.

25.

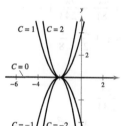

27. $y = x^3 + C$

29. $y = \ln|1 + x| + C$

31. $y = \frac{1}{3}\sqrt{(x^2 + 6)^3} + C$

33. $y = \frac{1}{4}\sin 4x + C$

35. $y^2 = \frac{1}{4}x^3$

37. $y = 3e^x$

39. (a) $N = 750 - 650e^{-0.0484t}$ (b) $N \approx 214$

41. $s = 25 - \dfrac{13}{\ln 3}\ln\dfrac{h}{2}$, $\dfrac{ds}{dh} = -\dfrac{13}{\ln 3}\left(\dfrac{1}{h}\right)$

So, the equation is a solution of $\dfrac{ds}{dh} = \dfrac{k}{h}$, where $k = -\dfrac{13}{\ln 3}$.

43.
$$y = a + Ce^{k(1-b)t}$$
$$\frac{dy}{dt} = Ck(1 - b)e^{k(1-b)t}$$
$$a + b(y - a) + \frac{1}{k}\frac{dy}{dt} = a + b[(a + Ce^{k(1-b)t}) - a]$$
$$+ \frac{1}{k}[Ck(1 - b)e^{k(1-b)t}]$$
$$= a + bCe^{k(1-b)t} + C(1 - b)e^{k(1-b)t}$$
$$= a + Ce^{k(1-b)t}[b + (1 - b)]$$
$$= a + Ce^{k(1-b)t} = y$$

45. True

Section 11.2   *(page 672)*

1. Yes; $(y + 3)\,dy = x\,dx$ **3.** Yes; $dy = \left(\dfrac{1}{x} + 1\right)dx$

5. No, the variables cannot be separated.

7. $y = x^2 + C$ **9.** $r = Ce^{0.05s}$ **11.** $y^4 = 2x^2 - 4x + C$

13. $y = \sqrt[3]{x + C}$ **15.** $y^2 = -\frac{1}{6}x^3 + C$ **17.** $y = Ce^{x^2/2}$

19. $y = \ln|t^3 + t + C|$ **21.** $y = 1 - \left(C - \dfrac{x}{2}\right)^2$

23. $y = C(2 + x)^2$ **25.** $y^2 = -2\cos x + C$

27. (a) $y = \frac{1}{2}x^2 + C$ **29.** (a) $y = Ce^x - 3$

(b)   (b)

31. $y^2 = 2e^x + 14$ **33.** $y = -4 - e^{-x^2/2}$

35. $y = 5\sqrt{x^2 - 16} - 17$ **37.** $y = e^{\sin x}$

39. $16y^2 + 9x^2 = 25$

41. $v = 34.56(1 - e^{-0.1t})$

43. $V = \left(\frac{1}{3}kt + C\right)^3$

45. 98.9%

47. (a) $w = 1200 - 1140e^{-kt}$
(b) $w = 1200 - 1140e^{-0.8t}$ $w = 1200 - 1140e^{-0.9t}$

$w = 1200 - 1140e^{-t}$

(c) ≈ 1.31 yr; ≈ 1.16 yr; ≈ 1.05 yr   (d) 1200 lb

Quiz Yourself   (page 674)

1. $y' = -\frac{1}{2}Ce^{-x/2}$ and $2y' + y = 2\left(-\frac{1}{2}Ce^{-x/2}\right) + Ce^{-x/2} = 0$

2. $y'' = -C_1 \cos x - C_2 \sin x$ and
$$y'' + y = -C_1 \cos x - C_2 \sin x + C_1 \cos x + C_2 \sin x = 0$$

3. $y' = -\dfrac{1}{x^2}$ and $y'' = \dfrac{2}{x^3}$; $xy'' + 2y' = \dfrac{2}{x^2} - \dfrac{2}{x^2} = 0$

4. $y' = \dfrac{3}{5}x^2 - 1 + \dfrac{C}{2\sqrt{x}}$ and
$$2xy' - y = \frac{6}{5}x^3 - 2x + C\sqrt{x} - \frac{1}{5}x^3 + x - C\sqrt{x} = x^3 - x$$

5. $y'' = -9C_1 \sin 3x - 9C_2 \cos 3x$ and
$$y'' + 9y = -9C_1 \sin 3x - 9C_2 \cos 3x$$
$$+ 9(C_1 \sin 3x + C_2 \cos 3x)$$
$$= 0$$
$y = 2 \sin 3x - \frac{1}{3} \cos 3x$

6. $y' = C_1 + 3C_2 x^2$, $y'' = 6C_2 x$, and
$$x^2 y'' - 3xy' + 3y = x^2(6C_2 x) - 3x(C_1 + 3C_2 x^2)$$
$$+ 3(C_1 x + C_2 x^3) = 0$$
$y = -2x + \frac{1}{2}x^3$

7. $y = -2x^2 + 4x + C$ **8.** $y = 1 + Ce^{x^2/2 + 2x}$

9. $y^2 = \ln|2x + 1| + C$ **10.** $y^3 + y = \dfrac{x^2}{2} + C$

11. (a) $y = \pm\sqrt{\frac{1}{3}x^3 + x + C}$ **12.** (a) $y = C(x - 3)$

(b)   (b)

13. $y = \frac{1}{2}e^{-2x} + \frac{1}{2}$ **14.** $y = -3e^{-(\cos \pi x)/\pi}$

15. $y = 2e^{x^3}$ **16.** $v = 20 - 20e^{-1.386t}$

Section 11.3   (page 678)

Skills Warm Up   (page 678)

1. $e^x + 1$ **2.** $e^{3x} + 1$ **3.** $\dfrac{1}{x^3}$ **4.** $x^2 e^x$

5. $2e^{2x} + C$ **6.** $\frac{1}{6}e^{3x^2} + C$ **7.** $\frac{1}{2}\ln|2x + 5| + C$

8. $\frac{1}{2}\ln|x^2 + 2x + 3| + C$ **9.** $\frac{1}{12}(4x - 3)^3 + C$

10. $-\frac{1}{6}(1 - x^2)^3 + C$

1. $y' + \dfrac{-3}{2x^2}y = \dfrac{x}{2}$ **3.** $y' + \dfrac{1}{x}y = e^x$

5. $y' + \dfrac{1}{1 - x}y = \dfrac{1}{x - 1}$ **7.** $y = 2 + Ce^{-3x}$

9. $y = \frac{1}{3}e^x(e^{3x} + C)$ **11.** $y = \frac{1}{2}x^2 + 3\ln|x| + C$

13. $5e^{-x^2}(e^{x^2} + C)$ **15.** $y = \dfrac{x^3 - 3x + C}{3(x - 1)}$

17. $y = e^{1/x^2}\left(-\dfrac{1}{2x^2} + C\right)$ **19.** $y = Ce^{-x} + 4$

21. $y = Ce^{x^2} - 1$ **23.** c   **24.** d   **25.** a   **26.** b

27. $y = 3e^x$ **29.** $xy = 4$ **31.** $y = 1 + 5e^{-x^3}$

33. $y = \dfrac{3}{4}x^2 - \dfrac{5}{3}x + \dfrac{7}{12x^2}$

35. $S = t + 95(1 - e^{-t/5})$

t	1	2	3	4	5
S	18.22	33.32	45.86	56.31	65.05

t	6	7	8	9	10
S	72.39	78.57	83.82	88.30	92.14

37. $v = \dfrac{1}{k}[9.8 + Ce^{kt}]$

39. (a) $N = 40 + Ce^{-kt}$ (b) $N = 40 - 30.57e^{-0.0188t}$

41. Answers will vary.

Section 11.4   (page 685)

Skills Warm Up   (page 685)

1. $y = \frac{3}{2}x^2 + C$ **2.** $y^2 = 3x + C$ **3.** $y = Ce^{x^2}$

4. $y^4 = \frac{1}{2}(x - 4)^2 + C$ **5.** $y = 2 + Ce^{-2x}$

6. $y = xe^{-2x} + Ce^{-2x}$ **7.** $y = 1 + Ce^{-x^2/2}$

8. $y = \frac{1}{4}x^2 + Cx^{-2}$ **9.** $\dfrac{dy}{dx} = kx^2$ **10.** $\dfrac{dx}{dt} = k(x - t)$

1. $y = \dfrac{360}{8 + 41t}$

3. $y = 1 - e^{-1.386t}$ **5.** $y = 200e^{-0.6931e^{-0.4397t}}$

7. $\dfrac{y(2 - y)}{(1 - y)^2} = \dfrac{19}{81}e^{0.50634t}$ **9.** $y = e^{(x \ln 2)/3} \approx e^{0.2310x}$

11. $y = 4e^{-(x \ln 4)/4} \approx 4e^{-0.3466x}$ **13.** $y = \frac{1}{2}e^{(\ln 2)x} \approx \frac{1}{2}e^{0.6931x}$

15. $\dfrac{dy}{dt} = ky$, $y = 20e^{-0.2231t}$ **17.** 269,972 people

19. ≈ 3.15 h   **21.** $S = L(1 - e^{-kt})$ **23.** 34 beavers

25. (a) $N = \dfrac{500}{1 + Ce^{-kt}}$ (b) $N = \dfrac{500}{1 + 4e^{-0.2452t}}$

(c) 121 deer   (d) ≈ 9.1 yr

27. (a) $Q = 25e^{-0.05t}$ (b) ≈ 10.22 min

29. $P = Ce^{kt} - \dfrac{N}{k}$ **31.** $A = \dfrac{P}{r}(e^{rt} - 1)$

33. \$10,708,538.49   **35.** (a) $C = C_0 e^{-Rt/V}$ (b) 0

37. (a) $C(t) = \dfrac{Q}{R}(1 - e^{-Rt/V})$ (b) $\dfrac{Q}{R}$

Review Exercises for Chapter 11   (page 691)

1. $\dfrac{dy}{dx} = \dfrac{1}{2}Ce^{x/2}$ and $2\dfrac{dy}{dx} = 2\left(\dfrac{1}{2}Ce^{x/2}\right) = Ce^{x/2} = y$

3. $y' = 6xe^{x^2}$ and $y' - 2xy = 6xe^{x^2} - 2x(3e^{x^2}) = 0$

5. $y' = 2x$ and $\dfrac{1}{2}y' - \dfrac{1}{x}y = \dfrac{1}{2}(2x) - \dfrac{1}{x}(x^2) = 0$

7. $y' = \dfrac{3x^2}{5} - 1 + \dfrac{C}{2\sqrt{x}}$ and

   $2xy' - y = \dfrac{6x^3}{5} - 2x + C\sqrt{x} - \dfrac{x^3}{5} + x - C\sqrt{x} = x^3 - x$

9. $y' = C_1e^x - C_2e^{-x}$, $y'' = C_1e^x + C_2e^{-x}$, and
   $y'' - y = C_1e^x + C_2e^{-x} - C_1e^x - C_2e^{-x} = 0$

11. Not a solution   13. Solution   15. $y = e^{-5x}$

17.

19. $y = \dfrac{1}{2}(x^2 + 1)$
21. $y = \dfrac{2}{3}x^3 + 5x + C$
23. $y = 3\sin x + C$
25. $y = x + 3\ln|x| + C$
27. Yes; $\dfrac{dy}{y} = \dfrac{dx}{x + 3}$
29. No, the variables cannot be separated.
31. $y = 2x^2 + C$

33. $y^4 = 5x + C$ 35. $y = \dfrac{1}{x^2 + C}$ 37. $y = Ce^{(x^2/2 + x)} - 1$

39. $y = Ce^{1/(4x^2)} - 2$ 41. $y^2 = 2\sin x + C$

43. (a) $y = x^3 + C$
    (b)

45. $y^2 = -2e^x + 6$
47. $y = e^{\sin x^2}$

49. $6x^2 - 5y^2 = 1$

51. $\approx 88.6\%$

53. $y' - \dfrac{y}{x^2} = -\dfrac{1}{4}x^2$

55. $y' - y = \dfrac{1}{2x^2}$

57. $y = Ce^{-4x} + 2$
59. $y = 2x^2 - 3x\ln|x| + Cx$
61. $y = e^{-6x}\left(\dfrac{1}{8}e^{8x} + C\right)$

63. $y = x^2 + 2x + \dfrac{C}{x}$

65. $y = 6 - 3e^{-x}$ 67. $s = 25 - \dfrac{13\ln(h/2)}{\ln 3}$, $2 < h < 15$

69. $y = Cx^{-k}$

71. $\dfrac{dy}{dt} = ky^{1/3}$, $y = \left(\dfrac{2}{3}kt + C\right)^{3/2}$, $y = (-5t + 9)^{3/2}$

73. About 383°F   75. About 50 pelicans

77. (a) $y = 10 - 8e^{-t/10}$ (b) About 7.1 gal

Test Yourself   (page 694)

1. $y' = -2e^{-2x}$ and $3y' + 2y = 3(-2e^{-2x}) + 2e^{-2x} = -4e^{-2x}$

2. $y'' = \dfrac{2}{(x+1)^3}$ and $y'' - \dfrac{2y}{(x+1)^2} = \dfrac{2}{(x+1)^3} - \dfrac{2[1/(x+1)]}{(x+1)^2} = 0$

3. $y^2 = x^2 + C$ 4. $y = Ce^{4x^2} - 2$

5. $y^3 = \dfrac{1}{\pi}\sin \pi x + C$ 6. $y = \dfrac{2}{5} + Ce^{-5x}$

7. $y = xe^{2x} + Ce^{2x}$ 8. $y = \dfrac{1}{3}x^2 + \dfrac{C}{x}$

9. $y = 1 - e^{-x^3/3}$ 10. $y = e^{e^{x^2}}$ 11. $y = \dfrac{1}{14}(\ln x)^2 - 2$

12. (a) $w = 200 - 190e^{-kt}$
    (b)

    (c) ≈ 1.7 yr
        ≈ 1.5 yr
        ≈ 1.3 yr
    (d) 200 lb

13. (a) $y = 1 - e^{-0.25t}$ (b) About 3 years   (c) About 63%

Appendix A

Section A.1   (page A7)

1. Rational   3. Irrational   5. Rational   7. Rational
9. Irrational   11. (a) Yes   (b) No   (c) Yes
13. (a) Yes   (b) No   (c) No
15. $x \geq 12$

17. $x < -\dfrac{1}{2}$

19. $x > 1$

21. $-\dfrac{1}{2} < x < \dfrac{7}{2}$

23. $-\dfrac{3}{4} < x < -\dfrac{1}{4}$

25. $x > 6$

27. $-\dfrac{3}{2} < x < 2$

29. $4.1 \leq E \leq 4.25$
31. $p \leq 0.4$
33. $120 \leq r \leq 180$
35. $x \geq 36$

37. (a) False   (b) True   (c) True   (d) False

Section A.2   (page A12)

1. (a) 51   (b) -51 (c) 51
3. (a) 14.99   (b) -14.99 (c) 14.99
5. (a) $\dfrac{128}{75}$ (b) $-\dfrac{128}{75}$ (c) $\dfrac{128}{75}$ 7. $|x| \leq 2$
9. $|x| > 2$ 11. $|x - 5| \leq 3$ 13. $|x - 2| > 2$
15. $|x - 5| < 3$ 17. $|y - a| \leq 2$
19. $-4 < x < 4$

21. $x < -6$ or $x > 6$

23. $3 < x < 7$

25. $x \leq -7$ or $x \geq 13$

27. $x < 6$ or $x > 14$

29. $4 < x < 5$

31. $a - b \leq x \leq a + b$

33. $\dfrac{a - 8b}{3} < x < \dfrac{a + 8b}{3}$

35. 16   **37.** 1.25   **39.** $\frac{1}{8}$ **41.** $|p - 33.15| \leq 2$
43. 20.75 oz and 19.25 oz
45. (a) $|4750 - E| \leq 500$,   **47.** (a) $|20{,}000 - E| \leq 500$,
$|4750 - E| \leq 237.50$ $|20{,}000 - E| \leq 1000$
(b) At variance   (b) At variance
49. $\$11{,}759.40 \leq C \leq \$17{,}639.10$

Section A.3   *(page A18)*

1. -54 **3.** $\frac{1}{2}$ **5.** 4   **7.** 44   **9.** 5   **11.** 9
13. $\frac{1}{2}$ **15.** $\frac{1}{4}$ **17.** 908.3483   **19.** -3.7798
21. $\dfrac{3}{4y^{14}}$ **23.** $10x^4$ **25.** $7x^5$ **27.** $\frac{5}{2}(x + y)^5, x \neq -y$
29. $3x, x > 0$ **31.** $2\sqrt{2}$ **33.** $3x\sqrt[3]{2x^2}$
35. $\dfrac{2x^3z}{y}\sqrt[3]{\dfrac{18z^2}{y}}$ **37.** $3x(x + 2)(x - 2)$ **39.** $\dfrac{2x^3 + 1}{x^{1/2}}$
41. $3(x + 1)^{1/2}(x + 2)(x - 1)$ **43.** $\frac{1}{3}x(5x^3 + 1)$
45. $x \geq 4$ **47.** $(-\infty, \infty)$ **49.** $(-\infty, 4) \cup (4, \infty)$
51. $x \neq 1, x \geq -2$ **53.** $\$19{,}121.84$ **55.** $\$11{,}345.46$
57. $\dfrac{\sqrt{2}}{2}\pi$ sec or about 2.22 sec

Section A.4   *(page A24)*

1. $\frac{1}{6}, 1$ **3.** $\frac{3}{2}$ **5.** $-2 \pm \sqrt{3}$ **7.** $\dfrac{-3 \pm \sqrt{41}}{4}$
9. $(x - 2)^2$ **11.** $(2x + 1)^2$ **13.** $(3x - 1)(x - 1)$
15. $(3x - 2)(x - 1)$ **17.** $(x - 2y)^2$
19. $(3 + y)(3 - y)(9 + y^2)$ **21.** $(x - 2)(x^2 + 2x + 4)$
23. $(y + 4)(y^2 - 4y + 16)$ **25.** $(x - y)(x^2 + xy + y^2)$
27. $(x - 4)(x - 1)(x + 1)$ **29.** $(2x - 3)(x^2 + 2)$
31. $(x - 2)(2x^2 - 1)$ **33.** $(x + 4)(x - 4)(x^2 + 1)$
35. $0, 5$ **37.** ± 3 **39.** $\pm\sqrt{3}$ **41.** $0, 6$ **43.** $-2, 1$
45. $-1, 6$ **47.** $-1, -\frac{2}{3}$ **49.** -4 **51.** ± 2
53. $1, \pm 2$ **55.** $(-\infty, -2] \cup [2, \infty)$
57. $(-\infty, 3] \cup [4, \infty)$ **59.** $(-\infty, -1] \cup [-\frac{1}{5}, \infty)$
61. $(x + 1)(x^2 - 4x - 2)$ **63.** $(x + 1)(2x^2 - 3x + 1)$
65. $-2, -1, 4$ **67.** $1, 2, 3$ **69.** $-\frac{2}{3}, -\frac{1}{2}, 3$
71. 4   **73.** $-2, -1, \frac{1}{4}$
75. Two solutions; The solutions of the equation are ± 2000, but the minimum average cost occurs at the positive value, 2000; 2000 units

Section A.5   *(page A31)*

1. $\dfrac{x - 4}{x + 6}, x \neq 3$ **3.** $\dfrac{x + 5}{2x + 3}, x \neq 2$ **5.** $\dfrac{x + 3}{x - 2}$
7. $\dfrac{x^2 - 3}{x}$ **9.** $\dfrac{5x^2 - 9x + 8}{(x - 3)(3x + 4)}$ **11.** $-\dfrac{x}{x^2 - 4}$
13. $\dfrac{1}{(x + 2)(x - 1)}$ **15.** $-\dfrac{x - 2}{x^2 + 1}$ **17.** $\dfrac{x + 2}{(x + 1)^{3/2}}$
19. $-\dfrac{3t}{2\sqrt{1 + t}}$ **21.** $\dfrac{x(x^2 + 2)}{(x^2 + 1)^{3/2}}$ **23.** $\dfrac{2}{x^2\sqrt{x^2 + 2}}$
25. $\dfrac{1}{2\sqrt{x}(x + 1)^{3/2}}$ **27.** $\dfrac{3x(x + 2)}{(2x + 3)^{3/2}}$ **29.** $\dfrac{\sqrt{10}}{5}$
31. $\dfrac{4x\sqrt{x - 1}}{x - 1}$ **33.** $\dfrac{49\sqrt{x^2 - 9}}{x + 3}$ **35.** $\dfrac{\sqrt{14} + 2}{2}$
37. $\sqrt{6} - \sqrt{5}$ **39.** $\sqrt{x} - \sqrt{x - 2}$

41. $\dfrac{1}{\sqrt{x + 2} + \sqrt{2}}$ **43.** $\$200.38$

Appendix B   *(page A39)*

1. 17.5 square units
3. Left Riemann sum: 0.518   **5.** Left Riemann sum: 0.746
Right Riemann sum: 0.768   Right Riemann sum: 0.646
7. Left Riemann sum: 0.859
Right Riemann sum: 0.659
9. (a)   (b) Answers will vary.
(c) Answers will vary.
(d) Answers will vary.

(e)

n	5	10	50	100
Left sum, S_L	1.6	1.8	1.96	1.98
Right sum, S_R	2.4	2.2	2.04	2.02

(f) Answers will vary.
11. $\displaystyle\int_0^5 3 \, dx$
13. $\displaystyle\int_{-4}^4 (4 - |x|) \, dx = \int_{-4}^0 (4 + x) \, dx + \int_0^4 (4 - x) \, dx$
15. $\displaystyle\int_{-2}^2 (4 - x^2) \, dx$ **17.** $\displaystyle\int_0^2 \sqrt{x + 1} \, dx$
19. 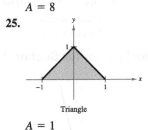   **21.**
Rectangle
$A = 12$ $A = 8$
23.   **25.**
Trapezoid   Triangle
$A = 14$ $A = 1$
27. 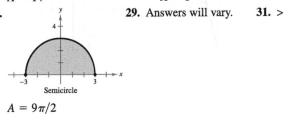   **29.** Answers will vary.   **31.** >
Semicircle
$A = 9\pi/2$

Answers to Checkpoints

Chapter 1

Checkpoints for Section 1.1

1

2

3 5   **4** $d_1 = \sqrt{20}, d_2 = \sqrt{45}, d_3 = \sqrt{65}$ **5** 25 yd
$d_1^2 + d_2^2 = 20 + 45 = 65 = d_3^2$

6 $(-2, 5)$ **7** \$87.5 billion

8 $(-1, -4), (1, -2), (1, 2), (-1, 0)$

Checkpoints for Section 1.2

1   **2**

3 x-intercepts: $(3, 0), (-1, 0)$, y-intercept: $(0, -3)$

4 $(x + 2)^2 + (y - 1)^2 = 25$

5 12,500 units   **6** 4 million units at \$122/unit

7 The projection obtained from the model is \$10,814.3 million, which is less than the *Value Line* projection.

Checkpoints for Section 1.3

1 (a)   (b)

(c)

2 Yes, $\frac{27}{312} \approx 0.08654 > \frac{1}{12} = 0.08\overline{3}$.

3 The y-intercept $(0, 1500)$ tells you that the original value of the copier is \$1500. The slope of $m = -300$ tells you that the value decreases by \$300/yr.

4 (a) 2   (b) $-\frac{1}{2}$ (c) 0   **5** $y = 2x + 4$

6 $y = 0.52t - 2.67$; \$2.01

7 (a) $y = \frac{1}{2}x$ (b) $y = -2x + 5$

8 $V = -1375t + 12,000$

Checkpoints for Section 1.4

1 (a) Yes, $y = x - 1$.   (b) No, $y = \pm\sqrt{4 - x^2}$.
(c) No, $y = \pm\sqrt{2 - x}$.   (d) Yes, $y = x^2$.

2 (a) Domain: $[-1, \infty)$; Range: $[0, \infty)$
(b) Domain: $(-\infty, \infty)$; Range: $[0, \infty)$

3 $f(0) = 1, f(1) = -3, f(4) = -3$
No, f is not one-to-one.

4 (a) $x^2 + 2x\,\Delta x + (\Delta x)^2 + 3$ (b) $2x + \Delta x, \Delta x \neq 0$

5 (a) $2x^2 + 5$ (b) $4x^2 + 4x + 3$

6 (a) $f^{-1}(x) = 5x$ (b) $f^{-1}(x) = x + 6$

7 $f^{-1}(x) = \sqrt{x - 2}$

8
$$f(x) = x^2 + 4$$
$$y = x^2 + 4$$
$$x = y^2 + 4$$
$$x - 4 = y^2$$
$$\pm\sqrt{x - 4} = y$$

Checkpoints for Section 1.5

1 6   **2** (a) 4   (b) Does not exist   (c) 4

3 (a) 5   (b) 6   (c) 25   (d) -2 **4** 5   **5** 12

6 7   **7** $\frac{1}{4}$ **8** (a) -1 (b) 1   **9** 1

10 $\lim\limits_{x \to 1^-} f(x) = 18$ and $\lim\limits_{x \to 1^+} f(x) = 20$

$\lim\limits_{x \to 1^-} f(x) \neq \lim\limits_{x \to 1^+} f(x)$

11 Does not exist

Checkpoints for Section 1.6

1 (a) f is continuous on the entire real line.
(b) f is continuous on the entire real line.
(c) f is continuous on the entire real line.

2 (a) f is continuous on $(-\infty, 1)$ and $(1, \infty)$.
(b) f is continuous on $(-\infty, 2)$ and $(2, \infty)$.
(c) f is continuous on the entire real line.

3 f is continuous on $[2, \infty)$.   **4** f is continuous on $[-1, 5]$.

5

6 $A = 10,000(1 + 0.0075)^{[4t]}$

Time (in years)

Chapter 2

Checkpoints for Section 2.1

1 3

2 For the months to the left of July on the graph, the tangent lines have positive slopes. For the months to the right of July, the tangent lines have negative slopes. The average daily temperature is increasing prior to July and decreasing after July.

3 4   **4** 2

5 $m = 8x$
At $(0, 1)$, $m = 0$.
At $(1, 5)$, $m = 8$.

6 $2x - 5$ **7** $-\dfrac{4}{t^2}$

Checkpoints for Section 2.2

1 (a) 0   (b) 0   (c) 0   (d) 0

2 (a) $4x^3$ (b) $-\dfrac{3}{x^4}$ (c) $2w$

3 $f'(x) = 3x^2$
$m = f'(-1) = 3$;
$m = f^{-1}(0) = 0$;
$m = f^{-1}(1) = 3$

4 (a) $8x$ (b) $\dfrac{8}{\sqrt{x}}$ **5** (a) $\dfrac{1}{4}$ (b) $-\dfrac{2}{5}$

6 (a) $-\dfrac{9}{2x^3}$ (b) $-\dfrac{9}{8x^3}$ **7** (a) $\dfrac{\sqrt{5}}{2\sqrt{x}}$ (b) $\dfrac{1}{4x^{3/4}}$

8 (a) $4x + 5$ (b) $4x^3 - 2$ **9** -1

10 $y = -x + 2$ **11** \$0.34/yr

Checkpoints for Section 2.3

1 (a) $0.5\overline{6}$ mg/ml/min   (b) 0 mg/ml/min
(c) -1.5 mg/ml/min

2 (a) -16 ft/sec   (b) -48 ft/sec   (c) -80 ft/sec

3 When $t = 1.75$, $h'(1.75) = -56$ ft/sec.
When $t = 2$, $h'(2) = -64$ ft/sec.

4 (a) $\frac{3}{2}$ sec   (b) -32 ft/sec

5 When $x = 100$, $\dfrac{dP}{dx} = \$16$/unit.
Actual gain $= \$16.06$

6 $p = -0.057x + 23.82$, $R = -0.057x^2 + 23.82x$

7 Revenue: $R = 2000x - 4x^2$
Marginal revenue: $\dfrac{dR}{dx} = 2000 - 8x$; \$0/unit

8 $\dfrac{dP}{dx} = \$1.44$/unit
Actual increase in profit $\approx \$1.44$

Checkpoints for Section 2.4

1 $-27x^2 + 12x + 24$ **2** $\dfrac{2x^2 - 1}{x^2}$

3 (a) $18x^2 + 30x$ (b) $12x + 15$ **4** $-\dfrac{22}{(5x - 2)^2}$

5 $y = \frac{8}{25}x - \frac{4}{5}$;
$y = \dfrac{x^2 - 4}{2x + 5}$

6 $\dfrac{-3x^2 + 4x + 8}{x^2(x + 4)^2}$ **7** (a) $\dfrac{2}{5}x + \dfrac{4}{5}$ (b) $3x^3$

8

t	0	1	2	3	4	5	6	7
$\dfrac{dP}{dt}$	0	-50	-16	-6	-2.77	-1.48	-0.88	-0.56

As t increases, the rate at which the blood pressure drops decreases.

Checkpoints for Section 2.5

1 (a) $u = g(x) = x + 1$, $y = f(u) = \dfrac{1}{\sqrt{u}}$
(b) $u = g(x) = x^2 + 2x + 5$, $y = f(u) = u^3$

2 $6x^2(x^3 + 1)$ **3** $4(2x + 3)(x^2 + 3x)^3$ **4** $y = \frac{1}{3}x + \frac{8}{3}$

5 $-\dfrac{8}{(2x + 1)^2}$ **6** $\dfrac{x(3x^2 + 2)}{\sqrt{x^2 + 1}}$ **7** $-\dfrac{12(x + 1)}{(x - 5)^3}$

8 About \$3.48/yr

Checkpoints for Section 2.6

1 $f'(x) = 18x^2 - 4x$, $f''(x) = 36x - 4$, $f'''(x) = 36$, $f^{(4)}(x) = 0$

2 18   **3** $\dfrac{120}{x^6}$

4 Height $= 144$ ft
Velocity $= 0$ ft/sec
Acceleration $= -32$ ft/sec²

5 -9.8 m/sec²

6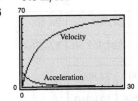

Acceleration approaches zero.

Checkpoints for Section 2.7

1 $-\dfrac{2}{x^3}$

2 (a) $12x^2$ (b) $6y\,\dfrac{dy}{dx}$ (c) $1 + 5\,\dfrac{dy}{dx}$ (d) $y^3 + 3xy^2\,\dfrac{dy}{dx}$

3 $\dfrac{dy}{dx} = -\dfrac{x-2}{y-1}$ **4** $\dfrac{3}{4}$ **5** $\dfrac{5}{9}$

6 $\dfrac{dx}{dp} = -\dfrac{2}{p^2(0.002x + 1)}$

Checkpoints for Section 2.8

1 9   **2** $12\pi \approx 37.7\ \text{ft}^2/\text{sec}$
3 \$1500/day   **4** \$28,400/wk

Chapter 3

Checkpoints for Section 3.1

1 $f'(x) = 4x^3$
$f'(x) < 0$ if $x < 0$; therefore, f is decreasing on $(-\infty, 0)$.
$f'(x) > 0$ if $x > 0$; therefore, f is increasing on $(0, \infty)$.

2 $\dfrac{dF}{dt} = -1.5348t + 2.872 < 0$ when $3 \le t \le 8$, which implies that the consumption of fresh fruit was decreasing from 2003 through 2008.

3 $x = \frac{1}{2}$

4 Increasing on $(-\infty, -2)$ and $(2, \infty)$
Decreasing on $(-2, 2)$

5 Increasing on $(0, \infty)$
Decreasing on $(-\infty, 0)$

6 Increasing on $(-\infty, -1)$ and $(1, \infty)$
Decreasing on $(-1, 0)$ and $(0, 1)$

7 Because $f'(x) = -3x^2 = 0$ when $x = 0$ and because f is decreasing on $(-\infty, 0) \cup (0, \infty)$, f is decreasing on $(-\infty, \infty)$.

8 $(0, 3000)$

Checkpoints for Section 3.2

1 Relative maximum at $(-1, 5)$
Relative minimum at $(1, -3)$

2 Relative minimum at $(3, -27)$

3 Relative maximum at $(1, 1)$
Relative minimum at $(0, 0)$

4 Absolute maximum at $(0, 10)$
Absolute minimum at $(4, -6)$

5

x (units)	24,000	24,200	24,300	24,400
P (profit)	\$24,760	\$24,766	\$24,767.50	\$24,768

x (units)	24,500	24,600	24,800
P (profit)	\$24,767.50	\$24,766	\$24,760

Checkpoints for Section 3.3

1 (a) $f'' = -4$; because $f''(x) < 0$ for all x, f is concave downward for all x.

(b) $f''(x) = \dfrac{1}{2x^{3/2}}$; because $f''(x) > 0$ for all $x > 0$, f is concave upward for all $x > 0$.

2 Because $f''(x) > 0$ for $x < -\dfrac{2\sqrt{3}}{3}$ and $x > \dfrac{2\sqrt{3}}{3}$, f is concave upward on $\left(-\infty, -\dfrac{2\sqrt{3}}{3}\right)$ and $\left(\dfrac{2\sqrt{3}}{3}, \infty\right)$. Because $f''(x) < 0$ for $-\dfrac{2\sqrt{3}}{3} < x < \dfrac{2\sqrt{3}}{3}$, f is concave downward on $\left(-\dfrac{2\sqrt{3}}{3}, \dfrac{2\sqrt{3}}{3}\right)$.

3 f is concave upward on $(-\infty, 0)$.
f is concave downward on $(0, \infty)$.
Point of inflection: $(0, 0)$

4 f is concave upward on $(-\infty, 0)$ and $(1, \infty)$.
f is concave downward on $(0, 1)$.
Points of inflection: $(0, 1), (1, 0)$

5 Relative minimum: $(3, -26)$

6 Point of diminishing returns: $x = \$150$ thousand

Checkpoints for Section 3.4

1

Maximum volume = 108 in.^{3}

2 $\left(\sqrt{\tfrac{1}{2}}, \tfrac{7}{2}\right)$ and $\left(-\sqrt{\tfrac{1}{2}}, \tfrac{7}{2}\right)$ **3** 8 in. by 12 in.

Checkpoints for Section 3.5

1 125 units yield a maximum revenue of \$1,562,500.
2 400 units   **3** \$6.25/unit   **4** \$4.00
5 Demand is elastic when $0 < x < 144$.
Demand is inelastic when $144 < x < 324$.
Demand is of unit elasticity when $x = 144$.

Checkpoints for Section 3.6

1 (a) $\displaystyle\lim_{x \to 2^-} \dfrac{1}{x-2} = -\infty$ (b) $\displaystyle\lim_{x \to 2^+} \dfrac{1}{x-2} = \infty$

(c) $\displaystyle\lim_{x \to -3^-} \dfrac{-1}{x+3} = -\infty$ (d) $\displaystyle\lim_{x \to -3^+} \dfrac{-1}{x+3} = \infty$

2 $x = 0, x = 4$ **3** $x = 3$

4 $\displaystyle\lim_{x \to 2^-} \dfrac{x^2 - 4x}{x - 2} = \infty$; $\displaystyle\lim_{x \to 2^+} \dfrac{x^2 - 4x}{x - 2} = -\infty$

5 2

6 (a) $y = 0$ (b) $y = \frac{1}{2}$ (c) No horizontal asymptote

7 $C = 0.75x + 25,000$

$\overline{C} = 0.75 + \dfrac{25,000}{x}$

$\displaystyle\lim_{x \to \infty} \overline{C} = \$0.75/\text{unit}$

8 No, the cost function is not defined at $p = 100$, which implies that it is not possible to remove 100% of the pollutants.

Checkpoints for Section 3.7

1

	$f(x)$	$f'(x)$	$f''(x)$	Shape of graph
x in $(-\infty, -1)$		$-$	$+$	Decreasing, concave upward
$x = -1$	-32	0	$+$	Relative minimum
x in $(-1, 1)$		$+$	$+$	Increasing, concave upward
$x = 1$	-16	$+$	0	Point of inflection
x in $(1, 3)$		$+$	$-$	Increasing, concave downward
$x = 3$	0	0	$-$	Relative maximum
x in $(3, \infty)$		$-$	$-$	Decreasing, concave downward

2

	$f(x)$	$f'(x)$	$f''(x)$	Shape of graph
x in $(-\infty, 0)$		$-$	$+$	Decreasing, concave upward
$x = 0$	5	0	0	Point of inflection
x in $(0, 2)$		$-$	$-$	Decreasing, concave downward
$x = 2$	-11	$-$	0	Point of inflection
x in $(2, 3)$		$-$	$+$	Decreasing, concave upward
$x = 3$	-22	0	$+$	Relative minimum
x in $(3, \infty)$		$+$	$+$	Increasing, concave upward

3

	$f(x)$	$f'(x)$	$f''(x)$	Shape of graph
x in $(-\infty, 0)$		$+$	$-$	Increasing, concave downward
$x = 0$	0	0	$-$	Relative maximum
x in $(0, 1)$		$-$	$-$	Decreasing, concave downward
$x = 1$	Undef.	Undef.	Undef.	Vertical asymptote
x in $(1, 2)$		$-$	$+$	Decreasing, concave upward
$x = 2$	4	0	$+$	Relative minimum
x in $(2, \infty)$		$+$	$+$	Increasing, concave upward

4

	$f(x)$	$f'(x)$	$f''(x)$	Shape of graph
x in $(-\infty, -1)$		$+$	$+$	Increasing, concave upward
$x = -1$	Undef.	Undef.	Undef.	Vertical asymptote
x in $(-1, 0)$		$+$	$-$	Increasing, concave downward
$x = 0$	-1	0	$-$	Relative maximum
x in $(0, 1)$		$-$	$-$	Decreasing, concave downward
$x = 1$	Undef.	Undef.	Undef.	Vertical asymptote
x in $(1, \infty)$		$-$	$+$	Decreasing, concave upward

5

	$f(x)$	$f'(x)$	$f''(x)$	Shape of graph
x in $(0, 1)$		$-$	$+$	Decreasing, concave upward
$x = 1$	-4	0	$+$	Relative minimum
x in $(1, \infty)$		$+$	$+$	Increasing, concave upward

Checkpoints for Section 3.8

1 $dy = 0.32$; $\Delta y = 0.32240801$ **2** $dR = \$22$; $\Delta R = \$21$
3 $dP = \$10.96$; $\Delta P = \$10.98$
4 (a) $dy = 12x^2\, dx$ (b) $dy = \frac{2}{3}\, dx$

(c) $dy = (6x - 2)\, dx$ (d) $dy = -\dfrac{2}{x^3}\, dx$

Chapter 4
Checkpoints for Section 4.1

1 (a) 243   (b) 3   (c) 64   (d) 8   (e) $\frac{1}{2}$ (f) $\sqrt{10}$
2 (a) 5.453×10^{-13} (b) 1.621×10^{-13}
(c) 2.629×10^{-14}

3   **4**

Checkpoints for Section 4.2

1

x	-2	-1	0	1	2
$g(x)$	$e^2 \approx 7.389$	$e \approx 2.718$	1	$\dfrac{1}{e} \approx 0.368$	$\dfrac{1}{e^2} \approx 0.135$

2 After 0 h, $y = 1.25$ g.
After 1 h, $y \approx 1.338$ g.
After 10 h, $y \approx 1.498$ g.
$\displaystyle\lim_{t \to \infty} \frac{1.50}{1 + 0.2e^{-0.5t}} = 1.50$ g

3 (a) \$4870.38   (b) \$4902.71
(c) \$4918.66   (d) \$4919.21
All else being equal, the more often interest is compounded, the greater the balance.

4 (a) 7%   (b) 7.12%   (c) 7.19%   (d) 7.23%

5 \$16,712.90

Checkpoints for Section 4.3

1 At $(0, 2)$, the slope is 2. At $(1, 2e)$, the slope is $2e$.

2 (a) $3e^{3x}$

(b) $-\dfrac{6x^2}{e^{2x^3}}$

(c) $8xe^{x^2}$

(d) $-\dfrac{2}{e^{2x}}$

3 (a) 0
(b) $3e^{3x+1}$
(c) $xe^x(x + 2)$
(d) $\frac{1}{2}(e^x - e^{-x})$
(e) $\dfrac{e^x(x - 2)}{x^3}$
(f) $e^x(x^2 + 2x - 1)$

4

5 \$18.39/unit (80,000 units); \$1,471,517.77

6

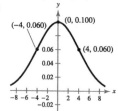

Points of inflection: $(-4, 0.060), (4, 0.060)$

Checkpoints for Section 4.4

1

x	-1.5	-1	-0.5	0	0.5	1
$f(x)$	-0.693	0	0.405	0.693	0.916	1.099

2 (a) 3   (b) $x + 1$

3 (a) $\ln 2 - \ln 5$ (b) $\frac{1}{3}\ln(x + 2)$
(c) $\ln x - \ln 5 - \ln y$ (d) $\ln x + 2\ln(x + 1)$

4 (a) $\ln x^4 y^3$ (b) $\ln \dfrac{x + 1}{(x + 3)^2}$ **5** (a) $\ln 6$ (b) $5 \ln 5$

6 (a) e^4 (b) e^3 **7** 7.9 yr

Checkpoints for Section 4.5

1 $\dfrac{1}{x}$ **2** (a) $\dfrac{2x}{x^2 - 4}$ (b) $x(1 + 2\ln x)$ (c) $\dfrac{2\ln x - 1}{x^3}$

3 $\dfrac{1}{3(x + 1)}$ **4** $\dfrac{2}{x} + \dfrac{x}{x^2 + 1}$ **5** $y = 4x - 4$

6 Relative minimum: $(2, 2 - 2\ln 2) \approx (2, 0.6137)$

7 $\dfrac{dp}{dt} = -1.3\%/\text{mo}$

The average score would decrease at a greater rate than the model in Example 7.

8 (a) 4   (b) -2 (c) -5 (d) 3

9 (a) 2.322   (b) 2.631   (c) 3.161   (d) -0.5

10

As time increases, the derivative approaches 0. The rate of change of the amount of carbon isotopes is proportional to the amount present.

Checkpoints for Section 4.6

1 About 2113.7 yr   **2** $y = 25e^{0.6931t}$

3 $r = \frac{1}{8}\ln 2 \approx 0.0866$ or 8.66%   **4** About 12.42 mo

Chapter 5

Checkpoints for Section 5.1

1 (a) $5x + C$ (b) $-r + C$ (c) $2t + C$ **2** $\frac{5}{2}x^2 + C$

3 (a) $-\dfrac{1}{x} + C$ (b) $\dfrac{3}{4}x^{4/3} + C$

4 (a) $\frac{1}{2}x^2 + 4x + C$ (b) $x^4 - \frac{5}{2}x^2 + 2x + C$

5 $\frac{2}{3}x^{3/2} + 4x^{1/2} + C$

6 General solution: $F(x) = 2x^2 + 2x + C$
Particular solution: $F(x) = 2x^2 + 2x + 4$

7 $s(t) = -16t^2 + 32t + 48$. The ball hits the ground 3 seconds after it is thrown, with a velocity of -64 feet per second.

8 $C = -0.01x^2 + 28x + 12.01$
$C(200) = \$5212.01$

Checkpoints for Section 5.2

1 (a) $\dfrac{(x^3 + 6x)^3}{3} + C$ (b) $\dfrac{2}{3}(x^2 - 2)^{3/2} + C$

2 $\dfrac{1}{36}(3x^4 + 1)^3 + C$ **3** $\dfrac{1}{9}(x^3 - 3x)^3 + C$

4 $2x^9 + \dfrac{12}{5}x^5 + 2x + C$ **5** $\dfrac{5}{3}(x^2 - 1)^{3/2} + C$

6 $-\dfrac{1}{3}(1 - 2x)^{3/2} + C$ **7** $\dfrac{1}{3}(x^2 + 4)^{3/2} + C$

8 About \$34,068

Checkpoints for Section 5.3

1 (a) $3e^x + C$ (b) $e^{5x} + C$ (c) $e^x - \dfrac{x^2}{2} + C$

2 $\dfrac{1}{2}e^{2x+3} + C$ **3** $2e^{x^2} + C$

4 (a) $2\ln|x| + C$ (b) $\ln|x^3| + C$ (c) $\ln|2x + 1| + C$

5 $\dfrac{1}{4}\ln|4x + 1| + C$ **6** $\dfrac{3}{2}\ln(x^2 + 4) + C$

7 (a) $4x - 3\ln|x| - \dfrac{2}{x} + C$ (b) $2\ln(1 + e^x) + C \, dx$

(c) $\dfrac{x^2}{2} + x + 3\ln|x + 1| + C$

Checkpoints for Section 5.4

1 $\dfrac{1}{2}(3)(12) = 18$

2 $\dfrac{22}{3}$ units^2 **3** 68

4 (a) $\dfrac{1}{4}(e^4 - 1) \approx 13.3995$ (b) $-\ln 5 + \ln 2 \approx -0.9163$

5 $\dfrac{13}{2}$ **6** (a) About \$14.18   (b) \$141.79

7 \$13.70   **8** (a) $\dfrac{2}{5}$ (b) 0   **9** About \$12,295.62

Checkpoints for Section 5.5

1 $\dfrac{8}{3}$ units^2

2 $\dfrac{32}{3}$ units^2 **3** $\dfrac{9}{2}$ units^2

4 $\dfrac{253}{12}$ units^2

5 Consumer surplus: 40
Producer surplus: 20

6 The company can save \$47.52 million.

Checkpoints for Section 5.6

1 $\dfrac{37}{8}$ units^2 **2** 0.436 unit^2 **3** 5.642 units^2

4 About 1.463

Chapter 6

Checkpoints for Section 6.1

1 $\dfrac{1}{2}xe^{2x} - \dfrac{1}{4}e^{2x} + C$ **2** $\dfrac{x^2}{2}\ln x - \dfrac{1}{4}x^2 + C$

3 $x\ln 2x - x + C$ **4** $e^x(x^3 - 3x^2 + 6x - 6) + C$

5 $e - 2$ **6** \$538,145   **7** \$721,632.08

Checkpoints for Section 6.2

1 $\dfrac{2}{3}(x - 4)\sqrt{2 + x} + C$ (Formula 19)

2 $\sqrt{x^2 + 16} - 4\ln\left|\dfrac{4 + \sqrt{x^2 + 16}}{x}\right| + C$ (Formula 25)

3 $\dfrac{1}{4}\ln\left|\dfrac{x - 2}{x + 2}\right| + C$ (Formula 21)

4 $\dfrac{1}{3}[1 - \ln(1 + e) + \ln 2] \approx 0.12663$ (Formula 39)

5 $x(\ln x)^2 + 2x - 2x\ln x + C$ (Formula 44)

6 About 18.2%

Checkpoints for Section 6.3

1 3.2608   **2** 3.1956   **3** 1.154

Checkpoints for Section 6.4

1 (a) Converges; $\dfrac{1}{2}$ (b) Diverges

2 1   **3** $\dfrac{1}{2}$ **4** 0.0013 or 0.13%

5 No, you do not have enough money to start the scholarship fund because you need \$125,000.   (\$125,000 > \$120,000)

Chapter 7

Checkpoints for Section 7.1

1

2 $2\sqrt{6}$ **3** $\left(-\dfrac{5}{2}, 2, -2\right)$

4 $(x - 4)^2 + (y - 3)^2 + (z - 2)^2 = 25$

5 $(x - 1)^2 + (y - 3)^2 + (z - 2)^2 = 38$

6 Center: $(-3, 4, -1)$; radius: 6

7 $(x + 1)^2 + (y - 2)^2 = 16$

Checkpoints for Section 7.2

1 x-intercept: $(4, 0, 0)$;
y-intercept: $(0, 2, 0)$;
z-intercept: $(0, 0, 8)$

2 xy-trace: circle, $x^2 + y^2 = 1$
yz-trace: hyperbola, $y^2 - z^2 = 1$
xz-trace: hyperbola, $x^2 - z^2 = 1$
$z = 3$ trace: circle, $x^2 + y^2 = 10$
Hyperboloid of one sheet

3 (a) Elliptic paraboloid   (b) Elliptic cone

Checkpoints for Section 7.3

1 (a) 0   (b) $\frac{9}{4}$

2 Domain: $x^2 + y^2 \le 9$
Range: $0 \le z \le 3$

3 For each value of c, the equation $f(x, y) = c$ is a circle (or point) in the xy-plane.

4 $f(1500, 1000) \approx 127{,}542$ units
$f(1000, 1500) \approx 117{,}608$ units
x, person-hours, has a greater effect on production.

5 (a) $M = \$421.60/\text{mo}$
(b) Total paid $= (30 \times 12) \times 421.60$
$= \$151{,}776$

Checkpoints for Section 7.4

1 $\dfrac{\partial z}{\partial x} = 4x - 8xy^3$

$\dfrac{\partial z}{\partial y} = -12x^2y^2 + 4y^3$

2 $f_x(x, y) = 2xy^3; \ f_x(1, 2) = 16$
$f_y(x, y) = 3x^2y^2; \ f_y(1, 2) = 12$

3 (a) $f_x(1, -1, 49) = 8$ (b) $f_y(1, -1, 49) = -18$

4 Substitute product relationship

5 $\dfrac{\partial w}{\partial x} = xy + 2xy \ln(xz)$

$\dfrac{\partial w}{\partial y} = x^2 \ln xz$

$\dfrac{\partial w}{\partial z} = \dfrac{x^2y}{z}$

6 $f_{xx} = 8y^2$
$f_{yy} = 8x^2 + 8$
$f_{xy} = 16xy$
$f_{yx} = 16xy$

7 $f_{xx} = 0 \quad f_{xy} = e^y \quad f_{xz} = 2$
$f_{yx} = e^y \quad f_{yy} = xe^y + 2 \quad f_{yz} = 0$
$f_{zx} = 2 \quad f_{zy} = 0 \quad f_{zz} = 0$

Checkpoints for Section 7.5

1 $f(-8, 2) = -64$: relative minimum

2 $f(0, 0) = 1$: relative maximum

3 $f(0, 0) = 0$: saddle point

4 $P(3.11, 3.81) = \$744.81$ maximum profit

5 $V\left(\frac{4}{3}, \frac{2}{3}, \frac{8}{3}\right) = \frac{64}{27}$ units^3

Checkpoints for Section 7.6

1 $V\left(\frac{4}{3}, \frac{2}{3}, \frac{8}{3}\right) = \frac{64}{27}$ units^3 **2** $f(187.5, 50) \approx 13{,}474$ units

3 About 26,740 units

4 $P(3.35, 4.26) = \$758.08$ maximum profit

Checkpoints for Section 7.7

1 For $f(x)$, $S = 10$. For $g(x)$, $S = 0.76$.
The quadratic model is a better fit.

2 $f(x) = \frac{6}{5}x + \frac{23}{10}$

3 $y = 16{,}194.4t + 132{,}405$
About 342,932,200 subscribers

Checkpoints for Section 7.8

1 (a) $\frac{1}{4}x^4 + 2x^3 - 2x - \frac{1}{4}$ (b) $\ln|y^2 + y| - \ln|2y|$

2 $\frac{25}{2}$ **3** $\displaystyle\int_2^4 \int_1^5 dx\,dy = 8$ **4** $\frac{4}{3}$

5 (a)   (b) $\displaystyle\int_0^4 \int_0^{x/2} dy\,dx$

(c) $\displaystyle\int_0^2 \int_{2y}^4 dx\,dy = 4 = \int_0^4 \int_0^{x/2} dy\,dx$

$R: 0 \le y \le 2$
$2y \le x \le 4$

6 $\displaystyle\int_{-1}^3 \int_{x^2}^{2x+3} dy\,dx = \frac{32}{3}$

Checkpoints for Section 7.9

1 $\frac{16}{3}$ **2** $e - 1$ **3** $\frac{176}{15}$

4 Integration by parts   **5** 3

Chapter 8

Checkpoints for Section 8.1

1 (a) 150°   (b) 30°   (c) 135°   (d) 30°

2 (a) $\dfrac{5\pi}{4}$ (b) $-\dfrac{\pi}{4}$ (c) $\dfrac{4\pi}{3}$ (d) $\dfrac{5\pi}{6}$

3 (a) 300°   (b) 210°   (c) 270°   (d) $-135°$

4 $\frac{1}{2}$ ft^2

Checkpoints for Section 8.2

1 $\sin \theta = \dfrac{1}{2}$

$\cos \theta = \dfrac{\sqrt{3}}{2}$

$\tan \theta = \dfrac{\sqrt{3}}{3}$

2 (a) $\dfrac{1}{2}$ (b) $-\dfrac{\sqrt{2}}{2}$ (c) $-\sqrt{3}$

3 (a) $-\dfrac{1}{2}$ (b) $\sqrt{2}$ (c) $\dfrac{\sqrt{6} - \sqrt{2}}{4}$

(d) 1   (e) 1   (f) 1

4 About 52.5 ft   **5** About 245.76°

6 (a) $\dfrac{\pi}{4}, \dfrac{7\pi}{4}$ (b) $\dfrac{2\pi}{3}, \dfrac{5\pi}{3}$ (c) $\dfrac{7\pi}{6}, \dfrac{11\pi}{6}$

7 $\theta = 0, \dfrac{2\pi}{3}, \pi, \dfrac{4\pi}{3}, 2\pi$

Checkpoints for Section 8.3

1

2

3

4

x	-0.10	-0.05	-0.01
$\dfrac{1 - \cos x}{x}$	-0.0500	-0.0250	-0.0050

x	0.01	0.05	0.10
$\dfrac{1 - \cos x}{x}$	0.0050	0.0250	0.0500

$$\lim_{x \to 0} \frac{1 - \cos x}{x} = 0$$

5

The predator population has an amplitude of 2500 and oscillates about the line $y = 12{,}000$. The prey population has an amplitude of 6000 and oscillates about the line $y = 18{,}000$.

6

Checkpoints for Section 8.4

1–3 (a) $-4 \sin 4x$ (b) $2x \cos(x^2 - 1)$ (c) $\frac{1}{2} \sec^2 \frac{x}{2}$

(d) $-6x^2 \sin x^3$ (e) $3 \sin^2 x \cos x$

4 (a) $4 \sec(4x) \tan(4x)$ (b) $-2x \csc^2 x^2$

5 (a) $-\dfrac{\sin 2x}{\sqrt{\cos 2x}}$ (b) $\dfrac{\sec^2 3x}{\sqrt[3]{\tan^2 3x}}$

6 (a) $-x^2 \sin x + 2x \cos x$ (b) $2t \cos 2t + \sin 2t$

7 Relative maximum: $\left(\dfrac{7\pi}{6}, \dfrac{7\pi + 6\sqrt{3}}{12}\right)$

Relative minimum: $\left(\dfrac{11\pi}{6}, \dfrac{11\pi - 6\sqrt{3}}{12}\right)$

8 Relative maximum: $\left(\dfrac{\pi}{6}, \dfrac{3\sqrt{3}}{4}\right)$

Relative minimum: $\left(\dfrac{5\pi}{6}, -\dfrac{3\sqrt{3}}{4}\right)$

9 About 1721 lb/day   **10** About $-3.9°$/h

Checkpoints for Section 8.5

1–2 (a) $-5 \cos x + C$ (b) $\sin x^4 + C$

3 $\frac{1}{5} \tan 5x + C$ **4** $-\csc 2x + C$ **5** $-\frac{1}{8} \cos^4 2x + C$

6 $\ln|\sin x| + C$ **7** 1   **8** 1

9 $\frac{1}{2} \ln|\sec 2x + \tan 2x| + C$ **10** $82.68°$

Chapter 9

Checkpoints for Section 9.1

1 (a) $S = \{(1, 1), (1, 2), (1, 3), (1, 4), (1, 5), (1, 6), (2, 1), (2, 2),$
$(2, 3), (2, 4), (2, 5), (2, 6), (3, 1), (3, 2), (3, 3), (3, 4),$
$(3, 5), (3, 6), (4, 1), (4, 2), (4, 3), (4, 4), (4, 5), (4, 6),$
$(5, 1), (5, 2), (5, 3), (5, 4), (5, 5), (5, 6), (6, 1), (6, 2),$
$(6, 3), (6, 4), (6, 5), (6, 6)\}$

(b) $E = \{(1, 6), (2, 5), (2, 6), (3, 4), (3, 5), (3, 6), (4, 3),$
$(4, 4), (4, 5), (4, 6), (5, 2), (5, 3), (5, 4), (5, 5), (5, 6),$
$(6, 1), (6, 2), (6, 3), (6, 4), (6, 5), (6, 6)\}$

2

3

4 7   **5** 2.37 units/day

6 $V(x) = 1.2,\ \sigma \approx 1.095$

Checkpoints for Section 9.2

1 $\displaystyle\int_0^2 \frac{1}{2}x \, dx = 1$ **2** $\displaystyle\int_0^\infty 2e^{-2x} \, dx = 1$ **3** $\dfrac{3}{16}$

4 0.4   **5** 0.148

Checkpoints for Section 9.3

1 2   **2** $V(x) = \frac{4}{5},\ \sigma \approx \sqrt{\frac{4}{5}} \approx 0.8944$ **3** 84.6%

4 Mean: 0.5; median: 0.35   **5** $\mu = 1;\ \sigma \approx 0.577$

6 About 0.567 or 56.7%   **7** About 0.159 or 15.9%

Chapter 10

Checkpoints for Section 10.1

1 (a) $a_1 = 2, a_2 = 5, a_3 = 8, a_4 = 11$
(b) $b_1 = \frac{1}{2}, b_2 = \frac{2}{5}, b_3 = \frac{3}{10}, b_4 = \frac{4}{17}$
2 (a) 0   (b) 2   **3** 0
4 $\frac{1}{n}$; converges   **5** $\dfrac{(-1)^{n+1}n^2}{(n+1)!}$
6 (a) $A_1 = \$1007.50$ (b) $A_{16} = \$1126.99$
$A_2 = \$1015.06$
$A_3 = \$1022.67$

Checkpoints for Section 10.2

1 $\displaystyle\sum_{i=1}^{4} 4\left(-\frac{1}{2}\right)^i$ **2** Converges to $\dfrac{1}{3}$

3 (a) 1   (b) $\frac{4}{3}$ (c) $-\frac{2}{3}$ **4** (a) Diverges   (b) Diverges
5 $S_5 \approx 5.556, S_{50} = 5.\overline{5}, S_{500} = 5.\overline{5}$ **6** $\$1021.17$
7 (a) Converges to $\frac{5}{3}$ (b) Diverges   (c) Converges to $\frac{5}{3}$
8 About 40,000 units   **9** 140 ft

Checkpoints for Section 10.3

1 (a) p-series with $p = \pi$ (b) p-series with $p = \frac{3}{2}$
(c) Geometric series
2 (a) Converges   (b) Converges   (c) Diverges
3 Converges to approximately 20.086
4 Diverges   **5** Diverges

Checkpoints for Section 10.4

1 (a) 2   (b) -3 (c) 0
2 Radius of convergence is infinite.   **3** $R = 3$
4 $\displaystyle\sum_{n=0}^{\infty} \dfrac{(-x)^n}{n!}$; radius of convergence is infinite.
5 $\displaystyle\sum_{n=1}^{\infty} \dfrac{(-1)^{n+1}(x-1)^n}{n}$
6 (a) $\displaystyle\sum_{n=0}^{\infty} \dfrac{(2x)^n}{n!}$ (b) $\displaystyle\sum_{n=0}^{\infty} \dfrac{(-1)^n(2x)^n}{n!}$
7 $(1 + x)^{1/2} = 1 + \dfrac{x}{2} - \dfrac{x^2}{2^2 2!} + \dfrac{3x^3}{2^3 3!} - \dfrac{3 \cdot 5x^4}{2^4 4!} + \cdots$
8 (a) $1 - \displaystyle\sum_{n=0}^{\infty} \dfrac{(-x)^n}{n!}$ (b) $e^2 \displaystyle\sum_{n=0}^{\infty} \dfrac{(-x)^n}{n!}$
(c) $\displaystyle\sum_{n=1}^{\infty} \dfrac{(-1)^{n-1}(x-1)^n}{n}$

Checkpoints for Section 10.5

1 $S_{12}(x) = 1 + 2x^3 + 2x^6 + \dfrac{4x^9}{3} + \dfrac{2x^{12}}{3}$

2 $e^{-0.5} \approx 0.607$ with a maximum error of 0.0003.   **3** 1.970

Checkpoints for Section 10.6

1 1.732143   **2** -0.453398
3 1.319074   **4** 0.567143

Chapter 11

Checkpoints for Section 11.1

1 Not a solution
2 Because $y' = 2Cx$, and $xy' - 2y = x(2Cx) - 2Cx^2 = 0$,
$y = Cx^2$ is a solution. Particular solution: $y = \frac{1}{16}x^2$
3

4

Checkpoints for Section 11.2

1 $y^2 = \dfrac{2x^3}{3} + C$ **2** $y^2 = (x+1)^2 + C$
3 $y = \pm\sqrt{-x^2 + C}$

4 $y^2 = 6 - 2e^x$ **5** $y = 65 - Ce^{-kt}$
6 $\$31,424,909.75$

Checkpoints for Section 11.3

1 $y = -10 + Ce^x$ **2** $y = x \ln x + Cx$
3 $A = 1 - e^{-0.05t}$

Checkpoints for Section 11.4

1 $y = \dfrac{80}{7t + 2}$ **2** About 440,000 people

3 About 76 wolves   **4** About 79%

5 About 17.6 gallons

Appendix A

Checkpoints for Section A.1

1 $x < 5$ or $(-\infty, 5)$

2 $x < -2$ or $x > 5$; $(-\infty, -2) \cup (5, \infty)$

3 $200 \le x \le 400$; so the daily production levels during the month varied between a low of 200 units and a high of 400 units.

Checkpoints for Section A.2

1 $8; 8; -8$ **2** $2 \le x \le 10$

3 $\$4027.50 \le C \le \$11,635$

Checkpoints for Section A.3

1 $\frac{4}{9}$ **2** 8   **3** (a) $3x^6$ (b) $8x^{7/2}$ (c) $4x^{4/3}$

4 (a) $x(x^2 - 2)$ (b) $2x^{1/2}(1 + 4x)$

5 $\dfrac{(3x - 1)^{3/2}(13x - 2)}{(x + 2)^{1/2}}$ **6** $\dfrac{x^2(5 + x^3)}{3}$

7 (a) $[2, \infty)$ (b) $(2, \infty)$ (c) $(-\infty, \infty)$

Checkpoints for Section A.4

1 (a) $\dfrac{-2 \pm \sqrt{2}}{2}$ (b) 4   (c) No real zeros

2 (a) $x = -3$ and $x = 5$ (b) $x = -1$

   (c) $x = \frac{3}{2}$ and $x = 2$

3 $(-\infty, -2] \cup [1, \infty)$ **4** $-1, \frac{1}{2}, 2$

Checkpoints for Section A.5

1 $\dfrac{x - 2}{x + 1}$, $x \ne -10$ **2** (a) $\dfrac{x^2 + 2}{x}$ (b) $\dfrac{3x + 1}{(x + 1)(2x + 1)}$

3 $\dfrac{3x + 4}{(x + 2)(x - 2)}$ **4** $-\dfrac{x + 1}{3x(x + 2)}$

5 $\dfrac{2(4x^2 + 5x - 3)}{x^2(x + 3)}$ **6** (a) $\dfrac{3x + 8}{4(x + 2)^{3/2}}$ (b) $\dfrac{1}{\sqrt{x^2 + 4}}$

7 (a) $\dfrac{5\sqrt{2}}{4}$ (b) $\dfrac{x + 2}{4\sqrt{x + 2}}$ (c) $\dfrac{\sqrt{6} + \sqrt{3}}{3}$

   (d) $\dfrac{\sqrt{x + 2} - \sqrt{x}}{2}$

Answers to Tech Tutors

Tech Tutor

Section 1.3   *(page 29)*

The lines appear perpendicular in the setting $-9 \leq x \leq 9$ and $-6 \leq y \leq 6$.

Section 1.6   *(page 61)*

Most calculators set in connected mode will join the two branches of the graph with a nearly vertical line near $x = 2$. This line is not part of the graph.

Section 4.5   *(page 287)*

Answers will vary.

Section 6.3   *(page 395)*

1.46265

Section 8.4   *(page 537)*

Answers will vary.

Section 8.5   *(page 546)*

Answers will vary.

Section 11.3   *(page 676)*

$y = x^2(\ln x + 1)$